THE WAR WITHIN

The FRED W. MORRISON

Series in Southern Studies

DANIEL JOSEPH SINGAL

THE WAR WITHIN

FROM VICTORIAN TO MODERNIST

THOUGHT IN THE SOUTH, 1919–1945

The University of North Carolina Press

Chapel Hill

© 1982 The University of North Carolina Press
All rights reserved
Manufactured in the United States of America

Library of Congress Cataloging in Publication Data

Singal, Daniel Joseph, 1944–
The war within.

(The Fred W. Morrison series in Southern studies)
Bibliography: p.
Includes index.
1. Southern States—Intellectual life—1865–.
I. Title. II. Series.
F215.S56   975'.042   81–16358
ISBN 0–8078–1505–5
ISBN 0–8078–4087–4 pbk

For Sarah

CONTENTS

ILLUSTRATIONS

PREFACE

Historians studying twentieth-century American thought repeatedly arrive at a quandary: they can detect no fundamental pattern within their subject that might help them to make sense of it. In part this problem reflects the peril facing all who try to understand the recent past. The stock notions and formulations that historians of earlier periods are able to rely upon simply have not been developed yet for this era. But there is also considerable doubt as to whether such formulations will ever be possible in twentieth-century intellectual history. To many, modern thought appears hopelessly chaotic, a realm of random rebellion and experimentation for its own sake.

Almost as soon as I started working in the field I began asking whether these doubters were correct. Could any underlying pattern be found? Or, to put the matter more concretely, are there characteristic qualities discernible in figures as diverse as Van Wyck Brooks, Walter Lippmann, Reinhold Niebuhr, Daniel Bell, and Norman Mailer that will identify them as twentieth-century American thinkers? Was there a common set of problems they addressed with their separate voices, a central tension they all sought to resolve?

I first explored these questions as I read William Faulkner, an author who struck me as patently twentieth century in character. If one could somehow come to terms with Faulkner's verbal pyrotechnics, I suspected, one would discover valuable clues. Before long, however, I realized that it would be difficult to comprehend Faulkner's thought if I treated him alone, that it would be necessary to set him in context and to look at southern intellectual life as a whole. As soon as I did so I saw that his work stood at the center of an immense cultural change that had taken place in the region between the two world wars. One could see that change at a glance in the shift from Ulrich B. Phillips to C. Vann Woodward as the dominant figures in the field of southern history, or from Ellen Glasgow to Robert Penn Warren in literature. In each case the earlier figures plainly belonged to the nineteenth century, while the later ones stood forth as intellectuals of our own time. Here, then, was a way to pursue my basic quest. If I could pinpoint the changes that southern thought underwent during this period, if I could determine precisely what beliefs and values were transformed, I would have that elusive, fundamental pattern I was seeking.

At the outset I expected to connect these intellectual and cultural changes directly to social changes in the South. The region, I believed, was shifting in these years from an agrarian to an industrial society, from a personal and localistic way of life to one far more urbanized, bureaucratic, and hurried. So suggested the concept of modernization handed down by Max Weber, a concept that at first glance seemed tailor-made for explaining the outburst of creativity in the South. Presumably southern intellectuals had been caught in an intense conflict of values between the agrarian world they were losing and the industrial world they aspired to join, and they had turned to writing in an attempt to work out that conflict. That was essentially what Allen Tate had declared in his famous essay of 1942 accounting for the origins of the southern literary renaissance. Virtually all subsequent histories of the renaissance have tended to accept Tate's analysis.

The problem with this thesis is that it does not accord well with the facts of southern history. The South did not industrialize significantly in the two decades between the wars. If anything, the region relapsed toward an agricultural society during the 1930s as a result of economic depression. Not until well after the Second World War did a majority of southerners take industrial jobs and begin to live in places that could plausibly be described as urban. In addition, the sort of agriculture practiced in the South had long been commercialized. Instead of the yeoman homestead, the predominant institution had been the plantation, based after Reconstruction on the sharecropping system. Committed to raising staple crops rather than food and supplies, such farming was always at the mercy of distant, impersonal capitalistic markets. Not until the New Deal support program inadvertently undermined this system by enabling planters to evict their sharecroppers in favor of day labor did the traditional forms of society in the South really start to break up. By that time the intellectual renaissance was already two decades old. Clearly one needed something other than social change fully to account for it.

Another place to look for the sources of intellectual change was within the realm of thought itself. This would of course be a problematic approach, at variance with the trend within intellectual history that rejected the practice of the late Arthur O. Lovejoy and his disciples, who argued in essence that ideas beget ideas. Such "neo-Platonism" has now been replaced by a reliance on various schemes of social causation, grounded in "objective" social facts. Regardless of this new dispensation, however, I could not escape my finding that in the particular instance I was studying, southern intellectuals had moved toward a new mode of culture largely by way of rebellion against the culture they had inherited. It was their deep dissatisfaction with traditional values and assumptions, and not social realities per se, that brought them to their best work (Faulkner in the 1920s being the clearest example). Nevertheless, the question remained, where did that dissatisfaction, that desire to rebel against the inherited culture, come from? Why did the writers I studied choose to prefer the new culture? Clearly the answers I was seeking could not be found solely within the realm of pure thought, either.

It was here that I turned to the concrete sensibilities of the intellectuals—to the structures of their minds and their ways of perceiving the world. For it is within their sensibilities, formed through individual life experiences, that abstract thought and social conditions must ultimately be fused. A sociologist may be trained in the most advanced social science theory, or a novelist may be steeped in the literature of his times, but in each case the beliefs and perspectives actually absorbed and utilized will depend on the constellation of formative experiences the person has undergone. And those experiences, in turn, will reflect the person's immediate social environment. Thus it was of immense importance that the southern writers in this book were recruited from social strata different from most of their predecessors, and so brought with them a set of attitudes that would strongly shape their work. It was of equal importance that they most often attached themselves to the small number of fast-growing university centers in the region, where they found gathered other young southerners who shared their intellectual concerns. These various facets of their experience, mediated through their sensibilities, played a major role in determining how they would respond to the intellectual circumstances they encountered during their careers.

To put the matter in more formal terms, my methodological conclusion is that one must not prejudge the relationship between culture and society. The lines of influence can flow either way: in some cases thought may follow upon social change, in other cases it may effectively reshape society, and in still other cases the link may be dialectical. The task of the intellectual historian is to approach each historical situation with an open mind to discover what the relationship actually is. The only assumptions one can safely make in advance are that the connection between culture and society will rarely be simple, and that it should be sought first of all at the level of individual sensibility.

These assumptions were chiefly responsible for my decision to employ a biographical method. Clearly this approach has some disadvantages from the standpoint of exposition. Continuity may be disrupted as the narrative proceeds from one biographical chapter to another; major themes may temporarily disappear among the details. But the fact remains that ideas are not created by eras, or generations, or even schools of thought; they are generated by individuals through a complex interaction between the mind, intellectual influences, and personal encounters with the world. To write the history of thought accurately, to avoid the large-scale reifications—such as the "American Mind"—that have plagued the discipline so often in the past, we must concentrate on individual thinkers as the first step toward our more thematic treatments. Moreover, a thematic focus has the disadvantage of obscuring the sweat and agony that so often accompany intellectual change. A person questioning or surrendering the concepts and values he was raised on will frequently experience great psychic anguish that may find expression in gestures of guilt or compensation. Twentieth-century southern writers casting off the remnants of traditional racism will provide a case in point. To leave out this inner warfare would be to omit an important part of the story and to oversimplify the process of intellectual change.

The choice of southern writers to include was a difficult one, since there was so much talent in the South during this time. My criteria of selection tended to be both conceptual and practical—I wrote on those figures who plainly illustrated the cultural transformation I was describing, and on whom I could obtain sufficient information, either through archival sources, oral history interviews, or autobiographical accounts. The influence of some major authors, like Faulkner, Howard W. Odum, or the Nashville Agrarians, was so important that they simply could not be left out. In many instances, though, several other figures could easily have been substituted for those I chose. My purpose never was to produce an encyclopedic narrative of southern intellectual history in the twentieth century, but to chronicle and in part explain the process of cultural transition in the region, and it seems to me that the individuals I chose allowed me to do that.

Two other points deserve mention. First, it is obvious that my emphasis falls on the fields of history, literature, and sociology. The reason for this is simple: those were the areas toward which the most capable southern writers of the period gravitated. Furthermore, it seemed wisest from the standpoint of continuity to follow developments in the same three fields rather than to cover many different disciplines. Second, it is true that no black intellectuals appear in my cast of characters. This was still the age of segregation, when black children in the South received virtually no education. Not surprisingly, talented blacks born in the region usually left it at an early age in search of a more hospitable environment. There were some exceptions to this rule—most notably the sociologist Charles S. Johnson at Fisk University. But they were few, and research materials on them are often hard to come by (in part because their situation forced them to adopt a public mask, which came off only when they communicated with their closest friends). An important study remains to be written on black culture and thought in the modern South, but the task will involve the use of sources quite different from those employed for the present book.

But again, my main concern was not the South per se, but Modernism. I have tried to suggest how this new culture came about and to describe something of its shape and structure. I would only add here that I consider the results of my exploration highly tentative. Surely the pattern of thought and values I have put forward to describe Modernist culture will be found wanting in many respects—so much has been left out, so much remains to be explained. I do hope, though, that I have helped establish the fact that there *is* a basic pattern beneath the various forms of intellectual endeavor in the twentieth century, that literature and social science and political thought have not proceeded autonomously, but that an underlying matrix of culture and experience unites them at the deepest level.

It would be impossible to thank adequately all who shared in the completion of this study. The project began as a doctoral dissertation at Columbia University under the late Richard Hofstadter; it was completed under the direction of Eric L. McKitrick to whom I am grateful for a careful editorial reading and many helpful suggestions. Others who read all or portions of the manuscript and offered important comments include John B. Boles, Wayne D. Brazil, James B. Gilbert, Nathan I. Huggins, Richard Latner, William E. Leuchtenburg, Michael O'Brien (whose many criticisms were especially useful), John S. Reed, Leo P. Ribuffo, Morton P. Sosna, and George B. Tindall. Professors Tindall and Leuchtenburg also supplied invaluable moral support along the way (something a first-time author badly needs), as did Raymond A. Esthus and the director of the University of North Carolina Press, Matthew Hodgson.

A number of the people I studied were still alive at the time I conducted my research and kindly agreed to be interviewed. In several cases I was able to complete full-scale oral history memoirs with them, thanks to an arrangement with the Oral History Research Office at Columbia University. Transcripts of those memoirs have been deposited both at Columbia and at the University of North Carolina at Chapel Hill. I am most grateful to William T. Couch, Jonathan W. Daniels, Guy B. Johnson, Broadus Mitchell, Arthur F. Raper, Robert Penn Warren, and the late Rupert B. Vance for cooperating in this project and giving so generously of their time. I am also indebted to C. Vann Woodward, Lambert

Davis, and the late Louis R. Wilson for sharing their recollections with me on a more informal basis.

Many other people provided invaluable aid and support. I would especially mention the staff of the Southern Historical Collection at Chapel Hill, including J. Isaac Copeland, Carolyn Wallace, Brooke Allen, Michael G. Martin, Jr., and Richard Shrader, all of whom made me feel thoroughly at home during my long stay there. Other librarians who took special efforts to help me were Mattie Russell of Duke University, William G. Ray and Gregory A. Johnson of the University of Virginia, Susan A. Haddock and Marice Wolfe of the Joint University Libraries in Nashville, Donald Gallup of the Beinecke Library at Yale University, and Wanda M. Randall of Princeton. I owe a great deal to my aunt, Mrs. Mary S. Hahn, who typed and retyped the manuscript with unusual speed, accuracy, and affectionate concern. Mr. Jack Cofield of Oxford, Mississippi, was extremely generous in supplying me with such a fine photograph of William Faulkner from his collection. Julia Morgan of the Johns Hopkins University Archives, Judith A. Schiff of Yale, and Kay Beasley of Vanderbilt all aided in the search for illustrations. And once the manuscript was completed, Sandra Eisdorfer of the University of North Carolina Press edited the text with great skill, sensitivity, and care for detail.

I am grateful to Tulane University and the Andrew W. Mellon Foundation for supplying me with time to write through a Mellon Postdoctoral Fellowship at Tulane from 1977 to 1979. I am also grateful to my colleagues at Hobart and William Smith Colleges for their patient understanding while I was engaged in the time-consuming task of revision.

My chief intellectual debt belongs to R. Jackson Wilson of Smith College, a master craftsman of intellectual history who not only guided me in reaching my formulations but taught me the art of writing about ideas. Although he probably would not concur with all I have said, he deserves a large part of the credit for what is best in the book. On the personal side, my parents offered constant encouragement and support throughout this endeavor. My greatest debt of all, however, surely belongs to my wife, Sarah, who endured the demands of scholarship over several years with a devotion that passeth understanding. This book would simply not have been possible without her. My two daughters, Hannah and Rachel, also helped in their own way.

Geneva, New York
June, 1981

THE WAR WITHIN

INTRODUCTION

In the years just after 1900, a new mode of thought appeared in the United States that we may call, for want of a better name, twentieth-century Modernism. In a relatively short span of time, it was to displace nineteenth-century Victorianism, that genteel cultural omnibus that had dominated the Anglo-American world with astonishing resiliency for nearly three generations. Of course the demarcation was not exact, for such arbitrary benchmarks as the turn of a century rarely coincide with the actual process of cultural transformation, especially when a change of this magnitude is involved. The questions that led to Modernism were first posed in America as early as the time of the Civil War; powerful remnants of Victorian culture still survived after World War I. Altogether the period of transition was to run a full half century, as men and women probed, with many backward steps and much confusion, toward a new framework of intellectual life.[1]*

Nevertheless, as the undercurrents of rebellion began to surface and gain intensity, the tempo of change picked up visibly in the decades surrounding 1900. The quickening started, writes Richard Hofstadter, "with the avant-garde reconnoitering of the 'pianissimo revolt' of the nineties, proceeded to the cannonading of the Little Renaissance of the pre-war era, and culminated in the unrestrained frontal attack of the 1920's." Hofstadter's military imagery is highly appropriate, for as the

*The usage of Modernism employed here, it should be noted, differs significantly from that usually associated with the word "modern," a vague term denoting something new within a given era (the work of a Victorian writer like Thomas Carlyle, for example, appeared "modern" in its time), or from "modernization," a social and economic process usually centered upon industrial development. For the possible connections between modernization and Modernism, see Marshall Berman, " 'All that is Solid Melts into Air,' " 54–73, and Peter Berger, Brigitte Berger, and Hansfried Keller, *The Homeless Mind: Modernization and Consciousness.* There is considerable debate over whether Modernist culture should be limited to the last century; to a conservative writer like Lewis P. Simpson it stretches back to that "profound discontent with civilization" that entered Western thought at the time of the Enlightenment. However, Simpson and others like him ignore the fact that the discontent with civilization largely dissipated during the nineteenth century, to reappear at century's end in the guise of Modernism. See his *The Man of Letters in New England and the South,* 167.

assault on Victorianism broke into the open, to those caught up in it on either side the conflict became nothing less than a fight to the finish. That note of militance was unmistakable in the work of H. L. Mencken, Van Wyck Brooks, and George Santayana as they took aim at "Puritanism" and gentility; it could be seen also in rebel authors like Upton Sinclair, Theodore Dreiser, Frank Norris, Sherwood Anderson, Max Eastman, and Floyd Dell, among many others, who were bent on introducing a new strain of critical realism into American letters. Their opponents, the entrenched literary critics of the time, were to charge them with a decadent fixation on sordidness inappropriate to the supposed wholesome simplicity of American life, but this exploration of the dark side of human existence was to continue until, spurred by postwar disillusion, it had developed into a genuine tragic sensibility. At the same time, a new contingent of social thinkers was gathering in the universities, connected most often with the fledgling social sciences. Edward A. Ross, Lester F. Ward, and Albion W. Small in sociology, Thorstein Veblen and Edwin A. Seligman in economics, William James and John Dewey in philosophy, Charles A. Beard, James Harvey Robinson, and Carl Becker in history—all were asking questions about the nature of man and the workings of society that could be answered only within the matrix of Modernist culture.[2]

To be sure, much disagreement still exists on the definition and meaning of Modernism. Most writers to date have followed the lead of Lionel Trilling in portraying it as an "adversary culture" essentially limited to the artistic avant-garde and dedicated to shocking the bourgeois sensibility by overturning all rules of social convention, proper form, and logic. At the heart of this rebellion, Trilling remarks, lies a deep "hostility to civilization," along with a concomitant "discovery and canonization of the primal, non-ethical energies." For many Modernism has seemed to lack a real intellectual center; Irving Howe, for instance, finds it based upon little more than an "unyielding rage against the official order," while to Daniel Bell "its very amorphousness or protean nature precludes a single encapsulating term" in describing it. Marshall Berman sees Modernism not as an entity in its own right, but as a "family of artistic and intellectual movements that have been radically experimental, spiritually turbulent and militant, iconoclastic to the point of nihilism, apocalyptic in their hopes and fantasies, savagely destructive to one another—and often to themselves as well—yet capable of recurrent self-renewal."[3]

Recently, however, this more or less pejorative view has come under challenge from those who regard Modernism as a major historical culture to be ranked alongside the Enlightenment, Puritanism, or its predecessor Victorianism. Peter Gay in particular has argued that the Modernist movement represents much more than an artistic or literary phenomenon, that it constitutes no less than a "pervasive cultural revolution, a second Renaissance," which has "transformed culture in all its branches." "A very troop of masters," according to Gay, "compelled Western civilization to alter its angle of vision, and to adopt a new aesthetic sensibility, a new philosophical style, a new mode of understanding social life and human nature." For Gay the prevailing interpretation errs by considering only the more sensational surface features of Modernist culture while ignoring the important intellectual transformation occurring below. If there has been occasional despair and emotional fireworks, there has also been a positive underlying purpose, a commitment to rationality, and a fundamental seriousness in Modernism. In his words, "its bursting of boundaries did not imply hostility to discipline; its vigorous aesthetic and social criticism did not involve a yielding to depression; its profound exploration of unreason was not a celebration of irrationality. The Modernists found almost as many ways of affirming life as they did of rejecting it, and they were equally modern in each of these postures." If Gay is correct—and the present writer strongly believes that he is—then Modernism and its origins clearly require a closer look by historians.[4]

To begin to discover how Modernism came about, there is no better place to start than the shift in meaning of the term "culture" itself. For the Victorians, culture was a quite specific concept—it stood for a traditional moral discipline, instilled in a child through education and a proper upbringing, which enabled him to keep his baser emotions in check. Whether it took the form of polite manners, a code of honor, or an acquaintance with the arts, the purpose of culture was to refine, inspire, and "elevate" an individual from the moral standpoint, raising him above the common herd. Those who possessed culture were thought to be "civilized," those who lacked it were "savages." The latter category, rarely well defined, was made to include an assortment of people the Victorian middle class feared or did not like—the lower classes, those whose origins were other than European, and races whose skin color was other than white. Most important of all, the barrier between civilization and savagery, between the cultured and the uncultured, was considered virtually uncrossable, except through the very gradual effects of multigenerational mobility. This radical dichotomy pervaded everything the Victorians said and did; even when they spoke optimistically of uplift and reform it was not far from their minds. This separation between the barbaric and the civilized, the animal and the human, became in fact the very bedrock assumption of their thought.[5]

Although it would take us too far afield to detail it here, it is fair to say that the steady erosion of this Victorian dichotomy under the onslaught of naturalism and social science constitutes the main story of Western intellectual history in the second half of the nineteenth century. The initial attack came with Darwin, whose findings showed that the separation between modern man and the jungle was less absolute than the Victorians wished to believe. Victorians learned to cope with evolution, however, by positing a series of developmental stages, running through man's simian ancestry up to savagery, barbarism, and finally civilization. Since each stage was said to be self-contained, it was still possible to distinguish sharply civilized beings from savages. Freudian theory presented a greater problem, because it declared the existence of a powerful animal component in human nature difficult to control and apparently inescapable, even for a proper Victorian. And for those who came in contact with it, Marxian sociology shook nineteenth-century thought further with its reductionist notion that high culture and noble ideals were in reality just a cover—a "superstructure"—for the predations of the bourgeois class.[6]

But the crowning blow to the dichotomy came from cultural anthropology. Its field studies proved consistently that "savage" life was not as different from civilized life as the Victorians had supposed. Civilization itself could no longer be construed as some vague spiritual quality cultured people possessed, but rather it was a set of traits and practices people invented to adapt to the particular environment they found themselves in. "All men are totally civilized," Alfred L. Kroeber declared in 1915; there could be "no higher or lower in civilization." Less easy to trace, but also of major consequence, was the influence of developments in the natural sciences, especially those discoveries concerning the microscopic structure of matter, the existence of invisible forces such as radiation, and of course Einstein's theory of relativity. The entire notion of solidity that the Victorians so admired—witness their architecture—now was called into question. In the physical world, men were learning, nothing was as it seemed. As Miklos Szabolcsi has written, this "revelation of hitherto invisible provinces—to see the hitherto invisible, to learn the hitherto unknown without having to resort to mysticism and irrationalism—this overwhelming experience is, among others, at the source of the avante-garde waves."[7]

As a result of these developments, culture, in its twentieth-century usage, has become completely detached from morality and has received a far broader definition than before. It has come to signify the interrelated system of ideas, attitudes, myths, and institutions that enable a given social group to make sense of its environment and to give order to its society. No longer the exclusive property of the upper classes, culture has now been attributed to everyone, including the most primitive Australian aborigine. Indeed, it has come to be seen as a necessity for psychological survival, providing, as Clifford Geertz contends, a "template or blueprint for the organization of social and psychological processes, much as genetic systems provide such a template for the organization of organic processes." In this way the concept has been democratized, with profound consequences for social thought—as we shall observe many times in this study. Moreover, where the Victorians saw (or tried to see) culture as an organic whole, each part of which harmonized with all the others, modern thinkers have viewed it as a construct of diversified elements that frequently conflict. Erik H. Erikson, for example, speaks of a nation's culture as "derived from the ways in which history has, as it were, counterpointed certain opposite potentialities," lifting them to a "unique style of civilization," or permitting them to "disintegrate into mere contradiction." To most Victorians, this image of a culture resting on shifting polarities that might possibly clash head-on would have been impossible to fathom.[8]

In sum, one might say that the Victorian concept of culture was based ultimately on a world view of radical innocence and that Modernist thought represents a deliberate flight from that innocence. The point is not that Victorians were in fact innocent people (or that Modernists have entirely escaped innocence), but that they established innocence as their cultural goal. Their impulse was to strive for purity in all things, to refuse resolutely to accommodate the presence of conflict or evil within the perimeter of civilization. Such was the purpose of their dichotomy between civilized and savage—to wall off as far as possible those irrational tendencies in the human personality that could lead to cruelty, excess, and pain. In truth their actual behavior saw frequent lapses from this lofty standard, most evident in that "other" life of prostitution and pornography that Victorian gentlemen commonly led. On the "spiritual" level, moreover, there were constant struggles of the moral will to keep the more acceptable domesticated emotions from degenerating into the forbidden passions, and the battle was often lost. The key point, though, is that these outbreaks of "animalism" were viewed precisely as lapses. The ideal of the Victorians remained a world governed by moral purity, and they tried hard to attain it.[9]

Modernists, it is clear, have pursued the exact opposite course. They launched their rebellion with the express intention of countering what they felt was an unnatural repression of human vitality ordained by Victorian culture. Following the insights of Darwin and Freud, they insisted on seeing man as the human animal and turned their attention to those darker reaches of his being that the Victorians sought to evade. For contemporary novelists especially, the human capacity for evil has become, not a source of shame, but rather the force that gives life its texture and significance. To borrow Lionel Trilling's terminology, the Victorian quest for "sincerity," in which personal integrity is achieved solely at the level of consciousness, has been replaced by a search for "authenticity," which requires nothing less than the effective reconciliation of the conscious and unconscious selves. In short, while Victorian moralists contrived to exclude man's irrationality from their conception of culture, their twentieth-century counterparts have tried to reclaim it. The barrier between savagery and civilization has been intentionally broken down in an effort to make man whole again. It is in this sense that Henry May was right in calling the coming of Modernism the "end of American innocence."[10]

Although no infallible litmus test exists for identifying Modernist culture, there are a number of signs one can look for. First is an author's willingness, even eagerness, to plumb the nether regions of the psyche. The Modernist imagination is not normally "propelled by an exploration of the demonic," as Bell would have it, but it does treat the irrational as an integral part of human nature that must never be ignored. Second, Modernists perceive the universe as turbulent and unpredictable, as opposed to the Victorians who believed in an orderly universe governed by natural law. Third, and closely related, is their positive view of conflict, whether personal, social, or political. The Victorian objectives of "bliss" and "peace" have become unpalatable to twentieth-century thinkers, notes Trilling, because they suggest the "negation of the 'more life' that we crave"; we have come to "dread Eden." Fourth, the true Modernist possesses an ability to live without certainty, either moral or epistemological. Such a person recognizes that moral standards inevitably fluctuate with historical experience and must always be considered tentative. Finally, a Modernist mind will typically display a critical temperament uninhibited by considerations of formal manners: gentility gives way to the necessity of making contact with "reality," no matter how ugly or distasteful that reality might be. The recognition of man's irrational nature, the acceptance of an open and unpredictable universe, the notion of conflict as inherently virtuous, the tolerance of uncertainty, and the drive toward probing criticism—all are part of the Modernist effort to reintegrate the human consciousness and thus to liberate man from the restrictive culture of enforced innocence with which the century began.[11]

Although the battle between Victorian and Modernist culture raged throughout Western society, nowhere can it be seen with greater clarity than in the American South. There Victorianism had settled in with a vengeance during the late nineteenth century, merging with the distinctive cultural patterns that had formed prior to the Civil War. The war had devastated southern society, wiping out the political and economic base, along with most major social institutions. By the end of Reconstruction all that southerners could salvage from their history was the sustaining conviction that, in its day, theirs had been an aristocratic culture infinitely superior to the crass materialistic culture of their enemy. This Cavalier myth, moreover, embodied traits of order, stability, and cohesion that southern society stood in desperate need of. The result was what Paul Gaston has called the New South Creed, a transposition of Cavalier mythology onto the framework of Victorian belief in morality and industrial progress, a fusion of ideological elements so formidable that it effectively blocked the arrival of intellectual Modernism in the region through the First World War.[12]

Thus when a new generation of southern intellectuals emerged after the war, theirs was a task of deliberately and rapidly catching up. Modernism, they soon discovered, was an accomplished fact in most of the Western world, of which the South had become a backward province. To escape that backwardness, they would have to assimilate a veritable galaxy of new ideas with unusual speed, recapitulating as they did the experience of their northern brethren during the previous half century. Far more self-conscious than the northern pioneers of Modernism had been, and operating, one might say, with the script already written, they were to follow a smoother and straighter path. As a consequence, by the time the United States entered the Second World War Modernism had been firmly installed as the predominant style of literary and intellectual life in the region.

That is why the South offers a special opportunity for studying the shift from nineteenth- to twentieth-century culture and for determining what the latter truly entailed. When it finally arrived, change proceeded there in far more concentrated fashion, with fewer false starts on the one hand, but with greater tension and drama on the other—making the process of transition easier to observe. The question of southern culture itself, past and present, became the most emotional issue of debate, sufficiently charged to make those who approached it critically fearful of retribution. When W. J. Cash, for instance, wrote in 1941 that the "intellectual and aesthetic culture of the Old South was a superficial and jejune thing . . . not a true culture at all," his were fighting words, aimed at the most sensitive beliefs of his opponents. In addition, nowhere else was the topic of race, a prime concern of Modernists, more explosive than in the South. Ever since the Civil War the Victorian dichotomy had supplied a principal bulwark for southern white supremacy, with blacks cast customarily as savages (or undisciplined children) and whites as the foremost paladins of civilization. Those hoping to alter southern racial thought through the concept of environmentalism would first have to deal with this residual belief in the dichotomy, rendering the struggle for Modernism still more dramatic and conspicuous.[13]

Lastly, not only was the clash of cultures fiercest in the South, it was also comparatively self-contained. The script was played out on a smaller stage than elsewhere, with far fewer characters and a more limited plot. Participants normally couched their arguments in terms of the region's specific dilemmas, leaving matters of national policy and abstract theory to their northern counterparts. The version of Victorian culture propagated by southern intellectuals was far simpler than that found in the North or in England. The subtlety, complexity, and contradictory tendencies of English Victorianism generally did not survive transplantation into the thin soil of southern bourgeois life. The mocking wit of Matthew Arnold, for example, was often lost on his disciples below the Potomac such as Edwin A. Mims, nor was much retained from Thomas Carlyle save for his defense of chivalric heroism. As a result, the basic framework of Victorian thought stood exhibited in the South in sharper relief than elsewhere, and, to a lesser extent, the same can be said of Modernism. For our purposes, in sum, the South may serve as an arena large enough to contain the chief contending forces, but small enough to make manifest what in essence was involved.[14]

The plan will be to trace this process of change in three rough stages, corresponding to the emergence of a Modernist intellectual generation in the South. The first stage, which might be called "post-Victorian," was made up of those southerners born in the wake of Reconstruction who tried consciously to break with the strictures of Victorianism, but whose underlying loyalty to nineteenth-century values dominated in the end. Next, there was a small contingent of transitional figures who managed to straddle both cultures, coming down ultimately on the side of Modernism, but by the barest margin. These "Modernists by the skin of their teeth" provide a chance to assess the special potentialities and pitfalls facing intellectuals who live at a time of rapid cultural change. Finally, a group of southerners unquestionably in the twentieth-century camp and displaying several of the varieties of southern Modernism will be considered. In examining them, one may gain a sense not only of what was won in the transition to Modernism but also of what was lost.

CHAPTER I

CAVALIER MYTH AND
VICTORIAN CULTURE:
THE NINETEENTH-CENTURY
BACKGROUND

We of the South," declared the elder Confederate statesman Robert Toombs, "are a race of gentlemen." Ever since the days of William Byrd, this notion of the South as the last refuge of aristocracy in America has dominated the region's cultural life. Nor has its appeal been limited to the South, as William R. Taylor has shown; Americans from all parts of the country have been anxious to believe that in at least one time and place of their history chivalrous lords walked the center stage immune from the normal American traits of ambition, practicality, and money-grubbing. "Plantation school" novelists from John Pendleton Kennedy to Margaret Mitchell have battened on the nation's seemingly endless appetite for tales of Old South grandeur. With his larger-than-life scale and his aura of romance, the Cavalier has in fact become the very symbol of the South, intimately bound up with the region's sense of identity, providing southerners with their predominant source of common pride in the perpetual struggle with Yankeedom. Twentieth-century southern intellectuals found that they had no choice but to confront this mythological view of their society before they could address themselves to the region's ills. Since the nineteenth-century myth became their starting point, it must be ours as well.[1]

Of course, judged by traditional European standards, no such entrenched aristocracy ever existed in the South. In both its Continental and British versions, the idea of aristocracy has presupposed a society in which a small number of families monopolize power, wealth, and land for generations, where class lines are consequently well defined and permanent, and where all emphasis falls on stability and continuity. Moreover, those born at the top of the aristocratic pyramid, freed by their inheritance from the necessity of earning their living, are required under the rules of noblesse oblige to assume the burden of leadership in their communities, especially in matters of social welfare. The product of careful breeding and an equally careful upbringing, the true patrician is expected to epitomize self-control, moderation, and refinement—the qualities he will need to bring stability to his domain. Although this ideal may never have been realized, at various times in European history it was at least approximated; there a real aristocracy did exist.

The nearest the Old South came to this sort of established nobility was the tobacco gentry of Tidewater Virginia, whose influence peaked about the time of the American Revolution. The Byrds, Lees, Pages, Carters, and other Old Dominion families could indeed trace their origins back to the colony's founders, and most of them actively shared their ancestors' dream of transplanting the life of the English country gentleman to the New World. After a century or so of tending to crops and pedigrees, the effort began to succeed: Tidewater planters could point to fine estates, sizable fortunes, and a high level of intellectual attainment among certain segments of the upper class. But even this set of well-born southerners was compelled by economic necessity to spend far more time at the hard work of growing tobacco than cultivating social graces. Furthermore, as children of the Enlightenment the Chesapeake squires of Jefferson's day preferred to advertise themselves as democrats, espousing an open "natural" aristocracy rather than one based solely on heredity. Likewise, in their aesthetic taste predilections ran to "homespun simplicity" rather than imported pretense. In short, judged by mid-eighteenth-century standards, the world of the Tidewater gentry struck a unique balance between contemporary notions of a well-structured society and the realities of American experience, between establishment and mobility; but it was not—and did not claim to be—a full-fledged aristocracy.[2]

Not until the early nineteenth century when cotton replaced tobacco as the region's chief staple did antebellum planters begin depicting themselves as Lords of the Manor. Cotton was never an important crop in the colonial South, but after Eli Whitney's invention of the cotton gin in 1793 made large-scale production possible, an extraordinary expansion of the plantation system took place virtually overnight. By 1830, the contrast between the old Virginia society and the new cotton areas of the Deep South was striking. Although the requirements of tobacco cultivation dictated small-sized units, cotton made no such demand, allowing the new plantations to grow to huge proportions with slave populations occasionally numbering in the thousands. Also unlike the Tidewater, these communities tended to be fresh and raw, carved out of the forest or swampland at the same time as the plantations themselves.[3]

The most important difference, however, was in the character of the planters themselves. Though some of the new cotton barons were sons of Upper South gentry who had moved southward for fresh land, many were ambitious men of lower- or middle-class origin taking advantage of the easy access to wealth afforded by the magic white staple. In fact, with frontier-like conditions prevailing over most of its territory, the antebellum black belt offered a case study in rapid social mobility. There were, reports Clement Eaton, "no hard-and-fast lines drawn between classes in white Southern society," and the records are replete with "success stories of hard-driving, horse-trading farmers who became plantation owners." Men on the make with sharp wits, few scruples, and no pedigree flocked to the booming cotton lands of Alabama, Mississippi, and Georgia in search of instant fortunes; with a few years of hard work and a little luck at marketing their crops (or at real-estate manipulation or card-dealing), they could soon elevate themselves to the stature of "gentlemen." A typical example is Samuel Davis, the father of Confederate President Jefferson Davis, who rose from a landless small farmer to an aristocrat in little over a decade. It was this breed of Lower South cotton planter above all others who became associated in legend with the glories of the Old South.[4]

Indeed, it was simultaneous with the emergence of the cotton parvenu in the early 1830s that the Cavalier myth first flowered. In part this timing was due to the increasing popularity of romantic literature, especially the novels of Sir Walter Scott, which soon became as much a southern staple as cotton itself. Landed southerners, finding it easy to identify with the medieval knights and lords portrayed in the Waverley tales, began acting out fantasies of feudal splendor. Southern summer resorts held jousting tournaments exactly as Scott described them, homespun simplicity gave way to rococo excess, and the *code duello* lent frontier gunplay a respectability it had never enjoyed before. But while the influence of Scott might account for a passing fad, it does not begin to explain the tenacity with which southerners grasped the aristocratic myth or the persistence the myth displayed for more than a century after the Jacksonian era. Why, after all, should early nineteenth-century southern Americans, the ideological heirs of Jefferson and Madison, suddenly develop exotic visions of establishing themselves as feudal barons on the southwestern corner of the American frontier?[5]

The answer to this question lies in the considerable social changes that accompanied the Age of Jackson and the special impact those changes had on the South. Historians have traditionally depicted the Jacksonian period as a time of unparalleled optimism, progress, and democratic reform. Yet recently they have discerned a very different note below the surface—an undercurrent of anxiety concerning the direction the country was headed coupled with a nostalgia for the supposed stability and decorum of the past. "The assertions of the orators might point to a bountiful future," William R. Taylor has written, "but locked in the syntax of their sentences lurked the lingering doubt, the scarcely noticed qualifier, the parenthetical 'if.'" Embarked on an unprecedented experiment in democratic politics and personal liberty and separated from the civilizing influence of Europe by three thousand miles of ocean, Americans were understandably fearful that their young nation might be too fragile to withstand the pressures Jacksonianism brought in its wake. According to David J. Rothman, such was the diagnosis of contemporary psychiatrists; to them the "style of life in the new republic seemed willfully designed to produce mental illness. Everywhere they looked, they found chaos and disorder, a lack of fixity and stability. The community's inherited traditions and procedures were dissolving, leaving incredible stresses and strains." Unless something could be done, they maintained, the country might easily collapse to become the derision of the entire world.[6]

What alarmed these Jacksonians most was the specter of excessive individualism tearing at the roots of social order. In both the political and economic arenas, the great American scramble for status and power was now on. Moreover, the rules had changed: the race now went to the man with the most stamina, ambition, and competitive skill, and not necessarily to those well-born or most deserving. That, of course, was exactly what the new democratic ideology called for. But to the middle-class citizens of this generation, reared on eighteenth-century values of order, restraint, and moderation, the spectacle was bound to be more than a little terrifying. In Taylor's words, "if men were naturally self-centered and rapacious, bent on pursuing their own private ends, and nature was an amoral or a neutral force, then what was there in the classless and open society of America to prevent its becoming a social jungle the equal of which the civilized world had never seen?" Without the binding ties provided by family and community, American society might rapidly break down into warring atoms and succumb to crime, violence, and barbarism. That was the apocalyptic scenario hidden beneath the hopeful rhetoric of the 1830s that Jacksonians carefully consulted before designing their engines of reform.[7]

How Americans responded to these tremors depended on which side of the Potomac River they resided. Northerners reacted by doubling their cheerful estimates of illimitable progress and by creating a variety of new social institutions designed to help hold their society together. As Rothman has shown, the most striking of these efforts involved correctional institutions—asylums, almshouses, and penitentiaries—built on the principle of supplying a well-ordered environment where the wayward person could regain his self-control. Those whom the temptations of an open society had made criminal or insane could thus be sent to the appropriate institution for a thorough schooling in restraint and emerge useful citizens once again. If the asylum and its sister institutions never lived up to these near-utopian expectations, what is important is the approach northerners chose to take—launching community endeavors with widespread participation to confront directly the perils of unrestrained individualism. Given the quantity and fervor of such reform campaigns, the steady growth of towns and cities, the start of the factory system, and the development of a vigorous two-party political system, all of which tended to promote communal endeavor, it may well be that the very process by which the asylums were built helped northerners gain that elusive sense of social cohesion they were seeking in the first place.[8]

If it was the Age of Jackson, however, in the South it was the Age of Nat Turner as well. Significantly, almost no benevolent institutions went up in the black belt, where slaveholders remained highly suspicious of the ultimate implications of reform. Besides, social services of this sort in the South usually fell under the rubric of plantation paternalism, which held the individual planter responsible for the care of his own slaves but not necessarily for the fate of his less fortunate white neighbors.[9]

Yet there can be no doubt that southerners of the 1830s more than shared their Yankee brethren's anxieties over social order. In addition to the perils of individualism, which was just as rampant below Mason-Dixon as above, the planters of this era faced—or thought they faced—ever-present threat of slave revolts, the accelerated attacks of northern abolitionists, bitter sectional cleavages over the tariff and Nullification, and a concerted challenge to their political control from Jacksonian Democrats within the South. No wonder Cassandra-like predictions, which were little more than a "scarcely noticed qualifier" in northern public rhetoric, became something close to an obsession for southern orators. "Ah, why should such a happy state of things—a society so charming and accomplished," wrote Hugh Swinton Legaré in 1832, "be doomed to end so soon, and perhaps so terribly! . . . My heart sinks within me often when I think of what may too soon be." Indeed, one senses in such pronouncements an almost morbid delight in foretelling disaster.[10]

Although the tensions inherent in slavery were in large part responsible for producing this state of mind, perhaps an equal cause lay in the peculiar character of antebellum society as shaped by the plantation system.

Few institutions in recent history have dominated a society so thoroughly as did the plantation in the Old South, becoming, in Edgar Thompson's phrase, "the molecular unit, the very quintessence, of the South and of southernism." The plantation's needs determined the South's pattern of settlement, its principal transportation routes, and the location, size, and vitality of its cities, all the while sapping life from any other institution that threatened to compete for power. In short, the plantation flourished at the expense of the development of the rest of southern society. By importing from outside the region whatever goods and services it was unable to supply itself, for example, the plantation effectively choked off the economic growth of southern towns and thus prevented the rise of an independent middle class. Likewise, public schools were nonexistent in many counties because of the planters' preference for teaching their children at home or sending them to a private academy.[11]

The result was a rural society spread over an immense territory with remarkably few focal points of population or commerce and with a frequent lack of those institutions one would normally expect to find in a settled community. Especially in the black belt, where the impact of the rapidly expanding plantation system was greatest, only a minimum of formal ties existed to bind together this scattered and insular society, a fact that no doubt troubled reflective southerners.* Clearly such a social order was at variance with the eighteenth-century ideal of a stable, cohesive community they still retained. And as everyone knew, this sort of loose and open society, where each individual was free to pursue his own ambitions, was the perfect environment for the virus of human greed (along with the rest of man's worst instincts) to develop and thrive. What, indeed, was to prevent the South from disintegrating into a social

*Frederick Law Olmsted, perhaps the most perceptive contemporary observer to tour the antebellum South, also noticed the deleterious effect of the plantation system on community cohesion: ". . . if all the wealth produced in a certain district is concentrated in the hands of a few men living remote from each other, it may possibly bring to the district comfortable houses, good servants, fine wines, food and furniture, tutors and governesses, horses and carriages, for these few men, but it will not bring thither good roads and bridges, it will not bring thither such means of education and civilized comfort as are to be drawn from libraries, churches, museums, gardens, theatres, and assembly rooms; it will not bring thither local newspapers, telegraphs, and so on. It will not bring thither that subtle force and discipline which comes of the myriad relations with and duties to a well-constituted community which every member of it is daily exercising. . . . There is, in fact, a vast range of advantages which our civilization has made so common to us that they are hardly thought of, of which the people of the South are destitute. They come chiefly from or connect with acts of cooperation, or exchanges of service; they are therefore possessed only in communities, and in communities where a large proportion of the people have profitable employment" (*The Cotton Kingdom,* 17–18).

jungle? How, in a wilderness insufficiently civilized, could natural human rapacity be kept within bounds?

I

Southerners began turning to the aristocratic myth to mask the apparent deficiencies in their society as early as the seventeenth century. To defend their young colony against charges of frontier crudeness, Virginia tobacco planters of that day sent back to England glowing accounts of a polished nobility. The capacity for mythmaking in this literature, notes Kenneth S. Lynn, was already quite remarkable: "A rural society, so isolated and decentralized that it did not produce even the villages that were springing up everywhere in the colonies to the north, is represented as having a social life as swirlingly active and gay as London itself could offer." However, these colonial efforts, lightened by occasional touches of self-mockery, seem little more than harmless puffery by comparison to what came later; by the nineteenth century, the southern legend was far more serious business.[12]

To be sure, there is nothing inherently pernicious in mythology itself. In fact, many students of the subject would insist that a vital mythology is essential to human well-being, even in the modern world. What makes myth indispensable—and what made it so attractive to the nineteenth-century South—is its power to enhance social identity. Myth is no mere literary device; rather, it is a means for members of a society to "share communally in the nature of inner experience." By projecting a people's deepest dreams and fears onto a series of external characters and events, myth can become the organizing framework for the society's shared emotions, providing its members with their most fundamental sense of unity and purpose. Yet despite its numerous positive functions, mythology can also become a source of danger. A healthy myth is always half-true; it lives, Jerome Bruner tells us, poised "on the feather line between fantasy and reality." Regardless of the shocks of history, this balance must be maintained, for if a myth descends into pure fantasy, it can become "fanatical and obsessive" and begin to serve as a substitute for reality. That, it appears, began to occur in the antebellum South.[13]

The Cavalier identity adopted in the 1830s spoke directly to the planters' deepest apprehensions about themselves and their society. By setting forth the heroic figure of the southern gentleman, with his heroic ability to bring order and culture to all he surveyed, it enabled southerners to convince themselves and others that the South enjoyed the *most* stable and civilized society in America. For the certifying mark of the true southern gentleman was his complete self-control; as Taylor puts it, he was a paragon of temperance whose "natural impulses" were successfully "held in check by a massive set of restraints," including his "concern for family and racial traditions," his "rigid standards of decorum," and the "complicated code of honor" by which he lived. Thus if the myth could be believed, the aristocratic planter was reined in by such extraordinary internal discipline that he *did not need* the conventional legal and institutional restrictions of society to save him from temptation. Moreover, the gentleman could use his great stature and remarkable personality to stop the drift toward chaos. To those who subscribed to the myth, Taylor continues, "the gentleman planter was not simply a Southerner, he was the principal civilizing agent in a society where everything tended toward anarchy and disorder. . . . Only the Cavalier possessed the heroic force of character which was required to hold back the restless flood of savagery that threatened to overflow the country."[14]

Such, for instance, was the argument made by proslavery apologists like George Fitzhugh. It was clear, Fitzhugh wrote, from the abundance of crime, poverty, and misery in the North that that section's experiment in liberty and democracy had failed. The reason was plain to see—in Yankee society, with its open competition for wealth and power, the "only motive of human conduct" was selfishness: "None but the selfish virtues are encouraged, because none other aid a man in the race of free competition. Good men and bad men have the same end in view, are in pursuit of the same object—self-promotion, self-elevation." By contrast the southern planter was "the least selfish of men," thinking only of family and community rather than self-advancement. "We are better husbands, better friends, and better neighbors than our Northern brethren," Fitzhugh insisted. "Love for others is the organic law of our society, as self-love is of theirs." This general diffusion of the Cavalier spirit resulted in a perfectly cohesive society, he alleged, making the South "wholly exempt" from criminals and paupers and so obviating the need for jails, almshouses, and similar badges of Yankee shame. Rather than fearing instability, Fitzhugh summed up, southerners could take immense pride in the superior civilization their distinctive social order permitted.[15]

Fitzhugh also maintained as an integral part of his thesis that southern society was arranged in a fixed hierarchy, with each person remaining more or less in the station to which he was born. An open social structure like that of the North, he claimed, violated the laws of nature, which decreed that all men subordinate their individual desires to the requirements of the social organism: "Man is born a member of society, and does not form society. Nature, as in the case of the bees and the ants, has it ready formed for him. He and society are congenital. Society is the being—he one of the members of that society; and that society may very properly make any use of him that will redound to the public good." Of course, this mythical image of a close-knit society in the South blatantly contradicted antebellum reality, but Fitzhugh and his colleagues, pursuing their Idealist premises, did not seem to care.* A semifeudal order was the kind of society they *wanted* the South to have, as opposed to the relatively fluid and competitive way of life they saw all around them.[16]

Fitzhugh's writings presented one side of the Cavalier ideal: the myth of lower-class violence depicted in the work of the Southwest humorists presented another. These stories, which began to appear in southern newspapers just after the Nullification crisis of 1833 and which grew in popularity up to the eve of secession, were designed primarily to warn readers of the dangerous men lurking at the bottom of southern society, especially in the raw frontier areas of the Deep South. As Kenneth Lynn has shown, the authors were all professional men, southern patriots, and conservative Whigs with a passionate hatred of Jacksonian democracy. Thus although grotesque characters like A. B. Longstreet's Ransy Sniffle or J. J. Hooper's Simon Suggs might have been entertaining, their antics were meant to convey an unmistakably ominous undertone, a foretaste of what might happen should the better sort of southerners lose their monopoly of political and social control.[17]

To drive their point home, writers in this vein always contrived to tell their tales through the eyes of a high-minded aristocrat, whose commitment to the Whig virtues of temperance and moderation stood in sharp contrast to the savage exploits of the characters he described. Here was

---

*Although it may be true, as Eugene D. Genovese has argued, that many nouveau planters were attempting to realize the ideal society set forth by Fitzhugh and other purveyors of the aristocratic myth, there were severe social and economic constraints on their ability to do so. The plantation remained an essentially capitalistic institution, tied intimately (not marginally as Genovese would have it) to the marketplace through the need to obtain credit, sell cotton, buy and sell land and slaves, and purchase a host of necessary supplies. Those planters who could not maintain an entrepreneurial role were doomed to bankruptcy—as the fate of many a planter's wastrel son attests. Nor would the future have brought any change, even had the Civil War not taken place, so long as the South remained wedded to that preeminent institution of frontier capitalism, the plantation.

Genovese is certainly correct in maintaining that the aristocratic ideal was beginning to modify the actual behavior of planters by the 1850s, especially in their increasingly paternalistic treatment of their slaves, and we must adjust our understanding of the Old South accordingly. But his contention that "their acquisitiveness did not make them bourgeois" makes no sense in the context of the times. The distinction between bourgeois and aristocrat drawn by contemporaries depended precisely on this fundamental issue of acquisitiveness, the one trait the planters could not dispense with if they wished to survive economically as planters. See his *The World the Slaveholders Made*, 139, 142.

the southern planter playing his familiar role as the "principal civilizing agent" of his society, a task that, from the evidence presented, was far from over. The reader was left to choose between the balance and discipline of the narrator ("the Self-controlled Gentleman," Lynn calls him), or the unrestrained viciousness and profanity of the low-born scoundrels. What is striking about this strategy—and about the Cavalier myth in general—is the absence of any middle ground. The pious, sober, industrious pioneer farmer, so central to the developing mythology of the frontier West at this time (and so frequently found in *actual* southern society), was largely ignored by the mythmakers of the South. For them a man was either a gentleman in total command of his emotions, or a hopeless boor or ruffian. Nothing less than aristocratic perfection was considered civilized.[18]

Plainly, the antebellum planter in real life was not always the exemplar of self-mastery portrayed in the myth. Although the Whig humorists spoke through the mask of the self-controlled gentleman in their fiction, most were known in private for unusually hot tempers. More revealing still was the widespread practice of dueling, justified by its defenders as a means of upholding the aristocratic code of honor. William W. Freehling's account of how conversation at a Charleston tea party could lead to a duel suggests that, for the low-country planters, violence was just a hair-trigger reaction away:

> The great social art was to slip, without ostentation, into an easy familiarity with all companions. The besetting social sin was to permit one's companion to take advantage of the relaxed cordiality. The balance often broke down. A jest which went a bit too far could be taken as an insult, a clever argument could be interpreted as an affront. Then came the inevitable challenge and often the tragic duel.

Journalists were the most duel-prone of all; their lives, in Lynn's words, "were often as violent as their columns." Several states tried to legislate against the *code duello*, with some public opinion in favor of reform, but those in the upper strata of antebellum society refused to settle their differences through the courts, and the custom continued.[19]

This impetuous use of pen and pencil, when set against the Cavalier standard of complete self-control, tells a great deal about the relationship between culture and society in the Old South. The writers and editors of that day who created the aristocratic ideal spoke for a generation of self-made men who had struggled to the top by conquering both the natural environment and other men. To solidify their precarious new status, they grasped at the identity of the Cavalier, a model of personal excellence that seemed easily accessible to those who could afford the trappings. At the same time, they vigorously divested themselves of the frontier wildness they associated with the lower classes. But in truth they were not men of composure; rather, their whole lives rested on ambition and conflict. Whether planters, lawyers, or editors, they were often, as Louis Hartz puts it, "very new, very raw, very fierce." Their craving for competition sat just below the surface of their store-bought personalities, stronger and less controllable for being repressed. Believing in their own mythology, they kept these strong passions hidden from themselves, instead projecting their anxieties onto the supposed violence of their slaves and backwoods neighbors. In the end—as some of their twentieth-century descendants would later perceive—the social volcano they thought they were sitting on may not have been as consequential as the secret volcano that rumbled inside.[20]

II

When the war was over, southerners of all social ranks began searching for a rationale to justify their attempt at secession and to explain their current predicament. It did not take them long to find an answer: their main purpose in going to war had been the preservation of an aristocratic way of life. This was the message of a new generation of plantation school novelists, led by Thomas Nelson Page, who took up literary arms almost as soon as the last Federal troops left the region. Further adding to the strength of the Lost Cause myth was the heroic figure of Robert E. Lee, who seemed the perfect example of the superior man antebellum society was supposed to have produced. With the rise of numerous patriotic societies in the 1890s, including the United Confederate Veterans and the United Daughters of the Confederacy, the myth obtained still another advantage it had not enjoyed before the war: an army of full-time perpetuators willing to suspend all disbelief in their effort to embellish history. Whatever proof might once have existed either to substantiate or refute the myth was now safely buried in the past, and the only limits placed on the Cavalier's splendor lay in the ample capacities of the southern imagination and in the requirements of the region's wounded pride.[21]

By 1880, however, a new and quite different spirit, dedicated to the rapid rebuilding of the South in the image of the North, had appeared alongside the aristocratic myth. What the South needed most, proponents of this New South Creed insisted, was to turn away from plantation agriculture in favor of manufacturing and commerce.* In their view, no other section of the country had been blessed with a more abundant store of natural resources; if only southerners could erect enough factories to process those resources at home, the region could soon reap fabulous profits. New South advocates also became strong supporters of national reconciliation, since only the North possessed the capital and technology needed to get this industrial development underway. It was time, they told their followers, to extinguish sectional antagonisms and unite all Americans beneath a common banner of capitalism. In short, theirs was an urban and industrial vision of the South, with progress and modernity the stuff their dreams were made of.[22]

To realize those dreams, New South leaders believed they would have to work a fundamental change in southern character. They would have to create a new personality model for the South based on the dynamic prototype of the northern captain of industry. As they saw it, the antebellum regime had fostered an air of lethargy, along with a glorification of wasteful consumption—both anathema to the architects of the new order. Drive and energy were to be the hallmarks of the new race of capitalists they had in mind; nothing less would permit southerners to beat the Yankees at their own game. Equally important, they thought, was an outlook of thoroughgoing optimism, an almost blind faith in the future essential for inspiring others to take up the difficult task of reconstruction. The man they wanted would be above all a convincing salesman for his community, a perpetual southern booster—precisely the kind of man H. L. Mencken and his followers would excoriate a generation later.[23]

At the same time, these southerners were hardly prepared to jettison their Cavalier heritage. For them, capitalism was a means to an end, but it did not define that end—the latter was to have a distinctively southern cast. Their New Model capitalist was to be a gentleman. A person of impeccable character, he was said to be ambitious, but not acquisitive; energetic, but not predatory; competitive, but never cutthroat. Unlike his northern counterpart, he was a man who subscribed fully to the paternalistic code, who opened factories primarily to provide poor whites with employment, and who cared deeply about their welfare. He was a

---

*The term "New South" has become increasingly difficult to pin down: for most people, the New South period has come to include all of southern history after Appomattox. Following Paul Gaston's suggestion, however, its use here will be quite specific. It will refer to the movement for southern industrialization and its accompanying ideology that flourished from approximately 1877 to the turn of the century. See Gaston, "The 'New South,'" in Arthur S. Link and Rembert W. Patrick, eds., *Writing Southern History*, 317.

philanthropist first and a capitalist second. It must be stressed that to the New South promoters, this portrait of the businessman as gentleman was not mere window-dressing. As Paul Gaston points out, these men clung to the Lost Cause legacy even when its archaic value system impeded the very changes they sought; to them, it was an "emotional and strategic necessity." Thus when Henry W. Grady spoke of the antebellum social order as "feudal in its magnificence" and invoked the Cavalier ideal to explain the course of southern history, he was expressing his conception of what the South really was and where its future development would surely return it.[24]

The New South movement also produced a full-scale mythology of its own. No sooner had the first cotton mills gone up and the first stretches of devastated railroad track been repaired than its spokesmen issued a "declaration of triumph." According to Gaston, southern promotional literature, which had initially taken a realistic view of the region's postwar condition, now boasted "wondrous descriptions of a people who had already achieved, or were on the verge of achieving, all that had been promised as fruits of long toil." Similarly in the sphere of race relations, southern leaders claimed a harmonious adjustment between the freedmen and white society that subsequent events disproved. By 1887, in other words, fantasy had taken over and the New South Creed had become transformed into a myth. As Gaston argues, this shift to mythology was in some respects to hurt the movement, lending it a large measure of self-deception that would infuriate many thoughtful southerners in the generation that followed. But in another sense, perhaps the myth was necessary, initially at least, to help compensate for the region's extreme poverty and helplessness after the Civil War—preventing southerners from giving up hope and allowing them to negotiate the difficult transition from defeat to the beginnings of recovery. Either way, there can be no doubt that the New South myth was widely diffused in the region by the turn of the century.[25]

To comprehend the full meaning of the New South Creed for southern thought, it is important to see it not only as something unique to the South but also as yet another species of Victorianism. Its central tenets represent little more than the essentials of Victorian belief wrapped in southern garb. One finds the same worship of material success, the same insistence on diligence and practicality, the same outlook of steadfast optimism. More striking still, these values associated with industrial progress were joined with and subsumed under the moral code of gentility, in the South as in England. "Things spiritual ranked higher than things material," notes David Hall of Victorian doctrine, "and it was the duty of civilized man to preserve this hierarchy." For southerners, of

course, "things spiritual" took the form of the Cavalier heritage, which
was to ensure that the emerging society would be "cultured," guided by
gentlemanly standards of honor, and run according to the principles of
paternalistic benevolence. That (in theory at least) was the goal of the
New South movement.[26]

Southern Victorianism, however, did differ significantly in terms of
timing. Although elements of Victorian culture could be found in the
antebellum South, a mature version did not appear in the region until the
1880s when Victorianism elsewhere was already on the wane. For this
reason the New South generation did not usually turn to the British
writers of their own time for inspiration, but rather to those who had
dominated the scene three decades earlier when Victorianism in England
was at its height. The aestheticism of Walter Pater or the reforms of
Fabian socialism clearly had less meaning for a people who had just
undergone Reconstruction than did the moral verities of Thomas Carlyle
with his "everlasting yea." Accordingly, New South Victorianism, even
though it flourished well into the twentieth century, corresponds most
closely with what students of British culture would describe as the
"middle Victorianism" of the 1850s. Partly as a consequence of this time
lag, and partly due to the lack of sophistication of most late-nineteenth-
century southern thinkers (whose educational opportunities had typically
been cut short by the Civil War), Victorian culture in the South tended to
be thinner, more derivative, and more simplistic than that found elsewhere. Certainly no important original thought was produced by southerners of this era; rather, their work at times seems almost a caricature as
they strained to imitate the style of the British authors they admired
without fully understanding the philosophic issues at stake. Though they
reproduced the basic structure of Victorian belief, it remained essentially
in skeleton form.[27]

The New South intellectuals most responsible for bringing Victorian
culture to the South came in two waves. The first, appearing about 1880,
consisted of journalists and publicists like Henry W. Grady and Joel
Chandler Harris of the *Atlanta Constitution*, Francis W. Dawson of the
Charleston News and Courier (who was born in England), Henry Watter-
son of the *Louisville Courier-Journal*, and Richard Hathaway Edmonds
of the Baltimore-based *Manufacturer's Record*—all strategically placed
to spread the gospel of progress. By and large, they were public men,
concerned with bringing about rapid improvement in the region's economic fortunes and not with contributing to the store of knowledge
about southern society. The second wave, by contrast, was composed of
young scholars and men of letters who arrived at southern colleges and
universities during the early 1890s. In addition to repeating the themes

of the Grady-style journalists, these New South academics also took a critical look at the sorry state of southern intellectual life and at what they saw as the high potential for instability in the region's social arrangements. Their ranks included Walter Hines Page, Edwin Mims, John Spencer Bassett, William Peterfield Trent, Edgar Gardner Murphy, William Garrott Brown, Philip A. Bruce, Edwin A. Alderman, and Andrew Sledd. Their headquarters, to the extent that they had one, tended to be the nest that the Duke family had feathered for them at Trinity College in North Carolina (now Duke University).[28]

A good example of this latter breed of New South intellectual is Edward Kidder Graham, who served successively as chairman of the English department, dean of the College, and finally as president of the University of North Carolina until his death in 1918. A frequent speaker, like most academic leaders of his day Graham habitually filled his talks with references to eminent men of learning. Yet, in reading through his texts one discovers that, aside from the sainted Woodrow Wilson, few of his American contemporaries are mentioned. Consistently his taste ran to nineteenth-century Victorian prophets, with the names of Carlyle, Matthew Arnold, and Thomas Huxley looming up most often. When moved to quote poetry, Graham turned to Browning and the early Tennyson. Furthermore, Graham's speeches, with certain minor adjustments, could have easily been delivered in the midst of the industrial revolution in England rather than in the twentieth-century South. "There is a spiritual uplift in every sort of material construction," Graham announced over and over, echoing that prime Victorian theme.[29]

Consider, for example, Graham's inaugural address of 1915, a speech whose rhetoric of commercial progress sounds to our ears strangely out of keeping with a solemn academic occasion, but which was greeted as a triumph by his listeners in Chapel Hill:

> And while [the South] is under the thrill of the prosperity within its grasp, it is not primarily because in the past ten years its bank deposits and the capital invested in its manufactures have increased tenfold, that half of the nation's exports originate in its ports, that a world treasure hidden in its oil, gas, coal, iron, waterpower, and agriculture makes certain the fact that the next great expansion in national life will be here, and that here will be "the focusing point of the world's commerce"; the summons that puts the eager and prophetic tone in Southern life today is the consciousness that here under circumstances pregnant with happy destiny men will make once more the experiment of translating prosperity in terms of a great civilization.

Here was an unmistakable specimen of early Victorian optimism, surviving intact into the new century.[30]

The immersion of Graham and his contemporaries in Victorian culture has many sources. For one, most of them were brought up on nineteenth-century British classics. Victorianism was then the staple fare of higher education throughout the United States, and, as Bruce Clayton points out, young southerners took it up with special gusto, showing a particular relish for Arnold and Tennyson. "Precociously absorbed in everything English," Woodrow Wilson, Clayton tells us, "hung a picture of Gladstone above his desk the year he joined the Presbyterian Church and enrolled at Davidson College." London was still setting the world's standards of refinement and intellectual polish, one reason it caught the eye of ambitious southerners in search of a culture. Moreover, for those bent on preserving some semblance of sectional identity in the wake of military failure, England had the further advantage of not being the North. Thus when William Trent founded the *Sewanee Review* in 1892, his stated purpose was not to create a southern imitation of *Scribner's* or the *Atlantic Monthly*, but "to supply the kind of literature that the English quarterlies gave England." But most of all, there was the remarkable convergence between the Victorian concept of the gentleman and the traditional southern identity of the Cavalier. Because of that fact, Victorianism seemed expressly tailored for the South.[31]

III

Along with the role of the gentleman, New South thinkers also perpetuated the underlying ethos of Victorian thought—its radical dichotomy between savagery and civilization. In truth, that dichotomy had long been present in Western culture and had received considerable attention during the eighteenth-century Enlightenment, but with a different moral emphasis. Enlightenment writers had depicted members of primitive societies as "noble savages" or "children of nature," free from the corrupting influence of civilized life. Some ambivalence about savagery had been present, to be sure, but the balance had generally tipped toward savage virtues rather than defects. In America especially one finds late eighteenth-century figures like Benjamin Franklin, Thomas Jefferson, J. Hector St. John de Crèvecoeur, John Bartram, and Philip Freneau avidly celebrating the untutored emotions of the American Indian in contrast to Old World oversophistication. But this hopeful conception of human nature, with its corresponding mistrust of society, could not withstand the tremors that shook Europe in the wake of the French Revolution. Nor could it withstand the conclusions of positivistic naturalism that by the early nineteenth century seemed to many to have shorn man of his claims to divinity, leaving him kin only to the beasts. It was this situation of apparent social and intellectual chaos—a chaos compounded by the dislocations of the industrialization process—that led to the great revivals of evangelical religion both in England and America, and it was out of those revivals that Victorian morality was born.[32]

What the emerging Victorian middle class did, in effect, was to stand the Enlightenment view on its head, placing everything they most valued under the heading of "civilization," while consigning the many things they loathed to the netherworld of "savagery." To the first they assigned all that was moral, pure, rational, advanced, and prosperous; to the second category went all that was backward, animalistic, irrational, and poor. This embrace of civilization, writes Michael Timko, along with "the emphasis on the qualities of man that distinguish him from 'natural' creatures and show him to be 'civilized,' moral, or ethical," became their "positive answer" to the crisis of the early nineteenth century. "This is the note that connects such disparate figures as Mill and Carlyle, Huxley and Tennyson," he explains. "It is the note that constitutes the Victorianism of Victorian literature; it is the essence of the charter of style of the period, the one response of all the writers that embodies the paradigmatic experience of their time."[33]

Of the many distinctions between the two categories, the chief one was the inability of the savage to master his instinctual drives. "The savage," according to John Stuart Mill in 1836, "cannot bear to sacrifice, for any purpose, the satisfaction of his individual will. His impulses cannot bend to his calculations." With its members thus at the mercy of their passions, savage society was ravaged by a "state of perpetual conflict" in which everyone became habituated to "the spectacle of harshness, rudeness, and violence, to the struggle of one indomitable will against another, and to the alternate suffering and infliction of pain." Only civilized man possessed the faculty of rational self-control (part of his "moral" or "spiritual" faculty, Mill thought), allowing him to cooperate with others to reap the benefits of technology. Even those later nineteenth-century writers like Matthew Arnold who chafed a bit at the restraints of Victorian moralism still upheld these basic tenets of the dichotomy. For Arnold the first need was always to achieve that "discipline by which alone man is enabled to rescue his life from thralldom to the passing moment and to his bodily senses," although once that discipline was in place Arnold hoped to temper it with the "sweetness and light" of high culture. In this sense Arnold was merely refurbishing the fundamental Victorian precepts: the "spiritual perfection" he advocated was founded, as he put it, upon "the growth and predominance of our humanity proper, as distinguished from our animality."[34]

This dichotomy, in turn, accounts for the inordinate stress Victorians placed on personal morality. There was a potential for savagery inside every individual, they believed. To maintain civilization, that potential must be strictly curbed, and eliminated if possible. Children must be taught at the earliest age to repress feelings that were "selfish, mean, or destructive"—those feelings that made up, in other words, the animal part of human nature. Once established, that repression must never be relaxed. Nothing illustrates this imperative better than Robert Louis Stevenson's famous novella of 1885, *Dr. Jekyll and Mr. Hyde*, in which the eminently respectable Dr. Jekyll transforms himself into an alter ego, the pleasure-seeking Mr. Hyde, in order to experience a few of the indulgences he had always denied himself. The experiment soon goes awry, however, culminating when Hyde commits a succession of unusually sadistic crimes purely on impulse. Jekyll, who had always assumed that he could regain control at will, finally resorts to suicide to stop the insatiable Hyde from usurping him forever. The lesson is clear: a civilized man must not unleash the animal within, even for a moment. As Masao Miyoshi comments: "In most societies men are not required to suppress the '*je*' [or hidden self] totally, and they agree to curb it. But in Jekyll's world, the '*je*' must be ruthlessly suppressed."[35]

This perpetual threat explains why the Victorians had such an excessive fear of sexuality. To them the world was filled with what one writer called "furious provocatives to unbridled sensuality and riotous animalism," any of which might undermine their elaborate efforts at self-mastery. One must accordingly drape the legs of chairs and pianos and in some instances carefully separate the works of male and female authors on library shelves to block out dangerous stimuli. Within marriage, where sexual relations usually could not be avoided, they could at least be minimized. If seventeenth- and eighteenth-century marriage manuals typically encouraged sexual pleasure (though in moderation), those published in the nineteenth century counseled separate bedrooms and suggested sex solely for procreation. The true purposes of marriage, warned a minister writing in one such book, "can be fulfilled only when the two parties in the relation are agreed to *make no provision for the flesh* in thought, desire, or practice." Victorian families doubtless departed somewhat from this advice in actual life, but again the point is that this sort of "purity" remained the widely held ideal.[36]

Plainly, this obsession with maintaining moral purity had a social dimension as well. Having achieved respectability, the middle class was taking no chances. "An unguarded look, a word, a gesture, a picture, or a novel," notes G. M. Young, "might plant a seed of corruption in the most innocent heart, and the same word or gesture might betray a lingering affinity with the class below." As for the lower classes, though Victorian thinkers often expressed optimism that they might in time be uplifted to a civilized existence, few expected this to happen soon. Indeed, when speaking of the working class most emphasis was placed on their sensuality, drunkenness, spendthrift habits, and imminent potential for violent revolution. Arnold, for instance, may have campaigned for better common schools to raise the general level of culture, but his descriptive passages on what he called the "populace" reveal his deep fear of how these "raw and unkindled masses" through their "monster processions . . . and forcible irruptions into the parks" would bring about "anarchy." In the United States, where social mobility was presumably easier and a long-standing democratic political tradition existed, the social implications of the Victorian dichotomy were just as stringent. "While Victorian didacticism assumed that everyone would benefit by acquiring Victorian culture," writes Daniel Howe of nineteenth-century America, "the stereotypes supposed that some people were incapable of doing so, at least beyond the elementary stage."[37]

Of course the basic aim was not new. People have struggled to master their emotions for centuries, and they have always held some notion of what was civilized and what was not. The difference lies in the Victorians' struggle to build an unassailable wall between themselves and the uglier aspects of life, and in their pre-Freudian conviction that human evil— what the twentieth century would call the unconscious and preconscious mind—could be held at bay by a firm act of will. Here was the basis of that incorrigible naiveté, that willful innocence, so commonly associated with Victorian life.[38]

In the case of the New South intellectuals, the Victorian dichotomy showed up most often in their tendency to divide the South into, as Bruce Clayton has put it, "two polar camps of the rational and irrational." The first camp naturally included the remnant of the old planter class as well as the growing middle-class elite—those actively involved in building the new order, such as lawyers, teachers, and the enlightened captains of industry. These were the gentlemen George W. Cable had in mind when he coined the term "Silent South." To him they were "brave, calm, thoughtful, broad-minded, dispassionate, sincere, and in the din of boisterous error . . . , all too mute." Always rational in their perception of the South's true interests, in their treatment of blacks, and in their attitudes toward the North, they constituted the nucleus of civilization in the South.[39]

On the other side of the dividing line stood the southern masses: the mill hands, dirt farmers, mechanics, and sharecroppers who formed the overwhelming majority of the southern population. Bigoted, ignorant, violent, and poor, they had a way of making themselves all too audible to suit the New South intellectuals. It was this group that had revived the barbarous practice of lynching, elected race-baiting demagogues to high political office, resorted to perpetual mayhem and cruelty, and launched vicious attacks on academic freedom. The height of their irrationality came during the Populist crusade of the 1890s, which the intellectuals viewed as an alarming portent of outright class warfare in the South. With the exceptions of William E. Dodd and Josephus Daniels, not one of them displayed the least sympathy for Populism, not even in its milder "Bryanesque" configuration.[40]

In fact, despite their commitment to calm rationality, these men became notably intemperate when discussing the behavior of the southern common folk. The masses, wrote John Spencer Bassett in 1902, "are not yet out of the stage of uncultured animalism." Bassett's colleague at Trinity College, John C. Kilgo, agreed. Lynching, he claimed, stemmed from a basic defect in the southern personality, its excess "emotionalism." The only permanent cure for this "temporary social insanity" was a thorough overhaul of the southern character, rendering it "less sensitive and excitable." Kilgo never specified which southerners he was talking about, but his friend Andrew Sledd was more direct: "Our lynchings are the work of our lower and lowest classes. What these classes are is hardly comprehensible to one who has not lived among them and dealt with them." Sledd, with his perception controlled by the Victorian ethos, wrote these words in total innocence of the malice implied; he was more amazed than anyone when a number of Georgia Populists took offense and succeeded in having him fired from Emory. Nor was Edwin Mims aware of his bias when he observed of a pair of newlyweds on a train in Arkansas: "It is interesting to watch them. They are ignorant, uncultured people, and marriage can mean but little to them. What a low conception of life they have! And so it is with marriage as with all other good things in the world."[41]

However, the New South generation did not pronounce the situation hopeless. Like good Victorians, they put their trust in industry and education to dampen southern emotionalism and dispel the atmosphere of social animosity. These two forces, Kilgo promised in a moment of ex traordinary optimism, could not only stop lynchings but all "partisanships, social distinctions, and religious antagonisms" as well. Work itself could be therapeutic in this sense; in Edgar Gardner Murphy's words, "The world at work is the world at peace." The intellectuals also took note of how the Populist uprising spread like wildfire among the rural population but skipped over the new class of mill workers. The countryside, it seemed, was full of bitter discontent, while the prosperous industrial society of their dreams, they felt sure, would be conflict-free.[42]

If the New South intellectuals could envision a segment of the lower-class white population some day crossing the line from savagery to civilization, they entertained no such hopes for southern blacks. On the contrary, the Victorian dichotomy became one of the chief props behind their willingness to support legally enforced segregation. In their eyes, preserving white supremacy was never a matter of regional tradition or social expediency; it was an ineradicable moral necessity. Edgar Gardner Murphy, for example, an Alabama minister turned social activist, was regarded by his fellow southern liberals as one of the Negro's "best friends"—a paternalist whose heart went out to those who were "helpless and defenseless." Yet, in writing of blacks, Murphy spoke of the "dark, vague, uncertain masses,—half-pitiful, half-terrifying, free forever from the white man's mastery, yet never free from the brooding and unyielding heritage of the black man's barbaric past." Because of that "barbaric past," Murphy argued, any attempt to break down the color line in the South would almost certainly result in black domination, with "many of those reversions of the standards of political and social life which have been exhibited in Hayti and San Domingo." A southerner like Murphy who cared about upholding those standards could never let that tragedy happen.[43]

Murphy's well-known program for achieving racial harmony in the South centered on education. Since black schools represented the first "upbuilding contact" between the "life of the civilized with the life of the uncivilized," he contended, white southerners could ignore them only at great peril. By education for blacks Murphy did not mean fancy book-learning, but rather a training in those skills, moral and industrial, that black children would need to get through life. Foremost of these was punctuality, "one of the rudimentary assumptions of civilization" and a subject that could inspire Murphy to his most eloquent passages:

> Is it not of importance to realize what a difference lies just here
> between the state of the savage and the state of the citizen? There
> is a moral idea and a moral achievement in the notion of punc-
> tuality, and the rural primary school stands for that.

After punctuality came order, which taught the child that "everything has its place" and that "even standing and sitting . . . are to be performed under the control and direction of another." In these and in the additional "virtues" he listed, Murphy's purpose was transparent; he wished to condition blacks for a permanent role of subservience. Even though he hoped to develop a Negro middle class to serve as a conduit for "civilized" values, his belief in the genetic inferiority of blacks was unshakable. Yet there can also be no doubt that his writings represented the most advanced southern racial thought of his times, a fact that testifies to the enormous power of nineteenth-century dualism in the South.[44]

Thus in the early years of the twentieth century a potent, highly tenacious complex of ideas had emerged that might best be referred to as New South thought. At its center was the venerable antebellum concept of the southern gentleman as the exemplar of self-control. But the gentleman's status had been somewhat democratized; while the Old South had tended to limit that rank to members of the planter class, in the New South middle-class citizens who demonstrated the prerequisite virtues (or appeared to demonstrate them) could now claim it. Although New South thinkers genuinely wanted to "uplift" the lower class of whites, they remained contemptuous and fearful of them. As for blacks, New South intellectuals regarded them with a mixture of traditional paternalism and Victorian moralism, sympathetic with their plight but preoccupied with preserving a strict separation between civilization and savagery.

"Civilization," in fact, was the key word, for beneath the entire complex of New South thought was the intellectuals' passionate concern for upholding some measure of civilization in a society they believed woefully undercivilized and bedeviled by conflicts that could tear it apart at any moment. This specter reappeared constantly throughout Murphy's major book, *Problems of the Present South*, and was stated in summary form in the conclusion:

> The vast stretches of rural territory, . . . the prevailing isolation, the few railways, the poor roads, the absence of strong centres of social organization, the remaining poverty, the comparative lack of diversity in industrial life, the schools,—inadequate and not effectively distributed,—and last, but not least, the two races dividing the lands, dividing the churches, dividing the schools—races to whom coexistence seems imperative, but between whom coalescence would be intolerable; here indeed is a task for stout hearts, a task in the presence of which men—if they are ever to accomplish anything— must learn to know, to think clearly, to be patient, and to love.

There was much truth in this diagnosis and much sincere benevolent intent as well. Yet the paradox remained that the fundamental cultural assumptions New South thinkers employed in viewing their society tended to perpetuate the very divisions of class and race they deplored. Their successors after 1919, accordingly, would have to break with the Victorian ethos first; only then could they begin finding solutions to the region's multitude of social problems.[45]

PART ONE

THREE SOUTHERN
POST-VICTORIANS

It would seem at first sight that Ulrich B. Phillips, Broadus Mitchell, and Ellen Glasgow had little or nothing in common. Their interests, modes of vision, writing styles, and personal lives could not have been more different. Phillips, the son of a less than successful storekeeper from the clay hills of Georgia, made his mark as a premier historian of the Old South, defending both the plantation system and, to a certain extent, the institution of slavery itself. Mitchell, on the other hand, lambasted the old cotton plantation as the primary cause of the region's downfall; he placed his hopes on the rise of industry to bring the South back into the American mainstream. In direct contrast to Phillips, moreover, Mitchell grew up on a university campus and never received more than a passing taste of southern rural life. Ellen Glasgow was also a city dweller. Born to an upper-class Virginia family that had retained its wealth despite the war, she wandered into a career as a novelist as part of her personal rebellion against the designated role of the Southern Lady. Treading a narrow line between irony and sentimentality, often lapsing into the latter, she attempted to reconcile the aristocratic values she had inherited and the demands of the modern world. Thus to all appearances the only thing uniting these three was the accident of birth that placed them in the same approximate chronological generation and brought them to the peaks of their respective careers just after World War I.

Yet one important similarity does emerge if we consider them as intellectuals, for all three clearly exhibit the traits associated with post-Victorian thought. In their work one finds a definite effort to break with the Victorian (or New South) mentality that they felt was inadequate to the task of rebuilding southern society and culture. They wished above all to free themselves from the romantic and chauvinistic view of southern history they identified with their predecessors. To accomplish this aim, they reached out for "realism" in one form or another, usually through the aid of some currently fashionable, all-inclusive style of thought encountered early in their careers. Phillips applied the Progressive cult of managerial efficiency to his studies of the antebellum South; Mitchell became a militant Socialist; and Glasgow turned to Darwinism as a virtual substitute for the teachings of the Bible. In each case the objective was to break through the limitations their southern birth had imposed on them, to view the region's problems in the cold light of modern science, and to establish contact with the most advanced thinking of their age.

What makes them post-Victorians, however, is not just their quest for realism but the fact that they ultimately failed to achieve their goals. Regardless of the potentially revolutionary ideas they had acquired, Phillips, Mitchell, and Glasgow could not manage to shake off the nineteenth-century values they had been raised on. The Cavalier myth, with its notion of the South's essential innocence from evil or guilt, remained firmly entrenched in the substratum of their minds and continued to control their life's work. They had grown up too close to the great trauma of Civil War and Reconstruction to escape the strong pull of regional chauvinism. For this and other reasons, they could not bring themselves to part with the mythology that gave them their principal identity as southerners and that embodied the cultural values most dear to them. Progressivism, socialism, and Darwinism—to the extent that they truly absorbed them—may have provided some perspective on their society, but none of these theories proved sufficient to overcome their most deeply grounded personal beliefs.

It is this peculiar tension that marks these writers and others like them as southern post-Victorians. Those who came before them in the saga of the South's intellectual development had by and large accepted New South ideology at face value; those who came immediately after them were better able to secure a beachhead in Modernist culture. But those who fall into the post-Victorian category could neither advance nor fully retreat. As Louis Rubin has written of Ellen Glasgow, "she never understood *what* it was that was displacing the old. She never comprehended the nature of the new." That was their common dilemma. It was their fate to be trapped in an intellectual no man's land between the thought of two centuries, a position that sometimes augmented, but more often crippled, their final accomplishments.[1]

CHAPTER 2

ULRICH B. PHILLIPS:

THE OLD SOUTH AS THE NEW

Most readers nowadays regard Ulrich B. Phillips as the epitome of Old South Bourbonism. Phillips, they say, was a fine historical craftsman who mastered his manuscript sources thoroughly, but whose manifest racism and overwhelming bias toward the planter class irretrievably marred his conclusions. The attack began in 1943 with Richard Hofstadter. "While Phillips certainly did not originate the plantation legend of the Old South," Hofstadter charged, "he did his best to continue it." A "reverence for the values and standards of the old planter class" pervaded Phillips's life and work, agreed Stanley Elkins. Even Wendell Holmes Stephenson, a writer on southern historiography highly sympathetic to Phillips, described him as one who "surveyed the southern scene from the hospitable atmosphere of the 'big house'; a patrician who saw only fringes of friction on a tranquil tradition."[1]

Plainly there is much truth to this view. Phillips's insistence on dedicating his second book "TO THE DOMINANT CLASS OF THE SOUTH," despite the strong objections of his publisher, gives ample evidence of his affections. Yet a close study of Phillips suggests that his critics have overlooked the most persistent theme of his work—his desire to place the South in the vanguard of progress. Most of all, they have failed to interpret Phillips within the context of his times. When Phillips is seen in historical perspective, as Eugene D. Genovese has pointed out, his social viewpoint is "neither nostalgic, nor reactionary, nor unreconstructed, but . . . cautiously forward-looking, humanely conservative, and deeply committed to social and racial justice." With his Progressive outlook, Phillips was prepared to turn a critical eye on the Old South when necessary. Young southern intellectuals in the 1920s looked to him, not as a bulwark of the old guard, but as an exemplar of what southern scholarship could produce at its finest. In brief, Phillips was a far more complicated thinker than his liberal detractors have usually depicted him; his role in the South's intellectual history warrants reassessment.[2]

To begin with, his bias toward the plantation system notwithstanding, Phillips deserves to be included among the New South school of historians who held sway over the field of southern history during the first two decades of this century. Led by Philip A. Bruce and Holland Thompson, these men spent much of their prose celebrating the supposed arrival of full-scale industrialization in the South, but, as Paul Gaston notes, their foremost concern lay always with the question of moral character. Ruefully they admitted that antebellum planters had made a cult of leisure, until the entire region had acquired a reputation for urbane inactivity. Now, they insisted, all that had changed. The South's great success in rebuilding its economy after the war along the lines of northern industry had proved, once and for all, that southerners were just as capable of hard work, thrift, and enterprise as other Americans. "Most of the real Southern colonels are dead," Thompson assured his readers, "and the others are too busy running plantations or cotton mills to spend much time discussing genealogy, making pretty speeches, or talking about their honor." The old affability was gone, he reported; these new captains of southern industry were "cold, hard, and astute, for the New South has developed some perfect specimens of the type whose natural habitat had been supposed to be Ulster or the British Midlands."[3]

This approach to southern history posed one major problem. In their effort to overturn the myth of the lazy South, writers in this vein were forced to disown the whole antebellum period as an unfortunate aberration from the South's true development. Slavery, they believed, had been the main culprit. Unscrupulous Yankee traders had fastened the slave system on the South, leaving southerners with the unhappy alternatives of either continuing slavery or coping with the dire racial dilemmas associated with an immense population of emancipated blacks. Reluctantly, according to the New South historians, the planters had chosen the former course and had been partially corrupted as a result. Thus the typical New South account would condemn slavery, castigate Old South indolence, add an obligatory compliment to antebellum "grace and charm," half apologize for secession, and then proceed as if the real history of the South began in 1880. In this fashion, two and a half centuries of southern development were cast to oblivion.[4]

Phillips's achievement was to reverse this historiographic process by showing that the antebellum period could be interpreted within the framework of New South values. His exhaustive research in plantation

1. Ulrich B. Phillips (circa 1930)
Courtesy Yale University Archives, Yale University Library

archives had convinced him that the Old South did not deserve its stigma as a land of industrial slackness and that the plantation system in particular had been badly maligned. He did not see the plantation as a latter-day version of the feudal manor, but rather as a highly efficient economic unit where southerners practiced "the application of manufacturing or capitalistic methods to agricultural production." Far from being an idle aristocrat, the antebellum planter had been a veritable captain of industry, a man whose primary claim to distinction rested not on his pedigree but on his remarkable skill as a manager. Phillips thus carried the New South argument about southern character to its utmost limits by applying it not only to the New South but to the Old South as well. The old regime in his hands turned into the embodiment of traditional Yankee virtues.[5]

In this way, although he surely had no such intention, Phillips became the first major southern intellectual to challenge the Cavalier myth. Like other New South writers, Phillips felt a keen sense of sectional chauvinism, and his emotional ties to the myth were strong. His books are strewn with the standard references to "the graciousness and charm of the antebellum civilization." Nevertheless, his vision of the Old South stood at odds with the myth at several key points. The efficiency-minded capitalist Phillips depicted at the center of plantation society, whatever his merits, could not be construed in any fashion as a romantic, devil-may-care aristocrat; nor did he eschew the profit motive at all times as did the planter of legend. Phillips may well have done his best to continue the plantation legend, as Hofstadter contends, but the net effect of his work in the long run was to help undermine it.[6]

Phillips was born in 1877 to a middle-class family in the small Georgia farming town of La Grange. His early years appear to have been uneventful. In 1891, however, his parents, evidently recognizing his intellectual gifts, sent him to a special preparatory school at Tulane. He attended the University of Georgia, where he received both his B.A. and M.A. under the aegis of John T. McPherson, a disciple of Herbert Baxter Adams. McPherson endowed Phillips with a lifelong zeal for "scientific history." For his Ph.D., Phillips chose Columbia University and its acknowledged master of southern studies, William Archibald Dunning. Phillips chafed somewhat under Dunning's preoccupation with political history and much preferred the social and geographical approach of Frederick Jackson Turner, whom he had encountered during a summer session at the University of Chicago in 1898. Turner's concept of sectionalism, he believed, was far more useful than Dunning's staid constitutionalism in making sense of the South's distinctive development. Still, his prizewinning dissertation, *Georgia and States Rights*, clearly bears Dunning's stamp.[7]

With his doctorate in hand, Phillips in 1902 made a fateful decision. Rather than returning to his native region or remaining in one of the conservative academic citadels of the Northeast, such as Columbia, Phillips plunged himself into a hotbed of Progressivism by accepting an offer from the University of Wisconsin. The presence of Turner, along with the sizable collection of materials on southern history available there, seem to have been the chief attractions. To be sure, Progressivism was a transitional movement within American cultural history and shared many traits with Victorianism. Nonetheless, with its strong bent toward empiricism as opposed to formal theory, its tendency to seek causal factors in the social environment rather than in personal character, and its sympathies toward social democracy, Progressive thought differed significantly from the characteristic beliefs of the nineteenth century. This was especially true of the midwestern variety that Phillips encountered at Wisconsin.[8]

Yet Phillips had no trouble whatever adjusting to the intellectual environment he found in Madison. He immediately struck up friendships with the high priests of Progressivism assembled there, including John R. Commons, Richard T. Ely, Charles McCarthy, and, of course, Turner. These friendships were as much professional as personal: Phillips had many common intellectual interests with these men, especially their concern for "industrial history." To the Progressives, that term meant something far broader than the study of factory production. How men worked—their routines, techniques, and relative efficiency—was thought to be among the most important ingredients in establishing their styles of life. Above all, the goal was to get away from the conventional focus on political and legal events, which the Progessives regarded as mere surface manifestations, to find the true economic and social wellsprings of American life. To this end, Phillips collaborated with Commons and several other reform-minded economists in editing the ten-volume *A Documentary History of American Industrial Society*. His *Plantation and Frontier Documents*, the first two volumes of the series, was designed to show how the new methods could be applied to the study of the South. Although he never fully adopted his colleagues' sympathetic view of trade unions and labor legislation, Phillips, while at Wisconsin, was open to the most advanced thought of his day. The Progressive theories acquired during his stay there would remain with him for the rest of his career.[9]

Phillips conducted his fervent defense of the antebellum plantation system along such Progressive lines. He began by rejecting the standard portrait of Old South life, which had centered on shiftless, ill-trained slaves performing their tasks in haphazard fashion while their helpless masters looked on in kindly indulgence. For Phillips, the key word was "routine." Antebellum southerners may not have exhibited the frantic pace of the Yankee peddler, he argued, but they did understand the need for routinized labor practices, the very basis of modern industrial efficiency. "Just as in the case of the factory system, which of course is entirely analogous as regards labor organization, the success of industry [on the plantation] depended upon its regularity and the constant repetition of similar tasks," he wrote. Over and over he quoted the maxim of Richard Corbin, a Virginia planter Phillips especially admired, who put the matter in a nutshell: "'The ways of industry are constant and regular, not to be in a hurry at one time and do nothing at another, but to be always usefully and steadily employed.'" In other words, southerners were not naturally slow of tempo or adverse to hard work, as the legend of their supposed laziness had it; they merely knew how to pace themselves for maximum productivity.[10]

At each opportunity Phillips implied that the Old South, in industrial matters, had been not backward but ahead of its time. It had in fact succeeded in anticipating Frederick W. Taylor's concept of scientific management by nearly a century. For example, Phillips often spoke of the plantation slave-gang system as a species of "time-work" and the task system as "piece-work." With obvious relish he swooped down on a series of articles in the *Southern Planter* in 1842 by a certain H. W. Vick whose "analysis of stance and movement" savored "of the most advanced industrial study in the twentieth century." Indeed, Phillips claimed, it was the incredible "routine efficiency" of the system that proved its undoing when the resulting overproduction periodically glutted the cotton market.[11]

Phillips drove this point home by including lengthy, detailed descriptions of plantation-work routines in all his books. As these passages wind on, occupying scores upon scores of pages, the list of chores to be done becomes almost staggering:

> From the end of May until as late as need be in July the occurrence of every rain sent all hands to setting the tobacco seedlings in their hills at top speed as long as the ground stayed wet enough to give prospect of success in the process. In the interims, the corn cultivation was continued, hay was harvested in the clover fields and the meadows, and the tobacco fields first planted began to be scraped with hoe and plow. The latter half of June was devoted mainly to the harvesting of small grain with the two reaping machines and twelve cradles; and for the following two months the main labor force was divided between threshing the wheat and plowing, hoeing, worming and suckering the tobacco, while the expert Daniel was day after day steadily topping the plants. In late

August the plows began breaking the fallow fields for wheat. Early in September the cutting and housing of tobacco began, and continued at intervals in good weather until the middle of October. . . . Two days in December were devoted to the housing of ice; and Christmas week, as well as Easter Monday and a day or two in summer or fall, brought leisure.

This account of a tobacco plantation in Virginia was repeated for each major southern staple, leaving the reader with the clear impression that life on a typical southern plantation consisted of continuous regulated motion with free time always a rarity.[12]

Although he realized how thoroughly labor-intensive plantation practice actually was, Phillips even tried to show that the Old South had kept in step with technological advance. He seized every chance to point to the planters' use of machinery, often straining to make his point and lavishing far more attention on the subject than it deserved. The chapter on cotton cultivation in *American Negro Slavery*, to take one instance, begins with a page and a half description of the gin house and baling press, which Phillips terms "the outstanding features of the landscape" on the upland plantation. However, only on the rice and sugar plantations, with their elaborate irrigation systems and refineries, could he find truly convincing evidence of a commitment to technology. Here he could discuss sluice gates, pounding mills, clarifiers, retorts, vacuum pans, and similar equipment to his heart's content, crushing all doubt that the antebellum captains of industry could cope with the most sophisticated apparatus of their era when necessary.[13]

Phillips found the old plantation system so modern and attractive, in fact, that he recommended it as a prime cure for the South's twentieth-century ills. Allowing the former slaves to shift for themselves as tenant farmers or sharecroppers after Reconstruction had been a dreadful mistake, he believed, since the "ignorance, indolence, and instability" of the average black would always "prevent him from managing his own labor in an efficient way." This pernicious arrangement was the root cause of postwar southern poverty in Phillips's view: "It is a dead loss for a good manager to have no managing to do. It is also a dead loss for a laborer who needs management to have no management." The only solution he could foresee was to restore the plantation on the basis of Negro wage labor secured through long-term contracts—"voluntary indenture," as he called it. If someone had charged that this proposal sounded suspiciously like a return to slavery, Phillips would doubtless have answered that his plan would at least raise southern blacks out of their current state of slothful penury into steady and gainful employment.[14]

This last point suggests one additional Old South virtue that Phillips commended to his own age—the tradition of plantation paternalism. Genovese, indeed, maintains that it was the patriarchal ethos above all that Phillips wished to preserve in southern life, that capitalism to him was no more than an adjunct to paternalism. Certainly Phillips placed great emphasis on the planters' observance of noblesse oblige. Equally certain, that precapitalistic set of customs, which held the master responsible for the welfare of his sick and aging workers, undercut the kind of hard-nosed business practice Phillips wanted the South to follow. How can we explain this apparent contradiction?[15]*

The answer is that Phillips saw no antagonism whatsoever between the patriarchal ethos and the profit motive. Rather, for him paternalism was indispensable to the proper functioning of plantation capitalism. Adopting a fatherly concern for one's slaves was the only feasible method of labor control available to antebellum planters, if they wished to preserve the morale of their work force. Phillips constantly repeated his formula: the "successful management" of slaves necessitated "a blending of foresight and firmness with kindliness and patience." Everything depended

---

*In his various pieces on Phillips, Eugene D. Genovese claims Phillips saw the antebellum regime as one in transition from an essentially "capitalistic enterprise" to a genuine "paternalistic community." According to Genovese, Phillips understood that the planters were rapidly becoming a full-fledged "ruling class" in the prebourgeois sense of the term, with their paternalistic ideology shaped by the obligations of the master-slave relationship rather than the ethos of profit-making. To be sure, Genovese is aware that Phillips never engaged in such analysis explicitly, but he argues that the evidence Phillips marshaled and the manner in which he presented it all lead unmistakably in this direction. "If he [Phillips] failed to draw the necessary conclusions from his extraordinary lifetime efforts," Genovese maintains, "we are under no compulsion to follow suit." Genovese is also aware that Phillips tried hard "to prove the Old South a capitalist society," but this, he believes, was mainly a tactical maneuver—the only way Phillips could get the ear of his generation for his espousal of patriarchal values.

My disagreement with this reading of Phillips is chiefly one of emphasis, although a crucial emphasis. Genovese thinks Phillips viewed capitalism as an accessory to paternalism, but in fact the opposite was true. Phillips exulted in depicting his southerners as hard-nosed, ambitious managers, not as models of benevolence; he saw them as captains of industry, not Lords of the Manor. Genovese himself is forced to acknowledge this fact on several occasions, as when he notes with surprise how Phillips, "having told us . . . that the Southern regime produced men of a special, high-spirited type, . . . proceeded to insist that their ultimate decisions would flow from economic calculation of the crassest sort." Most of all, I would contend that the focus must ultimately rest on Phillips's concern for efficiency and the discipline of work, and not on capitalism or paternalism as such, since that was always uppermost in Phillips's own mind, at least until the latter part of his career.

See Genovese, "Race and Class in Southern History," 347, 349, 353–54, 357, as well as Genovese's introduction to the paperback edition of *American Negro Slavery* (Baton Rouge, 1966), vii–xxi.

on the correct "blending." "The ideal in slave control," he wrote, "may perhaps be symbolized by an iron hand in a velvet glove. Sometimes the velvet was lacking, but sometimes the iron. Failure was not far to seek in either case." Those masters who performed this task well were rewarded with few disciplinary problems and great prosperity; those who did not met with continual instances of slave resistance and runaways, which could eventually lead to bankruptcy. Implicit in this view, of course, was Phillips's belief that blacks were inherently childlike in their dispositions and would respond accordingly to paternal treatment.[16]

To Phillips, this balancing act between firmness and kindness was closely akin to an art form. He would appraise the managerial skills of those planters and overseers whose records he examined with the eye of a connoisseur. There is the pointed story of John Palfrey of Louisiana, whose plantation account book revealed frequent whippings, truancies, and recurrent financial disasters during his first ten years as a master. Ultimately, however, Palfrey found the right touch. In Phillips's words, his eventual economic success "plainly tells that Palfrey had learned to be a much more considerate and effective master than the record of his runaways indicates for his first Louisiana decade." By contrast, a Georgia overseer, Rufus King, drew Phillips's praise from the start for his discretion in meting out punishments, his use of varied incentives, and his genuine concern for his workers' health, all of which resulted in a "brisk and willing performance" by the slaves. Phillips also liked to cite the example of Thomas S. Dabney, an "ideal" master, whose "continued prosperity proved his benign discipline effective."[17]

Nor was this advocacy of paternalism incompatible with Phillips's commitment to Progressive reform. Like others of his generation, Phillips was troubled by labor violence and the worst abuses of the factory system. Paternalism, by stressing the mutual obligations between employer and worker, seemed to speak directly to these problems. Labor relations in the old plantation regime, he delighted in reminding his readers, did not suffer from "that curse of impersonality and indifference which too commonly prevails in the factories of the present world." But whether or not the rest of the world chose to adopt these lessons, Phillips believed the racial makeup of the region's unskilled work force made them "essential" for the South.[18]*

---

*By the late 1920s, when he began to come under the spell of southern mythology, Phillips's portrait of paternalism came much closer to the plantation legend. Now he spoke of how slaves were "cherished" as "loving if lowly friends" and of how "benignity" was taken "somewhat as a matter of course." This sort of language does not appear in his earlier writings. See Phillips, *Life and Labor*, 214.

Thus Phillips's position came full circle: to place southern agriculture on a modern business basis, the captains of southern industry must resort to paternalism. To realize its most cherished objectives, the New South must recapture the values of the Old South. That, Phillips thought, was the only sure path to progress and reform.

I

Item number one on the liberals' bill of charges against Phillips has always been his benighted stand on race. Throughout his career, Phillips's attitude toward blacks remained highly condescending, if indulgent. As he wrote in 1904: "The average negro has many of the characteristics of a child, and must be guided and governed, and often guarded against himself, by a sympathetic hand." To his critics such a statement supplied incontrovertible proof that Phillips was at best a bigoted Old South Bourbon bent on resurrecting slavery.[19]

To judge Phillips this way is to ignore the historical environment in which he worked. Despite the impulse for reform that arose during the Progressive era, that period also witnessed the most virulent display of racism in American history. Nor was that display limited to the South—the anti-Negro pronouncements and calls for immigration restriction that issued from certain "respectable" circles in New York and Boston sounded almost as shrill a note as those heard in Dixie. To most reformers of that age racism did not necessarily violate the spirit of Progressivism. As they saw it, the campaign for racial purity was itself a reform. Keeping the Negro and others of dubious skin color at the margins of American life was indispensable to realizing the Progressive vision of a wholesome, homogeneous society.[20]

Moreover, until the mid-1920s, the notion of racial inequality represented conventional wisdom in academic circles as well. Categorical statements on Anglo-Saxon superiority appeared regularly in the works of the liberal economists Phillips collaborated with at Wisconsin, as well as in scientific journals, textbooks, and doctoral dissertations. Within the discipline of American history, highly regarded northern writers like James Ford Rhodes, John W. Burgess, and William Archibald Dunning may have evaluated the Civil War and Reconstruction from a pro-Union standpoint, yet each made clear his belief that blacks were genetically inferior to whites and that no evil could match the loss of white control over southern society. The anti-Negro bias so apparent in Phillips, then, was no more or less than the standard fare of his time. In fact, when compared with his fellow southerners in this respect, Phillips comes out looking much like a reformer.[21]

Far from being "solid" in its attitudes, the white South during most of this period was divided into two main camps on race, the bitter-end extremists and the New South liberals. The extremists, who usually held the upper hand until the First World War, consisted of three groups: political demagogues who made racism their bread and butter; survivors of the old planter class; and a number of highly vociferous polemical writers obsessed with the need for race purity, including Thomas Dixon, Ernest Sevier Cox, and Charles Carroll. These men believed that the very social fabric of the South stood in mortal danger as a result of emancipation and its aftermath. Blacks, they assumed, harbored intense animal passions that could easily be aroused by political agitators or sexual temptation, leading to general chaos. The strict controls of slavery had in their view effectively prevented that dire possibility, but now, with slavery gone, the door was left open to black criminality and aggression. To counter this threat the extremists took upon themselves the task of warning other southerners of the Negro's true nature, mounting, as George Fredrickson puts it, "an evangelical effort to transform the stereotype of the Negro" from the kindly image of Uncle Tom to the menace of the black beast. In addition, they advocated the strongest conceivable methods, including lynching, to keep the dread "beast" in his place.[22]

To a large extent, the liberals—or "moderate-liberals" as Phillips preferred to describe them—found their voice on this issue in response to the extremists. Beginning with New South prophets like Henry Grady and J. L. M. Curry and continuing down to Progressive activists such as Edgar Gardner Murphy and W. D. Weatherford, they chose to emphasize the black man's purported childlike qualities, focusing on the first half of the traditional child-beast dichotomy. In general, their program was built on an updated version of paternalism in which whites would offer blacks help, guidance, and protection in exchange for a commitment to the New South values of thrift and hard work, as well as a continued subservience. Often divided on the question of disfranchisement, the liberals all vigorously condemned lynching, supported Tuskegee-style industrial education, and promised economic opportunity for blacks with special talents. If pressed for a long-range prognosis, most liberals would have predicted a very gradual uplifting of the Negro race, although they would have quickly added that blacks could never attain full equality with whites. Regardless of the final outcome, though, they wanted racial peace and harmony for the present—not the constant turbulence stirred up by the extremists.[23]

In the 1920s, this New South approach to racial problems would eventuate in the formation of the Commission on Interracial Cooperation and the beginning of a southern movement for civil rights. Unlike the prewar liberals, the Interracial Commission's leaders would operate on the premise that blacks deserved full equality, even if they had to remain separate. In addition, a few members of the group would become ultimate integrationists, believing that at some distant time the South might finally accept a lowering of the Jim Crow barriers. But before this new set of attitudes could develop, the old child-beast dichotomy that controlled southern thought on race had to be cast aside, an advance that, for all their benevolence, remained far beyond the reach of New South liberals of the Progressive era like Phillips. Instead, they continued to assume that a permanent policy of segregation amended by paternalism was both desirable and inevitable.[24]

Hence the starting point of all Phillips's writings on race was the Negro's supposedly childlike temperament. "Typical negroes," he claimed, "are creatures of the moment, with hazy pasts and reckless futures" who, under suitable discipline, would respond to commands with an "easygoing, amiable, serio-comic obedience." Although "dilatory" and "negligent" when left to their own devices, when set to work they became "robust, amiable, obedient, and contented." This combination of traits, which had made them "the world's premium slaves" in the past, suited them perfectly for industrial exploitation in the present. Accordingly, Phillips insisted, it was time the South regarded its black population as an important economic asset rather than as a powderkeg.[25]

The intellectual capacity of blacks was not at issue here. Phillips was well aware that the race had produced many gifted leaders in America, from Benjamin Banneker to George Washington Carver and Booker T. Washington in his own day. What amazed him about these individuals was not their talent but their backbone, which he could never quite account for. As he put it, the "wonder of them lay in their ambition and enterprise, not in their eminence among scientific and literary craftsmen at large." In the last analysis, then, it was ambition, perseverance, and initiative—qualities he associated with maturity and manliness—that separated the two races for Phillips; and ambition, he believed, was an inborn racial trait that could not be learned from one's environment.[26]

If these assumptions about the Negro's personality were true, it also followed that southern whites had little to fear from their black neighbors, despite the alarms of the extremists. Phillips frequently served up historical evidence designed to establish this very point. He suggested on several occasions that antebellum southerners who saw slaves as a potential source of mass violence either did not comprehend the black personality or lacked the ability to discriminate fact from rumor. A great number during that regime had "held the firm belief that the negro population was so docile, so little cohesive, and in the main so friendly toward whites and so contented that a disastrous insurrection by them would be impossible." In his opinion, those few revolts that did occur were often blown out of proportion by overanxious southern newspapers. Clearly he was determined to give blacks every benefit of doubt in order to maintain his faith in their childlike character.[27]

Although Phillips generally upheld the orthodox New South position on race, he did introduce one important modification. Southerners had long explained the black man's distinctiveness just as they had answered all other basic questions—in biblical terms. They had assumed that God had shaped the Negro's physical and emotional makeup at the beginning of existence and rendered him forever inferior to whites. But Phillips was too heavily steeped in social science empiricism to accept such a vague, mythological explanation. Instead, he adopted a quasi-Darwinian theory, highly popular among contemporary anthropologists, which traced the racial characteristics of the Negro to his adaptation to the African environment. It was the hot, stultifying climate of Africa, according to this theory, which had arrested the Negro's evolutionary development, even as the comparatively cool climate of northern Europe had stimulated Anglo-Saxons to achieve higher and higher levels of civilization. "To live where nature supplies Turkish baths without the asking," Phillips wrote, "necessitates relaxation"; such an environment "not only discourages but prohibits mental effort of severe or sustained character." In this fashion Phillips planted—without intending to—a seed of Darwinian doubt that would in time prove fatal to the South's traditional racial views.[28]

Indeed, his adoption of environmentalism as an explanatory device often posed problems for Phillips himself, especially in regard to his cherished notion of how the antebellum plantation served as a "school" for its slaves. As he argued in a 1904 article entitled "The Plantation as a Civilizing Factor," blacks had been "heathen savages" when they first arrived in America, with their animal impulses always in danger of "breaking forth." To fit them "for life in civilized, Christian society," they had to be "drilled, educated in a manner, and controlled." The plantation was ideal for this purpose, Phillips contended, functioning much like a modern social settlement house by providing its residents a close-hand view of American life at its best—only in this case it was the master and his family who set the example for the newcomers rather than trained social workers. Since Negroes possessed a natural "imitative faculty" as part of their racial heritage, they were able to learn quickly. Thus the Old South succeeded by environmental means in transforming the African savage into the dependable, contented plantation "darkey."[29]

At this point, though, the reader might well ask some troublesome questions. If the plantation had been so effective in altering the black man's personality, why then did the South still require a thoroughgoing system of racial control in the twentieth century? Had not blacks become at least partially civilized? Phillips had no real answers, except to toy with words. In *American Negro Slavery*, for example, he claimed that the African's nature was "profoundly modified but hardly transformed by the requirements of European civilization." At times he seemed to be saying that blacks had made considerable progress and were becoming more like whites, at other times he described them as "still in the main as distinctive in experience, habit, outlook, social discipline and civilian capacity as in the color of their skins or the contour of their faces." His dilemma became especially keen when dealing with, in his words, the "exceptional negroes," the "high-grade intelligent, self-reliant negroes, mulattoes, and quadroons" for whom Phillips felt genuine sympathy. The failure of the slave regime to find a place for these "graduates" of the plantation school constituted its major defect, according to Phillips, and, like other southern Progressives, he strongly urged that the New South avoid a similar mistake. But again he left the main question unanswered: if these exceptional blacks had adapted so well to the American environment, why need they be segregated?[30]

To escape this logical thicket, Phillips fell back on the old child-beast dichotomy and its parent formulation, the radical Victorian distinction between savagery and civilization. Caucasians, he asserted, were innately civilized; they carried the germs of civilization in their blood as a matter of "natural inheritance." Negroes, however, could acquire civilized ways only by imitating whites. Accordingly, Negroes had to renew their acquisition in each generation or stand in danger of "lapsing back into barbarism." In Phillips's mind, these racial differences were so great that blacks could not even transmit such "lessons" to each other: "To contend that the educated negro is the best source of guidance and enlightenment for the average negro in the American system is to argue that the reflected light of the moon is brighter and more effective than the direct rays of the sun." Since the savagery in the Negro's blood could never be fully tamed, Phillips concluded, areas like the South, which harbored large black populations, would always require a permanent system of racial control, regardless of the economic or moral cost entailed.[31]*

---

*Phillips's use of the savage-civilized dichotomy was not limited to race relations. The imagery appears scores of times throughout his writings in a wide variety of contexts. For

Many writers on Phillips have tended to see a mellowing of his sectional attitudes in his later years, as if the simple passage of time and his continued residence in the North had brought him closer to the revised national consensus on race. In fact, just the opposite was true. When environmental theory began to displace scientific racism in the various social science disciplines after the First World War, Phillips became increasingly strident in his defense of southern policy. He appears to have realized that his primary values were under attack and that his strategy of accounting for racial distinctions on environmental as well as genetic grounds was rapidly falling apart. Little more was heard of the steam baths of tropical Africa. Instead, in "The Central Theme of Southern History," his famous essay of 1928, he adopted a new and far harsher tone on racial matters. What bound the white South together, he wrote, was "a common resolve indomitably maintained—that it shall be and remain a white man's country. The consciousness of a function in these premises, whether expressed with the frenzy of a demagogue or maintained with a patrician's quietude, is the cardinal test of a Southerner and the central theme of Southern history." The very fact that Phillips had broken with his previous practice of shunning generalization to offer up a "central theme"—and that he was willing to link himself as a southerner with political extremists like James Vardaman and Coleman Blease—indicates the degree of desperation he had come to.[32]

In sum, Phillips's environmentalist strategy did not work. Tying the orthodox southern position on race to evolutionary theory may have lent it intellectual respectability for a while, but such an expedient also let the genie of environmentalism out of the bottle. Likewise, Phillips's emphasis on the Negro's childlike qualities and his downplaying of black criminality could suggest a very different racial policy for the South from the one Phillips advocated. Assuming that blacks were indeed harmless, or at least that they posed no special threat to southern society, a new generation of southern liberals in the late 1920s would start to view the shackles of segregation as cruel and unnecessary and call for some to be removed. Assuredly Phillips did not join them. By that time he was already beginning to appear a conservative.

---

instance, he refers to early seventeenth-century Virginia settlements along the James River as a "ribbon of civilization thrown into a continent of barbarism" (Phillips, *Life and Labor*, 26). The metaphor, and the mode of perception it represented, were fundamental to Phillips's intellectual makeup.

II

A parallel shift toward a more conservative stance marked Phillips's general approach to Old South history during the last years of his career. When Phillips first came on the scene around the turn of the century, he had found his field of study dominated by the Lost Cause spirit. Those late nineteenth-century southern writers who were venturing into ante-bellum territory did so with a high degree of chauvinism. The South, they thought, needed loyal sons and defenders, not critics; for them, the sole function of a southern historian was to keep alive the South's memories of glory. Phillips, of course, had no use for this sentimentalism. He dismissed the work of what he called the "thick-and-thin champions of everything Southern," such as the United Daughters of the Confederacy, as "in keeping with the futility of propagandist efforts by patriotic societies in general." It was time, he thought, for the region to regard its history through the eyes of a detached professional scholar who could point to the defects along with the glories. Thus, although he never relinquished his allegiance to the Cavalier myth, Phillips often took on the role of critic of the old regime. And since he kept wishing the Old South had really been the New South, he had much to criticize.[33]

The chief target of his critical remarks was slavery. As Phillips saw it, chattel labor had made some economic sense through the period of initial settlement when workers of any kind were scarce, and it had been essential in gearing blacks to plantation routine when they first arrived from Africa. But afterwards slavery soon became that worst of all sins, a "clog upon material progress." It had tied up the region's capital, prevented the diversification of the southern economy, blocked the introduction of advanced machinery into southern agriculture, forced the South to base its entire industrial system on the crudest sort of labor, and trapped the planters into a cycle of chronic speculation over slave and land prices. In keeping with his New South penchant for technology, Phillips summed up the results with an image drawn from mechanics:

> The system may be likened to an engine, with slavery as its great fly-wheel—a fly-wheel indispensable for safe running at first, perhaps, but later rendered less useful by improvements in the machinery, and finally becoming a burden instead of a benefit. . . . This great rigid wheel of slavery was so awkward and burdensome that it absorbed the momentum and retarded the movement of the whole machine without rendering any service of great value.

Slavery, the South's foremost historian of the subject concluded, was "out of place in the modern, competitive world."[34]

What distressed Phillips most was slavery's "unfortunate fixation of capital" and the speculation it brought in its wake. "While the farmers of Ohio and Illinois . . . were investing their profits in land improvements, railroads, and local factories," he noted ruefully, "the planters of Alabama and Louisiana were applying their cash and straining their credit to buy slaves." Phillips considered this practice bad enough when the price of field hands was still reasonable. After the closing of the foreign slave trade in 1808 caused prices to rise far beyond the slaves' actual labor value, however, he thought it sheer madness. Equally mad was the economic cycle that soon came to dominate the South: "Prices of land and slaves would rise, at first slowly, then faster, and then with speculative acceleration, until another furor of speculation would be upon the community." The bubble would burst, he explained, when overproduction at last glutted the cotton market and the price for the staple plummeted. With most of their assets tied up in slaves, the planters would have little flexibility in coping with the crisis and many would go bankrupt. Phillips, who believed that "the ways of industry are constant and regular," deplored this "frenzied finance." This was not his style of capitalism.[35]

Phillips lodged still further charges against the slave system. He repeatedly condemned the way it restricted opportunity for nonslaveholding whites, who, "whether farmers, artisans, or unskilled wage earners, merely filled interstices in and about the slave plantations." He also faulted it for scaring immigrants away from the South (a common New South complaint) and for depleting the soil through wasteful methods of cultivation. In addition to these "industrial" flaws, Phillips deeply regretted the check slavery placed on freedom of speech in the Old South due to the need to guard against insurrection. He accounted the "death of southern liberalism" in the 1830s one of the major costs of maintaining the peculiar institution. Clearly, then, Hofstadter was wrong in describing Phillips's presentation of slavery as "a latter-day phase of the pro-slavery argument." To Phillips slave labor was a usage "civilized people had long and almost universally discarded as an incubus" whose sole value to the South lay in the area of racial control. He never really wavered from that judgment.[36]

Alongside his critique of slavery, Phillips also began to formulate an analysis of the plantation's impact on southern society similar to that put forth by writers such as Edgar T. Thompson in the late 1930s. This was a wholly different matter from slavery, since the antebellum plantation represented the very model Phillips wished to use in revitalizing the modern South. Phillips nonetheless could see its defects. "Unfortunately," he noted, "the plantation system was in most cases not only the beginning of development, but its end as well. The system led to nothing else." This had happened as a result of the system's inherent tendency to too rapid expansion, which had kept the population in most black-belt counties "too sparse to permit a proper development of schools and the agencies of communications." He fully understood that the speculative finance he abhorred stemmed not only from slavery, but from the very nature of the plantation itself, and that the consequent reliance on distant markets put the South in a quasi-colonial relationship with the North and Europe from which it had yet to obtain release. This willingness to acknowledge the more serious failings in a system he dearly loved indicates how objective a scholar Phillips at the height of his career could be.[37]

Furthermore, given his interest in putting to rest the myth of planter indolence, Phillips on occasion could even take direct aim at the Cavalier legend. Leisure had almost no place in his version of Old South existence. The haughty rice nabobs of South Carolina, so often depicted as the ultimate in antebellum decadence, appeared in Phillips's pages as men who "deliberately and constantly preferred the career of the useful captain of industry to the life of the idle rich." His typical planter was usually portrayed as a diligent, unostentatious businessman, more interested in what was "plain and comfortable" than in fancy display. Nor did he put much stock in the storied "big house" of plantation romance. Although a few such colonnaded mansions did exist, he reported, many planters lived in virtual log cabins; and the usual plantation domicile—as his own travels around the South had taught him—had been "commodious in a rambling way, with no pretense to distinction without or luxury within." Attacking another aspect of the myth, Phillips cautioned his readers about plantation size, reminding them that "slave industry was organized in smaller units by far than most writers, whether of romance or history, would have us believe."[38]

However, such departures from southern mythology remained the exception, never the rule. Despite Phillips's efforts to eradicate the image of Old South leisure, he could not resist upholding the planters' pretensions to gentility. Periodically he would speak of "the fine type of the Southern gentleman of the old regime," or those "considerate and cordial, courteous and charming men and women" of the antebellum South with their "picturesque life" who represented "the highest type of true manhood and womanhood yet developed in America." Later his critics would focus on these passages in their attempts to stamp him a Bourbon.[39]

Most often such compensatory gestures to the Cavalier hovered in the background in Phillips, to reappear in full force at the conclusion of his books. Equally striking is the way the space allotted the myth tended to increase as his career progressed. In *American Negro Slavery*, for example, it required only the final paragraph to reinstate the gentleman as the centerpiece of southern history, while ten years later, in *Life and Labor in the Old South*, Phillips devoted the full concluding chapter to an adoring description of "The Gentry." The effect of this arrangement was curious. Clearly the graceful, learned, temperate aristocrats he portrayed in his conclusions bore little or no relation to the hard-driving, competitive managers and speculators who occupy the stage through most of his work. Phillips might suggest in epigrammatic fashion that running a slave plantation was "less a business than a life" and that "it made fewer fortunes than it made men," but all the elaborate evidence he had marshaled to establish the planter as a "high-grade captain of industry" indicated just the contrary. It was almost as if, having proved his case that the Old South was actually the New South, Phillips wanted to take it all back in the end.[40]

The tightening of the myth's hold over Phillips was especially apparent in his treatment of the frontier—always a good touchstone for judging the power of the Cavalier on a southern writer's imagination. Initially Phillips had accepted the theory of his mentor, Turner, who saw the frontier as the wellspring of American democratic virtue. In his 1909 introduction to *Plantation and Frontier Documents*, Phillips argued that the plantation and frontier had been of equal significance in shaping southern character, with the frontier operating along Turnerian lines. In *American Negro Slavery*, published in 1918, he still spoke of the frontier in terms of "self-sufficing democratic neighborhoods," where the challenges of daily existence forced the inhabitants to develop the spirit of innovation and enterprise, along with a healthy taste for hard work. The frontier, in other words, was seen as a molder of New South values. As late as the 1850s, he observed, "the whole South was virtually still in a frontier condition."[41]

By 1928, Phillips had shifted his views decidedly. Now he contended that the southern frontier had been "tamed with considerable speed." A good thing, too. "Pioneers here as elsewhere," he explained, "left most of the apparatus of law and culture behind them when they plunged into the forest." The old aristocracy came swiftly to the rescue. Certain households headed by transplanted Virginians soon began "to radiate refinement instead of yielding to rough mediocrity; and the stratification of society facilitated the recovery of culture by those who had relinquished their grasp." Here was the Cavalier myth in its most dramatic form—the gentleman planter, that bulwark of civilization in the wilderness, redeeming his society from barbarism and possible dissolution. As for those backwoodsmen who escaped the planters' civilizing touch, Phillips now described them as "listless, uncouth, shambling refugees from the world of competition." No longer, it seems, did the frontier automatically instill the spirit of enterprise.[42]

Even the element of southern chauvinism—the one component of Lost Cause mythology Phillips had always successfully resisted—ultimately came to the fore in *The Course of the South to Secession*, an unfinished manuscript published by one of Phillips's friends after his untimely death by cancer in 1934. It is possible that Phillips might have revised this work heavily had he lived. It is true, in addition, that he had left behind the more neutral field of "industrial history" to write of the sectional conflict directly. Nevertheless, one cannot imagine the younger Phillips ever penning such an extended diatribe against the North. The strategy throughout was to turn the tables on New England by accusing it of all the evils the abolitionists had once heaped upon the South. Yankees were presented as religious fanatics, just as southerners had been called fanatics on slavery. Southern nationalism was seen as a defensive response to "predominant Northern selfishness." If a solid South existed, it had been called forth by an equally "solid North," which had used its power to undo the Missouri Compromise and the Compromise of 1850, cheat in Kansas, aid and abet John Brown, and array itself in a "phalanx" to crush the unoffending South. Whatever the merits of correcting the pro-northern bias in American historiography, this book plainly overstepped the bounds of objective scholarly debate.[43]

By the 1930s, then, when his fellow southern historians were just beginning to explore the insights of his earlier work, Phillips was beating a hasty retreat back to the nineteenth century. While others muted the race issue, "rediscovered" the southern frontier, analyzed the economics of slavery, charted the scope of Old South entrepreneurship, and generally played down the political antagonisms that led to the Civil War, Phillips was refighting the war, disowning the frontier, and passionately defending segregation.

Since so few of Phillips's personal papers have survived, the reasons for this retreat may never be fully known. However, the available evidence does suggest one likely explanation. In the sharp, assertive, occasionally bitter tone Phillips sustained in his last publications, one detects a pained reaction on his part to the intellectual changes then underway in the country, which brought him in turn to a fervent affirmation of those values under challenge. In addition to the mounting environmentalist attack on southern racial policy, which he responded to in his "Central Theme" essay, Phillips could not have helped but notice the inclination of so many postwar writers within the South to question regional pieties.

Although it was true Phillips himself had contributed to the launching of that rebellion by using Progressive standards to gain perspective on antebellum society, he had done so against a cultural backdrop in which the old verities of Cavalier and Lost Cause had been secure. The values and beliefs attached to those myths had remained intact at the deepest level of his mind, ready to make their customary reappearance in his conclusions. Now, with a new group of southern writers starting to tear those pieties apart, Phillips could only react by rushing to defend his heritage.[44]

It is in this sense that Phillips must be seen not as a true reactionary, but as a southern post-Victorian. Coming of age just after 1900, he had peered through the doorway of Modernism and, at first, liked what he saw. Attempting to bring the South's past into line with the new era, he had emphasized as best he could the continuity of the region's commitment to capitalism, technology, efficiency, and the work ethic, along with the velvet glove of paternalism in racial matters. But the Progressive movement was never more than a halfway station to the modern world. So many of the virtues Progressives championed, like industrial efficiency, really belonged to the high tide of Victorianism. Accordingly, when the main forces of change became apparent following World War I, Phillips started to pull back. His position on race hardened into a stern defense of the iron hand of segregation, while southern mythology occupied an increasingly larger place in his work. Confronted by a crisis, he was fast returning to the certainties of the century in which he had been born and raised.

In the end he arrived at the impasse that had always been implicit in his thought. On the one hand, Phillips desperately wanted his antebellum planters to appear as forerunners of modern businessmen; on the other hand, he did not have the slightest desire to dislodge the Old South myth. It was a dilemma that would have troubled him profoundly had he ever acknowledged it.

CHAPTER 3

BROADUS MITCHELL:
THE NEW SOUTH AS THE OLD

T hat Broadus Mitchell should be classed a southern post-Victorian at first presents a puzzle; almost every facet of his background and experience would seem to dictate against it. Raised in a lively urban environment, gifted with a vigorous and original mind, trained in the latest social science theory at Johns Hopkins prior to the First World War, and engaged in extensive social work activities from his graduate student days on, Mitchell should have emerged a leading figure within the Modernist generation of intellectuals in the South. Such, indeed, appears to have been his initial ambition, especially in terms of bringing a new realism to the region's thought. Yet clearly something went wrong. In both tone and substance Mitchell's books on the South have a distinctly archaic ring when compared with those of his contemporaries. As Paul Gaston notes, his work on the history of the southern textile industry, though published in the 1920s, belongs historiographically with that of the New South scholars who gained ascendancy at the turn of the century. Furthermore, few southerners looked to him for intellectual leadership after, say, 1927; most regarded him as occupying an orbit totally different from their own. Strangest of all, Mitchell himself appeared oblivious to this fact, convinced that he was pioneering new paths of endeavor that other southern writers would inevitably have to follow. How is one to account for this unusual performance?[1]

From the beginning Mitchell was different. Most southerners of his era bound for social science careers spent their childhoods in the countryside, the offspring of obscure families of modest means. If their fathers did not raise cotton or tobacco, they usually preached the gospel or taught country school. In short, their roots were sunk deeply into the way of life shared by the overwhelming number of their people, and their identification with the South was, as a consequence, complete and visceral. Not so Mitchell, who hailed from one of the region's few well-established academic families. His father Samuel Chiles Mitchell, a major figure in the South's "Education Crusade" during the Progressive era, was at once a professor of history at Richmond College, a minor New South prophet, and an ordained Baptist minister; he also served briefly as president of the University of South Carolina. On his mother's side Broadus Mitchell was descended from John A. Broadus, for many years the head of the Southern Baptist Seminary in Louisville. Thanks to his father's prominence, the men who dominated the region's cultural and industrial life at the time he was growing up, such as Daniel A. Tompkins, George Foster Peabody, and Thomas Nelson Page, were not just distant names to him; they were his parents' guests, who visited often. The talk he heard around the family dinner table did not center on the price of crops or the vagaries of the weather, but on the miraculous rehabilitation of the South through industrial progress. Thus it was a different South that Broadus Mitchell began to identify with and a different southerner that he became.[2]

It was this apparent headstart, however, that was to prove his undoing. For Mitchell learned his father's lessons all too well, steeping himself in New South ideology to the point where he would later be incapable of adapting to changing trends. No matter how much evidence might be adduced to the contrary, he could never bring himself to believe that the motives of the founders of the southern textile industry in the late nineteenth century had been anything short of selfless. Behind this belief lay an unshakable faith that the southern people shared at some basic level a moral character entirely free from evil or guilt that would manifest itself under the proper circumstances—a faith likewise inherited from his father. All the many contradictions in his work would flow, directly or indirectly, from this initial assumption. If the case of Ulrich Phillips, then, illustrates how easily the New South mentality, for all its talk of progress and efficiency, could revert to traditional mythology, that of Mitchell shows how its innocent point of view, even after it had been detached from its mythological base, could continue to blind the most sophisticated and conscientious researcher. An unparalleled example of the extreme tenacity of nineteenth-century thought once it had taken hold, Mitchell provides an opportunity to examine how the New South Creed exercised such remarkable power.

I

Born in 1892, Broadus Mitchell grew up in as stimulating a setting as vouchsafed to any southern youngster at the time. In effect, the campus of Richmond College (now the University of Richmond) became his playground, and its preparatory academy his school. His father, known throughout the state as one of the most popular teachers on the Richmond faculty, also held a reputation as one of the South's leading liberals, primarily for his spirited advocacy of public education and willingness to break with many regional shibboleths on race. Nonetheless, it was a strictly Victorian home, Broadus would later recall, filled with intense discussion of books and current events, with an atmosphere "almost painfully serious and earnest." Not surprisingly, both his younger brothers, Morris and George Sinclair Mitchell, would go on to distinguished careers in scholarship and public service. Such were the aspirations S. C. Mitchell tried hard to cultivate in his children.[3]

All went well for the family until 1913, when suddenly, under fierce political pressure, the elder Mitchell was forced to resign the presidency of the University of South Carolina after only four years in the post. The crisis arose when Governor Coleman E. Blease, whose lower-class constituency hated blacks and the state university with equal fervor, fulminated against Mitchell's recommendation that a $90,000 gift from the George Foster Peabody Fund earmarked for South Carolina go to a black college. Sensing a golden political opportunity, Blease chose to ignore the fund's by-laws, which stipulated that the money go to aid Negro education; nor did he heed the findings of a subsequent legislative investigation upholding Mitchell. In the end, Mitchell, having little taste for battle and fearing irreparable harm to the university, decided to step down. Perhaps that was the wisest act under the circumstances, perhaps not. Whatever the case, to Broadus, then in his final year as an undergraduate at South Carolina and thus a firsthand witness, the incident confirmed all he had been taught about the hopeless corruption of southern politics. The need to modernize the region through transforming its economic base could not have appeared more urgent to him.[4]

Upon graduating from college, Broadus applied for admission to the Columbia University School of Journalism in hopes of a career in that field. In selecting this profession he did not have in mind the kind of fact-finding, investigative reporting that had created such a sensation during the Progressive era, but rather the efforts undertaken by the original corps of New South publicists to make the South safe for industry following Reconstruction. He would become another Grady, cheering on the "constructive forces" in southern society and thereby continuing, in a slightly different manner, the campaign his father had begun. As a first step toward this objective, he took a summer job in 1913 writing business news for the *Richmond Evening Journal*. There he spent his time composing booster-style pieces on the fine economic climate in Richmond and singing the praises of southern dry goods. It was exactly what he thought he wanted.[5]

By summer's end, however, something was troubling him, even though he could not really pinpoint it. Later stints on Richmond papers would reveal to him what should have been obvious at the start—that this kind of journalism, kept simplistic by the necessity of aiming for a popular audience, was too superficial and dull for his vigorous mind. The scholar in him was not, and could not, be satisfied.* Significantly, though, Mitchell refused for some time to admit this to himself; instead, he believed that he had been caught unprepared. To cope with the complexity of modern conditions, he reasoned, to get at the underlying realities, he would require far more technical preparation than Grady had possessed. In particular, he would need a grounding in economics, a subject he had neglected to take at college. It was in this fashion that he made what would turn out to be the most fateful decision of his life. Continuing to believe that he was headed for a career in journalism, he entered graduate school at Johns Hopkins.[6]

The choice of Hopkins itself deserves comment. Mitchell went there on his father's strong urging that Baltimore was the proper locale for a young southerner seeking top-flight graduate training. Twenty years earlier, during the reign of Herbert Baxter Adams, that had certainly been true; but by the time Mitchell arrived Adams had long been gone, and the mecca for southern students had shifted either to Columbia University or the University of Chicago. Had Mitchell elected either of those schools, he would doubtless have encountered some of the talented contingent of southern students then present, such as Frank L. Owsley, Herman Clarence Nixon, John Donald Wade, or Guy B. Johnson. These young southerners tended to flock together in the unfamiliar urban environment, establishing relationships that would continue long after they returned home. Had he enjoyed the benefit of exchanging ideas with these men, it is possible they might have helped wean him away to some extent from

---

*While covering efforts for municipal reform for the *Richmond News-Leader* in the summer of 1917, he told his mother he was "discouraged." The problem "has to be studied calmly," he wrote, "and this takes not hours but days and weeks. I find myself losing self-confidence when I try to combine facts with ideas, and give it all, moreover, a popular turn" (Mitchell to his mother, July 19, 1917, SCM Papers, Series B).

his New South premises, which many of them were fast coming to question. At Hopkins, though, Mitchell was isolated from such influences. The only future southern scholar of consequence to pass through during his tenure there was the historian Charles S. Sydnor, with whom Mitchell had little in common. Following the beaten path of another era, in short, served to reinforce the differences his atypical upbringing had already implanted between him and his southern contemporaries.[7]

It soon became apparent to him that graduate work was no more fulfilling than his summer apprenticeship in journalism had been. The study of political economy, he wrote his parents, seemed "as hard as mathematics, as cheerful as this rainy day, and a great deal more dry." "It is a discipline, more or less conscious with me," he insisted. "I do not think I shall ever want to use it actively when I have gotten it." Above all, Mitchell was oppressed by the formal and stifling ambience he claimed to find at Hopkins. At times he thought his "spirit" suffocating as he longed to remove himself to some less analytical community, where men believed in action, not words: "I would rather be a savage and not have production goods and not know the laws of physics and chemistry, and be able to feel; here [at Hopkins] it is a rarity for men to be natural and actually laugh or frown." He persisted, though, because of his growing conviction that political economy supplied the key to understanding all of human affairs, especially in the later stages of evolutionary development. In modern society, he observed, the "economic factor" is "the center of the web, and conditions the radiating strands. Politics is a phase, history is the covering, but the secret lies, often concealed, in economics."[8]

Through his studies Mitchell was picking up a rudimentary economic determinism that would in time develop into his own brand of Marxism. In fact, his interest in socialism began as early as 1915 when he started attending meetings of the Baltimore Family Welfare Association, a small group attempting on a shoestring budget to ameliorate the suffering of the city's poor. Mitchell undertook various chores for the association, escorting children to eye clinics for examinations, finding homes for orphans, teaching a chronically hospitalized youngster how to read, and so forth. Determined to be of service to his fellowmen, as his parents had always encouraged him to be, and grateful for the chance to escape the strictures of academic life, Mitchell thrived on this work and soon became chairman of one of the association's district boards in east Baltimore. The more he became involved, the more his outrage at the poverty and helplessness he had discovered grew. "I wish you could hear some of the stories," he wrote home. "You cannot understand the facts of suffering of these people since unemployment set in without being horrified at the social system which permits such things to happen. The reason more people are not militantly reforming is that they simply do not know what goes on about them." Here, in the Baltimore slums, he believed, he was finding the reality absent from his textbooks.[9]

But strikingly, while this movement toward radicalism was taking place on one level, his commitment to New South boosterism remained intact on another. Nothing better illustrates this fact than his reaction when the Baltimore-based *Manufacturers' Record* offered him a staff position in 1917 with the understanding that he would succeed to the editorship shortly when the paper's founder, Richard Hathaway Edmonds, retired. The job was "just the thing" he wanted, because the *Record* was "the best medium through which to reach the South by writing in economic fields." That his credentials as a southern-born Baptist of good family trained in economics impressed Edmonds is understandable; but what is less easy to comprehend is Mitchell's interest in the *Record*, an ultraconservative trade journal for southern industrialists noteworthy for its fight against child-labor laws, its vigorous attacks on trade unions, and its wholesale opposition to social-reform legislation. The only conceivable reason Mitchell could have coveted the job was the paper's status as mouthpiece of the New South movement, a role it had filled since Grady's death. In any event, the negotiations were soon interrupted by American entry into the First World War and Mitchell's induction into the army, thus saving Mitchell and Edmonds from sealing an agreement both would quickly have come to regret.[10]

Not until mid-1920 after Edmonds had publicly attacked him did Mitchell finally revise his estimate of the *Manufacturers' Record*. Upon leaving military service, which was spent doing routine clerical work, he had actually tried to reopen the negotiations, but Edmonds, perhaps wary of Mitchell's increasingly evident participation in liberal causes, met the overtures with silence. By this time Mitchell had joined the economics faculty at Hopkins, where he was teaching courses on labor problems and social reform; he was also speaking out frequently against child-labor practices in the South and supporting strikes by textile workers. Still, the *Record* held back its heavy artillery until Mitchell announced plans to set up a labor college to promote workers' education in Baltimore. Suddenly, all of Mitchell's prounion pronouncements became a target of the paper's concern. For his part, Mitchell was stunned at this about-face; the same journal he had once called his best chance for serving the South now turned into "a most excellent example of economic narrow-mindedness and selfishness." "They do not want to be at all honest," he complained to his parents in genuine amazement.[11]

This abrupt shift in his relations with Edmonds reveals the extraordinary contradictions that had developed in Mitchell's thought as he arrived at maturity. Not only did the New South ideology he had inherited blind him to the political realities of the situation until the very last minute, but it kept him from seeing the inconsistencies in his own position as well. The paradox was also apparent in his published work: his scholarship had become an exercise in historical justification for southern capitalism and the status quo, while the sympathies in his political writing lay almost entirely with the militant working class. Indeed, it almost seemed as if there were two Broadus Mitchells at large in the 1920s—one an exact replica of his father, and another who, in his search for realism, was striving mightily to enter a realm of thought and endeavor no southerner had ever reached before. Most remarkable of all, these two personae coexisted side by side in perfect tranquillity. Broadus Mitchell the Socialist looked upon Broadus Mitchell the latter-day New South prophet with complete equanimity, and vice versa. It was a combination no other member of his generation in the South could conceivably have effected.

II

To see how Mitchell attempted to resolve these contradictions, one must start with his unique concept of the turn of the century as the great moral dividing line of southern history. Prior to that time, when the South had been "mustering every resource to stagger to its feet," rebuilding from its Civil War devastation, anything that helped provide the poor-white class with a regular income had been permissible in Mitchell's opinion, even if it entailed below-subsistence wages or seventy-hour work weeks. Child labor, for example, "was not avarice then, but philanthropy; not exploitation, but generosity and cooperation and social-mindedness." After 1900, though, as the southern textile industry emerged from its infant stages, these moral valuations began to change. Soon the use of children became "as cruelly unjust as at first it was natural." With the arrival of relative prosperity, the mill hands deserved to receive their long-deferred rewards, a goal attainable only through unionization. In this way Mitchell could reconcile, at least for his own purposes, his two divergent ideologies: although his father's teachings held true for the nineteenth century, the economic transformation that had occurred made socialism a moral imperative in the twentieth.[12]

The distinction hinged on more than the impersonal process of industrial evolution, however. For, despite his talk of economic causation as the key to understanding history, Mitchell's moral dividing line in the

2. Broadus Mitchell (1921)
Courtesy The Ferdinand Hamburger, Jr., Archives,
The Johns Hopkins University Library

final analysis depended heavily on his subjective assessment of southern character. His deepest beliefs told him that things had been different in the nineteenth century because a different breed of men had been in charge. Not the rough-hewn entrepreneurs one might expect to find on an economic frontier, but bona fide southern gentlemen, recruited largely from the old planter class, had made up the first generation of mill owners. Having tragically misled their people during the slave regime, these same individuals, perceiving the error of their ways, had determined to restore the region to well-being through industrialization; not for personal gain, but because they were "lovers and servers" of the South. To these "far-seeing, public-minded, generous-natured leaders" the "philanthropic incentive" had been "frequent and normal." As Mitchell saw it, they had built their factories "as much from altruism as from any other cause."[13]

Most important, Mitchell attributed this saintly behavior precisely to the fact that the mill builders were southerners. The "ingrained and living social morality" they practiced reflected nothing less than the "permanent character of the South." When tracing the origins of this instinctive paternalism back to the antebellum period, Mitchell's account became hazy. He spoke of the obligations imposed by slavery, along with a supposed inborn nobility that marked the planter class. But whatever the origins of the code, in Mitchell's schema nineteenth-century southern leaders automatically acted in accordance with it; their sense of responsibility to those dependent on them resided in their bones. Occasionally, of course, this benevolence was "very properly" joined to the "usual commercial promptings," but often "it controlled alone." This was why he could say that the "South of slavery, agriculture, and aristocracy" had in effect created the "South of free labor, industry and democracy." That the South had actually become industrialized, that it did enjoy free labor and democracy, he did not doubt. As he explained in the preface to his first book, his father had told him so.[14]

Little detective work is required to discern that Mitchell was relying here on the New South version of the Cavalier myth. In keeping with that myth, he was assuming that southern planters had been blessed with a special immunity from greed that remained intact even after they left their agrarian habitat and entered the capitalist arena. To support these contentions, Mitchell relied solely on legend and personal testimony, not the facts and figures an economic historian would normally employ. "The genuineness of altruism as a motive in the Cotton Mill Campaign," he wrote, "is supported by observation of Southern character in other particulars and especially as operative in this period." No other proof was offered. The fact that these early mills often turned an annual profit of between 30 and 75 percent, as he himself observed, did not alter his appraisal, even though he could produce no evidence that the dividends ever found their way to charity. Mitchell also accepted the myth's corollary—that the poor whites had understood the mill barons' generous intentions and reacted with childlike gratitude, "even asking, if one pleases, to be exploited." Again, no objective evidence backed this assertion.[15]

Having subscribed to the myth, Mitchell soon faced the problem of explaining why this happy state of affairs had eventually ended. If southern mill owners conducted their enterprises with unparalleled benevolence, and if workers responded in kind, why was the industry plunged into chronic struggles over child labor and other social issues? Mitchell's solution was to argue that, beginning around 1895, the old-fashioned gentlemen who had founded the mills were gradually replaced by a new type of hard-nosed managers who did not adhere to the old code. As a result, economic motives started to dominate, and the textile industry in the South lost its distinctive southern character. For approximately two decades, while the first generation of owners was in charge, the region had followed its own course, Mitchell suggested, but it then began to recapitulate the experience of England and New England, where employers sought to exploit labor and workers eventually organized for self-protection. Not only had the industry grown up, but the planter class had been pushed out.[16]

The Cavalier myth, then, exerted such a tenacious hold on Mitchell, that it was able to supersede his commitment to objective scholarship. For the sources of that tenacity one must look to the circumstances attending the writing of *The Rise of Cotton Mills in the South*, completed as his doctoral dissertation in 1918 and published without revision three years later, the work in which his first and most complete statement of his interpretation of New South history appears. Largely because it arrived on the scene at a time when dispassionate studies of regional topics by southern authors were in short supply, the book became an instant classic, praised by all for its mastery of academic technique. Gerald W. Johnson, for example, a man usually quite skeptical of the motives of capitalists, was convinced by what he called Mitchell's "carefully documented discussion" that in the case of the early mill owners "all the money return looked for was expected to accrue to the poor whites." The belief that the mills had been founded to exploit cheap labor "cannot survive the perusal of this work," Johnson claimed. As late as 1941 Wilbur J. Cash was still citing Mitchell's "celebrated monograph" with its "comprehensive and carefully documented proof" to substantiate his own account of the building of the mills. Yet, for all the praise of its scholarly technique, the writing of this study became an intensely personal experience for Mitchell. As his correspondence with his parents shows, his purpose was not merely charting the course of industrialization in the South, but tracking down that most elusive quarry, southern identity. It was this latter quest, as much emotional as intellectual, which led him to mythology.[17]

Most New South intellectuals, with their espousal of national reconciliation and Yankee values, felt this need to secure their identities as southerners, but Mitchell especially so. Raised in a household where the South had been largely an abstraction, he was seeking in his research to discover what the South really was and what connection, if any, he might have with it. His was the exuberance of a native son returning at last to claim his birthright, attempting virtually to imbibe "southernness." "I wish I could look at it coldly," he confessed, "but I cannot help entering in very enthusiastically when the human aspects are the theme; the subject is so absorbing in its dramatic and personal aspects, that considering it sympathetically is as tiring as sitting appreciatively through a great play at the theatre. Truly I am finding out what the Southern people are like. I cannot be analytical; it makes me want to feel it, and never have to write it." When the "subject-matter touches so importantly and really crucially the whole genius and hopes of your own people," he added, "you are calculated to be worn out by the process."[18]

It was this effort to find the "whole genius" of his people that led him directly to the leaders of the mill campaign. In them he saw a role model unmistakably southern in character that comported with his residual nineteenth-century ideal of innocence. From the start, he regarded them not as ordinary human beings living through especially trying times but as ahistorical supermen, bereft of all flaws, unsullied by ambition or greed, with seemingly unlimited public generosity. Capable of freely borrowing northern ways while preserving their essential southernness, they combined the most admirable Cavalier traits with a grounding in economic realism. This image, implanted in his mind well before he began his research, was reinforced and deepened in the course of the extensive interviews he conducted with those original mill owners still alive, interviews that in turn became the evidentiary basis for his thesis. Approaching his subjects with a mixture of awe, piety, and affection, Mitchell appears to have accepted at face value virtually all that they told him. "When the student of Southern industry meets one of the few surviving members of this company," he remarked in his book, "he at once feels himself in touch with the spirit that was the South's salvation."[19]

Furthering this process of identification was Mitchell's conception of the South as one united racial family, another part of his nineteenth-century ideological legacy. "The white population of the South is homogeneous and has always been so," he asserted flatly. This racial purity had given southerners the "best blood in America," producing a "stock which has no superior." An awareness of these genetic facts had been a prime source of motivation for those involved in the mill campaign, he believed, compelling members of the old aristocracy to create jobs for their poor-white cousins and extinguishing any glimmers of class consciousness among the workers. "No people less homogeneous," he maintained, "less one family, knit together and resolute through sufferings, could have taken instant fire, as did the South" in 1880. Clearly, this notion of southern kinship exerted a strong pull on Mitchell at the time he was composing this book. Since his own ancestry was impeccably southern for generations, presumably he too belonged to the "southern family." In 1918, that was a claim he was most anxious to make.[20]

Even during the 1920s, when his focus shifted primarily to the contemporary scene and his pronouncements on the southern textile situation became more militant, Mitchell was still trying desperately to get straight with his southern heritage. His purpose, he kept insisting, was to dwell on the region's "positive accomplishments," to be seen as a fullfledged member of the southern family and not as a detached, faultfinding intellectual. "As a native Southerner, an honestly admiring student of its [the region's] growing greatness, and one devoted to its interests," he wished "to be above all else helpful." It is also revealing that the two book-length works he produced during this decade dealt not with the struggle for unionization but rather with the Old South. Precisely because they run counter to what he considered the main trend of his work, *Frederick Law Olmsted: A Critic of the Old South* (1924) and *William Gregg: Factory Master of the Old South* (1928) deserve attention. Even as he was grasping for an alternative identity as a socialist, these books show, his New South mentality remained alive and well.[21]

More than anything else Mitchell wrote, the Olmsted book defies easy classification. Certainly not a biography of Olmsted, nor a study in economic analysis, nor a critique of Olmsted's writings on the South, the main impression it leaves is that of a therapeutic exercise for its author. Mitchell was using Olmsted as a vehicle to vent his considerable bitterness toward antebellum society without appearing to make direct attacks on the Old South himself. The peripatetic *New York Times* correspondent who had sent back voluminous reports from the South in the 1850s may not have anticipated the New South line exactly, but with his Whiggish predilections he came close enough. As Mitchell quickly discovered, with a little maneuvering he could find a sanction for nearly everything he wished to say about the old regime somewhere in Olmsted. He could excoriate secessionist politicians, for example, calling them "frenzied, deluded, selfish, and absurd," then attribute the epithets to Olmsted. Best of all, he could beat the slaveholders over the head for allowing the South to become backward, all the while absolving them from any true moral guilt.[22]

Consequently, *Frederick Law Olmsted* reads, on the one hand, like a catalog of antebellum errors. According to Mitchell's synopsis Olmsted had concluded that "the inertia of forced labor . . . [had been] the greatest fact in the life of the South," giving rise to "idleness and improvidence" among both races and thus producing "a system of social statics" without parallel in the modern world. Olmsted's frequent passages on the widespread existence of high-powered entrepreneurs within the planter class, of men on the make and unstable frontier conditions, received no mention in Mitchell's account. Slavery had caused stagnation, that was the book's theme. On the other hand, Mitchell contended that Olmsted had held the South blameless for this baleful condition: "The impression which grew upon him more strongly than any other . . . was that the section, as a consequence of slavery . . . was suffering a mental aberration which threw it into a pathological state and rendered it incapable of rational action or deliberation. . . . Withal, the South was to be regarded less as the criminal than as a patient; its very dignity and calm resentfulness of treatment was to be regarded as an affectation of frantic delirium."* Olmsted, that most objective of observers, Mitchell was saying, had understood that slavery was an "institution of accidental inception and long growth" and had accordingly "refused to the last to outlaw the South in his esteem."[23]

This was the familiar plea of not guilty by reason of insanity that New South intellectuals had used often to condemn and defend their society simultaneously. The tactic—pre-Freudian in conception—permitted them to "explain" slavery or lynching by arguing that circumstances had somehow conspired to paralyze the South's reasoning faculty, a situation presumably remediable through social and industrial progress, while at the same time enabling them to hurl charges like "frantic delirium" at the slaveholders. For older southerners such a strategy represented a psychological necessity: it allowed them to maintain their adherence to the Lost Cause while expressing their barely hidden hostility toward the ante-

---

*Unfortunately, the belief that the South had gone temporarily insane belonged entirely to Mitchell—Olmsted said no such thing. In the passage Mitchell cites to support this contention, Olmsted tells of a conversation with a Mississippi planter who happened to be an abolitionist. "*It seemed to him*," Olmsted wrote, "there was an epidemic of insanity on the subject" (italics added). Olmsted, who thought the prime motive behind slaveholding was the desire for profits, gave no sign of agreeing with the planter's opinion. Olmsted, *A Journey in the Back Country*, 185.

bellum regime for bringing the South to defeat. So long as they steered clear of any detailed investigation of the period prior to Appomattox, it worked reasonably well. The problem came when younger New South historians like Phillips and Mitchell did attempt to come to grips with the slave plantation system. How could one attack Old South social arrangements and still stay loyal? Phillips provided one solution to this impasse, retrieving the plantation system from moral limbo by emphasizing its modern industrial features. The other option, which Mitchell eventually took, was to break openly with the Lost Cause itself, while upholding the inherent innocence of the slaveholders. In 1924, however, he was not yet ready emotionally to repudiate Confederate romance on his own and so retained the old insanity plea and artfully employed Olmsted as his proxy.[24]

Mitchell's long-suppressed rancor toward the slave regime was unmistakably on display in an article he published five years later. Visiting a Robert E. Lee shrine in Virginia in early 1929, he noticed that a group of New Jersey tourists found the exhibits more moving than he had. "I was inclined to reproach myself," he admitted, "that they felt more tenderness for these souvenirs of the Old South than did I, a native son." By this time, though, Mitchell had been living away from the South for over a decade, and he had begun to think of himself more as a member of the socialist family than the southern. As a result, despite his traces of guilt, he was now prepared to throw one poisoned barb after another at the Confederates. Rather than "knights of the 'Lost Cause,'" he wrote, they should more aptly be termed "knaves of a lost South." Their "vaunted chivalry" was a "mockery," their culture a "myth." The most scathing passage was reserved for Lee himself: "Why embalm his remains and keep his few belongings like relics at the shrine of a saint? We paid him too much honor while he lived, and furthermore sad reminders of his handiwork are all about us in the South this long time afterward—poverty, race hatred, sterile fields, the childish and violent crowd gulled by the demagogue." The sense of betrayal here is almost palpable. In time, Mitchell would go so far as to propose melting down all Confederate memorials in Richmond for scrap metal; they would make "splendid gutters and downspouts," he would declare.[25]

Nonetheless, despite this savage attack on the Lost Cause, Mitchell's idealized conception of nineteenth-century southern character remained intact. That fact becomes apparent in his biography of the antebellum South Carolina industrialist William Gregg, published only one year before the Lee article. An unabashed piece of Victorian hero worship, the book is patently cut from the same cloth as his earlier treatment of the post-Civil War mill barons. "The reader may feel that the pages which follow contain too much praise of him [Gregg]," Mitchell announced defensively in the preface, "I can only say that the evidence which I have been able to collect lends little support to an unfavorable view of the man." This was, if anything, an understatement.[26]

In the adoring eye of his biographer, Gregg could do no wrong. Blessed with "a restless mind, an outreaching spirit, and eager, capable hands," Mitchell's Gregg personified the nineteenth-century virtues of industry, economy, punctuality, and faithfulness, standing in diametric contrast to the stereotype of the leisure-loving planter. Yet, Mitchell asserts, like a twentieth-century socialist Gregg always thought "in terms of public economy" and "the long-term advantage of the people." Gregg's advocacy of the use of slave labor in textile factories was excused as a tactical ruse to win southern backing for his industrial program. His willingness to join the secessionists as early as 1858 and his firm allegiance to the Confederacy during the war were said to reflect his loyalty to his homeland, a sentiment that made him "more human." Mitchell even went so far as to apologize for his hero's penchant for sarcasm. It was a "spirited sarcasm," he wrote, "not so bad in an unpretending man of sheetings."[27]

What intrigued Mitchell most was the undiluted paternalism Gregg had practiced in his isolated factory town of Graniteville. Existing in an age when industrial competition and trade unionism were virtually non-existent, Graniteville appeared to Mitchell a rare laboratory experiment in political economy, a unique opportunity for the southern system of labor relations to operate in its purest form. For Gregg was Mitchell's ideal capitalist:

> With William Gregg the human motive ran *pari passu* with the commercial. He acted, in all his plans for the life of the people of Graniteville, from a profound sense of social obligation, and a finer patriotism than answers to war trumpets. *Noblesse oblige* was his intuition. He set a pattern for the industry which, in our more complex day, can never be quite returned to.

The result, Mitchell enthusiastically reported, had been the achievement of a genuine southern community: "All at Graniteville formed one family under Gregg. Many intimate ties of work, frolic, fatherly discipline, and mutual gratitude and respect knit them into one uniquely happy little group." Moreover, he noted, the enterprise had been enormously profitable once it got into high gear.[28]

A striking resemblance exists between this picture of Graniteville and the portrait of the perfect antebellum slave plantation drawn by Phillips. Echoing Phillips, Mitchell described Gregg's rule as a "benevolent despotism" and suggested that Graniteville had been meant to serve as a school for civilization. That was why Gregg insisted on tidy houses, absolute punctuality at the workplace, abstention from drink and gambling, and a host of similar rules. Mitchell registered no complaint about this wholesale deprivation of workers' rights and intrusion into their private lives. Rather, he approvingly compared the town to a "feudal village" where the poor whites had huddled "for the protection of their overlord." "If they gave up something of an unmeaning freedom," he argued, "they gained in the substantial asset of security." This may or may not have been true, but nonetheless it was a startling statement for a self-proclaimed socialist to make in 1928. That Mitchell did make it, repeatedly and without self-consciousness, showed how firmly the New South mentality with its hankering for "benevolent despotism" and social stability continued to control his thought.[29]

As its impassioned conclusion makes plain, *William Gregg* was directed to a specific audience—the captains of southern industry in the twentieth century. Although the Graniteville scheme itself could not be resurrected, it was still possible, Mitchell thought, to recapture Gregg's "spirit." Now that cotton manufacturing in the South had achieved all Gregg had "hoped for in a material way . . . ," he observed, "it cannot fail to accomplish what he dreamed of in whole social betterment. . . . Those who are impressed with the story of his life, if they wish to honor him, ought to have a care that this process, on the human side, shall go forward in constant anxiety for justice." To insure that this message reached its intended audience, Mitchell carefully instructed his publisher to mail announcements of the book to all presidents of southern textile factories and to the members of the chambers of commerce in cities like Charleston, Augusta, and Columbia. Despite all his talk of new tactics to meet new objective conditions, it would seem that paternalism never lost its place in his affections.[30]

Put another way, Mitchell was attempting to carry New South belief to its purest, most logically consistent conclusions in the face of twentieth-century realities. That was bound to be a hopeless task. No matter what expedients he tried, the values underlying paternalism could not be reconciled with the modernization of southern society, nor could the goal of Americanization be coupled with the preservation of a distinctive regional identity. The congeries of ideas and attitudes that had comprised a coherent ideology in the time of Henry Grady failed to do so in that of Broadus Mitchell. The more Mitchell tried to extrapolate the New South Creed, the more he exposed its internal weaknesses, and the more he detached himself from contemporary southern life. Yet Mitchell seemed oblivious to this dilemma. Even as his interpretation of the mill campaign began to come under challenge, he staunchly retained his generational dividing line, cordoning off a historical era in which his New South precepts seemed, in his own eyes at least, to ring plausibly true. A large part of his mind had become trapped in the nineteenth century and, struggle as he might, he could not manage to extricate it.

III

All the while a very different Broadus Mitchell had begun to emerge. This Broadus Mitchell, who would one day run for governor of Maryland on the Socialist ticket, advocating the total abolition of private property, first appeared in print in a 1919 article condemning the Supreme Court's decision to strike down the Keating-Owen Child Labor Act. What bothered him was not the outcome of the case—he had always held that laws could not solve social problems, that one needed an economic remedy for an economic evil—but rather the duplicitous testimony of the southern mill owners when the bill had been pending before Congress. Although he understood their desire to maintain profits, he could not forgive them the "complex of transparent evasions" they had resorted to in stating their case. With their talk of states' rights, the manufacturers had been "so artless in their sidestepping of the perfectly clear issue" (that is, the children's welfare) that anyone could have seen through them. If the textile leaders took little joy from this attack, it was true that Mitchell's animus fell mainly on their tactics, not their motives. "One would like to believe," he added two months later, "that sometimes, in its adolescent quality, . . . Southern industrialism has not even known it was dissembling." In any event, the matter passed with little notice, and, except for those aware of his activities in Baltimore, Mitchell maintained his reputation as a friend of the mill owners.[31]

All that changed in 1927, however, when Mitchell let loose a bombshell in the staid pages of the newly established *Virginia Quarterly Review*. "Fleshpots in the South" represented one of the fiercest assaults on the textile magnates ever put forth by a southern intellectual. "If you thrust your fingers into the downy wool of the lamb," Mitchell said of them, "you feel beneath it the coarse bristle of the wolf." In no way did the current crop of mill men resemble their forebears: "They are not burdened with a sense of *noblesse oblige*. They are not aristocrats, but bourgeois. They are class-conscious and money-wise." Their actions revealed the "awkward driving fist of capitalism" flailing away without regard for truth, consistency, or the well-being of their workers. What elicited this outburst was a recent advertising campaign by southern industrialists promising would-be northern investors an unlimited supply of cheap white labor. To Mitchell, with his exalted conception of the South as one united family, this was the last straw. "The workers are being offered on the auction block pretty much as their black predecessors were," he noted in outrage.[32]

Also calculated to raise hackles below the Potomac was Mitchell's prediction in the article that southern distinctiveness was nearing an end. Since the exploitation of mill hands in his view constituted an inevitable, if painful, transitional stage in the region's economic evolution, the question arose of "whether these great industrial developments will banish the personality of the South as we have known it, or whether the old spirit will actuate the new performance. Will industrialism produce the same effects here as elsewhere, or will it submit to be modified by a persistent Southern temperament?" Since "Fleshpots" was written the same year as *William Gregg,* one would expect Mitchell's prognosis for the survival of the "old spirit" to have been, at minimum, hopeful. According to his estimate, however, not a shred of the South's "distinct culture" would be left. Instead, the region would "soon be . . . for the first time established as a part of the American achievement." At the conclusion of the article, he touched on the ultimate heresy. In a fictitious exchange with a hypothetical "doubter," he raised the possibility that the region's uniqueness had always been mythical. "[T]here has always been an unique inescapable *something* in the Southern people, in all the Southern people," the doubter insists. "I wonder if there has been," Mitchell replies, leaving the question open.[33]

This time, neither friend nor foe could avoid taking notice of the "new" Broadus Mitchell, which was exactly what Mitchell had intended. Shortly before the piece appeared he had told his father he expected "some come-backs from the South," and he was not disappointed. Protest letters were sent to both Mitchell and the *Virginia Quarterly Review,* asking, as one South Carolina textile executive snidely put it, "to learn something of the heredity and environments of Mr. Broadus Mitchell." No man born and raised in the South, they implied, could have composed such a scurrilous libel on his homeland. At Chapel Hill, on the other hand, William Terry Couch, the young assistant director of the university press, found the article "something I've been hoping to see now for some time." Personally anxious to publish similar manuscripts on contemporary southern problems, he confessed to Mitchell that he did not know whether the University of North Carolina "would be as courageous as the *Virginia Quarterly Review.*" In New York, Worth M. Tippy, a Social Gospel minister who looked after the cotton-mill situation for the Federal Council of Churches, thought so much of the piece that he mailed reprints of it to churchmen throughout the South.[34]

The net effect of this uproar was to alter instantly Mitchell's image and standing within the region. Prior to 1927 southerners had caught only occasional glimpses of Mitchell as a socialist realist. That was enough to make Howard Odum vaguely suspicious, causing him to pass over Mitchell when setting up a special committee to study the textile industry in 1924. But most people had long regarded Mitchell, in Couch's words, as a writer "very favorably inclined toward the promoters of the industry." Now those same promoters cast him out as a pariah. David Clark, the right-wing editor of the *Southern Textile Bulletin*, who had gladly aided Mitchell in his dissertation research, went so far as to refuse paid advertisements for *William Gregg*. "It should be a book of much interest to cotton mill people," Clark explained to the publisher, "but we do not think Prof. Mitchell would hesitate to misrepresent Mr. Gregg or his actions if he thought it would make his acts conform to his preconceived idea of the textile industry of the South." The man who had been considered a decade before as a possible editor for the *Manufacturers' Record* was suddenly perceived as a traitor; just as Mitchell felt betrayed by the mill owners, so they now felt betrayed by him.[35]

Why did Mitchell choose to bare his sentiments in a manner so plainly calculated to shock, with no advance warning? Again the answer lies in the Victorian base of Mitchell's thought and his attempt to compensate for it. Examined closely, his brand of socialism bore little resemblance to modern Marxism; the very idea of class conflict was abhorrent to him. Rather, Mitchell's radicalism resembled that of those late nineteenth-century writers like Edward Bellamy or Laurence Gronlund who led the first concerted attack on laissez-faire capitalism and styled themselves "socialists." Although somewhat advanced for its time, their social thought nonetheless depended at bottom on Victorian moral values. In keeping with them, Mitchell emphasized the virtue of cooperation in all things, called for the social use of wealth, supported trade unionism, and—in sharp contrast to the Marxists—downplayed the role of doctrine and group action. As he once explained: "I think cooperation is on the way to displacing competition. I am a collectivist. I may be a socialist or a communist, but about this I am not sure because particular doctrines interest me less than the obvious general economic drift." Above all he dreamed of a new *"mass religion"* to inculcate a new social morality, based on the premise that personally upright behavior, "however 'good' as such, may not contribute to the social 'good' at all." That was the chief lesson he would preach to the modern captains of industry from his socialist pulpit.[36]

The same assumptions informed Mitchell's sense of tactics. Despite the growing trend among those on the left to employ the machinery of government in dealing with social problems, Mitchell remained thoroughly skeptical. He had decided, based on his experiences in the South, that politics was invariably outright chicanery and the legal system a hopeless fraud. To bring about meaningful change, he believed, one must rely on constant propaganda and other forms of "education," accompanied by the organization of workers. Thus, when the National Association for the Advancement of Colored People approached Mitchell in 1930 to head a massive campaign of litigation, backed by a $100,000 war chest, to win more equal distribution of school funds in the South, he refused on the ground that the effort would be worthless even if successful. "The law does not secure rights, but simply confirms rights already established by education and economic competence," he argued, suggesting they spend the money "to attack the same evils in print instead of in court." The NAACP, needless to say, did not heed his advice.[37]

The project dearest to Mitchell was always workers' education. On his return to Baltimore after the war, he began teaching night courses for Jewish immigrant clothing workers under the auspices of their union. Before long, he was formulating plans for a citywide "Labor College" to be run in conjunction with the local universities, a scheme that never got off the ground because of opposition from both the Johns Hopkins administration and the *Manufacturers' Record*. His basic rationale was simple: to escape from poverty, the proletariat would have to arm themselves intellectually by mastering the principles of political economy; only then could they bargain successfully with their employers. As he put it in a paraphrase of a speech by the itinerant labor organizer William Z. Foster to a mass rally of the Baltimore unemployed: "My brothers and sisters, why are we in trouble this afternoon, with no work, no earnings? It is because we are boobs. If only we KNEW, were INTELLIGENT, comprehended the situation and could plan a way out of it. We are in trouble because we have not developed our brains!" If only the workers could be made *rational*—there lay his final aim. It is striking how squarely Mitchell's focus was always on the individual, on reforming the social conscience of the manufacturer through moral exhortation and on uplifting the worker through education. That, along with his participation in organizations such as the National Consumers' League and the League for Industrial Democracy, constituted the essence of his politics.[38]

As a result, by the time things began heating up in the southern textile industry in the late 1920s, Mitchell's stance seemed less militant every day. The violent strikes at Gastonia, Danville, and Elizabethton may have stirred radicals throughout the country, but Mitchell found them appalling and harmful to the workers' cause: "It is lamentable that the fanfare of emotional protest has been flung up to obscure industrial issues. Invective, reproaches and bitterness have been enemies to the calm thinking which is necessary where sharp conflict has sprung up in a section new to manufactures and newer to class cleavage." Late in 1929 he implored the American Federation of Labor to call off its announced mass-organizing drive for southern mills, preferring instead the "gradual infiltration" strategy of the United Textile Workers on the theory that "what the Southern employer stands most in need of is education." The objective, he claimed, should be "the establishment of confidence" with each mill president, with the union working out "what improvement it may in that mill by cooperation with him." Regardless of the wisdom of these tactics, in the context of the current explosive crisis in the mill villages they hardly represented the radical point of view—and Mitchell desperately wanted to be perceived as a radical. On the scholarly front, moreover, his account of the origins of the industry was coming under fire from scholars like Harriet L. Herring at Chapel Hill. Mitchell had put things exactly backwards, they had discovered: exploitation had come first, paternalism second. Mitchell's heroes, the original mill owners, had been "pretty harsh masters," Herring observed; it had been their successors, frightened by the specter of unionization, who had erected the schools, hospitals, recreational centers, and other institutions associated with village welfare work. Mitchell, she wrote, had concocted "a past that never was."[39]

One suspects, then, that Mitchell resorted to bombshell tactics in "Fleshpots" and the articles that followed in an attempt to compensate for his lack of genuine militance, to disguise how increasingly old-fashioned his position on southern issues had become. In snarling at the mill owners, the Lost Cause, or the Fundamentalists, he was at least able to look modern, even if the preconceptions on which his arguments rested belonged to the previous era. At the same time, the angry response these writings provoked among southern conservatives seems to have helped Mitchell cement his self-made identity as a Socialist, just as he was surrendering his efforts to retain his identity as a southerner. If his ideas drove David Clark to a frenzy, then they must have been at least partly radical. He was striving, in short, to convince himself that he had at last broken through the barriers to confront modern reality directly and was therefore in the intellectual vanguard. That had been a major purpose of his turn to socialism in the first place.

With the coming of the Great Depression, Mitchell's verbal pyrotechnics greatly intensified. "We must have a new system with production for profit abolished," he told his father in 1933. "I am giving my students socialism and communism hot and heavy." The next year he accepted the Socialist nomination for governor of Maryland, putting aside his normal objections to politics for an "educational propaganda" campaign. Delivering soapbox speeches in Baltimore and motoring through western Maryland with his close associate, the Christian Socialist Elisabeth Gilman, he managed to capture seven thousand votes, ironically becoming the only prominent southern intellectual to run for public office in the 1930s. At the same time he was busily revising his economics textbooks to conform to the new developments, despite contrary advice from his publisher who feared that a left-wing orientation would hamper sales. "Those who write the vapid, unrealistic texts are stultifying themselves, and will be compelled to put some iron in their blood soon," Mitchell insisted, for "time works with us."[40]

Yet, in all these endeavors, the substance of Mitchell's thought continued to reflect his nineteenth-century cast of mind. A puzzled economist reviewing the revised textbook, for example, could not help noticing how the "author sticks quite close to the conservative, orthodox position on certain vital phases of economic theory . . . only to break abruptly and completely with orthodox theory at other places." In discussing the role of capital, interest, and the general theory of value, Mitchell, he found, "carefully avoids some disturbing questions," but "it is a different man who speaks later for the single tax and socialism." Likewise, Mitchell's running critique of New Deal policy often came from the conservative side, as when he protested Roosevelt's decision to abandon the gold standard.[41]

But the best place to look for his unyielding New South bias remained his historical writings, which during the 1930s were largely concerned with the early Whig publicists, beginning with Alexander Hamilton in the eighteenth century and continuing with such figures as Henry and Mathew Carey, Daniel Raymond, and Georg Friedrich List in the nineteenth. What attracted Mitchell to these stalwart defenders of banks and high tariffs was their open dissent from laissez-faire, their declarations of concern for the public welfare, and, most of all, their expansionist optimism, that "sure characteristic of collectivist contention." These advanced policies, he claimed, entitled these men to be seen as forerunners of modern socialism—"American Radicals Nobody Knows," he called them, with only the slightest touch of irony. He was especially sure that Hamilton, had he returned to life during the depression to find the means of production fully developed but moribund, would have favored converting them instantly to national ownership.[42]

3. Broadus Mitchell in 1938
Courtesy The Ferdinand Hamburger, Jr., Archives,
The Johns Hopkins University Library

In time Mitchell would pursue this line of analysis to produce his most important scholarly contributions. First, however, he resigned from Johns Hopkins in a bitter protest over the university's refusal to admit a black graduate student—a gesture, it might be added, no other southern-born intellectual of that day would conceivably have made. After three stormy years at Occidental College in Los Angeles, where his fervent pacifism met with the displeasure of the prowar Board of Trustees, Mitchell in the fall of 1942 moved permanently to New York, serving initially as research director for the International Ladies' Garment Workers' Union and then as professor of economics at Rutgers University. Leaving Hopkins seems to have given him a clean break with the South; the suffering entailed in the temporary disruption of his career may have aided in confirming his status as a radical in his own eyes. Whatever the case, his work after the Second World War, especially his full-length biography of Hamilton and his critical account of New Deal economics, *Depression Decade*, shows a stability and consistency of perspective that had hitherto eluded him. Still believing himself a modern socialist, he would develop his unique interpretative synthesis in his own way, no matter how others perceived him.[43]

The intellectual odyssey of Broadus Mitchell, then, reveals the extraordinary power that could be wielded by New South ideology over one of the most intelligent, learned, and compassionate southerners of his era. Mitchell had set out earnestly to update his father's teachings and to apply them to the twentieth-century South. He had been determined to penetrate to underlying realities, to locate the economic secret at "the center of the web," to put some "iron" in his blood, with the ultimate intention of serving his native region. But the more he tried to recast New South thought, the more it came apart in his hands. When he turned to socialism as another possible route to the modern world, his residual New South beliefs held him captive. Above all, his ingrained ideology did not prepare him to deal with the forces that soon overcame his chosen object of expertise, the southern textile industry. The raw test of wills dividing one mill town after another, the owners' intense lust for profit, the strikers' passionate class hatred smoldering beneath the surface and erupting with sudden violence—all were beyond Mitchell's comprehension. He could posture as a radical, hurling rhetorical thunderbolts at the status quo, but he could not understand the dynamics or direction of the changes he sought to further.

In the end, he became an idiosyncratic figure, totally detached from the South, writing American history from a doggedly nineteenth-century viewpoint. His rebellion was restricted to periodic gentle probings designed to test the outer limits of his own innocence, to brief hesitations in accepting the values he was raised on, to questions that were not really questions. "I am less desirous of dissection of the social animal than inclined to dream of perfection for all its members and harmony in all its functioning," he wrote his parents in 1919 in an admission that sums up his post-Victorian thought. "The universe is expressed, after all, isn't it, in terms of love."[44]

CHAPTER 4

ELLEN GLASGOW AND
THE TIDEWATER RENAISSANCE

In the aftermath of the First World War, to the astonishment of everyone, a new literary vitality struck the South. Suddenly, and with great speed, the open rebellion against the genteel tradition in American letters that had broken out in Chicago and New York the decade before the war rolled southward past the Mason-Dixon line, bringing with it its characteristic panoply of "little magazines," local poetry societies, and regional theater groups. Just a few years after H. L. Mencken had proclaimed the region a "Sahara of the Bozart" he was forced to reverse his opinion. Thomas Nelson Page, James Lane Allen, John Esten Cook, Grace King, and others who had dominated the sleepy world of southern literature in the New South period now seemed like relics of another age; their chivalrous planters, colorful Cajuns, and faithful retainers would do no more. Scores of books by previously unknown southern novelists flooded the marketplace, most flying the banner of the region's new "realism." Southern plays, often depicting the lives of impoverished black tenant farmers, captured prize after prize on Broadway. Poems and articles from below the Potomac filled the major national magazines. Such were the beginnings of what was soon self-consciously styled "The Southern Literary Renaissance."[1]

For the most part, the rebellion came South initially by process of imitation, with southerners doing those things they thought necessary to call themselves literary and modern. Especially important in this respect was the influence of Mencken, whose mannerisms and beliefs became models *de rigueur* for young southern talents. The result was frequently a shameless copying of examples inappropriate to the real needs of the region's literature, ranging from Menckenian iconoclasm to the elegant sophistication of *Vanity Fair*, the disillusionment of the expatriates, and the bohemianism of Greenwich Village. Accordingly, one must take special care to distinguish these first stirrings from the cultural revolution that followed. Once it reached maturity, the literature of the twentieth-century South did not engage in a decorous free-for-all; rather, it centered on a tragic sense of the pervasiveness of human evil, a belief in the inexorable power of history to shape human events, and on a preoccupation with exacting artistic craftsmanship. Not until the late 1920s did these concerns predominate.[2]

On close inspection, therefore, the early rebellion appears more as the last hurrah of Tidewater culture than as the actual advent of Modernism. Based primarily in cities like Richmond, Norfolk, Charleston, and New Orleans, the movement continued to reflect the genteel amateurism long associated with the Tidewater. Nor was it usually able to free itself from the intellectual underpinnings that had controlled late nineteenth-century southern writing. If the Cavalier, with his cape and sword, had gone, the happy ending had not. A case in point is the Poetry Society of South Carolina, formed in Charleston in 1920 with a roster of 250 enthusiastic members. "Culture in the South is not merely an *ante bellum* tradition, but an instant, vital force, awaiting only opportunity and recognition to burst into artistic expression," announced the group's initial statement of purpose. To that end weekly meetings were held, a yearbook published, prizes offered, and "missionary" work undertaken to encourage the organization of similar bands throughout the region. But before long the upper-crust background and amateur inclinations shared by most members began to show through, causing one associate to term the gatherings "one-tenth poetry and nine-tenths society." Those with serious literary ambitions like Josephine Pinckney complained of an atmosphere that inhibited rigorous self-criticism of each member's work, with the consequence that most verse produced soon lapsed into the sentimental treatment of local scenes. John Crowe Ransom's summary judgment in 1935 was blunt and accurate: "Charleston poetry, like Charleston fiction, is built on local color; it has no Southern quality so far as I can see."[3]

At the opposite pole stood the New Orleans *Double Dealer*, indulging in such slavish imitation of Mencken that the Sage of Baltimore himself felt forced to disown it. Put out from a dilapidated loft atop the city's French Quarter by a diverse crew of would-be poets, local newspaper writers, and hangers-on, the magazine regarded itself as an embattled southern beachhead for the New York and Parisian avant-garde. "A musty garret of a world is being cleared out, its cobwebby cerebellum cleared for thought. Lend a shoulder to the wrecker," counseled its favorite refrain. But rarely did it say what it would put in place of the old world it was "demolishing." Speaking in short, snappy cadences, its editorial voice seemed to totter between a reflex celebration of art for art's sake and a highly sophomoric brand of social criticism plucked from the pages of *The Smart Set*. Although it did publish several pieces, mostly unremarkable, by four promising native writers—William Faulkner, Hamilton Basso, David L. Cohn, and James K. Feibleman—rarely during the six years of its existence did the *Double Dealer* address itself to the special problems, social or cultural, of its home region.[4]

This sort of frenetic, aimless cosmopolitanism was assuredly not what Mencken wanted. In "The Sahara of the Bozart" and similar essays he had attempted to refocus the attention of southerners on their own cultural roots—on what he called that "civilization of manifold excellences" that had perished in the Civil War. No group in American history drew higher praise from him than the antebellum planter class, those "men of delicate fancy, urbane instinct and aristocratic manner—in brief, superior men—in brief, gentry." The fall of this class from power accounted in Mencken's view for the region's present sorry state:

> The best blood of the South . . . is the best in the whole Republic— that is, taking account only of so-called Anglo-Saxons. But the best blood, save in a few areas, mainly along tide-water, is no longer dominant. The lower order of Southerners, having been lifted out of poverty by the general economic rise of the region, have got the reins of political power into their hands, and through the medium of politics they are trying to force their ignorance upon their betters.

With his hereditarian assumptions, strident elitism, and debunking of both the bourgeois class and poor whites, Mencken's tendency was to reinforce all the Tidewater's favorite prejudices. That he came to play a catalyst role for southern Modernism ranks among the major ironies of the region's intellectual history.[5]

Mencken's designs for southern letters can best be seen in *The Reviewer*, called by one writer "the nearest thing to a southern organ of expression he would ever have." Its editor, Emily Tapscott Clark, personified the very strain of Tidewater culture he most wished to save. Descended from an assortment of Virginia's first families but raised in genteel poverty as the daughter of an Episcopal clergyman, she was, in Gerald Langford's words, "something of a snob," with "all of the traditional Southern sense of propriety and most of the biases of her time and place." To her, art constituted an upper-class monopoly and intelligence a guide to correct behavior, not a tool for inquiry. When the critic Louis Untermeyer once sent her a letter on "dreadful scalloped paper," she was utterly shocked. "Isn't it queer that talent shouldn't give him good taste or make him a gentleman?" she asked a friend. "I can't understand it." Yet in many ways Emily with her restlessness and impertinence was a poor candidate for the subdued role of the Southern Lady. Strongly attracted to the glamour of New York's artistic society, she found nothing more exciting than a visit to the Algonquin Hotel, where the city's better-known literati customarily held court.[6]

As one might expect, the magazine Emily Clark helped to found in 1921 and sustained in Richmond for a little over three years closely reflected her own personality. Its tone resembled that of a perpetual garden party to which both the fashionable and creative had been invited, provided the latter watched their manners. For the moment at least, the old and new mixed easily in its pages. *The Reviewer* could without the slightest blush print the sentimental effusions of a hopeless Richmond dowager alongside the latest work of Greenwich Village regulars like Carl Van Vechten, Achmed Abdullah, and, on one occasion, Gertrude Stein herself. It could lavish strong praise on Eugene O'Neill's highly controversial play, *The Emperor Jones*, all the while describing it as "a convincing study of this particular type of darkey." It could offer its readers a survey of the latest developments in French sculpture, and in the same issue run a piece purportedly proving that Edgar Allan Poe had been a secret crusader for temperance because "every sheet of the beautifully penned manuscript he left shows a steady hand." Yet in the end its Tidewater roots predominated—even its more radical departures stayed within certain bounds. "Our most uninhibited contributors were oddly subdued when they wrote for us," Emily later confessed with puzzlement. "We constantly, wistfully, hoped for something rather more outrageous than we were ever able to get." *The Reviewer*, in short, remained a very chaste happening.[7]

Moreover, its ties to the South were minimal. Despite the magazine's stated aim of serving as a showplace for new southern writers, it is not unfair to say that Emily Clark was dragged into the Southern Literary Renaissance kicking and screaming by Mencken. Only through his persistence did *The Reviewer* "discover" Julia Peterkin, Frances Newman, Gerald W. Johnson, and Paul Green; only through his cajolery did it undertake an extended series on southern cities (where Mencken believed the region's new culture would arise). The same Tidewater upbringing that made Emily Clark so attractive to Mencken made her look down on the South, save for her own limited social circle. "Mr. Mencken's Southern talk is all very well," she wrote her confidante Joseph Hergesheimer in 1922, "but it won't fill the magazine—with much but slush. Whenever we grow really Southern we are stupid." A few months later she reported Mencken was sending "new and appalling Southerners every week."

Gerald Johnson, pursued under Mencken's "orders," took "life and the poor South very hard"; Frances Newman was "so fearfully erudite and full of shop." The only southern author to fare well in her esteem was DuBose Heyward, but then he was "part of the Charleston that every properly brought-up Virginian knows, quite outside the Poetry Society." Such comments amply illustrate the characteristics of the Tidewater sensibility as embodied in Emily Clark: haughty, superficial, disdainful of all but a tiny segment of southern society. Mr. Mencken's illusions notwithstanding, it would take a person of a very different cast of mind to lead the cultural revolution fast developing in the South.[8]

I

Richmond at this time was also home to two novelists invariably associated with the initial phase of the region's literary revival. In many ways, however, James Branch Cabell and Ellen Glasgow had only a coincidental connection to the renaissance movement. Both had established their reputations and laid down the major lines of their work long before the 1920s. Cabell by then was enjoying near-unanimous acclaim as one of the most important contemporary writers in the entire country. "Mr. Cabell is creating great literature," Vernon Parrington assured his readers in 1921, "one of the great masters of English prose, the supreme comic spirit thus far granted us, he stands apart from the throng of lesser American novelists, . . . individual and incomparable." Ellen Glasgow never gathered such inordinate plaudits, but in the immediate afterwar period her series of novels portraying middle-class life in Virginia—a "social history" of the state, she began to call it—drew considerable praise as the most "realistic" fiction the South had produced since the Civil War. Today the literary stature of both writers is open to question, but that is not the issue here. What is of concern is their common intellectual traits, for nowhere else can two finer specimens of the southern post-Victorian mentality be found. It is in this sense that the two are linked to the Tidewater renaissance.[9]

Theirs was a mode of thought dominated by skepticism, the quality their 1920s audience doubtless found most appealing. Born in the 1870s to prominent Tidewater families, both Cabell and Glasgow by the time they came of age had managed to cast away many of the conventional social and religious beliefs that had sustained their parents. Like their counterparts in the North, they had become acutely aware of advances in the natural sciences that seemed to undercut the old assumptions about a purposeful universe presided over by an Omnipotent Father caring for his human children. Accordingly, they became agnostics, adopting a world view that saw man as the helpless plaything of cosmic physical forces. "All about us flows and gyrates unceasingly the material universe," wrote Cabell,

> an endless inconceivable jumble of rotatory blazing gas and frozen spheres and detonating comets, where through spins earth like a frail midge. And to this blown molecule adheres what millions and millions and millions of parasites just such as I am, begetting and dreaming and slaying and abnegating and toiling and making mirth, just as did aforetimes those countless generations of our forebears.

From this relentlessly "naturalistic" viewpoint, man's history appeared to contain no more permanent significance than the life cycle of the lowliest ant—that at least was the reductionist conclusion toward which skeptics like Cabell were inescapably drawn. There seemed no middle ground between the old religious beliefs they had overthrown and the harsh "realism" of science. Furthermore, if science was right, the implications for morality were devastating. Without a God to lay down the laws of right conduct, men would be free to do as they wished. In sum, the whole Victorian value system was under siege.[10]

For most people raised in the traditional manner, this specter of a cold, meaningless universe shorn of absolute moral values could evoke sheer terror. Cabell's famed pawnbroker Jurgen spoke for the great majority when he simply refused to entertain the possibility that such a nightmare existed. "As it is," Jurgen observes, "plain reasoning assures me I am not indispensable to the universe: but with this reasoning, somehow, does not travel my belief. . . . I lack the requisite credulity to become a free-thinking materialist." But Cabell himself, along with Ellen Glasgow, fell in with that small band determined to stare the new reality in the face. Perhaps they could not go so far as their contemporary William James who, in theory at least, positively welcomed this new conception of an open, chaotic universe as *more rational* (i.e., more in accord with human reason) than the previous absolutist belief, but they did feel a compulsion not to ignore it.[11]

By and large, the course the two Richmond skeptics chose to follow was a gingerly one, betraying their strong, if unacknowledged, attachment to the past. Armed with the vision of irony, they would pierce through all illusion, spy out the brave new world science had decreed, take its measure, and, when possible, find a means to master it. In the process, they would also try to determine how much of the old world might be preserved. Above all, they would not admit fear. Whatever inner trembling they might feel, they would accept the changing conditions of existence displaying that personal courage and dignity the nineteenth-century Victorian mind prized so highly. They would, in a word, become stoics.

In practice, this gave them two options. The first was to strike a pose of total detachment and transcend the tragic predicament of man by laughing at it; the second was to endure it directly through stoic fortitude. The choice between the two rarely became absolute—Cabell and Glasgow adopted both expedients at different stages of their respective careers. But, as David Daiches astutely points out, which approach a post-Victorian skeptic tended toward most usually depended on whether or not his religious upbringing had been evangelical in character. In Daiches's formulation:

Scepticism + Nonconformist Conscience = Stoicism
Scepticism − Nonconformist Conscience = Wit

These "equations" applied in turn-of-the-century Virginia as well as in late Victorian England. Cabell, a casual Tidewater Episcopalian, embraced humor and fantasy as the mainstay of his arsenal, while Glasgow, never truly out from under the spell of her father's devout upcountry Presbyterianism, took recourse in her stoic "vein of iron" instead.[12]

The comic mode of post-Victorian skepticism dominates Cabell's eighteen-volume saga, "The Biography of the Life of Manuel." A satire on the pedantry of nineteenth-century scholarship, complete with prologues, epilogues, and genealogical appendixes (Cabell was a professional genealogist before he became a novelist), this mock-heroic work traces the story of Dom Manuel and his descendants for seven generations. The tale begins in the fictitious medieval kingdom of Poictesme, where Manuel, a common swineherd, saves his people from a usurper through a series of accidents and blunders. In time he becomes the legendary Redeemer of Poictesme, with his band of rogues transformed into the equally renowned Fellowship of the Silver Stallion. This obvious, irreverent parallel to Robert E. Lee, the Confederate cavalry corps, and the Lost Cause mythology in general seems to have been especially appealing to those young southerners ready to start questioning their heritage, but not quite prepared to abandon it. The epic continues through various historical eras, dallying on its way for numerous barely disguised erotic adventures (another pleasing feature for younger readers in the early 1920s) until it reaches Manuel's twentieth-century heir, the novelist Felix Kennaston of Lichfield, Virginia, who just might be a stand-in for Cabell himself.[13]

Regardless of the setting or time period, the action in these novels remains strikingly the same. A youthful male protagonist, intoxicated by his dreams, leaves the actual world to enter some sort of fairyland. There he vainly pursues an assortment of intensely seductive women, finds one illusion after the next shattered by his experiences, and returns home at novel's end strongly inclined to the skeptical point of view. Throughout the plot Cabell himself maintains a lofty, almost celestial detachment, looking down on his hero as each illusion becomes unmasked. This ironic detachment not only serves as the wellspring of his comedy but also provides both author and reader with a certain measure of safety. For, had Cabell attempted to identify with his characters in any respect, to see their disillusionment from within and share their discomfort at discovering themselves objects of ridicule, his novels would have immediately taken on tragic overtones. Viewed from a distance, however, the fate of man in an unfair world, as represented by the antics of a Jurgen or Gerald Musgrave, could become the occasion for laughter.[14]

Moreover, to a greater degree than one might at first suspect, Cabell remained a romantic. His irony was carefully designed to expose illusions momentarily, not to destroy them forever. It was as if a giant veil existed, dividing the world of romance from the mundane reality of the naturalists, with Cabell perched directly above. From his vantage, Cabell (and, vicariously, the reader) could view both sides of the veil simultaneously, while his characters, feet still on the ground, could see only their dreams and desires. The jest consisted in Cabell's periodically lifting the veil, revealing to those below the true commonplace nature of life on earth. In this fashion, Manuels' glittering statue turns out to be covered with colored glass, not exquisite jewels; Jurgen's beloved Dorothy De La Desirée is transformed into a hag at the stroke of midnight; and Felix Kennaston's potent charm, the Sigil of Scotia, becomes the lid to a cold cream jar in *The Cream of the Jest*. This, to Cabell, was realism: it involved knowing that the veil existed, that appearance and reality always differed, that the ordinary inevitably lurked behind man's idealist visions and must receive its due. Beyond such mild debunking he did not go, for he had no intention of removing the veil completely.[15]

Here, one suspects, lay the source of Cabell's immense popularity in his day. On the one hand, he appeared impeccably modern. He was a doubter, a skeptic, a writer whose delight in multiple meanings seemed to place him in the vanguard of world literature. On the other hand, his work added up to a comforting defense of romanticism. Myths, morals, high aesthetic standards, and all the other artifacts of nineteenth-century idealism and culture—along with Christian doctrines—were, he argued, essential to survival, since they alone could inspire man to better himself and his civilization. "The things of which romance assures [man] are very far from true," he wrote, "yet it is solely by believing himself a creature but little lower than the cherubim that man has by interminable small degrees become, upon the whole, distinctly superior to the chimpanzee." Such fictions must accordingly be maintained, even if they could not be empirically verified. That was the basic premise of his thought, which the findings of science could not begin to alter.[16]

What ultimately distinguishes Cabell from the Modernist writers, however, is his refusal to confront experience directly. His is a contrived allegorical world filled with masks, ambiguities, and incessant word play, highly reminiscent of that created by Oscar Wilde and other British post-Victorians in the 1890s. It is a world whose inhabitants never, under any conditions, show emotion. Put in situations of great fear or excitement, they react "without any particular enthusiasm"—a phrase Cabell uses repeatedly. Thus Jurgen, after happening on the bodies of his dead mistresses lined up side by side in a mysterious cave and noticing that the shadow of death is now tracking him, responds with proper stoic cool:

> "I do not exactly like this," said Jurgen. "Upon my word, I do not like this at all. It does not seem fair. It is perfectly preposterous. Well,"—and here he shrugged,—"well, and what could anybody expect me to do about it? Ah, what indeed! So I shall treat the incident with dignified contempt, and continue my exploration of this cave."

By comparison, one thinks of Katherine Anne Porter's heroine Miranda in her first encounter with the meaning of mortality, standing panic-stricken, "quietly and terribly agitated."[17]

Such a reaction, acknowledging man's essential helplessness before the forces of nature, was precisely what Cabell most wished to avoid. Rather than exploring the depths of human experience, he bent his efforts at somehow anesthetizing himself against it. Like Jurgen's friend, the seemingly complacent King Gogyrvan, he thought it better to "jeer out of season in order to stave off far more untimely tears." There, in one sentence, lies Cabell's secret.[18]

II

Unlike her Richmond neighbor, Ellen Glasgow could not take even temporary refuge in cosmic detachment; the inexorable conscience drilled into her at Presbyterian Sunday School would never permit it. In truth, the nineteenth-century evangelical tendency to view the world in intensely moral terms was always something of a burden to bear, but its discomfort was minimized so long as it was securely attached to its religious base. Then the injustice it so frequently found embedded in human life could be construed as the working out of God's inscrutable will. But for an agnostic like Glasgow, who saw the universe as governed by pure chance, this same Calvinist morality could have the approximate effect of an exposed nerve ending, registering the most excruciating stabs of pain whenever the least instance of suffering was encountered. Any report of illness, cruelty, or corruption hurt her deeply, even when she did not personally know the individuals involved; the sight of a stray dog or cat, homeless and hungry, could reduce her to tears. Her life became dominated, as she once put it, by "an instinctive, and no doubt illogical, feeling that I had no right to seek happiness for myself in a scheme of things where so many mortal creatures, both man and beast, were enduring even upon earth the extreme tortures of hell. Pain anywhere, without purpose and without hope, a single wilfully tormented animal, has denied, for me, the perfect harmony of the spheres." Nothing, it seemed, could make this excessive sensitivity go away. "The agony of the world has always pressed in upon me, even when I was a child," she wrote a close friend in 1935, "and the curious part is that my power of suffering, both personal and vicarious, has not diminished as I have grown older. I still blaze with rage at the injustice and cruelty of life." Under these circumstances, soaring to the heights of Cabellian irony would always be a difficult, and at times impossible, task for her.[19]

Yet Ellen Glasgow also possessed an unyielding determination to overcome her Victorian upbringing and forge ahead into the new mode of life and thought she had identified as modern. By age twenty she was in full-scale rebellion against her family, her society, her religion, and, most of all, her inherited culture, which she regarded as "false," "affected," "sentimental," and "pretentious." Passionately she wished to break through the intellectual limitations that culture imposed on her and make contact with the "reality" she was convinced lay just beyond her grasp. Her definition of that reality, in turn, was based on her extensive reading in contemporary European literature, which had taught her that the foremost truths of the new age were often psychological in nature. Becoming modern, then, would require not only a willingness to accept the existence of a purposeless universe but also, in her words, "a fearless exploration into the secret labyrinths of the mind and heart." Of course, nothing was better calculated to jangle her exposed moral nerve than that sort of endeavor.[20]

Thus Ellen Glasgow was caught both ways. Her commitment to the new culture focused her attention directly on those emotions, drives, and impulses that constituted the prime locus of human suffering, all the while depriving her of the relative comfort she might have derived from religious belief. It was a classic post-Victorian dilemma. "How," she asked plaintively, "can an oversensitive nature defend itself against the malice of life? How can one learn to endure the unendurable? Not the cruelty of civilization alone, but the cold implacable inhumanity of the universe." We should not be surprised, then, that Ellen Glasgow was afflicted with a severe, debilitating neurosis most of her life, lapsed into frequent depressions, and continuously sought psychiatric care. Nor should it cause surprise that, in her struggle to become modern, she often lost out, allowing her novels to degenerate into what one critic has called "soap opera," clinging persistently to the outward symbols of the Tidewater tradition, and, at the end of her career, turning her back on the very revolution in southern letters she had once helped to launch. Rather, the wonder lies in her forward progress, for, when all necessary qualifications are made, it is safe to say that no other member of her intellectual generation in the South dared explore the inner workings of the southern psyche as she did. If she ultimately failed, her failure was, as Louis D. Rubin, Jr., has suggested, "more than a little heroic in the old way."[21]

She was born in 1873, the next-to-youngest child of a decidedly unhappy marriage. Her father, a director of the Tredegar Iron Works, one of the largest industrial enterprises in the Upper South, combined a zeal for ruthless business competition with the stern personal morality and religious faith bequeathed him by his Scotch-Irish ancestry. A cold man, even within his own family, Francis Glasgow had little use for beauty, literature, or new ideas, and virtually no understanding of his highly temperamental wife and daughter. On one occasion he brought the latter to the brink of delirium by giving away her pet dog without notice or explanation. Ellen, for her part, came to hate him and his Calvinist God with equal fury.[22]

A delicate flower of the Old Tidewater upper class, Mrs. Glasgow could not have been more different from her husband. Conceivably, with her love of things cultural, she might have served as a source of succor as her daughter became interested in writing. Caring for eleven children through the hardships of Civil War and Reconstruction with almost no support or sympathy from her spouse proved too much for her frail constitution to bear, however, causing her to collapse from nervous exhaustion when Ellen was only three. Seven years later, after hearing apparently reliable reports that her husband was keeping a black mistress, Mrs. Glasgow turned into a chronic, helpless invalid. Afterward, when Ellen had steeped herself in Darwinian lore, she would diagnose her mother's illness as the predictable outcome of the "tragic conflict of types" that resulted when the rough-hewn Shenandoah pioneer stock of her father had been matched—or rather mismatched—with the genteel but weaker strain of the lowcountry aristocracy. She took this as her first object lesson in the overwhelming injustice of the universe, for how else could one explain why a paragon of "pure goodness," as she characterized her mother, should be subjected to such constant and undeserved punishment? The debilitation of this gentle, selfless person moved Ellen to pity, while also alerting her to the dangers faced by the traditional Victorian Lady when confronting a heartless masculine world.[23]

Too "nervous" to attend school, Ellen received all her education at home. She began with the novels of Scott and Dickens, but soon moved on to contemporary works in French, British, and Russian literature. She discovered the French naturalists, Balzac, Flaubert, and Maupassant, who would become such an important influence on her own writing, along with her perpetual favorites, Joseph Conrad and Thomas Hardy. Refused admission at the University of Virginia because of her sex, an exclusion she deeply resented, Ellen sought advice from George Walter McCormick, a philosophy professor at the University of South Carolina who was married to her sister Cary. With his guidance, she set herself a broad-based program of reading in political economy, current philosophy, and natural science. How much she truly absorbed this material is open to question, but the fact remains that this sheltered Richmond debutante, with only her willpower to sustain her, rapidly plowed her way through the major works of Adam Smith, Karl Marx, Malthus, Ricardo, Mill, Bagehot, Saint-Simon, Henry George, Herbert Spencer, Nietzsche, Schopenhauer, and, above all, her intellectual patron saint, Charles Darwin. Although still terrified by the conditions of life, gradually, through her studies, she was gathering up the means to defend herself, with Darwin her chief weapon.[24]

According to her own account, Glasgow first picked up *The Origin of Species* primarily to spite her father, who thought it a book for infidels, but it did not take her long to realize that the new biology spoke directly to her personal concerns. Here at long last was a view of life that seemed to comport with reality. Unlike the conventional wisdom of late nineteenth-century Richmond, which insisted blindly on the absolute fixity of tradition and social structure when both were undergoing patent transformation, the certainty of change and movement was the sole constant in the Darwinian world. As J. R. Raper observes, Darwinism "implied the total annihilation of southern ideology, replacing its emphasis upon hierarchical order, stability, uniformity, and protection of the innocent, with an emphasis on change, diversity, and struggle." Moreover, no longer was heredity regarded as the root cause of human character.

Darwinian thought introduced the added factor of the environment, both natural and social, allowing the individual considerable leeway to develop according to his own desires provided he was willing to undertake the necessary struggle. Such plasticity was especially important to Ellen Glasgow in her determination to avoid her mother's fate. Moreover, Darwinism had the glorious advantage of undermining her father's hardshell Calvinism, with its literal reading of the Bible. No wonder she fast came to see Darwinian thought as the perfect vehicle of escape from her southern heritage.[25]

Just as important to her was the new conception of human nature she found implicit in Darwinism. Prior to Darwin, most people had assumed the existence of a total separation between mind and body—a persistent residual notion harking back to the Great Chain of Being by way of Descartes and Linnaeus. The human body, it was thought, was composed of mere physical matter resembling that of the animals, while the mind or "soul" was made up of an entirely different "spiritual" substance that partook of the divine essence. Through its special attribute of rationality, the mind was capable of performing those "higher" functions, such as moral guidance, abstract thinking, and religious belief, that sharply distinguished mankind from the beasts below (and, in the Great Chain, connected human beings with the angels above). Humanity, in other words, was defined in terms of this discrete realm of "spirituality." Those "lower" impulses and passions that continued to plague human beings were assigned to the physical realm; they represented the automatic responses of the animal body over which the mind was required to establish control. From a religious standpoint, such impulses were habitually identified with man's inherent corruption, arising from original sin. To be cursed forever with lusts and hungers like other mortal creatures was, after all, the punishment visited upon Adam and his descendants. Thus in the dichotomy between mind and body lay the very basis of moral judgment, the criteria for determining good and evil, which was why the Victorians, faced with the onslaught of scientific naturalism, were so intent on preserving it.[26]

Darwin's findings, however, effectively shattered these bedrock beliefs. By demonstrating that man was part of the evolutionary process, on a continuum with apes, chimpanzees, and the rest of the animal kingdom, Darwin made it impossible to mark off a distinction between body and soul. The mind, he made clear, had evolved as an integral part of man's total makeup. To the late Victorians, this was a staggering blow. All the attributes they most treasured—willpower, intelligence, moral sense—were now seen to have developed from the lowliest origins, nor was there any way to wall off the base instincts they fervently loathed from man's fundamental nature. Raper spells out the profound moral implications:

> Formerly considered a little lower than the angels and higher than the beasts, man became, in the Darwinian arena, simply the human animal. Humanistic, as well as Judaic-Christian, values were placed in question. As an animal, man must acknowledge violent struggle and sexuality as part of his condition. Where Darwin was accepted, a vast ethical vacuum came into existence that the individual had to fill with whatever authority he might accept without deceiving himself.[27]

Such were the lessons of Darwinism that became, in turn, the foundation for the reconstruction of American thought in the twentieth century.

For Ellen Glasgow, these were not easy lessons to comprehend. As much as she professed her allegiance to Darwin, the assumptions that ultimately controlled her perspective on life remained those of conventional Victorian dualism. Try as she might, she could not escape her ingrained tendency to divide all existence into that which was human and civilized, on the one hand, and that which was animal and primitive on the other. Her deepest belief held that man's bestial instincts would soon overwhelm him if his higher, more civilized nature did not keep them in constant check. Perfect self-control continued to be the standard she applied to her characters and to herself, even if it had to be purchased in the stoic manner by a total suppression of human feelings.

Where Darwinism did begin to liberate Miss Glasgow, though, was in fastening her attention on the animal component in human nature to the point where she was willing to acknowledge its presence openly. The practice of genteel culture had long been to sweep the subject under the rug, or, when necessary, to consign it to ministers and other professional moralists properly equipped to handle it. Such a dangerous matter was certainly not considered a fit topic for a lady novelist of good family, who was expected to produce "sweet" and "uplifting" books to reinforce gently the strictures of civilization. But Ellen Glasgow, thanks in large part to her reading in Darwin, had declared war on that sort of "evasive idealism"—her term for the enforced innocence she thought dominated the Tidewater mentality—and it was precisely those inextinguishable "jungle" instincts in man that evasive idealism evaded. As she saw it, the only way to go was forward. "Heartily as one might regret the old ways, or hate the new," she later remarked, "one choice alone was offered the artist and the thinker. To advance or retreat, these were the only alternatives. One must either encounter reality or accept the doctrine of evasive idealism." Here lay her problem: she wished to dispense with gentility and stare the disturbing findings of the new biology straight in the face, all the while retaining her pre-Darwinian moral values. That, for Ellen Glasgow, was bound to be painful.[28]

The clearest illustration of this dilemma appears in *Virginia*, perhaps the best of her prewar novels. The heroine, Virginia Pendleton, is both "a perfect flower of Southern culture" and a perfect specimen of evasive idealism, brought up according to the "simple theory that the less a girl knew about life, the better prepared she would be to contend with it." Virginia's innocence in turn reflects that of her parents. Descendants of prominent antebellum families who lost all during the Civil War, Gabriel Pendleton and his wife now devote their lives to the systematic "white-washing" of reality:

> Both cherished the naive conviction that to acknowledge an evil is in a manner to countenance its existence, and both clung fervently to the belief that a pretty sham has a more intimate relation to mo-rality than has an ugly truth. Yet so unconscious were they of weaving this elaborate tissue of illusion around the world they inhabited that they called the mental process by which they dis-torted reality "taking a true view of life." To "take a true view" was to believe what was pleasant against what was painful in spite of evidence.

The product of this high Victorian mentality, Virginia turns out all "natu-ral sweetness and goodness," much like Glasgow's image of her own mother. But also like Mrs. Glasgow, Virginia is defenseless; she lacks the necessary biological instinct for self-preservation. The culmination of centuries of fine breeding, she has become so genteel she is helpless, especially when thrown into contact with the fast-paced competitive world springing up around her. Her undoing is her marriage to Oliver Treadwell, an aspiring playwright schooled in European Modernism, who ultimately leaves her for a glamorous Broadway actress. A victim of cultural changes she cannot comprehend, Virginia is incapable of fighting back.[29]

Yet, as Glasgow takes pains to make clear, a vestige of primeval sav-agery still survives in Virginia. This "small secret part" of her, dormant most of her life, awakens when she learns that Oliver is paying attention to another woman: "At the moment the civilization of centuries was stripped away from her, and she was as simple and as primitive as a female of the jungle. . . . Not Virginia, but the primeval woman in her blood, shrieked out in protest as she saw her hold on her mate threatened." Whatever her moral reservations, Ellen Glasgow in 1912 was determined to maintain her Darwinian perspective and see such "primitive" impulses as a source of strength. Thus she spoke of the animalism now suppressed in Virginia in terms of "that immemorial spirit of adventure which lies buried under the dead leaves of civilization at the bottom of every human heart—with whose rearisen ghost men have moved mountains and ploughed jungles and charted illimitable seas." It had been the same "lusty impulses" that had sent Virginia's Cavalier ancestors "on splendid rambles of knight-errantry." Plainly Glasgow tended to approve such hearty emotions in *Virginia*, setting them in contrast to the sterile artificiality that seemed to envelop Tidewater society in her account. "The natural Virginia had triumphed for an instant over the Virginia whom the ages had bred," she announced. Ellen Glasgow was exceedingly anxious to place herself on the side of nature.[30]

As her representative of the contemporary culture that was supplanting that of the Tidewater, Glasgow conjured up Margaret Oldcastle, the actress with the "flame-like personality" who steals Oliver away. Everything about Margaret seems to exude an incandescent energy, arising from a perfect merger of the biological and spiritual, for that was how Glasgow had come to conceive of the new century. At one "with evolution and with the resistless principle of change," this "elemental" force of "burning vitality" had arisen from poverty by "hard work, self-denial, and discipline," building her fierce independence "upon the strewn bodies of the weaker." Glasgow piles on the descriptives, but, revealingly enough, fails to render Margaret as an actual character. Our only glimpse of this magical creature comes in one brief scene, as Virginia gazes at the "glowing intellectuality" of Margaret's face and senses instantly that the contest is over:

> It took passion to war with passion, and in this she was lacking. Though she were wounded to the death, she could not revolt, could not shriek out in her agony, could not break through that gentle yet invincible reticence which she had won from the past.

In a larger context, this passage can also be read as Ellen Glasgow's epitaph for the Tidewater aristocracy, circa 1912. Burdened by overrefinement, stymied by archaic tradition, it was no match for the likes of the relentless, dynamic Miss Oldcastle.[31]

Through most of the text, *Virginia* leaves the impression that its author is also a citizen of the new age who views the action with considerable ironic detachment, but toward the end instances crop up when just the opposite seems true. Increasingly Glasgow begins to identify with Virginia, experiencing her tragedy from the inside and pointing out the

4. Ellen Glasgow in 1922
Courtesy Ellen Glasgow Collection (#5771),
Manuscripts Department, University of Virginia Library

virtues of her vanishing way of life. In a preface written a quarter century later, Glasgow confessed as much: "Although, in the beginning, I had intended to deal ironically with both the Southern lady and Victorian tradition, I discovered, as I went on, that my irony grew fainter, while it yielded at last to sympathetic compassion." One cannot escape the feeling of loss, for example, when Virginia's parents die. Previously condemned for evading reality, Mrs. Pendleton, on the occasion of her death, is eulogized at length for her noble altruism. "A child of ten might have demolished her theories," Glasgow explains, "and yet because of them, or in spite of them, she had translated into action the end of all reasoning, the profoundest meaning in all philosophy." Similarly when Gabriel Pendleton meets a heroic end attempting to rescue the grandson of his former slave from three drunken white tormenters, we discover that the hopelessly ineffectual minister had all along possessed a latent "spark of greatness in his nature." These Tidewater traits of selflessness, heroism, and paternalism may have become anachronisms in the modern world, but plainly Glasgow believed that something of irreplaceable value was being lost with their demise.[32]

One also finds indications in *Virginia* that Ellen Glasgow was less sanguine about the prospects of unearthing man's instinctual life than her Darwinian "realism" might lead one to believe. Such primitive impulses may once have endowed pioneers with the energy to move mountains and plough jungles, but in those same emotions, she notes elsewhere, lay "the seeds of that ancient lust of cruelty from which have sprung the brutal pleasures of men." Virginia, for her part, reproaches herself severely after momentarily giving in to the "primeval woman in her blood" by purchasing some expensive material for a blue silk dress (a perennial symbol of sin in Glasgow's works) and joining her husband for a fox hunt. "She had sacrificed duty to pleasure," Glasgow sternly comments, "and suddenly she had discovered that to one with her heritage of good and evil the two are inseparable." Moreover, to Ellen Glasgow, the desirability of reviving animal instinct depended directly on one's social status and race. If aristocrats like the Pendletons seemed too far removed from their jungle heritage, the "three hearty brutes" who killed Virginia's father out of sheer impulse obviously were not. As for the Negro, he was at best destined to be like "some trustful wild animal that man has tamed and only partly domesticated." Even when a black person appeared thoroughly assimilated, as did the Pendletons' faithful Aunt Mehitable, one could never tell how genuine the process was. "Was it development or mimicry," Glasgow asks, "that had brought her up out of savagery and clothed her in her blue gingham dress and her white turban, as in the outward covering of civilization?" The very phrasing of the question provides Ellen Glasgow's answer.[33]*

The clearest evidence of the apprehension Glasgow felt concerning the drift of her times, however, shows up in her sketches of Virginia's three children. Harry, the youngest, appears the most promising of the three, competitive like a Treadwell, charming and warm like a Pendleton. But unfortunately, little more is known of him, since Glasgow conveniently sends him away to pursue his "brilliant" studies at Oxford as soon as he becomes an adult. Jenny Treadwell, next in line, has acquired the "inflexible logic" and "serene infallibility" of science through her work in—naturally enough—biology at Bryn Mawr. She also appears to have acquired its clinical coldness. With her vestige of Pendleton altruism, she is capable of sympathizing on an abstract level with the misfortunes of the working class, but she cannot seem to comprehend the suffering of her own aggrieved mother. A "wandering goddess" with a "look of almost superhuman composure," Jenny wanders in and out of the final section of the novel, saying and doing very little.[34]

By far the most concrete glimpse Glasgow provides of her vision of the future comes in her depiction of Virginia's oldest daughter, Lucy. Cynical, worldly, ill-mannered, egotistical, "utterly emancipated from the last shackles of reverence," Lucy embodies the complete reversal of all the major personality attributes the nineteenth century most admired. She has no conception whatever of family, honor, or duty. On reaching the age of twenty-two, she impulsively marries a man twelve years her senior, a widower with two children "at that," whom she has known only casually. But, Miss Glasgow quickly and hopefully points out, Lucy is definitely "not a savage"; rather, we are to believe she represents "the perfect product of overcivilization." Because Lucy does not subscribe to the Victorian moral code—or, apparently, any other—she is thereby excused from following it. "The very simplicity and sincerity of her egotism," Glasgow insists, "robbed it of its offensiveness, and raised it from a trait of character to the dignity of a point of view." Brave words, indeed.[35]

If *Virginia*, then, marked Ellen Glasgow's sharpest attack on southern Victorian culture prior to the war, the book is also filled with hesitations and occasional retreats. Later she would call attention to her "applica-

*Not surprisingly, when other southern writers in the late 1920s praised the Harlem Literary Renaissance for at last enabling blacks truly to express themselves, Ellen Glasgow was not among them. His *Nigger Heaven*, she wrote Carl Van Vechten only half-facetiously, "seems to me the best argument in favor of African slavery that I have ever read" (Glasgow to Carl Van Vechten, July 28, 1926, in Glasgow, *Letters*, 80).

tion of modern theories in psychology" in the novel, which, she claimed, "were in advance of the period in which I was writing." She meant, of course, her willingness to give the animal component in human nature its due, to detail the primitive instincts residing even within the chaste bosom of a pedigreed southern lady. As we have seen, though, there were clear-cut moral limits to Ellen Glasgow's celebration of instinct. When she extrapolated what seemed to her the tendency of modern psychology and produced a creature who lived wholly by instinct in Lucy Treadwell, the results were not exactly encouraging. Perhaps she could still defend Lucy's behavior as "overcivilized" in 1912, but by a decade later, after the war and certain other events had done their work, Glasgow would have a new and less flattering name for such conduct—"barbaric."[36]

III

An assortment of forces—social, literary, and personal—combined to make the First World War an immense watershed in Ellen Glasgow's intellectual development. Given her extreme sensitivity to suffering, combined with her "biological" outlook, the war itself was bound to depress her and confirm her worst suspicions about human nature. "Had humanity been trying unwisely to hurry evolution," she asked soon afterwards, "and had the crust of civilization proved too thin to restrain the outbreak of volcanic impulses?" What worried her most was the fate of England. Like others raised in the Victorian mold, Glasgow viewed England and its culture as the vital center of world civilization, with America at most an overcommercialized outlying province. Now, drained by four years of constant fighting, that center seemed to be falling apart. Nor did the coming of peace bring relief; rather, it appeared to unleash many new and highly threatening currents of social change. The upheaval, she later wrote, "had disturbed the steady stream of experience, and from the shaken depths embryonic fragments of impulse had floated to the surface of consciousness. Everything was becoming—or so it seemed at the moment—nothing was finished, except the Great War and the great tradition." The effects were most dramatic in her own bailiwick of literature, where a thoroughgoing experimentalism in both form and content temporarily ruled the day. Glasgow could, with effort, accept the naturalism of a Theodore Dreiser, but the hieroglyphics of Ezra Pound and the bloody violence of Ernest Hemingway fell far beyond her ken.[37]

Personal problems compounded her dismay. For one, there was her abortive romance with Henry W. Anderson, a wealthy Richmond lawyer to whom she became engaged in July, 1917, at the age of forty-four. A few months later Anderson left to head a Red Cross relief operation in the Balkans, where he paid particular attention to the well-being of Rumania's attractive and flirtatious Queen Marie. Whether or not that affair became the point of discord between him and his fiancée is not exactly clear, although it is true that members of the Richmond bar with uncontrollable sexual appetites figure as objects of satire in two subsequent Glasgow novels. Whatever the case, the engagement did not survive the war and Glasgow was forced to resign herself to the growing likelihood that the "happiness" her mother's generation had defined as the capstone of every woman's existence would never be hers. Added to this realization was her advancing deafness, which further isolated her from human contact, and the continuing failure of her work to receive what she thought was its due critical acclaim. To Ellen Glasgow, then, in the early 1920s, the world seemed decidedly bleak.[38]

Her response to this situation took three forms. First, as the attack on the old aristocracy mounted in other quarters of the southern literary scene, Glasgow's defense of Tidewater values came more and more into the open. This heightened tolerance for the class of her birth may have stemmed in part—as McDowell claims—from her increasing disillusionment with the outcome of the New South movement, especially the filth and disfigurement industrialization had visited on Richmond, but it also presented an obvious grasp for some established certainties in a period of great flux. Second, Glasgow began speaking out vehemently against the trends of modern literature, culminating in her assault on the "Raw-Head-and-Bloody-Bones" school of southern fiction in 1932. Before long this constant tongue-lashing of Hemingway, Faulkner, and other "sophisticated barbarians" became a source of much embarrassment to many of her New York literary friends. "In the days of my youth," she retorted, "such degradation of intelligence before instinct would have been classified as simple derangement of the reasoning faculty." Finally, with her exposed moral nerve more vexatious than ever, she turned to the philosophy of stoicism, or, more precisely, to what Daiches calls "the stoic mood of agnostic heroism" so characteristic of late Victorians. Not merely endurance for its own sake, but endurance against the specific torture of "the cold implacable inhumanity of the universe" became her objective. Like Cabell she sought to anesthetize herself from the realities of a world she could not feel at home in.[39]*

*One might also list a fourth response to her dilemma—her extraordinary concern for the rights of animals and her often-commented-upon fawning over her pet dogs, which came to border on the pathological. It is most suggestive that this tenderness toward animals, although always with her, reached its apogee in the 1920s at the same time as her turn toward stoicism, suggesting a certain degree of emotional displacement. The affections she

Out of this pain and turmoil came *Barren Ground*, Glasgow's uncontested favorite among the nineteen novels she eventually wrote. Personal as well as literary reasons accounted for this choice. As she noted in her preface, the book "became for me, while I was working on it, almost a vehicle of liberation. After years of tragedy and the sense of defeat that tragedy breeds in the mind, I had won my way to the other side of the wilderness, and had discovered, with astonishment, that I was another and a very different person." The validity of this victory claim may be subject to dispute, but there can be no doubt that, in chronicling the progress of Dorinda Oakley from a weak and foolish young girl, filled with romantic dreams, to a self-reliant, unsentimental, "securely" middle-aged woman who has "learned to live without joy," Ellen Glasgow was attempting a spiritual autobiography. Little wonder she would later immodestly refer to it as "the truest novel ever written."[40]

The daughter of a middle-class farm family whose holdings have gone to weeds, Dorinda grows up in an isolated Virginia town longing for the "emotional realities" of life. She possesses, we are told, an agile mind, a sensitive nature, and a powerful "vein of iron," all apparently inherited from her great-grandfather, the celebrated Presbyterian missionary John Calvin Abernethy. At first misled by youthful dreams of romance, Dorinda allows a handsome but invertebrate young doctor named Jason Greylock to "ruin" her, getting her pregnant and then, under pressure from his family, marrying another woman. Although "caught like a mouse in the trap of life," Dorinda bravely refuses to give up. Instead she runs off to New York, suffers a convenient miscarriage, and spends the next few years learning to repress her natural impulses. Her stoic self-control perfected, she returns home intent on transforming the faltering

---

now denied to humans, it would seem, were lavished instead on animals.

On the intellectual level, this passion for animals appears directly tied to her Darwinism, representing yet another attempt on her part to establish continuity between the human and animal realms—yet carefully contrived not to undercut her Victorian values. Just as she had identified an animal component in human nature, she now began to find what one might call a "human" component in animal nature. To her, her beloved Scottish terrier "Jeremy" (note his Scottish ancestry and Calvinist name!) was far more than a dog; he was a spiritual being with a capacity for "higher" emotions like love only slightly less developed than that of a man. That was why Jeremy's death in 1929 became, as her biographer describes it, the greatest tragedy in her life. Desperately she wanted to believe that animals could, despite their vigorous instinctual lives, become at least partially civilized. Jeremy and the other domesticated animals in her retinue supplied daily proof for this fiction.

As James Turner explains, this sort of relationship with pets was a fairly common expedient for late Victorians in their effort to get right with Darwin, and specifically, in Turner's words, "to drain off some of the tension induced by man's kinship with animals." See Godbold, *Ellen Glasgow*, 153–57, and Turner, *Reckoning with the Beast*, 69–73, 76–78.

Oakley homestead into a prosperous enterprise. At novel's end, she has conquered the wild broom sedge that had overrun the land and established a successful dairy farm—at the cost of her own inner life. Aware of that cost, Glasgow nonetheless implies that Dorinda has made the best possible adjustment to the wreckage of civilized existence in the twentieth century. She has achieved "serenity of mind," which is all a woman of her disposition could have asked.[41]

The novel's imagery centers upon the metaphoric parallel Glasgow sets up between Dorinda's dual efforts to conquer nature, represented by the emotions within her and the broom sedge on the land. The "wild, free principle of nature" with its "inexhaustible vitality," Glasgow repeatedly advises, will overwhelm the human spirit if it is not brought under control. Or, as wise old Matthew Fairlamb puts it, "Thar's one thing sartain sure, you've got to conquer the land in the beginning, or it'll conquer you before you're through with it." The same maxim, Dorinda discovers, applies in the personal sphere. To root out the "wildness" inside her, Dorinda must stay on guard every minute, lest her "primitive impulses" and "blind instincts" burst forth from "the buried jungle of her consciousness" in the same way the weeds spring back to reclaim the land. Any emotion-laden event—her mother's death, Jason Greylock's funeral, or a concert of romantic music she attends in New York—can stir up "the hidden roots of her life," unleashing "the natural Dorinda" she has worked so hard to suppress. Only through constant application of her vein of iron can Dorinda keep the hostile and unremitting forces of nature at bay.[42]

This incessant war between man and nature suggests how much Ellen Glasgow had shifted ground since 1912. Her main concern in *Virginia* had been to find some means for retrieving Virginia Pendleton's buried instinctual life from its entombment beneath "the dead leaves of civilization." Now, in *Barren Ground*, she was taking the opposite tack, searching for a mechanism that would enable Dorinda Oakley to repress those same biological instincts forever. Plainly things had gone awry. In her earlier, more sanguine calculations, she had always expected that evolutionary change would sweep up and carry along the finer achievements of Victorianism as she saw them, including the emphasis on morality and good breeding, leaving the defects, such as evasive idealism, behind. Culturally as well as physically, the fittest would survive. By the mid-1920s, however, it was apparent that she had misjudged the course of events. Everywhere she looked, she complained, "old cultures were breaking up, codes were loosening, morals were declining, and manners, another aspect of morality, were slipping away. A whole civilization was disintegrating, without and within." In this world gone mad, where intelligence was openly degraded before instinct, the sole recourse that seemed available to her was a strategic retreat to the values of her father's nineteenth-century Calvinism, that stern moral code more deeply implanted in her than she was ever willing to admit. Only a return to this "moral fibre that had stiffened the necks of martyrs" could prevent human beings from falling apart at the seams. Fortunately, in Dorinda's case, such moral fibre was indeed present, "deeply embedded in her character if not in her opinions." "Though her mind rebelled," Glasgow assures us, "her conscience was incurably Presbyterian."[43]

In fact, Ellen Glasgow retained not only her father's moral sensibilities but much of his Calvinist cosmology as well. As her need for religious certitude increased after the war, one can detect her beginning to substitute Nature for God in her view of the cosmic plan, producing that strange amalgam of belief that Richard Hofstadter, writing in a slightly different context, has termed "naturalistic Calvinism." Gradually the tenets of Presbyterianism crept back into her thought—predestination in the form of a more purposeful working of the evolutionary process, the inscrutability of the Calvinist God in the power of accidental happenings over men's lives. Even though this pilgrim's regress would soon land her in a dead heap of intellectual and moral confusion, she was helpless to resist it.[44]

One sees the development of this naturalistic cosmology reflected in the spiritual progress of Dorinda Oakley. Like Glasgow herself, Dorinda experiences grace briefly during her youth, but then, "suddenly, as mysteriously as it had come, the illumination in her soul had waned and flickered like a lamp. Religion had not satisfied." Cast momentarily adrift, she turns, following her jilting at the hands of Jason Greylock, to the "elastic doctrine of predestination" for an explanation of her plight, realizing that "no matter how hard she had struggled she could not have prevented it." Soon she comes to understand that "invisible processes" rule her life, that she is caught "in the whirlpool of universal anarchy" and cannot "by any effort of her will bring order out of chaos." Having learned the truth about existence she can at least prepare for it. She can face the world with stoic heroism: "There was no self-pity in her thoughts. The unflinching Presbyterian in her blood steeled her against sentimentality. She would meet life standing and she would meet it with her eyes open." No doubt Glasgow conceived Dorinda's story as a parable of the forging of a twentieth-century woman, one capable of living in accord with the post-Darwinian framework of belief, but what this book really entails is not Modernism at all, but nineteenth-century theology got up in stoic dress.[45]

Moreover, the stoicism itself is far from complete. For all the steel in her blood and iron in her veins, Dorinda cannot down her longing for something better than agnostic realism. "Although it seemed to her that she had grown wiser with the years," we are told at the book's end, "she had never entirely abandoned her futile effort to find a meaning in life." Especially in times of stress there returns to her "the old baffling sense of a secret meaning in the universe, of a reality beneath the actuality, of a deep profounder than the deeps of experience." In short, she feels cheated in the matter of religious faith. Even if her parents had lived their lives in poverty, she reflects, they had

> possessed a spiritual luxury which she herself had never attained. She had inherited, she realized, the religious habit of mind without the religious heart; for the instinct of piety had worn too thin to cover the generations. Conviction! That, at least, they had never surrendered. The glow of religious certitude had never faded for them into the pallor of moral necessity.

This is the only passage of its kind in Ellen Glasgow's work—the only one in which she expresses a comprehension of what had happened to her. Given the anguish this insight clearly caused her, it is remarkable that she put it into print at all.[46]

The worst part, though, was that the contradictions inherent in her naturalistic Calvinism left her without a fixed moral code to guide behavior. As Glasgow well knew, it had been the same "strong impulses" that had caused Dorinda's downfall that later "enabled her to rebuild her life out of the ruins." On the naturalist side, all such impulses were accounted normal biological processes, morally neutral if not a positive good; by the lights of Calvinism they were evil and must be suppressed. How could one resolve this paradox from the viewpoint she had adopted? The answer is that no resolution was possible. "Good and bad, right and wrong, they were all tangled together," Glasgow comments in exasperation. At times she hints that sinfulness can no longer exist in the post-Darwinian universe—that the sole standard of judgment has become success or failure, survival or death. Thus Dorinda decides Jason cannot be blamed for his actions; for congenitally weak characters of this sort there can only be pity, described, of all things, as "a detached impulse." "Good failure and bad failure," it was all the same because "nature abhorred both."[47]

Here, though, one suspects Glasgow was at least in part dissembling. Whenever she speaks of the weak and the strong, a careful inspection of her words reveals that she is referring specifically to moral stamina, to the strength to resist temptation. In addition, as Dorinda goes about her long ruminations on this subject, there are adumbrations of a still more orthodox concept remaining in effect:

> [W]hy had she, in whom life burned so strong and bright, wasted her vital energy on the mere husk of a man? Why, above all, should Nature move so unintelligently in the matter of instinct? Did this circle of reasoning lead back inevitably, she wondered, to the stead-fast doctrine of original sin? "The truth is we always want what is bad for us, I suppose?" she concluded, and gave up the riddle.

Plainly, Ellen Glasgow could no more escape a sense of sin than Charles Darwin could accept the Mosaic account of creation. Only in her case, the Calvinist conscience, detached from its religious base, had been permitted to float freely through her thought, infesting every nook and cranny. The world has scarcely devised a more exquisite form of torture—nor one less congenial to the intellectual temperament of the twentieth century.[48]*

I V

As her biographer depicts it, Ellen Glasgow's house at One West Main Street in Richmond had become by the 1920s an accurate reflection of her personality. "Downstairs," he writes, "was the world of wit and

---

*Following *Barren Ground*, Glasgow completed four additional major novels (along with one of minor significance), all of which reflected her continuing but unsuccessful effort to reconcile Darwinian naturalism with her native Calvinism. The first two works in her Queensborough trilogy, *The Romantic Comedians* (1926) and *They Stooped to Folly: A Comedy of Morals* (1929), both poke gentle fun at members of the Richmond aristocracy by revealing their unacknowledged sexual appetites and outdated mores. In *The Sheltered Life*, the third work in the trilogy and perhaps Glasgow's best novel artistically, the comedy turns to tragedy once again as the Tidewater world is portrayed on the brink of extinction—its beauty and nobility succumbing to the forces of an inferior industrialized society, its fine manners and sustaining illusions shattered by the new cult of egotism and impulse. Finally, *Vein of Iron* (1935) represents in essence a rewriting of *Barren Ground*, with Ada Fincastle replacing Dorinda Oakley as the young girl from the Shenandoah valley who learns through life's hardships the need for a stoic persona.

Beneath that persona, however, Glasgow's central questions went unanswered. As General David Archbald, a character whose consciousness closely reflects Glasgow's own, muses to himself in *The Sheltered Life*: "Everywhere people are loving, suffering, hating, hoping, going into hospitals, coming out of hospitals, laughing, weeping, trying fruitlessly to make life what it is not. All the striving for an impossible happiness, for an ecstasy that endures. All the long waiting, the vain prayers, the hope that is agony! And who knows what the end of it is? Who knows that the end ever comes? But what we see and touch

gaiety, bright colors, and elaborate parties, the world where a public image was created and external history recorded. Upstairs was a world of despair and self-pity, the place where novels were written for escape and companionship." The metaphor may easily be extended to fit the state of Tidewater culture in the postwar era. On one level could be found the playful formality of a Cabell, on another the stoic "realism" of a Glasgow, attempting in vain to reconcile her Calvinist heritage with the dictates of science and, in her words, with the "artistic impulse we call Modernism." Certainly it was possible to move between these levels—Cabell assuming the stoic mode when writing of more recent times, and Glasgow, with *Barren Ground* behind her, turning to the comedy of manners in the first two volumes of her Queensborough trilogy. What was not possible was to leave the house, which, for all its southern trappings, could have been located in any number of places where Victorianism had taken deep root.[49]

For those who cared to see it, the shape of southern Modernism was being limned out by the North Carolina playwright Paul Green the same year that Ellen Glasgow was at work on Dorinda Oakley. Writing in *The Reviewer*, whose move from Richmond to Chapel Hill in 1924 neatly symbolized the cultural transfer of power, Green demanded that southern letters liberate itself completely from the strictures of the nineteenth-century sensibility. His prime example of what to avoid was *The Library of Southern Literature*, a seventeen-volume collection of the region's verse and prose assembled with obvious reverence but little taste by the New South generation of literary scholars. If this extravaganza faithfully represented southern literature, Green argued, it left out too many important truths: "In this Library's thousands of pages there is no hint that times are ever out of joint, that evil is among us, that there are ultimate and absolute dramatic conflicts in which a man can lose his soul. With the exception of one or two figures (and they are no more Southern than national), it has had nothing to do with richness, with spontaneity, with vitality." To break through these limitations, Green continued, all the southern writer need do is look about him at the ordinary lives of sharecroppers, mill hands, or small-town shopkeepers. There he would find "an abundance of crude, unshaped material" from which to draw a "dynamism of emotion terrible enough in its intensity for the greatest art."[50]

---

cannot be the whole of it. There must be a plan, there must be a meaning, he insisted, still faithful to a creed he had forsaken." Likewise, Glasgow remained in the impossible position of being faithful to a creed she had forsaken—and that in the end was her tragedy. See *The Sheltered Life*, 195.

For Ellen Glasgow and others brought up in the Tidewater tradition, the path Green was charting was clearly an impossible one. No matter how much they may have desired to appear "modern," the values that ultimately controlled their work stood firmly opposed to the "absolute dramatic conflicts" and "dynamism of emotion" that Green wished to place at the center of the region's artistic consciousness. On the contrary, as post-Victorians their efforts were bent toward creating a stoic barrier to shield themselves from the darker side of life. But in the mid 1920s a new vision of the South was starting to appear, a vision that would leave the genteel Tidewater far behind. It would not take long before William Faulkner, Thomas Wolfe, Erskine Caldwell, Katherine Anne Porter, Carson McCullers, and so many others would make good on Green's bold prophecy.

PART TWO

MODERNISTS BY THE
SKIN OF THEIR TEETH

In the southern post-Victorians one sees writers of considerable talent hedged in by historical circumstances, tied to an outdated morality and disabled by a radical innocence they were but vaguely aware they possessed. The result in most cases was to limit their work to a playing out of old ideas in a new context, rather than a striking out in original directions. The breakthroughs they ardently hoped to achieve all fell short. Such is often the fate of those unfortunate enough to get caught on the wrong side of cultural change.[1]

For those southern intellectuals in the early 1920s whose sensibilities fell closer to the Modernist than to the Victorian camp, however, just the opposite was true. Straddling two cultural eras, theirs was an unparalleled opportunity to view the South with fresh eyes, using the conceptual tools made available by the social sciences and the perspectives afforded by Modernist literary culture in bringing to light facets of southern society previously ignored. "For the first time in the history of the South," W. J. Cash later wrote of these pioneers, "they dimly felt the thing was there, and groped to make out its shape and form and nature and to comprehend how it came to have so much power over themselves, as a child gropes to grasp the far-away woods and hills through the pane of his nursery window." As Cash suggests, the work of these writers was marked by a certain tentative quality; never would they obtain the sure apprehension of their subject enjoyed by those starting fully Modernist in the mid 1930s. Nonetheless, these transitional figures also possessed a chance for broad-ranging exploration far more extensive than their successors. Those capable of taking advantage of this unusual status, such as Howard W. Odum, William Faulkner, and various members of the Agrarian group, were thus able to set the agenda for southern culture, becoming seminal figures of such magnitude that the course of intellectual development in the region was permanently altered in their wake.[2]

Often this opportunity was purchased at a high personal price. For what their fresh vision of the South frequently revealed was a society ridden with pathology, pervaded by social hatreds, sectional animosities, and a sense of failure and defeat. In rapid succession they were to witness the peak of Klan activity, the Fundamentalist crusade, the Scopes trial, the bitter 1928 presidential campaign, a series of pitched labor battles in the textile industry, and the Scottsboro case—along with many less visible, but equally unattractive symptoms of social change. The New South generation had assumed that the forces that gave rise to such events had been only temporary, the unfortunate aftermath of Reconstruction, which industrialization would soon sweep away; but now it was clear this was not so. Instead, the sources of pathology would have to be traced to defects in the region's social order and culture. The South's history, customs, and character would need to be reexamined to discover what had gone wrong. To men who still harbored a sizable remnant of Victorian belief, who remained attached to the South's traditional mythology even as they acted to vitiate it, such explanations were painful indeed. A keen sense of their own vestigial innocence and the necessity of overcoming it was not the least source of that pain.

Therefore it should come as no surprise that the hallmark of their writing on the South was a thoroughgoing ambivalence. Compulsively they tried to erect barriers between themselves and what they were in fact saying. For Odum, this distancing took the form of what he termed "portraiture"—a depiction of southern society that laid bare the pathology and many of its causes without analyzing or identifying it by name. Faulkner, as his means of searching out the unspoken attitudes that shaped southern life, pursued a trance-like exploration of his own consciousness, periodically counterbalancing his advances with displays of allegiance to regional mythology. Like Quentin Compson at the conclusion of *Absalom, Absalom!*, he was torn by both an intense love for and an equally intense alienation from his homeland, feelings he could never begin to resolve. The Agrarians, by contrast, attempted to circumvent that ambivalence by an act of fiat, declaring that the South, whatever its imperfections, represented the last hope for realizing their ideal social vision, and pretending at times that the vision had already come into being. Within the realm of metaphor, this strategy might succeed temporarily, but confronted with actuality, their suppressed ambivalence sprang back with renewed vigor. In no way could the Agrarians escape their lot as intellectuals of transition.

The writers who followed these men built on their achievements, facing southern ills with a measure of detachment and working steadily to help correct them. Those fully Modernist understood that the irrational could never be wholly eliminated from human existence; that, on the contrary, its presence was often to be desired. Those Modernist to a lesser degree could not acquiesce in that conclusion: the blemishes they saw in the society they loved would torture them all their lives and prod them to feats of immense creativity.

CHAPTER 5

HOWARD W. ODUM AND
SOCIAL SCIENCE IN THE SOUTH

Ever since his death in 1954 the name of Howard Washington Odum has been slipping slowly into obscurity. To those southern liberals of his day who have survived him, this eclipse of reputation must surely seem strange. Odum, the region's first modern sociologist, was their beacon of light, their most reliable guide to a genuinely new South, the one man, they thought, whose work would prove indestructible. In 1940, for example, when Lillian Smith and Paula Snelling, the coeditors of the *North Georgia Review*, compiled a list of one hundred influential southerners, Odum stood at the very top. "Warm-hearted, cool-headed, far-visioned, steady-armed man of dreams and action," they wrote of him, "he drew up the blue-prints and laid in solid rock the foundations on which the South may establish realistic and constructive regionalism in stead of defensive and lethal sectionalism." Nor was Odum's influence necessarily limited to the intellectual elite. A few years earlier Jonathan Daniels reported visiting a lawyer's office in the tiny Arkansas town of Marked Tree. On learning that Daniels was from North Carolina the lawyer grew quite excited: "Do you know Odum?" he asked.[1]

Students of southern history have not forgotten Odum, and for good reason. Both at the University of North Carolina, his home base for thirty-five years, and in the South generally, the man's accomplishments were prodigious. At Chapel Hill, Odum not only created a Department of Sociology from scratch, the first such department in the South, and brought it to national attention in less than a decade, but in addition he founded an Institute for Research in Social Science that is still very much in existence, started the *Journal of Social Forces*, set up a School of Public Welfare (later the School of Social Work), and lent indispensable aid to the establishment of a university press. To these brick-and-mortar achievements one must add his immense bibliography, comprising twenty-three books and over 150 articles if joint authorships are counted. By the late 1920s, these publications, together with his service for the President's Research Committee on Social Trends during the Hoover administration, had catapulted Odum to the height of his profession. His tenure as president of the American Sociological Society in 1930—he was the only southerner so honored up to that time—cemented his status as one of the country's leading social scientists.[2]

But such tangible measures of success tell only half the story; the other half concerns the remarkable breadth and acuity of Odum's vision of the South. As George B. Tindall puts it, Odum was "the most perceptive observer of the Southern scene during the first half of the century. He saw it whole, the old and the new, the folk and the academic, the agrarian and the industrial, the spiteful and the generous—and saw it all with a profound sensitivity and respect." Here, in his ability to see the region in entirely original terms, lay the real source of Odum's power over his generation, and also, paradoxically, the seeds of his future obscurity.[3]

For Odum's was a special vision of the South, one born of the particular historical moment when southern cultural life was poised on the brink of Modernism. Precisely because Odum came along at this time of transition his work had a potential for enormous scope, encompassing a far broader view of the South than anyone arriving either before or after him could achieve. And Odum, as the region's first modern social scientist, was strategically endowed by temperament, training, and position to take advantage of this opportunity. He was able to look both ways, at "the old and the new," to see not only the strengths and moral virtues of southern society but the conflicts, tensions, and evils as well. Furthermore, unlike his Victorian predecessors, he was willing to depict many of the latter characteristics in print—carefully balanced against the good. But Odum's all-embracing portraiture approach also had its limitations. When younger sociologists, many of them his disciples, began moving beyond mere description to analyze specific southern problems like lynching, mill villages, and sharecropping with an eye to drawing causal connections and assigning responsibility, Odum could encourage but not join them. Willing to acknowledge the evil in his society, he consistently stopped short of exploring its roots; the same cast of mind that brought him to his initial vision of the South prevented him from doing so. It was this failure to pursue his own leads that eventually made his sociology seem out of date.

In Howard Odum, then, we may see the unique possibilities open to a man whose work spans a period of transition. We can find instances of great success and great failure, for Odum certainly knew both. We can also find, if we look closely enough, the agonizing struggle of one of the first southerners to become a Modernist intellectual, for Odum knew that, too.

I

To understand Odum's thought, one must not lose sight of Odum himself. For the Howard Odum who arrived in Chapel Hill early in 1920 brought with him not only a mind trained in social science theory but a personality formed through an intense experience with rural poverty, childhood tragedy, southern defeatism, and death. His father, William Pleasants Odum, owned a small truck-and-dairy farm near the tiny Georgia village of Bethlehem, where Howard was born in 1884. The Odums had always been of yeoman stock, content to lead a peaceful, humble, religious existence close to the earth—indeed, the very name "Odum" is derived from the Anglo-Saxon word for "earth." On Howard's mother's side, however, things were quite different. His maternal grandfather, Philip Thomas, a moderately successful slaveholder prior to the war, had served as a major in the Confederate cavalry, but by the end of Reconstruction the family's possessions had been virtually wiped out. All that remained was a bitter hatred of the Yankees and a visceral desire, felt most keenly by Odum's mother, to regain something of the family's lost standing. Here Mary Ann Odum's hopes rested on her children; in direct contrast to her husband, who cared little about such matters, she was determined to see that they, through education, rose to positions of social leadership. Moreover, to insure that they grew up with proper gentility, she diligently attempted to maintain for them a special environment, free from the cruder and uglier aspects of life, where their aesthetic sensibilities might be nourished. Thus from his earliest days, the two predominant strains of traditional southern culture, yeoman and Cavalier, were competing for young Howard's attention.[4]

Odum would later romanticize his youth as a time of family warmth and old-time pleasures, but the evidence indicates that the prevailing mood was far from sanguine. Tragedy struck the household repeatedly. The worst instances came after Howard, weakened by a bout of typhoid, had been excused from farm chores and assigned to watch over his younger siblings. In short order, despite his best efforts to save them, three of the children died—one by accidentally walking into a brush fire, another by falling from a tree, and a third by diphtheria. Although not his fault in any way, the three traumas left Odum ridden with powerful feelings of guilt and inadequacy the rest of his life. Adding to his sense of self-doubt was the presence of his grandfathers, Confederate veterans who had returned home in physical and psychological shambles. Howard was especially close to his paternal grandfather, John Wesley Odum, with whom he identified strongly and whose deep pessimism he came to share. In time he would perceive John Wesley Odum as a symbol of the South's defeatism—as the embodiment of the precise attitude that had allowed the region to wallow in underdevelopment. He would later devote much of his career to battling that sense of defeatism, but for the moment his grandfather's talk of futility only reinforced his own apprehensions about the future. It was a lonely and despondent Howard Odum, then, who entered Emory College in 1900 and passed through without attracting anyone's notice. Hurt by his inability to join a fraternity, beset by mediocre grades (a result of his poor preparation), and with few friends, he thought of himself, as he later put it, as "A.U.I.P., or Awkward, Ugly, Ignorant, and Poor." Small wonder that his intellectual interests centered on classical Greek tragedy, in which he seems to have found a resonance of his own and his family's suffering. For Odum, the tragic mode was to be part of his personal life.[5]

It was against this backdrop of despair that Odum discovered social science. Upon graduating from Emory he had gone to Mississippi, at first to teach school and later to continue his studies in classics at the University of Mississippi. There he came under the influence of the psychologist Thomas Pearce Bailey, Jr., a specialist in race relations, whose tutelage, writes Odum's biographer, was to become "the most important single experience in Odum's intellectual life." Like most Progressive social scientists, Bailey viewed the potential of his new discipline as virtually limitless. Applied to social problems, the methods of social science could lead to ultimate truths, providing infallible guidance in shaping public policy and serving as the final arbiter in any conflict situation—that was the lesson Bailey impressed on Odum. To the young student so unsure of himself, yet aspiring to a role of leadership for his people, this lesson came as a revelation. Science, it seemed, could place in his hands a mighty lever for directing the course of rural reconstruction in the South, one available regardless of his personal inadequacies. With the authority of science, it would not matter if he were awkward, ugly, or poor. In addition, scientific method would permit him to retain his preferred style of aloofness, since detachment was its one inescapable requirement. Later in his career Odum was to be accused, with some justice, of overvaluing sociology, of regarding it in quasi-religious fashion as a source of salvation rather than a mere technique for research; here, in the convergence of Bailey's teachings and Odum's inner needs, lies the reason why.[6]

It would take a little more than a decade, however, before Odum began putting his plans for the South into full practice. First came his formal training in social science, beginning with a field study on the folk culture of southern blacks done under Bailey's guidance from 1906 to 1908 and continuing with two doctorates in rapid succession, one directed by Bailey's old teacher, G. Stanley Hall, at Clark University in 1909, and the second under the noted sociologist Franklin Henry Giddings at Columbia University the following year. Both dissertations were based on the research into Negro life Odum had completed before going North. Unable to find a teaching job in the South, Odum spent the next two years working for the Philadelphia Bureau of Municipal Research as a consultant on race relations in the public schools. From there he moved to the University of Georgia in 1913 as an assistant professor of education, concerned mainly with upgrading teacher training and fighting for higher school budgets in rural districts. Although he found this work satisfying—improving country schools would always be among his favorite projects—it soon became apparent to him that Georgia possessed neither the will nor the resources to back his designs for a regional social science center. And so, following his wartime service as state director of social work for the Red Cross, he accepted an offer in December, 1918, to become dean of the School of Liberal Arts at Emory.[7]

Because of a misunderstanding, however, this decision soon proved ill-fated. Somehow Odum had gathered the impression that he had been hired to turn Emory into a southern replica of Harvard or Columbia. He was apparently unaware before he arrived of the school's limited finances or of the arch-conservative views of its chancellor, Methodist Bishop Warren A. Candler. As the Board of Trustees rejected his elaborate proposals for expansion, one after another, Odum became increasingly frustrated. "Odum wanted to build a University overnight and build it his own way," Candler later explained.[8]

Then, in the spring of 1920, Odum's long-awaited opportunity finally came. Through the initiative of Harry Woodburn Chase, his classmate and close friend at Clark, Odum was appointed to head both the new School of Public Welfare and a new Department of Sociology at Chapel Hill. Odum was elated, for it seemed that he was moving into the one southern state that might appreciate his work. "North Carolina," he pointed out to a correspondent, "has very advanced social legislation and the University is fitting into the state program with commendable service and dispatch." Unfortunately, there is no way of knowing how thoroughly Odum had been apprised of the difficulty Chase had experienced in getting the appointment approved by the trustees, many of whom could not differentiate between a sociologist and a socialist. Whatever the case, Odum was soon to discover that the sailing in North Carolina would be anything but smooth; if it was to become a liberal state, he would have to help make it so.[9]

Prior to Odum's coming, social science at Chapel Hill, and in the South generally, had usually fallen under the rubric of Rural Social Economics, a field presided over by Eugene Cunningham Branson. Branson had moved to North Carolina in 1914 from Georgia with his novel scheme of organizing students from each county into study groups to survey the utilization of natural and economic resources in their home communities. Branson also set up a North Carolina Club, made up of the members of the county clubs, which chose a topic of statewide interest each year for its bimonthly discussion meetings and published its findings in a well-documented *Yearbook*. These ventures drew Branson into a number of areas like farm tenancy, soil conservation, taxation, rural housing, and county government, which Odum and his students would explore in greater depth the following decade. Yet, while Branson's work did serve to sketch out the dimensions of rural poverty in the South, it went no further. Never did he attempt to link the conditions he found with anything beyond mistaken techniques of husbandry. Reduced to its essentials, Branson's message represented the principles of the 4-H Club applied to southern agriculture, with scientific, diversified farming his answer to almost every ill. Moreover, Branson was a gentle soul who kept clear of controversy and paid careful obeisance to southern tradition. "A fine stimulator and progressive spirit," Odum once called him, "but withal an unreconstructed southerner of noble mien."[10]

By contrast to Branson, Odum's arrival in Chapel Hill resembled the onslaught of a cyclone. "He was an agent of social change, and at times the area around him seemed charged with ozone," one colleague remembered. To the more conservative faculty especially, Odum's countless projects seemed willfully and perversely fashioned to land the university in the maximum amount of trouble. For one, there was the School of Public Welfare itself. It was true that an active citizens' lobby, the North Carolina Conference for Social Welfare, had pushed a relatively progressive reform program through the state legislature in recent years, culminating in the adoption of a county unit welfare system in 1917. But these accomplishments had been instituted primarily from above. "The social legislation of North Carolina today," observed Gerald W. Johnson in 1923, "is miles ahead of public opinion in the state"; anyone working in the field, he warned, would be well advised to proceed with caution. Thus when Chase sent his memorandum to the trustees proposing the new school, he spoke in vague terms of promoting good citizenship through the development of a "spirit of socialmindedness which leads the individual to look beyond himself and to think of himself in relation to his community." The situation plainly required slow, well-considered steps, done with little or no fanfare, taking care always that the society's basic values did not appear threatened.[11]

Odum, however, was irrepressible. No sooner did he receive his appointment than he began spinning plans to raise funds for a new social science building, recruit expert faculty from all over the country, call scores of conferences on every conceivable topic, invite Herbert Hoover to speak at the school's dedication ceremony, and, in general, turn out an army of eager welfare agents on the unsuspecting backwoods precincts of North Carolina. Although Odum unquestionably regarded good citizenship as a worthy aim, the curriculum he promulgated for his school was far more oriented to encouraging social criticism than Chase's nebulous "spirit of socialmindedness." In addition to standard courses in social theory, community health, family case work, educational sociology, child welfare, recreation, and statistics, students could choose from offerings in social pathology, juvenile delinquency, labor problems, Negro problems, and "Problems of the Small Town and Mill Village"—courses that started out by assuming some conspicuous defect in southern society. It was a bill of fare unavailable anywhere else in the South at that time.[12]

In 1924 Odum greatly stepped up the investigative dimension of his work with the launching of his Institute for Research in Social Science. Funded entirely by the Laura Spelman Rockefeller Memorial, the institute was created specifically to sponsor interdisciplinary study of those areas in southern life undergoing the most rapid change. Some of this research was to be done by senior faculty at Chapel Hill and elsewhere, but the bulk of it was placed in the hands of eight full-time "research assistants" chosen to pursue particular tasks. At the start, Odum seems to have anticipated a fairly steady turnover of personnel. Within a few years, though, a group of about fifteen young southerners had assembled who were to comprise the core of the institute for its initial two decades. Attached in varying ways to the institute and the Department of Sociology, these were Odum's chief disciples, the men who received his unqualified support when their work aroused controversy and whose stream of publications put Chapel Hill on the map of American social science. Their personal interests in turn would play the major role in setting the institute's agenda.[13]

These researchers soon began attacking a multiplicity of pressing southern problems head-on. First in importance came the studies of Rupert B. Vance and Arthur F. Raper on farm tenancy, of Guy B. Johnson and Thomas J. Woofter, Jr., in what Odum called the "Negro field," and of Harriet L. Herring, Jennings J. Rhyne, and George S. Mitchell on labor relations in the textile industry. Touching on three of the most highly charged issues facing the South, these projects got Odum's closest attention. Slightly more independent of Odum, but still tied directly to the institute, were Roy M. Brown, Wiley B. Sanders, and Gordon W. Blackwell, working on problems of public welfare, H. C. Brearley on crime, Paul W. Wager and Samuel H. Hobbs on local government, Clarence Heer on taxation, and Fletcher M. Green, Guion G. Johnson, and Julia C. Spruill covering topics in southern history. Many previously proscribed subjects were investigated, including the North Carolina chain gang, the problem of rural illegitimacy, corruption in county government, the abuses of sharecropping, Negro child welfare, illiteracy, and the convict lease system. In the first phase of his leadership of the institute, then, Odum was anything but cautious.[14]

Odum's boldest efforts of the early 1920s, however, came not in his sociology curriculum or in his policies at the institute, but in the pages of the *Journal of Social Forces*, the periodical he founded in 1922 to revitalize southern intellectual life. Here Odum and his comrade-in-arms, Gerald Johnson, let loose one of the most devastating editorial assaults on southern society and culture that the region had ever experienced from critics in residence. Although many southerners in the past had attacked their homeland from exile, those still living in the South had usually kept their criticisms to themselves, or aired them with discreet indirection, as did James Branch Cabell in his allegories. But Odum, with his declared intention of making *Social Forces* into a medium for southern self-criticism, was different. Characteristically, he wanted his new journal to say everything, do everything, and offer something to just about everyone. Its objectives, he wrote on various occasions, were to promote the study of southern problems, to discover new southern writers, to influence popular opinion by exposing it to science, to help establish social values, to encourage the organization of reform groups in the South, and to smooth the course of social change by "making democracy effective in the unequal places"—the latter a phrase he repeated constantly. *Social Forces* would, he hoped, contribute to the development of social theory, but it would also have "practical utility"; it would be academically respectable, but not wholly dominated by experts. The publication was aimed primarily at the South, but it would contain articles of interest to readers elsewhere, and many of its authors would be non-southerners. "Its ideals," he summed up, "are the ideals of those who work hard, believe in folks, set standards, accept limitations, and look ahead with directed optimism unafraid."[15]

Needless to say, Odum had trouble keeping these different promises, but the extent to which he did succeed was remarkable. By 1924, *Social*

Forces had 1,700 subscribers, about half in the South, ranging from sociologists to social workers to professional reformers to interested citizens. It was printing abstruse theoretical contributions from many of the country's leading social scientists alongside reports on prison conditions in North Carolina, statistical studies of poverty in the South, and the magazine's regular "departments," in which a reader could find the latest news of local interracial and social welfare organizations throughout the region. There was also an elaborate book review section, edited by two Mencken disciples, Harry Elmer Barnes of Smith College and Frank H. Hankins of Amherst. "The whole program of the Journal amazes me," Gerald Johnson told Odum in early 1923. "You are making it enormously more powerful than I had believed it could be made." No southern intellectual of that day would have disagreed.[16]

Most powerful by far were Odum's own editorials. "We seem to be in a period now," he wrote to the head of a southern women's group, "where the next immediate step is a sort of frank, honest, scientific, stock-taking of ourselves, giving full recognition to strong points but also to weak points and deficiencies, with a view to starting out at once upon a more creative and articulate South." To get this process underway, Odum in his editorials took special aim at what he referred to as "the present coercive, intolerant, reactionary religious and intellectual tyranny." He bore down heavily on the Klan, calling it "un-American, un-democratic and un-Christian," and sharply attacked the Fundamentalists for their hypocrisy and parochialism, which, he suggested, spilled over into other areas of southern life as well:

> The religion that boasts much, complains continuously, seeks motes in other people's eyes, klans together for persecution, mobs the weak, has little respect for truth, is selfishly self-centered, is emotionally and lazily inclined toward the easiest way, would hardly be expected to produce distinguished creative contributions in any field. So long as the majority of leaders and the great group of followers are rich in that spirit of self-righteousness, of sensitive antagonism toward things not our own or of our way of thinking, so long will the South be thrice not blessed.

Of course, despite the obvious intensity of this passage, Odum was not entirely breaking new ground here. Much of his critique merely restated the familiar themes New South intellectuals had been offering for thirty years. Like them, Odum was blaming the region's backwardness on (in his words) the "hot-headed, emotional, unthinking" attitudes of its people and their willingness to follow false leaders. His argument that the "atmosphere of fear" they had created was primarily responsible for stifling southern intellectual development was the same diagnosis Cable had made in his book of 1885, *The Silent South*.[17]

But Odum did move significantly beyond his predecessors in two ways: in his tendency to view this excessive irrationality of the masses as the logical result of insufferable social conditions, and in his considerable distrust of the New South mentality itself. To him the Klansmen were more than just another proof of the South's appalling irrationality:

> They, too, represent part of the people. . . . They are fathers and brothers and American citizens with representative rights; with potential through their children of this and the next generations of intellectual and social progress or of other possibilities. They are of the folks 'folksy,' and in proportion as they fail American democracy and civilization fail.

Furthermore, Odum thought he knew exactly where the source of this failure lay—in the South's lack of adequate social institutions, arising organically and working in harmony with one another to form a genuine human community. According to his basic theoretical premises, institutions such as the home, school, church, factory, state, and voluntary associations performed an essential function as a "buffer between the individual and social change"; when they did not, people in situations of rapid change would invariably react with fear, anger, and even violence. Through a "wholesome" institutional life one could develop a "perfected social individual," capable of joining in cooperative endeavors to improve his community; without it, the result was the "unthinking so-called mass freedom." Thus in the South, where a succession of historical shocks had supposedly undermined the stability of local institutions, Odum believed the appearance of "pathological conditions" should surprise no one. "Have the institutions stood by them in their time of growth and stress," he asked of the Klansmen, "or have some of the institutions . . . failed them in their time of need?"[18]

In short, Odum departed from the New South line by portraying the southern social order as fundamentally defective. He did not see the problem in terms of a few lower-class wild men obstinately refusing to become civilized, nor did he place much stock in paternalism to restore stability. Rather, he viewed the social landscape as a scene of perpetual conflict, at times verging toward anarchy, all because the institutions of southern society had fallen apart. In his description, the region had become a New South intellectual's nightmare, with "conflict between races, between classes, between denominations, between visible and invisible government." Odum loathed these various social antagonisms as much as any nineteenth-century southerner did, but, unlike the latter, he was too well trained a social observer to pretend them away. If he was not ready to go as far as his students and identify the plantation system as the culprit, he was at least prepared to dispense with the myth that the South was a land of continuous harmony. Southern society, he said in effect, was not more civilized than the rest of America, but possibly less so.[19]

Odum also challenged the New South outlook at other points. He saw straight through New South public rhetoric, finding it full of the "prideful boast of mediocrities" and the product of "small-town adolescent zest." "The time ought soon to arrive," he counseled, "when we cease to boast of the little things we do in comparison with a crippled past, rather than to judge critically in terms of standard values and standard maximum progress elsewhere." Moreover, Odum assuredly did not perceive the new business elite as potential saviors. Increasingly he suspected that their ultimate role in southern history would not be as agents of advancement, but as allies of conservatism, a point he reiterated often: "Here are some of our southern groups, perfecting themselves in the technique of business, in the mechanism of economic progress, breeding a gross spirit of materialism with ecclesiastical dogmatism and joining political demagoguery in unholy alliance with religious fervor, and producing a mongrel barrenness the despair of classification." Finally, on a few occasions Odum even hinted that those priceless intangibles, southern character and culture, might not be as close to perfection as the orthodox maintained. In many ways, he wrote, the region was deficient "in the finer things of the spirit for which Southerners have such an excellent background"; and "in some parts of the South" people had tended "to face adversity with bitterness and cowardice." But these were specifically limited criticisms, meant to apply only to certain sectors of the contemporary South and not to the region's history as a whole.[20]

With each passing year, it seemed, the attack on southern pieties grew bolder as Odum's confidence in his North Carolina constituency rose. At the outset, he was hesitant when an article by Gerald Johnson referred to several North Carolina political leaders by name. Three months later, however, he was urging Johnson to oversee a series on industrial relations in the South that would begin "quietly" but soon move to such topics as the "psychology of servitude" and the "social mechanisms that underlie the present tendencies toward radicalism." In late 1923 Odum was delighted when an article by Johnson drew fire from newspapers in Asheville and Wilmington; it "adds to the value of your contribution," he wrote his friend. Nor was he unduly worried when *Social Forces* became a prime target for David Clark, the extreme right-wing editor of the *Southern Textile Bulletin*, in January, 1924. By the end of that year, heartened by his success, Odum began planning his "baker's dozen project," which consisted of locating thirteen or more especially trenchant young writers in each southern state to fill the pages of *Social Forces* and to form a "nucleus for producing in the South." Only Chapel Hill, he felt, could supply the leadership needed for such a project. "It is, of course, the North Carolina and the University atmosphere, as opposed to other Southern States, which enables *The Journal* to function," he boasted to Mencken in October.[21]

Then, in January, 1925, disaster struck. Two articles in that month's issue brought down a storm of controversy on Odum, *Social Forces*, and the university that would transform each permanently—a controversy entirely within the journal's home state. In most respects, the offending pieces could not have been less similar: one was a flippant, sarcastic tour de force by Barnes, the book review editor, mocking Christianity and Victorian ethics; the other, by the sociologist Luther L. Bernard, attempted to treat the psychological origins of religious belief in a serious, scholarly way. But in the eyes of North Carolina Fundamentalists, both seemed the epitome of scientific arrogance and infidelity.[22]

What made these articles so explosive was not only their content but the unfortunate timing of their appearance. Purely by chance, the fateful issue had come out at the very peak of a statewide battle over the teaching of evolution in publicly supported schools, including the university at Chapel Hill. That same month a certain David Scott Poole had introduced in the North Carolina legislature a bill to ban the Darwinian hypothesis altogether. Well-organized, primed for attack, and especially eager to secure any evidence to support their charge that the university was ridden with atheists, the Fundamentalist leaders pounced on Odum's magazine as Exhibit Number One. Almost overnight, ministerial associations throughout the state adopted resolutions condemning the journal, some petitioning the governor to cut off its funding. Worse still, to Odum's great discomfort, he and his journal became front-page news for months in both the religious and secular press. One irate citizen, writing to the *Raleigh Times*, urged that Odum be shipped to the Soviet Union forthwith. "What I have long feared has at last happened," Gerald Johnson noted wryly, "Somebody has read the *Journal of Social Forces*."[23]

As Wayne Brazil points out, this catastrophe was in many ways Odum's own fault. Odum was well aware that Barnes's continual sneers at Christian belief might cause trouble among southerners, and just a year earlier he had explicitly asked Barnes to tone down his style, adding "we are determined . . . to establish a long-term career for the *Journal of Social Forces*." In the same letter Odum had also indicated his personal disagreement with Barnes's approach, suggesting that they undertake a joint debate on the subject of science and religious certitude, using *The American Mercury* as their forum. But Odum soon became so absorbed in the affairs of his institute that he let the matter drop and stopped paying attention to the copy Barnes and Hankins sent in. When two of his assistants at Chapel Hill, Guy Johnson and Wiley B. Sanders, tried to warn him of possible problems with the book review section, Odum apparently ignored them. Thus through a combination of editorial negligence and false complacency Odum wandered into the political minefield that was to cost him so many of his dreams.[24]

Bewildered by the suddenness of it all, a distraught Howard Odum searched in vain through the spring of 1925 to find some means of retrieving his position. His first response was an open telegram to the protesting ministers, taking full responsibility for the contents of *Social Forces* (but disclaiming all liability for its authors' opinions) and accusing his opponents of magnifying a trivial incident for ulterior political motives. When these tactics only further infuriated the orthodox, Odum turned to conciliation, in some cases personally inviting his most outspoken adversaries to spend a weekend in Chapel Hill to "talk it over." In addition, contrary to his proclamations of 1922, he now began to insist that *Social Forces* was in reality a "technical publication," circulated "largely with libraries and the larger universities and with the most mature scientific groups." "If God and Christianity cannot stand against discussions, intended solely for specialists and advanced students," he argued, "our faith is pretty weak."[25]

Above all, Odum lost no opportunity to reaffirm his loyalty to the South or his ties with the common folk. "It is rather startling," he wrote one Gastonia minister, "to be devoutly working for a greater southern Christianity, to find oneself at break-o'-day a sort of outcast in the minds of a group which I have believed in and stood by all my life." In the letters to the editor he sent North Carolina newspapers, to take another example, he would speak repeatedly of the "old days in our rural community, from vantage point of log cabin and school house and generations of native folk back of me." Nor were such professions strictly for public consumption. "I have been a regular, orthodox, almost professional, Southerner," he maintained to his sociology colleague Bernard, "and I am one of those specimens who actually believes in the common folks." What is striking about these declarations and the way they were strewn through his writings is that Odum had totally confused the issue. No one had questioned his southern patriotism; no one had raised the slightest complaint against his critical editorials on the South. The dispute in 1925 was limited to the alleged slurs on religious faith that Odum had allowed to appear in an official university publication. Yet in March of that year we find him deliberately rescheduling his most brilliant editorial, "A Southern Promise," because it was "so very, very critical."[26]*

Clearly Odum had been badly wounded, the most significant effect of which was the stirring up of those powerful feelings of guilt and insecurity that had dogged him since childhood. Ever since his first encounter with social science at Mississippi he had managed to suppress those feelings, assuming instead the identity of a hopeful intellectual Moses leading his people back to the promised land through the authority of science. Beginning with his success at Georgia, he had been riding an upward trajectory, which he was certain corresponded to actual southern progress. In North Carolina, evidence of this movement could be seen all around, he thought. But now it appeared he had missed the danger signs; his own persistent innocence had blinded him to the realities of southern life. Unlike the post-Victorians, Odum was acutely aware of that innocence and regarded it as an obstacle to be overcome. The whole incident, he confessed to Bernard, had been a "revelation to me of how little I knew and of how earnestly I hoped and believed that the facts were different." There was also the fear that he had taken criticism too far, that he had in fact stepped over the bounds of southern loyalty. Others younger than himself caught in the same situation might have gone the other way and become detached intellectuals, but not Odum; had his roots become severed he would have been lost.[27]

Thus after 1925 a new unmistakable note of caution and ambiguity entered Odum's work. There were to be no more editorials in *Social Forces*, no more baker's dozen projects, no more open clashes with the proponents of the status quo. Instead there was to be indirection, much asking of unanswered questions, and a concentration on finding the "facts." At its worst, this change would give rise to the murkiness and equivocation many have noticed in Odum's mature writings; yet in other instances, as we shall see, it could also lead to a remarkable sharpening of insight. Joined with his critical spirit and concern for the future, this

---

*Those orthodox religious leaders who were also personal friends kept reminding Odum that southern patriotism was not the issue. Livingston Johnson, editor of the *Biblical Recorder* (and the father of Gerald W. Johnson) explained that the "point of my criticism in everything I said . . . was that such views should not be permitted to be expressed in a publication sent out from the University press." Likewise, Rev. William P. McCorkle, author of the widely read pamphlet *Anti-Christian Sociology as Taught in the Journal of Social Forces*, noted that the "only issue presented in the pamphlet" was "whether publications of the University ought to be permitted to purvey arguments against the fundamental verities of the Christian religion." See Livingston Johnson to Odum, May 22, 1925, and Rev. William P. McCorkle to Louis Graves, September 24, 1925, September 26, 1925, Odum Papers.

heightened consciousness of "the old in the new" would help produce Odum's unique portrait of the South as a land of incessant paradox.

II

Judging by scholarly output, the decade following the Fundamentalist debacle was by far the most fruitful of Odum's career. With his activism temporarily restrained by his desire to remain quiet in the state, Odum turned to writing instead. Beginning with the popular "Black Ulysses" trilogy of the late 1920s, he was to publish his most enduring and influential books on the South, including *An American Epoch* in 1930 and *Southern Regions* in 1936. At the same time, however, his work was now filled with an elaborate array of diversionary devices, all designed (one suspects) to shield him from those unpleasant truths about the South he had acquired. Caught in what was for him an impossible dilemma, Odum was responding in the only way he could—by retreating into himself, taking one step back, as it were, from his previous, full, wide-eyed confrontation with the world.

This change took many forms. A semimystical quality suddenly appeared in his thought, his prose style became more and more convoluted, and there was a growing tendency to hide his main conclusions amid a barrage of statistical data or technical jargon. George S. Mitchell, for one, found these traits unmistakably displayed in an Odum lecture he attended in 1931. "He has a queer way of doing Sociological incantations for a couple of minutes," Mitchell reported, "and then producing a sort of orange-tree of a beautiful idea, all set out in understandable words—then another trance." Whole paragraphs in his books were filled with nothing but interrogatories, and, as Arthur Raper recalled, it was often the same in his classroom:

> Odum . . . he was just so full of questions—we had a course with him when he frankly the whole way through . . . hardly made a single statement. Asked questions. Now, when the textile industry comes to the South, what kind of wages will they pay in connection with what they were paying up there? What will they do with the Negro? Will he work at all or if he does work, what jobs will he work at? How about labor unions? Will they permit labor unions here? If they won't permit labor unions here, why won't they permit labor unions here? . . . Question, question, question, the whole way through.

5. Howard W. Odum (circa 1930)
Courtesy North Carolina Collection,
The University of North Carolina Library

Of course, these questions were not asked at random. Rather, they all pointed in a particular direction, generally a "most uncomfortable" direction for southerners, as Edwin Mims once suggested. Thus it was not surprising that Odum himself was unwilling or unable to answer them.[28]

The device he resorted to most frequently, though, was what he termed "descriptive studies" or "regional portraiture." This technique, which Odum seems to have originated, consisted in a sort of word-painting, a presentation of facts and descriptions with a minimum of interpretation, but with an emphasis, as he put it, "upon representative samplings and vividness." It was designed to leave the reader with a "comprehensive picture" of the subject that left out no details but which was carefully balanced between favorable and unfavorable impressions. First appearing in *Rainbow Round My Shoulder* in 1927, the technique was perfected a few years later in *An American Epoch* (subtitled *Southern Portraiture in the National Picture*). In fact, by the 1930s portraiture had clearly emerged as Odum's indelible style, never to be supplanted—not even by the "regional analysis" he later espoused.[29]

Plainly, the method had both strengths and weaknesses. There was its grand, encyclopedic scope, combined with an emphasis on rendering the South a visual, almost palpable entity. On the debit side one must cite Odum's near-compulsion for achieving "balance" at the expense of analysis and his proclivity for drifting off into his own private dreamworld. These characteristics can be found in innumerable passages throughout his works, but perhaps none would illustrate them better than the truly remarkable set of instructions he sent the artist working on the endpapers of *An American Epoch*. Because the design for those endpapers— a two-page map showing the South's resources and problems—represents his southern portraiture in microcosm, Odum's description of what he wanted included is worth quoting in full:

1. A colonial home here and there, e.g., Monticello in Virginia, one in east Carolina, one at Charleston, one in Georgia, one around Montgomery, one at Natchez, and one somewhere in Louisiana

2. Here and there a sample of the common man, small farm house and of Negro cabins

3. Mill Villages—one each at least in Virginia, North Carolina, South Carolina, and Georgia, Piedmont area

4. Chimney stacks, other manufacturing, Muscle Shoals, and touches of power development would make another unit

5. The Cotton Belt, the farms, especially cotton and cattle in east Carolina, southern Georgia, Mississippi, Alabama, etc., and don't forget the mules. And here and there a handsome barn

6. Resorts starting in Virginia and circling the whole coast

7. A unit of fruit and flowers in the tropical part along with the resorts would be good

8. Birmingham and Texas show coal and oil

9. You could indicate skyscrapers where all the major cities are, especially in Texas

10. I should put the old-time Negro and the new Negro as a unit

11. Somewhere I should put Lee on traveller and somewhere else Ku Klux Klan riding horses robed [Note the careful balance here]

12. And I should run a ribbon of highways here and there, showing a curve and hill in the mountains or a drive under hanging moss for detail

13. We ought perhaps to have on the coast border also considerable pictures of ships indicating commerce and exports

Having indulged his vision of the South, Odum added a final suggestion: "If it could be done, I believe I should border the whole thing with question marks." That, too, was an integral component of his portraiture.[30]

When the artist experienced difficulty in complying with these instructions, Odum was terribly distressed. There was so much left out, he complained to his editor—sugar canes in Louisiana, razorback hogs in Arkansas, dairy cows in Texas, and a seacoast resort "to fill that aching void on the white coast of North Carolina." As always, he was especially concerned about the balance of his presentation. In North Carolina, he insisted, the artist "must put a package of cigarettes . . . with a smoking cigarette at least equal to the moonshine." Likewise, he demanded a city with a blast furnace to appear directly above the cotton pickers in Alabama. "This is very important," he wrote. "I shouldn't dare face the South without Birmingham."[31]

Given his abiding commitment to southern self-criticism, it was inevitable that Odum would become defensive about his new method. A part of him continued to regard portraiture, whatever its intrinsic merits might be, as a surrender to the enemy, and he repeatedly vowed to his friends to do better. "I think that by next year we may have to break loose again and start on some more critical studies after we have put out these descriptive efforts," he assured Gerald Johnson in December, 1926. His research plans, he told Beardsley Ruml of the Rockefeller Foundation a short time later, would center on a "critical inquiry and analysis of our culture patterns and progress, or lack of it." But the aggressive critical studies never really came, at least until his disciples at the institute began pursuing independent projects during the 1930s. Thus in mid-1929 we find Odum admitting to Johnson that the institute's publications on the textile industry represented "tame affairs" at best and that "we have got to do something a little more than that." Eventually Odum began to rationalize his descriptive studies by invoking the name of science, claiming that they constituted the essential "first stage" toward the scientific study of the South, but one suspects that his reservations about such nonanalytical work, although suppressed, always remained.[32]

In truth, however, portraiture did have its roots in Odum's early scientific training, and it did fulfill certain very specific artistic needs for him. The turn-of-the-century organic social theory he had imbibed from Bailey, Hall, and Giddings had fixed in his mind once and for all the value of balance and harmony. That theory had depicted society as a species of natural organism, developing through the progressive "differentiation" and "integration" of its various institutions—much as the higher biological organisms were both more complex and better integrated than those below them on the evolutionary scale—until it would become at last a perfectly integrated whole. The key to the entire process of social evolution, he was taught, resided in the need for mutual interdependence among a society's constituent parts; without such mutuality there could be no social harmony and no progress. It was this grounding in organicism that helped guide Odum to portraiture, making him attempt to see the region in its totality while at the same time dutifully tracing the growth of its different "parts." Everything about the South was separate and distinctive for Odum; everything was related and combined. Each state, for example, had "its own peculiar institutional character and challenging portraiture which at once recapitulates and integrates the story of the South and yet differentiates it." This was why, in composing *An American Epoch*, he was particularly afraid "to leave out any aspects of the picture"; although his final aim, of course, was to "present the picture without calling attention to it in detail."[33]

Yet the most fundamental reason Odum turned to portraiture was artistic. Put simply, once he began to fathom the complexity of the South, no other method could have enabled him to express his conception of southern society with such exactitude. In his own words, "any adequate picture of the South must combine the poetic with the scientific. It is as if a new romantic realism were needed to portray the old backgrounds and the new trends and processes." Like its literary counterpart, the stream-of-consciousness technique employed by Faulkner, portraiture allowed Odum to say all he knew and felt about the South at once; he did not have to choose between the potentially painful alternatives of praise and blame, conformity and detachment, the mythical and the real. As in a cubist painting all lines of perspective went down on the canvas simultaneously, with no effort to sort them out.* It was, in short, a most useful vehicle for a southern intellectual like Odum struggling on the brink of Modernism.[34]

Thus to make sense of Odum's portraiture we must extend Odum a measure of artistic license. For if the basis of poetry is metaphor, and if metaphor consists in joining together two or more contradictory elements to achieve a deeper level of significance than ordinary rationality would permit, then Odum was writing, not sociology per se, but what might be called "poetic sociology." One sees this sensibility at work, for instance, when he writes of the two races in the South as "white and black, separate and mixed, inseparable and unmixable," or in his description of monuments erected to the Lost Cause as "numerous, noble and pathetic." Empirical analysis was never his true stronghold; rather, the ultimate purpose of his writing was akin to that of a novel, helping the reader penetrate beneath external features to the inner characteristics of the South, fostering sensitivity toward southern problems, and capturing some of the majesty Odum beheld in the region's history. These same artistic motives encompassed even his abundant use of statistics, aptly characterized by Brazil as a "kind of subtle photography which exposed facts that were difficult for the unaided eye to see."[35]

Odum's greatest achievements, then, came precisely when he surrendered himself to his artistry. Then his vision of the region's immense diversity provided southerners of his era with a view of their society that was fresh and imposing:

> Both the old and the new culture abounded in sharp contrasts and logical paradoxes. There were many Souths yet *the* South. It was preeminently national in backgrounds, yet provincial in its processes. There were remnants of European culture framed in intolerant Americanism. There were romance, beauty, glamor, gayety, comedy, gentleness, and there were sordidness, ugliness, dullness,

---

*In his recollections of Odum, Guy B. Johnson also makes the comparison to cubism: "his work reminded me of one of those paintings, which doesn't mean much if you get too close to it. You've got to stand off at some distance and then it begins to come in focus" (Oral History Memoir of Guy B. Johnson, 57).

sorrow, tragedy, cruelty. There were wealth, culture, education, generosity, chivalry, manners, courage, nobility, and there were poverty, crudeness, ignorance, narrowness, brutality, cowardice, depravity. The South was American and un-American, righteous and wicked, Christian and barbaric. It was a South getting better, a South getting worse. It was strong and it was weak, it was white and it was black, it was rich and it was poor. There were great white mansions on hilltops among the trees, and there were unpainted houses perched on pillars along hillside gullies or lowland marshes. From high estate came low attainment, and from the dark places came flashing gleams of noble personality. There were strong men and women vibrant with the spontaneity of living, and there were pale, tired folk, full of the dullness of life. There were crusaders resplendent with some perpetual equivalent of war, and there were lovers of peace in the market place. There were freshness and vivacity as of a rippling green-white rivulet, and there were depth and hidden power as of gleaming dark water beneath an arched bridge.

Here was Odum's poetic sociology at its best, exploiting his unique status as a transitional figure to see the whole South at once. What it revealed was a paradoxical South, racked by the trials of change, possessed by its past but still very much open to transformation in the future. To the generation raised on the certainties of the New South ideology, Odum's vision seemed strikingly new, and it is a testimony to the vision's persuasiveness that it soon became the dominant conception of the region in the twentieth century. It is on these grounds that Odum may be placed in the Modernist camp.[36]

III

On one level, Odum's portraiture was characterized by a precise, formal balance among its component parts, good and bad, progressive and backward, hopeful and fateful. But at another and deeper level, the hallmark was an extraordinary ambivalence. Not evasiveness or distancing but the clash of strongly felt emotions became the rule whenever he turned to the three main groups he saw as comprising southern society, the aristocrats, yeomen, and blacks. This ambivalence, in turn, reflected one additional and highly important facet of Odum's status as an intellectual living at a time of transition—his shifting and oftentimes confused understanding of the idea of "culture." Straddling two eras, he was torn between the

Victorian and Modernist definitions of that word, with profound consequences for his thought.

The nineteenth-century conception of culture, which Odum had fully absorbed as a child, centered upon a set standard of morality and learning to which all men must aspire. There was only one "Culture"— indivisible and unassailable, the product and sign of civilization, representing the highest stage of evolutionary progress yet attained. Culture to the Victorians was above all conscious and rational, the instrument that enabled man to shed the blind customs of his primitive past and to curb those baser instincts he shared with the animals. In theory, the goal was to make culture seep downward, touching more and more individuals at the lower end of the social scale in order to attain a more peaceable, "civilized" society. To most Victorian intellectuals, however, this seemed a distant prospect at best; even when they sympathized with democracy, as many did, the inescapable logic of their belief in "Culture" turned them elitist when put to the test. A good example is Josiah Morse, a psychologist at the University of South Carolina and a contemporary of Odum's who reacted in the traditional manner when the Klan became active in his state:

> The masses know not what they do; they never have and probably never will, unless there shall be a miracle of eugenic and educational reform and development. That is the great tragedy, and the danger of democracy. The problem, as I see it, is not one of race or creed, but of Culture. Given Culture and we shall be able to dwell together in peace and good-will and mutual helpfulness; without it there will necessarily be friction, conflict and war, in spite of all the leagues and courts that may be set up. And how hard it is and how long it takes to culture the human animal!

For the Victorian, then, a fear of the mob became the corollary of his concept of culture.[37]

By contrast, the Modernist view made culture accessible—in fact unavoidable—to everyone. First appearing around 1900 in the field of anthropology, especially in the work of Franz Boas at Columbia, it assumed the existence of many cultures, each formed as different peoples attempted to make sense of their particular histories and environments. Operating through the same customs and folkways the Victorians had regarded as hopelessly "irrational," culture was now seen as performing an essential social function. It was, to borrow George W. Stocking's phrase, the medium a society used to impose a "conventional meaning on the flux of experience," a meaning *all* members of the society could share, thus helping to maintain social cohesion. Clearly, cultures arising to meet the needs of specific societies, or of specific groups within societies, would conflict with one another repeatedly, and each would have its own notions of truth and falsehood. Accordingly, the dictates of science would hereafter require that all cultures, including those of the most "savage" tribes, be accorded respect regardless of their intellectual or moral content.[38]

By installing cultural relativism as a scientific imperative in this way, the new definition of culture did succeed in breaking down the ethnocentric, antidemocratic bias inherent in the Victorian concept, but at a price. Since culture was now looked upon as omnipresent, embedded in the least custom or habit, it quickly became all-powerful as well. Every thought, attitude, or perception was believed to be conditioned by the hidden cultural framework below. In short, just as elitism accompanied the Victorian view, a new determinism was the adjunct of Modernist culture.[39]

For his part, Odum did his best to keep these two notions of culture separate. He was drawn to the anthropological concept early in his career, primarily because the idea of cultural conditioning seemed so useful in accounting for southern deficiencies. "Every major problem," he was able to argue, was "bound up" with the "regional folk culture"—that amalgam of "race, state and sectional loyalties" that came "nearer conditioning all the culture of all the groups of the region than any [of the] other forces." In addition, Odum appears to have found the Modernist assault on Victorian snobbery most congenial. "Don't you brilliant folk," he once taunted Gerald Johnson, "posit a superior type of intelligence and culture, belonging to the few, throwing this in bold contrast to the many, and then insist that the many in Moronia be expected to conform to a civilized code which the superior themselves are desperately trying to agree upon?" Yet, like many intellectuals of his generation throughout the country, Odum remained attached to the older view of culture as well. There were " 'culture patterns' of the Old South," he informed his readers, that "were not in the nature of anthropological culture but of manners and breeding." Despite his best efforts to sort them out, the two concepts frequently overlapped in the recesses of his mind, giving rise to both confusion and ambivalence.[40]

Nowhere was this problem more evident than in his treatment of the Cavalier myth. Having grown up in the nineteenth-century South, Odum continued to regard the antebellum planter as the bearer and symbol of the only bona fide cultural tradition (in the old sense of "culture") that he, as a southerner, could ever claim. That was why he devoted an entire chapter of *An American Epoch* to "The Glory That Was the South" and included in it passages of pure piety:

Whatever else [the plantation houses] were, they were reflections of glory and grandeur, vivid, beautiful, and distinctive. In these pictures one sees southern men and southern women as the perfect flowering of American personality, and the plantation life as the best of American culture. Even a Walter Hines Page with his keen criticism of southern deficiencies, could see the romance and virtue of the big house in the midst of the groves and the hundreds of surrounding acres, burdened with crops white for the harvesting by black folks, musical in their rendering of old spirituals, cheerful in song and story, polite, gracious, artistic beyond measure.

Odum was at particular pains to establish the planters' personal and intellectual qualities. "Volumes of Shakespeare, Scott, George Eliot, Johnson, Goldsmith, Greek and Latin classics, were often a part of the culture of these plantation masters," he maintained, and the "discussion of philosophy and literature" stood among their favorite pastimes. Whatever else he may have been, the "old Southerner" was a "gentleman and an aristocrat, whose character could be told at a glance."[41]

Then, in an ensuing chapter entitled "The Glory That Was Not," Odum completely reversed himself. Now he portrayed the Old South as a virtual frontier society dominated by upstarts and pretenders, its intellectual life a thin veneer contrived to cover massive social defects. The culture of its "unthinking aristocracy" had been based not on Shakespeare, but on a "superficial acquaintance with the classics, an overemphasis upon luxuries and physical life, hard drinking and dueling." As for the vaunted plantation houses, in most cases they had begun as bare log cabins, with wings eventually added in back and on the sides, capped by the "finishing of it all in boards and columns and paint and its gradual evolution into the 'big house.'" The planters' gravest sins, though, had resided in their attempt to establish a false social barrier between themselves and the majority of their fellow southerners, an attempt Odum described in distinctly Modernist terms:

The extreme snobbishness which the imitation-aristocracy manifested [has] left its mark, and remained as a conditioning influence. . . . Later bitterness and antagonism of the common folks and the poorer whites . . . [have] manifested themselves in politics, religion, education, intersectional and interstate quarreling and conflicts. A modern cultural region in which one class could not mingle socially with the other, or recognize its existence socially, although sprung from the same ancestry, could not thrive in that form.

As so often with Odum, the jumbled syntax betrays a measure of guilt, for these were decidedly heretical views, holding the Old South itself responsible for the region's failures. That was the painful conclusion toward which his "anthropological" concept of culture mercilessly drove him.[42]

Clearly Odum could find no logical way to reconcile these contradictory images of the Old South. That case was hopeless. He could, however, make his amends to the Cavalier myth, and, in a manner strikingly reminiscent of Ulrich B. Phillips, he did so at the very end of *An American Epoch*:

> The White House, that was the perfect symbol. That was indeed
> southern portraiture in the national picture. Stately and grace-
> ful with its fine lines and white columns, it was symbolic of all that
> the South had contributed to the Nation, yet it appeared utterly
> national and oblivious of all origins or sections. Imposing, quiet,
> peaceful, powerful as the home of the Nation's President, who knew
> no North or South, it combined the beauty and dignity of the Old
> South with the vigor and strength of the new Nation. Yes, that
> was the picture for him, symbolic alike of old origins and na-
> tional transcendence.

Only by taking refuge in this idealized vision of ahistorical innocence, it seemed, could he resolve his confusion about southern history.[43]

The same ambivalence, the same conceptual confusion, pervaded his writings on the white yeomanry, with similar results. That was the class Odum came from and with which he most strongly identified; those were the people he wished to champion. Hence, forgetting the miseries of his own rural childhood, he tended on most occasions to romanticize their lives, downplaying their poverty and embracing the age-old agrarian mythology that saw the farmer's existence as closer to the soil, more "natural," and thus superior to any other. When rhapsodizing about southern farm life, in fact, Odum easily kept pace with the Nashville Agrarians. But what he professed to value most was the life-force within the people themselves, their "sheer organic vitality" that, he believed, represented the South's greatest resource in the long run. "Whatever else may be deduced from the vast array of evidence," he concluded in *Southern Regions*,

> the general culture of the region, including the people, their tradi-
> tions, and their behavior reflected great vitality of many sorts. There
> was rugged and rural vitality of the pioneer; there was fertility, vi-
> tality of reproductive stocks; there were intensity, emotional drives,

loyalties, patterns of struggle and conflict; there was vitality in the stubborn survival values of the people, in their humor and recreation, in their stubborn bantering threats to outsiders, and in their defense mechanisms.

Odum's celebration of southern vitality here plainly hinged on his adoption of the Modernist conception of culture. The same "animal" energy a New South intellectual like Morse would have found the ultimate threat, Odum now considered a subject for boasting.[44]

Odum broke further with New South practice, it should be noted, in attributing this impressive vitality to the persistence of the southern frontier. Where Ulrich Phillips had hesitated in applying the term "frontier" to the South because of its implications of crudeness, Odum had no such reservations. "The South has always been a frontier," he gladly admitted, "rich in struggle and conflict, romance and adventuring, victory and tragedy." The twentieth century "saw it still a frontier country." Far from being a badge of shame, the survival of a frontier way of life, Odum wrote, might well prove to be the South's chief contribution to the nation by inspiring Americans in other regions to recapture their own frontier past and replenish their store of pioneer strengths. Similarly, where New South thinkers had tended to downgrade southern folk music, dismissing it as the relic of a less-than-civilized past, Odum regarded the same songs and dances as "literally setting culture patterns of a people" and devoted whole chapters to them in his books.[45]

Yet Odum could as easily view this frontier vitality another way. The old standard of culture, with its unceasing terror of animal impulse, still operated in him, and the potential of the southern masses for unpredictable violence was never far from his mind. The average southerner possessed an unstable temperament, "hot-headed" and "ready to fight at the drop of a hat," he sadly observed, a fact especially visible whenever race and politics intersected. Then unscrupulous demagogues like Tom Watson could produce a "fanning of mass emotions" similar to that which occurred in wartime. "No one who has not heard the murmur of a vast mob swell into some terrifying roar could understand the power of this sort of leader," Odum observed feelingly. When one colleague protested that such statements were overdrawn, Odum adamantly refused to back down, again citing firsthand empirical evidence. Anyone "who drives through the South, as I did last year, and enjoys the men at the garages and other places," he insisted, would find the pictures "not so extreme."[46]

The tug and pull of Odum's dual conception of culture was also visible in his writings on race, although with a somewhat different outcome. There the postulates of cultural anthropology allowed him to break free, ever so slowly, of the traditional southern attitudes he had inherited, while his Victorian biases alerted him to aspects of contemporary Negro life in the South that more consistent Modernists tended to overlook or ignore. As a result, Odum, though he never fully overcame his ambivalence toward blacks, nonetheless became the first white southerner to make a lasting contribution to the modern study of black folk culture—a remarkable accomplishment considering the point he started from.

Odum's first approach to the subject, published as *The Social and Mental Traits of the Negro* in 1910, reads almost like a parody of the scientific racism of its time. Although submitted as a doctoral dissertation at Columbia University, the manuscript was in fact researched and written from 1906 to 1908 when Odum was still at the University of Mississippi studying under Bailey. Thus its conclusions did not reflect his experience at Clark University in 1909, where he attended the famous seminar on psychoanalytic theory given by Sigmund Freud, or his exposure to the ideas of Boas at Columbia the following year. What the book unmistakably did reflect was Bailey's efforts to defend white supremacy through social science, as well as Odum's own unquestioned Victorian moralism based on the premise of a radical dichotomy between savagery and civilization, with rational self-control the highest aim. That was the standard Odum first applied to southern blacks.[47]

Like most sociologists of the period, Odum began by assuming that the Negro's status and behavior were determined exclusively by inherited biological traits, foremost among which was the utter inability to master his "animal impulses." Few whites understood this fact, Odum claimed, because blacks always put forward their best behavior when whites were present. Consequently, the only way to discover the truth was to study the Negro in his own habitat, like some species of wildlife; to observe him in his home, church, and social club "as he struggles—or more exactly does not even struggle—against the onrush of his animal nature." This was the research agenda Odum set for himself, but it was not, he soon found, an easy one. "Many incidents growing out of the efforts to secure . . . information are repulsive, not to say nauseous and gruesome," he reported in his preface. "Only the hardiest scientific interest in discoverable facts can sustain the investigator."[48]

When Odum did penetrate the Negro's "natural" environment he was hardly encouraged by what he saw. "Individual character is inseparably connected with pure homes," he postulated, which made his findings on the blacks' domestic life all the more dismal:

> The Negro has little home conscience or love of home, no local attachment of the better sort. He does not know in many cases for

months or years the whereabouts of his brother and sister or even parents, nor does he concern himself about their welfare [a particularly salient fact for Odum because of the tragic death of his own younger siblings]. He has no pride of ancestry, and he is not influenced by the lives of great men. The Negro has few ideals and perhaps no lasting adherence to an aspiration toward real worth. He has little conception of the meaning of virtue, truth, honor, manhood, integrity.

The conclusion was inescapable: southern blacks could never qualify as proper Victorians. That diagnosis was more than reconfirmed when Odum turned his attention to black folk songs, which he had collected by the hundreds. "Openly descriptive of the grossest immorality and susceptible of unspeakable thought and actions rotten with filth," the songs, he adjudged, represented "the superlative of the repulsive." "Saddest" of all, these songs provided the most reliable candid expression of the intrinsic characteristics of the race, the Negro's "true nature." "Must he continue as the embodiment of fiendish filth incarnated in the tabernacle of the soul?" Odum gravely asked.[49]

In addition to this moral outrage, Odum's account of the black man's "mental traits" also betrayed a measure of barely concealed fear. Following a theoretical framework first laid down by Herbert Spencer a half century earlier, Odum claimed that the Negro possessed "the accepted characteristics of the savage mind"—that is, his emotions were "little more than impulses," which, set off by some "accidental" stimulus, would run their course "with little inhibition, thus giving rise to many violent forms of expression." Of all these "inherited impulses," none troubled him more than black anger, a "passion easily excited, running riot, uncontrollable, insatiable, expressing itself in a blind instinct to destroy." It was this "tendency and facility for violent explosions"—and not social and economic circumstances—that rendered blacks "peculiarly liable to crime," though luckily, he was quick to add, the violence was almost always directed at other blacks, rarely at whites. But despite this disclaimer, one plainly senses his uneasiness here. This belief in the inherent predisposition of blacks toward crime and immorality was the reason for his adamant insistence on maintaining segregation. "In the keeping of it is the highest culture, education, religion and conduct"; he explained, "it underlies purity, virtue, traditions, ideals."[50]

Over the next decade and a half, as he closely followed the ongoing debate between the environmentalists and hereditarians, Odum's attitudes gradually shifted. His primary concern remained the threat blacks posed to upholding the standards of white society; but his organic social theory also suggested to him that some means would have to be found to "integrate" blacks into the southern social order if the society was to function properly. This latter imperative made him particularly attentive to the work of the cultural anthropologists, led by Boas, who were rapidly striking down the notion of hereditary racial traits by demonstrating that even those physical characteristics thought absolutely fixed by race, such as the size and weight of the brain, could be altered over the span of one generation through a change in environment. Not prepared to join the environmentalists, or to abandon his belief in segregation, Odum nevertheless was slipping into a halfway stance by the early 1920s, loosening his grip on his earlier ideas and opening himself to new ones. As he told a northern acquaintance, "I think it is good for us the country over to think about the Negro in terms of simple description and objective facts for a while." He would wait patiently for the verdict of science.[51]

Important in this respect was the influence of Guy B. Johnson, a southern-born cultural anthropologist in all but name, who had come to Chapel Hill as a sociology graduate student in 1924. No sooner did Johnson arrive than he and Odum teamed up to publish two book-length collections of black folk songs, drawing mostly on the materials Odum had gathered in 1906 and roundly condemned in *Social and Mental Traits*. This time, however, Odum's estimate of their worth was quite different. Even if the songs did not conform to the genteel canons of literary taste, the authors commented, these ballads and blues still constituted genuine poetry, perhaps even superior to "what the white man calls culture." "Here may be seen much of the naked essence of poetry," they wrote, "with unrefined language which reaches for the Negro a power of expression far beyond that which modern refinement of language and thought ordinarily approach." On the matter of possible immorality, moreover, there was now a social and environmental, not a racial, explanation—"it must be constantly borne in mind that this collection of songs is representative only of what may be called the Negro lower class." Whether Johnson or Odum originated these thoughts is impossible to say, although it is probably safe to assume a case of the student leading the teacher. Whichever it was, by 1926 Odum's view of black folk culture was clearly casting free of its nineteenth-century moorings.[52]

Under these circumstances, with his ideas on race very much in flux, Odum started composing his Black Ulysses trilogy. This saga of "primitive man in the modern world," as he once put it, revolved around the tales and travels of John Wesley "Left-Wing" Gordon (so nicknamed because he had lost his right arm), a real-life casual laborer with exceptional story-telling abilities who had been working on a road construction crew near Chapel Hill when Odum met, befriended, and plied him with whiskey sometime around 1924 or 1925. Left-Wing's embellished accounts of hustling his way through thirty-six states and World War I instantly seized Odum's imagination; by June, 1925, Odum was already thinking of turning them into a book. The story would be of epic proportions, for Odum had begun to see Left-Wing, in all his wanderings, as a modern specimen of the classic folk hero—a "Black Ulysses." In time there would be three books: *Rainbow Round My Shoulder* (1928), telling of Left-Wing's childhood, adventures, and philosophy; *Wings on My Feet* (1929), his experiences during the war; and *Cold Blue Moon* (1931), a set of ghost stories Left-Wing told about a haunted antebellum southern mansion. Riding a wave of public interest in the "New Negro" set in motion by the Harlem Renaissance, the three were to sell more copies than any of Odum's other works.[53]

The trilogy, representing Odum's then-evolving portraiture technique applied to blacks, displayed the same ambivalence that marked his treatment of Cavalier and yeoman. For Odum was not merely painting a portrait of Black Ulysses; he was taking on his subject's persona as well—placing himself inside Black Ulysses' skin to explore the exotic but forbidden world of black culture. Although Black Ulysses does in some ways fit the 1920s image of the black man as "natural primitive," it must be stressed that Odum was not at all engaged in moral or intellectual "slumming," the kind of deliberate "cultivation of the perverse" Nathan I. Huggins has attributed to white writers connected with the Harlem movement. Odum did not have the least desire to invert the moral values of white society. On the contrary, throughout his spiritual journey he retained much of his older Victorian perspective on blacks, with the result that one detects him alternately frightened, fascinated, amused, shocked, sympathetic, sermonizing, and secretly envious as he describes his hero's adventures.[54]

The result was an immense change from 1910. All that Odum had once termed "vulgar" now seemed to him the embodiment of the "natural," emanating from the "organic forces and essence of life" required to sustain a vigorous culture. Even if much of this "natural" behavior still did not meet his approval, viewed from the inside it was at least vaguely explicable. The product of a broken home, cheated and exploited by white labor contractors as he drifted from one odious job to the next, with police constantly on his back and women forever two-timing him, Black Ulysses' very survival became a wonderment for Odum, bespeaking the extraordinary folk vitality his black soul mate was endowed with. In *Social and Mental Traits*, Odum had denounced the Negro's "bragging, handling of knives and pistols, boasting, singing, love of criminal notoriety, abuse of the weak, hoodlumism, and extreme feelings of mega-lomania" as "touches of the morbid pleasure." Black Ulysses does in-dulge in gratuitous violence at times, shooting up dances or church meet-ings out of "jes' pure meanness," and Odum registers his disapproval. More often, though, it is clear from Odum's account that Black Ulysses' fighting stems from necessity, brought on by the conditions under which he is forced to live. "Sometimes seems like boys in [work] camp jes' ain't civilized," Left-Wing explains. "Folks say they do anything, an' I guess some time they do. Fellow can't hardly git nothin' to eat less'n he fights for it. Got to fight if he eats, got to die if he don't eat."[55]

In commenting on these escapades, Odum abstained dramatically from his earlier outright moralism. Epithets like "animal impulse" and "savagery" are conspicuously missing from the trilogy, replaced instead by a series of loosely connected impressionistic phrases suggesting ad-miration for or apprehension of Black Ulysses, or both: "Holding his own with zest in the midst of sex conflict and strife—heat, passion and ruthless survival. Blood and pearls, razors and hearts. Now New Orleans, now Vicksburg, now Memphis. . . . Black man and blind urge." Similarly, the songs depicting this nether-life, formerly "the superlative of the repulsive," now became "a sort of superhuman description of the folk-soul." Above all, the element of moral loathing, the fear of contamination that had rendered his previous research "nauseous and gruesome," had entirely disappeared. "There are a great many places in his life," Odum wrote his publisher, "when there is poignancy and sometimes poetry. I have sat beside him, admired his profile, his face with blood vessels standing out and perspiration bursting out and his physical earnestness. While we do not sentimentalize over him, we do treat him as a human being rather than as the mere Negro." The stereotype was giving way to a sensitive appreciation, which alone made the soul-sharing possible.[56]

In the final volume of the trilogy, *Cold Blue Moon*, Odum essayed what for him was the most dangerous territory of all—using his black persona to take a fresh look at the culture of the Old South. More like a novel than its predecessors, its plot centered on the stories Black Ulysses' slave ancestors had supposedly told him about Big House Hall, a leg-endary plantation mansion whose occupants had met a succession of mysterious and tragic ends and had returned to haunt it. Using a black raconteur to narrate ghost stories about the old planter class held several advantages for Odum, not the least of which was the ambiguity it permitted him to place between himself and his Old South subject. "Wus told to me, don't know if I believes it, don't know does I disbelieve it," Left-Wing keeps saying. It also meant that Odum could dispense with historical reality altogether and portray the southern past exactly as he wished it had been. A genuine "lover of thoughts and literature," his Old Colonel could live in a society "confident of the superiority of its culture" because it possessed "a certain beauty and artistry which seemed indestructible and fine."[57]

But instead of his usual practice of "balancing" the myth with an alternate image of the planter as noveau riche, this time, thanks to his narrative device, Odum was able to depict the flaws within the picture of mythical innocence itself. Thus we discover that the colonel, far from being a paragon of gentlemanly self-control, was "so hot-tempered till [he] had trouble all his days, gonna have it till he die." "Like a storm if he gits mad," the old man lashes out cruelly and impulsively at blacks and certain whites, causing great destruction to those around him. His eldest son, cursed with an equally violent and unpredictable temper, goes the route of drinking, gambling, and miscegenation, meeting an ignominious death apparently at the hands of his mulatto son. By framing this story within the overall epic of Black Ulysses, Odum was now in effect ascribing the "savage" character traits traditionally associated with blacks directly to the Cavalier, shattering the rigid dualism that separated white southern culture from black. Even *at his best*, Odum implied, the planter was a frontier creature less than civilized, harboring a potential for evil that, as the hovering ghosts signified, continued to haunt the present-day South. No thought, of course, could have been more heretical, at least by the standards of southern writing in the 1920s, which was why it was hinted at only through the ambiguous medium of Black Ulysses' unsubstantiated tales. Yet, Odum felt, it was "a story that has got to be told before we can ever get a clean slate for the South of the future."[58]

If he could surmount his ambivalence only with the greatest difficulty when it came to the Cavalier, the story was somewhat different in the area of race relations. For by the late 1920s the verdict of science had come in, and Odum, freed from many of his Victorian shackles, was prepared to deliver it to his southern readers. Thus in *An American Epoch* he spoke of the South's "first tragic consciousness" that, "conditioned by [the] white environment, conditioned by his own limited environment," no southern black ever had "a fair chance to develop to full capacity." If the concepts of anthropology applied to southern whites, explicating and, to some degree, exonerating their behavior, then, Odum was saying, the same concepts must also apply to blacks. If that were true, the same environmentalism would be in force, opening the way to unlimited, if gradual, development. Odum made this still more explicit in *Southern Regions*. "Modern social scientists," he reported, had reached the "general conclusion" that race was not "an entity in itself, a purely physical product," but rather "the result of long developed folk-regional culture." The assumption that the "Negro was an inferior race" was equally in "error," he added. On the contrary, "ample evidence" indicated "many manifestations of superiority, of extraordinary personality and survival qualities, of capacity for intellectual and social achievement." Although it would be "asking too much of a region to change overnight the powerful folkways of long generations," there could be "hard-boiled, realistic, evolutionary hope for the future." Nowhere in the book did Odum make the slightest plea for preserving segregation. Not yet ready formally to renounce Jim Crow, Odum had become, perhaps without even realizing it, an "ultimate integrationist."[59]

"Objective" evidence, theoretical advances, and a deeper subjective transformation—all had worked together inextricably in bringing Odum to this position. Slowly his initial Victorian belief that the world must be divided into airtight compartments of savage and civilized had given way to the realization that, in the empirical world, no such dichotomy was possible. He had made his own ambivalent peace with the animal component of human nature, still terrified of it when out of control, but accepting it otherwise as a "natural" feature of life and an indispensable source of vitality. It had been these basic intellectual changes, serving as the precondition for his acceptance of the modern scientific view of race, that had produced the virtual turnabout in his image of blacks. "I hope that I have gone a long way since that was written," he told a correspondent in 1936, disowning *Social and Mental Traits*. Indeed he had.[60]

I V

One further objective, more or less political in nature, lay behind Odum's portraiture—his persistent desire to counter the popular image of the Solid South with, in his words, a South of remarkable "power and range and variety." "The South was anything but homogeneous at any time," he contended, and, to prove it, he piled on detail after detail as in his design for the endpapers of *An American Epoch*. Clearly this was far more than an academic exercise for him. Homogeneity implied a belligerent South connaturally united in defiance of the rest of the nation, and Odum, as an organicist, found any form of sectional conflict intolerable. Nonetheless, Odum faced a serious problem here. Evidence of the existence of a Solid South was everywhere at hand, a fact he was continually forced to acknowledge. "The South, yet many Souths" was the refrain that echoed through his books. But how could this paradox be explained? How could the region be both homogeneous and heterogeneous, united and yet riven with conflict? What had made the southern people so thoroughly American in their origins and fundamental attitudes, as Odum maintained, yet so different from their fellow countrymen in political and social behavior? These were the questions his portraiture raised again and again, but which it could not help him answer.[61]

To the extent that Odum did try to resolve these paradoxes, he did so through a Lamarckian environmentalism that permitted him to hedge his bets carefully. As Stocking has shown, Lamarckianism—the theory that acquired traits may be passed on to one's offspring by genetic means— was still highly popular among American social scientists as late as the 1920s, despite its repudiation within the field of biology itself. Prewar liberals who could not escape the hereditarian assumptions of their elders found the doctrine particularly appealing because it seemed to offer the sole escape from biological determinism and thus the best hope for social progress. The danger, though, was not a lapse into determinism, but rather a drift into the opposite—what Stocking calls a "vague sociobiological indeterminism" that thoroughly obscured the roles heredity and culture actually played in forming social character. In short, Lamarckianism could provide its adherents so much room for maneuver that their accounts of social causation came close to being meaningless.[62]

Precisely because it was so indeterminate, Odum was to find Lamarckianism indispensable to his entire career. It was perfectly suited to the needs of his portraiture, allowing him to paint his picture on a presumably "scientific" basis without stopping to give exact causal explanations. Thus he was able to contend that the folk culture that conditioned southern life had originally been heterogeneous in its essence, "of such variety and mixture that later biological and cultural homogeneity reflects remarkable power of physical and cultural environment quickly to develop social patterns and regions." In other words, the South's climate, its living habits, the experience of slavery, and the crises of Civil War and Reconstruction had combined to produce the present distorted culture that Odum held responsible for the region's pathological state. Since this new culture was rooted in biology it would be no swift or easy task to alter it. But as a Lamarckian, he was convinced that if attitudes, ideas, and habits were changed through proper training, a significant and durable modification of the culture pattern would follow. In this sense he could go on to argue that the South's cultural deficiencies, including its homogeneity, were "not due to organic limitations," but were perforce "temporary" and "remediable through the normal processes of development." In all his writings on the region, that was the central point he wished to convey.[63]*

Regionalism, the concept Odum worked so hard to popularize in the 1930s, began from this premise that the South's backwardness could gradually be corrected if only its culture could be changed. While recognizing "the logical, inevitable, evolutionary nature of the South's culture," it sought to neutralize its worst aspects by "blending" it with the national culture, all the while "making the national culture and welfare the final arbiter." At the opposite pole stood sectionalism, whose proponents, at least in Odum's view, were bent on strengthening and intensifying the defective homogeneous culture that had brought the South to grief. Characteristically, Odum explained this distinction by resorting to a biological analogy. Sectionalism he compared to "cultural inbreeding, in which only home stocks and cultures are advocated, whereas regionalism is line-breeding, in which the regional cultures constitute the base but not the whole of the new evolving cultures." Under regionalism, in other words, the South would become organically interconnected with the rest of the country to form a coherent "integrated" whole while still retaining part of its identity; under sectionalism it would become hopelessly separate and isolated, engaged in constant skirmishing with an "inevitable coercive" federal government.[64]

Others, of course, might see political implications here, but not Odum. Indeed, one of the chief charms of regionalism for him was its seemingly apolitical character. As "component and constituent parts" of a "larger national culture," his ideal regions would be capable of working together with little or no friction. This fact would open the way for cooperative regional planning, administered by a corps of social science experts. Sectionalism, by contrast, implied selfishness, competition, and conflict. "The point," he wrote, "is that we need to shift to the real regional, interregional balanced economy and society rather than an individualistic sectionalism just as we need to turn from the old individual, unlimited, competitive processes to the newer designed order." In the case of the South, the reasons for doing so were especially compelling. If only the region could forswear its outdated sectionalist preoccupations, Odum

---

*As further evidence for his optimism on changing southern culture Odum often cited his research into "social prepotency," a distinctly Lamarckian concept he defined as "persistency and continuity in the power of transmitting biological and cultural qualities from one generation to another." His studies on the prepotency of the southern people, he reported, indicated a human stock "adequate for the utmost in cultural achievement." See his "Notes on Regional and Folk Society," 169–70, and *Southern Regions*, 25.

was saying, it could end the appalling waste of its resources and at last realize its true potential.[65]

In practice, however, this distinction between regionalism and sectionalism proved impossible for Odum to maintain, and its sole consequence was to keep him embroiled in senseless semantic wrangling with his southern liberal colleagues from the mid-1930s on. As Donald Davidson of the Agrarian group astutely pointed out, regionalism in essence was sectionalism depoliticized. One might distinguish the two briefly for academic purposes, but as soon as one moved to the realm of action they were bound to converge. If Odum thought he could preserve the distinction indefinitely, Davidson concluded, he was only fooling himself: "Odum, I am sure, must realize that pure politics, pure science, pure art never remain pure very long. Politics runs into economic considerations, and economics finally runs into politics. Odum will not escape the political aspects of Southern economic and cultural problems simply by insisting that he has a regional, not a sectional, program."[66]

But Odum *did* believe in pure science. Especially after his devastating experience at the hands of the Fundamentalists the least sign of politics that invaded his world was sufficient to make him cry with alarm. It was his fear of politics, for instance, that kept him at arm's length from the Tennessee Valley Authority, an agency ostensibly carrying out the exact kind of regional planning he had espoused. The same fear prevented him from ever getting his pet project in the late 1930s, the Council on Southern Regional Development, off the ground. The council, he told everyone, was to be "analagous to a great university or research coordinating and integrating agency, which knows no party or specialism," and it could function only in an atmosphere of "relative unanimity." When other, more politically minded organizations such as the Southern Policy Committee and Southern Conference for Human Welfare refused to vacate the field, Odum delayed his plans again and again. Predictably he soon began to intimate that one of their leaders, H. C. Nixon, an ardent New Dealer, was hell-bent on "secession."[67]

His advocacy of regional planning in the 1930s, moreover, was closely tied to his fear of the southern populace, a fear that predictably intensified following the Nazi takeover in Germany. By January, 1934, he was already drawing up "deadly parallel columns" between the South and Germany that showed how the region was "revivifying an emotional culture" and displaying "possible trends, now toward unsuspected fascistic principles and now symptomatic of revolution." Odum, who liked neither alternative, quickly retreated to a transparently Victorian elitism—with social science substituting for culture as his mechanism of polite social control. Through scientific planning, he wrote, "certain tech-nical procedures" could be devised to initiate new customs and "prac-tices" among the people that would lead in turn, through the Lamarckian process, to a gradual change in southern folkways. In effect, he was calling for a directed program of cultural conditioning in which the people being conditioned would have little to say. Frustrated and scared, he revised his maxims: "Love the people, yes, but don't let them misrule by ruling in technological situations. Worship them, yes, but don't let them rule or ruin. Slave for them, yes, but do it by standing in their interest and not their mob psychology." A nineteenth-century British reformer could not have agreed more.[68]

The same apprehensions about political action appear in his involve-ment with the Commission on Interracial Cooperation, the organization formed by southern liberals just after the First World War to help fore-stall lynchings and foster interracial goodwill. Odum did not even be-come a member until Will W. Alexander, the group's director, cornered him into doing so in 1927. In 1933, though, Odum volunteered to head the commission in his state and four years after that was elected national chairman. The work proved something of an education for him, exposing him to southern racial problems in all their unlovely particulars and putting him in touch for the first time with the region's sizable black elite who, Odum discovered to his surprise, largely shared his sentiments on the need for cooperation, gradualism, and statesmanship. However, to-ward the latter part of the decade, fearful as always of those younger "restless forces with whom we must deal in the future," Odum floated a scheme to subsume race under the general heading of regionalism by merging the Interracial Commission with his proposed Regional Devel-opment Council. "More and more," he argued, "it seems to me that our race problem needs to be handled as a regular integral problem of the region and the nation, since many of the basic difficulties are economic, education, etc." But his attempt to defuse and depoliticize a controversial issue was no more successful here than elsewhere, and nothing came of his plan. In fact, aside from his teaching at nearby North Carolina Col-lege for Negroes beginning in 1939, one finds few tangible results to show for his decade's service in interracial activities.[69]

The bankruptcy of regionalism, then, reveals the limits of Odum's unique sensibility. "I am trying hard to present a picture of the South," he wrote in 1930, "but also to make an honest analytic diagnosis to see what the trouble with us is." But, though he might encourage his disciples to do so, Odum himself was not equipped to risk the dangers of full-scale analysis. He was prepared neither to face the political implications such analysis might reveal nor to follow through with the sort of realistic proposals it might demand. In advancing his idea of regionalism it appears Odum was attempting to circumvent these limitations by offering a program that left partisanship far behind—an effort obviously doomed to fail. As George Tindall reported in 1958, regionalism has had "scarcely any effect at all" on the actual life of the South, and intellectually "the whole concept has somehow fallen into disuse." At best, Odum's regionalism must be seen as an overlay on his fundamental mode of expression, his portraiture. One might well argue, in fact, that because of its enduring value, portraiture, rather than the nebulous and transitory concept of regionalism, deserves to be most closely associated with his name. In the end, Odum was an artist, not an activist; a teacher, not a planner; a Modernist, but by the skin of his teeth.[70]

CHAPTER 6

WILLIAM FAULKNER
AND THE DISCOVERY OF
SOUTHERN EVIL

Although no evidence suggests that William Faulkner ever read Howard Odum, Odum certainly read and admired Faulkner. He found a special resonance in the Mississippi novelist, a shared perspective that proceeded from the close resemblance of their respective backgrounds—and perhaps from something more. In Faulkner, Odum could detect the same studied ambivalence, the same concern for the irrational forces lurking beneath the apparent calm of southern life portrayed in his own work, but drawn with unmatched vividness, even ruthlessness. "I myself have known Yoknapatawpha and it is no purely imaginary fantasy," Odum testified. ". . . I have been close enough to Faulkner's quicksands to sense something of its terrors and have often imagined, behind the cedars and columned houses, that anything could happen there." In creating Yoknapatawpha, he went on to explain, Faulkner had depicted the South as a "frontier echoing both primitive and civilized heritage," raising the most crucial question of all for southerners: "Suppose there *is* a barbaric past, merged with a 'flowed and cherished past melting into one desolation, one hopelessness,' so what?" Odum had put his finger on the central issue in Faulkner's work, the matter of whether the South's history was, in essence, as civilized and innocent as the Cavalier myth maintained.[1]

Like Odum, Faulkner was engaged in a fresh exploration of southern culture, but instead of cataloging the objective manifestations of that culture, his method was to probe deep inside his own mind. There he found drives and attitudes he shared with so many southerners, along with fragments of historical identity that, pieced together, gave the southern personality whatever distinctiveness it might have. Once having reached this innermost psychological stratum, Faulkner's great achievement was to pour his subconscious freely onto paper, bringing to daylight all those problematical impulses and instincts banished by the Victorians but endemic to human nature as they took shape in the southern psyche. His immediate predecessors, Ellen Glasgow in particular, had recognized the presence of that instinctual life, but had been inhibited by the strictures of an implacable moral dualism from going further. With Faulkner, the floodgates broke open. As Paula Snelling put it in 1938, it was "as if all the emotional force stored up during a century in which the pendulum has been held against the laws of nature suspended at the point of its furthest righthand swing has suddenly . . . burst its bonds and with accumulated momentum pushed . . . through the leftward arc." Whatever image one chooses to describe it, the explosive power of Faulkner's effort was terrific.[2]

What stood revealed was a South tormented and paralyzed, trapped in an intricate web, largely of its own making, which tied together sexuality, avarice, and aggression with the "higher" facets of southern life until they were all hopelessly tangled. Instead of a repository of glory and innocence, the past was now seen as a fatalistic curse upon the present that no southerner could wholly escape. The existence of a barbaric past *did* matter, for in Faulkner's novels so many of the region's best sources of hope, its young men in their prime, were removed from society one after the other, driven to insanity and senseless death by the demons of history. Likewise the young women, "flowers" of southern womanhood, were lost to defilement and corruption. Little wonder, then, that critics North and South at first identified Faulkner as a sensationalist purveyor of degeneracy and pessimism. "That man!" a Memphis bookseller exclaimed to David Cohn, "He ought to be run out of the country, writing about the South the way he does." Far more than any other writer of his generation, Faulkner made southern evil visible; after him, the region's perception of itself could never be the same again.[3]

Assuredly, Faulkner did not undertake this pursuit joyfully, as his detractors seemed to believe. Enough of a Modernist to see through the mask, he was Victorian enough to be shocked by what he saw. An intense inner compulsion seemed to drive him. An artist is the captive of his own imagination, he once told an interviewer: "He has a dream. It anguishes him so much he must get rid of it. He has no peace until then." To free himself from the dream, Faulkner maintained, a writer must first surrender himself to it. "I listen to the voices," he explained to Malcolm Cowley, "and when I put down what the voices say, it's all right. Sometimes I don't like what they say, but I don't change it." In Faulkner's case, those voices were usually southern voices, and the demonic vision was most frequently the image of southern innocence violated. Once that image became implanted in his mind, he was helpless to do anything but trace out the story it contained. The result was a career-long compulsion to unravel the mystery of the South that those images suggested; to diagnose what had gone wrong, why it had happened, and to discover how some shred of lost innocence might be restored. Such was the quest that led him to immense triumphs of perception in his major works: *The Sound and the Fury, Light in August,* and, above all, *Absalom, Absalom!.* Yet if living through a period of cultural transition helped make those triumphs possible, it ironically prevented the completion of his quest. His attempts, mostly after World War II, to deal with southern problems in the straightforward terms of cause and effect and to formulate a new identity for the South met with invariable and, occasionally, clumsy failure. The magic had almost disappeared.[4]

As with Odum, then, one sees in Faulkner the advantages and drawbacks peculiar to an intellectual straddling a time of transition. Like Odum, Faulkner could perceive the intricate relationships binding past and present; his, also, was a range encompassing every layer of southern society. But we also find in Faulkner the same thoroughgoing ambivalence, the same fear of arriving at final conclusions we found in Odum. To some extent this ambivalence arose from the necessities of Faulkner's craft, but even literary critics have been constantly struck by the way Faulkner kept his judgments suspended. As early as 1930 Conrad Aiken noticed a "persistent offering of obstacles" in Faulkner, "a calculated system of screens and obtrusions, of confusions and ambiguous interpolations and delays, with one express purpose . . . to keep the form— and the idea—fluid and unfinished." More recently Walter J. Slatoff has written on what he calls Faulkner's "polar imagination," the tendency "to view and interpret existence in extreme terms and to see life as composed essentially of pairs of warring entities." The oxymoron was always Faulkner's favorite rhetorical device, Slatoff observes, because it allowed him to place these polarities "in a state of deadlock" where they could "neither be separated nor reconciled." This construction, he notes, "has often been used to reflect desperately divided states of mind." Odum, of course, was equally enamored of the oxymoron.[5]

Many other telling resemblances exist between the two men's styles. Both frequently indulged in their own versions of psychological word-painting to convey their most sensitive impressions of the South, using words, "almost independent of meaning," as Hugh Holman writes of Faulkner, "so that out of them emerges not a clear statement of fact but an aura of feeling." Both strove for flexibility in their handling of time, shifting their narratives freely between different historical periods to establish interconnections. Lastly, both men were determined to capture the totality of the South, often within the limits of one page or paragraph. "It is as if Mr. Faulkner had decided to try to tell us everything," Aiken suggests, "absolutely everything, every last origin or source or quality or qualification, and every possible future or permutation as well, in one terrifically concentrated effort." Aided by his extraordinary fluency with words, Faulkner's technical experiments almost invariably succeeded, while Odum's did not. Moreover, Faulkner as a novelist was working in a medium obviously better suited to impressionism than sociology, one in which ambivalence could be turned to aesthetic advantage. But these differing outcomes of their respective attempts at generating new and appropriate styles should not obscure the similarity of their underlying objectives.[6]

Thus it is just as imperative to avoid any flat characterization of Faulkner's thought as it is of Odum's. To label Faulkner a traditionalist, moralist, nihilist, sensationalist, Christian, Stoic, atheist, or naturalist, as various critics have done, represents a fruitless effort. Partially accurate at best, none of these labels does full justice to Faulkner's awesome complexity. One can only comprehend Faulkner by viewing his work in terms of ongoing process, as a continuing search to resolve the mysteries that presented themselves as he probed deeper and deeper into the southern consciousness, discovering, as he went, occasional moments of stable insight but more often a furthering of paradox. Perhaps no one has put this better than Robert Penn Warren:

> Clearly, "absolute knowledge" is not what Faulkner's work springs
> from, or pretends to achieve. It springs from . . . a need—not a
> program or even an intention or a criticism of society—to struggle
> with the painful incoherences and paradoxes of life, and with the
> contradictory and often unworthy impulses and feelings in the self,
> in order to achieve meaning; but to struggle, in the awareness that
> meaning, if achieved, will always rest in perilous balance, and
> that the great undergirding and overarching meaning in life is in
> the act of trying to create meaning through struggle.

We must see Faulkner, then, for what he was—an immensely gifted intellectual living through an experience of intractable cultural change, a southerner just over the threshold of Modernism.[7]

I

For years William Faulkner cultivated the public image of a literary bumpkin, growing up isolated from the main currents of modern writing in a small southern town. When his New York publisher sent him a few books in 1927, to take one instance, Faulkner thanked him profusely and spoke wistfully of someday starting a library. "I possess no books at all, you see," Faulkner told him. The charade would continue through countless interviews in which Faulkner would insist with straight face that he had never read James Joyce, Sigmund Freud, or any other contemporary whose work seemed to have influenced his own. The strategy worked: as late as 1970 an otherwise astute author would describe him as "alone in the Mississippi countryside, with Shakespeare and the Old Testament" his sole companions, reaching his vision through some indeterminable alchemy of intuitive genius and regional savvy.[8]

Faulkner did spend his life in the small Mississippi town of Oxford, but we now know that his schooling in the avant-garde was more complete than that of any southerner of his generation. Beginning at age eight, he embarked upon an intensive reading of western literature that would take him through all the classical and modern masters up to Joyce, Pound, and Hemingway. First he tackled Cooper and Dickens, and then, encouraged by his mother and grandfather, Cervantes, Balzac, Flaubert, Shakespeare, Fielding, and Conrad. By the eighth grade he was immersed in *Moby-Dick*. Three years later, in 1914, a stroke of good fortune brought this patently precocious boy under the tutelage of a family friend, Phil Stone, a recent graduate of Yale who much preferred the role of literary counselor to his actual profession of law. Stone gave Faulkner, in Joseph Blotner's words, "a kind of college seminar in modern literature," introducing his apt pupil to Swinburne, Housman, the Symbolist and Imagist poets, Yeats, Eliot, and Conrad Aiken, along with Sherwood Anderson, Hardy, Tolstoy, Dostoevski, Oscar Wilde, James Branch Cabell, and many more. The relationship continued for some time: it was Stone who handed Faulkner a copy of Joyce's *Ulysses* in early 1924 and who served as business agent for his first two novels. Whatever Faulkner may have missed in his sessions with Stone, he made up for during his brief forays in New York, Paris, and New Orleans throughout the 1920s. In short, his exposure to Modernist culture was so extensive that by the time he started his own writing in earnest about 1927 Faulkner was perched on the furthest reaches of the literary frontier, with nothing left to assimilate. Only then, realizing that "I had read too much," that his learning from others was beginning to cramp his spontaneity, did he stop his long, deliberate training in his craft.[9]

Faulkner's earliest published work, most of it poetry, conspicuously showed the influence of this vast reading, particularly that of Swinburne, Housman, and the French Symbolists, those late nineteenth-century bohemian poets in whom the Modernist sensibility had first taken root. Faulkner prized the Symbolists for many things—for their stripping away of artifice, their economy of expression, and their calculated use of obscurity to achieve an effect of mystery. But what seems to have appealed to him most was their attempt to detach the senses from rational control, giving rise to a subtle, lyrical sensuality entirely absent from the British and American verse of the time. In imitation of their practice, nymphs, centaurs, satyrs, and fauns—creatures part human and part animal with well-known sexual proclivities—sported through the pastoral landscapes of Faulkner's poems, involved in activities the poet only alluded to. The classical setting and imaginary characters, combined with the technique of suggestiveness, were meant to preserve a veneer of innocence that made the eroticism all the more tantalizing and which, incidentally, may have proved of special comfort to a young man of old-fashioned upbringing venturing into forbidden territory. At the same time, Faulkner was discovering in Housman what he thought was the "secret after which the moderns course"—namely, the spiritual and aesthetic value of stoicism. Intently studying "A Shropshire Lad," he was struck, he said, by the "splendor of fortitude, the beauty of being of the soil like a tree about which fools might howl and which winds of disillusion and death and despair might strip, leaving it bleak, without bitterness; beautiful in sadness." It was all so bittersweet, this cold indifference of the universe, a point on which Ellen Glasgow, then writing *Barren Ground*, would surely have agreed.[10]

His first two novels, *Soldier's Pay* and *Mosquitoes*, written in 1925 and 1926 respectively, display Faulkner's simultaneous desire to appear unmistakably au courant and to place himself, as he put it, well above the "yelping pack." He had never stood in awe of the Greenwich Village lions, speaking of them in a 1922 review as those "aesthetic messiahs of our emotional Valhalla who have one eye on the ball and the other on the grandstand." Now, experimenting with a new and more congenial form, he set out to show himself superior. Consequently, both novels are packed with literary allusions, to Cabell, Eliot, and Joyce especially, and contain the requisite number of purple passages, all designed to give the reader the impression that the author was a very knowledgeable young man indeed. On occasion, this effort succeeded brilliantly; at other times, it became *too* obvious, leading Faulkner to many false notes and inconsistencies. As Michael Millgate observes of *Soldier's Pay*, through most of the text Faulkner assumes an "attitude of pseudo-sophisticated bitterness, self-consciously enrolling himself among the wastelanders, but elsewhere in the book he creates an almost Hardyesque sense of life's ironies." Moreover, these apprenticeship novels exhibit a curious evasion of the subject to which he would eventually devote his career. Faulkner was putting everything he had learned into them, but leaving one thing out—the South.[11]

Although set in Georgia, *Soldier's Pay* could as easily have taken place anywhere in the country, for the action centers on the general problem of the First World War veteran coming home to a changed American society. As Faulkner portrays them, all of these men have somehow been wounded, physically or psychologically, installing them in the "comradeship of those whose lives had become pointless through the sheer equivocation of events, of the sorry jade, Circumstance." Their plight is epitomized by Donald Mahon, a once-glamorous aviator mortally shot in the head who returns blind and comatose to face a slow death. This was, of course, a familiar theme in the 1920s, but Faulkner was determined to handle it in a different way. For Hemingway and others, this wartime experience of disillusionment enabled the individual to surmount his initial innocence, making his wound a veritable badge of Modernism, a token that he had met the irrational nature of existence face-to-face. Not so with Faulkner's veterans; their service overseas has, if anything, cemented them in innocence. They have become frozen in time, cut off from the modern world of speed, poise, and sensuality that sprang into being while they were gone. At an elegant dance—perhaps the best scene in the novel—we find them looking on helplessly "like eternal country boys of one national mental state" while those a few years younger glide by "locked together, . . . drifting like a broken dream." This new style of life leaves the veterans bewildered:

"We can't do them dances. It ain't just going through the motions.
You can learn that, I guess. It's—it's—" he sought vainly for words.

"Where I come from," another puts in, "you'd have to have a license to dance that way." "Dat's de war," a Negro driver explains to them, as if they had never heard of it. A lifetime of American Legion meetings awaits these men; they, and not Hemingway's Jake Barnes, are the real walking wounded of the decade.[12]

Faulkner's account of life among the artists likewise strayed from literary convention. Based on an actual incident involving Faulkner and some of his *Double Dealer* friends, *Mosquitoes* depicts an assemblage of New Orleans art-colony types, most nonsoutherners, marooned aboard a disabled yacht a few yards offshore on Lake Pontchartrain. But instead of following the 1920s formula of portraying these artistically inclined characters as creative nonconformists, Faulkner shows them indulging in an endless drone of inconsequential conversation, punctuated with hidden barbs—a drone resembling that of the ever-present mosquitoes who swarm about the boat. On board one finds a varied dramatis personae: Mrs. Maurier, the ship's owner, a wealthy would-be patroness of artists who disapproves of the drinking and philandering taking place but realizes that "after all, one must pay a price for art"; her niece, an athletic girl modeled on Faulkner's lady friend of the time (to whom the book is dedicated), who tries to run off with the ship's steward; Ernest Talliaferro, a clear-cut Prufrock figure with thinning hair chasing unsuccessfully after every woman in sight; and Mark Frost, "a poet who produced an occasional cerebral and obscure poem in four or seven lines reminding one somehow of the function of evacuation excruciatingly and incompletely performed." Some halfway serious discussion of aesthetic philosophy does occur, but the main thrust is satirical. The book even includes an offstage appearance by Faulkner himself, described as a shabbily dressed "little kind of black man" who "said he was a liar by profession."[13]*

Whatever Faulkner may have intended, one detects in these early works more than a little brashness, a deliberate flaunting of newly discovered powers almost as if the author's ego were running out of control. The impression is reinforced by Faulkner's habit about this time of informing his New Orleans acquaintances that they were standing in the presence of a "genius" who would one day surpass Shakespeare. Yet alongside this bravado, which doubtless served to sustain him through a difficult period of his career, Faulkner had also come to believe that without professional humility an artist was lost, a theme he dwelt on often in *Mosquitoes*. "Strangle your heart o israfel," the sculptor Gordon warns himself, "winged with loneliness feathered bitter with pride." But Gordon—and, by implication, Faulkner himself—can curb his haughtiness only by finding a passion consuming enough to engage his talents fully, a subject so compelling and all-absorbing that it, not the artist, became master.[14]

Although in retrospect it seems inevitable that Faulkner would turn to the South at this juncture, this was not immediately apparent to him at the time. He was, he insisted, seeking general, not provincial truths, and a beauty that, like Keats's Grecian urn, would remain absolute and unimpaired forever. Only gradually did he perceive that the familiar land-

---

* It is entirely possible that *Mosquitoes* may have had an additional personal dimension— Faulkner may have had in mind the best-selling novel published in the 1880s by his great-grandfather, William C. Falkner, entitled *The White Rose of Memphis*, which concerns a shipload of grotesque characters aboard a Mississippi side-wheeler wending its way to New Orleans. The parallels are too interesting to overlook.

6. William Faulkner in the late 1920s
Courtesy Jack Cofield © 1978

scape he had grown up in might contain these qualities and so represent his salvation, as he indicated, almost by way of notation to himself, in a critical essay of April, 1925: "The beauty—spiritual and physical—of the South lies in the fact that God has done so much for it and man so little. I have this for which to thank whatever gods may be: that having fixed my roots in this soil all contact, saving by the printed word, with contemporary poets is impossible." For the next year and a half, however, Faulkner continued to rely on topics currently in vogue, recasting them, as we have seen, in his personal idiom.[15]

The breakthrough came in late September, 1926. With *Mosquitoes* just finished, Faulkner suddenly shifted focus, writing furiously at not one, but two southern novels simultaneously, the first of eleven major works he would publish on southern themes during the next fifteen years. Approaching his native region with the Modernist perspective acquired through his reading, a whole new world opened before him, one not in the least provincial or shopworn. Most significant of all, as this change took place, the problem of pride disappeared. Into his mind, he would later report, streamed a seemingly interminable procession of "half formed" images crying for completion, "by reason of whose labor I might reaffirm the impulses of my own ego in this actual world . . . with a lot of humbleness."* Writer and subject had begun to fuse, exactly as Symbolist theory postulated, leaving him to wonder "if I had invented the (teeming) world to which I should give life or if it had invented me, giving me an illusion of greatness." Immersed in the subject he cared about most, Faulkner was now embarked on a journey into the southern interior that would sustain his period of maximum creativity.[16]

II

The first fruits of that expedition came in *Flags in the Dust* (published in a severely cut version as *Sartoris*),[17] at once a working out of regional and family pieties and a reconnoitering of new terrain. Because of its exploratory nature, the novel is marred by considerable confusion and

---

*To be precise, Faulkner did not so much extirpate his pride as provisionally submerge it in his work, and a certain tension was always evident. In 1944, for example, he wrote Malcolm Cowley on how he had labored diligently at his craft "with pride but I believe not vanity, with plenty of ego but with humility too." Five years later he carried this a step further, claiming it was now his ambition "to be, as a private individual, abolished and voided from history, leaving it markless, no refuse save the printed books; I wish I had had enough sense to see ahead thirty years ago and, like some of the Elizabethans, not signed them" (Faulkner to Cowley, May 7, 1944, February 11, 1949, in Cowley, *Faulkner-Cowley File*, 7, 126).

ambiguity, including lapses into the old romantic stereotypes, but the overall impression remains one of a society caught up in pathology. "It is a book heavy with the air of sickness," writes Irving Howe, "but neither diagnosis nor cure is suggested; the characteristic tensions of Faulkner's world begin to emerge, but they are still incipient and undefined." Certainly the novel's most striking feature is its portrayal of the South's younger generation in the early 1920s as, not degenerate, but psychologically disturbed. Degeneracy was no stranger to southern fiction; embodied in the stock figure of the planter's dissipated son, it implied a personal failure of moral weakness or an understandable response to a family's loss of fortune during the Civil War. A pervasive incidence of neurosis, on the other hand, indicated a judgment on the society as a whole, a deeper malady whose root cause went beyond the individual to the region's most treasured cultural values, a defect that portended social catastrophe.[18]

This sense of inner doom manifests itself most clearly in Bayard Sartoris, the book's main character. Last scion of one of Yoknapatawpha County's most prestigious families, he has returned from combat as an aviator in France obsessed by the wartime death of his twin brother, John, and determined to seek death himself. The war, however, has not produced Bayard's urge to self-destruction; it has only served to intensify it. Even before he left home he had been given to terrorizing the townfolk with reckless stunts, including a celebrated jump from a ninety-foot water tower in which he swung by a rope over the railroad freight yard and landed in a small concrete swimming pool. Gripped by forces he neither understands nor controls, Bayard on his return proceeds to drive his powerful sports car at breakneck speeds along narrow, unpaved country roads, on one occasion taking deliberate aim at an approaching mule-drawn wagon, then swerving past "with not an inch to spare, so close that the yelling negro in the wagon could see the lipless and savage derision of his teeth." These exploits give him no pleasure, he admits to Narcissa Benbow, the aloof, quiet girl he eventually marries, yet he cannot restrain himself, even when Narcissa is with him. The denouement comes when he skids off a muddy embankment down a steep ravine with his grandfather, "old Bayard," in the car, causing the old man a fatal heart attack. After fleeing in panic and shame, Bayard finally meets his desired end test-piloting an airplane no one else dared to fly. He crashes the same day his son, Benbow Sartoris, is born.[19]

The source of Bayard's addiction to violence becomes a prime topic of speculation in the novel, most of it focused on the violence-prone history of his family. "It's in the blood," claims Miss Jenny Du Pre, Bayard's great-aunt and the first of a line of wise-grandmother figures in Faulkner.

"Savages, every one of 'em. No earthly use to anybody." Old Bayard seems to second this interpretation, attributing the problem to the family dream of a "Sartoris heaven in which they could spend eternity dying deaths of needless and magnificent violence while spectators doomed to immortality looked eternally on." Faulkner himself offers a variation on this thesis, suggesting that Bayard is adhering to an obsolete code designed for grander times but out of place in the present. Lastly, there is the opinion of wise old Aunt Sally Wyatt, who thinks Bayard should have been locked in an asylum years ago.[20]

As usual in Faulkner, all of these explanations are meant to be partially correct; none can stand by itself, but perhaps Aunt Sally's is the most pertinent with which to start. For whatever its origins, Bayard's behavior is plainly pathological. Unlike his Civil War namesake, the gallant "Carolina Bayard" who went on madcap raids with Jeb Stuart "in a spirit of pure fun" and found the war a "holiday without restrictions," this Bayard performs his violent antics solely out of compulsion; he gets no pleasure from them. His obsessive feelings of guilt over his brother's death stem not from normal grief, but from the latent incestuous homosexual love existing between them that Faulkner repeatedly alludes to. The most revealing symptoms, though, are the recurring nightmares of aerial dogfights that wake him even in periods of relative contentment and that closely resemble old Bayard's description of the Sartoris version of heaven:

> Then, momentarily, the world was laid away and he was a trapped
> beast in the high blue, mad for life, trapped in the very cunning
> fabric that had betrayed him who had dared chance too much, and
> he thought again if, when the bullet found you, you could only
> crash upward, burst; anything but earth. Not death, no: it was the
> crash you had to live through so many times before you struck
> that filled your throat with vomit.

The Sartoris dream of forever "dying deaths of needless and magnificent violence," in other words, has turned into a vicious psychological entrapment for Bayard. What was once glamorous has become a neurosis.[21]

In psychiatric terms, Bayard appears to be a classic case of secondary narcissism. As defined by Freud, a narcissist is a person who treats himself as the object of his own sexual desires and thus fancies himself omnipotent. In secondary narcissism, however, the individual suffers from feelings of utter emptiness, and regards his own body as worthless. To overcome these feelings, which usually arise when the person compares himself to a powerful parent or legendary ancestor, he adopts the expedient of "introjecting" their supposed omnipotence into his own personality, borrowing, as it were, their magical powers for his own self-esteem and protection. For Bayard Sartoris, that borrowed identity belongs to his great-grandfather, Colonel John Sartoris, the fiery soldier, political leader, and railroad magnate who established the family dynasty in Mississippi, and whose ghost continues to pervade the Sartoris household. Since Bayard's sense of omnipotence is borrowed, he must test it constantly in death-defying acts, always barely averting disaster—and always in his great-grandfather's "presence." That is why his various driving incidents—the confrontation with the mule-drawn wagon and the accident that kills old Bayard—take place on a bluff just below the cemetery where a larger-than-life statue of Colonel Sartoris looks down "in pompous effigy." That is why his jump from the water tower takes him over the railroad yards his great-grandfather built. This also helps explain his peculiar relationship to his twin brother, whose name, one recalls, was also John Sartoris.[22]

The significance of Bayard's neurotic syndrome becomes apparent when we realize that the character of Colonel Sartoris was modeled, with only a few major discrepancies, on Faulkner's own great-grandfather, the man on whom, as his younger brother later put it, Faulkner "more or less unconsciously patterned his life." Like his fictional counterpart, Colonel William C. Falkner arrived in Mississippi in the 1840s, acquired a large plantation, served in the Mexican war, raised an infantry company in 1861 and rode at the head of the column as it marched out of town, fought with unusual courage—some said recklessness—at the First Bull Run, was voted out of his command (apparently because of his recklessness) by his troops soon afterward, returned home to organize a guerilla band to snipe at Yankee lines, assembled a local railroad system after the war (using convict labor), and was shot down in the middle of town by his estranged business partner after announcing he would no longer carry a gun. Colonel Falkner's fourteen-foot-high monument still stands, exactly as Faulkner described it in *Flags in the Dust*, in the Ripley, Mississippi, cemetery, a short distance from Oxford.[23]

But the differences between the two men, actual and fictional, are worth noting, too. Falkner came to Mississippi penniless and on foot by way of the Tennessee mountains, where, rumor had it, he had killed a man in a fight. A frontier lawyer of fierce ambition and, in Blotner's words, of "violent and impulsive" temperament, he continued to embroil himself in bloody and often fatal altercations, somehow managing to get himself acquitted each time he was hauled into court. His heroism on behalf of the Confederate cause was unquestionable through 1863, but during the last years of the war there are strong indications that he was engaged in infiltrating supplies to the northern troops besieged at Memphis; that, it appears, was how he accumulated the capital to build his railroad. Finally, in his later years, this soldier of fortune turned New South entrepreneur began writing novels, producing one book, *The White Rose of Memphis*, that sold over 160,000 copies and secured him a minor place in the region's literary history. Little wonder, then, that his great-grandson had strong but decidedly mixed feelings about this man, or that those feelings were inextricably linked in Faulkner's mind with southern mythology.[24]

In this sense, *Flags in the Dust* may be seen as Faulkner's initial skirmish against the Cavalier myth—with the myth still far from vanquished. In Bayard Sartoris he was attempting to portray how the weight of such a perplexing, violence-ridden heritage pressed down on southerners of his class and generation, leading to possible further violence and self-destruction. The element of compulsion that had entered into the Cavalier tradition is graphically illustrated by means of Bayard's crippling neurosis. At the same time, in John Sartoris, Faulkner was trying to keep the romantic tradition alive. Wistfully he wrote of these swashbucklers as resembling "prehistoric" creatures "too grandly conceived and executed either to exist very long or to vanish utterly when dead from an earth shaped and furnished for punier things." In deference to the myth, Faulkner amended historical actuality when necessary. The Sartorises hail not from the Tennessee mountains but from the South Carolina lowland aristocracy. Colonel Sartoris does kill several men, but *after the war*, eliminating northern carpetbaggers and assorted brigands as a service to his community. Faulkner, in short, was trying to have it both ways, to assail the myth and keep it too.[25]

That was a difficult chore, as Faulkner's treatment of the other John Sartoris, Bayard's deceased brother, plainly shows. John is meant to be a twentieth-century Sartoris exhibiting all the Cavalier's better traits but free of neurotic disturbance. In contrast to Bayard's "cold, arrogant sort of leashed violence," John's, we are told on several occasions, "was a warmer thing, spontaneous and merry and wild." Significantly, though, John appears only indirectly in *Flags in the Dust*; we glimpse him through remarks made by others and in a description of a miniature painting of his face done when he was a child. When Faulkner later tried to bring this chimerical character to life in a short story, the results were less than successful. "Something had failed to fall into place," Blotner writes of the manuscript. "Sartoris came through not as a doomed hero but as an even more violent self-centered ruffian than he had appeared" before. The tensions that the Cavalier identity aroused in Faulkner's mind could not be more obvious. Faulkner would never repudiate the Sartorises. He would always use them as a sort of rod by which to measure other Yoknapatawpha families, but hereafter he would keep them locked safely in the past.[26]

Following the dictates of his "polar imagination," Faulkner paired the Cavalier Sartorises with an antithetical family, the delicate, withdrawn, peace-loving Benbows who represent the South's alternate legacy from the nineteenth century, Victorianism. Their cultural origins are explicit in Faulkner's description of their home. Designed by "an English architect of the 'forties who had built the house (with the minor concession of a veranda) in the funereal light Tudor which the young Victoria had sanctioned," the Benbow mansion and everything surrounding it bespeak the early Victorian period, right down to the "mullioned casements brought out from England." The two remaining occupants of the house, Narcissa and her brother Horace, likewise reflect this transplanted tradition. Horace, after graduating from Sewanee, has pursued his love of things British as a Rhodes Scholar at Oxford, finding there "a perfect life, a life accomplishing itself placidly in a region remote from time and into which the world's noises came only from afar." He leaves Oxford only with the greatest reluctance. Narcissa, for her part, comes close to being a caricature of the ideal Victorian maiden. Dressed always in gray, her facial expression conveying "that serene repose of lilies, objecting even to Shakespeare because, unlike a gentleman, he 'tells everything,'" she seems the least likely match for Bayard Sartoris. "All of her instincts were antipathetic toward him," Faulkner observes, yet by novel's end, primarily through her own initiative, Narcissa has married Bayard and borne his child.[27]

What brings this strange pair together is their complementary pathologies. For just as Bayard displays the symptoms of secondary narcissism, Narcissa, as her name unsubtly implies, is a primary narcissist. Raised as a virtual orphan in near-complete social isolation, with no powerful parent or ancestor figures to introject, she has fallen in love with her own ego. "I hate all men," she tells her brother, and she means it. Yet, her ego always seeking enhancement, Narcissa cannot resist keeping the anonymous and obscene love letters Byron Snopes has sent her. Nor can she turn down the "romantic glamor" of carrying the Sartoris name, or the chance to exercise her prized maternal skills in taking care of Bayard. But above all, Victorian as she is, she cannot overcome her secret fascination for Sartoris animality: ". . . on occasions when she had seen them conducting themselves as civilized beings, had been in the same polite room with them, she found herself watching them with shrinking and fearful curiosity, as she might have looked upon wild beasts with a temporary semblance of men and engaged in human activities." Narcissa finds gratification in associating with a man like Bayard so long as she can preserve her "inviolate serenity" by staying within "her walled and windless garden." Given his compulsive need for "cold sufficiency," such an arrangement suits Bayard fine. Thus an invisible barrier, which both desire, remains between them. The force of his violence may shake her briefly, "like a lily in a gale," but it leaves her ultimately intact, "without any actual laying-on of hands." The Cavalier and Victorian traditions are joined, but they do not truly merge. The South's historic culture, Faulkner implies, rests on a profound contradiction.[28]

Faulkner was also engaged here in a deliberate attack on Victorianism itself. This becomes apparent in his treatment of Horace Benbow, that Prufrock-like creature with an "air of fine and delicate futility" whose drive toward spiritual suicide parallels Bayard's route to physical self-destruction. A narcissist like his sister, Horace, as is often the case with male narcissists, feeds his ego by projecting his self-love onto others— especially his sister. This leads to an incredibly tangled relationship, as we discover when "he sat beside her on the couch and took her hand in his and stroked it upon his cheek and upon the fine devastation of his hair." His projected narcissism also leads to his ecstatic hobby of glass-blowing, in which he sublimates his incestuous feelings by producing "one almost perfect vase of clear amber, larger, more richly and chastely serene . . . which he kept always on his night table and called by his sister's name in the intervals of apostrophising both of them impartially in his moments of rhapsody over the realization of the meaning of peace and the unblemished attainment of it, as Thou still unravished bride of quietude." The vase permits Horace the fantasy of permanent possession of his sister as well as a guarantee of her continued virginity. Clearly, Victorian innocence has become as compulsive for him as Cavalier violence is for Bayard.[29]

According to Freud, male narcissists may be especially attracted by the "charm of certain animals which seem not to concern themselves about us, such as cats and large beasts of prey," and they may show a fatal weakness for women who display similar characteristics. The objects they choose to project their self-love on, in other words, are usually creatures who appear self-sufficient—and who may well be narcissists themselves. Whether Faulkner acquired this insight through reading Freud or arrived at it by himself,* he certainly made ample use of it in creating

---

*On the perennial question of what direct influence Freud may have had on Faulkner, John T. Irwin is probably closest to the truth in suggesting that Faulkner attempted to disguise the insights he found in Freud to prevent anyone from thinking that he was borrowing ideas. The two seem to have arrived at similar discoveries independently, although Freud of course published his work some twenty years before Faulkner. See Irwin, *Doubling and Incest/Repetition and Revenge*, 5.

Horace Benbow. Horace's most vivid childhood memory, for example, concerns an old, toothless circus tiger yawning in its cage which he had seen at age five. Most little boys, Faulkner tells us, took the tiger in stride, regarding it as just another interesting sight at the circus, but not Horace: "in him a thing these many generations politely dormant waked shrieking, and again for a red moment he dangled madly by his hands from the lowermost limb of a tree." The animality that his Victorian upbringing had tried to suppress had been rekindled, causing Horace unexpected pleasure. Later in his life, tiger-like women would have an identical effect.[30]

That is why, to the puzzlement of everyone, Horace picks for his wife Belle Mitchell, a tasteless, petulant, "preeningly dictatorial" divorcée whose strong perfume smells of "tiger-reek." To listen to her maid describe her, remarks Belle's first husband, "you'd think Belle was some kind of wild animal, wouldn't you? A dam tiger or something?" And, indeed, that is exactly how Horace sees her. Prior to this time, Horace had been happy in "his winged and solitary cage," much like Narcissa in her walled garden. His sexual impulses, when they surfaced, had taken the shape of sensual pastoral fantasies, strikingly similar to those in Faulkner's early poetry, with nymphs and unicorns prancing "about meadows nailed with firmamented stars to the ultimate roof of things." But, as in his encounter with the circus tiger, his involvement with Belle has aroused a buried part of his personality he no longer can or wants to control. There is "something there," he tries to explain to Narcissa, "something you must go after; must; driven":

> That may be the secret, after all. Not any subconscious striving after what we believe will be happiness, contentment; but a sort of gadfly urge after the petty, ignoble impulses which man has tried so vainly to conjure with words out of himself. Nature, perhaps, watching him as he tries to wean himself away from the rank and richly foul old mire that spawned him, biding her time and flouting that illusion of purification which he has foisted upon himself and calls his soul. But it's something there, something you—you—

Horace cannot finish the sentence, for, in *Flags in the Dust*, he knows only that the secret exists. He cannot yet see its shape, but pursue it he must. One is reminded of the advice the merchant Stein gives to Conrad's Lord Jim—"in the destructive element immerse"—for Horace too senses the inadequacy of his Victorian innocence and is determined to reestablish contact with the repressed, animalistic side of human nature.[31]

Horace finds that reality, of course, in *Sanctuary*, Faulkner's sixth published novel, but one apparently begun as early as 1926. The book stemmed from an incident that year when a certain young woman came by Faulkner's table at a Memphis nightclub to tell a horrific tale of how she had once been abducted by a notorious local gangster known as "Popeye"; how, since he was impotent, he had raped her with a cruel mechanical device; and how he had kept her in a brothel more or less against her will for several weeks. Faulkner could not put this image of innocence rudely violated out of his mind. Time and again he reworked the material, even undertaking a massive and costly revision of the original galley proofs, until it finally took shape as the story of an alluring University of Mississippi coed named Temple Drake, "no longer quite a child, not yet quite a woman," who stumbles by chance into a bootlegger's hideout where Popeye lies lurking. The couple in charge of the operation, Lee Goodwin and his common-law wife, Ruby Lamar, warn Temple to leave, but she ignores them, choosing instead to race crazily about the premises half terrified and half fascinated by her first view of the underworld. Her actions set off a long chain of nightmarish events: Popeye's shooting of the kindly half-wit Tommy, her deflowerment by Popeye using a dried-out corncob, her stay in a Memphis whorehouse, Goodwin's mistaken arrest for Tommy's murder, her perjured testimony at Goodwin's trial saddling him with both the killing and the rape, culminating in Goodwin's violent death at the hands of a lynch mob. These events are recounted in full lurid detail, making *Sanctuary*, in Hyatt H. Waggoner's words, "less an implicit judgment of experience than a compelling and almost unbearable subjection to it."[32]

If *Sanctuary* represents the "discovery of evil," as Cleanth Brooks has termed it, it is Horace Benbow who does the discovering. It is the assault on his innocence, rather than Temple's, which the reader is made to feel most keenly, and it is his ultimate defeat that creates the overwhelming sense of despair. Put another way, in *Sanctuary* the Victorian dichotomy between savagery and civilization, morality and sin, on which Benbow had based his life is bludgeoned to pieces by a blunt, heavy instrument— too blunt, perhaps, for the book's aesthetic good.[33]

Horace becomes a direct participant in the tragedy when he volunteers to serve as Goodwin's lawyer, partly out of sympathy for the ever-suffering Ruby Lamar, but mainly because of his abstract conception of moral duty to defend an innocent man. With "the law, justice, civilization" all on Goodwin's side, Horace feels sure that his client will go free, but as the case proceeds it becomes clear that he has not reckoned with the hidden malice and corruption that infests every layer of Jefferson society. He is shocked when so many of Goodwin's longtime, if surreptitious, customers now feel obliged to denounce him, when the Baptist minister uses Goodwin as the text for a sermon, and when a delegation of church ladies forces the local hotel to throw Ruby and her sick child into the streets because she is not legally married. "Christians, Christians," Horace mutters as he pays the hotel bill "with shaking hands." The worst outrage, however, comes at the trial, where Goodwin is falsely convicted by Temple's surprise testimony and the ambitious district attorney's inflammatory charge to the jury that the case rightfully belonged to a lynch mob. Just the previous night Horace had assured Goodwin all would go well, that God might be "foolish at times, but at least He's a gentleman." Afterward, Horace wanders about dazed, not even hearing the mob when it almost turns on him. As one critic points out, the bitter lesson Horace has learned is ironically embedded in Goodwin's name—in *Sanctuary*, the good do not ever win, nor is there any such thing as a sanctuary.[34]

Thoroughgoing as it is, this exposé of small-town bourgeois hypocrisy, so common a literary theme in the 1920s, is meant only as an overlay, a kind of social counterpoint to Horace's simultaneous discovery of evil at a far more personal level. As the novel opens, we find him leaving home after ten years of marriage, telling himself he can stand Belle's noxious habits no longer, while in truth his motives have more to do with his growing unease over the ripening sexuality of his teenage stepdaughter, Little Belle. He becomes further disquieted when he accidentally encounters Popeye a few days before Temple Drake does; like her, he is immediately taken by some unfathomable quality of Popeye's presence, a shadow "monstrous and portentous" hovering over the landscape "in black and nameless threat." Both curious and repelled, Horace begins searching for the meaning of what he has seen, attempting initially to confine it within the framework of his Victorian beliefs. "There's a corruption about even looking upon evil, even by accident," he remarks to Aunt Jenny the following week, "you cannot haggle, traffic, with putrefaction." The experience sticks in his memory—much as the nightclub girl's story did in Faulkner's—and accounts in large part for his persistence in seeing the case through.[35]

It is these two elements—Horace's compelling need to believe in the existence of childlike innocence, specifically that of Little Belle, and his exposure to evil in his meeting with Popeye—which fuse with cataclysmic force when he learns of Temple Drake's involvement. "She was all right. You know she was all right," he begs Ruby Lamar to tell him as he first hears of the incident. That same evening he watches in "quiet horror" as his photograph of Little Belle's "sweet, inscrutable face" appears to change before his eyes into a "face suddenly older in sin than he would ever be." His anxiety is compounded as he frantically searches for Temple, building to fever pitch when he finally locates her in Memphis, listens to her story, and realizes she is "recounting the experience with actual pride, a sort of naive and impersonal vanity." As Cleanth Brooks points out, the interview makes clear to him not only that a sweet young girl can come in contact with evil, but also that she might actually invite and enjoy it, thus shattering the bedrock belief in unassailable innocence on which Horace had constructed his entire view of the world. Once again his photograph of Little Belle is transformed by his imagination from "sweet chiaroscuro" to "voluptuous promise," but this time the fantasy descends into a nightmare vision of Little Belle substituted for Temple atop the corn shucks raptly watching "something black and furious go roaring out of her pale body." Sick to the very core of his being, Horace barely reaches the bathroom in time.[36]

Horace does not, it should be stressed, arrive at instant worldly wisdom here. Rather, what is at stake is the destruction of his Victorian concept of radical purity, the same concept he had symbolically invested in the "almost perfect" vase he keeps on his night table and in his idealized image of his sister. Although always in tension with his desire to explore the "petty, ignoble impulses" of human nature, his belief in purity remains the standard by which he determines meaning in the world. That is why he is so devastated to learn, as Olga Vickery puts it, "that good and evil do not live in separate compartments," for he has no alternative culture to replace his Victorianism with. Faulkner underscores Horace's dilemma through his paradoxical description of Temple's appearance at the trial. Her dress and trappings are those of a prostitute, yet she sits with a demeanor of "childish immobility" as she tells the court sotto voce how her assailant found her "in the crib." Having finished her vicious testimony, which amounts to Goodwin's death warrant, this "defenseless child," as the prosecutor refers to her, leaves holding her father's hand. Horace Benbow had once consoled himself with the thought that at least "there is a logical pattern to evil," but after witnessing Temple's performance he has no consolation left at all. His value system in shambles, his life in effect ruined, he returns in complete submission to Belle.[37]

Compared with Faulkner's later works, both *Flags in the Dust* and *Sanctuary* seem relatively uncomplex, their plots and style more or less straightforward and at times cliché-ridden, implying that some distance remained between author and subject matter. Faulkner had used two variants of narcissism, Sartoris and Benbow, Cavalier and Victorian, to focus on two predominant traits of the southern personality as he observed it—the tendencies to impulsive violence and radical innocence, the one hyperactive, the other hyperpassive. For the most part, he had stayed outside his characters, content to portray their behavior and occasional reflections, but not attempting to follow the train of association within their minds. Moreover, he had essayed no suggestion of how these two traits might be connected, or how they might develop in the future. As *Flags in the Dust* closes, Dr. Loosh Peabody and his son speculate on the prognosis for the newborn Benbow Sartoris. "Maybe that Benbow blood will sort of hold him down," Loosh, Jr., maintains. "They're quiet folks, that girl, and Horace sort of. . . ." "He's got Sartoris blood in him, too," his father quickly reminds him. Faulkner leaves the question unanswered, and the book ends on a high note of ambiguity.[38]

III

In *The Sound and the Fury*, Faulkner's focus sharpened considerably. Leaving the semimythical Sartorises temporarily behind, he pressed on to a family that came far closer to representing a prototype of the southern experience as he knew it. The Compson's "solid square mile," once virgin wilderness, stands "almost in the center of the town of Jefferson." The piecemeal sale of their property, down to the last stick of furniture, epitomizes the steady dissolution of the Old South following the Civil War—"the spectacle," as Henry Nash Smith puts it, "of a civilization uprooted and left to die"; and the Compson children, in all their neurotic complexity, symbolize the central tensions Faulkner perceived in southern life just prior to the Great Depression. Because the book constitutes such a laying-bare of the region's deepest ills, it was, Faulkner said later, the one he "anguished the most over" and "worked hardest at." For six months, through the spring and summer of 1928, convinced by publishers' repeated rejections of *Flags in the Dust* that he was writing only for himself, he sustained an "ecstasy" he would "never again recapture." The result was an unparalleled portrait of the South's buried subconscious rendered in the Modernist vein, containing only the barest hint of possible future redemption. "In this fictional counterpart of *The Waste Land*," Hyatt Waggoner correctly sums up, "a situation is presented and diagnosed; no remedy is proposed."[39]

The process of composition began, Faulkner always insisted, with a "mental picture" that became the "only thing in literature which would ever move me very much"—the image of Caddy Compson, age seven, climbing a blossoming pear tree to peek into the room where her grandmother, "Damuddy," lay dying, while her three brothers looked up from below at the muddy seat of her drawers she had soiled playing in a creek that afternoon. Later the family's devoted black servant Dilsey would try to remove the stain, but to no avail. "It done soaked clean through onto you," Dilsey says. Faulkner claimed he understood the symbolism immediately—the pear tree standing for sexuality, Damuddy's death for the death of the Old South, and the dirty drawers for Caddy's lost inno-cence—as soon as he imagined Dilsey

> with the mudstained drawers scrubbing the naked backside of that doomed little girl—trying to cleanse with the sorry byblow of its soiling that body, flesh, whose shame they symbolised and prophe-sied, as though she already saw the dark future and the part she was to play in it trying to hold that crumbling household together.

Five different times Faulkner attempted "to rid myself of the dream" by unfolding the story the image contained, each time working from a dif-ferent perspective, but even after the completion of an "appendix" in 1945 he was still far from satisfied. The cause of the Compsons' chil-dren's doom, so intimately tied to the historical context in which he lived, would remain an irresistible mystery for him and for an entire generation of southerners as well.[40]

To gain some insight into that mystery, we would do well to view the problem in terms of Erik H. Erikson's concept of identity, defined by Erikson as the "immediate perception of one's self-sameness and con-tinuity in time." Such an identity depends directly on one's social and historical environment. As children grow up, Erikson writes, they begin to identify with "those *part aspects* of people by which they themselves are most immediately affected." At the stage of "identity crisis," usually in late adolescence, those "part aspects" must come together to form a "functioning whole." However, he adds, the "historical era in which a person lives offers only a limited number of socially meaningful models for workable combinations of identity fragments." Thus the individual must not only select worthy and mutually compatible ego identifications from the past; he must be capable of transforming them into a viable identity for the present and future. Failure to achieve identity is known as "identity diffusion," with its foremost symptom a "diffusion of the time perspective." The symptom becomes manifest in an overwhelming con-cern for things that tell time, accompanied by an inability to act in a temporal situation.[41]

Throughout his narrative, Quentin Compson is desperately trying to find an orientation in time. His first action on waking up is to break his watch, gently cracking open the crystal and prying off the hands so that the watch continues running but can no longer tell time—just like Quen-tin himself. On leaving his Harvard dormitory, his first chore is to visit a watchmaker, ostensibly to inquire about repairing his own watch but in reality to indulge his fascination with the unset watches on display in the shop window, showing a "dozen different hours" yet "each with the same assertive and contradictory assurance that mine had, without any hands at all." The watch Quentin has broken once belonged to his grand-father, implying a tie to his historical tradition. On presenting him the watch, his father had advised him: "I give it to you not that you may remember time, but that you may forget it now and then for a moment and not spend all your breath trying to conquer it." The irony is, of course, that Quentin does spend *all* his breath trying to conquer time when he commits suicide at the day's end.[42]

Quentin's anguish does not derive from a misguided attempt to live by an obsolete code of behavior, as so many critics have contended, but rather from his inability to coalesce the diverse and often antithetical identity fragments he has inherited into a workable whole. Those frag-ments include elements of the Cavalier tradition that he has acquired from his Compson ancestors, especially its assigned role of southern gentleman and its values of honor, courage, and strength. From his al-coholic father, whose loving nature has succumbed to a bitter fatalism at the sight of his family's decay, Quentin has received both his intense intellectuality and idealism and the cynical view that man "is the sum of his misfortunes." "No battle is ever won," Mr. Compson proclaims. "They are not even fought. The field only reveals to man his own folly and despair." Lastly, from his rigid, insecure, hypochondriac mother Quentin has been endowed with a fanatical devotion to purity and peni-tence. The mere fact that fifteen-year-old Caddy has kissed a boy can send Mrs. Compson into a paroxysm of mourning, dressing herself in black and telling everyone that her daughter is dead. "Thank God I dont know about such wickedness," she remarks on another occasion, "I dont even want to know about it." Translated into cultural terms, the still-powerful Cavalier and Victorian traditions, previously segregated in Faulkner's work in the Sartoris and Benbow families, have come together in the Compsons—converging with particular force within Quentin's personality.[43]

Trapped in this situation, Quentin desperately tries to save himself by adopting the tactic of isolation, strenuously partitioning in his mind those elements over which he feels some measure of control from those over which he does not. Two antipodal categories result—one best sym-bolized by the concrete image of the dirty drawers, containing all those forbidden instinctual qualities Quentin associates with sex, femininity, and natural processes in general; and the other, symbolized by his ab-stract concept of virginity, which comes to include rationality, mascu-linity, gentlemanly self-control, purity, and Compson honor. For Quentin, everything depends on his ability to maintain this isolation mechanism. When it breaks down, as it inevitably must, he will find himself helpless in a welter of confusion where

> all stable things had become shadowy paradoxical all I had done shadows all I had felt suffered taking visible from antic and perverse mocking without relevance inherent themselves with the final denial of the significance they should have affirmed thinking I was I was not who was not was not who.

Then only one meaningful identity choice will be left him—that of a suicide. If the principle Quentin employs here looks familiar, it should: it is the Victorian dichotomy carried to its extreme, divorced from its historical context, and thus gone mad.[44]

Such isolation would be difficult to maintain under any circumstances, but it is impossible for Quentin with a sister like Caddy. Caddy suffers from nymphomania; there have been "too many," she says. Not pleasure but "something terrible in me" compels her to pursue sexual gratification, causing her great shame: "sometimes at night I could see it grinning at me I could see it through them grinning at me through their faces." Like Quentin's, the roots of Caddy's compulsion lie in her twisted identification with the Compson past. Out of deserved hatred for her mother, she has deliberately repudiated the identity of a Southern Lady, yet she still feels the moral strictures associated with that identity. The penalty for violating a taboo is death, and, as she confesses to Quentin, "When they touched me I died." Caddy's identification instead runs to her powerful male ancestors, one a governor, the other a Civil War general. She is forever taking charge of situations, giving her brothers orders, and asserting her will. In their childhood fantasies, Quentin recalls, "she was never a queen or a fairy she was always a king or a giant or a general." Her special attraction to military men as sexual partners stems from this identification; only after she has passively surrendered to their power can she feel herself feminine again.[45]

In short, Quentin and Caddy, in their failure to combine their identity fragments into workable wholes, have partially reversed sexual roles. Quentin has fixated on the "honor" aspect of the Compson legacy, while Caddy has based her personality on the assertive part. As a consequence, Quentin is forced to repress his sexuality in order to preserve his masculinity, while Caddy must overindulge her sexual impulses to remain feminine. History has laid a cruel psychological trap for the Compson children, reversing for them what had long been the conventional moral order, as Caddy plainly senses: "theres a curse on us its not our fault is it our fault."[46]

As the tragedy moves toward its almost inevitable conclusion and Caddy becomes pregnant by an unknown suitor, Quentin can think of only one way out. He proposes that they announce to their father that they have committed incest, that the child belongs to Quentin. Incestuous overtones have in fact characterized their relationship all along. Caddy's fall into the creek the day of Damuddy's death, for instance, came as the result of Quentin's slapping her for flaunting her sexuality before another boy. "It was all your fault," she insisted afterward, implying that Quentin had been responsible for "soiling" her. Quentin's strategy, therefore, is designed to expiate his guilt and simultaneously to restore Caddy's purity by turning an *actual* evil into a *pure* and *imaginary* one. That way, he and Caddy would be isolated in their own special hell, "the two of us amid the pointing and the horror beyond the clean flame." Besides, within the confines of his tortured imagination, the incest *is* real for Quentin. "[Y]ou thought it was them," he pleads with Caddy,

> but it was me listen I fooled you all the time it was me you thought
> I was in the house where that damned honeysuckle trying not
> to think the swing the cedars the secret surges the breathing locked
> drinking the wild breath the yes Yes Yes yes

Caddy, of course, cannot afford the luxury of such fantasies. Nonetheless, even before her baby is born and its sex known she names it Quentin.[47]

With Caddy's purity irretrievably lost, Quentin clamps down even harder on his own identity as a virgin, his final gambit in his effort to find an identity that will match the imperatives of Compson honor and Victorian morality with the requirements of concrete experience. His father tries to warn him that this strategy will not work either, but Quentin will not listen. "Purity is a negative state and therefore contrary to nature," Mr. Compson tells him. "It's nature is hurting you not Caddy and I said That's just words and he said So is virginity and I said you dont know." Two months later, on the day of his suicide, Quentin realizes that his father was right, that his isolation tactics are doomed to fail:

> I thought about how I'd thought about I could not be a virgin,
> with so many of them walking along in the shadows and whisper-
> ing with their soft girlvoices lingering in the shadowy places and
> the words coming out and the perfume and eyes you could feel not
> see, but if it was that simple to do it wouldn't be anything and if
> it wasn't anything, what was I

Only death, as he sees it, can keep his purity alive. Only death can provide the viable masculine identity that the terms of existence in 1910 will not permit him. With meticulous care Quentin packs his bags, removes all stains from his clothing, combs his hair, and brushes his teeth in preparation for his fatal plunge into the river. Although he alone will know it, he will die a gentleman—and intact.[48]

If Quentin, in his intellectual paralysis, symbolizes one response to the South's cultural crisis in the early twentieth century, Jason Compson, the materialist New South businessman, represents another. "There are too many Jasons in the South who can be successful," Faulkner once remarked, "just as there are too many Quentins in the South who are too sensitive to face its reality." Instead of trying to sort out the various conflicting elements in his Compson identity, Jason attempts to regain mastery of the situation by rejecting them wholesale through a process Erikson calls "distantiation"—defined as "the readiness to repudiate, to isolate, and, if necessary, to destroy those forces and people whose essence seems dangerous to one's own." With perverse glee Jason sets out to erase every last vestige of his family's existence, "since to him," as Faulkner notes in the appendix, "all the rest of the town and the world and the human race too except himself were Compsons, inexplicable yet quite predictable in that they were in no sense whatever to be trusted." Thus it is Jason who triggers the incident that leads to his brother Benjy's castration by deliberately leaving the gate open when a group of schoolgirls pass by. It is Jason apparently who destroys Caddy's marriage by informing her husband that Caddy's child could have been fathered by anyone. And it is Jason who eventually sells the family's run-down mansion to a man intent on subdividing it into a cheap boardinghouse. "I haven't got much pride, I can't afford it," Jason says. In this way, Jason stands for the South's other alternative—to repudiate its history and traditions totally and forever.[49]

Ostensibly the one "sane" and "practical" Compson of his generation, Jason on close inspection shares all his brother's compulsive neurotic traits, except that they are directed toward money rather than time. "For all the differences between them," Michael Millgate points out, "both brothers display a similar obsessiveness and fundamental irrationality." Although many critics have mistakenly seen Jason as the archetype petty capitalist, maximizing his profit at each turn, that is hardly so. Jason, in Erikson's terms, has no firm control over the basic personal modalities of "holding-on" or "letting-go"; he can neither retain nor "lose" money properly. Instances of his stinginess over paltry sums abound. He maliciously burns two tickets to a carnival rather than giving them free to his black houseboy, Luster. Secretly and illegally he squirrels away the money Caddy has sent for her daughter's support. Yet at the same time Jason thinks nothing of tossing away forty or fifty dollars on his Memphis whore or of embarking on numerous ill-chosen ventures in the stock market. In his own incredible words: "After all, like I say money has no value; it's just the way you spend it. It dont belong to anybody, so why try to hoard it. It just belongs to the man that can get it and keep it." For Jason, money has become isolated from its true value and is either accumulated or squandered solely to gratify his ego. Even in his chosen role as a capitalist, then, he is far from "sane."[50]

Jason's neurosis manifests itself in other ways. He suffers, we discover, from splitting headaches and blind rages; he is at war with all women except his mother and those he can deal with on a strictly cash basis. Above all he lacks a sense of personal autonomy. "I guess I dont need any man's help to get along I can stand on my own feet like I always have," Jason boasts, but the portrait Faulkner draws of him constantly undercuts his claim. Like his Uncle Maury Bascomb, with whom Jason strongly identifies and from whom he derives his trait of keeping his hands in his pockets at all times, Jason's autonomy is a matter of mere posturing. Faulkner vividly demonstrates this in a tableau scene when Jason is still a child:

> Uncle Maury straddling his legs before the fire must remove one hand long enough to drink Christmas. Jason ran on, his hands in his pockets fell down and lay there like a trussed fowl until Versh set him up.

Here is the New South's swaggering pride and essential helplessness, its greed, pretension, and utter dependence, captured by Faulkner in one instant of timeless motion.[51]

This mentality, as Faulkner depicts it, carries within it the seeds of its own destruction, for letting-go, the opposite modality of holding-on, likewise becomes compulsive for Jason. When his niece runs off with the four thousand dollars he has stolen from her, and with three thousand dollars of Jason's own money to boot, Jason appears to get an "actual pleasure out of his outrage and impotence" when the sheriff refuses to help catch her. As Jason pursues her himself, we get the impression of a personality rapidly coming apart, until at the conclusion of his chase in the neighboring town of Mottson, Jason the childless bachelor comes to the dead end of his life, while the people of that village look on: "Some looked at him as they passed, at the man sitting quietly behind the wheel of a small car, with his invisible life ravelled out about him like a worn-out sock." The New South, in sum, is not Uncle Maury straddling across the hearth; it is Jason lying helpless on the floor, his hands in his pockets.[52]

When Jason, Quentin, and Caddy have been pared away, each meeting an inglorious end, what have we left for the white South's future? Faulkner's answer in *The Sound and the Fury* is Benjy, the ultimate example of identity diffusion, the final extension of the isolation and lack of continuity afflicting the other Compson children. Benjy's very physical attributes reflect his inability to coalesce as a person. He is described as a "big man who appeared to have been shaped of some substance whose particles would not or did not cohere to one another or to the frame which supported it." He gropes at the identity of the white southerner, telling us how "my shadow was higher than Luster's on the fence," but his identity never moves beyond that of a shadow and he must finally rely on Luster to organize his life. His mother, Caddy, and Versh all order him to keep his hands in his pockets, implying a Bascomb identification, but Benjy cannot consistently coordinate even that simple action; he can hardly hold a flower. He can grasp neither the Compson nor Bascomb identity fragments his siblings isolate and cling to. The best he can do is sit narcissistically before a mirror, which provides the immediate if temporary answer to his identity question.[53]

Yet it would be wrong to dismiss Benjy as a simple idiot. Bereft of a viable ego, he escapes the neurotic obsessions that distort the lives and perceptions of his brothers. His narrative of the family's downfall, although severely scrambled in time, is also marked, in Millgate's phrase, by a "camera-like fidelity," free of bias or interpretation with only one exception—his tendency to leave himself out. Incapable of selfishness, he achieves an innocence often compared to that of Adam in the Garden, or to a small child, or, as Faulkner himself later put it, to that of an "animal." However one describes it, one must agree with Lawrance Thompson that Benjy's innocence gives him "particular and extraordinary powers of perception," allowing him to cut through the calculations of rationality to sense directly those qualities that are life-sustaining as opposed to those that signify decay and death. In this way, Thompson goes on, Benjy serves as a "moral mirror" for the rest of the family by wailing at the top of his lungs at each step of the family's degradation. Although his role is limited to that of witness rather than participant, he is rightly described by Waggoner as a "kind of modern Christ, impotent to save us but supplying a standard by which we are judged, and, perhaps, may know ourselves lost." Once more the irony lies in Faulkner's inversion of Victorian values, for it is in the animal-like character of Benjy's nature, in his pure instinctual response to events, that the source of his Christ-like innocence may be found.[54]

Moreover, in his capacity as "moral mirror," Benjy insists on preserving a continuity with the past. Every Sunday he is driven out to the cemetery to visit the family gravesite, all the while keeping his head locked firmly to the right to avoid the Civil War memorial in the main square of Jefferson, which the carriage always passes on the right. But in the very last scene of the book, Luster makes the mistake of passing the monument on the left, "where the Confederate soldier gazed with empty eyes beneath his marble hand into wind and weather." Here is the heroic past looking down on him, judging him. Benjamin, the "last of my sons," can only bellow in shame: "There was more than astonishment in it, it was horror; shock, agony eyeless, tongueless; just sound." All the terror and shame lying just below the surface of the southern consciousness is embedded in Benjy's cry. When its complexities have been unraveled, *The Sound and the Fury* is that very bellow placed between the cloth-covered bindings of a book.[55]

I V
_____

Faulkner's novels of the late 1920s touched on all major aspects of contemporary southern life save one. Race, as an issue, occupied a distinctly peripheral place among Faulkner's concerns. Blacks appeared in his work primarily as stock comic figures such as Simon, the Sartoris's house servant in *Flags in the Dust*, or as a kind of moral and religious counterpoint to whites, the role played by Dilsey in *The Sound and the Fury*. At times, especially at the close of *Soldier's Pay*, Faulkner seemed to envy blacks their simple fervent Christianity, magnificent in its primitive power and lack of doubt, but he rarely explored their racial problems.[56]

By the start of the depression, however, the relationship between the races in the South had turned far too problematic for Faulkner, with his great sensitivity, to ignore. In addition to the more formal challenges mounted by organizations like the NAACP and the Interracial Commission, the caste system was slowly being undermined by certain spontaneous changes taking place almost unnoticed at the local level. Younger blacks, in particular, restless with the prescribed codes of behavior, were beginning to see through the white mask and assert themselves. The depression added further momentum to these stirrings by uprooting hundreds of thousands of poor farm folk, converting them into an army of migrants tramping the roads in desperate search of jobs. Towns that had been relatively stable suddenly experienced a sizable influx of strangers whose origins were wholly unknown. Where once it had been highly unlikely for a resident to have "black blood" without the town knowing of it, the system of community genealogy was now doomed. As one character in *Light in August* remarks of Joe Christmas, "These country bastards are liable to be anything."[57]

Written between August, 1931, and March, 1932, *Light in August* examines these new developments through Faulkner's favorite strategy of reversing a popular literary convention. The "tragic mulatto"—a creature torn between the dictates of his civilized "white blood" and savage "black blood," whose black blood invariably wins in the end—was a stereotyped character transparently freighted with racist belief, a character whose mixed biological origins unmistakably sealed his destiny. Joe Christmas, by contrast, thinks and acts as if he were a "tragic mulatto," but ironically he is not, or at least the supposition of his "black blood" rests on the flimsiest of evidence. Rather, he has been conditioned by white southern society to accept the negative identity of the Negro with all it implies. In him we see, magnified for greater visibility, nothing less than the cultural apparatus the South has used to distort and destroy the personalities of its black inhabitants. For this reason, as Robert Penn Warren observes, the moral and critical dimensions of this novel are enormous: "Faulkner here undercuts the official history and mythology of a whole society by indicating that the 'nigger' is a creation of the white man." In this connection it should be added that Faulkner was not trying to probe the Negro consciousness, as Odum had done in the Black Ulysses trilogy, but rather to look inside himself for the roots of that pernicious identity that whites had projected onto blacks and that had come in part to determine black behavior. As such, *Light in August* represented an exploration at a deeper level of consciousness than any Faulkner had previously essayed.[58]

To be precise, not one but two pathological and conflicting identities destroy Joe Christmas. The first, the traditional black identity originating in slavery, operates through oral sensuality to render him submissive to the will of others, while the second, that of white southern Calvinism, is based on a denial of all sensual gratification to achieve the virtues of self-sufficiency and control. In theory, these two identities were supposed to remain separate, with the black identity serving as a negative projection of the white man's forbidden desires, telling him what he must not become, and at the same time helping to cement the Negro in his inferior status. But for Joe Christmas, both identities have become equally compelling. In keeping with the "tragic mulatto" syndrome, his mind has turned into a battlefield over which the two identities fight for dominance while he, so to speak, stands by helplessly watching. Repeatedly his black self seeks oral-erotic gratification in food and sex. Just as often his white self, powered by a fierce castration anxiety, forces him to dam up his impulses. The effect of this whipsaw action is to pervert his psyche, transforming him into a being whom black and white people alike regard as Satanic. In the end, no simple moral assessment of him is possible; he is, as Robert D. Jacobs writes, "both heroic and pathetic"—"heroic in his struggle to define himself as a human being existing in his own right, outside the categories and stereotypes of Southern Protestantism and racism; but . . . pathetic as a victim of soul-warping forces beyond his control."[59]

The "soul-warping" begins during Joe's early childhood, spent in a white orphanage where he has been placed by his fanatic racist grandfather. Somehow Doc Hines has concluded that Joe's father, an itinerant Mexican circus worker, was actually part black. Convinced he is God's chosen instrument to combat earthly evil, Hines has murdered the father, permitted his daughter to die giving birth, and secured a job as boilerman at the orphanage in order to prompt the other children to start calling Joe "Nigger." Joe, troubled by the name-calling and deprived of maternal care, attaches himself to the orphanage dietician, the first of several women in his life with one thing in common—they dispense food in an impersonal manner. Hiding in her closet to taste her toothpaste, he accidentally witnesses her having an affair with a staff doctor. Excited by what he sees, he squeezes far too much toothpaste into his mouth, vomits, and is discovered. The trauma is compounded when the dietician, in her fury and embarrassment, picks up the refrain Doc Hines has initiated among the children, pronouncing Joe a "little nigger bastard." This terrifying incident, combined with other experiences at the orphanage, implants in him a permanent oral fixation, associated with an identification as a Negro. By age five, in short, the irrational interconnections between race, sex, religion, and identity that will dominate his life have already become established in Joe's mind.[60]

His white Calvinist identity arises when the orphanage director, suspicious of Joe's origins, arranges to have him adopted by an orthodox Presbyterian farm family named McEachern. It is McEachern, the stern rural Fundamentalist, who metes out punishment whether it is deserved or not until he and Joe come to share a "very kinship of stubbornness like a transmitted resemblance" in their respective characters. Joe comes to value McEachern's credo for its harsh masculinity, even taking a certain stoic pleasure in the punishments he receives. At the same time McEachern's strict paternal injunctions, which in Oedipal fashion carry for him a veiled threat of castration, force him to suppress, or at least conceal, his ever-powerful oral-erotic impulses. Thus he steadfastly rejects Mrs. McEachern's maternal overtures, going so far on one occasion as to dump a tray of food she has brought him onto the floor. When he is alone later that evening, though, he slips out of bed "and above the outraged food kneeling, with his hands ate, like a savage, like a dog." In the presence of the McEacherns he is a white man with his impulses held in check; in private, in the dark, he is a black man giving himself over to uninhibited gratification.[61]

As one might predict, these tensions begin to dominate his sexual life as soon as he reaches adolescence. On learning about the anatomy of women at age fifteen, he attempts to conquer his castration fears by shooting a sheep and exploring its genitals. He arrives at a sort of truce with himself: "It was as if he said, logical and desperately calm *All right. It is so, then. But not to me. Not in my life and my love.*" But such a truce, contrived by logic, cannot last. When some friends a short time later invite him to join them in meeting a young black girl at a deserted sawmill, Joe panics and begins fighting with the other boys until they finally subdue him. "None of them knew why he had fought," Faulkner notes, "And he could not have told them." Finally, Joe establishes a liaison with a "safe" woman, a combination waitress-prostitute at a cheap diner whose very name, Bobbie Allen, suggests her lack of true femininity. Not only does she exchange food and sex for cash, most important of all she is flat-chested, the very opposite of Joe's image of a "womanshenegro." "It was because of her smallness that he ever attempted her," Faulkner tells us. Although in time they develop a relationship as satisfying as any he would achieve, like all such relationships for Joe Christmas this solution to his problems is only temporary. The momentary balance between his inner conflicting compulsions ends the night McEachern finds them at a dancehall and Joe beats his stepfather unconscious with a chair. "I have done it! I have done it!" he shouts euphorically in the belief that he has killed his father at last, though whether or not he has is left unclear.[62]

The "killing" of McEachern proves another turning point for Christmas—it resolves his identity conflict temporarily in favor of his black identity and sets him "on the street which was to run for fifteen years" through cities North and South. During this interval he does everything in his power to make himself black, living in black ghettos, sleeping with black women, and asserting his sense of identity through violence: "Sometimes he would remember how he had once tricked or teased white men into calling him a Negro in order to fight them, to beat them or be beaten; now he fought the Negro who called him white." In one instance he attempts to incorporate his chosen identity in a strikingly oral way, sleeping next to a "woman who resembled an ebony carving" and trying "to breathe into himself the dark odor, the dark and inscrutable thinking and being of Negroes." But again his efforts fail, primarily because to all appearances he looks like a white man. His dilemma is inescapable: in the North he can act like a Negro, gratifying his impulses, but people will not accept his black identity; in the South, people will call him "nigger" when he insists, but they will prohibit his impulses. Only Joanna Burden, a northerner living in the South, can bridge the contradiction. Descended from an old abolitionist family, a spinster living in isolation from the town of Jefferson, she will treat him like a Negro and provide him with a sexual outlet as well.[63]

Almost consciously Joanna plays upon the oral-erotic component of Joe's personality. She keeps the front door of her house locked, forcing him to enter through the kitchen where she nightly leaves out food, as he comes to realize, "*Set out for the nigger. For the nigger.*" She then waits for him to climb the stairs to her bedroom "like a thief, a robber," as if "to despoil her virginity each time anew." She is gripped by a "sensuality discovered too late and pursued too far," in Millgate's words, rendering her sexual life as perverted in its own way as that of Christmas himself. Her still-vigorous conscience, born of a New England Calvinist ortho- doxy, requires her to maintain the fiction of being the passive victim of an unsought "rape," lest she participate in the sin. The belief that her assailant is black makes the debauchery all the more delectable for her.[64]

This stormy relationship between Joe Christmas and Joanna Burden, depending on a delicate balancing of their respective pathological needs and requiring constant readjustment, ends when Joanna passes menopause. Suddenly her religiosity returns to the surface, with fevered talk of prayer, salvation, and plans to have Joe attend a black college in order to take over her missionary work in Jefferson. Her revived Calvinism instantly renews Joe's castration fears. The extraordinary climax, tying together a myriad of symbolic threads Faulkner has woven through the novel, comes when Joanna asks Joe to kneel and pray with her, which brings back memories of McEachern, kneeling over the dead sheep, and all the other moments of trauma in his life. When he refuses, she attempts to kill both of them with an archaic cap-and-ball revolver that misfires; he in turn decapitates her with a razor in symbolic castration. As Faulkner's imagery ironically suggests, the fact that her pistol failed to fire scares him more than the actual threat of death.[65]

The murder of Joanna Burden, then, is fraught with the most complex psychological entanglements Faulkner's ample imagination could conjure up. Christmas's precise motives are beyond rational comprehension. Thus the ultimate ironic twist of the screw is the community's simplistic, stereotyped reaction to the event. The crowd that gathered to view the body, Faulkner writes with obvious sarcasm, "believed aloud that it was an anonymous negro crime committed not by a negro but by Negro . . . and hoped that she had been ravished too: at least once before her throat was cut and at least once afterward." Those who refused to associate with her during her life cry the loudest for vengeance. All the while, their picture of the Negro rapist hell-bent on violence is juxtaposed with the actual thoughts of Joe Christmas as he contemplates his eventual decision to surrender: *"Yes I would say Here I am I am tired I am tired of running of having to carry my life like it was a basket of eggs."* Even after he peacefully surrenders, the community cannot revise its stereotype. As one bystander remarks: "He dont look any more like a nigger than I do. But it must have been the nigger blood in him. It looked like he had set out to get himself caught like a man might set out to get married." Another tellingly refers to him as "that white nigger."[66]

Up to this juncture everything in *Light in August* points the accusatory finger at the community, and specifically its Fundamentalist Protestantism, as the root cause of Christmas's tragedy. All the major figures in his life—Hines, McEachern, Joanna Burden, up to the protofascist mob leader Percy Grimm—employ him as a scapegoat on which to pile their own intense feeling of sin, their secret repressed longings for sex and violence. The result is what Hyatt Waggoner has called a "terrible indictment of Southern Christianity." In the book, this judgment is summed up by the Reverend Gail Hightower, the defrocked minister living in isolation from the community who, as he becomes involved with Joe Christmas, hears echoes of the congregation singing hymns in his former church:

> Listening, he seems to hear within it the apotheosis of his own
> history, his own land, his own environed blood: that people from
> which he sprang and among whom he lives who can never take
> either pleasure or catastrophe or escape from either, without
> brawling over it. Pleasure, ecstasy, they cannot seem to bear: their
> escape from it is in violence, in drinking and fighting and pray-
> ing; catastrophe too, the violence identical and apparently in-
> escapable. *And so why should not their religion drive them
> to crucifixion of themselves and one another?*

Hightower, in his strange disembodied existence, represents the moral vision of southern Calvinism that, Faulkner seems to be saying, has become detached from normal religious practices for whites. Hightower's reflections on white Protestantism stand in clear and condemnatory contrast to Faulkner's descriptions of black religion in his previous books.[67]

Yet the force of this critique of his own society must have proved overwhelming for Faulkner in 1932, for at the end of the novel he abruptly retrenches to a position far less explicit. Almost as if he has emerged from the trance that made the writing of *Light in August* possible, he introduces in deus ex machina fashion a new character, the lawyer Gavin Stevens, to speculate at length on how Christmas's "black blood" had finally become the master of his soul. In subsequent interviews Faulkner would always disclaim Stevens as a spokesman, which may well be the case, but the effect of the monologue nonetheless is to muddle considerably the moral thrust of the novel just as it peaks, allowing Faulkner to hedge his bets. This wariness, moreover, also appears in Faulkner's horrific account of the castration of Christmas's dying body at the hands of Percy Grimm:

> from out the slashed garments about his hips and loins the pent black blood seemed to rush like a released breath. It seemed to rush out of his pale body like the rush of sparks from a rising rocket; upon that black blast the man seemed to rise soaring into their memories forever.

"Black blood" can be interpreted here two ways—literally, as the traditional racist stereotype would have it, or as a symbol for the unconscious evil identity Christmas carries all his life and from which Grimm's act at last liberates him. Given the language of crucifixion and resurrection, confirming the image of Christmas as a modern black Christ that counterpoints his growing pathology all through the book, one would assume Faulkner intended the symbolic meaning. It is a striking mark of his unyielding ambivalence that one cannot be sure.[68]

V

Although General Jason Lycurgus Compson II, Quentin Compson's revered grandfather, was Thomas Sutpen's only friend in Jefferson, Sutpen's name is not mentioned in *The Sound and the Fury*. Nor, despite the fact that Sutpen served as John Sartoris's second in command at the start of the Civil War and in time replaced him as head of the regiment, does Sutpen appear even for the briefest moment in *Flags in the Dust*. For until the early 1930s Sutpen still lurked deep in Faulkner's consciousness, a "dark inheritance from the Southern past," in Millgate's phrase, too threatening to bring to the surface. Yet the importance of Sutpen to Faulkner's quest was too overwhelming for him to stay submerged indefinitely. When Quentin in *Absalom, Absalom!* is beleaguered by his Harvard friends to tell about the South, he responds, as John Hunt notices, not with the saga of his own family or the Sartorises, but with that of Sutpen. "In some way," Hunt writes, "Sutpen's story holds for him the key to the whole Southern experience. If he could explain Sutpen, if he could account for the fact that a Sutpen could exist . . . he could also explain the South." The point holds for both Quentin and Faulkner himself.[69]

Certainly Faulkner always knew Sutpen was there: the problem was how to articulate him safely. One finds much of the basic plot of *Absalom, Absalom!* spelled out, for example, in the short story "Evangeline," drafted in 1926 and heavily revised in 1931. "Evangeline," though, focuses primarily on the Sutpen children, especially Henry's murder of his half-brother Charles Bon, with the Colonel himself relegated to the shadows as a "florid, portly man, a little swaggering, who liked to ride fast to church of a Sunday." Not until the winter of 1934, when he finally hit upon a device for holding its emotional impact at bay, was Faulkner able to expand this material to novel length and extract its full meaning. His masterstroke, arrived at by much trial and error, was to employ four separate narrators, each of whom would rehearse the key events in Sutpen's life with a different slant of interpretation. The reader would thus be forced to surmount an elaborate set of narrative hurdles, dodging false leads, piecing together scattered bits of information, evaluating each attempt at speculation in light of all the others—ending up with a reconstruction of history that is probably true, but that can never be made certain. Nor could Faulkner's own views ever be pinned down with precision. That this purposeful ambiguity greatly enhanced the book's aesthetic value should not obscure its imperative psychological function for Faulkner. Only under those conditions could he cope with the subversive implications of Sutpen's story.[70]

For Sutpen represents the total negation of the mythical Cavalier. He is the planter as nouveau riche, the southern aristocrat as self-made man, whose every action hinges on his self-centered, calculating ambition. Far from having stable roots in his community, Sutpen rides into Jefferson "out of no discernible past" and acquires his vast tract of barren swampland "no one knew how." Indeed, even his tombstone four decades later "did not divulge where and when he had been born." As the people of the quiet country village watch in fascination and outrage, this mysterious stranger with his twenty wild slaves and imported French architect proceed to "overrun suddenly the hundred square miles of tranquil and astonished earth and drag house and formal gardens violently out of the soundless Nothing." Their amazement heightens as wagonloads of crystal chandeliers, mahogany carvings, and antique furnishings pull up to complete the mansion, which its proprietor has modestly named "Sutpen's Hundred as if it had been a king's grant in unbroken perpetuity from his great grandfather." Most onlookers, like the frustrated spinster Rosa Coldfield whose older sister Ellen was to marry Sutpen, assume their new neighbor to be the offshoot of a fallen Tidewater family trying to recoup his fortunes in North Mississippi, "a man that anyone could look at and see that, even if he apparently had none now [i.e., at the time of his arrival], he was accustomed to having money and intended to have it again." Thus, as F. Garvin Davenport, Jr., observes, in *Absalom, Absalom!* "the Cavalier myth contributes to and encourages the very exploitation and crass worship of material goods which . . . Southern traditionalists claim that it opposes." In 1936, the year the book was published, this was still a highly charged insight for a southern writer to put forth.[71]

Here, however, Faulkner added an ironic twist that made his attack on the myth more devastating, for as the tale unfolds it becomes clear that the source of Sutpen's raw and ruthless materialism lies not in his greed, but in his innocence. It is the innocence of the southern frontier, stamped on him indelibly by his childhood in the West Virginia mountains where conditions were primitive and men untamed, but where no trace of class stratification had yet set in. Growing up in this backwoods Eden, he had come to believe the possession of wealth a matter of mere chance: ". . . it had never occurred to him that any man should take any such blind accident as that as authority or warrant to look down at others, any others." Nor, in this mountain fastness, was conventional morality to be seen. Eye gouging, heavy drinking, and other acts that the Victorians would consider sure indications of savagery seemed to young Sutpen the normal course of life.[72]

All this changed with fateful rapidity when the family drifted back to the Tidewater, where Sutpen's father found employment as a plantation overseer. There at age thirteen Sutpen came in contact with a different kind of society, a land "all divided and fixed and neat with a people living on it all divided and fixed and neat because of what color their skins happened to be and what they happened to own." At first blithely unaware of these class distinctions, he was to learn their meaning with traumatic impact the day his father sent him to the mansion on an errand, only to have a haughty black house servant turn him away from the front door. Totally unexpected, the incident triggered shock waves in his mind, shock waves not of anger but of shame, that all-encompassing emotion in which a person senses his identity shattered and his whole being exposed to the world without warning. So it was with Sutpen—all he had experienced was now cast in a new light, everything he had counted on as certain seemed in flux. His family appeared to him "as the owner, the rich man . . . must have been seeing them all the time—as cattle, creatures heavy and without grace . . . who would in turn spawn with brutish and vicious prolixity." The situation, he decided, was intolerable, yet he refused to blame either the planter or Tidewater society for it. He believed the problem lay in his own innocence, "that innocence he had just discovered he had, which (the innocence, not the man, the tradition) he would have to compete with." To live with himself and face his posterity, he would have to shed that innocence by the only means he knew how—by becoming a planter, too.[73]

In depicting Sutpen as principally a victim of naiveté, Faulkner was touching the most sensitive southern nerve of all. The story suggests that the Cavalier identity as associated with the men who dominated the region just prior to the Civil War was born in response to a painful consciousness of backwoods crudeness and isolation, that the pose of aristocratic sophistication was created to cover up an essential provinciality. As Sutpen confided to General Compson, "I was that green, that countrified, you see." To Faulkner, even the South's evil partook of this quality. "There is still a kind of clumsy heartiness to our corruption," he once wrote a friend, comparing gangsters North and South, "a kind of chaotic and exasperating innocence." If a curse did lie on the South, then, one could trace its origin not to slavery or racial segregation—important though these were—but to this trait of stubborn, pervasive, disabling innocence that arose through the frontier character of southern society and caused southerners to adopt identities hopelessly inauthentic, based on mythology rather than actual historical roots. Here, in short, was the wellspring of that paralyzing identity diffusion Faulkner had found so widespread in twentieth-century southern life.[74]

The effects of this fatal flaw in Sutpen—and, by symbolic extension, the South—become apparent in Faulkner's portrait of Sutpen's children. Many critics, like Ilse D. Lind, have correctly reported those children "drawn with a curious flatness; their gestures . . . formalized, almost choreographic," but that was exactly what Faulkner intended. The three, Judith, Henry, and Charles Bon, are meant to be symbols, not human beings in their own right, for they are in fact the constructs Sutpen has fashioned to fill his cultural vacuum. As Henry is said to have told Bon, *"the three of us are just illusions that he begot, and your illusions are a part of you like your bones and flesh and memory."* Thus we will not be remiss in interpreting them symbolically: on one level, as the three chief components of Sutpen's self-made personality; and on another, almost allegorical level, as representations of the three main forms of social order in the South, the frontier, the town, and the Tidewater, each of which Faulkner judges and finds wanting.[75]

Of the two children Sutpen has fathered by Ellen Coldfield, Judith most nearly embodies his true self, his frontier heritage. "Judith was the Sutpen," Quentin's father remarks, "with the ruthless code of taking what it wanted provided it were strong enough." Energetic and unquestionably brave, she is the "hoyden who could—and did—outrun and outclimb, and ride and fight both with and beside her brother." It is Judith who, hidden in a loft, thoroughly enjoys the spectacle of her father wrestling naked with his slaves, no holds barred, while Henry, forced by his father to watch, takes sick and vomits. Yet for all her backwoods energy, Judith is also portrayed as a creature oddly devoid of substance, a kind of reflecting mirror her brothers use to perfect their own personalities—a "blank shape, the empty vessel in which each of them strove to preserve, not the illusion of himself nor his illusion of the other but what each conceived the other to believe him to be." Like her father, she is a medium in which cultural illusions can grow and thrive.[76]

Henry, on the other hand, "was the Coldfield with the Coldfield cluttering of morality and rules of right and wrong." Embedded in him are the virtues and faults of the nineteenth-century southern small town. In this respect he symbolizes the stability and Victorian-style probity Sutpen had sought to incorporate into his being by marrying Ellen Coldfield, the daughter of a Methodist steward "with a name for absolute and undeviating and even Puritan uprightness in a country and time of lawless opportunity." But this identity also carries its limitations, for Henry is described repeatedly as the "provincial, the clown almost" in his utter lack of knowledge of the wider world, as the "grim humorless yokel out of a granite heritage." It is this provinciality in turn that draws him to Charles Bon, the urbane law student from New Orleans he meets at the University of Mississippi and who, unknown to Henry, is also his half-brother.[77]

Bon, the child Sutpen refuses to acknowledge, ironically personifies the elusive aristocratic ideal Sutpen grasps for all his adult life. The son of Sutpen's first marriage to the daughter of a wealthy sugar planter on Haiti, that "halfway point between what we call the jungle and what we call civilization" where Sutpen had initially gone to make his fortune, Bon and his mother had been repudiated when Sutpen learned that his wife's ancestry included a trace of Negro "blood." Mother and child subsequently moved to New Orleans, the city that always stands for southern urbanity in the Faulknerian cosmography, just as Memphis is the constant symbol of sin. In this environment, where Latin and Anglo-Saxon cultures freely mix, Bon grows up a cosmopolitan, a "young man of a worldly elegance and assurance beyond his years." But even more than Judith he seems to lack substance. Again and again he is referred to as a "myth, a phantom . . . some effluvium of Sutpen blood and character, as though as a man he did not exist at all." He is a person "who in the remote Mississippi of that time must have appeared almost phoenix-like, fullsprung from no childhood, born of no woman and impervious to time and, vanished, leaving no bones or dust anywhere." To Henry, the small-town provincial, Bon resembles a "hero out of some adolescent Arabian Nights," an identity model possessing all the characteristics required by a prosperous planter's son that he feels missing in himself. The two become fast friends, with Henry, to his father's horror, inviting Bon home one Christmas as a likely suitor for his sister. The past, Sutpen discovers, has its own way of exacting revenge.[78]

Having assigned symbolic meaning to the Sutpen children, Faulkner proceeds to set them in a triangle of incest. In addition to the hetero-sexual incest that arises when Bon and Judith fall in love, there are unequivocal indications of platonic incest between Judith and Henry as well as homosexual incest between Henry and Bon. As the various nar-rators detail the ramifications of these relationships in their speculations, the complications become mind-boggling:

> In fact, perhaps, this is the pure and perfect incest: the brother real-izing that the sister's virginity must be destroyed in order to have existed at all, taking that virginity in the person of the brother-in-law, the man whom he would be if he could become, metamor-phose into, the lover, the husband; by whom he would be despoiled, choose for the despoiler, if he could become, metamorphose into the sister, the mistress, the bride. Perhaps that is what went on, not in Henry's mind but in his soul.

In short, the incest signifies how each of Sutpen's children must look to the others for qualities necessary to complete his being. In this way Henry and Judith both covet the elegance of Bon: ". . . it would be hard to say to which of them he appeared the more splendid—to the one with hope, even though unconscious, of making the image hers through pos-session: to the other with the knowledge of the unsurmountable barrier which the similarity of gender hopelessly intervened." Bon, for his part, envies Henry and Judith the "life, the existence, which they represented. Because who knows what picture of peace he might have seen in that monotonous provincial backwater." He also, of course, envied their as-sured paternity and inheritance. Except for Judith in her later years, after she has lost her brothers, the three remain totally dependent on their "curious relationship" with one another to achieve any kind of personal fulfillment.[79]

On the level of individual personality, therefore, the existence of this incest triangle suggests that the three principal modes of antebellum southern culture—backwoods vitality, small-town probity, and Cavalier identity—were incapable of coalescing into a meaningful identity. In

Sutpen himself, we find an attempt to overcome this difficulty by forcing a synthesis, fusing these identity elements into an uneasy union, resulting in a series of ruthless actions and empty, extravagant gestures that succeed solely in deceiving his own self-absorbed, incestuous mind. In his children we see the same drama, the same inability to achieve wholeness, acted out with three separate characters and likewise ending in incest. Used in this fashion, the incest metaphor undercuts nineteenth-century southern mythology at the deepest possible level. It stands, for instance, in ironic contrast to the interpretation of the Sutpen tragedy offered by Quentin's father, who repeats the traditional claim that antebellum southerners, for all their failings, at least possessed a measure of heroic integrity by comparison with the present generation:

> victims too as we are, but victims of a different circumstance, simpler and therefore, integer for integer, more heroic . . . not dwarfed and involved but distinct, uncomplex who had the gift of loving once or dying once instead of being diffused and scattered creatures drawn blindly limb from limb from a grab bag and assembled.

The plight of Sutpen's children, with their incestuous interdependence, indeed the entire thrust of *Absalom, Absalom!*, is meant to belie this commentary.[80]

On the level of social allegory, the incest triangle appears to indicate Faulkner's belief that the predominant social institutions of the Old South failed to reach maturity, producing a society lacking in cohesion. Such a critique is implicit in the way Bon, symbolizing the Tidewater, needs the small-town roots and family heritage he finds in Jefferson to make his mythical personality real; in how Henry must seek the romance of the aristocratic ideal to offset his provincial rigidity and boredom; in how Judith requires a minimum of Coldfield morality to discipline her more animalistic impulses. Neither Tidewater, small town, or frontier has, in this allegory, developed the values and inner coherence necessary to exist by itself as a viable form of social organization. In this sense, the portrait of antebellum life revealed in *Absalom, Absalom!* stands very close to the contemporary observations of Frederick Law Olmsted and constitutes a refutation, almost a parody, of the familiar conception of the South as a stable, well-structured organic society. The metaphor of incest, that most antisocial form of conjugation, seems to mock the pretension of organic interdependence. At the same time, Faulkner equally rejects the opposing notion of the Old South as a society of pure frontier atomism—as stated by Cash, an "aggregation of self-contained and self-sufficient monads each of whom was ultimately and completely responsible for himself." In *Absalom, Absalom!*, the members of the incest triangle may all feign self-sufficiency, but they are not in any manner self-contained. Thus, in his most penetrating vision of southern society, Faulkner cuts through the region's two most flattering mythological perceptions of itself—as both organic and self-sufficient—at once.[81]

In arriving at these insights, Faulkner relies not only on his understanding of modern psychology and social thought but also on a distinctly Modernist view of history. Here a comparison with Ellen Glasgow may be helpful. Wavering between her ingrained Calvinist determinism and her belief in the prevalence of blind chance in the universe, Glasgow could detect little or no meaning in the sequence of human events and was forced to take refuge in an ice-cold stoicism. As the narrators in *Absalom, Absalom!* try to decipher the significance of Sutpen's downfall, two arrive at positions similar to Glasgow's. Quentin's father for one, a confirmed stoic, thinks he sees the malevolent hand of "Fate, destiny, retribution, irony—the stage manager, call him what you will," striking the set on Sutpen purely for sport. One is reminded of Mr. Compson's equally cynical speculations in *The Sound and the Fury*, which at times seem so close to Faulkner's own viewpoint, or the allusions to the "Player and the game He plays" strewn through *Flags in the Dust*. Stoicism held its temptations for Faulkner, too. In addition, there is Rosa Coldfield, speaking for the Calvinist tradition in which Faulkner had been raised, believing the South a "land primed for fatality and already cursed with it." Although she admits she does not know the source of this curse or comprehend its machinations, Miss Rosa is convinced Sutpen is both its victim and agent.[82]

Against these positions Faulkner sets the interpretation of Quentin and Shreve. As they begin their reconstruction of the tale, it quickly becomes apparent that, whatever the explanation may be, it is to be sought not in the heavens but in the normal transactions of human life. Sutpen himself puts in motion the series of events that will spell his doom by repudiating Bon and his mother. In telling Henry of Bon's racial ancestry, the act that leads to Henry's murder of his half-brother, Sutpen is virtually springing his own trap. To be sure, what had brought Bon to the university at a time when he was sure to encounter Henry Sutpen is never made clear—it may have been part of a scheme hatched by Bon's aggrieved mother, or by his legal guardian, or an effort by Bon himself to regain contact with his father and possibly to reclaim his patrimony. What is certain is that human action, not the powers that be, allow the past to exact its due from Sutpen. As Ilse Lind sums up: "Arbitrary rejection from those most binding of all ties, familial and marital love, breeds psychic outrage, and psychic outrage breeds personal revolt. The human psyche has its own mechanics of vengeance."[83]

In short, for the idea of a barren universe devoid of moral sanctions, which drove Ellen Glasgow to despair, Faulkner has substituted human history, to him the locus of moral meaning—in fact, the extent of his entire cosmos. The Great Player might strut and fret in some outer galaxy, but by the time of *Absalom, Absalom!*, history for Faulkner was the only stage that mattered. By contrast to the Victorians, his gaze was not outward and broad-ranging, but inward and intense. Moral significance was to be found in consciousness, not in some abstract code based on natural or supernatural law. Consciousness in turn depended on memory, which encompassed not only a man's personal history, but his society's history as well. Thus, writes Jean Pouillon, in Faulkner's work the "past is not so much what determines the present and future as it is the sole reality. Being the past, it is untouchable, and that is why it is also destiny." Any event in time, such as Sutpen's rejection of his first wife, will reverberate through the consciousness of generations until its full moral implications have been worked out, just as Sutpen's act reverberates for Quentin. Faulkner had explored these questions in his previous novels, but not until *Absalom, Absalom!* did he break through to his final conception of history's meaning. It supplied, one suspects, the moral center he needed to make sense of his inner world, allowing him to reach in this novel the pinnacle of his vision into southern life, the furthest point he would attain in his quest to resolve the enigmas of his region.[84]

V I

Faulkner's probe into the depths of southern consciousness was accomplished at enormous personal cost and did not continue much beyond *Absalom, Absalom!*. Indeed, the book he wrote simultaneously with his masterpiece tells a great deal about the tensions that were always present in his mind. Perhaps he was right in claiming that financial necessity forced him to churn out the Civil War stories he sent the *Saturday Evening Post* in mid-1934 and published with only minor revision three years later as *The Unvanquished*. Perhaps he really did regard this material as "trash," a "pulp series," and "third-rate Kipling," as he repeatedly called it. But one cannot escape the impression that his disclaimers were a little too vehement. Moreover, the timing of *The Unvanquished* is too suggestive to be ignored—Faulkner's return to the Sartoris clan came just as he was halfway through his novel on Sutpen, and in the same month Stark Young's *So Red the Rose* appeared, with its reverent treatment of antebellum Mississippi. Like Odum, it would seem, Faulkner felt compelled to pay homage to the Old South even as he was assaulting it. Any attempt to puncture the myth had to be carefully balanced by a concurrent gesture of expiation.[85]

As the book's few admirers point out, *The Unvanquished* does portray Colonel John Sartoris with a degree of moral ambiguity. The romantic figure he cuts in the early chapters, deftly evading Yankee patrols, is undermined in the latter part of the book by his habitual, excessive resort to violence. The bloodshed he has participated in through the war and Reconstruction begins to corrupt him, a fact even he comes to realize in the end as he provokes a needless fight with his former business partner. "He was wrong," his son Bayard reflects afterward, "he knew he was when it was too late for him to stop just as a drunkard reaches a point where it is too late to stop." The colonel has succumbed to the professional hazard of being a Cavalier in wartime. Yet, unlike a drunkard, he *does* restore his gentlemanly self-control before it is too late. Before going to meet his enraged opponent unarmed, he takes care to forewarn Bayard of the dangers of addiction to violence. The moral ambiguity may be there, but the myth stays substantially intact.[86]

The real problem in *The Unvanquished*, though, is Faulkner's handling of young Bayard. As an adolescent coming of age in a wartorn community, he has not escaped his share of searing experiences. He has seen his grandmother killed by a band of desperadoes, then witnessed the capture and mutilation of the gang's leader by members of his family and their friends. Yet, somehow he has managed to float above the surface of history, emerging as an apostle of nonviolence. When the pressure mounts on him to revenge his father's death, he chooses to face the killer unarmed and orders him to leave town, a strategy that succeeds presumably because the villainous Redmond cannot bring himself to shoot a child (why he does not simply ignore Bayard is not explained). Having upheld the family's honor, Bayard at the conclusion of the book goes off to law school, following his father's instructions to help bring order to the society peacefully. The choices Bayard faces are thus relatively simple ones. Gone are the impossible moral complexities that hamstring adolescent characters such as Quentin Compson or Henry Sutpen in Faulkner's more tragic fiction. In Bayard's case, the myth has not only been restored intact, it has been modernized and sanitized.[87]

The tenor of *The Unvanquished* unfortunately anticipates much of Faulkner's writing following *Absalom, Absalom!*. In Chick Mallison, who saves the innocent Lucas Beauchamp from a lynch mob in *Intruder in the Dust*, or Linda Snopes in *The Mansion*, one finds young southerners like Bayard capable of sensitive but decisive action in the most complicated situations. "Young folks and women, they ain't cluttered. They can listen," Lucas Beauchamp claims, giving voice to Faulkner's new philosophy. As many have observed, these post-World War II novels are filled with explicit political statements of the kind Faulkner had avoided in the past, yet, in a manner again reminiscent of Odum, they are curiously apolitical. "It is really strange," notes Warren, "that in his vast panorama of society in a state where politics is the blood, bone, sinew, and passion of life, and the most popular sport, Faulkner has almost entirely omitted, not only a treatment of the subject, but references to it." Even Faulkner's style in these later works reflects his turn away from the depths of consciousness to surface matters—a "regression to lucidity," R. W. B. Lewis has called it. It was as if Faulkner had fulfilled his quest in *Absalom, Absalom!* and so had little more of burning importance to say.[88]

The Unvanquished and the novels that followed it, then, show how compelling nineteenth-century southern mythology continued to be for Faulkner. No matter how thoroughly the discoveries made on his journey of exploration may have discredited it, no matter how severely it may have clashed with historical actuality as exemplified in his great-grandfather, the Sartoris ideal was too comforting for him ever to let go. Indeed, both visions of the southern past, Modernist and traditional, became inescapable for him, giving rise to the profound ambivalence that runs through his best writing. For this reason perhaps the most revealing moment in all of Faulkner's work comes when Colonels John Sartoris and Thomas Sutpen lead their regiment out of Jefferson at the beginning of the war. We must picture them, the myth and the reality, riding side by side in Faulkner's mind: Sartoris on the right, and Sutpen, that scion of no known family, riding appropriately on the left.[89]

CHAPTER 7

THE AGRARIAN RESPONSE
TO MODERNISM

In 1930 a book appeared that was to reshape the intellectual life of the South in the twentieth century. *I'll Take My Stand: The South and the Agrarian Tradition*, a defiantly chauvinistic symposium by "Twelve Southerners," made the explicit defense of southern culture respectable again for the first time since the antebellum proslavery apologists. It vehemently attacked the New South shibboleths of national reconciliation, industrialism, and the modernization of southern society, and called instead for the supremacy of tradition, provincialism, and a life close to the soil. "All tend to support a Southern way of life," the authors declared in their common Statement of Principles, "against what might be called the American or prevailing way; and all as much as agree that the best terms in which to represent the distinction are contained in the phrase, Agrarian *versus* Industrial." With one stroke the Agrarians thus countered the tendency to regard the rise of a new class of southern intellectuals as commensurate with the development of liberalism in the region. Now there suddenly was—or appeared to be—an active conservative voice ready to affirm Old South values in twentieth-century terms.[1]

That indeed was the paradox, for in most cases the Agrarians were young southerners whose work as poets, critics, historians, and social scientists seemed to place them in the Modernist camp. The four former "Fugitive" poets who made up the core of the group—John Crowe Ransom, Allen Tate, Donald Davidson, and Robert Penn Warren—were all identified with the national vanguard of their craft. Tate, for example, contributed regularly to the *Nation* and the *New Republic*; his verse, heavily influenced by that of T. S. Eliot and Ezra Pound, was considered among the most "advanced" being produced on either side of the Atlantic. Thus the key question: what moved these writers suddenly to reverse direction and initiate such an ostensibly backward step? With their literary and scholarly reputations at stake, why did they choose to cast themselves as—to borrow the title of Ransom's essay—"Reconstructed but Unregenerate?" What, in short, did their rebellion really signify?

Certainly, no indication of that rebellion was evident in the *Fugitive*, the amateur poetry magazine of extraordinarily high quality published in Nashville from 1922 to 1925, despite the fact that its principal editors would spearhead the Agrarian movement just a few years later. On the contrary, as Louis D. Rubin, Jr., observes, the "Fugitives rather thought of themselves as representatives, on the literary plane, of the idea of the new, modern, progressive South." Their first editorial struck precisely this note, declaring that "THE FUGITIVE flees from nothing faster than from the high-caste Brahmins of the Old South." In practice, this policy meant a virtually complete absence of references to the South in Fugitive poetry and criticism. When Harriet Monroe, the editor of *Poetry*, suggested in 1923 that southern poets should avail themselves of local subjects, "so rich in racial tang and prejudice, so jewel-weighted with a heroic past," members of the group took umbrage. The Fugitives, Tate explained to Monroe, "fear very much to have the slightest stress laid upon Southern traditions in literature; we who are Southerners know the fatality of such an attitude—the old atavism and sentimentality are always imminent."[2]

In their flight from sentimentality, the Fugitives turned to the comparatively neutral issues of poetic craftsmanship and aesthetic theory. These technical matters became the prime topics of discussion at their fortnightly Saturday evening meetings when the brethren, composed mainly of faculty and students from the Vanderbilt Department of English, gathered to criticize vigorously one another's poems and to select those for publication. Much debate took place as to the value of contemporary experiments in poetic form, the relative roles of intellect and emotion in the creative process, and the possibility of universal standards for judging art. From these exchanges emerged something one might cautiously identify as a Fugitive style, reflecting this preoccupation with technique. Poems in this mode were tightly constructed, spare of flourishes or clichés, and above all built upon a series of concrete images rather than the grandiose abstractions of nineteenth-century verse. Often ironic in tone, they made their point by allusion. As one member of the group put it: "it is the Fugitive habit never to name the Thing, to paint all the picture except the central figure." It was, in a word, difficult poetry that made the reader struggle to unravel the poet's intent, thus serving to obscure whatever romantic inclinations the poet harbored.[3]

Yet, for all this intense intellectuality, the old romanticism was still present in the *Fugitive*. One sees it in the magazine's very name, which, Tate later explained, denoted "quite simply a Poet: the Wanderer, or even the Wandering Jew, the Outcast, the man who carries the secret wisdom around the world." Presiding over the group's meetings one finds the embodiment of such a "Fugitive," Sidney Mttron Hirsch, a widely traveled mystic philosopher who, at least at the beginning, held the young poets fascinated with his apparent worldliness and exotic knowledge of the occult. Little wonder, then, that all sorts of overwrought emotions and fantastic beings found their way into Fugitive verse. One reads of young maidens mysteriously drowning, lovers tragically separated, dragons venting their wrath, and of nymphs and satyrs gamboling through the landscape. Clearly these men retained a large measure of the nineteenth-century poetic sensibility that their technical experiments only partially masked. Nonetheless, this lingering sentimentality never became openly associated with the South or its history. The striking fact was their utter obliviousness to their native region.[4]

In 1925, however, just as the *Fugitive* ceased publication, this situation began to change rapidly. Late that year Davidson started composition on *The Tall Men*, his full-length epic poem recounting the heroism of the Tennessee pioneers. The following year Tate produced the first of many versions of his "Ode to the Confederate Dead" and started reading extensively in the South's history, while Davidson researched a proposed study of the region's literature. By the spring of 1927 Ransom had joined them in discussing plans for a "Symposium on Southern matters," the book that would eventually become *I'll Take My Stand*. Meanwhile, Tate was touring Civil War battlefields in preparation for a biography of Stonewall Jackson and closing his letters to Davidson, "The Stars & Bars forever!" This shift to southernism came about so fast that even the future Agrarians themselves were taken by surprise. "Nobody would have dreamed that Allen Tate's first volume would be a narrative about Stonewall Jackson," Davidson wrote in a 1928 review. "One would think him more concerned about the French Symbolists, say, than the battle of Chancellorsville."[5]

Many writers have unfortunately connected these events to the Scopes trial, which took place at nearby Dayton, Tennessee, in the summer of 1925. Here, they suggest, was simply a case of the "old atavism" bursting forth in response to the infamous mockery of the South by northern journalists covering the trial. But, although Davidson and Ransom were outraged by Mencken's tactics, this explanation does not begin to account for the sudden emergence of their southern consciousness. The fact remains that Davidson had already drafted his seminal article, "The

Artist as Southerner," by May 1925, two months before the trial began, although a year passed before he sent the piece off for publication. Something deeper than a mere patriotic reflex was involved.[6]

For insight into what was happening inside these men the best place to look is "The Artist as Southerner" itself, an essay that Davidson later claimed had brought him to "spiritual 'Secession.'" The piece is devoted mainly to a complaint, a complaint of how the contemporary southern writer steeped in Modernist culture suffers from "a set of complex inhibitions that make him extremely self-conscious in his attitude toward his own habitat. And the more completely he is aware of the phenomena of modern literature—the more nearly he approaches a perfection of his technical equipment—the greater these inhibitions will become." Most revealingly, he cites the Fugitives themselves as examples of this tendency toward paralysis. The only real solution, he remarks, is to immerse oneself in the "hot-blooded nature" of southern life and cry "Dixie," but this is something the Modernist writer by his very nature cannot do. Davidson's lament, along with Tate's similar outcry in his "Ode," makes manifest the true source of the Agrarian mentality. Not chauvinism as such, but the effort to escape this deadlock of ambivalence arising from the clash of their nineteenth-century heritage with their equally powerful Modernist values, led these writers to construct their own special myth of the South. That myth would permit them, temporarily at least, to resolve the psychic and literary dilemmas they felt.[7]

What at bottom distinguishes the Agrarians from other southern intellectuals of their generation, then, is this attempt to overcome the anguish of cultural transition by *fiat*—to reconcile their conflicting beliefs by an act of sheer will. Odum and Faulkner, beset by the same painful ambivalence, had responded in ways ranging from the precarious balancing acts and frequent verbal obfuscations of Odum's portraiture to Faulkner's stream-of-consciousness technique. Although both paid due allegiance to the Cavalier myth, neither defended it as a positive good. The Agrarians, by contrast, declared flatly that the ideal embodied in the Cavalier was indispensable for social happiness and artistic creativity. For them the Old South became quite consciously a symbol—what T. S. Eliot would call an "objective correlative"—that could fuse together their disparate tenets and values at the metaphoric level. Precisely because it was consciously created, however, constant effort was necessary to sustain that symbolism. "No American writers ever worked harder at inheriting their inheritance than the Agrarians," Lewis Simpson observes astutely. "If ever they gave the appearance of being securely possessed of it, the appearance, as Henry James might say, is their little secret." When that effort became too exhausting in the late 1930s, when the component parts of the mythology would no longer hold together, the Agrarians one by one sought other solutions and the movement fell apart.[8]

Put another way, the Agrarians, in their resort to Old South symbolism, were attempting to recapture the unified structure of belief that had characterized Victorian culture, and with it the capacity for religious faith they felt they had lost—all the while preserving the intellectual advances of Modernism. As Louise Cowan writes, they had grown up "in a world where there was no doubt of the universals. They had made their acquaintance with learning in a university which had as its ideal the coherence of knowledge into one vast scheme, the nature of which was ultimately religious." Yet, infected by post-Darwinian skepticism, they could not get beyond agnosticism. Nothing, it seemed, could fully engage their religious instinct before their commitment to critical rationality cast a pall on it. They yearned for the ability to transcend empiricism and to subscribe wholeheartedly to a creed or cause in the old-fashioned religious way. Agrarianism represented only one response they took to this crisis: at other times, they would make a religion out of art, conceiving of the poet as a modern priest. Tate, in whom this yearning for a solid faith was strongest, eventually converted to Catholicism, much as his mentor T. S. Eliot had joined the Anglican church. But no solution would completely suffice. The cultural division that bedeviled them proved inescapable, no matter what expedient they tried.[9]*

This desire to overcome their divided sensibilities and to reach a firm ground of belief was what united them in 1930, but beyond this the members of the group had little in common. Indeed, their philosophical outlooks and conceptions of the South could hardly have been more diverse, ranging from the Mississippi Cotton Snobbery of Stark Young to the backwoods bravado of Andrew Nelson Lytle to the New Deal-style reformism of Herman Clarence Nixon. Even among the leaders of the group one finds different styles of Agrarianism. At the center of Ransom's vision stood the gentleman and the tranquil country life of England. Davidson's ideal Agrarian was always the hard-fighting frontiersman who tamed the Tennessee wilderness. Tate, when he came down from his mountaintop of abstract theory, had a taste for Confederate Generals and Virginia First Families. Nonetheless, despite these variations, the inner forces that led these men to Agrarianism were much the same, and none of them ever truly escaped the dilemmas of cultural transition.

---

*Of course, Victorian culture in actuality was not as unified or stable as it often appears from the perspective of the twentieth century. But to the Agrarians, so keenly aware of the perils of Modernist relativism, it seemed solid indeed.

I

"I am the son of a theologian, and the grandson of another one, but the gift did not come down to me," confessed John Crowe Ransom in 1930. There, perhaps, lies the key to understanding this enigmatic poet and critic who stood first among equals within the Fugitive group. Born in 1888, his father and grandfather both Methodist ministers in central Tennessee, Ransom was raised in the thick of late nineteenth-century southern evangelical culture. Sanctity and churchgoing, along with moralism and gentility, were taken for granted in the Ransom household. But certain agencies soon conspired to subvert John Ransom's piety. For one, the arduous curriculum in classics and philosophy, which he pursued first as an undergraduate at Vanderbilt and then during three years as a Rhodes Scholar at Oxford, strongly reinforced his tendency toward rationalism, fashioning his mind into a razor-sharp instrument. Logic became, in Allen Tate's words, the "mode of his thought and sensibility," and Ransom never felt comfortable straying far beyond it. In addition, his grounding in post-Darwinian science served to undermine for him the benevolent deity of his father, replacing it with the agnostic view of a cold, unpredictable universe. Throughout his adult life Ransom longed for the kind of faith his fathers had enjoyed, but to no avail. The "gift" of his family forever eluded him.[10]

Coupled with this religious crisis was a cultural one, brought on by his considerable exposure to Modernism. At Oxford he had made an initial acquaintance with contemporary European literature and thought. Then, following his wartime service in France as an artillery instructor (the mathematical aspects of firing ordnance fascinated him), he spent several months at the universities in Grenoble and Nancy studying Symbolist poetry. These influences were capped soon afterwards on his return to Vanderbilt, where, as a member of the English department and a Fugitive, he developed fast friendships with younger poets like Tate who forced him to pay attention to the literary experiments of the period. In this way, Ransom created an intense conflict for himself. Although he had once subscribed to the Victorian view of art as a vehicle for moral didacticism, such overt moralizing now repelled him. Instead, his standard of aesthetic achievement became the ability to express in their full complexity the feelings and perceptions of the human psyche. As he well understood, the rational faculty, with which he was abundantly endowed, interfered constantly with the spontaneity required for this sort of art. Yet he could do little to lessen his commitment to logic and order. Once again, as in his failure to achieve religious belief, Ransom felt blocked, stifled, incomplete.[11]

Caught in this predicament, Ransom responded by adopting an attitude of stoic detachment. Stoicism held many advantages: it was in keeping with his Victorian upbringing, it followed his bent toward cool rationality and self-control, and most of all it allowed him to conceal his inner turmoil from others—and from himself. On the surface this strategy worked well. Ransom seemed self-possessed and content, a gentleman in the old sense still in command of his world. Again and again acquaintances would comment on his lack of emotion, perfect manners, ironic wit, and dry but deadly logic. At times, however, Ransom took this demeanor too far, betraying his true unease. His "formality of manner" could become "so pronounced," his biographer observes, that "some of his best friends would accuse him of indifference and aloofness." Tate in particular became infuriated, complaining to Davidson in 1923 that Ransom was "so damned prissified with his Oxford culture that he won't bat his eye for fear it isn't good manners." Tate, who suffered from the same cultural divisions himself, later came to understand the reasons for his old mentor's pose; Ransom, he noted in 1974, harbored an "intolerable burden of conflict that only occasionally, and even then indirectly, came to the surface."[12]

In retrospect, one can find signs of that "burden of conflict" as early as 1919 in Ransom's initial book of verse, *Poems About God*. His intention, he explained in the preface, was to write about those instances "in which I could imagine myself pronouncing the name God sincerely and spontaneously, never by that way of routine which is death to the aesthetic and religious emotions." But, as various critics have noticed, when the words "God" and "Christian" appear in the book they seem almost to have been inserted as an afterthought. "It is just possible," suggests Vivienne Koch, "that there was a deliberate irony in the very *absence* of a religious tone in contexts where 'God' occurred." Equally striking is that stoicism, not faith, is the theme of the book's lead poem. In "The Swimmer" we learn of an adolescent who, unable to bear the heat of emotion, escapes his torment by drowning himself in a deep pond:

> And what if I do not rise again
> Never to goad a heated brain
> To hotter excesses of joy and pain?
> Why should it be against the grain
> To lie so cold and still and sane?

Ransom was not yet prepared to endorse the swimmer's solution: in the final line he calls the swimmer "*wicked*" and orders him to emerge. Clearly, though, to be "cold and still and sane" was already a great temptation.[13]

7. John Crowe Ransom in 1927
Courtesy The Fugitive Collection, Special Collections,
Vanderbilt University Library

In the main body of his poetry, almost all of which appeared in the *Fugitive*, a major change takes place—the poet himself becomes the stoic. Terrible things happen in these poems. Small children die suddenly and unaccountably, a beautiful plantation house goes to ruin, gallant warriors are slaughtered in battle and their bodies are left to the vultures. The emotions one would normally expect on such occasions are present, but in each case they have been cooled down, removed to a safe distance, by being filtered through the poet's nearly complete air of detachment. Thus, in "Bells for John Whiteside's Daughter," the family, after recalling the vitality of the dead girl, contains its grief:

> But now go the bells, and we are ready
> In one house we are sternly stopped
> To say we are vexed at her brown study
> Lying so primly propped.

There is no doubt that the family, with whom the poet is identified, is shocked at the tragedy, but its members do not weep uncontrollably. Rather, they are "vexed" and "sternly stopped." Through ritual ("the bells") and formality ("primly propped") they have managed to control their emotions and to accept their loss in the approved stoic manner.[14]

This exercise of stoicism in the face of tragedy constituted Ransom's "program" for his poetry, the formula he repeated over and over. As he informed Tate, his method was to find a vehicle that could symbolize the "dearest possible values" and then "to face the disintegration or nullification of those values as calmly and religiously as possible." Like the troubled medieval friar in "Necrological" surveying the bloody corpses on the battlefield, Ransom knows the awful secret that God has left the universe and that human existence has no discernible meaning, but again like the friar he must, to keep his sanity, act as if he does not know and conceal his fear. Two lines from the preface to *Chills and Fever*, Ransom's second book of poems, effectively sum up his position:

> Assuredly I have a grief,
> And I am shaken; but not as a leaf.

The loss of faith had struck deep, but never would he reveal his agony publicly.[15]

At first sight, Ransom's stoicism would seem to place him in the ranks of the post-Victorians, and perhaps that is where he ultimately belongs. One crucial difference, however, separates his stoic posture from that of Cabell and Glasgow. If he, like them, felt constrained to shield himself from the pain of experience, he was Modernist enough to rail against the fact. One does not find Ransom contending, as did Glasgow in her later works, for a total suppression of emotional response. On the contrary, Ransom, in his letters and critical essays, began by 1923 to argue vehemently for a heightening of perception, a deepening rather than a deadening of the sensibility—especially for artists. "The obligation to be aesthetic is the obligation to open our eyes very wide," he insisted to Tate in 1926. Good poetry in his estimate was that which plumbed "our passionate history" and expressed that which "needs expression from our private deeps." Only in this way could poetry become a truly "spontaneous and expressive art." So fully had Ransom assimilated these Modernist tenets that, by the mid-1920s, he could even put aside his concern for regular rhyme and meter and concede that Hart Crane was the preeminent poet of the day since Crane had the "free-est mind" of any contemporary.[16]

But the more he came to prize spontaneity, the more he was distressed at his own lack of it. He could not praise Crane for being "most free from abstractions," yet fail to recognize the high degree of abstraction in his own work. He complained increasingly about self-consciousness and rationality blocking poetic inspiration and hampering the proper response to art. "Our souls," he told the readers of the *Fugitive*, "are not, in fact, in the enjoyment of full good health. For no art and no religion is possible until we make allowances, until we manage to keep quiet the *enfant terrible* of logic that plays havoc with the other faculties." Ransom, however, could not "make allowances" with his highly trained mind; the *"enfant terrible"* would not stay quiet. Even in his best poetry (and some of it was very good indeed) critics would discover, as one put it, an "oddly abstractionist tendency." In short, Ransom was torn between the cultural values of two eras. Convinced that men required a firm and unified set of beliefs to live by, he was destined to suffer from an insurmountable ambivalence.[17]

Partly in hopes of resolving this dilemma, and partly as a result of his continuing dialogue with Tate, Ransom as of 1923 turned his attention from poetry to prose. Indeed, by 1926, when he embarked on a book-length study of aesthetics, his poetic career was at an end. He would write only six more poems in the remaining half century of his life, none of them of real significance. From this time on his reputation would rest on his considerable achievements as a critic and theorist of poetry, a role in which he explored many diverse concerns, from the function of form and structure in art to the poet's moral responsibility to society. But whatever the subject at hand, Ransom's central quest in these essays remained the same: his effort, never completely successful, to reason himself back to an intellectual bedrock where thought and feeling would be fused.[18]

Significantly, it was the question of poetic form—the technical side of poetry—that brought Ransom to criticism. The free verse experiments of Tate, and particularly of Tate's idol, T. S. Eliot, at first troubled him. He could not understand, for example, how a sensible gentleman like Eliot favored a "poetic vernacular that is utterly irrationalized." He did not approve of their innovations, but could not yet say why. By 1924, after much heated discussion with his fellow Fugitives, however, he was ready to defend his position logically. Form, he now argued, was not just an obstacle placed arbitrarily in the poet's path. Rather, it represented an essential element of the poem that, by supplying a constraint to the poet's emotions, gave rise to the drama and excitement of the art. Not only must the poet convey his meaning; he must contrive to express himself within a "uniform objective structure of accents and rhymes." The consequent tension between form and feeling was the source of the special "ecstasy" poetry could produce. For Ransom the magic was as much moral as aesthetic: it constituted nothing less than a "miracle of harmony, of the adaptation of the free inner life to the outward necessity of things." In slightly different terms, poetic form stood for the rational discipline that kept spontaneity from getting out of control, which was why Ransom prized it so highly.[19]

This tension between rationality and emotion, control and expression, became in turn the basis for Ransom's emerging aesthetic theory. Relying heavily on the conceptual scheme of Immanuel Kant, whose *Critique of Pure Reason* he had read at Oxford, Ransom began to posit two separate faculties of human thought, reason and sensibility. The former was inherently abstract, systematic, and theoretical, and led directly to modern science; the latter was concrete, spontaneous, metaphoric, and manifested itself principally in art and religion. For previous generations, he believed, the two had stayed roughly in balance, enhancing each other's functions, but at present they had become warring entities, with science at times threatening to overwhelm sensibility altogether. Given this threat, poetry's task was to free modern man from the tyranny of abstractions, enabling him to recover the endangered half of his psyche. Ransom was convinced that the mind itself instinctively sought such a deliverance. In his words, the "world of science and knowledge which we have laboriously constructed is a world of illusion; . . . we suddenly appear to ourselves as monsters, as unnatural members of humanity; and we move to right ourselves again." In fact, Ransom was again generalizing to the whole society the conflict he felt so acutely. *His* excessive rationalism bedeviled *his* sensibility. The assumption that all men shared the same distress was grounded primarily in his own experience, interpreted through the metaphysical categories of Kant.[20]

In late 1926, Ransom, given a semester's leave from Vanderbilt, launched into a book that, he hoped, would allow him to get his "philosophy" straight once and for all. Tentatively titled "The Third Moment," it traced the development of man's aesthetic consciousness in three dialectic stages. The first stage, corresponding to early childhood, was that of pure sensibility; the second, pure rationality. The "Third Moment"—the stage of maturity—was characterized by the effort to integrate the initial two stages. In the Third Moment, the mind, rebelling against the strictures of cognition, attempted to "reconstitute the fugitive first moment" and so regain its spontaneity. Through dreams, fantasies, religion, morals, and art, it retrieved the images and sensations from the First Moment that rationality had banished to the unconscious, blending them with the analytic concepts it had acquired during the Second Moment, and created a "sort of practicable reconciliation of the two worlds." The third stage, in other words, somehow transcended the separateness of Kant's two faculties. This was the blessed state Ransom longed for, in which the liberated sensibility would coexist with the discipline of rigorous logic—much as the poet's feelings were to harmonize with the requirements of meter and rhyme. The whole mind would thus be engaged and the rift in the modern psyche healed, at least temporarily.[21]*

This scheme sounded fine in theory, but how was it to be realized in actuality? After all, the reconciliation of the Third Moment was meant to be "practicable"—Ransom was always striving to connect his thought to real life. Whenever he did so, however, he found not the integration he sought but the shifting sands of dualism. The world he saw consisted of embattled opposites locked in perpetual tension, with the "miraculous" alchemy of Art relieving that tension only for the briefest moments. At times in the mid-1920s he would veer toward the Modernist pole and declare that Art in fact depended on this dualistic tension for its vitality. At other times he would pull back slightly, contending that poetry had to exhibit "Opposition" and "Reconciliation" at the same time. Ransom was, of course, anticipating the main thrust of twentieth-century literary criticism, which would explore the workings of symbol and metaphor in terms of the very tensions he was describing. But that fact did not help Ransom in 1926: for a man who sought certainty in his belief system and whose personality abhorred tension, dualism offered precious little comfort.[22]

Yet he could not escape that dualism. With his Modernist values pushing him toward liberation, and his underlying Victorian moralism forcing

---

*The phrase "to reconstitute the fugitive first moment" invites speculation. It clearly suggests Ransom's longing to return to that "first moment" when he was a Fugitive and producing poetry.

him to check himself through rationalism, the best he could do was to counterpose the contending parties of intellect and passion. Thus his striking poem, "The Equilibrists," in which two would-be lovers, stymied by the principle of "Honor," are doomed to dance around each other endlessly without touching:

> At length I saw these lovers fully were come
> Into their torture of equilibrium;
> Dreadfully had foresworn each other, and yet
> They were bound each to each, and they did not forget.
>
> And rigid as two painful stars, and twirled
> About the clustered night their prison world
> They burned with fierce love always to come near
> But honor beat them back and kept them clear.

The "torture," the dynamic stasis, was also in large measure Ransom's. By the late 1920s he had come to a dead end. Although convinced that writing poetry was essential to his "health and sanity," as he wrote his friend Merrill Moore, he now sensed that the muse had left him permanently. Moreover, after three years of fruitless attempts to complete it, he felt compelled to abandon "The Third Moment." Judging the manuscript far too abstract, he sadly consigned it to the flames.[23]

II

It was precisely at this juncture that Ransom discovered the South and Agrarianism. Prior to March, 1927, when Tate first proposed a defense of southern culture, Ransom had barely contemplated the issue at all. "I don't write consciously as a Southerner or non-Southerner," he had remarked to Tate a month earlier, adding that his work would probably become "less and less local." Some critics, it is true, have detected glimmerings of a nascent southern chauvinism in "Antique Harvesters," a poem written in late 1924, but as Robert Buffington has demonstrated, that chauvinism was weak and ironical at best. For the most part Ransom's attitude toward the region and its rural character had been reflected in the warning he once gave his family to beware of "Tennessee myopia." "Country conditions," he explained, "operate to produce in country people the qualities of stability, conformity, mental and spiritual inertia, callousness, monotony"—none of which met with his approval. Moreover, in the spring of 1927 Ransom had just finished assuring Tate that he had renounced "Cosmology" and "Mythology" of all kinds forever. "I am a desperate Positivist, Nominalist, Philistine, Sensationalist, and Skeptic," he maintained. Espousing a radical empiricism that would have done a modern scientist proud, Ransom argued that artists must constantly reject "entities which cannot be perceived" by the senses, or else "tell lies and fall into disrepute and lose even our own self-respect." Presumably an intangible like southern tradition would fall under this ban.[24]

Yet Ransom jumped at Tate's suggestion. Here, it seemed, was a chance to gain liberation at a fell swoop. By giving the South his passionate allegiance, he could at once still the *enfant terrible* of his logic, break through his painful ambivalence, sweep aside his protective barrier of stoicism, and face the world with a consciousness integrated around a cohesive set of beliefs. In short, the importance of the South for Ransom did not lie in the actual region or its history (a subject he knew remarkably little about), but in its availability as something to which he could devote himself wholeheartedly, even religiously. What drew his excitement was not the possibility of transforming southern society so much as the prospect of a group of talented young writers "manifesting themselves in the capacity of a Cause; about which they have Convictions." In this way Agrarianism served, for a while, as a substitute for the faith he had lost.[25]

To be sure, Ransom's image of the Old South as a place where the "life aesthetic was actually realized" did speak to his personal needs. The society he portrayed in *I'll Take My Stand* was a world of minimal tension, where the functions of intelligence and sensibility blended easily. It was controlled, not by haughty aristocrats or high-powered intellectuals, but by a gentle "squirearchy" much like that supposedly found in the English countryside. The pace of life these men administered was leisurely, orderly, and comfortable, and at the same time urbane, with balance and moderation suffusing all activities. Even the arts were "not immensely passionate, creative, and romantic; they were the eighteenth century social arts of dress, conversation, manners, the table. . . . The South took life easy, which is itself a tolerable comprehensive art." Defeat in the Civil War had ended this blissful state, but the region had still managed to retain its "European principles" and agrarian economy. Now industrialization threatened to replace those principles with "American" ones. If the industrialists succeeded, people would be cut off from healthful contact with nature, leisure would give way to the incessant demands of efficiency, spontaneity would be overwhelmed by calculation, and life would turn into mere mechanism. In more general terms, the powerful current of rationality that so tormented Ransom would be unleashed upon that last preserve of tranquillity: the hitherto resistant rural South.[26]

Such was Ransom's version of southern Agrarianism. Its sources, for the most part, were highly derivative and nonsouthern in origin. The ideal antebellum existence it described surely owed as much to his readings in English literature as to his native Cavalier mythology. His critique of industrialism was largely appropriated from that originally put forth by Carlyle and other nineteenth-century romantics. As for remedies, Ransom candidly admitted he had few to offer. He did hope for a new corps of leaders to "arouse the sectional feeling of the South to its highest pitch of excitement," provided of course that they did so "with discretion." Perhaps an alliance between southern and western agrarians within the Democratic party would be in order. That said, Ransom had nothing more to add about the South. It is highly revealing that his symposium essay (made up of two previously published articles) stands as his sole statement on the Old South and sectionalism; subsequent pieces would mention these subjects only in passing. From a substantive standpoint, Ransom's Agrarianism was neither very agrarian nor very southern.[27]

Equally revealing is that Ransom's main work during the period of his active participation in the Agrarian movement was a book of theology. Written "hot and hasty" (as he described it) during 1929, when his ideological passion was at its peak, *God Without Thunder: An Unorthodox Defense of Orthodoxy* does not mention the South at all, but rather was intended as a vindication of Fundamentalist religion against liberal Protestantism and contemporary science. Writers on Ransom have invariably seen the work as a delayed response to the Scopes trial, with Ransom cast as a latter-day, scholarly version of William Jennings Bryan. Certainly the book *can* be read that way. Ransom does call for a return to the thundering inscrutable Jehovah of the Old Testament through a revival of ritual and tradition. He does assail science as a false prophet. As he summarized his thesis for Tate: "Little by little the God of the Jews has been whittled down into the spirit of science, or the spirit of love, or the spirit of Rotary; and now religion is not religion at all, but a purely secular experience, like Y. M. C. A. and Boy Scouts." Ransom was trying to reverse this process by assaulting naturalism at its philosophic roots and thus restoring the potential for belief in the transcendent and mysterious.[28]

But there is more here than first meets the eye. Despite the lavish praise of Fundamentalists, the book can also be read as an attack, often an embittered one, on the Christianity and civilization those Fundamentalists were upholding. The battle lines do not run between liberal and orthodox Christians, as one might expect, but between "Occidentals" and "Orientals"—terminology Ransom had used since 1926 as an extension of his reason-versus-sensibility dichotomy. And Occidentalism, in Ransom's view, was essentially Protestantism. It possesses a "hard" mind (which he acknowledges as his own), operates almost exclusively in terms of rationality, and is "devoted either to authenticated facts or to sober generalizations about these facts." Ransom does not look kindly on this mentality or its works. Of all Satan's "grand triumphs," he writes, the "most extensive . . . was the setting up on earth of the vast historic polity which we may describe as Occidentalism." By contrast, the "Hebraic, Oriental, symbolistic cast of mind" was characteristic of "Poets, religionists, Orientals," and other "sensitive people" who "insist upon their contemplation and their freest inner development." Since only they possess the imagination to transcend the evidence of their senses and the rules of logic, Orientalists alone, according to Ransom, have access to real religious faith. Yet, though his sympathies lay obviously with the Orientalists, he did not endorse them carte blanche. "Aestheticism and Moralism would be good names for Orientalism and Occidentalism," he once told Tate in a letter, and Ransom, for all his yearnings toward the aesthetic, was hardly prepared to forego morality.[29]

As a result, *God Without Thunder* proceeds along an incredible zigzag path of abstract philosophizing as Ransom strains haplessly to find some sort of equilibrium for these two polar mentalities. The book begins by extolling the Orient, "peculiarly the home of superior religions," and by damning Protestantism, which "has always figured to itself as a determination to rationalize the antiquated religious doctrines." Several non-Christian religious groups receive commendation, including the Jewish Talmudists and Cabbalists, the ancient Greeks ("as much Oriental as they were Occidental"), and Rosicrucians. What these faiths share, we discover, is a reliance on mythology, which Ransom defines much as a cultural anthropologist would. Far from constituting a falsehood, myth for Ransom becomes an all-embracing form of knowledge that can "express truths which are not accessible to science." In particular, myth, through its resort to metaphor, captures the dynamic *"fullness of the natural"* as the static, abstract methods of science never can. Myth represents the ultimate functioning of the sensibility, the aesthetic capability of man raised to its highest pitch. But Ransom's conception of myth also includes a crucial psychological component, for it is myth—especially religious myth based on a powerful God—that provides man with a concrete, "sensible" entity to believe in, an image around which the mind and emotions can readily fuse. Such a myth, if successful, is comforting, stabilizing, an anchor for man in the constant flux of life; it is the fleeting resolution of the Third Moment made tangible and durable. Most of all, it is an acceptable means of expressing passionate conviction. "Evidently we are not playing when we participate in our religious myth," Ransom notes, "we *mean* it intensely, and perhaps fiercely."[30]

Ransom clearly envies such fierceness of belief, but he is also sure that Occidentals like himself have lost the capacity to attain it. Indeed, the less "civilized" a people are, it would seem, the more open they become to the mythological imagination: "Evidently this procedure is one in which the so-called 'primitive' thinkers are well versed, but it is nevertheless a rather subtle one, and far from the animal order of mentality. In fact, it would seem to be a trifle advanced by comparison with the acts of the naturalistic temperament, which fails to understand it." Ransom's chief source of inspiration here, it might be noted, was not modern anthropology, but rather Sidney Mttron Hirsch, whose influence on Ransom has been consistently underestimated. The scion of a prominent Jewish family in Nashville, Hirsch had garnered a wide if superficial knowledge of occult and Far Eastern religions during his world travels. Nothing pleased him more than holding his young votaries spellbound by displaying this knowledge, especially by tracing the secret symbolic meaning of words through the system of Rosicrucian etymology. As Davidson later recalled, Hirsch impressed upon them the importance of mythologies and religion, along with the "high eminence of poetry." One suspects, then, that Hirsch came to embody the "Oriental" sensibility for Ransom; at a minimum he made Ransom acutely aware of the limitations of "Occidental" culture. Whatever the case, *God Without Thunder*, which carries an open letter to "S. M. H." in place of a preface, unmistakably bears Hirsch's imprint.[31]

After presenting his theory of myth, however, Ransom suddenly reverses gears. He turns to Christ, the "New God" science has created to take Jehovah's place. Although this "Logos" or "patron of science" had nobly refused to become a God during his life, his overzealous disciples, we learn, made him a God anyway, thus placing him in the same category as Lucifer, another patron of science with unfounded pretensions to divinity. Surely Ransom, the preacher's son, sensed the sacrilege implicit in this argument. Surely he knew that such an irreverent devaluation of Christ ran directly counter to his declared support of Fundamentalism and undercut his call for maintaining the integrity of myth. Yet Ransom could not seem to help himself. His rhetoric—and suppressed bitterness at the church that had failed him—appeared out of control:

> The Church likes to say, Believe on Christ; and I am far from dissenting from the saying except that history shows it is a dangerous one. I would always add a qualification which the Church

sometimes forgets to make: Believe on him as he directed, that is, as Incarnate Reason *who was inferior to the God* that had sent him.

Christianity and science, then, were the same. Both rested on the deification of human reason and sought to control nature for man's benefit. Doubtless the Tennessee Fundamentalists, had they read Ransom's book, would have found this defense of orthodoxy "unorthodox."[32]

Throughout the latter half of *God Without Thunder* Ransom pursues his quarrel with science. "The scientific processes are terribly confining," he complains. "They crucify our organic sensibility while they drive furiously toward their abstracts . . . Science as a mental habit is an obsession which is quite unhealthful." Science cares solely about using the object, not appreciating it aesthetically. It picks out only those aspects of the object that are of value in formulating generalizations, leaving aside the infinite detail the object invariably possesses. Moreover, science ignores all that is "contingent, outside of expectation and prediction, irrelevant to the [abstract] pattern, and distracting." Plainly Ransom was thinking of the grand theories of eighteenth- and nineteenth-century science. He knew little of contemporary experimental method, which often errs on the side of too much absorption in concrete detail rather than too little. In any event, his polemic, so highly abstract itself, had more to do with his ongoing interior battle against the "obsession" of rationality than with the actual workings of physics or biology.[33]

The chief problem, though, was the direction this argument took. Citing the unlikely combination of David Hume and Henri Bergson as his guides, Ransom contends that the explanations of science are partial and illusory because they are not based on real sensory perception. No one has ever seen Gravity, or Cause and Effect, or Evolution. Consequently, scientific thought traffics primarily in "supersensibles"—concepts and images that lack concrete substance and cannot be verified empirically. As examples, Ransom mentions the state of Pennsylvania, the Catholic church, the Nordic race, the Crusades, and the twentieth century. Such entities must always be regarded as fictions, and not as fit subjects for veneration: "In vain we celebrate it [the supersensible] in ceremony and song; or feel intense emotions as we contemplate it; or even die for it. It is also in vain that we agree unanimously among ourselves about its sensible existence. . . . It remains a supersensible object and cannot be penetrated by the senses like a historical or sensible one." In short, Ransom was back to his radical empiricism. It was a position he could, to be sure, defend with pristine logic, but it was also one that stood totally at odds with the mythological imagination he had championed in the first half of *God Without Thunder.* After three hundred pages of intricate reasoning, he ends with the same contradiction he had set out to resolve.[34]

By the final chapter—a prolonged attempt to construct a case for the Holy Ghost through logic—Ransom seems to know how trapped he is. Almost apologetically, he acknowledges that his Occidental Protestantism has triumphed, that the schism he had hoped to heal remains as gaping as ever:

> An effort, such as this is, to work out a natural history and a logic of ghosts is doubtless a pure Occidental performance that would seem to Orientals a strange and tedious labor of love. But while this performance was appearing superfluous to the eyes of quick Orientals, their energetic play with [mythological] figures would be at the same time appearing very fantastic to me. They are as incapable of my Puritanical rigor as I am incapable of their freedom of imagination.

In his prefatorial letter to Sidney Hirsch, Ransom had justified his "policy of frankly analyzing the religious experience" and of subjecting myth to the "cold and not very fastidious terms of an Occidental logic" on the grounds that the religionist party had "not much more to lose." If Ransom had felt a degree of desperation when he began the book, he must have felt even more desperate at the end. Nonetheless, he could not resist leaving the reader with some practical proposal in the epilogue. Rejecting Catholicism and Anglicanism as foreign faiths unavailable to anyone of his ethnic stock, he settled on a simple set of injunctions that may fairly be paraphrased as "Restore orthodoxy to the church of your choice."[35]

God Without Thunder seems to have puzzled nearly everyone who encountered it in the early 1930s. Most reviewers could not square Ransom's stated objective of defending orthodoxy with his patent atheism—"Thunder Without God," one critic called it. Perhaps Kenneth Burke put the trouble most succinctly when he wrote Tate: "Imagine a Fundamentalist papa bringing up his child to believe that the whole thing was an *as if.*" Ransom himself was puzzled by the book; shortly after publication he commented to Warren that he was far too much of an unbeliever to have authored such a work. Yet, strikingly enough, Ransom was infuriated when critics pointed out the book's obvious contradictions. It was one of the few times his friends ever recalled him showing open anger.[36]

Ransom's attempt to implement his proposals five years after *God Without Thunder* was published is also instructive. Upon moving to the countryside some ten miles from Nashville, he began attending services at the local Methodist church for the first time since his youth. He also taught Sunday School, employing the same analytic method of close textual reading that he used in his poetry classes at Vanderbilt. But a controversy soon arose when the church fathers discovered that he refused to recite the Apostle's Creed to his class. As a result, the champion of ritual and orthodoxy was forced to leave the church. Thereafter Ransom spent his Sunday mornings reading or playing golf. Never again would he write on the subject of religion, orthodox or otherwise.[37]

Ransom was not prepared, however, to abandon his search for the elusive means to unify his thought, and for the remainder of his years as an Agrarian he sought it in social and economic theory, territory hitherto incognita for him. Following the publication of *I'll Take My Stand*, Ransom was more than ever determined to be practical. The frequent charge by reviewers of the symposium that he and his friends were embarked on a fairy-tale mission bothered him considerably and served as a spur to his new studies, but in fact his logic had been moving him in this direction anyway. The faith he was seeking, and which he thought he had found in Agrarianism, would have to extend into the minutest particulars of everyday life; there could be no contradiction between it and the way one made one's living. Thus in a 1929 essay (never published) he attacked the New Humanists for failing to deal with the political and economic aspects of their model society. In the ancient Greece they so admired, he reminded them, the existence of the gentleman depended on an economic order that made gentlemanly behavior possible. The "superstructure" may have been "aesthetic and philosophical," but the "base of the edifice" had been "moral and economic." The lesson was clear: if humanist-minded "schoolmasters" like himself wished to save culture, they had better become teachers of economics, too.[38]

As usual, once Ransom's mind set to work on an issue, it could not rest until, in Louis Rubin's words, all loose ends "were linked up in an ordered and rational system." He began a diligent reading in economic theory and devoted his entire year as a Guggenheim Fellow from 1931 to 1932 to a treatise on behalf of subsistence farming. But the work did not go well. No publisher would take the manuscript, and besides, the more Ransom learned of economics the more he drifted away from Agrarian tenets. The farmer's current plight, he concluded, was due to the collapse of foreign markets in the depression. Agriculture, however, was fortunate in being able to operate on either a commercial or subsistence basis. The farmer should thus take advantage of his status as an "amphibian" by reaping profits in the money economy during good times, then retreating to feeding his family in crises like the present. Subsistence agriculture, in other words, was valuable mainly as a stand-by. "The farmer needs income," Ransom asserted in 1936 in a startling reversal of Agrarian doctrine, "he should not be expected to live as a self-subsistent primitive" all the time.[39]

Once started on this heretical track, Ransom was of course helpless. To achieve a respectable income, he reasoned, farmers would need new domestic markets, which meant the further development of industry and cities, even in the South. "I do not know anybody in the South who thinks that industrialization can be stopped where it is, or wants it stopped there," he claimed. At one point, expanding on a plan suggested to him by Sidney Hirsch, Ransom went so far as to propose combatting unemployment by building a new national capital on the banks of the Mississippi, "more modern, and more beautiful than any city on earth." It was true, he admitted, that Agrarians like himself were supposed to abhor cities, but "they too go to cities and are influenced by cities, and it is a matter of fact that the city focuses all the features of a culture as nothing else does." Ransom's logic even led him to chastise one Agrarian-minded writer who wished to lower tariffs "no matter what it means to American industry." Needless to say, these changes in Ransom deeply upset his friends. "It seems that John has found the virtues always latent in the Tariff," Tate remarked sardonically to Davidson. "I'm sure it is a great triumph of John's dialectic even though it may be the death-knell of true agrarianism."[40]

By the mid-1930s Ransom himself knew that the Agrarian god had failed him. Whatever passion he had initially brought to the movement had long since evaporated. His contribution to *Who Owns America?*, the 1936 symposium edited by Tate and his English Distributist friend Herbert Agar as a sort of follow-up to *I'll Take My Stand*, fell exceedingly flat; it was, in Rubin's words, "all logical deduction," and sounded like nothing more than a rehash of New Deal policy toward the South. By versing himself in social science, Ransom was rapidly turning into an ordinary liberal.[41]

With infinite relief, Ransom now reverted back to his position of 1927, when he had written Tate that he was through with "cosmologies" forever. Henceforth, he decided, he would occupy himself solely with those questions of literary technique, like form and style, which constituted his real abiding interest. The signal for this shift came in late 1936 in a pair of heartfelt letters to Tate setting forth a plan for an "*American Academy of Letters*" (to be called the "Institute of Literary Autonomy and Tradition"), which would devote itself to upholding high "objective" standards in literature. Above all it would concern itself with style—that "symbol of personal individuation, which is the real object of the American tradition and of any literary tradition." But the "main thing," he added, would be the "*purity, autonomy, anti-Platonism of the poetry*," pure not only of political content but of obvious intellectuality as well. "Our intentions would be two," he explained, "and they would look contradictory: to have our literature created by persons of philosophical capacity; to have its pure forms without taint of explicit philosophy." "You will be able to phrase that," he confidently concluded.[42]

Ten years earlier in a *Fugitive* editorial Ransom had spoken of the "mature" poet's need to become a "dualist with a difference." He was referring to the poet's ability to accept the inherent dualism between reason and sensibility, mind and body—but with great reluctance. The poet's lingering desire to heal the schism would be the mark of his humanity, while his realization that it was impossible to do would be the mark of his sophistication. During the interim Ransom had surrendered to the temptation of actually resolving the dualism through the Agrarian myth and "Fundamentalist" religion. Now, in 1937, although aware of its inadequacies, he hastened back to his former philosophical base. Others, particularly his younger disciples, might find ways of reconciling thought and emotion under contemporary conditions, and Ransom would strongly encourage them ("You will be able to phrase that"); but for himself the dualism, with all its tension and ambivalence, would be inescapable.[43]

To minimize the pain—and to shed his southern and Agrarian connections forever—Ransom moved in late 1937 from Vanderbilt to Kenyon College in Ohio. There, as professor of poetry and editor of the *Kenyon Review*, he was able to isolate himself from all but literary concerns, save for his avocations of bridge-playing and golf. His friends noticed immediately how much happier he seemed. It was true that the muse never favored him again, and there is reason to believe that this fact continued to trouble him more than he revealed. "The physical death of Keats at an early age is painful to us," he wrote in 1955, "but worse, perhaps, is the death of the poet in the living Matthew Arnold, and I for one . . . will not be consoled by thinking of the value of the public man who emerged from the ruin." Nonetheless, Ransom's masterful analysis of the formalistic aspects of literature in his continuing flow of essays brought him recognition as one of the foremost critics of his generation and as a founder of the New Criticism. That recognition doubtless helped to compensate for the death of his poetic impulse. As for religion, it seems that Ransom returned to an earlier stance. "For you and me and the elite whom I know," he had told Tate in 1926, "art is the true religion and no other is needed." To borrow one of his favorite words, Ransom may have "consented" to live by that tenet, but one suspects that he did so without passion and with a haunting sense of loss.[44]

III

No such secret battles raged inside Donald Grady Davidson, who in many respects stands as an exact opposite of his friend Ransom. Davidson's father had been a country schoolteacher, not a minister. When Methodism gave way to a mild atheism, Davidson did not feel cheated in the least. "I seem to be bothered less by religious matters than by anything else," he reported to Tate. Moreover, stoicism played no part in Davidson's makeup; on the contrary, the forceful, direct expression of his feelings became the hallmark of his writing. What did upset Davidson, though, was ambivalence of any sort. The tension that Ransom gradually made his peace with and which Tate turned into high art were beyond the limits of Davidson's tolerance. Agrarianism for him, then, served the purpose of banishing ambivalence once and for all. In Rubin's phrase, his commitment to the Cause "came to dominate everything he did and thought." Once he had developed this Agrarian world view, he would cling to it without the slightest trace of self-doubt precisely in order to protect himself from doubt. This strategy had consequences for both his poetry and intellectual life, which, by the late 1930s, became simple, visceral, and extremely limited.[45]

Given Davidson's later stance as a stalwart neo-Confederate, bewailing the sins of the contemporary world, it is all too easy to forget that he began his career as a harbinger of southern Modernism. During his Fugitive days one finds him open to all kinds of new and outside influences—lining up most frequently with Tate and Ransom against the more traditional faction of Fugitives, introducing Tate to the *New Republic*, keeping his eye fixed hopefully on the twin capitals of national culture, New York and Hollywood, and alone of the group choosing a northern-born wife (a native of Oberlin, Ohio, the old abolitionist stronghold). As late as 1928 his published writings were filled with New South rhetoric commending the South's progress toward national standards. To be sure, Davidson's embrace of twentieth-century literary innovations was not unqualified. He did not like the more advanced works of Eliot, Crane, Pound, or Joyce, nor did he always approve of Tate's experiments in that direction. But he would inform Tate, "I am equally afraid of being dogmatic about anything artistic, and assure you that I am quite humble and ready to receive all manner of information and theorizing." His hope, he said, was "to strike a balance between the best of the old and the new." Thus he could, without contradiction, sign himself in 1922, "Yours for the Moderns (excluding the Dada's, the Vers Librists, the Secessionists, and the other ultra-ultra's)."[46]

Davidson's early poetry reflects this desire to install himself among his

8. Donald Davidson in the late 1940s
Courtesy The Fugitive Collection, Special Collections,
Vanderbilt University Library

literary contemporaries. Like Fugitive verse in general, it tends to be allusive, economical of phrase, often cerebral and ironic in tone, and devoid of reference to the South. However, Davidson was far more inclined to romanticism than either Ransom or Tate, a characteristic that appeared in his lush imagery and in a strong note of eroticism veiled through the usual conventions of demons, satyrs, tiger-women, and other exotic creatures. In "Naiad," for instance, a nymph-like girl bathing in a river with friends is enticed by some mysterious force to wander away, strip off her bathing suit, and drown herself in the fast-moving water. Davidson manages simultaneously to heighten and mask the sensuality by leaving it ambiguous whether this is a naturalistic event ("madness stung her blood") or a mythological one (a Naiad is a river nymph in classical myth). Perhaps, he suggests, the god of the river has seduced her:

> The penumbral depths received her slim trunk's thrust,
> Like lover gesturing, "Come, O Long-expected!"

Although still essentially romantic, this poetry was fairly advanced and even daring at that time for the South—more or less equivalent to what Cabell was attempting in prose. No wonder that when Tate arrived in Greenwich Village in 1924 he found Davidson's work well known and admired.[47]

Yet by the following year Davidson was already shifting toward a strident provincialism. Rubin is probably correct that the breakup of the Fugitives was partly responsible for this change, and doubtless the fusillade against the South at the Scopes trial hastened the process. But the root cause appears to have been that knot of dissatisfaction building up inside over what Davidson in "The Artist as Southerner" called the "inhibitions" of Modernism. As he understood it, the Modernist aesthetic required an intensely introspective style of poetry, informed as much by the intellect as the emotions, heavily symbolic in its language, and addressed principally to a tiny coterie of fellow literati. Most important, because of its strict ban on sentimentality, Modernism severed the poet from his native subject matter, particularly if he happened to be a southerner. The role of "place" must remain "incidental" and "subordinate," Davidson cautioned in a 1924 *Fugitive* editorial; at best "it is merely a picturesque addition, not the inner substance of poetry."[48]

Davidson bravely endeavored to live up to these dicta, but with growing discomfort. He was a man of vigorous passions, often of a chauvinist cast, who had little patience with ambiguity, indirection, or complexity. His anguish found expression in "Swan and Exile," a minor but poignant poem of 1924 in which the Modernist poet is portrayed as a swan floating in "exile" on a "strange lake" lamenting the death of his "wild soul":

And drifting sees the pale shadow
Of himself, as I have seen
My forgotten self in a cold pool
Dangerously serene.

Swan, where is the flock of eld?
What sorcery keeps us here
Circling within a rim of eyes
Silent in fear?

Ransom's image of nirvana took the form of lying at the bottom of a cold pool free of passion, which symbolized his stoic tactic for escaping the tensions of a divided psyche. But for Davidson, the cold pool was "dangerously serene." He would surmount ambivalence the opposite way by giving vent to his chauvinistic feelings, thus breaking out of the critical "rim of eyes" that kept him so painfully self-conscious, so "silent in fear." He would resuscitate his "dead" soul by deliberately cultivating the wildness within it.[49]

To achieve this liberation Davidson sought the "flock of eld." By that defiantly archaic phrase he meant to denote his Scotch-Irish backwoods ancestors, those fighting frontiersmen who, he believed, had not known doubt, despair, or introspection. Sometime in 1925 he began to celebrate them in a lengthy epic poem, published two years later as *The Tall Men*, and as he wrote it his resolve to identify himself with this tradition grew stronger by the day. With this new subject matter came an equally dramatic shift in technique. Gone were the packed lines and precise word choices that the "rim of eyes" had enforced on him at Fugitive meetings. Instead, Davidson drew on his expertise in southern folk music to devise a lyrical style, based on blank verse and colloquial speech, which at once emancipated him from formal restraints and tied his epic to the ancient oral tradition in poetry. Such art, he hoped, would appeal to common people, especially in the South, and not just to the intellectual elite.[50]

In taking these steps, Davidson was convinced that he was moving daringly backward, rejecting twentieth-century culture decisively. To the extent that he was countering the threats of skepticism and relativism, this was true. But paradoxically, his glorification of primitivism and attack on cultural elitism sprang directly from the Modernist strain in his thought. Certainly no nineteenth-century southern writer would have willingly claimed the violent frontier as his heritage. In this respect, Davidson stands closer to the neo-Populism of the 1930s and 1940s, which restored the plain folk to the center of southern life, than to any true conservatism.

What Davidson valued most in the frontier was precisely its violence.

For his heroic tall men, who "talked with their rifles bluntly," killing was as natural and frequent as speaking or breathing. Their "words were bullets." Davidson repeats this refrain so often that his forebears seem nothing short of trigger-happy. But that is exactly why he admires them—the tall men were brave enough to act before they thought, and their actions took place on the grand scale of life and death. They stand in sharp contrast to the poem's narrator, a modern southerner obviously meant to be autobiographical, who does nothing more daring than to take the streetcar to work in Nashville:

> And my soft proud body is borne on the smooth
> Parallel rails into a city hoarse
> With nine o'clock which brings the swivel-chair
> And to the hungry brain the pelt of typewriters.
>
> Some sort of a battle, would you call it, where
> Words pass for bullets, dabbed in a scribble of ink?

This vivid juxtaposition of the pioneers with their weak-kneed, bookish descendants becomes the main theme—in fact, the only theme—of the poem. But despite the imagery reminiscent of Eliot's *Waste Land*, Davidson did not wish to be pessimistic. Rather, he wrote his publisher, his intention was to help his reader overcome the desolation of modern life by returning to "deep sources of racial experience." In that way, it would be possible (as he phrased it in *The Tall Men*) to erect "a wall against the confusions of this night."[51]

Davidson sustains this simplistic racial vision through most of his poem, but with one striking lapse. It comes just prior to the conclusion when the narrator suddenly feels compelled to justify his marriage to a daughter of the North:

> You are Ohio. I am Tennessee.
> And in being faithful to you I have been unfaithful
> Maybe, this once, to my own.

Davidson might have excused this apostasy in a number of ways—perhaps his wife came from pioneer stock herself, for example. But instead he chooses a rationale wholly at odds with the main thrust of the poem. It was his wife's powerful and sensitive intellectuality, he claims, that overwhelmed him:

> The supple, reaching mind that leaps and conquers
> Vital and passionate after knowledge, spurning
> The weak and easy, an intellectual flame.

The passage suggests that the life of the mind, with its complex values, still held a place in Davidson's affections. The radical shift to wholesale primitivism, in other words, represented an act of will on his part that was accomplished at the price of suppressing much of his basic intellectual makeup.[52]

Tate, with whom Davidson had long been in the habit of exchanging poems for criticism, was predictably appalled by *The Tall Men*. Despite his own burgeoning southern patriotism, Tate could not endorse so facile a solution to the problems posed by Modernism, and he repeatedly advised his friend to abandon the work. "You are really trying to write a history of your mind," Tate correctly observed, "but this mind is not so simple as you think; it cannot be homogeneously accounted for as your schematism would lead one to believe." Davidson would always insist that Tate's harsh criticism did not mark a break in their friendship, but in fact it did, with Davidson increasingly committing himself from this time on to a strident, unabashed, and unambiguous celebration of the provincial South.[53]

One can also see this change reflected in Davidson's attitudes toward New York and the North generally. As late as November, 1925, the city still seemed a mecca to him. When Tate mentioned a possible appointment for him at Columbia, Davidson was quite enthusiastic. His willingness to move North diminished steadily through 1926, however, as he worked on *The Tall Men* and read extensively in southern history and literature. By March, 1927, we find him fuming to Tate about "midwestern jackasses" and "Yale-Harvard-Princeton pretty boys" dominating the New York literary scene. "As a Southerner, egad, and a gentleman (I hope) of independent mind, I hate these cliques and Star Chambers," he informed his friend. "I propose to fight 'em like hell." The occasion for this outburst was the *Nation's* choice of a Modernist poem over one of Davidson's for its annual poetry prize. That a major northern publisher was about to issue *The Tall Men* made no difference; Davidson was taking refuge in his simple southernism and nothing could qualify his emotions. By May, as he, Tate, and Ransom discussed plans for the symposium, the same Donald Davidson who a year and a half earlier was contemplating making his career in New York was now virtually foaming at the mouth about the terrible North. "There are so many things which make me mad," he wrote Tate in this context. "Good God, what is a man to do to remain decent?"[54]

It was in this mood—so different from Ransom's—that Davidson approached the Agrarian movement. Early plans for the symposium had called for a book of detached scholarly articles on southern culture past and present, but by 1929 Davidson was insisting that only a "group of openly partisan documents" would suffice. Above all he wanted "action," not mere intellectualizing. Military rhetoric and an air of conspiracy permeated his correspondence with his friends. In his eyes, *I'll Take My Stand* was to be the first shot in a prolonged campaign to bring the North to its knees, culturally and politically. This was war against an entrenched, well-equipped, cunning, and particularly noxious enemy, and no amount of vigilance was excessive. Still, Davidson was not yet prepared to abandon everything to the cause. He retained much of the old Fugitive belief that literature should be kept separate from politics and judged by its own standards. When Tate in late 1929 upbraided him for condemning the work of Ernest Hemingway as anti-Agrarian, Davidson was most contrite. "I've felt for quite a while that I was in danger of losing balance and becoming merely a cantankerous localist," he admitted, "and your admonishment warms my conscience to its task." In addition, Davidson, with his precarious personal finances, did not wish to jeopardize his standing at Vanderbilt, where New South ideology continued to reign and Agrarianism came to be looked upon as only slightly more respectable than Bolshevism. Hence, no matter how strong his private feelings, Davidson at this time exercised caution in his public utterances.[55]

As John Stewart notes, Davidson's contribution to the symposium can be read as an apologia for his growing militance. "A Mirror for Artists" begins by recasting Matthew Arnold's familiar critique of industrial society into agrarian terms. The chief complaint is that art, under industrialism, is divorced from the real business of life and relegated to the status of mere entertainment. Moreover, Davidson points out, an inherent conflict exists between the efficiency ethic of industrialism and the leisure and stability required for the artistic life. At this juncture, however, he parts company with Arnold and with Arnold's latter-day disciples, the New Humanists led by Irving Babbitt, whose remedy is to restore High Culture to its former eminence. Museums, libraries, and concert halls only heighten the dissociation between life and art in Davidson's view; they represent the "mark of a diseased, not a healthy civilization." The only abiding solution, we are told, is to transform the economic base of society from industrial to agrarian, thus creating a world in which culture again becomes part of everyday life. And it is the artist who must take the major responsibility for effecting this change. He must drop everything, "step into the ranks and bear the brunt against the common foe" despite the immense personal cost, for his sole alternative is continued spiritual exile.[56]

Curiously, though, the South is mentioned only briefly in "A Mirror for Artists," and then in rather indirect fashion. The region is "worthy of the most heroic effort that men can give in a time of crisis," Davidson claims, not for its own sake, but because it stands as a "living example" of the kind of society he has in mind. Industrialism has not fully taken hold there, and its people, still relatively "homogeneous," live close to the soil. The South may yet resist the temptations of modernity if native writers can be persuaded to do battle for their tradition—again, not for chauvinistic reasons, but because the southern way of life just happens to be an agrarian one. These disclaimers make one suspicious. For all his talk of championing agrarianism, for instance, it is noteworthy that he gives the agrarian existence far less concrete and detailed treatment than one might expect. Compared with the symposium essay by Andrew Nelson Lytle graphically entitled "The Hind Tit," Davidson's piece is cast primarily in abstract terms. We find nothing like Lytle's injunction to "throw out the radio and take down the fiddle from the wall." For in actuality Davidson cared little about rural life—unlike Lytle he never had nor would reside on a farm. What concerned him most was resolving the cultural conflict inside him, along with the fervent southern patriotism he was barely able to suppress.[57]

These deeper issues prompting Davidson's Agrarianism surfaced a few years later in an essay significantly titled "Southern Literature: A Partisan View." Although he still spoke dutifully about the artist maintaining an "equilibrium between interest and detachment," his essential thesis now was that loyalty to the region constituted the sine qua non of the southern writer and must be preserved at all costs. A critical or unflattering treatment of southern society represented apostasy, he claimed. Writers who indulged in such exercises were allowing a "cosmopolitan, denaturizing" national culture to rob them of their "rightful inheritance." To be sure, Davidson recognized that the dilemma he had complained of in "The Artist as Southerner" had not disappeared, that the clash of two cultures could still lead to a paralyzing ambivalence:

> The southern writer finds himself inhibited at the very moment when the greatest opportunities seem to open before him. The social programs that emanate from the metropolis, bearing in their train a host of powerful aesthetic ideas and literary modes, urge him in one direction. His sense of loyalty to his own tradition, indeed his fidelity as an artist to his subject-matter, pulls him in an opposite direction. There is a tragic contradiction, which results in painful self-consciousness, in split personalities, in dubious retreats, in Hamlet hesitations.

In 1925, Davidson had offered no solution to this quandary, but in the early 1930s he did—partisan involvement in the Agrarian movement.[58]

But the problem was that Davidson, for all his disdain of doubt and inner division, possessed a thoroughly divided mind. He might take comfort in conceiving of himself as a literary Tall Man, filling his correspondence to Tate with military rhetoric and boasting proudly of how he had inherited all the "bellicose tendencies" of his ancestors—"that much, at least." But alongside this bravado he complained incessantly of chronic depression, of having the "fighting spirit and vitality knocked out of me." This refrain became so constant during the 1930s, in fact, that it helped cool his relationship with the other Agrarians. Davidson, Tate once remarked to John Gould Fletcher, was a man "temperamentally incapable of action" who loved to spin plans, but who "invariably, and unconsciously, frames them so that they will never be tested out." Ransom noted repeatedly how Davidson was fast "developing into Hamlet" with his "moping melancholia" and inability to make decisions. "His trouble is pretty deep," Ransom submitted. The deeper that depression—the more Davidson engaged in "dubious retreats" and "Hamlet hesitations"—the more intense his sectional militance became. Verbal warfare served a compensatory function for him. Within his own frame of reference, he was not in the least a Tall Man, but a weak-kneed intellectual taking the streetcar to work each day in Nashville. Only a fusillade of Agrarian polemics could hide that stubborn fact from his view and enable him to banish his deep-rooted ambivalence from his consciousness.[59]

In 1932 Davidson started a series of articles, later collected as *The Attack on Leviathan*, in which he argued the case for southern sectionalism with mounting boldness. One stimulus was the appearance of Frederick Jackson Turner's *The Significance of Sections in American History*, a book that seemed to lend Davidson's position a degree of intellectual respectability. At a deeper level, as Michael O'Brien points out, his deteriorating relationship with his Agrarian friends—worsened by the Puritanical streak in his nature that would not permit him to drink or socialize with them—helped erode his previous caution in avoiding extremist postures. Moreover, his fear that northern liberals who seemed to be taking charge of the New Deal would soon tamper with southern race relations made him more combative. But again the prime motivation was his desire to overcome inner doubt, to wall off forever the "confusions of this night." If other members of the group were wavering or even retreating, then he would take *his* stand alone, whatever the opprobrium.[60]

In these essays Davidson tried hard to preserve his objectivity and reasonableness. Sections arose from the varying geography of the American continent, he wrote, and it was only natural that their "organic" social and cultural differences be reflected in politics. In the past the sections had engaged in constant warfare, most conspicuously the massive violence of the 1860s, with the Northeast exercising uncontested "sectional imperialism" ever since Reconstruction. However, now that the depression had undermined the Northeast's dominance Davidson hoped a new "equilibrium" could be achieved allowing the sections to live together peacefully under a loose federalism. Davidson even reached out to embrace southern social scientists like Howard Odum and the concept of regional planning so long as the planning took local mores into account. Above all Davidson strove to present himself as a pluralist whose advocacy of the South represented part of a broader effort to foster American diversity. "We are a heterogeneous people," he explained, "who in sheer consistence of democratic principle have learned to tolerate a mixture of religions and races." In this formulation, ironically, sectionalism became the very essence of Americanism.[61]

But as soon as Davidson turned to the characterization of specific sections, this hopeful pluralism quickly broke down. Aside from some polite comments about northern Vermont (where he spent his summers), the only part of the country he praised continuously was the South. The Northeast, it seemed, had long been embarked on a sordid campaign of industrial aggression. The "sucking tentacle-tip" of its "money octopus" had been "flung far" across the land so that the "Northeast may walk in silk and satin." The Middle West he described as a land of mindless mass production and mechanized farming, an area beset by "ugliness, drought, congestion, stockyards, slums, duststorms," its literature an artistic desert of dull realism and its culture the "spirit of Rotary." So much for a region whose farmers Davidson was ostensibly trying to woo to the Agrarian cause. As for the West, Davidson confessed he knew little about it and so paid it almost no attention at all.[62]

More striking still, what Davidson admired in the South was precisely its success in avoiding the melting pot. There one found the largest concentration of "old colonial stock" left in America, he boasted, as opposed to the "foreign strains" that were coming to predominate elsewhere. New York was "already a foreign city" in his estimate, full of "motley immigrant groups." Thanks to its demographic good fortune, the South had been able so far to reject the decadent cosmopolitan culture of "modernism" that New York had imported wholesale from Europe and that was now spreading through the rest of the country like a dread disease. Modernism had made some inroads in the South: one could see it in the way ancient folk ballads had been replaced by "a 'mammy song' devised in Tin Pan Alley by the urbanized descendant of a Russian Jew." But Davidson was confident that the region's "fighting tradition" would ultimately stave off this alien peril. Let the Modernists and reformers beware, he warned, for the southerner "will be ready with his rampart of cotton-bales and mud, and his line of rifles that do not miss." So much for heterogeneity.[63]

The South he arrived at in his prose writings, then, was the same South of stalwart certainty he had celebrated poetically in *The Tall Men*. The frontier had gone, but its "heroic tradition" survived in the "intensity of conviction" embedded in the southern character. The southerner has "little capacity for being intellectually disinterested," Davidson explained. "He must take sides, he must be a partisan, . . . doubt runs against his grain." Other sections might succumb to Modernist dissolution, but the South "offers its people belief rather than doubt, conviction rather than skepticism, loyalty rather than distrust." Such traits were of particular importance to the poet, who "must believe or perish." With such words Davidson summarily dispatched—or tried to dispatch—the chronic ambivalence that had dogged him ever since he had found himself suspended between two cultures. This mythical South was to be his anchor, his simple solution to the perplexing problems of his age, and he would cling to it fiercely the rest of his life.[64]

As the years passed, the xenophobia, paranoia, and racism in Davidson's thought became increasingly pronounced. He had always displayed a special sensitivity about racism, as witnessed by his heated attempt to keep Robert Penn Warren's essay on southern blacks out of *I'll Take My Stand* because it seemed too liberal. The legal attack on segregation beginning in the late 1930s brought out the worst in Davidson. Although he had remained a New Dealer through Roosevelt's first term, endorsing such programs as progressive taxation and aid to sharecroppers, after 1936 he became frightened by the Democratic party's efforts to woo black voters in northern cities. The South, he realized, would soon face political isolation. Now the New Deal appeared to him as yet another manifestation of New York imperialism bent on creating the Leviathan state:

> We keep the fiction of democracy, but behind the fiction, what do we see? The strongest central government we have ever known; the most elaborately restrictive and regulative laws; a continually increasing tendency of the government to call for and indeed to exact unanimity of opinion, to brook no criticism, to demand almost servile obedience. The Democratic party itself, still invoking the name of Jefferson, has taken these steps, using the idea-men of the North as its Dorian knights and the Southern politicians as its willing helots.

Such outbursts became still more frequent after the Second World War. By the 1950s, one finds the sad spectacle of this former Agrarian writing propaganda pamphlets for the Southern States Industrial Council and heading up the Tennessee Federation for Constitutional Government's campaign to spur massive resistance against federal civil rights enforcement in the state.[65]

With his activities and pronouncements becoming steadily more embarrassing to them, many of his former comrades started to draw away. Also contributing to his growing isolation was the change several noticed in his personality. The enthusiastic young poet of his earlier career was fast turning into an embittered polemicist with a one-track mind. Tate would warn him that "you have put such a dense barrier between your friends and your private life that we cannot penetrate it," but to no avail. Davidson replied to such criticisms that he too felt this keen sense of "intellectual isolation, this lack of communion," and that it had begun "before any of you left these parts," but its cause was a "mystery I can't solve." Thus while Ransom, Tate, Warren, Lytle, and Owsley went on to greater national recognition after the mid-1930s, Davidson drifted steadily away from national attention until he had become little more than a local curiosity at Vanderbilt, an angry old man keeping the Agrarian flame burning long after the movement had died. In his own terms Davidson had succeeded: he had indeed managed to put the confusions of the Modernist night safely behind a wall. But at how immense a price.[66]

CHAPTER 8

THE DIVIDED MIND
OF ALLEN TATE

If John Crowe Ransom attempted to embrace the Agrarian faith but could not long sustain it, and if Donald Davidson took his stand all too well by act of will, then Allen Tate might best be described as one who became an Agrarian by the most delicate intellectual balancing act. With scrupulous, often tortuous logic Tate edged his way toward a position from which he could give himself over to passionate belief. Thoroughly steeped in Modernist culture and aesthetics, more so than any of his Nashville colleagues save Warren, Tate could not put aside the imperatives of his cosmopolitanism and relativism. At the same time he yearned for a simple, absolute system of thought with an intensity greater even than Davidson's. Moreover, because of his Modernist tendencies to introspection and candor, Tate proceeded in his search for a fixed faith with complete self-consciousness. As one writer notes, Tate was not only aware of what he was trying to do, he "even seems to be aware of his awareness." In this respect, precisely because his inner divisions were sharpest and his struggle to surmount them the most complex and heroic, Tate may stand as the epitome of the Agrarian mentality. Certainly others in the group sensed this fact, referring to him as their intellectual "nucleus," the true spiritual leader of their movement.[1]

The deep cultural division in Tate developed directly from his family background. He was born November 19, 1899, in Winchester, Kentucky, the third son of parents whose troubled relationship reflected the predominant social tensions of the South. His father, from middle-class Piedmont stock, was a ne'er-do-well businessman whose fortunes ebbed steadily through his life, causing Tate to speak afterwards of how his father "had humiliated us." His mother, by contrast, could, and frequently did trace her origins to the Virginia Tidewater aristocracy. Her family, the Varnells, had been moderately prosperous slaveholders in Fairfax County before the war and could even claim a distant lateral relationship to George Washington. Lest her children forget this heritage, she would take them on ritual summer pilgrimages to the ruins of Pleasant Hill, her family's old plantation, where they would stand for a time surveying the remnant of the foundation and chimneys. In this way strains of Old South and New South mingled in Tate's background, with defeat, decline, and compensatory fantasy strongly coloring each.[2]

Nor did the circumstances of his childhood help mitigate the effect of what he would later call "my terrible family." As relations between his parents deteriorated, he frequently found himself living with his mother apart from his father, absorbing her increasingly mythological account of his ancestry. On some occasions, he reports, the family would move as often as two or three times a year as his mother tried frantically to protect herself and her sons from reality. To a certain extent she succeeded: not until after her death, when he was thirty years old, did Tate learn that he had actually been born in Kentucky, and not in Fairfax as his mother had told him. Everything, in fact, came to seem shifting and impermanent to him. The family's migratory habits did not permit him to develop friendships with other children, or even to attend school regularly. Indeed, it is striking how Tate in his youth enjoyed anything but the stable community life he would later champion as an Agrarian.* The psychological sources of his lifelong quest for rootedness (along with his great discomfort whenever it came within reach) are not far to seek.[3]

Tate's existence changed dramatically in 1918 on entering college at Vanderbilt. There he met Ransom, Davidson, and others of a literary bent whose influence soon led him to abandon his intention of becoming a classicist in favor of poetry. Thanks to Davidson, he was invited to join the Fugitives in November, 1921, becoming the only undergraduate among the magazine's founders. Surely this was a decisive event for him, for the group provided him not only with close personal friendships and a lasting sense of intellectual community, but also with a secure tie to the South. Whatever else he might become, he could always fall back on his initial professional identity as a Fugitive poet.[4]

To be sure, the role Tate played within the Fugitives was that of young

---

*It is noteworthy that the other two leading Agrarians, Ransom and Davidson, also spent their childhoods moving from town to town. Ransom, whose father as a Methodist preacher was constantly transferred from one church to another, moved with his family no less than eight times. Those critics who have portrayed the Agrarians as men looking back nostalgically on the rooted community life they had supposedly enjoyed as youths are obviously mistaken.

rebel, casting himself as the solitary embattled Modernist marooned among provincial conservatives. He delighted in perplexing the brethren with his difficult verse, employing obscure imagery, highly esoteric vocabulary, and irregular rhyme and meter. "The unique virtue of the contemporary revolt," he argued in a 1922 editorial, "is its break, in a positive direction, with the tyranny of representation." Since the "world as it is doesn't afford accurate correlatives of all the emotional complexes and attitudes," he explained, artists were "justified in not only re-arranging . . . but remaking, remoulding, in a subjective order, the stuff they must necessarily work with—the material world." When this theory of poetry drew fire from others in the group, especially Ransom, it only served to embolden Tate in his experimentalism. As he once commented to Davidson, he could not resist his inclination "to sympathize with almost anything revolutionary, sensible or not."[5]

Most importantly, Tate arrived at this position essentially on his own. Before he "was really reading . . . the moderns," recalls Robert Penn Warren, "he had become a modern, his whole sensibility." Through Ransom's influence Tate had been exploring the French Symbolists, along with various Elizabethan poets of the metaphysical school, and he had found that their vision comported well with his own experience of flux and impermanence. He thus traveled a parallel route with other literary rebels of his generation, a fact he remained unaware of until the early summer of 1922 when Hart Crane, writing to praise one of Tate's poems in the *Double Dealer*, compared it to the work of T. S. Eliot. Tate promptly discovered Eliot and realized that he had a new master to set alongside Ransom. Soon Crane was shipping him copies of the *Little Review* and otherwise helping to put him in touch with his contemporaries. However, this new contact with the wider world did not produce any radical change in his poetry or outlook. On the contrary, its main effect was to cement tendencies already present, making Modernism his instinctive mode of thought and expression. "I defend modernism just as I would defend legs and arms if somehow they came after abdomens and necks," he wrote Davidson. It was that automatic and inescapable.[6]

Ever the self-conscious intellectual, Tate assiduously sought out the philosophical premises to undergird his developing sensibility. Vanderbilt left him with abiding interests in philosophy and psychology, two fields in which he now read widely. As early as August, 1922, he arrived at the insight that would lie at the center of all his subsequent thought: that the profound "dissociation of sensibility" (in Eliot's phrase) that afflicted modern man must be cured by closing the breach between reason and emotion. Emotion, Tate flatly insisted to Davidson, "is not a real division of the mind, but only an aspect of it, inseparable from any mental state,

9. Allen Tate in the early 1920s
Courtesy The Fugitive Collection, Special Collections,
Vanderbilt University Library

however 'intellectual' that state may seem." As Tate well knew, this concept of emotion thoroughly undercut Victorian moral dualism by making man's animality an integral part of his nature that one could not evade or disguise:

> If the brutal is sentimentalized into a scheme of pretty flowers and birds, the ladies like it, for that adequately justifies a human element the unadorned truth of which they will not face. Sentimentality excuses all. The Moderns know that passion is vestigial of the brute and tell us so.

But here, having reached the crux of Modernist thought, Tate beats a slight, though most revealing, retreat. If the "Moderns" feel obligated to acknowledge human passion, he adds, they

> do not love it. Since Irony is the keynote to life, they throw, for this effect, the bare flesh into sharp contrast with the mind. The flesh is the scourge of intellect, but art takes no sides, and so the result is simply spirit and body juxtaposed.

Achieving the full integration of sensibility he desired would plainly require more than leaving "spirit and body juxtaposed." Beset by the nineteenth-century values instilled during his upbringing, Tate, like Odum and Faulkner, was half appalled at the direction in which he was moving and, again like them, would periodically halt midway to his destination.[7]

On the whole, however, Tate's aesthetic theory was firmly Modernist. He described poetry as the "expression of the whole mind," an attempt by the poet to capture "successive instances of the whole rhythm of thought, and that includes reason, emotion, [and] extralogical experience." In practice this meant free association, the technique through which the poet mingled imagery and visions from the subconscious mind with the more calculated productions of the rational intellect. Poetry written in this manner might be difficult, violent, or ugly, but at least it would be honest: it would express real and "objective" emotions rather than the contrived sentimental ones of the Victorians. This was why the Symbolists were so important, for they had shown how poets could use external objects as symbols for the subterranean feelings they discovered inside themselves—in Tate's words, as "sign-posts upon which the poet may hang his attitudes, his sensibility." Tate fully realized the limitations of such art, but felt that under the conditions of the twentieth century, with its fragmentation of beliefs and values, the modern poet had no choice. The best he could do was to transcribe his sensibility accurately, even though "from the data of his experience he infers only a distracting complexity."[8]

By mid-1924 Tate was living in New York City, leading the existence of the Greenwich Village literati. After graduating from college he had toyed with the idea of pursuing an advanced degree in English, but he could not obtain the needed fellowship because of the opposition of Edwin Mims, chairman of the Vanderbilt department and a prime example of the sort of nineteenth-century mentality Tate detested. Convinced that the South was a "region none too friendly at best" for a young poet, he taught high school for a semester in Lumberport, West Virginia, then used the proceeds to make his way North. His reaction to the city is striking in view of his future Agrarianism. Put simply, he loved New York at the outset. He was overcome by the excitement of the place, marveled at the technology, and thoroughly enjoyed the company he found among Hart Crane's friends. He became a full-fledged member of this circle, which included Malcolm Cowley, Kenneth Burke, E. E. Cummings, Matthew Josephson, Edmund Wilson, John Dos Passos, and James Light, the director of the avant-garde Provincetown Theater. He thought these people congenial, serious about their work, and "much less theory-ridden than we Fugitives." They did not haggle about Modernist experimentation, but accepted it as a basic fact of literary life. Tate thrived in this atmosphere. "I'm enjoying life tremendously and have never felt better," he reported to Davidson. "It's great to get up at eight and feel so good you have to take calisthenics to calm yourself."9

Within a few years, however, Tate's attitudes toward the city began to shift. Even at the height of his exuberance he had complained of the frantic pace and cultural anarchy. By early 1926 these discontents had greatly intensified. As John Stewart explains, the license and vitality Tate had once valued so highly in New York now seemed to endanger his very being:

> Rebellion had some meaning when the opposition was so clear [in Nashville], and a rebel was a rebel. But in New York City, anything went—and in such freedom, nothing was. The poetic license to explore the farthest reaches of his inward experience which he had demanded among the Fugitives was taken for granted as part of a bewildering total freedom that threatened to undermine all values and identity.

Tate thought that he had reached intellectual bedrock with his Modernist beliefs; he had reconciled himself to the Modernist portrait of reality as one of "distracting complexity." So he had written in the *Fugitive*. But two years in Greenwich Village left him grasping for a new anchor, for some device to give him a chance for stability amidst the fast-flowing current of cultural change. Instinctively he moved his family out of the city to a country house in Patterson, New York, where he spent much of his time tending to manual chores. And, just as instinctively, his thoughts turned increasingly to the South.[10]

Tate would later place the crucial moment of transformation in the fall of 1926 as he began work on "Ode to the Confederate Dead," by far his best-known poem. He had not at first realized that the poem was to be anything out of the ordinary, but as the verse took form in his mind with its imagery of the "inscrutable infantry rising" and the "furious murmur of their chivalry," he knew that he had touched on material of immense significance for him. The poem, he told Davidson, "came out of God-knows-where (as most poems do); and after it was on paper it served to bring up a whole stream of associations and memories, suppressed, at least on the emotional plane, since my childhood." Once the "Ode" started the flow, the stream proceeded at floodtide until, by March of 1927, Tate had become preoccupied with reestablishing his link with southern tradition. Yet he knew from the start that he would fail, that the heritage he wished to repossess would always elude him. He could immerse himself in southern history, explore his genealogy, and announce to the world that he had become an unabashed sectional chauvinist; no matter, his Modernist self-consciousness stood irrevocably between him and the identification with the region he sought. His fate was to become perched on the precise balance point of ambivalence between the two cultures—a position he found alternately excruciating and delicious.[11]

This very dilemma forms the main subject of the "Ode." The narrator is a modern southerner standing by the gate of a Confederate cemetery on a gray autumn day oppressed by the thought that the heroic tradition represented by the dead buried there can never be his. He tries to picture the soldiers charging in fury at "Shiloh, Antietam, Malvern Hill, Bull Run," but his strict empiricism enables him to see only the dead leaves blowing about him, symbolizing in their fall the ultimate futility of existence to which modern man stands condemned in the naturalistic universe. His is a world governed by a positivism that undercuts the possibility of sustained faith or inspired action:

> You who have waited for the angry resolution
> Of those desires that should be yours tomorrow,
> You know the unimportant shrift of death
> And praise the vision
> And praise the arrogant circumstances
> Of those who fall
> Rank upon rank, hurried beyond decision—
> Here by the sagging gate, stopped by the wall.

Tate's narrator envies the fierce convictions that impelled the Confederates to hurl themselves at the enemy oblivious of danger while for him there is only the "unimportant shrift of death." Yet even as he commemorates their heroism his skeptical mind suddenly realizes that they might not have charged out of conviction at all, but may merely have been "hurried beyond decision" in the heat of battle. Thus he is stymied, "stopped by the wall" that exists both at the cemetery's edge and within his mind.[12]

In contrast to Davidson in "The Tall Men," Tate ends his poem on a markedly pessimistic note. His narrator asks plaintively:

> What shall we say who have knowledge
> Carried to the heart? Shall we take the act
> To the grave? Shall we, more hopeful, set up the grave
> In the house? The ravenous grave?

The key to this passage lies in the double meaning of the word "grave." By taking the "act to the grave" the narrator would be allowing his yearning for a durable faith to go the way of a naturalistic death. That is a grim choice, but the ostensibly "more hopeful" alternative of setting up the "grave in the house" and worshiping at the altar of regional pieties is hardly more palatable, for that kind of chauvinist "grave" is "ravenous" and can easily consume the spirit. Tate, one recalls, knew well the perils of the "old atavism." As he later put it in an essay explicating the poem, there is "no solution offered" in the "Ode"; rather, his intention was "to make dramatically visible the conflict, to concentrate it." He was, he now realized, the man at the cemetery gate with "knowledge carried to the heart" who might hope to gain integrity by entering the cemetery and immersing himself in all it represented on the mythological level, but who at the same time would forever be stopped by the implacable "wall" within his consciousness.[13]

Nonetheless, though aware there was no solution, Tate soon started searching for one, plunging into southernism in a determined effort to break through his ambivalence once and for all. He began by writing a biography of Stonewall Jackson, to be followed by similar volumes on Jefferson Davis and Robert E. Lee. His reading now encompassed large quantities of southern history, including war memoirs, official records of the Confederate government, and highly technical military accounts of Civil War battles. His spare moments were spent delving into his genealogy, touring battlefields, or discussing southern matters with John Gould Fletcher, the Arkansas-born Imagist poet who shared Tate's prejudices and briefly became a father-figure to Tate during this phase of Tate's career. Yet the inner divisions did not go away; they only became more complicated. The more he learned about the South, the more trouble-some he found the conflicts between Tidewater and frontier, aristocrat and yeoman, which were reflected so vividly in his own family. Equally important, the revulsion he had long felt toward the region for its back-wardness remained, despite his attempts to suppress it. "The stupidity of our people turns me in rage against them, and I wheel in greater rage against their enemies. In this state of mind it is hard to be coherent," he admitted to Fletcher in 1927. Only a firm act of will, a resolute leap into southern chauvinism, seemed to offer hope of escape from this quandary.[14]

Sustaining that act of will proved relatively easy in Tate's first endeavor as an unreconstructed southerner, the writing of *Stonewall Jackson*. The book was not only, as Tate wrote Davidson, a "stirring partisan account of the Revolution," it was also a psychological portrait of the sort of man Tate secretly wished he could be. Unlike the enervated narrator of the "Ode," Old Stonewall in this treatment does not suffer from inner doubt at all. Rather, he is a man of ironclad self-certainty whose historical circumstances afford him boundless opportunities for taking decisive action. Guided by simple, fixed principles, and fortified by an intense introspective religiosity, he pursues his objectives with a splendid ruth-lessness. At the same time, Tate's Jackson curiously exhibits characteris-tics one might normally associate with a Greenwich Village intellectual. We are reminded often of Jackson's formidable mind, with its "intellec-tual power of a high order," and of his aloof and eccentric behavior, which his associates continually puzzled over but which, Tate pointedly remarks, is the sure sign of "character" in both generals and poets. Here, in sum, was a man for whom intellect and action coexisted easily, who did not suffer from cultural disarray and paralysis. Here was the model Tate was looking for in his foray into the southern past.[15]

However, problems arose as soon as Tate began describing antebellum society. Until this time Tate in his social philosophy had generally favored the same liberal program of social "progress" advocated by New South writers like Edwin Mims, although Tate usually added a touch of in-tellectual elitism to the formula. "Dr. Mims' viewpoint is liberal and I like it," he commented to Davidson in June, 1926, even though Mims "doesn't see that . . . the first duty of a society is to produce first-class minds, liberal or illiberal." To embrace southern tradition wholeheartedly thus required a sharp turn to the right, which is exactly what Tate pro-ceeded to do in *Stonewall Jackson*. Echoing George Fitzhugh, he con-tended that the South had entered the Civil War to defend its virtuous "existing order of a stable, landed society." He especially praised the discipline and organization of the Confederate army, picturing it admiringly as moving "with the precision of a machine." Even Jackson's home "was run like a battalion of artillery. There was a time for everything and everything had its place." The North, by contrast, was in the midst of a massive cultural revolution based on the fateful concept of freedom:

> When such a revolution triumphs, society becomes a chaos of self-interest. Its freedom is the freedom to do wrong. This does not mean that all men will do the wrong thing; only that no external order exists which precludes the public exercise of wrong impulses; too much, in short, is left to the individual.

The Old South, Tate insisted, protected the individual against this nightmare. It offered community in place of self-interest, order instead of chaos.[16]

Unfortunately for Tate, though, the Modernist half of his sensibility instinctively rebelled against discipline of any kind, whether in art or life, and his empirical bent brought him repeatedly to evidence that undermined his thesis. Tate might esteem Jackson's personality on one level, but he could not help noticing how his hero was in fact a "humorless, unimaginative man, exact as a multiplication table." Given the discipline supposedly inherent in antebellum southern character, moreover, it was noteworthy that Jackson had to labor mightily to control his troops, for, as Tate conceded, "they were free men; they had been brought up to believe in personal liberty." The very landscape, he found, was anything but orderly—in most cases it was a "jungle," with roads "crooked and uncharted." "Tidewater Virginia after two hundred fifty years of European culture was a desolate wilderness," he sadly concluded.[17]

Yet, in the face of these contrary insights, Tate still clung to his vision of the Old South as a unified, stable, and civilized society struggling against a turbulent, individualistic North. Michael O'Brien puts it succinctly: "This view of the Civil War was the mirror image of the warfare in Tate's mind between a religious temperament and an atheist mind, a conservative view of culture and a modernist training. Tate was as divided against himself in 1928 as had been the Union in 1861. The Confederacy stood for what he wanted to be, the Union for a pessimistic diagnosis of what he feared he was." The further he immersed himself in southernism, the more divided he became, and the harder he would struggle in turn to perfect his belief in the southern myth. But he could not like Davidson simply submerge himself in the myth, nor could he like Ransom preserve a degree of stoic detachment from the whole business. Trapped in his illimitable ambivalence, he could only battle helplessly onward knowing that he was doomed to fail.[18]

I

In late September, 1928, with his grandfather's gold-headed cane in one hand and Jefferson Davis's two-volume history of the Confederacy under the other, Tate boarded ship with his family for a prolonged stay in Europe courtesy of the Guggenheim Foundation during which he was to complete his book on Davis. Although the Tates spent the bulk of their visit in Paris, getting to know the more celebrated expatriates like Ernest Hemingway, F. Scott Fitzgerald, Ford Madox Ford, and John Peale Bishop, they first lived for two months in London, a period critical to Tate's development because it finally gave him the chance to meet Thomas Stearns Eliot. Eliot, along with Ransom, had served as Tate's chief literary mentor since 1922. Despite a Midwestern childhood and a New England education, he had covered much the same ground and encountered the same perplexities as had Tate—his was a sensibility divided between Modernist liberation and Victorian moralism. Eliot's solution had also been an attempt to embrace a traditional culture that bespoke order and stability, that of the British upper class. Just as Tate, upon his return from Europe in early 1930, was to seek to live his myth by moving to the Tennessee countryside, Eliot had set himself up as a gentlemanly man of letters in London and had joined the Anglican church. Eliot was bound to make a significant impact on his young admirer, intensifying Tate's search for a moral and philosophical bedrock.[19]

First, however, came a resurgence of Tate's democratic liberalism reminiscent of his original enthusiasm for New York. As an American discovering the Old World he initially felt "quite superior" to the class-ridden society he encountered and pronounced himself a "confirmed democrat." In November, 1928, he reported that his favorite among the presidential contenders was the socialist Norman Thomas, though he also liked the progressive governor of New York, Al Smith. Indeed, what he most admired about Eliot at this time, he claimed, was the "very American" way Eliot had worked himself up, Horatio Alger-style, in the British literary establishment. But, almost predictably, a polar shift soon took place. As in New York, the apparent chaos of the intellectual scene began to oppress him, and increasingly he turned rightward for relief. By the spring of 1929 one finds him agreeing with Fletcher on the need for an aristocracy and horrifying Davidson by talking of entering the Catholic church "to find some ultimate discipline of the soul." By August the course was complete: he was counseling his friends that they would have to "go the whole hog of reaction" and champion feudalism in order to save the world. "We must be the last Europeans," he insisted, "there being no Europeans in Europe at present."[20]

The deep cultural divisions in Tate responsible for this political pendulum swing showed up equally vividly in his biography of Jefferson Davis, his most comprehensive statement of his Agrarian view of southern history. It begins boldly enough with the assertion that the Old South had represented the "last stronghold of European civilization in the western hemisphere, a conservative check upon the restless expansiveness of the industrial North." Indeed, by 1850 the South had become "more European than Europe." But there were difficulties sustaining this claim. Tate knew too much about the areas where his ancestors had lived—the Tidewater and the Piedmont backwoods—to mythologize them in this fashion. Thus he found it necessary to locate his feudal ideal exclusively in the Lower South. Tate also knew, however, that throughout the antebellum period the Deep South was controlled principally by parvenus much like Jefferson Davis's father Samuel who had started off as crude frontiersmen. If that was so, how could one call this society, or the South generally, a feudal domain—the last bastion of civilization in America?[21]

In circumventing this problem, Tate, the would-be reactionary, ironically anticipated the thesis that the Marxist historian Eugene D. Genovese was to propound forty years later in his writings on the South. Like Genovese, Tate contended that the enormous wealth made possible by cotton planting had produced "rapid stratification" in Deep South society, with the result that an authentic "agrarian ruling class" had sprung up "almost overnight." "Like *nouveaux riches* everywhere," he noted, these men "speedily took on the customs and manners of the local *haute noblesse*" until, by the time of secession, many had acquired a "knowledge of the humanities superior to the New Englanders." An excellent example of this transformation was the way in which "Samuel Davis, a plain man, became the symbol of knightly grace." Simultaneously this new aristocracy was becoming conscious of its class interests, repudiating "Jefferson's moment of heresy" and formulating a "new philosophy of inequality" more appropriate to its situation.[22]

Most important, that philosophy rested solidly upon what Tate termed the "patriarchal idea" and Genovese "seigneurialism," a sense of social responsibility arising directly from the ownership of tangible property. In Tate's view, such a relationship was the only sure antidote to capitalist greed:

> This identification of power and responsibility is the best basis for
> a society; in the Lower South it produced a genuine ruling class.
> Men were bound by their responsibility to a definite physical
> legacy—land and slaves—which more and more, as Southern
> society tended to become stable after 1850, checked the desire for

mere wealth and power. Men are everywhere the same, and it is only the social system that imposes a check upon the acquisitive instinct, accidentally and as the condition of a certain prosperity, that in the end makes for stability and creates the close ties among all classes which distinguished a civilization from a mere social machine.

Here was the crux of Tate's interpretation of the Old South, and the basis upon which he built his Agrarian theory. In his search for certainty he had arrived at a belief in philosophical materialism in which the ownership of property determined social relations and even, to some extent, human nature. It was this materialism that brought him so close to Marxist thought.[23]

Whatever merit this rendering of southern history might have in Genovese's hands, it was a strange one for Tate to adopt. Few men took more pleasure in distinguishing between pretension and nobility than he. To stake his claim for the South on the Cotton Snobs violated many of his most cherished sentiments, whether derived from his Virginia or Kentucky backgrounds. In addition, as he would acknowledge in subsequent writings, he was taking grave liberties with historical accuracy by underplaying evidence of the planters' inescapable ties to the capitalist market through their need to sell cotton and obtain credit, as well as their constant speculation in land and slaves. Nor was Allen Tate by any means capable of becoming a consistent materialist given his commitment to the power of human consciousness. In 1929, however, he was willfully giving himself over to his new mythology, as much to convince himself as his reader. He knew full well, as he accurately put it, that the world of Jefferson Davis had in fact been "new and expansive, unbound by strong local tradition," yet a few pages later he could argue that that same society had spearheaded secession to "perpetuate a stable and deeply rooted way of life."[24]

Tate's portrait of Davis himself also deserves comment. If Stonewall Jackson epitomized for Tate the man of bold action, Davis was the opposite: a hopeless intellectual whose decisiveness was undermined by the "curious separation of his intellect and his feelings." Again and again Tate held that the South might well have won the war had it been led by men of "fierce unreasoning Southern patriotism" like Robert Barnwell Rhett instead of those like Davis who suffered from a "divided mind." When the Confederacy needed a demagogue to rouse the people to sacrifice, it got in Davis a "studious, neurotic egotist" who cared only about vindicating his abstract principles. "The theory of state may be learned in the cloister," Tate lectured Davis, "but politics only in the street." Tate was clearly projecting many of his own apprehensions about himself onto Davis, intent that he would not make the same errors.[25]

In mid-1929, as *Jefferson Davis* was being published, Tate reached the crescendo of his attempt to will himself into a fixed and unified set of beliefs. When Davidson and Ransom sent word of developing plans for the southern symposium, he responded with a far more drastic proposal for an "academy of Southern positive reactionaries" founded upon a "long and elaborate philosophical constitution." The document would be signed by all members and would set forth a "complete social, philosophical, literary, economic, and religious system." Only in this way, he maintained, could they create an intellectual dialogue *"internal to the South,"* one that would smoke out those "muddling and *unorganized"* southern liberals who so irresponsibly mixed foreign ideas with those appropriate to their region. To achieve this goal *"organization and discipline* would be *indispensable."* "We must crush minor differences of doctrine under a single idea," he wrote, even though doing so would violate the hallowed southern tradition of personal independence. "Emotionally this [suppression of individuality] does me considerable violence because I am, emotionally, a Jeffersonian," he explained. "This is what I mean by discipline."[26]

By early 1930, when he returned to the United States, Tate was firmly resolved to live his beliefs. Thanks to his older brother Ben, a successful businessman in Cincinnati, he was able to buy a large antebellum farmhouse complete with pillars and verandas overlooking the Cumberland River in Clarksville, Tennessee, not far from Nashville. Tate and his wife, a fine novelist in her own right who wrote under her maiden name Caroline Gordon, spent most of their time at their typewriters, but a tenant family was employed to tend with intermittent success to the hundred acres. Visitors from the North were duly impressed, and those from Nashville suitably entertained.* But for Tate this was more than a mere gesture: rather, it was an attempt to take his social philosophy literally, despite his realization that the effort was probably as quixotic as the loaded rifle and Confederate flag over his mantlepiece. When a minor critic named Robert Shafer claimed to find "deliberate misrepresentation" and "impudence" in Tate's essay on the New Humanists, Tate took it as a personal affront rather than normal literary warfare and, to the

---

*Tate's attempt to install himself as a practicing Agrarian occasionally met with discouraging results. Soon after arriving in Clarksville, the Tates loyally attended a Confederate memorial service, only to hear the local Baptist preacher inform them that God had brought about the South's defeat in order to set the region on the New South path of industrial development! Tate to Davidson, June 5, 1930, Davidson Papers.

horror of the brethren at Vanderbilt, threatened to challenge Shafer to a duel. Northerners who learned of the controversy assumed that Tate was role-playing, but in his own mind he was dead serious. "I wished, I still wish, to do the man violence," he insisted to John Peale Bishop a year later. In short, Tate in 1930 was on fire with Agrarianism, perhaps more so than any other member of the group: he was prepared to take on the whole world if necessary.[27]

It is in the context of this intense striving for commitment that one must interpret "Remarks on the Southern Religion," Tate's contribution to the symposium. Given the circumstances, one would have expected an impassioned statement of belief from Tate, a doctrinaire treatise with claps of chauvinist thunder on every page. Instead, after five months of agonized rewriting, Tate produced a searching philosophical inquiry noteworthy for its constant refusal to alight on any firm conclusion, its confessions of the author's own religious bankruptcy, and its heretical implication that the South might be hostile ground for the development of religious faith. This was hardly what he had intended. In a preliminary sketch sent to Davidson he had assured his compatriots that his subject would be "Fundamentalism defended, and Dayton explained histori-cally" in a "plain" and "bellicose" manner. But, just like Ransom in *God Without Thunder*, Tate in the end managed to prove exactly the contrary of what he had set out to prove. Unlike Ransom, however, Tate was supremely self-conscious of his failure. Because this piece was perhaps the most self-revealing he ever wrote, it is worth a close look.[28]

"Remarks on the Southern Religion" can be divided into two main parts—the first depicting the spiritual crisis in which Tate found himself, the second asking how, if at all, the South's history might relate to the resolution of that crisis. The starting point is a condemnation of the rational intellect much akin to Ransom's. Abstraction, we are told, de-bases the human sensibility: it turns the mind into a mere machine and blocks it from apprehending concrete experience. Thus the modern ab-stract mind values the horse only for his horsepower, rather than appre-ciating him on his own terms. It uses history to demonstrate particular abstract concepts, like the idea of progress, instead of viewing the past in all its infinite variety and specificity. Most important of all, rationality and its attendant self-consciousness destroy the possibility of maintain-ing an authentic social tradition. Such a tradition, in Tate's judgment, "must be spontaneous to count at all"; it cannot be deliberately created or preserved. And since religious faith in turn depends on the existence of a living tradition, abstraction becomes the "death of religion no less than the death of anything else."[29]

To understand this essay, it is essential to realize that Tate was using "tradition" and "religion" almost interchangeably and that both were remarkably close to the Modernist definition of "culture." A tradition, he explained to Fletcher, was an "image of concrete living which fills the minds of enough people to constitute a basis of action," while by religion he meant not belief in a deity but a "profound conviction about the way life should be lived." In other words, religion for Tate meant a culture so instinctively held that its precepts were not only routinely practiced but capable of arousing the most passionate "latent" emotions. It was a psychological state in which a person felt ultimate certainty in his beliefs, full integrity within his personality, and, in Tate's phrase, a "deep unity of mind" with the other members of his society. Such a harmonious adjustment between life and thought could exist only in a relatively stable society; hence the need for tradition. Beyond this Tate vaguely hoped that religion would partake of the supernatural, or at least sur-mount the realm of naturalism, and that it would encompass a church and dogma, but he did not fare well in describing these aspects of faith. The fact that he was an "enforced atheist," as he once told Fletcher, did not make the task easier. Of one thing he was sure, though: it was impossible to contrive a genuine religion or tradition by abstract means. Both had to be completely unself-conscious to survive.[30]

It was here that Tate's spiritual crisis arose. "I am trying to discover the place that religion holds with logical, abstract instruments," he ad-mitted to his reader, "which of course tend to put religion in some logical system or series, where it vanishes." But since his was the divided sensi-bility of the modern era, he could do no other. Perhaps the "Russian or eastern European mind" could grasp the bounty of "naive religion," but an Occidental like himself was doomed to perpetual anguish since he could not escape "the existence of those halves that render our sanity so precarious and compel us to vacillate between a self-destroying natural-ism and practicality, on the one hand, and a self-destroying mysticism, on the other." Here were the two poles of his polar thought (for "mysticism" read "irrationality") that he was trying so desperately to integrate. How could a divided and overly self-conscious individual like himself find the path back to spontaneous tradition? That was the puzzle to which he de-voted the second half of the essay.[31]

The answer, he suggested, might be found in the antebellum South, but first it would be necessary to unravel the contradictions of the region's history. The chief contradiction was that the Old South had been a "feudal society without a feudal religion." It had inherited Protestantism, a "non-agrarian and trading religion," indeed "hardly a religion at all," whose tenets of rationalism and materialism ran counter to the region's true culture. Before the Civil War this mismatch had not mattered much because the South's agrarian way of life neutralized the worst effects of Protestantism, but after Appomattox the destruction of the old order left the region spiritually helpless before the inroads of industrial capitalism. "Southern nationalism would have survived a couple of centuries if Southern religion had been more in accord with Southern politics and society," Tate observed to Ransom, "(vide Ireland)."[32]

Still, despite this flaw, Tate insisted in his essay that the Old South had enjoyed a culture approaching perfection that could serve as a model for modern man. Although ostensibly Protestant, its denizens had possessed an authentically religious frame of mind: "They were virtually incapable of abstracting from the horse his horsepower, or from history its historicity." Nor did they suffer from tension or ambivalence: "The Southern mind was simple, not top-heavy with learning it had no need of, unintellectual, and composed; it was personal and dramatic; rather than abstract and metaphysical; and it was sensuous because it lived close to a natural scene of great variety and interest." In sum, Tate here depicts antebellum southerners as representing all he wished to be—spontaneous, self-possessed, liberated from the harsher demands of the intellect, and in close communion with nature.[33]

Or were they? For at this juncture Tate changes gear. No sooner does he make his ardent leap into the mythological than empiricism suddenly reclaims him. The contemporary southerner might wish to tamper with the facts, he notes, but there is no escaping the hard truth that "he inherits a concrete and very unsatisfactory history." To believe that the planters were blessed with an integrated sensibility is to descend into chauvinist fantasy: "In fact, their rational life was not powerfully united to the religious experience, as it was in medieval society, and they are a fine specimen of the tragic pitfall upon which the Western mind has always hovered." Just as, one is tempted to add, Tate's essay becomes a fine specimen of the tragic ambivalence upon which his mind had hovered and would continue to hover.[34]

This failure to find a final meaning in the southern past sets the stage for Tate's conclusion. For twenty pages he had indulged in the most intricate argumentation, to the point where Eliot would later accuse him of "refuting yourself by exhibiting that gift for abstractions which you rather depreciate when employed by a Northerner." One senses him constantly wrestling with himself, knowing full well that his performance was vitiating the message he wished to convey. Then, seemingly out of nowhere comes his famous dictum:

> We are very near an answer to our question—
> How may the Southerner take hold of his Tradition?
> The answer is, by violence.

To some extent Tate wished this remark to be taken literally, though perhaps not as literally as it was taken in the late 1930s when various critics charged him with advocating a Fascist coup d'etat. He did want to believe himself capable if necessary of decisive violent action in the manner of Stonewall Jackson. But surely Louis Rubin is closer to the mark when he interprets "violence" to mean that the modern southerner "must consciously and even abstractly *will himself* back into his tradition" even though doing so may automatically destroy that tradition. Tate was proposing, in other words, an act of cultural fiat to end his tormenting inner dualism forever by creating from his mythological heritage what he conceived of as a religious faith. Impetuous, defiant, and desperate, it was a strategy that contained within it the entire thrust of the Agrarian movement. "We are agitators trying to make a political creed do the work of religion," he told Fletcher. But as his closing paragraph indicates, Tate knew it would never work:

> The Southerner is faced with a paradox: He must use an instrument, which is political and so unrealistic and pretentious that he cannot believe in it, to re-establish a private, self-contained, and essentially spiritual life. I say that he must do this; but that remains to be seen.

Tate was still the man standing wistfully at the cemetery gate, unable to bring himself to enter.[35]

II

In the years following the publication of the symposium, Tate followed a peculiar zigzag course in regard to Agrarianism as the nineteenth- and twentieth-century halves of his sensibility tugged at each other. His recoil in fact began before the ink had properly dried on his article. He complained bitterly about Ransom and Davidson's decision to title the book "I'll Take My Stand"—a phrase lifted from the Confederate marching song "Dixie"—on the grounds that it represented an "emotional appeal to ill-defined beliefs," while the essays, he said, "justify themselves *rationally* by an appeal to principle." After long debate Tate was allowed to place a footnote at the start of his essay disclaiming the title. So much for "violence."[36]

But Tate worked hard in many ways to keep the faith during the next five years. He embarked on a book based on the history of his family, attempted a biography of Robert E. Lee, fired off a number of pro-Agrarian articles, and produced some poetry of a mildly Agrarian cast. Though most of these endeavors failed, and despite dire financial distress, Tate persisted in them out of his immense hunger for cultural rootedness. Well aware of the successful career he might have enjoyed in New York, he was convinced at this time that southerners who left the South, either physically or spiritually, "sacrifice some great part of their deepest heritage." And as he wrote Bishop, his choice was clear: "There is no other 'culture' that I can enter into . . . and of course I assume that one needs the whole pattern of life: I can't keep half of it and live on another style the other half of the time."[37]

On the political front, Tate diligently advertised himself as a fire-eating reactionary. He tilted with liberalism at every opportunity, accusing it of drifting without a comprehensive philosophy and of relying solely on the marketplace for its values. In place of its "system of money references" he wished "certain absolutes—points of moral and intellectual reference by which people can live." The only way to create such stable values, he insisted, was by first establishing a "physical background in which morality, economics, religion and art are simply different expression forms for the total mentality of society." Presumably this meant an agrarian society, but increasingly Tate chose to cast his discussion in terms of a general traditionalism with little or no mention of the South. This tendency to put the South aside became especially marked after 1933 when he struck up a friendship with the journalist Herbert Agar, who in turn introduced Tate to the work of the English Distributists and the members of the Catholic rural-life movement. Through Tate, these right-leaning groups formed a brief alliance with the Agrarians, eventuating in the symposium *Who Owns America?* coedited by Tate and Agar in 1936 and intended, in Tate's words, to "define what at present we are calling a genuine Conservative Revolution."[38]

The trouble was that throughout this period Tate's actual pronouncements on social policy closely resembled those of New Deal liberals, while his rhetoric often came out sounding quasi-Marxist. It was Tate, for example, who urged Warren and Davidson to join in protesting the arrest of a radical writers' delegation by Kentucky authorities during the Harlan County coal strike of 1931. "The protest would do much towards establishing in the public mind the existence of a disinterested class of leaders," Tate wrote them in his best Progressive voice, "since politicians are bought off, writers, i.e., students of economics, politics, science, philosophy, and literature, are taking their place. This is definitely part of our program." Davidson, who had little taste for either "disinterested" politics or the defense of radicals, refused to go along. He must also have winced when Tate supported the southern labor movement, called for programs to give blacks economic security by providing them land, and unreservedly backed the Chapel Hill concept of regional planning as an "excellent recommendation that ought to be the basis of restoring southern life." Instead of the New Deal goal of a "planned economy," Tate explained, he favored a "planned society." In practice it was hard to tell the difference.[39]

When Tate launched his polemics on the evils of capitalism, it was harder still to tell him from a contributor to the *New Masses*. With relish he attacked the American system of "middle class–capitalist hegemony" by means of which "productive property, or capital, is constantly taken from the people" until they are reduced to a "state of abject economic dependence, which approaches servility." Like a typical 1930s Marxist, Tate took special pride in exposing capitalist mythology, revealing, for instance, how democracy under the present system was purely a "rationalization" to give the masses an illusion of power while the "real political masters are the bankers and industrialists." Even the investors were being duped: relying on the economists Adolph A. Berle, Jr., and Gardiner Means, Tate pointed out that the purchase of stocks no longer constituted "effective ownership" because the shareholder "has no control over the portion of the means of production that he owns." It was all a grand conspiracy in which the "money power rules." No wonder Malcolm Cowley, after reading Tate's *Reactionary Essays on Poetry and Ideas* in 1936, was impressed at how Tate, "writing from an apparently opposite point of view . . . arrived at the same sort of social judgments that a good radical critic might reach."[40]

Of course Tate's position was not identical with that of the Marxists. Instead of transferring the ownership of the means of production to a collective state, he wished to parcel it out in the form of small enterprises (of which the most numerous would be medium-sized farms), thus giving the majority of citizens both genuine security and a sense of moral responsibility for their economic conduct. Such was the "Agrarian-Distributist" scheme. It is striking, though, that Tate set forth this vision only once in detail—in his contribution to *Who Owns America?*—and that he found that piece unusually difficult to write. What really engaged his passions was his radical animus against capitalism, a subject on which he was never at a loss for words; his advocacy of the corner grocery store, or even the family farm, was little more than a perfunctory technical exercise by contrast. All of this suggests how difficult it is to pin down Tate's politics with any precision. If he appears a true conservative at times, he may also stand as a forerunner of the revival of Populist sentiment among southern intellectuals in the late 1930s. As for his attempt to label himself a rabid reactionary, that should probably be seen, along with his Agrarianism, as yet another paradoxical manifestation of his troubled transition to Modernist thought.[41]

That commitment to Modernism was certainly as evident as ever in the literary realm. Though seeking absolutes in social thought, he continued to explore the slippery shoals of consciousness in his art. Though advocating traditionalism as a way of life, in the realm of letters he favored experimentalism and persistently praised controversial writers like James Joyce. Tate saw no contradiction here: he simply insisted that literature and politics remain separate, even when a crisis like the present one made it necessary for literary figures to involve themselves politically. Nothing made him angrier than to discover his Nashville colleagues violating this injunction by judging contemporary authors along provincial or conservative lines. "If our Southern provincialism cannot assimilate the technique of Joyce and understand it, I am ready to move away," he warned. On occasion he would try to gain acceptance for the new literature by pointing out how Modernist writers shared the Agrarians' distress over unbelief. "Theirs is the right kind of modernism," he assured Davidson, "which by opposing everything modern is reactionary." Joyce, for example, was a "provincial Irishman" whose work comprised a "history of the moral horror in the individual when he is confronted with Modernism in all forms." Whether or not this analysis applied to Joyce, it clearly held for Allen Tate.[42]

As with Ransom, the Modernist part of Tate's sensibility served him best in his literary criticism, an area of endeavor in which his rational faculty could stay in complete control. In the early 1930s he moved steadily toward the insight (perhaps the most important of his career) that the very tension he so often complained of, the tension arising from "modern unbelieving belief," might constitute an invaluable literary asset. Tate began groping toward this realization as early as 1927 when he argued in "Poetry and the Absolute" that the test of the successful poem was the achievement of a "signification of experience that becomes absolute" within the poem itself. But Tate could not at the time describe what the "signification of experience" consisted of; he knew only that it involved an "intensification of perception into 'something rich and strange,'" and that it somehow represented the "unique quality of all good art." Similarly in a 1928 essay he had spoken of Emily Dickinson as a poet lucky enough to be born into the "equilibrium of an old and a new order," but again he had failed to draw the full implications of his remark. Not until the Agrarian movement heightened his own polar tensions, it seems, was he ready to formulate these thoughts into a comprehensive theory.[43]

That theory first came to light in 1932 when he thoroughly revised the piece on Emily Dickinson. What she had so fortunately enjoyed, he said, was the experience of rapid cultural transition, brought about in her case when New England's Puritan heritage gave way to a secular, distinctively American culture centered on material progress and science. This, according to Tate, provided her the "perfect literary situation," much like that which obtained for Shakespeare and John Donne in Elizabethan England. The cultural "clash of opposites" within her became the wellspring of her creativity, but only because she was able to resist the temptation to resolve the conflict intellectually. Caught midway between faith and rationality, Dickinson was incapable of giving herself to either. Instead her mind came to function at that exact level of integrated perception where thought and emotion are miraculously fused:

> Miss Dickinson and John Donne would have this in common: their sense of the natural world is not blunted by a too-rigid system of ideas; yet the ideas, the abstractions, their education or their intellectual heritage, are not so weak as to let their immersion in nature, or their purely personal quality, get out of control. The two poles of the mind are not separately visible; we infer them from the lucid tension that may be most readily illustrated by polar activity. There is no thought as such at all; nor is there feeling; there is that unique focus of experience which is at once neither and both.

"Lucid tension"—that, rather than absolute dogma, was now the basis of the integrated sensibility, and to achieve it required cultural change rather than stability. Tate's literary theory now stood in diametric contrast to his pronouncements on the good society, and it was literature he cared about most.[44]

In short, Tate had arrived at an unequivocally Modernist conception of art in which the primary concern was the *process* of artistic creativity rather than the moral beliefs the work of art might happen to express. Poetry in this view was "merely a way of knowing something," and the individual poem the "fulness of that knowledge." By comparison to positivistic knowledge, which proceeded in terms of direct rational statement, the essence of poetic knowledge resided in tension—specifically, a "tension between abstraction and sensation in which the two elements may be, of course, distinguished logically, but not really." If that metaphoric tension were present in sufficient degree, the poem would qualify as art, regardless of its literal subject matter or the mode of expression it was written in. The only criterion was that the poet reach down to the deepest levels of experience, "facing its utmost implications," and that rationality did not short-circuit the act of creation:

> Serious poetry deals with the fundamental conflicts that cannot be logically resolved: we can state the conflicts rationally, but reason does not relieve us of them. Their only final coherence is the formal re-creation of art, which "freezes" the experience as permanently as a logical formula, but without, like the formula, leaving all but the logic out.

No matter what his other intellectual inconsistencies, Tate would henceforth hold to this theory of literature in all his future critical writings—it was to become the one constant in his wavering thought.[45]

III

Having arrived at these insights, Tate was left with the question of how they might bear on his relationship to the South and on his own art. By the mid-1930s he had come to perceive that the South of his day was undergoing the same sort of cultural transit Emily Dickinson had experienced in New England and that it was this "crossing of the ways" that had given rise to the "curious burst of intelligence" so evident in southern letters. But with this discovery came the unhappy corollary: the same self-consciousness that enabled him to analyze the situation so accurately was preventing him from taking advantage of it. In effect, he had uncovered the secret of Faulkner's great success (which Tate was among the first to recognize), and of his own ultimate artistic failure. Moreover, the knowledge that he was living through a renaissance period made his relationship to the region's past even more problematic. If this was the optimum time for a southern writer to be at work, what was the value of the traditional society he longed to recapture? How, in other words, to reconcile his Modernist and "reactionary" beliefs—his equal desire for change and stability, flux and certainty—in the context of his legacy as a southerner? This was the puzzle in his mind as he worked on his only novel, *The Fathers*, in the late 1930s. The book consequently represents his last heroic effort to square himself with his heritage, relying this time not on his Agrarian solution of "violence" but on his concept of poetic tension.[46]

As the title suggests, *The Fathers* was bound up closely with Tate's powerful filiopiety, and it began in fact as an investigation into his ancestry at the peak of his Agrarian enthusiasm. Its origins can be traced to the "Genealogical Statement of Reasons for Entering the Symposium" with which Tate surprised his friends in 1931. Following this exercise Tate embarked on a scheme to write a social history of the South as seen through his family's experiences. Entitled "Ancestors of Exile," the book was to be dialectic in nature, pairing two figures from each generation to demonstrate, in his words, the "fundamental contrast" between the stable civilization of the Tidewater and the enterprising existence of the pioneer who "made modern America." He and his brother Ben were to stand for this contrast of types in the present. But, as so often with Tate, the project soon ran into rough shoals with the usual protestations of "agony," and in October, 1933, he nearly abandoned it. The fact that Tate's own father died in a car accident that month is probably not coincidental. By the following spring he was back to work on the book, this time as a historical novel. More delays and agonies ensued, including a two-year stint of full-time teaching at Southwestern University in Memphis brought on by financial pressures. In this way the novel spent seven years in gestation, with the result that when it was finally completed in July, 1938, the original filiopietistic impulse had become transmuted into something noticeably different.[47]

The book that emerged from this long process replicated the structure of Tate's thought to perfection. At its core stood a finely wrought balance, setting off the Tidewater gentleman against the driving entrepreneur, or more generally the traditionalist way of life against what Tate conceived of as Modernist. Representing traditionalism is Major Lewis Buchan, a character modeled on Tate's favorite antebellum ancestor Major Benjamin Lewis Bogan. With his perfect manners, constant regard for the feelings of others, and automatic adherence to the "rules of a rigid life," the major personifies Tate's ideal conception of Old South culture. Everything Major Buchan does is determined by the code he was born into; never does he think to assert himself against that code. He virtually lacks an ego. His opposite is George Posey, a city-bred businessman married to the major's daughter Susan and a close friend to the major's sons Semmes and Lacy. Because Posey has no inherited code, his behavior is governed solely by his impulses. His is the old frontier vitality made modern, but devoid of social purpose, causing him to appear to others as a "tornado" whose "one purpose is to whirl." The tension of the novel arises when this man of unbounded ego enters the hitherto tranquil Buchan household on the eve of the Civil War, a harbinger of the Yankee invasion to come.[48]

Clearly this match-up should have left no room for choice in the mind of an Agrarian. Here was Tate's model society under assault from unscrupulous capitalism. Here also was his prided ancestry on the verge of destruction (the novel ends with smoke rising from the charred ruins of "Pleasant Hill," the Buchan's plantation). Yet Tate endeavors throughout to suspend his judgment. He does so by viewing the action through the eyes of Lacy Buchan who, we are told, is a retired doctor reflecting back on the time when he was just approaching manhood. Lacy, as Tate's surrogate, takes "no sides" in the conflict between the Buchan and Posey ways of life. Indeed, as Louis Rubin points out, both the major and George Posey become Lacy's "fathers" in a sense—hence the novel's title. Tate thus leaves the central issue unresolved, in keeping with his concept of tension in art and with the actual ambivalence he felt between the two competing cultures.[49]

Given his strong feelings toward his Virginia forebears, perhaps Tate's greatest triumph in the novel is his evenhanded portrait of the Buchans. To be sure they exemplify the unself-conscious traditional life Tate always claimed to admire. Isolated from the financial and political marketplaces, free of greed, ambition, or pretension, they exist in a self-contained world where their inbred code of honor suffices for meeting every trial of experience. Because of that code, moreover, they are able to maintain almost complete control of their natural impulses. Never does the major display the least emotion; never does he lose his dignity or fail to project an air of self-certainty. Even at his wife's funeral, Lacy notices, "every muscle of his face kept its place." Yet, as Lacy discovers, there is another way of regarding Buchan virtues. By 1860 the major already appears old-fashioned, provincial, rigid, and hopelessly "innocent"—a man whose entire mode of being was static, who had divorced himself from the intensely dynamic reality around him. This becomes especially apparent to Lacy during the secession crisis, when his father keeps insisting that if men would only be calm and statesmanlike the whole trouble would go away. Such defects in the major explain why his children instinctively turn to Posey for an alternative vision of life, much as the Sutpen children in Faulkner's *Absalom, Absalom!* are drawn to Charles Bon.[50]

Despite his positive attributes, however, Posey does not win Tate's complete approval. Handsome, tall, affable, and invariably competent, a man of "great energy and imagination," he pursues his various enterprises less for profit than for the pleasure of the game. Most important, he is clearly riding the tide of history. "I admired George Posey even when I did not understand him," Lacy reflects, "for I shared his impatience with the world as it was." But Posey's grave defect stands revealed whenever his character is tested. Here Tate performs a curious chronological inversion. Instead of casting his nineteenth-century entrepreneur as a typical "inner-directed" figure, to borrow David Riesman's terminology, Tate construes him as a twentieth-century hollow man, an "outer-directed" creature who "received the shock of the world at the end of his nerves." Since there is nothing inside him, he is left to sway with the political winds or the vicissitudes of the market. "I am not choosing sides," he informs an astonished Major Buchan during the secession crisis. "I am chosen by circumstances." He is, in short, not a true representative of his times but rather Tate's portrait (close to a caricature) of a rootless modern liberal.[51]

Posey is also a Victorian's nightmare. His lack of substantive belief leaves him at the mercy of his impulses—in Tate's imagery, the "abyss" lurking inside every man. Whenever an emotion wells up inside him he must react immediately and often violently. Vaguely sensing his predicament, Posey gravitates toward the Buchans, Lacy later surmises, in the hope that they could restore his "forfeited heritage" and give him "what the Poseys had lost: an idea, a cause, an action in which his personality could be extinguished." But the contrary occurs: Posey's violent actions set off a chain of events that culminates in the murder of his slave half-brother Yellow Jim, the death of Semmes Buchan, the insanity of Susan, and the major's tragic suicide.[52]

Clearly Tate had to treat this emotionally laden material with special handling. Unable to suspend his consciousness like Faulkner, he took the opposite and for him inevitable tack: he displaced his consciousness onto Lacy Buchan, an old man recollecting the distant past in tranquillity. This device allowed Tate the luxury of describing the clash between the Buchans and Posey with relative detachment and balance. But Tate's reliance on intellectual control often went too far, spilling over into direct manipulation of the reader and snapping the effect of the tension. For all its dramatic circumstances, observes Richard King, the novel "remains rather cerebral and without passion . . . We never experience Lacy's world in any but an intellectual way." Again and again Tate has his narrator explain directly the significance of a character's action or remark, rather than letting the incident speak for itself. In addition, Tate's symbols all too frequently seem contrived: having Posey arrive at Pleasant Hill clutching a carpetbag in one hand and a telescope in the other does not smack of subtlety. *The Fathers*, then, constantly violates Tate's own aesthetic canon by having direct statements, mechanical symbols, and unassimilated abstractions do the work of the metaphoric imagination.[53]

The reasons for this failure to relinquish rational control must be sought, as usual with Tate, in the warfare between his Victorian and Modernist sensibilities—a conflict objectified in the very plot of *The Fathers*. The treatment of George Posey reveals how much force the old dichotomy between savagery and civilization still retained for Tate. No matter how valiantly he tried to emphasize the more attractive side of Posey, the reader cannot help concluding that Tate found this character morally appalling. The only solution Tate could envisage for countering Posey's savagery was a traditionalist civilization based on absolute standards. As Lacy Buchan puts it, victims of excessive personalism like Posey "have a communion with the abyss," and "is not civilization the agreement, slowly arrived at, to let the abyss alone?" Although aware that such an "agreement" amounted to an outright evasion of the problem of human evil, Tate, or at least a substantial part of him, sympathized with the effort to sustain the illusion. All "highly developed societies" must rely on an "ostrich-like code" to keep their sanity, he explained to John Peale Bishop shortly after *The Fathers* was published. "At present we live in a world where the disorder is at the surface. So all honor to Major Buchan!"[54]

But the other part of Tate had no intention of letting the abyss alone. The Modernist Tate found that Victorian practice an escape from reality, a denial of life itself. From this perspective *The Fathers* becomes not a tragic account of the demise of traditional society, but Lacy's narrative of his own struggle to shed his innocence and reach maturity. "Why cannot life change without tangling the lives of innocent persons?" he asks at the beginning. "Why do innocent persons cease their innocence and become violent and evil?" Lacy repeats these questions throughout the novel, attempting to fix blame for the terrible things he witnesses. In time he comes to perceive that innocence itself constitutes the mortal flaw in both his "fathers." The major is doomed through his failure to comprehend human irrationality, and Posey falls prey to violence because of his complete lack of self-consciousness. The only (albeit slender) defense against man's condition, Lacy discovers, is to confront one's own evil directly, to learn how "to hear the night":

> to hear the night, and to crave its coming, one must have deep inside one's secret being a vast metaphor controlling all the rest: a belief in the innate evil of man's nature, and the need to face that evil, of which the symbol is darkness, of which again the living image is man alone.

The insight embodied in this passage—surely one of the most feelingly written passages in the book—could not be more at odds with Tate's endorsement of civilization and its "ostrich-like code."[55]

At the time Tate seems to have believed that his juxtaposition of these two alternate visions fulfilled the requirements of his theory of literary tension. "I do see the subject in terms of unresolvable conflict," he told Bishop; "looked at closely enough, all human situations have that aspect;

hence the necessity of literature." Tate was unfortunately mistaking the unresolved ambivalence that arose through his own cultural polarity for the genuine metaphorical tension that the integrated sensibility could achieve. Metaphorical tension, he once wrote, is "so focused that it is destroyed." In *The Fathers*, however, the tension was often so polar and unfused that it was palpable. What kept it unfused was the intervention of Tate's excessive rationality that repeatedly stymied the metaphoric process within his mind beyond a certain "safe" level. As he well knew, the same inhibitions dogged his poetry. "I have really let myself go only once," he admitted to Fletcher in 1933, "in the Ode."[56]

To put it another way, Tate, like Odum and Faulkner, could never quite surmount his innocence. One sees this clearly in Lacy Buchan who, despite the ordeal he experiences in *The Fathers* and his expressed desire "to see the night," emerges with his innocence intact. Lacy strikingly shies away from the various sexual temptations offered him. Likewise he is never more than an innocent observer of the violence that occurs. He enjoys this privilege of detachment from the world's more sordid business because he is still young, just as he is able as narrator to look back upon the crisis dispassionately because he is so old. Although probably unaware of the fact, Tate had portrayed his surrogate figure at those two stages of life when such detachment is most possible. As a consequence, though, the wisdom Lacy obtains comes through his status as a spectator, and not from any personal encounter with the abyss. By contrast when Robert Penn Warren placed himself inside the consciousness of Jack Burden, the narrator of *All the King's Men*, he did not hesitate to plunge Burden into what Warren calls the "convulsion of the world." Burden learns through immediate experience the hard existential lesson that "all knowledge that is worth anything is maybe paid for by blood." And although Warren clearly employed much conscious intelligence in crafting his novel, it was intelligence guided by a sustained metaphoric vision, leading to the sort of "focused" tension that Tate had been striving for. The differences between Warren and Tate in these respects measure the distance between the fully Modernist southern writer and one in the midst of transition.[57]

As for the South, the completion of *The Fathers* effectively marked Tate's leave-taking of the region. The god of the Old South had failed, and he would have little more traffic with it except for occasional essays. In 1939 he accepted a position teaching poetry in the Creative Arts Program at Princeton, a setting he told his Nashville friends he detested because the Yankee mind was "all abstraction," but which in fact he found quite pleasurable. Various appointments followed, with two brief stays in the South, but not until after his retirement in 1968 from eighteen years as professor of English at the University of Minnesota did Tate really return home again.[58]

For the South had never been the real focus of Tate's concern. He had used it beginning in 1927 because it appeared to offer a means of healing the deep cultural divisions that his intense self-consciousness kept raising to the surface. He had hoped briefly that Agrarianism as an intellectual and social movement might eliminate that division by one bold stroke, but never did he truly believe it would succeed. When he criticized the New Humanists in 1930 for their "attempt to get the social results of unity by main force, by a kind of moral Fascism," he may have sensed that the critique applied to himself. In spite of his internal dilemma—perhaps because of it—he became a master critic and theorist who saw as clearly as anyone what was happening in twentieth-century literature, but who for that very reason was blocked from the artistic spontaneity he craved. Though he relished the Modernist world of paradox and relativism, at the same time he persisted in seeking the certainty of a religious faith—a search that culminated, as one might have predicted, in his decision of 1951 to join the Catholic church. Whether he ever found the solace he sought is questionable, for the war of cultures within him raged to the end. Agrarianism in retrospect appears to have been one fierce short campaign in that long and relentless war.[59]

PART THREE

THE MODERNIST GENERATION ARRIVES

By the late 1920s the process of intellectual change in the South entered what might be called its third stage. An increasing number of writers appeared whose sensibility and style of thought could be identified beyond doubt as Modernist. For them, the debate that had started in the late nineteenth century was largely over. They began with the assumption that man was the human animal, that the universe was inherently irrational, that morality was embedded in history and not in immutable natural laws, and that personality was primarily determined by one's culture. All of these beliefs and more went essentially unquestioned for them, just as the dichotomy between civilization and savagery had gone unquestioned for the Victorians. As Modernists, their concern was not to maintain the old moral dividing line, but to find new ways of integrating thought and emotion and to bridge the existing gaps between classes and races within the South, as well as the gap between the South and the rest of the nation.

Unlike the transitional figures like Tate and Odum, these Modernist writers were not torn within by two opposing cultures, with all the paralysis and compensatory gestures such inner conflict entailed. To be sure, they were puzzled by the many contradictions they found in southern society and were uncertain how best to proceed toward social change. But these dilemmas existed for the most part outside themselves and could be dealt with in objective fashion. Most important, they did not expect to find epistemological certainty; just the opposite. Usually full-fledged relativists, they believed that knowledge was at best a shifting affair. As the Tennessee poet and journalist James Agee put it in his *Let Us Now Praise Famous Men*, "nothing can be held untrue. A falsehood is entirely true to those derangements which produced it and which made it impossible that it should emerge in truth; and an examination of it may reveal more of the 'true' 'truth' than any more direct attempt upon the 'true' 'truth' itself." Existence, they thought, was chaos, and man's understanding of it highly imperfect. Under these conditions it was necessary for man to face his plight without the illusion of certainty in order to make what small improvement he could.[1]

The new contingent of Modernist southerners was above all distinguished by its ability to see the region clearly. Theirs was an empirical approach that gathered in significant details unencumbered by the requirements of traditional mythology or moralism. In particular, they were able to explore that "dark side" of the region, the vast area of ugliness and pathology that had often gone unacknowledged in the past. There they would find their most important insights concerning southern character. Agee, for instance, sought revelations in the everyday lives of Alabama sharecroppers, depicting his subjects' existence in almost infinite detail and discovering consummate beauty even in their illiteracy and slovenliness. However, it must be pointed out that, although avidly empiricist, these new writers and thinkers were not positivists in the nineteenth-century meaning of that term. Although they plainly believed in using their senses to apprehend reality, reality for them was not limited to the physical world. Rather, their desire to integrate all levels of the psyche led them to pay as much attention to consciousness as to the more "objective" realm of behavior. They resolutely looked inside their own minds to find the dynamics of southern identity, and with equal resolution researched the subjective states of the people they were writing about. The new sociologists no less than the poet Agee wished to delve inside the thought processes of sharecroppers. Such intangible evidence, which the true positivist would abhor, was as important to them in understanding the South as were statistical indexes of income or mobility.

Yet if the Modernists achieved a clearer vision of the South thanks to their new cultural tenets, it is also true that their vision lacked the scope and solidity of their predecessors. Instead of attempting to comprehend all the South at once, as Odum had, their technique generally caused them to focus on one small facet of it. Rather than seeking universal truths, their search was usually limited to temporary solutions of immediate problems. Minute detail frequently absorbed them, while grand visions typically eluded them. It was a price they were willing to pay in their effort to achieve empirical honesty.

If those of us living in the late twentieth century now find their philosophic outlook less satisfying, if we yearn for a stable base on which to construct our knowledge and ethics, we must keep in mind the intoxicating sense of liberation that accompanied Modernist belief a half century ago, especially in a hitherto backward province like the South. All modes of thought in time outlive their usefulness, but for southern intellectuals in the 1930s the dynamic, critical precepts of Modernism seemed exactly what their society needed most.

CHAPTER 9

THE CRITICAL TEMPERAMENT
UNLEASHED:
WILLIAM TERRY COUCH AND
SOUTHERN PUBLISHING

One otherwise tranquil morning in May, 1927, an event took place in Chapel Hill, North Carolina, that forever changed the course of publishing in the South. The occasion was an emergency session of the Board of Governors of the newly created University of North Carolina Press, called on less than one hour's notice in the office of the school's president, Harry W. Chase. Assembled in a circle around Chase's desk that day sat the elite of the university's faculty, the nucleus of that determined band of scholars then engaged in transforming Chapel Hill from a sleepy intellectual backwater into an oasis for modern thought in the region. Howard Odum was present, as was James Finch Royster, dean of the Graduate School, the historian J. G. de Roulhac Hamilton, the noted biologist W. C. Coker, R. H. Wettach of the Law School, and Louis R. Wilson, the librarian and director of the press.[1]

The purpose of the gathering was to decide the fate of a book entitled *Congaree Sketches*, newly arrived from the bindery. This collection of tales told by black raconteurs living along the Congaree River in South Carolina had been assembled by a wealthy white physician, planter, and sometime politician from Columbia named E. C. L. Adams; it had been solicited by Odum as part of his institute's effort to collect and publish black folklore. Since the stories themselves contained nothing offensive to southern prejudices, their publication had won easy approval by the press board. The problem resided in what the board had not seen or even heard about—an emotional introduction appended to the book at

Adams's request and written by Paul Green. A member of the philosophy department, Green was one of the boldest of the Young Turks on the Chapel Hill faculty and recipient the previous month of a Pulitzer Prize in drama for his play on southern Negro life, *In Abraham's Bosom*. In the introduction Green had observed how, having lived together in America for two hundred years, "black and white are inextricably mingled in blood and bone and intention." For the moment, he went on, the black man stood "in the ditch doing the dirty digging" while the white man above gave orders, but like all social arrangements this was bound to change. The white man's obligation was thus to extend a helping hand, enabling his black brother to get out of the ditch faster. By all this, Green assuredly did not intend an assault on the doctrine of "separate but equal," an issue he never addressed. Beneath his semimystical rhetoric his purpose was simply to bring about more humane treatment of blacks in the South and to laud the achievements of the Harlem Renaissance, of which his own work was considered a part. Still, in 1927 these were strong sentiments for a southern university press to contemplate publishing.[2]

Although proud of what they had accomplished at their institution since the First World War, the press's Board of Governors, having just weathered a pitched battle between the university and North Carolina Fundamentalists over the teaching of evolution, were in no mood for taking chances. At the outset, their choice of action seemed clear. The meeting opened with Royster, head of the manuscript committee, contending that the appearance of the introduction under the university's imprint in the existing political climate could set off a massive explosion of adverse criticism in the South, causing the school irreparable damage. The only solution, he declared, was to destroy all existing copies of the book forthwith and to reprint it without the introduction. One by one the board members registered their agreement. The vote was predictably unanimous.[3]

Then a young man barely twenty-five years old spoke up. As assistant director of the press, William Terry Couch had been running its day-to-day operations for almost two years following the illness of his ostensible superior, Louis Wilson. He had chafed constantly at what he saw as the board's excessive caution. As the only major nonreligious publishing house in the South, the press, in his opinion, was wasting a golden opportunity by confining itself to bibliographies of Argentine literature and treatises on the typology of local mushrooms. If men like Odum really meant what they said about reinvigorating southern culture, this was hardly the way to go about it. Such, however, was not his line of argument in Chase's office. Instead, in as matter-of-fact a tone as he could muster, Couch explained certain facts the board did not know: on his special instructions, more than a hundred advance copies of *Congaree Sketches* had already been distributed to reviewers, leading literary figures, and major bookstores throughout the country. The *New York Times* had a copy, as did the *New York Herald-Tribune*, along with Walter Lippmann and Oswald Garrison Villard, editor of the *Nation*. If the press stopped publication of the book now, Couch asked, wouldn't some of these people suspect foul play and start inspecting the book closely to see what was wrong? Would not their eyes soon fall on the introduction? Perhaps it would be best to do nothing, he suggested. Again a vote was taken, this time with each member agreeing in turn to follow Couch's advice.[4]

What happened next—or, more accurately, what did not happen—was equally important. The Klan did not march on Chapel Hill, the legislature did not vindictively cut the university's budget, nor did the press, despite the book's heavy sales in the South, receive so much as one protest letter. A critic writing for Adams's hometown newspaper, the conservative *Columbia State*, thought Green's essay the "most inexpert, unrelated, alien thing we can recall ever seeing attached to something else," but reviewers for other southern papers tended to ignore the piece when they did not gently praise it. To James Weldon Johnson of the NAACP, on the other hand, the introduction represented "one of the finest approaches by the written word to interracial understanding and good will ever made." Most of the national media taking notice of the book echoed Johnson's opinion. In short, by publishing *Congaree Sketches* the University of North Carolina Press lost no ground in its home territory while it garnered valuable prestige elsewhere.[5]

Two key developments stemmed from this incident. First, it became clear that the press's prior policy had erred on the side of circumspection. "When Paul Green's Introduction . . . did not produce a convulsion, not even a tremor," Couch later recalled, "this was a demonstration that something thought to be not possible was possible." Second, as a result of his daring, Couch was able to consolidate his control of the press. Having shown himself shrewd and unpredictable, few save Odum would dare challenge him again over what he could publish. "I have found it necessary to compromise and to be cautious," he wrote Walter Lippmann in triumph just after his coup, "but I do not compromise or exercise caution merely to avoid criticism. I think this organization should take the ground that one of its prime functions is to provide a way for free and informed discussion of important subjects." This, in a nutshell, was

Couch's policy throughout his twenty years' tenure as head of the press, a policy that was to make the press the single most influential institution in launching Modernist thought in the South.[6]*

I

Alone among the men who put Chapel Hill on the academic map in the interwar period, Couch had deep personal roots in the community. His father's family had lived in the New Hope Creek area, a few miles from the university, since the mid-eighteenth century, prosperous farmers but not slaveholders. Yet Couch himself did not set foot in North Carolina until he was seventeen years old.

He was born in December, 1901, the son of a Baptist country preacher in Pamplin, Virginia, a tiny town bordering Prince Edward County where his mother's family, the Terrys, had been well-to-do planters and professionals prior to the Civil War. The South's defeat, however, had wiped out the family's entire fortune; Couch would always vividly recall wading in Confederate currency up to his knees during childhood visits to his grandmother's attic. Thus, despite their origins, his parents were forced to scramble constantly to make ends meet all their lives, and they were never able to situate themselves permanently in one place. Rather, their wanderings took them back and forth across the Upper South to small towns like Pearisburg and Natural Bridge in Virginia and to cities like Louisville and Roanoke. Finally, in 1918, Couch's father decided to abandon the ministry and attempt to return to farming at New Hope Creek to give his family some stability at last and to permit his children to attend the nearby university. Young William was coming home to the only community he would ever feel tied to, but which he in fact had not yet seen. His experience, then, was a curious blending of peregrination and rootedness.[7]

*There is an interesting sequel to the *Congaree Sketches* story. Following the book's publication, Adams ran for lieutenant governor in the South Carolina Democratic primary, only to find the Paul Green introduction used as an issue against him. As a consequence, he arranged to have Scribner's take over his book and reissue it with no introduction. Couch pleaded with Maxwell Perkins, at the time the country's leading literary editor, to leave the book alone, arguing that the "significance and value of these sketches are greatly enhanced by their being published by a University Press in the South." But it was to no avail. In 1928 Scribner's published the text of *Congaree Sketches* unrevised under the incredible title *Nigger to Nigger*. Couch had learned something about northern liberalism, too. See Henry R. Fuller to Couch, December 14, 1927, Couch Papers; Couch to Charles Scribner's Sons, March 28, 1928, Maxwell S. Perkins to Couch, March 16, 1928, and Couch to Edward C. L. Adams, April 27, 1928, in "Adams, *Congaree Sketches*" file, UNCPP.

As we have seen, most southerners recruited into the intellectual class before the First World War tended, in one fashion or another, to be plucked from the mainstream of everyday life and set off in a special world of their own at a comparatively early age. For the New South generation, from Walter Hines Page through Ulrich B. Phillips, this process normally took the form of attendance at private academies, followed by scholarships at leading universities. Some, like Ellen Glasgow or Emily Clark, came from wealthy families; others, like Odum, were protected from mundane existence by parents with ambitious hopes for them; a few, like Faulkner, found their own shelters. Whichever the case, a separation soon became apparent between their lives and those of the overwhelming majority of southerners. Even before they assumed their roles as academics or writers, they had become more or less self-conscious members of an elite.[8]

Not so for Couch and most of his contemporaries. Those future intellectuals arriving at southern colleges after 1919 had generally undergone some form of immersion in the living conditions of the common people that would drastically affect their ultimate perspectives. As soon as he was old enough, for instance, Couch took a summer job in a factory to supplement his family's income. In North Carolina he spent a year doing heavy labor—clearing fresh land, chopping firewood for sale, and plowing on hire—aiding his father in what proved to be a vain effort to revive New Hope Farm. The following year Couch worked at a generating station of the Southern Power Company, often on a twelve-hour, seven-day per week basis. The necessity of supporting himself and his family continued after he entered the university, causing him at one point to drop out and enlist in the army in the hope of earning an appointment to West Point. In sum, Couch was hardly sheltered from the hardships of life. Even if he could claim descent from the Virginia planter class, he was not about to identify himself as a gentleman.[9]

The experiences of this difficult period were to have many significant effects on Couch's later thought, perhaps the most important of which was to neutralize whatever vestiges of elitism lingered from his upbringing. Others might look upon the lower classes with condescension, or, in the reverse procedure, sentimentalize them, but for Couch neither was possible. His observation of existence at the bottom of southern society was grounded in extensive personal participation; his perceptions accordingly were *internal* as well as external. One detects the resultant sensibility—so different, say, from that of an Odum or a Broadus Mitchell—in this description given to Erskine Caldwell in 1932 of his job as an operative in a furniture factory:

The thought uppermost in my mind, so long as I was fully conscious of myself, was the desire for release. I could look out
my window now and then—at the risk of an arm, a hand, or a
finger—and see other boys running around, going swimming or
fishing or anywhere but to work, I would think. After a time,
I would lose consciousness of myself, and become absorbed in the
mechanical motions required by my machine, avoiding pullies, saw
teeth, and threatening jaws by motions which had become in-
voluntarily careful, sure, habitual, only after hours and days of
extreme caution. I once entertained the ambition of learning to play
a violin and the fear that I might lose a finger on my left hand was
a nightmare to me. A careless moment and I might easily lose
more than one. . . . While in the state of semi-consciousness hours
passed like minutes, and finally I would suddenly become aware
of the closeness of the noon or closing hour. Then the minutes
would drag like hours, until finally the whistle would blow, the
machines would be stopped, and a dead stillness, broken only by
the seemingly quiet rush for the exits, would take the place of
the violent roaring and rasping.

There is a clarity and power of expression here, a freedom from any
ambivalence, which we have not seen before. The issue of working-class
savagery has vanished, replaced by a straightforward curiosity for detail,
a concern for understanding the actual quality of the worker's experience. Given this perspective, Couch would not pity or romanticize the
white southern masses, and (with the one crucial exception of their racial
attitudes) he would not fear them.[10]

Coupled with this new social outlook, Couch brought to the press an
innate sense of candor, a belief that the truth must be spoken regardless
of consequences. In time this trait would land Couch in considerable
trouble, but at the outset it served to land him a job. His frankness first
went on display in 1924 when Couch became editor of the *Carolina
Magazine*, a previously obscure student publication that soon became a
prime topic of conversation not only on campus but out in the state as
well. Along with his own articles attacking southern conservatism, Couch
began printing letters from Fundamentalists condemning the teaching of
evolution, letters that made the authors look ridiculous. The resulting
furor even called forth speeches in the North Carolina legislature. "I did
not have any policy, so far as I was aware, of creating controversies,"
Couch later explained, "but somehow they spawned around me all the
time." Whatever the university's administrators thought of the performance, it was sufficient to catch the eye of Louis Wilson, who in May,

1925, was looking for an assistant to run the press while he was away on a medical leave of absence. Wilson hoped Couch would help make the press as lively as he had made the *Carolina Magazine*. In that respect, Wilson was not disappointed.[11]

The operation Couch took over had indeed been a timid one. The men who founded the press in 1922—Odum, Chase, Wilson, Coker, and Edwin Greenlaw, a literary scholar soon to depart for Johns Hopkins—had done so with grandiose visions of turning it into a major publishing center for the region, but their subsequent actions had not kept pace with their intentions. In their initial memorandum, for example, Wilson and Greenlaw had outlined plans for the press to issue its version of the *New Republic*, relying primarily on southern writers and aimed at educated laymen rather than scholars in an effort to "gain wide influence on the thought of the entire South Atlantic section." To some extent Odum's *Journal of Social Forces* fulfilled this mission up to 1925. But, though technically published by the press, the journal was in reality the creature of the Institute for Research in Social Science, and its character was far more scholarly than the periodical Wilson and Greenlaw had had in mind. The idea of a southern *New Republic* never got beyond the blueprint stage. No doubt their wish to start such a magazine was sincere, but, even had the funding been available, one cannot imagine the early leaders of the press courting the risks the venture would inevitably have entailed. It was simply not their style.[12]

Caution, rather, was their watchword. One sees it in the choice of books they published initially—all of them staid, highly scholarly, not destined to leave the library shelves very often. When a book did touch on a current regional problem, as did Edgar W. Knight's *Education in the South* (1924), controversial statements were carefully avoided and the emphasis fell on Progress. When, on the other hand, a Columbia University professor delivered a set of lectures at Chapel Hill in 1923 containing critical remarks on Prohibition, the press board, after much discussion, refused to publish them. Because the subject matter was "in certain particulars highly controversial," Wilson wrote the author, the manuscript did not "fall within the scope of the policies of the Press." The founders' caution also led them to set up their institution as a separate, nonstock corporation owned wholly by its Board of Governors, rather than as an integral part of its parent university. If the press did get into trouble, they reasoned, this arrangement would make it possible for the university to disclaim all responsibility. As things turned out, this legal fiction did not convince many of the press's enemies, but paradoxically it helped give a director like Couch unusual freedom from the university's trustees. That was not really what the founders had intended.[13]

Entering this situation in mid-1925, Couch immediately began to bridle at the conservative attitudes he found. Wilson, on hiring him, had told him that the press could never publish anything that dealt in substance with race, religion, or economics. "He said this merely as an observation of what appeared to him to be a fact," Couch recalled, "and he said it in a way that made it clear to me that he regretted the fact." Even a proposed series of translations of modern European drama had ·been vetoed as potentially too dangerous. But as chance had it, one book that stood as an exception to Wilson's rule was arriving from the printer just as Couch came aboard. Had William Louis Poteat's *Can a Man Be a Christian Today?* been submitted as an unsolicited manuscript, it would unquestionably not have passed the press board in 1925. However, Poteat, president of Wake Forest College and an outspoken advocate of Darwinism, had been invited the previous year to give a set of endowed lectures on the relationship between science and religion with the understanding that the press would afterward publish them. This had been done as a gesture of friendship to the denominational colleges in the state and in appreciation for Poteat's role battling Fundamentalism within the Baptist ranks. By the time Poteat had finished his talks, the university itself had come under fire from the champions of religious orthodoxy in the *Social Forces* controversy; still, the press had no real choice but to issue the book. This gave Couch his first opportunity to test his situation.[14]

His efforts were intense but short-lived. All through the summer of 1926 he traveled the state in Odum's Model T Ford, placing a few seed copies of Poteat's book in each small town with no expectation of ever being paid for them. If only a handful of people would read the book and spread the word, he figured, orders would start to pour in. The stratagem worked: in no time the entire first printing of three thousand copies had sold out and Couch exultantly requested a second printing of five thousand. "The fact that we have been allowed to continue to exist after publishing this book makes us feel somewhat superior to certain other southern states," he boasted to a New York critic. To help sell the second printing, he contracted with Nell Battle Lewis, a well-known columnist for the *Raleigh News and Observer*, to write a biographical sketch of Poteat for newspaper syndication throughout the South. Then, in January, 1927, precisely when the promotional campaign was to start, the Fundamentalists staged a brief resurgence in the legislature. The university business office sat for months on Couch's order for additional books until all interest in Poteat's volume had died. At the same time instructions came down to stop circulating the Lewis article immediately. Couch was, to say the least, downcast. "The Press has certain limitations in its directorate," Wilson counseled his young assistant, "in the type of manuscript which it is publishing, and in a number of other ways. It probably cannot become the University of Chicago Press or the Harvard Press; but, by realizing its limitations, by sticking to certain standards and procedures, . . . it can go a good long distance."[15]

Couch, however, was in no mood to accept this advice. "I am wondering if there is anyone here who has a backbone," he wrote Nell Lewis, "that is, any one in an executive position who is willing to take a fairly intelligent and informed position and stand or fall by it." Besides, he did not want his press to become like Harvard's:

> I can see no reason whatever why this institution should take Harvard or Yale or Columbia as its pattern. On the contrary, it seems to me that there is much in them which should be a warning and an example to us. Just for example, if the University Press, like Harvard or Yale, is to devote itself to bringing out nice inoffensive books—perfect examples of modern scholarship—it seems to me that the legislative gentlemen who protest at our expenditures have a real reason for their protests.

Odum felt a measure of this sentiment, believing that his work belonged at Chapel Hill rather than at one of the prestige universities that periodically offered him appointments, but he had always looked to the name institutions for his standards. To Couch, those standards, based on the old gentility, constituted the enemy. "Please do not worry about me and my job at all," he told Lewis ominously, "on the contrary, I should like to see somebody really do something about this miserable situation." Four months later, with the publication of *Congaree Sketches*, he struck his decisive blow.[16]

From that time on, as he consolidated his control over the organization's management and increasingly put his stamp on its affairs, it became apparent that Couch represented something new on the Chapel Hill scene—a man who invited contention rather than evaded it. He did so not simply out of temperament but on the basis of his most fundamental philosophic assumptions. Conflict for him, as for other Modernists, was a positive good; it was not a threat to scholarship but rather its lifeblood. Without conflict cultural life would rapidly degenerate into sterility and inertia, as it had in the nineteenth-century South. The life of the mind, as Couch saw it, was not supposed to take place in a refuge, shielded by "objectivity," devoid of passion, and aiming at some putative state of perfection. On the contrary, what made the intellectual game worth playing was the chance to move to the cutting edge, to make the sparks fly. Over and over he counseled his authors to break with politeness and become *more* critical of the South rather than less. "No well-

10. William Terry Couch in the mid-1930s
Courtesy William Terry Couch

bred person in the South," he noted sarcastically to the journalist Clarence Cason,

> would ever be so boorish as to insist, to the point of unpleasantness, that opinions should be based on facts and tempered with a little measure of justice. . . . It is neither possible nor desirable always to preserve the amenities while doing such work. It inevitably becomes unpleasant to those who profit from the old system or those who do not wish to be bothered.

Nothing, he went on, was more important than to bother people, to wake them up and get them activated. If that required stepping on some toes, so much the better.[17]

In his eyes, inculcating a critical attitude among southerners at all social levels became the press's central mission. Though others at Chapel Hill might despair when press books met unfavorable receptions in southern newspapers, Couch welcomed thoughtful criticism as a sign of health. "If you should find anything about any one of our books which you think ought to be criticized," he constantly told small-town editors, "I would appreciate it very much if you would go to it. Instead of your paying us for the book when you criticize it [the editors did not always receive complimentary review copies], according to my way of thinking, we should do all the paying." When the press itself came under attack, Couch's response was not to try and smooth the situation over diplomatically, as Chase and Odum were wont to do, but to take the offensive, often joyfully. On one occasion Wade H. Harris, editor of the powerful *Charlotte Observer*, protested to the president of the university concerning derogatory remarks about his newspaper in a recently published press book by the Richmond journalist, Virginius Dabney. Couch characteristically hurled the challenge back. "The record is there in your news and editorial columns for Mr. Dabney or anyone else to see," Couch told him, suggesting that Harris and Dabney debate the matter in public. Harris quickly backed down.[18]

A quick glance at the publishing schedule the press maintained during Couch's tenure gives a good indication of how successful he was in using the institution to stimulate the region's intellectual life. In that time, Chapel Hill issued over 450 titles, of which 170 dealt chiefly with southern topics. There were, naturally enough, many volumes on the South's history, including major works by Thomas P. Abernethy, E. Merton Coulter, Philip S. Foner, John Hope Franklin, Fletcher M. Green, Francis Butler Simkins, Vernon L. Wharton, and Louis B. Wright. There were books on the contemporary South, several written for a general audience and often specially commissioned by the press, such as Dabney's *Liberal-*

ism in the South (1932), Clarence Cason's *90° in the Shade* (1935), Herman Clarence Nixon's *Forty Acres and Steel Mules* (1938), Donald Davidson's *The Attack on Leviathan* (1938), and two volumes edited by Couch himself, *Culture in the South* (1934) and *These Are Our Lives* (1939). Also published were important works of literary criticism by Cleanth Brooks, Norman Foerster, Howard Mumford Jones, and René Wellek; collections of white and black folklore by Arthur P. Hudson, George Pullen Jackson, and others; and books by nonsouthern authors like Bronislaw Malinowski, Frank Tannenbaum, and Harold Laski whose ideas did not always find favor in the region. This was an unusual fare for any university press at the time, especially a southern one.[19]*

The heart of the press's publishing schedule, though, the work that brought it the most public notice and drew the greatest critical fire, consisted of the regional social science studies it brought out on behalf of Odum's institute. The titles bespeak the range and controversial nature of this series: Arthur F. Raper's *The Tragedy of Lynching* (1933), Roy M. Brown's *Public Poor Relief in North Carolina* (1928), Clarence Heer's *Income and Wages in the South* (1930), Jennings J. Rhyne's *Some Southern Cotton Mill Workers and Their Villages* (1930), Harriet L. Herring's *Welfare Work in Mill Villages* (1930), J. H. Chadbourn's *Lynching and the Law* (1933), Duane McCracken's *Strike Injunctions in the New South* (1931), Wiley B. Sanders's *Negro Child Welfare in North Carolina* (1933), and Horace R. Cayton and George S. Mitchell's *Black Workers and the New Unions* (1939). Although some reflected Odum's cautionary approach, these and many similar volumes clearly dealt with subjects southerners had not been accustomed to discussing. Perhaps most would have found their way to publication anyway, but, given the prevailing attitude on the press board prior to the time Couch gained control, and given the lack of other publishing outlets in the region, it is doubtful that so many of these books could have been issued in the South save for Couch. And the fact that they *did* emanate from a southern publisher,

---

*The University of North Carolina Press under Couch also published books designed for specific practical purposes. To raise the quality of children's books available in the South, for instance, Couch engaged some talented teachers in the Chapel Hill school system to write *The Find Out Book*, a two-volume work that answered the questions preschool children asked most. For elementary and high school students in North Carolina, the press issued a series of four books covering the history and the present social and economic conditions of the state. Part text and part reference work, the set sold tens of thousands of copies over the years, helping to finance some of the press's more chancy ventures. There were also books on farming techniques aimed at 4-H Clubs and individual farmers to encourage diversified husbandry, a very successful textbook for adult illiterates, and a number of works on gardening and local architecture to promote appreciation of the aesthetic environment. Again, no university press in America had entered such fields before.

carrying the imprimatur of a prestigious southern university, was, as Arthur Raper later testified, of incalculable advantage in gaining acceptance for them below the Potomac.[20]

By the late 1930s, then, Couch could claim a considerable measure of success for what he called his "experiment in 'cultural' publishing." Not only had he subdued virtually all his opposition in Chapel Hill, he had also made considerable headway in his larger purpose of creating a tolerance for such publishing in the region. So he observed, not without pride, in late 1941:

> In spite of the fact that during the last sixteen years we have published numerous books which have been extremely critical of the South, which have antagonized many of our people, which at first aroused bitter opposition to us, which secured for the University exactly the opposite kind of publicity which university presses are supposed to get, we are now winning ground rapidly with our own people. The best evidence of this is in the increase in support given to this organization in recent years by the legislature of North Carolina and the wide use of our books throughout the South.

Put another way, the press had managed to develop a constituency, consisting mainly of middle-class, well-educated professionals holding positions of some influence in southern society. These men, who could and did exert strong counterpressure against the likes of David Clark or Wade Harris, responded with gratitude to the press's willingness to tackle difficult topics. Included in this constituency were countless southern newspaper editors who valued freedom of publication as keenly as Couch did and who appreciated having Chapel Hill as a lightning rod. "The increasing usefulness of the University of North Carolina Press to this section deserves more attention than it has received from Southern newspapers," said the *Mobile* (Alabama) *Press Register* in a typical encomium. "It is a brave work that is being undertaken at Chapel Hill." Such statements of support in turn gave Couch even more leeway in conducting his "experiment."[21]

Nor was the appreciation of Couch's work or the publishing revolution he had started limited to the South. Older members of the Chapel Hill faculty stood amazed as their brand-new university press, scarcely a decade old, received national recognition for its pioneering work. In the judgment of Allan Nevins, for instance, North Carolina as of 1934 was "easily at the head of the university presses of this country." "You are publishing better and more interesting books than any other University Press," echoed Henry Steele Commager a few years later. More flattering still was the fact that other university presses, which, with the sole exception of Yale, had previously confined themselves to "perfect examples of modern scholarship," now began to follow Chapel Hill's lead, bringing out high-quality trade books aimed at the general reader. For many it was a strange sight: the publishing arms of institutions like Harvard and Chicago struggling to keep pace with a southern university press. Instead of always being backward in matters cultural, the South was suddenly cast in the role of initiator. Above all, Couch's triumph was a sure indication that the Modernist movement had finally arrived in the region. In the final analysis, that was the significance of that tense moment in 1927 when the fate of *Congaree Sketches* was decided.[22]

II

Many elements of this unusual success story had little to do with Couch himself. One cannot discount, among other things, the importance of Odum's institute, with its continuous flow of good manuscripts, or the unquestioned support given the press by Frank Porter Graham after he became president of the university in 1930. In addition, the press enjoyed a virtual monopoly in southern publishing during its first fifteen years of existence, a fact that had great bearing both on book sales and the availability of foundation support. This state of affairs could not last for long. In the mid-1930s, Louisiana State University and the University of Georgia started presses of their own, with Vanderbilt following in 1940. Simultaneously, more or less dormant presses at Duke University, the University of the South, and the University of Texas came back to life. Often endowed with far more generous subsidies than Couch had ever been allotted, these new competitors began aggressively searching out the same sort of manuscripts on which the North Carolina Press had thrived. Indeed, Couch's decision to leave the South in 1945 to become director of the University of Chicago Press was partly related to this development.[23]

But the real secret of Couch's achievement lay in his willingness to follow the dictates of his Modernist sensibility as he went about his work. That fact was apparent not only in his effort to seek out books that he knew would generate controversy, but in the prodigious amount of editorial counseling he engaged in trying to coax southern authors away from nineteenth-century conventions. His correspondence of the period is filled with instructions to authors, much of it going well beyond the normal prerogative of a publisher, at times amounting to an informal seminar on Modernist standards.

What Couch wanted most was detail, striking and plentiful. "This is fresh, vivid, and carries the conviction of authenticity," he noted of one paragraph in Clarence Cason's 90° *in the Shade*, "more of such fresh illustrative matter ought to be included." Put another way, his was the documentary imagination that, according to William Stott, dominated American cultural expression during the 1930s with its concern for the "texture of reality" and the "particularity of the common man's life." In Couch's case, this cast of mind definitely predated the depression, representing not so much a reaction to hard times as the onrush of curiosity released after the floodgates of Victorian elitism had crashed open. "I want to read [a book] by some one who has eaten at the cotton mill hand's table and felt of his bed," he wrote Broadus Mitchell early in 1927. "I would like to know what he [the worker] thinks and what he wants." Over and over Couch pounded his authors with this sort of question, prodding them to tell more about the circumstances and inner lives of sharecroppers, blacks, factory workers, members of lynch mobs, and others, pressing for books that would expose middle-class southerners to conditions beyond their normal experience.[24]

However, Couch was never satisfied with the mere recitation of fact. Having surveyed the output of the first generation of American sociologists, he had little faith in the capacity of social science by itself to arrive at meaningful truths, nor did he believe that complete objectivity was possible. A story he told the annual meeting of the Association of American Universities in 1934 wryly expresses his skepticism on this point:

> The truth concerning the present state of the social sciences was almost given in a textbook a few years ago. In the first few pages the effort was made to define social science. A number of definitions were quoted, and among these was one that should have read "Science is knowledge which is verifiable and cumulative." However, the book was dictated to a stenographer, and in going through her hands this passage was transmuted to read "Science is knowledge which is very feeble and cumulative." Surely she was guided by an invisible hand. If she had only said "social" science, we should then know that the truth in this field was at last discovered by disinterest and indirection.

For Couch the facts had to be explained, their underlying meaning extracted, even if this necessitated a sacrifice of objectivity. "The excessive desire to avoid emotive terms may lead to ambiguity," he advised the writer of a 1933 book on lynching in what might stand as his cardinal editorial principle—one directly in contrast to Odum's. In Couch's view, detail had to be evocative, analysis explicit, and the author's own bias and belief openly set forth.[25]

Three books published by the press during the 1930s may serve to illustrate Couch's methods in action. The first two, Dabney's *Liberalism in the South* and the symposium, *Culture in the South*, were originally intended as part of a series on "The Old and New South" commissioned by the press in 1929 but never completed because of inadequate finances during the depression. *These Are Our Lives* grew out of Couch's service as regional director of the Federal Writers' Project during the latter years of the decade. All three immediately secured a place among the classic works about the region.[26]

Liberalism in the South seems a relatively tame work today, but in 1932 the practice of identifying by name the persons it was criticizing represented a new departure for books published by a southern press. From the start Couch hoped to produce a model of candor that would induce other southern writers to follow suit. As he observed to Dabney in 1932, that was why he considered the book "epoch-making":

> I believe this is the first time any book has been written and published in the South embodying an undiluted liberal philosophy.
> I know to my sorrow that this book could not have been published here three or four years ago, and I doubt whether there are many educational institutions in the South today that would be willing to have their names connected with the volume, even at the present time. That is, the majority of our institutions will have this attitude until they discover that the calm and honest statement of decent and humane attitudes toward public problems can occur in the South without disastrous results.

Although Dabney, the descendant of a notable Virginia family, was somewhat reluctant to depart from his Tidewater manners, the book thanks to Couch did take a distinctly critical approach toward southern problems, thus helping to smooth the way for the still harder-hitting publications that followed it.[27]

Indeed, most of the more outspoken passages in *Liberalism in the South* can be attributed directly to Couch's influence. It was at his urging, for instance, that Dabney included a discussion of the then highly sensitive Scottsboro case, raising the question of whether the nine black youths convicted of raping two white girls in Alabama had received a fair trial. Couch was anxious that the book cover recent labor troubles in the South, in particular the bloody coal miners' revolt in Harlan and Bell counties, Kentucky, and the violent textile workers' strikes in North Carolina and Virginia. The problem in those disputes, he pointed out to Dabney, was the failure of local law enforcement officials to remain impartial. Since justice for workers could not be had in the South, the only solution Couch could see was federal intervention. Dabney, a states' rights man, was not willing to go that far, but his treatment of the strikes plainly mirrors Couch's position. Most important of all, Dabney's conclusion was based almost verbatim on a long letter Couch had sent him setting forth the principles of modern liberalism. Its argument, closely anticipating one of the main tenets of the New Deal, was that all the liberals' traditional talk of civil liberties became meaningless if people did not first possess economic security. It might be more accurate to say, in fact, that Couch drafted the chapter and Dabney edited it—surely an unusual role for a publisher.[28]

A still more dramatic demonstration of Couch's propensity for putting his stamp on press books can be found in the long, tortuous history of *Culture in the South*, a volume first proposed by Couch in late 1928 that did not see publication until five years later. Modeled on Harold Stearns's 1922 symposium, *Civilization in the United States*, the book was to survey southern society critically in a broad array of areas, including politics, journalism, education, religion, literature, and so on. Like the Stearns volume, it was supposed to convey a mood—a sense of disenchantment and impatience on the part of the upcoming generation of southern intellectuals. At first Couch toyed with the idea of editing the book himself, but, realizing that he did not have sufficient stature to corner good contributors, he turned to an ambitious younger member of the Chapel Hill English department and a close personal friend, Howard Mumford Jones, who accepted the job provided that "editorial responsibility" would be "fixed with the editor solely." It was an arrangement that almost cost Couch and Jones their friendship.[29]

The problem was simple: Jones did not care much about the project, but Couch cared intensely. Jones, Couch was convinced, fully understood that "we want a first-class book" and that "he should row with his contributors if necessary" to get one. But when Jones in late 1930 finally submitted the articles he had gathered, the misapprehension of intentions was clear. To Couch the book seemed lifeless and soporific, its article on southern education "painfully dull," while that on religion (which Jones had praised as "good, solid stuff") was "utterly incompetent." Only the piece by Donald Davidson analyzing trends in southern literature met Couch's litmus test of requisite intellectual acerbity. For his part, Jones considered Couch's critique "tactless." The manuscript, he maintained, was filled with a "wealth of information and of sober discussion" even if it did lack "literary finish." The tone of debate continued to decline until Jones, angrily citing the "obvious desire exhibited on your part to edit this book," officially quit. Couch was willing to sacrifice anything, including a friendship, to get the "first-class book" on the South he had in mind.[30]

Besides the issue of quality, the other major reason why Couch took the reins from Jones was that his conception of the book had changed. Originally he had been content with Jones's plan to survey key areas of southern society, such as agriculture, industry, and education. But as he read over the articles that had come in, he found himself increasingly disturbed by their New South emphasis on "physical development and the acquisition of wealth." "I feel that there are other values of equal, if not greater, importance which ought to be defined and discussed," he told John Donald Wade in February, 1931. "If we cannot show some of these other values, I for one have serious doubts as to the excellence of our culture." He meant by this the folk values that determined everyday life in the region. Thus by April, 1931, he had decided that the "inclusion of at least one chapter directly describing the Southern people and their ways of living is imperative." A year later his entire notion of the project had been reshaped along those lines: "The purpose of the book is to discuss all of the more important phases of culture in the southern states, using the term 'culture' in its widest sense. The book should describe the varieties of life in the South, with emphasis on those ways of living which are most generally followed and on the influences which are changing the present patterns of life." Jones had tentatively titled the book "Civilization Below the Potomac"; Couch soon amended that to "Culture in the South." He was referring, of course, to the anthropological—or Modernist—sense of "culture."[31]

Like a cultural anthropologist, Couch was trying to capture the normally unnoticed "patterns" of southern existence, especially those unspoken values and attitudes that, precisely because they were unexamined, often controlled behavior. To this end he solicited a whole new set of articles, dealing with the daily lives of farmers, industrial workers, mountaineers, coal miners, city dwellers, professionals, and aristocrats. The emphasis, he kept insisting, should in each case fall on "human values." As he told the prospective author of a piece on southern workers, the reader should derive

> a clear picture of the daily routine of the laborer in industry, of his working and leisure hours—his rising in the morning, what he eats and how important eating is in his life, his attitude toward his work, his home and his neighbors, toward the levels of life which he considers beneath himself, toward religion and the church, education and the schools,—toward all the more important factors which in any way impinge upon his life.

The article on the region's middle class would follow a doctor on his rounds, or a shopkeeper plying his trade. In addition, Couch now sought a further set of articles covering the more direct expressions of southern culture in folk songs (white and black), tall tales, speech patterns, humor, fine arts, and handicrafts. In some cases these topics had been so little explored that great persistence was required to find a capable author— it took over fifty letters of inquiry for the chapter on fine arts alone— but Couch was determined not to leave out any subject he deemed significant.[32]

Equally crucial was his watchful editing. On occasion his efforts were directed at toning a piece down, as when he persuaded one ardent Mencken disciple writing on southern religion to avoid a condescending approach to the Fundamentalists. More typically, though, Couch found himself trying to convince apprehensive southerners that the region's former restraints on free expression need no longer be heeded, that "emotive terms" could and should be used. "I should like especially to have a description of a mob," he told H. C. Brearley, an Odum-trained sociologist whose draft chapter on southern violence was predictably weighted down with statistics,

> —how it gathers, becomes excited, starts a chase (possibly with dogs), gets on a trail, catches a Negro, and then proceeds to indulge in barbarous cruelty, pulling off toe and finger nails, cutting off toes and fingers by joints, pulling out chunks of flesh with corkscrews, and finally burning and shooting and gathering bones, teeth, or remnants of clothing as souvenirs. The cruelty of our mobs is, I believe, unique, and should be remarked upon in some detail.

Here was an entirely new sensibility in the South approaching the problem of lynching in all its ugliness. As it happened, Brearley took Couch's suggestions for bringing his essay to life, with markedly beneficial results.[33]

The quality Couch most insisted upon was candor. The survey of southern colleges and universities, he wrote Herman C. Nixon, should deal fully with the question of "academic subservience to economic and political pressures," not failing to "cite particular instances and name names." The chapter by Edd W. Parks should cover the "less attractive as well as the more attractive" neighborhoods of southern cities. The most extreme implementation of this policy, however, came in the chapter on journalism. There Couch wanted to know about the "connection between editorial and news policies and the business interests of the papers." "Is news of public interest and importance ever suppressed at the behest of private and selfishly interested parties?" he asked. If so, the article should include "specific examples" with "names and dates." When Robert Lathan, editor of the *Asheville* (N.C.) *Citizen* and contributor of the original article on journalism submitted to Jones, protested that such a treatment would call down more criticism than he could handle, Couch turned instead to John D. Allen, a young journalism professor from Georgia. Lathan had recently received a Pulitzer Prize, Allen was unknown, but upon receiving Allen's article Couch could not have been more pleased with his decision. Thoroughly critical, yet well-balanced and comprehensive, it ranks among the strongest in the book.[34]

With the exception of Allen Tate (who seems to have been miffed that he was not invited to contribute), *Culture in the South* won nearly unanimous praise from reviewers. Although most of the contributors had in fact been prominent figures for a decade or more, the comment was repeatedly made that the symposium heralded the arrival of a new generation of southern intellectuals with a voice easily distinguishable from their predecessors, one thoroughly in tune with their era but directed squarely at the South. "Their heritage is more nearly that of the Populists than the Confederates," Jonathan Daniels accurately observed. "They speak in truth more of the times than of the South. Their regionalism is purely geographic. It is their problem and not its solution that is southern." Constance Rourke, writing for the *New York Herald-Tribune*, was struck by the prevailing "unromantic and salty view." "The whole volume may be construed as an effort to break up the fixed notion of a 'solid South,'" she wrote, "and it succeeds because the many facets of a complex life are so brilliantly classified." What the reviewers were really praising, without knowing it, was the impact of Couch's informal seminar with his authors. The full extent of his labors remained hidden behind the scenes, as he apparently preferred it.[35]

In the symposium, Couch employed experts to write on southern culture viewed from the top down; in the late 1930s, as the trend toward documentary expression in America peaked, he attempted to let people living within that culture speak for themselves. *These Are Our Lives* evolved from an urgent plea to Couch by Henry G. Alsberg, director of the Federal Writers' Project, to rescue the stagnated program in the South. Couch responded in April, 1938, with a proposal for collecting life histories from all major social and occupational groups in the region, with special emphasis on the farm population. This would give the project's southern staff an immediate sense of purpose and possibly provide the press with some interesting material to publish. Various sources provided the inspiration for this idea, including the chapter devoted to case studies of farm tenants in Rupert Vance's *Human Factors in Cotton Culture*, Erskine Caldwell and Margaret Bourke-White's immensely popular venture in photojournalism, *You Have Seen Their Faces*, and John Dollard's *Caste and Class in a Southern Town*. But most of all, Couch was guided by his own ever-present curiosity about the South. What went on, what attitudes were held, at the different levels of southern society? Did the recollections of his childhood still hold true, or had ordinary life in the region irretrievably changed? The life-histories method seemed an ideal means of answering these questions.[36]

The basic approach was simple—perhaps too simple. Staff writers were sent out to interview literally hundreds of people, ranging from mill executives to migrant farm workers. In effect, the interviewers were told to transform themselves temporarily into recording machines. "If the subject's head is filled with wrong notions, foolish thoughts, and misinformation," read Couch's instruction sheet, "record it. Let the subject's mind speak for itself." The writer was to work this raw material up into a short story, using the subject's own language as extensively as possible, but also striving for "literary excellence." It was here, as Stott and others have pointed out, that problems set in, for the writers involved were not trained sociologists but would-be journalists and literary types in search of employment. Their practical need to have their abilities noticed caused them to intrude their opinions and style into the stories repeatedly, vitiating the documentary accuracy of the approach. Couch conceivably might have taken steps to control this tendency, possibly by publishing the life histories in their raw form, but he did not. In part, he wanted to help members of his staff find jobs, but mainly he was insufficiently sensitive to questions of objectivity to cope with the situation. His previous efforts over the years had been spent tearing down the barriers of formality in southern social science, getting investigators to put aside artificial constraints and view their subjects in an immediate and personal fashion. In *These Are Our Lives* he overshot his mark and could not reverse direction fast enough.[37]

It must be remembered, though, that *These Are Our Lives* was meant primarily as a preview of things to come. A series of sixteen volumes was to follow it, each volume focused on a specific occupational group in the South, with the subjects selected in accordance with orthodox social science sampling procedures. The larger project was to be conducted, if possible, with the close cooperation of sociologists and other pertinent experts, and with the added financial backing of private foundations. Couch had hurriedly assembled *These Are Our Lives* and filled it with what he believed were the most poignant stories he had available in hopes of attracting this widespread backing. As he explained in his preface, the goal was to feel his way toward a new kind of social research that would reveal the "real workings of institutions, customs, habits" by taking into account the "whole life experience" of the individual. Such studies would fill in the "living context" that Couch thought sociology had hitherto ignored and, through their human interest content, appeal directly to the general reader.[38]

Unfortunately, Couch never had the chance to test this ambitious scheme. By the time *These Are Our Lives* appeared, congressional conservatives had succeeded in forcing Alsberg out of the Writers' Project and otherwise gutting the program. After six months of petty wrangling with the WPA bureaucrats in charge, Couch resigned in disgust. Equally devastating was the reaction of the social science community, which steadfastly ignored the book. Ellsworth Faris, editor of the *American Journal of Sociology*, pompously refused even to have *These Are Our Lives* reviewed, claiming that it belonged in the same category as *Tobacco Road* and *Gone With the Wind*. Complicating the situation further was the long-simmering personal feud between Couch and Odum, two prima donna competitors vying with each other for national attention and financial support. Odum, who lived in terror that Couch would someday set off a firestorm comparable to the *Social Forces* furor of 1925 and so jeopardize the institute, prevented the members of his department from giving Couch aid and comfort.* This, in 1939, was enough to deal the crowning blow to Couch's plans.[39]

Whether Couch could have turned the life-histories project into a genuine success, even had he received the help he wanted, remains an unanswerable question. One suspects his talents more suited to editing a symposium like *Culture in the South* than to appraising the authenticity and poetic value of the materials such an undertaking would gather. Still, his preface to *These Are Our Lives* makes one wish he had gotten his chance:

> To those who glance at a page [of this book] and imagine they have
> absorbed its contents, to those who are fixed in their ideas as to how

---

*There is a temptation to make more of the Couch-Odum rivalry than it is worth. Although it is true that Couch was willing to take more publishing risks than Odum, by the 1930s the differences between them on this score were not that great. Odum was perfectly happy to see the press publish potentially controversial studies done by his own disciples like Arthur Raper—provided the books appeared under Odum's sponsorship. Rather, this was a contest between two strong personalities, each guarding his respective institutional domain. For a review of the situation from Couch's perspective, including details on Odum's efforts to keep anyone in the institute from cooperating with Couch on the life-histories project, see Couch, "Memorandum to President Graham," July 13, 1938, as well as Paul Green to Henry G. Alsberg, July 11, 1938, and Frank P. Graham to Alsberg, July 12, 1938, Couch Papers. Unfortunately, almost no information on the dispute appears in the Odum Papers—either Odum scrupulously avoided committing such matters to paper, or his literary executors chose to excise the relevant materials from the collection.

writing should be done, to those who are already certain how people think and feel, to those who are not genuinely interested in the rich variety of human experience, to those who cannot for a moment look at the world and people as if they were seeing them for the first time, pushing aside all patterns and doctrines that might be obstructive, this book will have no meaning. I ask only that the reader take the time to consider and understand why and how it has been written. I shall appreciate greatly any suggestions or criticisms which might lead to improvement of the method used here, or to a better method of revealing the people as they are.

This paragraph concisely embodies the openness, curiosity, and innovative quality Couch brought to his work at the press. It was these characteristics, all flowing from his Modernist sensibility, which made him not an ordinary publisher but rather an intellectual force in the region.[40]

III

In addition to his accomplishments at the press, Couch's Modernist values were also manifest in his willingness to participate in the rough-and-tumble ways of political activism. For the intellectuals of the New South generation, politics was always a source of contamination, unfit for the gentleman scholar to engage in (save for voting on election day). Those in the academic profession especially regarded political involvement as a breach of objectivity. If a faculty member held strong views on a partisan issue, he was expected to keep those views to himself. Odum, as we have seen, did make sorties into the public arena, but reluctantly, cautiously, and quietly, working behind the scenes for prison reform or serving on the staff of the President's Commission on Recent Social Trends. Odum could blink at, if not condone, the firing of a University of Texas professor because the man was, in Odum's words, in "open public speaking rebellion." And Chase, considered the most liberal university administrator in the South at the time, could in 1928 draft a policy statement (for internal consumption only) that read:

No faculty member has any right to allow his personal sympathies for any controversial cause to involve his colleagues and his institution in a situation that means general embarrassment, restricted educational opportunities for students and threatened careers for his colleagues. Such conduct is a fundamental denial of what should be his prime loyalties. If his sympathy for such a cause becomes sufficiently strong to raise in his mind a real conflict with his

institutional loyalty, he should obviously sever his connection with the institution.

As examples of controversial causes, Chase went on to mention "advocacy of particular forms of taxation, of the organization of labor, of
social equality between the races, of a socialistic regime, etc." Such was
the prevailing opinion when Couch began his career in the late 1920s.[41]

He did not take long to challenge this policy. In April, 1927, just as he
was preparing his surprise for the press board over *Congaree Sketches*,
he made his presence known on the editorial page of the *Durham Morning Herald* in a fashion that sent shudders through the community. Incensed by an editorial in the paper praising Massachusetts officials for
their handling of the Sacco and Vanzetti case and denouncing radicals in
general, Couch penned a fierce rejoinder that took swipes at southern
conservatism for good measure:

> If Jesus Christ were to come to earth today and come into a
> Southern community and start preaching as we are told he did
> 2000 years ago, if he suggested again his teaching of the brother-
> hood of man, and instead of a parable were to preach against
> the condition that negroes cannot ride on busses in North Carolina
> and that they were in many things treated in a somewhat un-
> brotherly way, what would happen to him? If he came as a college
> professor, white or black, he would probably be promptly fired.
> If he kept up his agitation the mob would rise and demand his
> blood. Would you care to be a member of such a mob? Jesus
> Christ was a radical; his teachings, though professed, can hardly
> be seriously mentioned in public in the South.

The language is surely that of a headstrong young man, reminiscent in
ways of Broadus Mitchell as he tried to establish his claim to be a socialist. Couch would later learn to use political rhetoric with greater maturity,
avoiding gratuitous insults. But, as this early incident reveals, public
controversy for Couch represented the meat and drink of intellectual life,
a moral imperative for any man who pretended to care about social
affairs. That belief he would never abandon.[42]

Couch's eagerness to jump into the political fray was predicated on his
conception of the structure of southern society, a conception not unlike
that of Odum or the Agrarians but much more sharply defined. Where
the New South generation had seen the region in terms of polarities—
aristocrats versus poor whites with a small bourgeoisie tucked precari-
ously in between—Couch envisaged a sizable middle class, running the
gamut from professionals to the more substantial variety of tenant farm-

ers, comprising the "majority" of the southern population. This middle class was not composed of mythical yeomen drinking in virtue from the soil but rather of average, hardworking, sober citizens, many of them living in towns and cities. Couch identified with this middle class even more strongly than did Odum with his. Their very existence, he believed, had been hitherto "ignored" by writers on the region, an error he continually tried to correct through his work at the press. Atop the social scale he placed a small contingent of planters, bankers, merchants, and industrialists who, because they controlled the South's economy, bore "chief responsibility for our present miseries." Although he admired some members of this class for their paternalistic concerns, Couch was also convinced that the "mere fact of their class membership" and especially "their notions of respectability, of what one can and cannot do," prevented them from saving the region "from disaster." At the bottom of the heap he tended to see a mudsill class, considerable in number, but impoverished, illiterate, and powerless. In his estimate, only the mill workers could provide material for a real proletariat in southern politics; sharecroppers of both races he likened to an inert, hopeless "peasantry."[43]

The key to the South's social and political problems, Couch believed, was the failure of the middle class to take politics seriously. "Well-intentioned but authority worshipping," too often given to the "complacent acceptance of long-standing habits and attitudes," the plain folk had as a class "abdicated its leadership." By not asserting its numerical superiority, it had allowed first the antebellum planters and then the commercial elite—all the same to Couch—to dominate the political system and impose its self-serving ideology on the whole society. Even rabble-rousers like Heflin and Bilbo were in his eyes agents of the elite, their antics contrived to "fool and pacify the masses while the old gang continues to carry off the loot." Couch was turning the diagnosis of earlier southern liberals upside down. He was pinning the blame for the region's barbaric politics on the upper, not the lower, class, while holding the middle class guilty as an accessory by reason of its inaction. Accordingly, his prescription for the middle class was not to remain aloof, unsoiled, nonpartisan, as New South liberals had counseled, but to become reinvolved in the political process. "The spectacle of Heflin, et al., is funny," Couch noted in 1934, "but the middle-class is going to discover one of these days that it is not only funny."[44]

This desire to wake up the middle class accounts for the shock tactics Couch frequently used. The extreme language of his letter to the *Durham Morning Herald*, his readiness almost alone among southern liberals to denounce publicly the injustice done at Scottsboro and Gastonia, his willingness to adopt less celebrated causes such as that of ten strikers railroaded into prison for allegedly dynamiting a textile mill in Burlington, North Carolina—all reflected his effort to stir things up, to break down the old complacency, and to move public opinion leftward. At times these tactics made Couch look more radical than he really was. This was especially true in the area of race relations where Couch stood ready to champion better treatment for southern blacks while retaining the traditional belief that segregation was imperative. In truth, Couch's basic political thought differed little from that of most American intellectuals of his era: it was New Deal liberalism applied to the South. His program for the region encompassed aid to tenant farmers, unionization and collective bargaining for workers, a gradual redistribution of wealth through progressive taxation, and the creation of producers' and consumers' cooperatives when feasible.[45]

Couch did part company with most of his southern contemporaries, however, in his eagerness to join political organizations. He was among that small group of southerners whose names appeared again and again on the letterheads of the political correspondence of that decade, a group that included Frank Porter Graham, Herman Clarence Nixon, Charles W. Pipkin, Francis P. Miller, Mark Ethridge, and Brooks Hays—the "younger upper bracket folk" Odum once called them. These were the friends Couch stayed closely in touch with, and with whom he helped to form the Southern Policy Association and Southern Conference for Human Welfare, the two most noteworthy attempts by southern liberals to mobilize a constituency in their region on behalf of the New Deal.[46]

To be sure, the Southern Policy Association accomplished little during its short-lived existence, but it deserves mention as the first attempt ever made by intellectuals in the South to organize expressly for political purposes. Formed as an offshoot of the Foreign Policy Association in mid-1935, its guiding light and indispensable link to Washington was a genial Virginian named Francis Pickens Miller, whose wife Helen held a strategically placed position in the Department of Agriculture. Miller's idea was to set up committees in each southern state composed of academics, politicos, and sympathetic businessmen to debate current policy issues. Their recommendations were to be funneled into an annual region-wide meeting, which would adopt a final report and plan for its implementation. The association held its most important meeting in May, 1936, at Chattanooga on the general topic of "Social Security for the South," endorsing such proposals as federal aid to education, removal of the poll tax, and reapportionment of southern state legislatures on the basis of population. The gathering was highlighted by a fierce verbal duel between Couch and Allen Tate. Tate argued that only widespread ownership of private property could preserve democratic institutions, while Couch contended that some "effective means of controlling in the public interest large aggregations of wealth" was needed. The SPA also lobbied with indifferent success for strengthening the Bankhead-Jones Farm Tenancy Act and published through the North Carolina Press a series of pamphlets on social issues affecting the South. But mainly, it provided a chance for activists like Couch to get acquainted with one another, acquire a modicum of political skill, and refine their policy objectives.[47]

If the Southern Policy Association helped bring the intellectual elite together, the Southern Conference for Human Welfare represented what many believed was the obvious next step—a mass organization drawing in labor, blacks, and the poor. Plans for such a coalition had floated about for some time, but little was done until late 1936 when the Louisiana Coalition of Patriotic Societies, an ultra-right wing group in New Orleans, mounted a campaign to have Herman Clarence Nixon, then chairman of the Southern Policy Association, and certain other Tulane faculty members fired. Unlike so many of his southern predecessors faced with similar threats, Nixon knew how to fight back: discreetly he contacted a syndicated writer for the *St. Louis Post Dispatch* and within a few days the story of how the Tulane administration was about to commit a gross violation of academic freedom appeared, among other places, in the leading New Orleans newspapers. Although the pressure against him soon subsided, Nixon began thinking about forming a new organization of progressive elements in the region, as he confided in a letter to Couch:

> I am convinced that we need a strong liberal organization in the South for action, not one balanced between agrarians and industrialists, between academicians and "men of affairs," or between capital and labor, but a group of persons in approximate agreement as to what should be done and said. Such a movement would include . . . a large contingent of the Southern Policy group. It would not be in opposition to Southern policy and would go along with it in many ways but would be more militant and more in contact with labor.

Couch readily agreed that intellectuals should be advocates, not neutral mediators, in social disputes. As it happened, he had just raised $95,000 for the press from various sources to finance innovative projects, and he could imagine nothing more innovative than using part of the sum to send Nixon through the South researching a book they had discussed on rural reconstruction and, coincidentally, laying the groundwork for the proposed conference.[48]

For the most part, the first meeting of the conference, held in Birmingham's Municipal Auditorium in November, 1938, turned out as planned. Nearly twelve hundred delegates and as many onlookers, representing farm groups, labor unions, women's clubs, civil rights and social welfare organizations, and academia, assembled to hear a succession of impassioned speeches and to agree that the South required generous federal aid to solve its myriad ills. The National Emergency Council's *Report on Economic Conditions of the South* had appeared fortuitously just three months before, allowing Nixon to instate it as the centerpiece of discussion at the conference. This led many to believe that the conference had been called expressly to follow up the report with specific proposals, a supposition Nixon astutely did all in his power to foster. Also emphasizing this unofficial connection with the New Deal was the roster of speakers, including Eleanor Roosevelt, Aubrey Williams of the National Youth Administration, Senators William B. Bankhead of Alabama and Claude Pepper of Florida, and Supreme Court Justice Hugo Black. As Couch, who served as program chairman, proudly observed in a report for the *New Republic*, nothing like this had ever happened in all the South's history. It looked like the movement was off to an auspicious start.[49]

Two clouds darkened the horizon. First and foremost was the segregation issue, fastened on the conference by the actions of the Birmingham police. As was the custom at such conclaves by the late 1930s, delegates had been sitting in racially mixed fashion for nearly two days when the city's police chief, Eugene "Bull" Connor, informed them they were violating a local ordinance prohibiting integrated seating in public buildings. The question of what to do was brought to Couch, who decided the only sensible course politically was to resegregate. Since mixed meetings had been held in the auditorium before, he reasoned, someone was deliberately trying to sabotage the conference, and resisting the ordinance could only compound the damage. To pacify delegates unhappy with this choice, a resolution was passed condemning the police and instructing conference officers in the future to avoid similar situations "if at all possible." But, as Couch had anticipated, this was bad enough. Several southern newspapers interpreted the resolution as a general attack on Jim Crow (an inaccurate United Press dispatch contributed to this misinterpretation), spreading the impression that the gathering had gone on record in favor of racial equality. Many liberals like Jonathan Daniels who might otherwise have become strong supporters of the conference began scurrying for the exits as a result.[50]

The second storm cloud, which began descending early in 1939, involved the presence of members and fellow travelers of the Communist party in key leadership roles. The party, then in its popular front phase, was seeking to infiltrate groups like the Southern Conference for Human Welfare and to work in tandem with the New Deal. It was especially interested in the South, where extreme poverty, a comparatively well-defined class system, and easily exploitable racial tension seemed to offer it a potential American base. Thus, while the liberals headed by Nixon and Couch had remained in thorough control at Birmingham, in February, 1939, a fellow traveler named Joseph S. Gelders, former physics professor at the University of Alabama and southern representative for the National Committee for the Defense of Political Prisoners, became effective head of the influential civil rights committee; and a few months later Howard Lee, a full-fledged party operative, replaced Nixon as executive secretary after the latter returned to full-time teaching. As the real locus of power became obscure, more liberals deserted. "I have no intention of being used as a front by forces which elude inquiry," wrote Francis Miller, explaining his refusal to accept election as vice-president. Soon it was a vicious cycle—the initial exodus creating a vacuum that the Communists moved to fill, leading to more departures and thus insuring that the conference would never obtain sufficient financial backing to do its work. That it did not collapse entirely was due to the decision of Frank Porter Graham to stay on as chairman in the face of much contrary advice.[51]*

*This account, it should be pointed out, differs from that of Thomas A. Krueger on both the origins of the SCHW and the matter of its infiltration by Communists. Krueger maintains that the prime mover in convening the conference was Gelders. Gelders was indeed pursuing independent plans for an organization to champion civil liberties in the South, but by mid-1938 it is clear that he had hitched his work to the ongoing efforts of Nixon. This fact helps explain why Gelders played such a minor role at the Birmingham meeting while Nixon and Couch ran the show. On the primacy of Nixon, Couch, and Graham at Birmingham, see Charles S. Johnson to Howard W. Odum, November 25, 1938, Odum to Johnson, September 21, 1938, Odum Papers; and Lucy Randolph Mason to Frank P. Graham, November 24, 1938, folder 1938–78, Graham Papers. None of these documents concerning the organization of the conference so much as mentions Gelders, nor was he listed on the conference letterhead.

As for the Communist issue, Krueger argues that, even though the party did control the most important conference leadership roles by late 1939, this did not matter since the "insipidity of the Communists' popular-front policy rendered them nearly innocuous" (p. 67). Here he fails to understand the political climate of the era. The policy differences separating liberals and Communists at the time, such as support of the Soviet Union following the Nazi-Soviet Pact, were real and vital to those living through the period. Besides, few people then or now care to belong to an organization in which a small, tightly disciplined minority exercises clandestine control, in which one can never be sure of the true allegiances of one's coworkers. Few enjoy being duped. By infiltrating this way the Communists managed to stop dead whatever momentum the SCHW might have achieved had it remained in liberal hands. Their impact cannot be ignored, here or in similar organizations like the Southern Tenant Farmers' Union.

While these events were taking place, Couch was becoming preoccupied with international affairs. In all probability no one else in the South watched the rise of nazism with greater care or trepidation. Capable of reading German, he had subscribed to German periodicals from the late 1920s onward trying to decipher what was happening in that country, particularly in regard to race. "I was specially interested in Hitler's racial attitude," he later recalled, "because the South had a racial problem that could, with malign leadership, be made worse than that which Hitler was trying to make the German people feel that they had." What struck him most was the fact that it had been the German middle class that proved so susceptible to fascism: "I had for years been saying to myself that Nazism could never succeed in Germany, that the German people were probably the best educated people in the world, best universities, best science—nothing of the sort could possibly happen there. But it did happen." The very existence of a *race problem*, he concluded, had opened the door for Hitler; whenever two races lived side by side with a degree of antagonism, a Fascist demagogue could find ready kindling. It could happen in the South "in a few years' time."[52]

With the signing of the Nazi-Soviet Non-Aggression Pact in August, 1939, these apprehensions rose markedly. Like most left-leaning American intellectuals of the 1930s, Couch had looked upon Russia as a rough approximation of the world's future. A society once as dismally backward as the South that had raised itself to economic stability through planning, it was a measuring rod to gauge the progress or stasis of other nations and, above all, a bulwark against fascism. Thus in 1935 he had lectured the author of a book on contemporary Germany on

> the extreme difference between Communist and Nazi doctrine,
> between internationalism and nationalism, between tolerance for all
> races and the cult of the Nordic, between a system designed to
> destroy and one designed to maintain capitalism, between a system
> that gives women a wide scope and one that puts them back in the
> home, between one that encourages everyone who has the ability to
> get as much educational training as possible and one that limits
> training. . . . If there are any such things as different and op-
> posed systems, I think Germany and Russia have them.

But by 1938, this distinction, crucial to his inner map of political and moral geography, was well on its way to breaking down. Compared to Germany, he wrote a friend that year, "Russia has at least expressed decent sentiments from time to time. I admit this is cold comfort in the face of what she appears to practice." The final blow came with the Russian invasion of Finland in November, 1939, an act Couch branded the "most criminally insincere conduct that has occurred among nations in a long time." His disillusionment was now complete.[53]

By this time Couch was coming to feel directly and personally threatened by the course history was taking. Just as he had previously tried to make southern social issues come alive for others through tying fact to emotion, so the foreign policy dilemmas facing the country now came alive for him. "Here and in Britain it has been and is still possible for me to work for the things that I value," he explained, "whereas if the Nazis win this will not be true anywhere in Europe, and I am certain the same condition will soon come to exist in this country." As a southerner engaged in a long-term battle for freedom of thought and expression in the region, he was well aware of what a Fascist suppression of civil liberties might mean. In addition, Couch was incensed at the way a number of his former political friends continued to defend Stalin even after the alliance with Hitler had been struck. Once again Couch replicated the pattern of so many American liberals of the time as his sense of betrayal pushed him rightward.[54]

His response to the crisis took several forms. He became a fervent interventionist, firing off letters to newspaper editors, circulating petitions to Congress, and serving as de facto southern secretary on behalf of Fighting Funds for Finland and the Committee to Defend America by Aiding the Allies. His most successful effort was the publication through the press of a short volume, Reuben H. Markham's *The Wave of the Past*, meant as an anti-isolationist rejoinder to Anne Morrow Lindbergh's *The Wave of the Future*. The book sold over seventy thousand copies in four months, enough to make the bestseller list in mid-1941. His opposition to fascism was matched by his animus toward communism, an ideology he now called the "worst hodge-podge of snivelling hypocrisy" he had ever seen. Since Communists resorted to such underhanded tactics, no longer did he believe that they deserved the full protection of the First Amendment. At the same time, as the world order disintegrated, the problems of the South seemed to pale for Couch. This fact was dramatically illustrated by his reluctance to attend the second meeting of the Southern Conference for Human Welfare in April, 1940, lest his stand on intervention provoke a battle with the Communists and isolationist liberals. "I am, to be frank, thoroughly rabid on the subject," he warned a conference organizer about his feelings on the war issue. But in the end he did go, largely through Frank Porter Graham's persuasion.[55]

The confrontation that erupted at the meeting revealed the same outspokenness and activism that had characterized Couch's entire career. Unable to leave foreign affairs aside even temporarily, Couch moved at the opening session to amend a resolution passed unanimously at Birmingham condemning Nazi aggression to include Soviet aggression as well. His motion also called upon the United States government to adopt "any measures that can be taken within legal neutrality" to save democratic Europe. Certainly these were not idle matters. A month earlier the Russians, after a winter of bloody war, had forced Finland to capitulate and were busy consolidating their hold on eastern Europe. The previous week the Nazis had invaded Denmark and Norway. For over an hour the angry words flew, Couch and his antagonists denouncing one another with mounting vehemence, many accusing him of trying to split the conference, until three large men—whether Earl Browder's or John L. Lewis's minions is not clear—dragged him from the microphone and compelled him to be silent. Badly shaken, Couch left the following morning and resigned from the conference soon after—even though a watered-down version of his resolution was eventually approved at Graham's insistence. The incident marked the end of Couch's participation in the southern liberal movement, though it was hardly his last involvement in public affairs.[56]

I V

In 1944 another incident occurred that clearly displays the limits of Couch's Modernist thought. It concerned the one issue that was to prove most difficult for Modernist intellectuals in the South, the question of whether or not to maintain racial segregation. Like most southern thinkers, Couch had long assumed that black leaders favored continuing the color line in such areas as education, at least in the foreseeable future. That was what black spokesmen in the 1930s had consistently said. Accordingly, Couch felt no compunctions adopting a suggestion by Guy B. Johnson to have Rayford W. Logan, a black historian at Howard University, edit a symposium in which (in Couch's words) "Negroes would state what they believe and indicate what the Negro wants and what he ought to have." To be sure, Couch stipulated that Logan solicit articles representing the entire spectrum of black political opinion, from radicals like Richard Wright and Paul Robeson to conservatives like Frederick D. Patterson of Tuskegee. Logan readily agreed to this procedure; otherwise he was given complete freedom. When the manuscript arrived, however, Couch went into immediate shock. He had hoped that Logan's contributors would pick up some of the ferment brewing in the black community as a result of the war, but he had not anticipated that all of the writers, conservatives included, would report that the Negro wanted mainly one thing—an end to segregation. The controversy that ensued thus entailed not only the possibility of great jeopardy for the press, but a deep personal crisis for Couch.[57]

For years he had been considered among the most advanced southerners, white or black, on questions of race. His reputation was based largely on his essay on the Negro in *Culture in the South*, a piece Couch had revised along more liberal lines from an original draft by Will Alexander to the point where a cautious Alexander had disowned it. As Charles S. Johnson observed, the article broke "new ground" by openly decrying Jim Crow in public transportation and accommodations and by viewing the plight of southern blacks primarily as a class problem. The issue, Couch had declared, was not just race prejudice but an "economic system that is running in the wrong direction, that thrives on struggle between the poor and the less poor, that forces on the white laborer the fear that he will lose his job to a Negro." No progress could be made until the "community of interest of Negro and white labor is recognized and given orderly expression." However, while arguing for economic solidarity and ridiculing the Jim Crow laws at length, Couch also claimed that blacks preferred residential segregation and contended with some vehemence that segregated schools would have to be maintained indefinitely. In the 1930s, these latter propositions constituted baseline assumptions for southern liberals. As Dan T. Carter has pointed out, virtually no one within the South at that time was calling for an integrated society. Even Charles Johnson, writing in 1939 for a black publication, did not begin to broach the subject of desegregating the schools.[58]

Heightening Couch's standing as a racial liberal was the press's early and consistent policy of opening its doors to manuscripts from black authors. In 1929, Odum had remarked that he did not believe this would be possible for the press, but five years afterward, at Couch's urging, the board approved a book on *Early Negro American Writers* by a black literary scholar named Benjamin Brawley, and in July, 1936, again on Couch's advice, it adopted a resolution stating that the "decision to publish or not to publish black authors should be made entirely on the basis of the merits of the work." Following the adoption of this resolution (all the more meaningful because it was kept entirely private), the press issued a flood of books by prominent black writers, including Ira de A. Reid, Saunders Redding, Charles Johnson, Arthur Fauset, and Rayford Logan. That the publishing arm of a segregated southern state university should embark on such a program did not pass unnoticed at the time. A northern foundation, for example, agreed to finance one of Brawley's books out of "appreciation of the significance of the University of North Carolina publishing a work by a Negro scholar."[59]

In short, following his Modernist views, Couch had characteristically jumped out to a relatively progressive position on race and had proceeded to translate his beliefs into action. At the same time, he remained very much a segregationist; the prejudices instilled in him as a child did not entirely disappear. Always he would remember his experience having lunch at the home of a black playmate, whose parents carefully placed the five-year-olds at separate tables. The blacks themselves *wanted* to preserve "racial integrity," he had concluded. Moreover, his general impressions of the race remained unfavorable. Frequently he would remark on the "negro's loose and nonconforming habits in speech as well as otherwise." Not even his awareness of the impact of social and economic conditions in producing these behavior patterns could shake his fear that blacks might somehow pose a threat to white culture if they received full equality. That fear lay more or less dormant until 1938, when the Supreme Court's decision in the Gaines case opened up the possibility of blacks applying for admission to graduate school at Chapel Hill. Suddenly Couch saw all his work of the previous fifteen years in danger. If blacks tried to enter the university, "extremely serious troubles might ensue," he predicted, although he did not spell them out. Nor was he dogmatic: "I feel no certainty that my opinion is right," he added.[60]

It is with this background in mind that one must assess Couch's conduct in the *What the Negro Wants* controversy. As he wrote Logan after first reading the manuscript, he could concur that segregation should be limited to "those areas where it is more clearly required" and that the "inequalities arising out of it" needed to be "sharply curtailed," but publishing a book calling for its immediate and total abolition was a different story. In addition, he was greatly troubled by the authors' failure to pay attention to the "dilemmas involved"—by which he meant principally the dilemmas of the white South. If blacks were in fact creatures of their environment, he asked, with "mechanism of one kind or another" determining their fate, why should white southerners not be considered victims of a similar determinism in their racial prejudice? "Surely you and the other contributors must know," he noted, "that the same discipline, sociology, which has revealed and documented the folkways of the South also has supported the view that the folkways cannot be changed by rational or ethical ideas; that, on the contrary, rational and ethical standards are themselves products of the folkways." Even assuming the elimination of segregation was a desirable goal, in his opinion it would take a minimum of fifty or a hundred years to achieve the changes that *What the Negro Wants* seemed to demand overnight. Couch offered to spend "hours and weeks" working with Logan to reshape the volume along these lines. "All I ask," he pleaded, "is that you not expect me to do anything that I think would damage race relationships and hurt the chances for a better life for everybody in this country."[61]

Several months of acrimonious correspondence followed. Apparently, Couch had expected Logan would respond as other press authors had to his extensive criticism of their manuscripts, but this time more than editorial changes were at stake. The upshot came when Couch finally proposed the book go to another publisher and Logan fired back one devastating sentence: "In reply to your letter of Dec. 14 I have to say that I am consulting my attorneys." Couch was stunned—on an intellectual level he fully accepted Logan as his equal, but on a more personal level he had never imagined that a black man would dare deal with him in this fashion. In desperation he consulted with his friends, who were also confused and deeply troubled by the sudden, unexpected changes in American race relations brought about by the war. "The bellicosity, the almost pathological sensitiveness of the educated Negro nowadays is something which I had not known existed," wrote Virginius Dabney, adding:

> Your letter to Logan reveals that you were under the delusion, when you arranged for this book, that the Negro does not want the abolition of segregation, establishment of complete social equality, etc. That was my own view in, say, 1941, but I have abandoned it completely. The dead cats which have been mine during the past couple of years have made me realize all too vividly that the war and its slogans have roused in the breasts of our colored friends hopes, aspirations and desires which they formerly did not entertain, except in the rarest instances.

Everywhere he turned, Couch received similar advice. Nor should this fact surprise us. No matter how intellectually liberated these men were, they were bound to flinch when such a momentous social and cultural transformation stared them in the face, with the prospect of massive and potentially violent disruption of their region. The 1940s for this reason was an extraordinarily difficult decade for southern intellectuals, and it called forth strange reactions.[62]

Among those strange reactions was the "Publisher's Introduction" Couch wrote for *What the Negro Wants* supposedly presenting the white South's view. Suggested by N. C. Newbold, a local expert on race relations in North Carolina, this device was seized upon by both Couch and Logan as a compromise solution. It is revealing that Couch's main target in the essay was not the Logan book, but Gunnar Myrdal's massive *An American Dilemma*, which had just appeared, setting off a furor among southern intellectuals. It had been modern social scientists like Myrdal, Couch charged, who had spread the doctrine of cultural relativism—the belief that all cultures must be judged equal in moral value regardless of their content; this in turn supplied the operating framework for Logan and his authors. But here Couch fell into a quandary, for he was too much of a Modernist himself to dispense entirely with relativism. His only defense was to postulate a distinction between "culture" and "civilization," defining the latter as an "accumulation of universal values from various cultures" against which each individual culture must be measured. Worse still, he began equating "culture" and "race." "At any particular time," he wrote, "one race may embody values higher than those embodied by any other race, and so long as it does this, a race may rightly be regarded as superior." Since white culture stood closer to civilized thought and behavior than did black culture, it followed that the white race must, for the moment, be regarded as superior and its integrity protected by separate education. As proof of his assertion that universal moral values existed, he pointed to the biases so readily evident in Myrdal. If there were no such standards, he asked, "how do the anthropologists and sociologists and social engineers (not to mention the rest of us) explain their zeal to reform the South?"[63]

Many of the questions Couch raised were pertinent enough had his essay not been marred by its confused notion of race. If white culture did embody the universally valid standards of civilization, one could retort, why was it not essential to provide blacks with as thorough an exposure to white culture as possible through an integrated school system? The answer was that his thesis rested ultimately on the belief that racial—and therefore cultural—characteristics were largely fixed by heredity, that the mental abilities of southern blacks were relatively unchangeable. The Modernist part of his mind knew, of course, that this proposition was untrue. Ten years earlier he had maintained the environmentalist position on race both with conviction and at some personal risk. But, had he accepted fully the logic of his Modernism, he would have been forced to entertain the possibility of racial integration in the South. In the crisis atmosphere of 1944, that was something he could not do. Hence his resort to whatever intellectual structure was necessary, even if, as he acknowledged, it was "no longer intellectually respectable." Though it was a losing battle, he could not help waging it.[64]

By no means was Couch alone in this difficulty. Rather, the unusual situation regarding *What the Negro Wants*, along with his personal candor, had trapped him into saying what other southern intellectuals of his generation felt at this time but refrained from putting in print. Journalists like Dabney and Mark Ethridge, for instance, told Couch in private letters they thought the introduction excellent, singling out the assault on Myrdal for special praise. "Mr. Logan and his contributors know about Myrdal's work—in fact some of them were on Myrdal's staff," Dabney observed, "and now that this work [Myrdal's] has been published they may go the limit as it does." Gerald W. Johnson, by now a staff editor for the *New Republic*, thought the essay the "nimblest foot-work I have seen in a coon's age," while the historian Fletcher M. Green lauded it as "one of the clearest and best statements of the problem I have ever read." All seemed grateful to Couch for rushing into the breach; few were eager to follow in his footsteps. Even Couch himself confessed that, while he stood by everything he had said in the introduction, "I would rather not have to say it."[65]

In time, Modernist intellectuals in the South would make their peace with the race issue one by one. For those who came of age in the 1930s, like C. Vann Woodward or Ralph McGill, it would be a relatively easy task; for others like Couch, just a few years older, it would take a long and hard struggle. But at least they were able to face the conflict squarely. As Couch put it in 1944,

> modern modes of thinking—modes characteristic of current so-
> ciological and anthropological thinking—have penetrated the South
> as well as other places. Many of us would agree with Myrdal and,
> as he says, this leaves us divided in our own minds and, so far, we
> have been unable to overcome this division and see our way
> clearly to a place where we can stand.

Modernism did not exempt its adherents from contradiction or ambivalence; it did not supply all the answers to the problems of twentieth-century life in the South or anywhere else. But the blinding effect of Victorian innocence had gone. The Modernist did not expect harmony and certainty, a fact that enabled him to examine his own beliefs critically and candidly, as Couch was long in the habit of doing. If he could not simply put aside the prejudices instilled in him as a child, Couch could at least recognize them and perceive their conflict with the rest of his thought. In the end, this critical spirit so apparent in Couch represented the most significant contribution Modernist culture brought to the region, for eventually even the ingrained biases of racism would succumb to it.[66]

CHAPTER 10

THE NEW SOCIOLOGY
AND THE SOUTH

Modern social science arrived late in the South, but when it did cross the Potomac it quickly made up for lost time. In the early 1920s it was still possible to count the number of books by southern social scientists appearing in any given year on the fingers of one hand; by the mid-1930s a diligent reader trying to keep up with the literature would have found the task nearly impossible. As late as 1925 only ten institutions of higher learning in the region employed a full-time sociologist; by the following decade nearly all did, and several had bona fide departments in the discipline. This growth was the more striking because it came at a time of economic depression, when university budgets were being slashed and when foundation money was tight. Nonetheless, when the Southern Sociological Society held its first meeting in April, 1936, nearly one hundred and sixty members from various southern states attended—a surprising figure to the organizers who had expected fifty at most. Southern professional associations in political science, economics, and history, all founded around the same time, enjoyed a similar success.[1]

Many factors contributed to this development, but in sociology one suspects that the primary motivation lay in the lure of the South itself as a territory ripe for research. Southern society seemed so different from the American mainstream and harbored so many intractable problems that any capable investigator armed with scientific method could find an embarrassing oversupply of subjects to study. Sharecropping, mill villages, chain gangs, lynchings, paternalism, legalized racial segregation, backwoods folk culture—these and more awaited sociological survey and explication. That writing on topics of this sort was closely tied to reform made the enterprises all the more appealing to young southerners of a liberal bent. What was not generally noticed, however, was that this sociological onslaught depended on the existence of a generation of southern sociologists for whom the Modernist sensibility had become a matter of course. Having encountered the critical and empirical precepts of Modernist thought as undergraduates, they did not believe the world could be viewed accurately any other way. Their work in turn helped spread and legitimate those precepts among middle-class southerners generally.[2]

As it did in publishing, Chapel Hill served as the center of this activity, at least through the depression era. The only significant competition came from Fisk University, where Charles Spurgeon Johnson, a contemporary of Odum and a disciple of Robert E. Park at the University of Chicago, carried out important studies on the lives of black tenant farmers and on comparative race relations. The University of Virginia did attempt to imitate North Carolina by founding an Institute for Research in Social Science in 1926, but despite a level of foundation support equal to its Chapel Hill rival the excessive timidity of its first director, Wilson Gee, hampered its accomplishments. "When things got tough, dealing with Negroes, why, he kind of wanted to be excused," Rupert B. Vance recalled of Gee. Well-trained sociologists could also be found at several other southern universities by the mid-1930s, especially Edgar T. Thompson at Duke, Ernest T. Krueger at Vanderbilt, and George P. Wyckoff at Tulane, but aside from Thompson these men engaged in little except teaching unless they were connected to Odum's network. In the 1930s it was Odum's students who got the grants, conducted the research, and wrote the key publications, thereby creating a new discipline in the South.[3]

As the members of Odum's group rapidly learned, being a sociologist in the South required a mixture of courage and restraint during this period. Far more than Odum they were anxious to identify the root causes of southern deficiencies, an effort that often brought them to challenge the region's most treasured values. Nor were they inclined to camouflage their more provocative findings in murky prose as did their master. Yet at the same time they sensed the limits of their situation. A frontal assault on segregation, even if buried in the middle of a scholarly monograph, might arouse public opinion against the university and, worse still, eliminate their chance to get a hearing in the South. As long as they exercised caution, they knew they could count on the support of Odum and of both Harry W. Chase and Frank Porter Graham, Chase's successor as president of the University of North Carolina. Chapel Hill had loyal alumni in prominent places, especially in the state legislature, and Chase and Graham could be skillful lobbyists when necessary. But that alumni loyalty could not be counted on indefinitely. "So far North Carolina's attitude toward her university is liberal, tolerant and wise," remarked Gerald W. Johnson in 1928. "But let the President appoint more than about 30 percent. of his Faculty from the North and she would have his head tomorrow." Thus the Chapel Hill sociologists invariably walked a fine line—not out of inner ambivalence, but out of an all-too-clear understanding of tactical necessity.[4]

The dangers they faced became manifest in their investigation of the textile industry, the first item on the institute's agenda when it started in 1924. At the suggestion of Gerald Johnson, Odum decided to conduct the study through Harriet L. Herring, a personnel officer at a nearby North Carolina mill with academic credentials from Radcliffe and Bryn Mawr. A good choice for the assignment, Herring sensibly proposed that she and Odum approach the mill owners beforehand to gain their trust; otherwise the statistical data they needed might not be available. Three times the institute asked the mill owners for help; three times the hypersensitive executives threatened retaliation against the university if a study were made without their right to prior censorship. The request inspired David Clark of the *Southern Textile Bulletin* to charge the institute with radicalism and meddling, and before long stories about a controversy between the industry and the university were being carried by newspapers across the state. It was exactly what Odum and Chase hoped would not happen. Soon the original ambitious plans were scaled down to a narrow study of welfare work in North Carolina mill villages, which Herring completed for her dissertation. "The University of North Carolina has got its orders from the cotton manufacturers of that state," wrote Nell Battle Lewis in the *Nation*, "and has accepted them without protest."[5]

The pressure took its toll on Harriet Herring's work. Although a product of obvious expertise, *Welfare Work in Mill Villages* left the impression of an author bending over backwards to demonstrate to the owners that they had nothing to fear from sociology. An entire chapter, for example, detailed how the mill managers had actively promoted schools for children in their villages, yet it failed to mention the same men's longstanding opposition to child labor laws. Another assured readers that the companies provided more than adequate housing for their workers, since the "average mill family seems to want a house no larger than is quite necessary and is inclined to take boarders if there is any extra space." Even Odum had to admit that the book appeared "over generous to the mill people." The tragedy was that the book did not fairly represent Herring's actual views. In a series of highly perceptive articles on the explosive labor situation in the mills written in the late 1920s, she showed a clear understanding of the workers' plight and the need to move beyond paternalism. She also showed, however, an acute awareness of the perils facing (in her words) those "occasional moderate souls" intent on "serious" study of the industry, and too frequently she took refuge in equivocation:

> This may be philanthropy; it may be paternalism; it may be the much sought after personal touch in industry; it may be unwarranted interference and control [in the workers' lives]. One may hate it or use it, admire it or scorn and despise it, according to his point of view or his experience with it.

This sort of overcaution constantly beckoned to the southern sociologists of the interwar period when they encountered the sacred cows of their society. In so many different ways, studying the South at firsthand would not be easy.[6]

Three of Odum's prized disciples who did survive the crossfire are treated in this chapter. By the 1930s Rupert Vance was recognized as the foremost student of the cotton tenancy system and was playing a pioneering role in the field of southern demography. Guy B. Johnson stood as a leading authority on black folk culture and race relations. Arthur F. Raper produced a classic book on lynching, then documented in more graphic detail than any predecessor the condition of sharecroppers in the South. The three are atypical in their talent, productivity, and recognition received, but in terms of their backgrounds and the thrust of their work they are fully representative of the generation of southern sociologists of which they were a part. Although all trained under Odum, their closeness to him varied—Vance remained at Chapel Hill working continuously with the master; Johnson established a degree of detachment, leaving for temporary projects elsewhere; while Raper went off entirely on his own, relying on Odum for occasional consultation. What they shared was a determination to understand southern society by probing to a deeper level than had ever been attained before through social science. Unlike Odum, they felt few personal qualms about this endeavor.

I
_____

If, as Faulkner once put it, Quentin Compson was "trying to get God to tell him why" the South had come to such suffering, Rupert Vance framed the same question in less cosmic terms. Vance's study of the region's failure proceeded not from the tragic sweep of southern history but from the heartbreaking experiences of his father. The senior Vance, a small-time planter, storekeeper, and abstractor of title in the central Arkansas town of Morrilton, wanted desperately to become prosperous and possessed all the requisite New South qualities of drive, talent, and diligence to achieve his goal. Seeking the best technical advice from his local county agent, he tried everything from cotton to cantaloupes to short-horned cattle. Nothing worked. Again and again he would hopefully ship a crop to market, only to have his transportation and handling bill exceed the paltry payment he received for his produce. "I don't think I ever saw a man that worked harder to become rich," Vance later remarked, "and came a cropper with practically every new idea he tried." The final reward came in the early 1920s when the agricultural depression then blanketing the South brought him to bankruptcy and the loss of his land. It could not have been plainer to young Rupert that New South maxims would not by themselves save the South. Some fundamental defect was embedded in southern life, he reasoned—whether in the region's geography, social structure, economy, or culture he did not yet know. He would devote his career to discovering the nature of that defect.[7]

Along with his father's troubles, something else in his personal background caused Vance to focus on the image of a crippled South. At age four he contracted polio, although it took the country doctor who treated him more than a year to diagnose the disease. "It was hell to live in the backwoods then," he would recall. By the time his family got him to an orthopedic sanitarium in St. Louis, he had permanently lost the use of his legs and would be condemned to crutches for life. This affliction affected his development in several ways. For one, it turned him away from the active existence of his family to a regimen of intensive reading. Although he did not attend school until he was ten years old, he was already acquainted by that time with many classic works of nineteenth-century literature. Second, by his own testimony, it made him more combative, more willing to speak his mind—partly because he realized that others would hesitate to strike back. "I was kind of privileged, like hitting a guy with glasses," he explained. And third, the frequent references one finds in his writings to the region struggling against its handicaps make it clear that Vance projected his own plight onto the South. If he could beat the odds, it could as well.[8]

For Vance himself, overcoming handicaps proved relatively easy. At Henderson Brown College, a Methodist school in Arkansas, he served as president of the YMCA chapter and as editor of both the campus newspaper and yearbook. There he also encountered a most influential teacher named B. S. Foster, a biblical scholar steeped in the heresies of the New Criticism who weaned Vance away from the last vestiges of his religious faith and, more importantly, introduced him to the major strands of Modernist thought. "He had his understanding of Freudianism and Darwinism and Socialism," Vance remembered, "and if you just listened to him you'd get a whole lot of ideas, and I learned to listen to him." Armed with these advanced ideas, Vance in 1921 went on to Vanderbilt for a master's degree under the orthodox classical economist Augustus Dyer. His thesis showed how high cotton prices had stimulated overproduction in the South and thus destroyed the market from the producer's standpoint. Written to Dyer's specifications, this was hardly a novel interpretation of the region's ills; what is significant is Vance's great dissatisfaction with it. If the laws of supply and demand prevailed in this situation, then why, he asked himself, did not southern farmers act rationally by leaving the cotton business in droves? Perhaps the new field of sociology that Foster had taught him about might hold the answer.[9]

Vance at first considered graduate study at Columbia or the University of Chicago, the two foremost centers in the nation for training in the discipline at that time, but in 1924 he took the somewhat daring step of choosing Chapel Hill. What attracted him to the fledgling department was the editorial barrage Odum had been maintaining in *Social Forces* against the region's problems. Odum's emphasis on the discrepancy between the South's potential and its actual deficiencies, he said, was the "thing I guess subconsciously brought me. Why nothing in the South ever turned out—going back to my father's experiences. You could think up a good business idea in any other part of the country and it would work. Why the hell didn't any of them ever work in the South?" Nor did Chapel Hill disappoint him. He found Odum "always paradoxical, somewhat reserved," and "different from anybody else that I'd ever studied with." Most of all, he was impressed with the way Odum forced him to look at familiar subjects with a new perspective. Odum, he noted, "used objectivity . . . to cut us off from our tradition with its prejudices and give us a fresh view, with the criteria of economics and psychology, the group factor, to help reorient us." No specific theory was offered, no mystical key to southern reconstruction. Rather, for Vance and his contemporaries the encounter with Odum meant intellectual liberation—a chance to see the South "objectively," free from the blinders of convention and moralism. That, in most cases, was what they most needed.[10]

With Odum's strong encouragement, Vance returned in his dissertation to his foremost question of how cotton had enslaved the South. Published in 1929 as *Human Factors in Cotton Culture*, the work relied on a theoretical mix of human geography and cultural anthropology to establish the existence of what Vance called the southern "cotton culture complex." From the French school of human geographers came the con-

11. Rupert B. Vance in 1928
Courtesy Mrs. Rupert B. Vance

cept of a "natural region" characterized by distinctive patterns of soil, climate, and terrain. But geography, powerful as it was, did not by itself determine how men lived within a given region. Rather, Vance argued, it was the "adjustment of previously existing cultures" to the "natural environment" that gradually gave rise to a new cultural system as the territory became inhabited. That cultural system or "complex," in turn, ultimately controlled men's behavior. In the case of the South, the capitalist economy of the original settlers, the chance introduction of the cotton plant, and the availability of black slaves all combined with environmental factors to create a "complex whole" whose "parts fit together so perfectly as to suggest the fatalism of design." Though it was "intangible," Vance cautioned his readers, the culture he was describing was a "very real thing" responsible for much of the South's pathology and seemingly unsusceptible to change.[11]

What Vance found most striking about this cotton culture was its pervasive irrationality. Classical economic theory argued that each economic actor was rational, he observed, but in the cotton system that theory simply did not hold. The problem lay in the immense risks that all participants in cotton production faced, from bad weather to the boll weevil to wild fluctuations in the market price. Given these uncertainties, it was impossible to make rational calculations at all—a fact that accounted for the strange behavior one often found in the cotton South. The tenant, for example, received his income once a year when his crop was sold and could never be sure in advance of what he would earn; hence he had little incentive to develop habits of thrift or budgeting, and he would often indulge in foolish spending in those rare years when he came out ahead. Even worse was the speculative mania that overtook landlords and owners. Speculation might look rational to a theorist viewing it from the macroeconomic standpoint, but from the perspective of the "human factors" in the cotton system it was sheer madness blocking any possibility for reform:

> One almost comes to feel that the speculative element in cotton possesses a fatal fascination for the farmer. One good year offers balm for several bad ones. Many intelligent farmers can be found who prefer to risk their crops on outguessing their neighbors in planting and producing cotton rather than join with them in cooperative determination of cotton acreage.

Plainly Vance was writing with an intimate understanding of the psychology of cotton culture, based on his father's experiences. He had seen what the gyrations of the market could do to a man.[12]

Vance knew well the effects of the cotton system on the region's everyday life. Although he cited an abundance of government and scholarly studies, he needed little research to describe how devotion to cotton could lead to inadequate diets, poor housing, and disease. From his own observations he recounted the drudgery of the work routine and the monotony of existence—the backbreaking task of harvesting the crop, the conversations repeated endlessly at the country store, the jokes told over and over. One read of families without running water in their homes, whose walls were covered with newspapers and whose windows lacked screens, allowing the house to fill with insects. In addition, Vance included case studies he and Odum had collected. One story concerned the disasters that befell a particularly ambitious tenant farmer, a good man who had no chance; another told of a cotton merchant ruined through speculation. Though a few tales of better fortune accompanied the bad, Vance's presentation persuasively conveyed a sense of how the system entrapped its victims.[13]*

Although Vance thoroughly understood the croppers' lot, his greatest empathy was reserved for the managers and supply merchants caught in the middle of the system. Like Ulrich B. Phillips, a writer whose influence on him was second only to Odum's, Vance admired sound business judgment and the skill to supervise others, qualities he felt the South needed badly. Vance differed from Phillips, however, in seeking those qualities in the middle strata of society rather than at the top. His account of the antebellum plantation in *Human Factors*, for example, made almost no mention of the planter but dwelled extensively on the role of the overseer whose "good practical sense" so often went unappreciated. Clearly the Cavalier mythology had faded for Vance, while the firsthand recollection of his father's patient dealings with tenants loomed large in his consciousness. Tenants, he noted, might leave unexpectedly in the middle of the growing season, or demand more money in advance than they could possibly repay. "These contingencies," Vance wrote in words closely echoing Phillips, "require in the plantation manager a skillful blend of tact and firmness." Even the high interest rates charged tenants could be defended. Such rates might appear as "merciless exploitation," he acknowledged, but they could also be viewed as "inherent in the speculative

---

* A draft of the original letter that Vance sent out under Odum's signature to gather his case studies appears in the Odum Papers at n.d. [April 1928]. Although it asks the informants for stories of success as well as failure, the emphasis was clearly on getting evidence of the latter: "Does human tragedy follow in the wake of cotton? Why do we ask this question? Simply because we have run upon so many instances of cotton brokers, buyers, bankers, factors, and business men whose dealings in cotton have resulted in bankruptcies, failures, broken families, suicides, and resort to drink and opiates."

nature of cotton growing." "It has been observed that many credit merchants fail," he added, "while but few grow rich."[14]

This tone of unrelieved pessimism pervades *Human Factors* and sets it off sharply from Odum's work. Odum endeavored always to balance good news against bad, but there is little trace of uplift here, no talk of the region's infinite potential. Instead, the book with its recurrent themes of entrapment and doom at times verges on sociological tragedy and provides no ready way out. Political gestures Vance saw as futile, nor did he place the least faith in cooperative schemes among farmers themselves given their ruinous individualism. Phillips's plan for developing more efficient corporate plantations based on wage labor seemed to Vance only a surer path to overproduction. And though he favored the most obvious remedy, crop diversification, he was highly skeptical of achieving it. "No canon has been more persistently preached and more consistently breached than diversification," he reluctantly concluded. The very nature of the cotton culture complex, in which the various elements of indebtedness, climate, tradition, and race continued to reinforce one another, made any escape from its "vicious circle" unlikely. It was a bleak vision, but Vance did not shrink from it—unlike Odum's, his prose was always eminently readable, with no attempt to dodge the question of causation. Victorian optimism had given way to a dogged empirical realism in Vance, producing an image of the South that belonged unmistakably to the twentieth century.[15]

The gloom lifted somewhat in Vance's next book, *Human Geography of the South* (1932), primarily because of a shift from geographic to historical explanation. Although attracted by the objective, scientific character of geography, Vance was also becoming increasingly uncomfortable with its determinism; history seemed to offer more scope for human initiative. "The map may cradle man and mold him," he now observed, "but man is also shown remaking the map." His survey of southern history, emphasizing the formative roles of plantation and frontier, again relied heavily on Ulrich Phillips. But at one crucial juncture Vance broke with Phillips: where the latter drew a sharp line between plantation and frontier once the plantation system had become established, Vance saw the two as part of a continuum in which their characteristics "fused." Furthermore, Vance made no apologies for the frontier:

> it must be remembered that the folkways of the frontier were
> not only adjustments to conditions of crude culture, they were also
> expressions of human nature. Rough and tumble fighting was, it
> is true, the kind of fighting required for survival against In-
> dians and rough men in an area of sparse settlement and mag-

nificent distances, but it also served as an outlet for impulses possessed by us all.

Given these post-Freudian assumptions, Vance felt no need to compensate for the South's frontier heritage as Phillips had by quickly reminding his readers of planter gentility. On the contrary, he was free to argue that the plantation had remained in essence a frontier institution and that it had passed those frontier traits on to the present-day South. There, he now claimed, was the most important source of the cotton culture complex.[16]

Almost everywhere he turned in surveying the modern South Vance discovered that the basic patterns of the frontier still prevailed. The region continued to make its living by exploiting its natural resources heedlessly, applying little capital, skill, or technology, with dramatically low levels of income and living standards the result. When he turned to other southern staples like tobacco, he found the same conditions as in cotton. "The habits and knowledge of those actually on the land, the existing credit policies, and the lack of organized markets handicap change," he wrote. A patent sign of trouble was that livestock raising, the surest route to agricultural prosperity, was making virtually no headway in the region, in part due to problems in growing pasture grasses in a hot climate, in part through a lack of dependable local markets, but mainly due to the persistence of frontier ways. "The close attention to duty, the habits of steady, skillful routine accepted by butter fat producers of Wisconsin as a matter of fact are traits not yet present in southern culture," Vance sadly admitted. The situation was even worse in the highlands and piney woods sections, where a continued frontier existence occasioned both hopeless poverty and the depletion of valuable timber reserves.[17]

The one bright spot for Vance was the industrialization of the Piedmont, a subject accorded the longest chapter in the book. Here, he thought, was the wave of the future that might at last break the cycle of southern backwardness. The tobacco industry elicited his special pride, for its success proved how "keen business acumen in exploiting a native product could be developed in the South." But when he turned to textiles the current organization of the industry bore too much resemblance to the structure of a frontier economy. Southern firms relied too much on the North for capital, technology, and management skills, and depended too exclusively on mining the South's abundant resource of cheap labor just as staple agriculture mined the soil. Given that enormous reservoir of surplus manpower, Vance feared that unionization would have no chance for years to come. Moreover, the chaotic competition among a host of small firms gave rise to the same cutthroat individualism that Vance decried in southern agriculture. In short, despite the promise of industrial growth, the South remained in deep trouble. In every conceivable area of comparison, Vance noted, the statistical indexes for the region showed the "lowest rankings in the Union." "One may take the *Statistical Abstract*, the *World Almanac*, the latest census, and manipulate the slide rule to his heart's content," he wrote. "The Southern states always come out behind."[18]

In the final third of the book Vance methodically reviewed a series of environmental factors to determine if some natural cause could account for this poor showing. The region's store of resources, he found, the quality of its soils, its transportation capabilities, and its supply of minerals were all sufficient for prosperity. A lengthy section on the southern climate rebutted writers who claimed that warm weather bred human lethargy. Recent scientific experiments proved otherwise, Vance claimed, and besides, viewed from the standpoint of commercial activity, the long, hot summer imposed fewer hardships and required less adjustments than the wintry climate of the Northeast. The South's "so-called climatic handicaps," he concluded, were "lodged in the culture rather than in the climate" and could accordingly be modified.[19]

The charge that the South's troubles could be traced to the supposed biological inferiority of its people seemed to arouse Vance's temper. He could not agree that blacks were to blame for the region's backwardness. "No race has come further against greater handicaps," he maintained. Nor was he willing to accept the common hypothesis that the poorer class of whites were genetically predisposed to laziness. Their lethargic behavior, he pointed out, could be fully explained by the incidence of certain chronic "concealed diseases" like hookworm, malaria, and pellagra, which sapped the energy of their victims and which were attributable to the "survival of frontier conditions" in such areas as diet and home sanitation. Whenever public health officials attempted to combat these scourges, southerners often became highly defensive—a reaction that Vance, in contrast to the New South generation, readily understood: "It is not necessary to credit this resentment to any excessive provincialism. It is natural and to be expected in all diseases implying low social and economic standards. To say that an ailment indicates ignorance, filth, poverty, or undernourishment of an area has never been known to provoke a lively outpouring of gratitude." Nonetheless, because the root problem was cultural rather than biological, Vance believed the public health campaigns would in time succeed, bringing about a "notable release of the energies" of the South's population.[20]

By this time Vance had absorbed enough of Odum's enthusiasm for regional planning to hope that it just might work a transformation of southern culture. But, unlike Odum, he understood that planning would succeed only if it had teeth in it. Compulsory acreage reduction, the forced migration of farmers from what Vance called "submarginal" lands, and other coercive government measures would be imperative in any reform of the cotton system. Any program to rebuild the South would also have to take cognizance of the South's status as a colonial economy in relation to the rest of the country, an issue freighted with political tensions. Here his differences with Odum were especially striking, for Vance never envisioned regionalism or planning as divorced from politics: "Policy making is the task of statesmanship; it involves ofttimes the clash of interests; and its goals must be defined through the traditional political processes. Science as technics or engineering is the handmaiden of policy." There is little trace of residual innocence in Vance's position, no illusion that science might constitute a refuge from the world's battles. Nor was there false optimism. Vance's advocacy of planning was based on the hard-boiled realization that the changes he sought for the South might never be accomplished, or that they might at best be partially accomplished through some rough-and-tumble political battles. Perhaps that was why he could never bring himself to join Odum in campaigning actively for Regionalism.[21]

Instead, Vance increasingly turned his attention to demography. The figures emerging from the 1930 census, which revealed a continued high birthrate in the South in the face of an existing population surplus, convinced him that the only realistic answer for the region was mass migration. Thus, even when he supported measures like the Bankhead bill of the mid-1930s, which was designed to help displaced tenants buy their own farms, Vance remained highly skeptical. The southern economy simply could not support that population, he pointed out, no matter what government aid was available. As many as six million people would have to leave the region, he predicted—an estimate that, if anything, turned out to be on the conservative side. Instead of trying to put these people back on the land under hopeless conditions, Vance preferred programs that would ease their adjustment to new lives in the cities. His other recommendation, a highly controversial one at the time, was for a region-wide birth control program, as set forth in his pioneering demographic work, *All These People, The Nation's Human Resources in the South* (1945).[22]

In sum, Vance was a sociologist of Modernist persuasion able to regard the South with a straightforward critical realism. He did not, as had Odum, feel compelled to balance his portrait of southern problems with optimistic platitudes about the region's promise, and he did not shy away from expressing his opinions. He was even willing to turn his critical gaze on Odum's work, in private if not in public. Upon reading the manuscript of *American Regionalism* in 1938, Vance wrote a scathing memorandum complaining that the book was "hastily done" and lacked a "point of view." Most strikingly, he attacked the theory of regionalism itself for evading inescapable realities:

> I believe I must be wanting a more hardboiled view of social conflict. Conflict we will always have with us. How does Regionalism take it out of the realm of hard knocks and place it in the realm of discussion and reasonable 'due process' of policy making? And what about class conflict? Is the resolution of regional views an alternative to an increase of such conflict?

Vance himself would offer no broad-ranging theories to take the place of Regionalism. His work would never attain the vision or poetry of Odum's; it was always specific, empirical, and, to borrow his favorite term, "hardboiled," in the approved fashion of twentieth-century social science. In this way his books set the standard for other sociologists of his generation in the South who wished to train their new discipline relentlessly on the region's manifold dilemmas.[23]

II

Among the South's problems, few seemed more intractable than race relations. By the 1920s segregation was firmly implanted in the region, and challenging the system appeared a quixotic gesture at best. Members of the new cadre of southern intellectuals like William T. Couch had absorbed the ethos of segregation as part of their childhood experiences and consequently regarded it as normal and natural. Nonetheless, there were troubling questions to be met. In American social science the concept of race was undergoing a thorough transformation, with environment replacing heredity as the explanation for racial traits. Within this changing framework blacks were seen no longer as inferior beings but as victims of repression and prejudice. The implications for the South were obvious. At the same time the artistic avant-garde was coming to venerate the "New Negro." Those same animalistic qualities supposedly exhibited by blacks that had elicited such intense revulsion in the Victorians were now being extolled by northern intellectuals as the mark of self-liberation. As Nathan I. Huggins explains, blacks were coming to represent "that essential self one somehow lost on the way to civility, ghosts of one's primal nature whose very nearness could spark electric race-memory of pure sensation untouched by self-consciousness and doubt."

In short, the status of blacks within American culture was undergoing a reversal.[24]

Although these changes were not lost on young southern writers and academics, it was not easy for them to respond. Race relations remained a dangerous topic in the South, to the point where its very mention could jeopardize one's employment. The safest and most comfortable course by far, almost everyone concluded, was to agree that the matter of segregation was closed and that any discussion of southern racial mores was fruitless. Under the rules of this tacit consensus, liberals could concern themselves with social problems like poverty, poor schools, or disease among blacks if they wished, but never in the specific context of racial oppression. There could be no openly acknowledged "race problem" in the South, only a "task" of "adjustment" that could be readily met through the "cooperation" of leaders of both races. This philosophy guided the Commission on Interracial Cooperation in the early 1920s and informed the writings of those few southern social scientists of the era like Thomas J. Woofter, Jr., who wrote directly on race. The handful of black writers within the region likewise abided by this consensus.[25]

These ground rules, however, did permit discussion of black character and folk culture, topics that drew increasing attention from southern scholars after the First World War. Although the authors' intentions were usually sympathetic, the image of black life conveyed in the earliest of these writings seems clearly racist by later standards. For example, Newbell Niles Puckett's influential *The Magic and Folk Beliefs of the Southern Negro* cataloged a multitude of bizarre superstitions ranging from the belief in conjure charms, signs, and taboos to the outright practice of voodoo. Puckett made no attempt to treat his findings along the environmentalist lines of cultural anthropology, but instead he attributed the seemingly barbaric behavior to a "well-nigh inscrutable Negro soul." Newman I. White at Trinity College in North Carolina studied Negro poetry and songs to discover "racial traits," only to find a tendency to "depravity" in sexual matters, a "lack of logical sequence of thought," and a distaste for work and responsibility. At the same time White assured his readers that these poets revealed little animosity toward whites or the South, along with a strong disposition to accept their allotted racial roles. The lines of one George Marion McClellan, he claimed, represented the attitudes of the "typical Negro":

> But I forgib my in'mis, my heart is free from hate
> When my bread is filled wid cracklins/
> an' dais chidlins on my plate.

Such was the state of black studies in the South in the mid-1920s.[26]

It is essential to keep in mind that Guy Benton Johnson began his work in this atmosphere of fear, caution, and traditional racism. Johnson would himself proceed carefully, developing over the years a finely tuned sense of how far a southern-based scholar could go in criticizing the region's system of race relations. Lingering traces of racism appear in his work, moreover, especially in his emphasis on primitivism in his initial treatment of black culture. Nonetheless, Johnson, protected by the institutional backing Odum provided at Chapel Hill, became something new on the southern scene: a major scholar specializing in the problems of race relations. The subject that had remained off-limits to southerners for two generations became his prime territory, and he surveyed it with a liberated perspective rare among his contemporaries. That he never openly advocated racial integration prior to the Second World War should thus surprise no one, given the intellectual environment at the time. The wonder was that he moved as far as he did in opposing Jim Crow during the 1930s.

To a certain extent, Johnson was born, raised, and educated on the periphery of the South. He was a Texan, descended from families who had pioneered the state in the early nineteenth century in part out of a desire to escape the evils of slavery. The small town of Caddo Mills he grew up in was just outside the plantation belt of east Texas, had few black residents, and in many ways resembled a Midwestern farming community as much as a southern one. Born in 1901 to a moderately prosperous family by local standards, he did not experience the bitter poverty or sense of lost social status so common among his southern colleagues. Hard work, Baptist piety, inadequate schools, and rural insularity were all part of his childhood, but a liberating influence was also present in the form of his father, a village skeptic with a sharp wit who possessed a sizable library for that time and place and who kept a steady stream of national periodicals flowing into the home. Although these early years were generally a comfortable and secure time, Johnson did suffer recurrent health problems, most notably two bouts of rheumatic fever that left him with a serious heart condition. This illness was to leave its mark on his personality: on his doctor's advice, Johnson learned to pace himself, restricting his scholarly output to short books and articles and avoiding emotional embroilments whenever possible.[27]

This relaxed attitude, in fact, was apparent in the way Johnson became a sociologist. Unlike those contemporaries like Vance who entered social science through an intense desire to remake the South, Johnson wandered into the field almost by accident . After attending a junior college near his home, he had gone to Baylor University with hopes of becoming a minister. By chance, however, he took a sociology course his first semester to fill out his schedule, only to find that the instructor, a certain G. S. Dow, was friendlier and more stimulating than his rather crusty Bible professor. Johnson soon decided to major in the field and, on Dow's advice, to pursue a graduate degree at the University of Chicago, perhaps the foremost sociology department in the country at the time.[28]

One might have expected a country boy from Texas to have encountered some difficulties, both personal and intellectual, in adjusting to Chicago, but this does not seem to have been the case. Johnson enjoyed working under Robert E. Park and Ellsworth Faris, readily accepting their racial liberalism and the advanced social science theory they taught him. Without difficulty he appears to have absorbed Park's enthusiasm for the sociological study of race relations, along with the environmentalist assumptions that underpinned it. Nor did the polyglot culture of a large northern city trouble him. At the invitation of his roommate Nells Anderson he would periodically spend weekends living in flophouses, observing the Chicago hobo community and acquiring an understanding of lower-class life. In this atmosphere, whatever social biases Johnson had arrived with rapidly dissipated, clearing the way for a Modernist cast of thought.[29]

These intellectual changes were readily apparent in his master's thesis on the Ku Klux Klan, an organization then at the peak of its influence nationwide. The Klan's revival, he argued, could be traced directly to the social and cultural transformation overtaking the country in the wake of the world war, a transformation most evident in the emergence of a new moral order that Johnson termed "Modernism." In his definition, "Modernism" meant essentially the breakdown of parental and institutional authority, with the concurrent decline of absolute moral standards in favor of more "individualistic" ones. "The Puritanic home of yesterday, with its unspared rod, its altar, and its taboos, is now a mere joke," he proclaimed. Though Johnson himself seemed to welcome this change, many Americans, he pointed out, found this shift in values a nightmare. Confused and frightened, they became prime recruits for the Klan, especially in the South where traditionalism was so firmly entrenched and the race issue was ever-present. Above all, Johnson refused to denounce the Klansmen for their alleged "animalism," as New South writers had always done. Rather, he insisted on the need for maintaining a cool scientific objectivity toward his subject. Since the Klan movement arose from "natural" forces, sociology's job was neither to "condemn or to fear it," but to "examine critically and scientifically the conditions that produced it, and to meet intelligently the problems which it has tried to meet with violence and force." In 1922 this was indeed a novel approach to the Klan.[30]

It was his work on the Klan that put Johnson in contact with Odum and eventually brought him to Chapel Hill in 1924. At the suggestion of another graduate school roommate Wiley B. Sanders, a former student of Odum's at Emory University, Johnson sent a summary version of his thesis to the *Journal of Social Forces*, where it was immediately accepted. Obviously impressed with the piece and with another Johnson sent the following year on black migration to northern cities, Odum offered Johnson one of the initial fellowships at the institute and even arranged an additional fellowship for Johnson's wife, the future historian Guion Griffis Johnson. After two years of teaching at small colleges in Ohio and Texas, Johnson was delighted to return to graduate school, even though he had planned on doing so at Chicago. Although he did not at the time realize it, he was moving to the place where he would spend his entire career.[31]

At the outset, however, Johnson doubted the wisdom of his move. Odum's enthusiasm was infectious, to be sure, but the style of sociology Odum practiced seemed haphazard, untheoretical, and often outdated to someone who had recently studied at Chicago. Moreover, no sooner did Johnson arrive than Odum asked him to collaborate on two books of black folk songs utilizing the materials Odum had collected in Mississippi in 1906. Although Johnson enjoyed the project, especially the collection of new songs for the second volume, he was also convinced that this sort of exercise did not qualify as true sociology. When Johnson made the mistake of telling these thoughts to Odum, a serious breach opened between the two men, the most serious consequence of which was Odum's temporary withdrawal of interest in Johnson's work. Left to devise a dissertation topic on his own, Johnson ultimately hit upon the idea of administering standardized tests to some three thousand black schoolchildren and college students to determine their innate musical ability by comparison with whites. Although his positive findings that blacks did possess special musical talent came as no surprise, his graphs and statistics at least allowed Johnson to feel that he had done something scientifically rigorous.[32]

Although the dissertation was never published, the research and reading Johnson was doing during these years was to have a major effect on his future work. Especially important in this regard was the influence of Bronislaw Malinowski, the famed British social anthropologist whom Johnson was assigned to escort around town during a visit to Chapel Hill in 1926. Following this encounter Johnson began reading widely in the field, beginning with Malinowski's own works. These explorations gave him a lasting insight into the functions of myth and symbolism in a folk culture, specifically into the way in which behavior that seemed absurd or immoral to an outside observer could fulfill crucial psychological purposes within the culture. This steeping in anthropological theory, combined with his travels to black schools for musical testing and various other contacts with the black community, began to give Johnson a perspective shared by almost no other white southern intellectual at the time—a view of black culture from the inside.[33]

That fact soon became evident in Johnson's writings. In a short piece surveying advertisements in black newspapers, for example, he reported that the majority of items for sale were useless potions or tawdries such as hair straighteners or good-luck charms. Presumably poor people were irrationally squandering their meager resources, but to Johnson the findings were perfectly understandable. "No matter how pathological the whole situation may appear when viewed from the outside," he explained, "the things advertised have subjective values and a certain efficacy for the Negroes who buy them." Johnson took pleasure in pointing out in another article the implicit sexual meanings of the lyrics in popular blues songs. Lines like "My man rocks me with one steady roll" or "I'm busy and you can't come in" had an unmistakable significance to the blacks who originated them, he insisted, no matter how steadfastly white musicologists tried to ignore the fact. Most of all, it was essential not to judge this language according to middle-class standards or perceptions. Many of these terms "were not indecent in their intention, for they were in ordinary and semi-respectable usage among Negroes."[34]

In early 1927 Johnson applied this relativist perspective to a study of the black folk hero, John Henry. A few years earlier H. L. Mencken had suggested to Odum that someone look into the question of whether Henry, the steeldriver who supposedly matched his strength successfully against that of a drilling machine, had been real or fictitious. Johnson took up the challenge, rummaging through old newspaper files, uncovering early versions of the ballad, and interviewing the few surviving workmen on the tunnel where the contest was said to have taken place. Though the evidence he assembled strongly indicated that Henry had actually existed, perhaps the most important part of the resulting book was Johnson's description of how the original story had evolved into myth. Painstakingly he surveyed over thirty versions of the John Henry ballad, leaving the reader thoroughly impressed by how subtle and complex black folk culture could be when approached correctly. He did not, as others had, decry the frequent lack of logical sequence within the ballads as the mark of a defective Negro intellect. Rather, Johnson was

12. Guy B. Johnson in the early 1950s
Courtesy North Carolina Collection,
The University of North Carolina Library

willing to dispense with "rationality" to find the intrinsic order of his material. "The stanza, not the song, is the unit," he wrote, and a given ballad was "likely to be composed of any combination of stanzas" arranged according to the individual taste of the balladmaker. To Johnson such works had to be approached as a species of poetry with aesthetic rules and standards of their own.[35]

After completing his research for *John Henry* in late 1927, Johnson suddenly found himself sidetracked onto another project that was to lead him to some different questions concerning black culture in the South. That summer an incoming member of the Chapel Hill sociology department, Thomas J. Woofter, Jr., was, to Odum's deep consternation, arrested for drunken driving. Aware that he would need to remove Woofter from the scene temporarily, Odum resourcefully and rapidly convinced the Social Science Research Council in New York to finance a study of St. Helena, a small island off the South Carolina coast where a black society had survived in virtual isolation from the white South ever since Reconstruction. A bridge from the mainland to the island then under construction threatened to end the isolation and thus allowed Odum to argue that the research had to begin with all possible speed. Woofter was appointed director of the study, with headquarters on the island. Johnson, who had slowly been returning to Odum's good graces, was chosen to accompany Woofter in order to research black spirituals and other folk music on St. Helena, while his wife went along to track down manuscript records of the community's history.[36]

The five months he spent on the island produced a significant change in the way Johnson viewed black culture. He had arrived with the conventional belief that the spirituals and the distinctive Gullah dialect spoken on St. Helena represented a remarkable survival of the blacks' African heritage. But the more he listened, the more he became convinced that he was hearing echoes of hymns and speech patterns he recalled from his Texas boyhood. A systematic comparison with white hymnals from the early nineteenth century confirmed this impression—whole phrases, sentences, and even verses had been borrowed. An analysis of the melodic structure of the spirituals and hymns revealed a strong musical resemblance as well, although the spirituals did differ, he decided, in meter and syncopation. Gradually Johnson began to conclude that the songs did not trace back to Africa at all, but had been adopted from the religious music of the whites at a time when slaves often attended white revivals and camp meetings. Gullah seemed to Johnson a relic of the dialect speech found among the lower-class whites whom the slaves had labored beside upon arriving in the United States during the seventeenth and eighteenth centuries. Again only the rhythm was different—the rapid pace and musical intonation of Gullah appeared to Johnson West African in origin. The slaves, he was saying, having lost their native culture following transplantation to a distant land, had acquired a new culture from the dominant whites, but had made that culture their own through the medium of rhythm.[37]

This thesis, set forth in *Folk Culture on St. Helena Island*, was bound to be controversial. Most of the uproar came from black critics, who accused Johnson of stealing the spirituals away from their race. A fierce scholarly debate ensued over the persistence of African influences, with writers like Melville J. Herskovits and Lorenzo Dow Turner charging that Johnson and others who agreed with him displayed a shameful ignorance of the African past. That debate, which still rages, need not be settled here. For the crucial point is not that Johnson was attempting to claim the spirituals for the white South—a ridiculous charge given his solicitude for black folk culture—but rather that he was underscoring how thoroughly black and white cultures in the South had *mixed*. The standing rationale for segregation held that the two cultures had to be kept free of contamination from each other, that the radical nineteenth-century moral dividing line had to remain in place. As a reviewer castigating Odum and Johnson's *The Negro and His Songs* in the *Memphis Commercial-Appeal* put it: "These opposites of the chroma, black and white, do not merge except in putrid, useless gray. It is difficult for polar opposites to understand each other." According to Johnson's account, however, this was not an instance of savagery on one side and civilization on the other, but of two peoples sharing essentially the same culture:

> Where does one find the old-time Southern oratory at its best? Among the Negro religious and educational leaders in the South. Where does one find the old-style manners of the Southern gentleman best exemplified today? Among the Negro aristocracy of the South. And so it goes for practically every culture trait that one might mention.

Even black folk beliefs and superstitions, he maintained, were of European descent originally. The subversive implications of this sort of argument are obvious.[38]

Nonetheless Johnson's work did not really fall in the danger zone until the early 1930s when he began speaking out directly on policy questions. Interpreting black folk culture was not considered a threat to maintaining the society's system of race relations, but addressing the issues of social or economic discrimination surely was. In 1933, to take one of many examples, a young sociology professor at Birmingham-Southern College in Alabama was dismissed for paying too much attention to the social pathology in Birmingham's black community and for attending a rally protesting the state's handling of the famous Scottsboro rape case. The fact that the president of the school, Guy T. Snavely, was himself a prominent southern social scientist indicates how sensitive the issue was at the time. Nor was Johnson free from such attacks in North Carolina. In September, 1932, three hundred leading citizens of the state calling themselves the "Tatum Committee" filed a petition with the governor asking that something be done about the "heresies" taught at the university, including those concerning race. Although little came of this complaint, and although Johnson felt no personal pressure, it doubtless served as a reminder of the climate of opinion he faced.[39]

It is with these facts in mind that one must read Johnson's 1934 essay, "Does the South Owe the Negro a New Deal?" Surely the most influential piece he ever wrote, the article attracted widespread notice in the southern press and was reprinted as a pamphlet in a print run of two hundred thousand copies by a black newspaper editor in Virginia. Ever since Emancipation, it began, the South had "pursued a policy of repression toward the black fourth of its population." Unfortunately, "few voices from within" had denounced "the folly and futility of that policy," and the price had been enormous for the entire society. With more than a hint of outrage Johnson reviewed the facts of black existence in the South—the all-enveloping poverty, the prevalence of sharecropping (that "vicious system of farming"), the wage differentials exacted against black workers, the blatant inequalities in administering federal relief, the disfranchisement of blacks and their inability to hold public office, their exclusion from jury service. "Is it not asking too much of a people so situated to be cheerful, contented, patriotic?" he asked. Pointedly he observed that there was "no guarantee" that blacks would remain patient; already a "militant school" of leaders had started to battle for legal rights. Johnson was not proposing an end to segregation, but he was arguing for the need to "take the inequalities out of the bi-racial system." Still, there could be no mistaking the profound changes he had in view when calling upon the South to "give the Negro a new deal."[40]

Throughout the 1930s, as he kept up a drumfire on this subject through lectures, articles, and radio talks, Johnson moved tentatively toward an openly integrationist position. By this time there was little ambivalence in his private position—he favored a racially integrated society in the South, though he did not expect to see it anytime soon. For the present he considered the chief objective reducing the "psychic distance" between the races, especially through combating white prejudice. Aware that he was unlikely to have much significant impact on the South as a whole, he focused his efforts primarily on higher education, pushing and prodding for closer contacts between white and black institutions.

Thus at a 1936 conference on regional development, Johnson chided his white colleagues for adopting a "patronizing and condescending air" toward their black counterparts. He urged them to invite more black lecturers to visit their classes, to hold joint seminars with teachers and students from neighboring black schools, and to help faculty members from those colleges obtain access to libraries and other research facilities. Johnson also proposed on that occasion that white southern universities respond to the increasing litigation concerning the admission of blacks to graduate schools by voluntarily abandoning Jim Crow at the graduate level. Although he acknowledged that it was "certainly a violation of the usual etiquette" even to make this suggestion, and though he thought it feasible only in the Upper South at the outset, he argued that integration would ultimately be the "simplest and most economical solution of the problem." It is safe to say that no other southern academic of Johnson's stature put forth a comparable proposal prior to the Second World War.[41]

Yet it was also true that Johnson's remained a voice of caution. The specter of white backlash always haunted him, as it did all other white southern liberals in the 1930s. Like them he tended to counsel blacks against radicalism. The surest strategy toward the "final and ultimate goal" of integration, he told black audiences, was to avoid inflammatory situations and temporarily to "make the best of segregation." He did not side with either the gradualism of the Booker T. Washington school or with the more militant tactics of the National Association for the Advancement of Colored People, but he hoped instead that a middle way might be found. Although essentially liberated from prejudice himself— he once described himself as "a free white man"—he could not escape the conclusion, born of his experiences in the region, that the fight to free other southerners of racism would have to be waged slowly and carefully. "I doubt if there *are* any short cuts," he explained in 1935. "Time itself is apt to prove the most decisive factor in the situation. If I were a dictator, I could think of several things I'd like to do, but I ain't."[42]

However sensible Johnson's forecast may have been at the time it was made, the rapid change in racial attitudes that occurred during and after the war soon made his position appear timid. That change was most noticeable within the ranks of black writers themselves. Prior to the war, most black intellectuals within the South had been even more reluctant than Johnson to attack Jim Crow. By the late 1930s a few exceptions had appeared within the social sciences, such as Horace R. Cayton and Ira De A. Reid, both of whom vigorously assailed racial injustices toward blacks while stopping short of denouncing segregation. Charles S. Johnson documented the evils of the sharecropping system with a balanced approach somewhat reminiscent of Odum's. For the most part, though, black writers in the South exhibited a Victorian abhorrence of conflict, suggesting a cultural time lag behind their white southern counterparts similar to that which the whites had displayed in the early 1920s relative to the North. But beginning in 1940, this situation began to change swiftly. That year, for example, saw the publication of Richard Wright's first novel, *Native Son*, a clearly Modernist work in which the hero, a young black man named Bigger Thomas, allows his anger at living in a segregated society to explode into an orgy of violence and murder. As Bigger's lawyer warns at his trial, the fury Bigger has displayed can be attributed directly to white civilization and can be found inside virtually all other black youth:

> "Every time he comes in contact with us, he kills! It is a physiological and psychological reaction, embedded in his being. Every thought he thinks is potential murder. Excluded from, and unassimilated in our society, yet longing to gratify impulses akin to our own but denied the objects and channels evolved through long centuries for their socialized expression, every sunrise and sunset make him guilty of subversive actions."

The same sentiments, although cast in less dramatic terms, appear in the black symposium of 1944, *What the Negro Wants*. Johnson's moderate stance, so effective in the 1930s, would not fare as well in this changed atmosphere.[43]

Johnson's dilemma became evident in 1944 when, as the first director of the new Southern Regional Council, he found himself clashing with younger liberals like Lillian E. Smith over whether the council should adopt a bold public stand against Jim Crow. In an exchange of views in *Common Ground*, Smith charged that the council was dominated by old-line Interracial Commission activists who proclaimed their continuing loyalty to segregation in order to compensate for the guilt they felt in periodically breaking the South's racial taboos privately. Whatever its merits, this analysis assuredly did not hold for Johnson. But, as he explained, he felt compelled "as any anthropologist might do" to take account of the tenacity of white southern folkways. It was thus a matter of tactics for him. "Personally," he wrote, "I should rather help to capture the foothills which have to be captured sooner or later than merely to point out the distant peak and urge my comrades to storm it at once! I, too, can see the peak, but I see no particular virtue in starting an association of peak-gazers."[44]

Unfortunately, Johnson's strategy was outdated: it was time to prepare for storming the peak. As Gunnar Myrdal, for whom Johnson had worked as a staff assistant prior to the war, pointed out in *An American Dilemma*, southern liberals needed to learn how to take chances politically, even when the immediate result might involve a white backlash. Though such gestures might seem futile or dangerous at first, Myrdal counseled, in the "long view" they might be "tremendously important as powerful stimuli to progressive thinking." Johnson did not appreciate this insight until much later, and besides, his temperament, his concern for his health, and his scholarly inclinations suited him poorly for the kind of battle Myrdal wanted. His career in the political arena was accordingly brief; after three years of coping with perpetual warfare and shaky finances at the council, he returned happily to Chapel Hill in 1947 to resume his academic career. When the great civil rights campaigns of the 1950s and 1960s commenced, he cheered quietly from the sidelines. And when the University of North Carolina itself came under pressure to desegregate, he was not directly involved.[45]

This failure as an activist should not, however, obscure the role Johnson played before the war in the struggle to change southern attitudes on race. For more than twenty years he had served as a major conduit for the new anthropological concepts of race, bringing the environmentalist and relativist approaches of Modernist thought to the attention of academics, newspaper editors, and educated laymen throughout the region. Having someone of his persuasion conspicuously stationed at Chapel Hill was crucial in convincing southerners of the legitimacy of the new attitudes. Moreover, many of the graduate students Johnson helped train at North Carolina subsequently took teaching jobs at southern colleges and proceeded to influence an entire generation of undergraduates to view racial questions in a different light. It is impossible to trace exactly what effect all of this had during the crisis of the 1960s, but one suspects that the presence of a substantial group of middle-class citizens weaned from the worst excesses of racism was of more importance than has generally been recognized. "I have always looked on it," Johnson would later say of his career, "as one little drop of oil maybe in the whole machinery of educating and changing attitudes and preparing people to accept change." Given the magnitude of the change involved, this seems far too modest.[46]

If Guy Johnson and Rupert Vance rarely ventured beyond the university, Arthur Franklin Raper never stayed within it any length of time. Another of Odum's prized flock of graduate students in the mid-1920s, Raper was lured away from Chapel Hill in 1926 by Will W. Alexander who, Raper recalled, had been looking for someone to "go down to Georgia and study sociology among the people." Raper happily accepted the assignment as research secretary of the Commission on Interracial Cooperation, a position that allowed him to travel continuously through the region during the next fifteen years investigating topics like lynching, race relations, and the breakup of the plantation system. Where Vance's work provided an overall analysis of southern life in the depression era, Raper's gave vivid empirical detail enabling the reader to view the region's problems from within the typical community. And because of his willingness to grapple with the South's pathology directly, his books ranked among the most controversial that the University of North Carolina Press published that decade.[47]

Raper's roots stretched back to the sort of rural community he would eventually write about. His father was a moderately successful tobacco farmer in upper Davidson County, North Carolina, where Raper was born in 1899. With its devotion to staple crops, its relative lack of social institutions, and the absence of a town center where people might gather, the area was characteristic of southern farm life save for the large number of Moravians in its population. A German pietist sect dating from the fifteenth century, the Moravians in 1753 had settled a large tract of land just above Davidson County, establishing the town of Salem (now part of Winston-Salem) as their headquarters. They moved there not as individuals but as a highly structured community, bringing with them all necessary skills and trades and imposing a rigid set of rules whereby each member of the society was expected to contribute to the general welfare. Long after their experiment had ended, their communitarian ethos persisted in the surrounding territory, often clashing with the equally strong individualistic creed of their nonpietist neighbors. Those tensions, in turn, were embodied in Raper's own family, for while his father was a Methodist of Welsh descent, his mother was a devoted Moravian.[48]

The clash in values between his parents became most evident in deciding on their children's education. His mother believed only a minimum of formal schooling necessary, since she expected her children to remain in the community as farmers. Her husband, by contrast, was determined to see his offspring escape the life of drudgery he knew. Beyond dispute the father won: at a time when few Davidson County youngsters went beyond high school, all eight Raper children completed college, and three continued for doctorates. To accomplish this feat required a virtual destruction of the family's land. A beautiful stand of white oaks was cut to fashion wagon spokes that were sold to pay for fertilizer. The intensive cultivation of the soil left it washed out and rent with gullies, but enough tobacco was raised to pay the college tuitions. "My mother saw all this washing away and thought it was very tragic," Raper remembers. "Dad saw it wash away, was sorry about it but thought it was the best he could do." Yet in another sense the mother won as well, at least in Arthur's case, for it is clear that many of her communitarian beliefs entered deeply into his thought, to be called upon later as a standard for judging the rural South.[49]

Raper's undergraduate education at Chapel Hill need not detain us, though he did well and graduated Phi Beta Kappa, since the most important learning he did in those years took place outside the classroom. Inspired by the social service ideals of his history teacher, Frank Porter Graham, he became active in the campus YMCA, participating in its many interracial and charitable activities and traveling under its auspices to distant conferences. More significant still, he cut hair. Setting up as an amateur barber was more than a means of earning income for Raper; it also became a workshop in sociological method. As he soon discovered, he could take the community's pulse simply by conversing with his customers: "I knew what the students were thinking when they left. I knew pretty well what they would say yes to and what they would say no to, what they would fight about, what they would give their lives for, because [there was] just this continuous flow of them, and I was just sampling in on them live, all the time." He had come upon what would in time be his most valuable research technique.[50]

After finishing college in 1924, Raper decided to try graduate work in sociology in anticipation of a career in social service. He began at Vanderbilt, where he studied under Ernest T. Krueger and Walter C. Reckless, two sociologists fresh from their training at the University of Chicago. Despite their presence, Raper was disappointed with the program and, after completing a master's thesis on "Negro Dependency in the Southern Community," returned in the fall of 1925 to Chapel Hill to complete his doctoral work with Odum. Like Vance and Johnson, he found Odum a source of counsel and support and above all a teacher who opened new and vastly broader perspectives. At the same time, Raper worked closely with Jesse F. Steiner, a specialist in community studies who introduced Raper to the sociological literature on the subject. Raper in return interviewed black convicts for Steiner's study of the North Carolina chain gang and composed a chapter on his home community for another of

Steiner's books. Then in 1926 came the invitation from Alexander. By then Raper had absorbed all the social science background he would need, yet he always kept his ties to Chapel Hill secure. "I wasn't divorced from the Institute," he once explained, "I was just sort of one of their fellows on leave down in the boondocks."[51]

However tame its work may seem in retrospect, in the 1920s the Interracial Commission constituted the cutting edge of racial progress in the South. Merely belonging to it marked a man as something of a dissident in southern circles, which was why Odum delayed joining until 1927. Its achievements came primarily through its eight hundred local interracial committees set up to forestall lynchings and to promote heightened contacts between whites and blacks. Of equal significance were its research efforts, its success in getting colleges throughout the region to offer courses on race relations, and Alexander's behind-the-scenes accomplishments through the Rosenwald Fund and later the New Deal. Although the NAACP may have pursued a more militant policy, especially through its legal challenges to segregation, the New York-based organization could not match the Interracial Commission in terms of grass-roots activities within the South. And, unlike the NAACP, the commission managed to retain sufficient respectability to make its voice persuasive to most white southerners. In this sense, then, it is best to think of the two organizations working in tandem, one inside and one outside the South, both laying the essential foundation for the civil rights movement that was to follow.[52]

Raper's most important contribution, in turn, was surely his report on lynching. Published in 1933 as *The Tragedy of Lynching*, it instantly became the authoritative treatment of the subject—a book that leaders of the antilynching campaign referred to repeatedly in their effort to stamp out the practice. Although relatively few copies were sold, literally hundreds of southern newspapers accorded the work prominent and favorable reviews. Its thesis was summarized and distributed in pamphlet form, discussion clubs took it up widely, and Raper himself traveled the region broadcasting his findings through speaking engagements. Perhaps no other social science book written about the South during this decade received as much serious attention from southerners, and perhaps none has had a greater impact on changing southern behavior.[53]

The project began in 1930 when Alexander, disturbed by the sharp increase in lynchings that year, formed a Southern Commission on the Study of Lynching as an offshoot of the Interracial Commission to locate the root causes of the problem. In addition to Alexander, the principal members came to include Odum, George Fort Milton of the *Chattanooga News*, William J. McGlothlin of the Southern Baptist Convention, and

13. Arthur F. Raper in the mid-1930s
Courtesy Margaret R. Hummon

Charles S. Johnson of Fisk University. Raper, as the chief investigator, was to visit each of the towns in which lynchings had occurred during 1930 and piece together a "case history" of what had actually happened. The commission could not have found a better choice for this assignment. By this time Raper had become a master at prying out information informally, whether by chatting with the folks in front of the county courthouse, or patronizing the local barber shop, or contriving to take a long taxi ride into the countryside in order to strike up a conversation with the driver. On one occasion he had the good fortune of spending an entire day with a ringleader of a recent lynching who had hitchhiked a ride to Atlanta with Raper and repaid the favor by providing a grisly, detailed account of the event. The sole information Raper did not have access to—the attitudes of the black community—was gathered by Walter R. Chivers, a black sociologist from Morehouse College who ran a parallel investigation on the other side of the Jim Crow line.[54]

Above all Raper and the members of the commission wanted the book to be persuasive to southerners. They knew that a frontal assault would never work with such an emotionally loaded subject. For that reason interpretation was kept to a minimum; the facts were arranged to speak for themselves. A report on a multiple lynching in Mississippi, for example, did not state outright that the townspeople had approved of the crime. Instead evidence was piled atop evidence to leave no doubt as to the proper conclusion: "What the people of Scooba and other communities in Kemper County felt concerning the lynchings can be judged by the fact that the local papers carried only a brief mention of it, the preachers did not mention it, a woman's organization refused to have it discussed, and people in general, although not convinced of the Negroes' guilt, found no fault with their fate." Rather than castigating local newspapers for their frequent silence on lynchings, Raper without comment compared their coverage to that of more prestigious urban papers in the South like the *Atlanta Constitution*. Nothing further was needed to shame local editors for their failure to maintain journalistic standards.[55]

Nonetheless, a close reading of *The Tragedy of Lynching* reveals certain interpretive threads. Through its twenty-one case studies, the book was designed to underscore what Walter White of the NAACP had insisted a few years earlier in *Rope and Faggot*—that the majority of lynchings did not stem from the rape of white women, but instead had to do with economic competition between whites and blacks, or a desire to "keep the Negro in his place." But the *Tragedy* also differed in important ways from *Rope and Faggot*. White, whose sensibility was far more Victorian than Raper's and who viewed southern whites with the animus of a black northerner, took obvious pleasure in indicting a savage, benighted South in the manner of Mencken. Lynching, he asserted, reflected the unrestrained animalism of the white southern masses who acted "with a bestiality unknown even in the most remote and uncivilized parts of the world." Raper, by contrast, made no mention of a conflict between savagery and civilization—the terms of the old dichotomy never entered his mind. As a trained sociologist he centered his analysis on the social conditions that gave rise to lynchings, and what he discovered was a clear correlation between the prevalence of lynching and the absence of stable community institutions.[56]

Raper's book, in fact, was as much about the nature of the southern community as about lynching. Each case study ended with a lengthy section entitled "Facts about the Community," which described the state of local social institutions. Repeatedly the facts demonstrated the hypothesis set forth on the first page of the book that "lynching rates have been highest in the newer and more sparsely settled portions of the South, where cultural and economic institutions are least stable," and that most lynchers "were from that unattached group of people which exercised least public responsibility and was farthest removed from the institutions and agencies determining accepted standards of conduct." Almost like a litany Raper showed how the communities involved had low school budgets, weak churches, an absence of health and welfare facilities, and a minimal sense of communal life. The standing critique of southern society in the 1920s, as articulated by Mencken or Walter White, had held that the South, like Sinclair Lewis's Gopher Prairie, suffered from a too closely knit and organic small-town life. The mob mentality, according to White, arose directly from this intensely self-contained local culture. But Raper, who gauged the South with both his mother's Moravian ideals of community and with the sociological theory Steiner had taught him, knew better. For Raper the mob was a parody of the communal spirit that was all too conspicuously missing. Like his contemporary Edgar T. Thompson, a southern-born sociologist at Duke University, Raper was discovering that the chief legacy of the plantation system had been a rural South still in the "belated frontier" stage, as Raper put it, and woefully lacking in social cohesion.[57]

This theme became more prominent still in *Preface to Peasantry*, Raper's second book which appeared in 1936. Originally his doctoral dissertation at Chapel Hill, the work might have sat on the library shelf indefinitely had not Couch suggested in 1934 that it be updated and published. Raper's concern in the dissertation had been the rural migrants pouring into Atlanta in the mid-1920s. Where were these desperate people coming from, he asked, and why had they left home? The exodus, he soon found, could be traced directly to the breakdown of the plantation system. He documented this conclusion by comparing two Georgia black belt counties, Greene and Macon, the first of which had been losing population drastically and the second of which had not. Through an old friend from Vanderbilt who happened to be a scion of one of the area's leading families, Raper gained invaluable contacts in both counties. In addition, he relied again on his informal techniques for striking up acquaintanceships, as well as extensive research in archival records and the back files of local newspapers. What was most interesting to Couch, however, was not Raper's explanation for migration but the treatment of black belt life he presented. In a sense, Raper was supplying the causal analysis and moral evaluation that Odum's carefully balanced portraiture so obviously left out.[58]

Although the plantation represented the "seed-bed of the South's people and her culture," in Raper's view it had not served as a school for civilization, as Ulrich Phillips had claimed, but as a school for dependency. By its very nature, the system required that its labor force remain subservient and irresponsible: "The improvidence and dependence of plantation workers rest primarily upon the demands of the plantation; they must be amenable to instructions, must live in the houses provided, must accept the merchant's and landlord's accounting, must remain landless. The very life of the plantation system is threatened when tenants accumulate property, exhibit independence." It was in this fashion that the plantation functioned as a "preface to peasantry," fostering a set of cultural attitudes more suited to the existence of a serf than to that of an independent yeoman farmer. In fact, Raper noted, the sharecropper's plight was worse than the serf's. In Europe the manor had at least been stable, remaining in one place for generations and therefore practicing a style of agriculture that conserved the land. In the South, the plantation had operated with a "reckless exploitation of resources unknown to European feudalism," leaving in its wake a devastated landscape, an impoverished people, and a community life shattered by constant migration.[59]

Raper's indictment of race relations in the black belt followed similar lines. Again the emphasis fell on how the system undercut community and deprived blacks of initiative and self-pride:

> The general peaceful relations between the two races in these counties rest, to no small degree, upon the Negro's acceptance of a role in which he is neither moral nor immoral—just nonmoral; neither saint nor sinner—just a rowdy; neither deceitful nor trustworthy, just lazy and easygoing; neither slave man nor free man— just an inferior man, just a "nigger."

Throughout his text Raper hovered on the brink of explicitly criticizing segregation. He described conditions in the black schools, with their minimal budgets, dilapidated buildings, unqualified teachers, and abbreviated school terms, implying that separate but equal had not and could not work. He spoke with feeling of the psychological gulf between the races that segregation created:

> The white child and the Negro child go their separate ways
> to school and church and graveyard before they are old enough
> to wonder why. They already are separated by the assumption of
> innate difference, already accept the dogmas which underlie caste
> distinctions. That the white man and the Negro are fundamen
> tally and unalterably different will scarcely be questioned.

Well aware of southern sensitivities on this issue, Raper always stopped short of drawing the obvious conclusions, leaving that task to the reader.[60]

By the late 1930s, Raper had taken his place as one of the most strident of the South's new generation of social critics. Donald Davidson complained angrily in 1938 of Raper's "bald equalitarianism" and classed him among the "militant school of sociologists" in contrast to Odum and Vance, for Raper had clearly outdistanced his former Chapel Hill colleagues in attacking both the plantation system and southern racism. To an extent, he could more easily afford his militance than they because he had no university affiliation to protect. Although he was forced quietly to resign his teaching post at Agnes Scott College after the school's president was deluged with letters demanding his dismissal, his appointment there was only part-time and not crucial to his work or income; the latter continued to be provided mainly by the Interracial Commission. But just as important, Raper felt no internal inhibitions about exposing the South's pathology. Indeed, rather than feeling disloyal for writing as he did, Raper believed he was performing a service to the region. His only real limitation was his sense of how much candid criticism the society could bear.[61]

Raper consciously pushed to that limit in his third book, *Sharecroppers All*, coauthored with a black sociologist from Atlanta University, Ira De A. Reid. In 1938 the two had approached Couch with a proposal for a popularized account of the collapse of the tenancy system complete with human interest stories and photographs. After a conference with Odum, Vance, Edgar Thompson, and others, the focus was expanded to include not just agriculture but all of southern society. The culture of dependency generated by the plantation was just as conspicuous in southern cities, they decided, and even in the way the South related to the rest of the country. Hence their title, *Sharecroppers All*, was meant to refer to the whole population of the South as it was shackled by the defective culture arising from the "feudalistic" plantation regime.[62]

As Raper fully expected, the manuscript set off a vigorous internal controversy at Chapel Hill. For Samuel H. Hobbs, Jr., head of the Department of Rural Social Economics, the graphic accounts of decay, violence, and exploitation were too much; he argued strongly against publication on the grounds that there was "virtually nothing constructive" in the book. "I may be wrong about my conclusions," Hobbs wrote, "but I have heard Raper speak several times and I feel that from his speeches and from this manuscript he doesn't miss much of advocating things that are highly repugnant to Southerners." Another reader, Federal District Judge Orville A. Park, complained that the authors had misrepresented the state of southern race relations and were too pessimistic in their conclusions. However, Margaret J. Hagood of the Department of Sociology, doubtless reflecting Odum's views, viewed the matter differently. The book, she reported, helped to document the "waste and inequalities" revealed in *Southern Regions* by discussing "present pathologies in a consistent [sociological] framework." She warned, though, that it would rouse tempers: "The content of some of the revelations, as well as their interpretations make the 'Report on the Economic Conditions of the South' and the Birmingham Conference for Human Welfare seem mild. Perhaps it is fortunate that Mr. Raper no longer has a job in a Georgia college to lose, for there is certainly dynamite in his book." Since Odum and Couch both favored publication, the manuscript's fate was never seriously in doubt. For his part Raper refused to make changes, insisting that the picture he and Reid had presented was, if anything, "too optimistic."[63]

Where *Sharecroppers All* broke new ground for the Chapel Hill group was in connecting the region's problems to a larger "national pattern" of economic exploitation. In effect Raper and Reid were dismissing the long-standing myth that southerners enjoyed a special immunity from avarice. "Whatever there is distinctive in Southern character," they claimed, "is little more than the regional expression of the typical American's assumption that it is good business to get more out of land and men than is put back." To them the slave plantation was "America's first really big business," based upon a method of exploitation that differed from that found in the North only in being more "obvious" and "extreme." No vestigial sense of innocence prevented them from reaching harsh judgments as to men's motivations. The South's soil fertility had been destroyed, and the nation's reserves of mineral and petroleum resources were being depleted, they contended, so that profits would continue to flow to "financial manipulators." The only excuses they could see for the low wages of southern industry were "greed or ineffective business organization," not paternalism. In sum, their analysis located the root cause of all the country's pathology in capitalist rapacity:

> America's unexcelled rates in lynching, homicide, kidnapping, and unemployment are the product of no deep and dark mysteries. They are as American as the cotton plantation, as the dominating and aggressive population elements, as the acquisition of wealth through exploitation of natural resources and people, as the chain store and the assembly line.

However accurate or inaccurate this thesis might be, it plainly shows that southern writers had finally exchanged the scruples of Victorian gentility for candid criticism.[64]

This sort of rhetoric and belief, premised on an economic determinism resembling that of Marxism, was far from uncommon among American intellectuals in the late 1930s, but that is just the point. The fact was that writers like Raper in *Sharecroppers All*, Herman Clarence Nixon in *Forty Acres and Steel Mules*, and C. Vann Woodward in *Tom Watson: Agrarian Rebel* had at last caught up with their contemporaries in the North and were writing about their society with a twentieth-century sensibility. Furthermore, the measures they advocated for the South did not rely on the nation's leaving the region alone to work out its troubles through a gradual process of evolution. In addition to the Bankhead-Jones Farm Tenant Act, Raper in *Sharecroppers All* endorsed the rapid unionization of southern labor, efforts to "deal realistically and constructively with Jim Crow laws and residential segregation," and New Deal relief programs in which the "federal government exercises its full authority" to see that benefits reach the intended recipients. All in all, it would be hard to imagine a more thorough reversal of the stand taken by turn-of-the-century southern social critics like Edgar Gardner Murphy. For the new leaders of the region's intellectual life just prior to the Second World War, in other words, the New South Creed had been consciously and vehemently repudiated.[65]

Another aspect of this new sensibility was that men like Raper could easily liberate themselves from the South. Following a year spent as an assistant to Gunnar Myrdal, and a further stay in Greene County writing *Tenants of the Almighty*, a report on the success of a Farm Security Administration project there that Raper had helped arrange, he left the region permanently. He served briefly as a rural sociologist for the Department of Agriculture, then beginning in the mid-1940s he worked for various agencies of the State Department as an expert on rural development. Unlike the "exiles" of the New South era, however, Raper did not break with his past entirely. On the contrary, wherever he was sent, in Japan, Taiwan, Iran, Afghanistan, Ethiopia, and the former east Pakistan, he applied the lessons he had learned in the South to the problems at hand.[66]

More important, he would later insist, his experience in the region had provided him with a philosophical basis that proved invaluable in his two decades overseas. To Raper the South was not a burden or an embarrassment or a quandary but a source of insight, precisely because its history demonstrated the need for struggle and change. As he reminisced toward the end of his life:

> The world is in crisis and always has been in crisis, and the only
> time it was worse off than when it was in crisis was when it wasn't
> in crisis, because it was when we weren't in crisis that we tried
> to accommodate ourselves to slavery. We tried to accommodate
> ourselves to the superiority of the male. We tried to accommo-
> date ourselves to some other fool inconclusive or incomplete
> idea. So crisis—there's strength in it.

His words may serve as a fitting epitaph to his own career, and as a summation of the Modernist cultural movement in the South of which he was a part.[67]

CHAPTER 11

ROBERT PENN WARREN:
THE SOUTHERNER AS MODERNIST

I
t has become a commonplace of
critical writing on the southern literary renaissance to regard Robert
Penn Warren as the immediate heir of William Faulkner, and with much
justification. The two have much in common: a keen sense of human
irrationality, along with a penchant for extravagant rhetoric, grotesque
characterization, and subtly interweaving plot. Yet the differences between them deserve equal attention. The thoroughgoing ambivalence
that marked Faulkner's thought as a figure of transition gives way in
Warren to a consistent philosophical approach akin to existentialism.
The archetypal tragedies of *The Sound and the Fury* or *Absalom, Absalom!* turn into the concrete historical dramas of *Night Rider* and *All
the King's Men*. Above all, the social tensions so often represented on an
oblique, symbolic level in Faulkner take explicit political shape in Warren.
Indeed politics—a subject Faulkner rarely treated—comes close to serving as the controlling metaphor for Warren's conception of the South.[1]

Populist emotions almost invariably throb beneath the action in Warren's novels. Excited crowds, demagogic leaders, and corrupt hangers-on
fill the landscape. Instead of stagnation or decay, whether of the big
house or the backwoods variety, one finds conflict, violence, and incessant change. Typical is the opening scene of *Night Rider*, set on a train
packed with angry farmers on their way to a mass rally to protest the
hated tobacco trust. This was the dimension of southern life that New
South authors had so studiously ignored, but which became for Warren
the lifeblood of his fiction. For him, politics became an instance of the
corruption man *must* plunge into, the destructive element in which he
must immerse himself in order to realize his full nature. It is precisely in
this respect that, although he worked almost entirely in the literary realm,

he shared a common sensibility with figures like Couch, Vance, and Raper whose essential orientation was in the social sciences.[2]

What most interested Warren, however, was not public turmoil as such, but the ability of the morally sensitive individual, deprived of all certainty by the conditions of modern existence, to make his way through the maelstrom. Invariably the principal test for Warren's characters becomes the capacity to respond to the unceasing, unpredictable pressure of events—"the blind ruck of history," as he calls it. Those who fail find themselves swept away on a floodtide of violence. Clinging in the Victorian manner to a rigid code of behavior or to a set of abstract ideals proves no defense. Nor does stoicism. Rather, the only sure path to stability lies in the attainment of self-knowledge. To save himself, the denizen of Warren's turbulent world must attain a sense of personal identity, taking into account the animal component of his nature, the innate human proclivity for evil, and the relentless flux of history. He must take his own measure by exploring that seamy, transient, emotional side of life that nineteenth-century culture pretended away. He must, in a word, surmount his innocence. This, of course, had been the underlying quest of protagonists in southern fiction ever since James Branch Cabell. The difference in Warren is that the battle has become a conscious one— both for the author and, to a certain extent, for the people in his fiction as well. "Innocence" and "identity" are words he and his characters frequently employ.[3]

Just as intriguing as the final result is the route Warren took in developing his Modernist sensibility, which assuredly did not suddenly descend on him as he started composing his major novels in the late 1930s. On the contrary, Warren reached intellectual maturity by following the same pattern of development we have been tracing for the South generally during the interwar period. The most important character Warren created, Jack Burden in *All the King's Men*, replicates virtually the same pattern in his struggle for identity. Personal and intellectual growth, self-knowledge and regional awareness, perceptiveness and literary skill, were all mingled together in Warren's writing, causing the forces reshaping southern thought to stand forth with special clarity. There we may see one of the fullest expressions Modernist thought was to obtain in the South before it too—like Victorianism before it—began its decline.

I

One may date the start of Warren's career as early as his sophomore year at Vanderbilt when, under the influence of John Crowe Ransom, Donald

Davidson, and Allen Tate, he decided to put aside his original intention of becoming a chemical engineer and to cast his lot with literature and the Fugitives. Members of the group immediately recognized his unusual talent—and his equally pronounced sensitivity. The product of a protected childhood in a small Kentucky town, Warren in college attached himself to compatriots far older and more experienced than he was. As a consequence, he was to have a difficult time as an undergraduate, particularly in terms of reconciling his growing exposure to contemporary cultural trends with the precepts of his old-fashioned upbringing. To all appearances boyish, naive, countrified, and helpless, he could also be found busily painting wall murals in the room he shared with Tate depicting scenes from Eliot's *Waste Land*. These disparate influences had their effect: at times he would seem a virtual basket case of adolescent romanticism combined with fin de siècle despair, arousing constant anguish in his friends. "Such a frail leaf," Tate once called him, suggesting to Davidson that Warren "must be handled like old china cups that have nitro glycerin in them."[4]

These tensions in Warren found their immediate outlet in his poetry. Images of death, violence, and eroticism abounded; in addition to the influence of Tate, one readily detects the world-weary cynicism of Eliot, the verbal excess of Mencken, and especially the masked sexual symbolism—nymphs, satyrs, and deep, dark pools—which Warren borrowed from his favorite writer at the time, Cabell. Throughout his verse ran the slow ticking of doom, as in these lines from "Death Mask of a Young Man":

> But now forgetful of slow pomp the clock
> With slavering fangs and like the haggard dog
> Harried the minutes in a desperate flock;
> Dully the bell in the cathedral tower
> Mouthing the death of the expiring hour,
> Bayed the white moon down to its lair of fog.

Warren was determined to deal directly with the most intense passions; poets who confined themselves to the "minor strains of emotional experience" were already receiving his critical scorn. But he had not yet broken through nineteenth-century convention. He was standing, in the familiar pose of the post-Victorian, still separated from the world of spontaneous feeling he wished to explore, and the separation was causing him much discomfort.[5]

His family had been typically bourgeois in many ways, but endowed with a powerful romantic streak and an abiding love for literature. His father had originally hoped to be a man of letters and had even published some poetry in his youth, but financial exigency forced him to settle instead on managing a bank in the busy tobacco market town of Guthrie, Kentucky, just over the Tennessee border. Warren would remember his father as an exceptionally quiet and gentle person, beholden to duty, who in good Victorian fashion never showed the least sign of pain or emotion. Indeed, despite the strictness with which they brought their children up, his parents would rarely raise their voices in anger. It was "not the way the world is, not what you saw in life," Warren later commented. Not all the family was as conventional. One uncle, an adventurous soul with whom Warren's father was especially close, went to Mexico as a mining engineer and later lost his life during the 1913 revolution. Above all there was his maternal grandfather, on whose tobacco farm Warren spent his childhood summers. A former Confederate cavalry officer, still gallant in his bearing, Gabriel Telemachus Penn was also overcome by a sense of personal defeat and remorse. Withdrawn from most social contact, he would sit beneath a cedar tree reciting poems, telling war stories, and reading history to the enraptured grandson for whom he was to become a symbol of the virtues of the old regime.[6]

Along with his family background, something else of a personal nature helps account for Warren's often puzzling behavior during his Fugitive days, as well as his subsequent literary development. In 1920, just as he was preparing to enter college, he received an accidental injury to his left eye—an injury that compelled him to give up an appointment to the Naval Academy at Annapolis and with it his dream of following in his grandfather's footsteps of military heroism. At first the actual loss of sight was relatively minor; but then, four years later in his junior year at Vanderbilt, the deterioration of vision sharply accelerated, and at age nineteen Warren feared that he would soon become totally blind. Worse still, he could not tell anyone of the problem, resolutely denying it even to himself. By the spring of 1924 he had fallen into a severe depression. "Everything connected with Vanderbilt or Nashville seems night-marish to me now," he wrote Tate in March. "Only Guthrie is worse." In May he attempted suicide, leaving behind a cryptic note stating he no longer wished to live because he could never be a poet. The fear was to fester inside him nine more years, until the possibility of losing his right eye as well caused him to have the condition corrected by surgery.[7]*

---

*Warren never told his Vanderbilt friends the reason for his strange behavior, causing them to speculate wildly about his problems. Lyle Lanier, for one, was convinced that the suicide attempt stemmed from Warren's romantic relationships and a particularly taxing psychology examination; Tate attributed everything to the baleful influence of Edwin Mims. Lyle H. Lanier to Tate, March 18, 1924, Tate Papers; Tate to Donald Davidson, May 24, 1924, Davidson Papers.

14. Robert Penn Warren in 1924
From *Nashville: The Faces of Two Centuries, 1780–1980,*
by John Egerton (Nashville: PlusMedia Incorporated, 1979)

By his own report this imminent peril of blindness was a "very power-ful determinant of all sorts of things for me." Imagery having to do with eyesight, blindness, darkness and light, night and day would recur fre-quently in his writings. It gave him a sense (in his words) "of deprivation and degradation and woundedness," a violation of his youthful perfec-tion that at times took on sexual overtones: "this was seen as a deep wound, you see. This disqualified you from life and all sorts of things accreted around this fact. And everything flowed into that to affirm it. But that was something that I kept denying, so deeply ingrained, that even then I would say, 'No, I wasn't one.'" Had the accident not hap-pened, it is likely Warren would have coasted for years as a brilliant student for whom all went right. As it turned out, he found it necessary to look inward to the deepest sources of motivation in order to cope with his secret crisis. Like Hemingway, with his "unreasonable wound" dur-ing the First World War, Warren was forced to come to terms early with unanticipated tragedy, and this doubtless served to deepen the resonance Modernist culture would have for him later.[8]

After graduating from Vanderbilt in 1925, Warren entered a long for-mative period characterized by extensive travel, close attention to his graduate work in English literature, and occasional skirmishes with his parents about his independence. First came two years at the University of California at Berkeley. Going west to see the country had been another of his childhood dreams, but once there the university greatly disappointed him. As he would later observe, members of the Berkeley English depart-ment did not sit up all night reading Baudelaire as his friends at Vander-bilt had; indeed, news of the twentieth century barely seemed to have reached them. Somewhat surprised at finding a part of the United States more provincial than the South, he spent his time reading widely in American history and perfecting arrangements to transfer to Yale. These were also years when he indulged frequently in earthly pleasures, hosting spirited drinking parties that landed him in trouble with the local police. This, too, represented an essential element in his self-education, a delib-erate breaking away from the shielded existence he had led at home and college. "I have learned certain things about myself at a perhaps not too exorbitant price," he reported to Tate, accurately summing up his stay at Berkeley.[9]

By contrast, his move to New Haven in 1927 brought Warren in contact with the mainstream of American literature. Primarily through Tate he met figures like Kenneth Burke, Mark Van Doren, and Malcolm Cowley; these acquaintances in turn opened other doors. Cowley, for example, solicited Warren's reviews for the *New Republic*, while the critic Paul Rosenfeld exposed him to twentieth-century painting by taking him on tours of New York galleries. At Yale, meanwhile, he was getting a grounding in contemporary poetic theory and in Elizabethan writing, the subjects that interested him most in graduate school. From 1928 to 1930 he pursued these interests further and learned something of the European literary scene as a Rhodes Scholar at Oxford. In short, he was absorbing new ideas and influences at a rapid pace—so rapid that it would take him almost a decade fully to assimilate them.[10]

Where he was heading, however, is apparent in the one book-length work he produced in these hectic years, a life of the abolitionist John Brown. Warren did not choose the subject himself: anxious to try his hand at Civil War biography like his friends Tate and Lytle, he had had vague notions of doing research on the frontiersman John Sevier when a publisher approached him about Brown. But once the book was launched, many of the themes that would concern him in subsequent works started to surface. Surely the critics have been right in pointing to the confusion and contradiction strewn through the narrative—evidence enough that Warren's ideas had not yet formed. Still, *John Brown: The Making of a Martyr* provides insight into Warren's more mature writings.[11]

Most striking is Warren's obvious fascination with political violence. To some extent this was attributable to literary considerations; Brown's bloody guerilla campaign in Kansas and his raid on Harper's Ferry gave Warren countless opportunities to display his skill at making violent action come alive for the reader. But other purposes are discernible, too. Over and over Warren seemed to be asking what motives might lead a man to indulge in cold-blooded killing for a distant, abstract political end. Was such violence ever politically or socially justified? How could the perpetrator desensitize himself from the human implications of his act? And how was the peace-minded individual to preserve his principles in a violent society?[12]

These questions—clearly central for any twentieth-century writer— had special relevance for Warren. Guthrie, far from being a tranquil agrarian community, had through most of his childhood been the head-quarters for an association of desperate tobacco farmers attempting to break the monopoly-buying power of the American Tobacco Company by holding crops off the market. When some growers had refused to join, thus undercutting the boycott, a wave of terror had ensued. Plantings were dug up, barns burned, and a row of warehouses in the nearby town of Hopkinsville was dynamited. Before long, beatings and killings, initi-ated by both sides, became all too commonplace. Eventually state militia troops were stationed in Guthrie—a sight Warren would never forget— in an attempt to halt what had come to be called the Black Patch War. He would also remember the fate of his grandfather, who, on pulling out of the association, had lost a barn full of uninsured tobacco to the night riders.[13]

Of equal importance with this mass violence was the generalized tension that pervaded the community, adding to the frontier restlessness already present. Life took on an unpredictable quality, as Warren vividly recalled:

> . . . there was a world of violence that I grew up in. You accepted violence as a component of life. . . . You heard about violence, and you saw terrible fights. . . . not violence of robbery, you see; it was another kind of violence in the air: the violence of anger, what sociologists call status homicide. . . . there was some threat of being trapped into this whether you wanted to or not and being stuck with it.

All sorts of things happened: a neighbor was known for having once shot a man to death, fights leading to serious injuries broke out in the schoolyard, his father met a nighttime intruder with a fireplace poker. And then there were fresh memories in the town of Civil War and Reconstruction violence, again personified for Warren by his grandfather. In particular, there had been an incident at the close of the war in which Captain Penn had executed a gang of brigands whose survivors later succeeded in having him indicted for murder. The affair always weighed heavily on his grandfather's mind. In sum, Warren's boyhood afforded him a thoroughgoing initiation into the less "civilized" aspects of southern life.[14]

Thus the utility of John Brown. An incessantly violent man whose politics were unambiguously tied to the antislavery North, Brown gave Warren the chance to explore the roots of fanatical behavior without bringing into question his own still-vigorous southern pieties. Brown, in this respect, was perfectly "safe." Indeed, dissecting Brown's motives and depicting him in the (often-conflicting) guises of calculating profiteer, opportunist, commonplace criminal, and bloodthirsty madman, could serve to exercise those pieties. The main case, moreover, rested on Brown's affiliation with the cultural tradition of New England. There Warren located the ultimate source of Brown's violence, "his elaborate psychological mechanism for justification which friends called Puritanism and enemies called fanaticism." Brown, it was argued, was abnormal only in the vehemence with which he pursued the logic of this inveterate Yankee creed; his was only an extrapolated instance of what Warren described as "that tight especial brand of New England romanticism which manifested itself in stealing guinea niggers, making money, wrestling with conscience, hunting witches, building tea-clippers, talking about Transcendentalism, or being an Abolitionist."[15]

The specific danger Warren saw in the Puritan mentality was its inordinate tendency toward self-deception. Every time he looked behind the facade of righteousness he found self-aggrandizement and the potential for mayhem. New England philanthropy, in his view, was never far removed from the desire for personal profit, as exemplified in Eli Thayer's decision to bankroll antislavery settlers in Kansas to serve God and himself at once. Repeatedly Warren would note how the lofty sentiments of Boston oratory could have "strange and brutal repercussions" when men like Brown were on the prowl. To be sure, this was not a case of hypocrisy—it was the very sincerity of the Yankees that made them so alarming. Believing totally in their abstract precepts, guided solely by their inflexible logic, they had cut themselves off from the real core of human experience. They had become incapable of understanding that men were "motivated by a confusion of passions, desires and beliefs" that did not necessarily make rational sense, that the world accordingly could not be reordered overnight in conformity with some neat and perfect plan. Worst of all, Yankees of this stripe, though possessed of absolute self-certainty, were unaware of the role played by their own passions. Once embarked on a crusade, Warren claimed, they could perpetrate limitless damage. As Charles Bohner puts it, Warren's John Brown is a "man blissfully untroubled by self-knowledge."[16]

In this attack on nineteenth-century New England culture, of course, Warren was repeating the prevalent misconception of the 1920s that all evil in America could be traced back to something broadly labeled "Puritanism." The real target, however, was Victorianism, specifically Victorian innocence. This fact became unmistakably clear in his treatment of that notable rebel against the old Puritan orthodoxy, Ralph Waldo Emerson. If Brown, the avenging angel, occupied one end of the New England spectrum for Warren, Emerson, the cloistered, self-absorbed rationalist who praised Brown's deeds without comprehending their consequences, occupied the other:

> Emerson was a man who lived in words, big words, and not in facts. . . . it is only natural that once or twice when he tried to deal with matters of fact words made him a common demagogue. And it is only natural that Emerson, in his extraordinary innocence, should have understood nothing, nothing in the world, about a man like John Brown to whom vocabulary was simply a very valuable instrument.

In innocence, then, Warren had found the cultural taproot of violence. It remained for him to discover that the same nineteenth-century innocence could be found below the Potomac as well.[17]

First, though, came his participation in the Agrarian symposium. As with the others in the group, Agrarianism for Warren became a shortcut for resolving the conflict between the Victorian values of his upbringing and the Modernist culture he had absorbed, all the while preserving his southern chauvinism. In addition, Warren found the Agrarian emphasis on establishing a closer relationship between man and nature especially attractive. Still, Warren for the most part remained on the margins of the movement, and his enthusiasm for the cause proved temporary. In time he would talk of how Agrarianism required a "conversion," akin to religion, which he could not quite achieve. His essay for *I'll Take My Stand* reflects this special relationship to the movement. Written in mid-1930 when he was abroad at Oxford, a period when he was homesick for his childhood haunts, it emphasizes the virtues of a simple, unhurried rural existence, which he thought was most readily available in the South. As he told Tate, his sole desire on returning from England was to "live in the South, in the country, and in your locality," the better to "watch the seasons, read, write, talk, play cards, and raise vegetables." Yet Warren by this time had also become a creature of the twentieth-century urban world. The pleasantness of rural life in the South, he added to Tate in the same breath, had "certain advantages which do something to compensate for the distance from New York."[18]

In retrospect his contribution to the symposium seems a curious piece, out of step with the general scheme of the book and so schematic in its presentation that one almost doubts Warren as the author. The topic, which Warren chose after all the other planned topics were taken, concerned the role of blacks in an agrarian South. "It's up to you, Red, to prove that negroes are country folks—'bawn and bred in a briar-patch,'" Davidson counseled at the start. But despite its title, "The Briar Patch" was to leave Davidson and the others baffled. In short order Warren called for improved vocational training for blacks, better opportunities for black professionals in the South, and the organization of white and black labor. "The fates of the 'poor white' and the negro are linked in a single tether," he insisted. Most of his prescriptions, in fact, aimed at giving blacks fuller participation in urban and industrial life, and most were in keeping with contemporary liberal opinion on race. His closing argument that country life provided more direct personal contact between the races came virtually as an afterthought. Nor did Warren ever defend segregation outright; instead one finds demands that blacks receive equal treatment within the separate-but-equal system. "There is all the difference in the world between thinking of a man as simply a negro or a white man and thinking of him as a person," he wrote.[19]

Needless to say, the essay brought no joy in Nashville. It "smacks a

little too much of the Inter-racial Commission . . . to suit me," Lyle
Lanier opined. A sharp debate soon erupted over whether the piece
should be published at all, with Davidson most strongly against it. Warren, he maintained, must be "protected from himself" if he ever wished
to teach in the South. Tate agreed that the essay suffered from a "sociological taint" and that the " 'solution' proposed at the end is appallingly
weak," but nonetheless fought for its inclusion, mainly, one suspects, out
of affection for Warren. Ultimately, Davidson was permitted to make
certain changes (as Warren had earlier authorized him to do), and "The
Briar Patch" appeared toward the back of the symposium. Hardly an
event of immense significance, the incident does illustrate the gap opening between Warren and his former colleagues. Although he would borrow much of their critical attack on Modernism, his criticism would
come from a position securely within the ambit of that culture, not from
its periphery. He would remain intensely loyal to his Nashville friends
and continue to identify himself with their movement, but, by the early
1930s, he was already moving beyond them.[20]

II

At Oxford Warren also began writing fiction, a step with enormous
consequences for his intellectual development. Once again, the impetus
came from outside when Paul Rosenfeld, a coeditor of the *American
Caravan* yearbook, suggested Warren try a short story based on the
Kentucky night riders he was always talking about. The timing was op-
portune, for Warren had recently been discussing the craft of fiction with
Katharine Anne Porter and Caroline Gordon, and he had just come upon
Faulkner's *Soldier's Pay*. Faulkner, he immediately recognized, "was
making a novel about the Southern small town world in a different tone
of voice," a fact that intrigued him. When he followed suit in "Prime
Leaf," Warren discovered a mode of expression he had been only dimly
aware of before—a mode combining concrete historical events with the
subjective reality of personal emotion he had explored in his poetry. "It
was a new way of looking at things," he would remember, "and my head
was full of recollections of the way objects looked in Kentucky and
Tennessee. It was like going back to the age of twelve, going fishing and
all that. It was a sense of freedom and excitement." This journey of self-
exploration differed from Faulkner's, however, in its constant reference
to a social and political context, and in its comparative freedom from a
pervasive ambivalence.[21]

In "Prime Leaf," the journey's starting point, the autobiographical elements are all on the surface. Dominating the plot is a noble grand-father figure who happens to be a former Confederate cavalry officer. Strong and independent, always capable of living up to the expectations of his idolizing grandson, Joseph Hardin has learned through a long trial by fire how passions rapidly overcome civilized restraints once blood has been shed. At the first sign of violence he keeps to his principles by re-signing from the board of directors of the tobacco-growers' association, even though he still supports the farmers' cause. His son Thomas, by contrast, is depicted as a weak man, who follows his father's lead. When their barn is burned, it is Thomas, acting out of his weakness of charac-ter, who impulsively retaliates by shooting one of the night riders, only to be ambushed himself the next day. In Warren's world, violence always proceeds out of weakness and innocence. In this novella it was his grand-father's generation that was strong; compared with the mere mortals who succeeded them, the men of the Civil War era were truly giants stalking the earth.[22]

On his return home in late 1930 Warren entered a difficult period of personal rootlessness and instability. Until 1934, when he landed a regu-lar appointment at Louisiana State University, he was forced to subsist on a succession of temporary teaching jobs, mostly at Vanderbilt. His wife took ill, his father's bank failed, the two novels he wrote went unpublished, and in 1933 his left eye became so badly infected it had to be removed. Also disorienting was the immense and unexpected social change he discovered taking place in the 1930s South: "as soon as I got back to the South I began to have all of these shifts of feeling, you see—just the stresses and also the Depression made the fixed order of a few years before change. It was changing before your eyes. . . . It was catastrophic change, not just the South. All the world was changing." Whether the pace of history did accelerate in the South or not in the 1930s, the salient fact is that Warren was now looking at these problems from his newly acquired perspective as a writer of fiction. Cut off from his earlier moorings, both personal and cultural, *he* was in the process of being transformed.[23]

It was under these conditions that Warren attempted his first two novels. Of the two, "The Apple Tree," written between 1931 and 1933, seems primarily a technical exercise, undertaken to learn how to master the form. As Warren later observed, he somehow became obsessed with making each scene self-contained, as in a play, with the result that little sustained development of character or ideas occurred. The second novel, however, was a different matter. Completed in early 1935, "God's Own Time" tells the story of a tall, skinny, intellectually inclined boy coming of age in a small Kentucky town not unlike Guthrie. Yet one must be cautious in using the label "autobiographical," for the transposition of experience was highly selective. What the reader finds in "God's Own Time" is a gathering up of all those less-than-pleasant memories of Warren's youth—the moments of weakness, pathos, and defeat—which he had previously left out of his picture of flawless childhood innocence. Before Warren had dealt with this material solely in his poetry, and then in oblique fashion; now, in this period of self-exploration, he was beginning to set it down in concrete prose.[24]

The central figure of the book, Steve Adams, is seen just as he is about to graduate from a rural high school in Tennessee. Tense, unattractive, his shoulders hunched, his hands covered with warts, called the "walking dictionary" by his schoolmates, Adams appears almost a caricature of adolescent awkwardness and self-consciousness—an apparent attempt by Warren to recapture the worst image he had had of himself during that earlier trying stage of his life. Steve wants desperately to achieve maturity, which he identifies with a world of adventure and passionate emotion. When the "pain of insufficiency and unworthiness" wells up inside him, he escapes to the woods and conquers all through his potent imagination:

> Sometimes, alone like this in the country, he was filled with his
> own power and competence, all his weaknesses of body and spirit
> having been cleansed. On such occasions he might think of striking
> some opponent, gigantic and anonymous, with his fists, almost
> feeling the flesh give under the impact; then he would strike out
> in the air, savagely, or stop on the road or path and assume the
> stance of a boxer. He, now, was strong like that, and savage.

Here Warren was rediscovering the other side of his youth and finding that it contained within its very innocence a reciprocal impulse toward savagery.[25]

The novel's plot revolves around Steve's efforts to pry off the restraints of bourgeois civilization and peek into the netherworld his parents have tried to protect him from. He listens intently, for example, when his one friend at school tells of experiences with railroad tramps and prostitutes. He is fascinated by Mrs. Elsie Beaumont, a woman once seduced by an itinerant tobacco buyer whom Steve regards as the "high-water mark of passion in the community." His curiosity is drawn by anything seemingly corrupt, decayed, or forbidden, as symbolized by his nightly ritual of forcing himself to look at the unwashed dinner plates, which the family cook has assured his mother are clean:

> The dishes had not even been scraped. They were submerged with
> hunks of food still clinging to them. Pieces of bread floated on
> the water, where the grease, slowly congealing, made a dull bloom
> like algae. He pulled the decent cleanliness of the cloth over the
> sight, and smoothed it with his hand. He had known they would
> be that way, for when ever in the evening alone in the kitchen
> he lifted the cloth the spectacle beneath it visited him with
> the nausea he now felt climbing in his throat. His mother al-
> ways asked [the cook], but never lifted the decency of the cloth;
> and he never told her.

This minor domestic foray into knowledge of the world is typical of the
headway Steve makes in the novel. Though dramatic events take place in
the community involving raw emotions, Steve participates in them only
as an observer, with the consequence that their impact on his growth is
limited. The novel's end finds him weeping "deliciously" over the supposed loss of his childhood self, but one feels strongly that the scene is
contrived. Warren had not yet learned how to put the innocence of his
fictional surrogates to a real test, nor was he ready to dispense entirely
with the protection of his own innocence.[26]

The same effort toward self-analysis found in his apprenticeship novels
appears in Warren's literary criticism during this period. One observes
him, for instance, speaking poignantly of the plight of the "contemporary writer" who feels "his latent powers" but "must first discover a
theme, unless he is content to project in symbol after symbol the frustra-
tion and confusion he suffers because he is *not* in possession of a theme
that will afford him an appropriate canalization of his powers." Novelists
of previous centuries, Warren claimed, had for the most part found their
themes ready-made in the structured, traditional beliefs of their societies,
but the present-day writer faced the cultural chaos of a world changing
so rapidly that it was fast losing touch with its past. This, he noted, left
the writer two choices. He could attempt to bring order to his material by
starting with a fixed doctrine arrived at through his intellect—the practice, in effect, of the New York proletarian novelists and of the writers
associated with the "regionalist" movement. Both groups attempted to
"reason" themselves into an "appropriate relation" with their respective
subjects. To Warren, however, this approach carried the fatal danger of
lapsing into abstraction, of short-circuiting the creative process and producing propaganda, not art. Although he did not mention Agrarianism by
name, the implied critique was there.[27]

The alternative was to accept the tumultuous condition of modernity as a given, acknowledging from the outset that one might never, in the traditional sense, find a "theme." Instead, the writer was obliged to develop his capacity for aesthetic and psychological perception, and to present the life he had experienced on its own terms and with a maximum of intensity. He would not precisely celebrate chaos, but he would steer true with it. He could certainly deal with ideas, but only when they had been given what Warren called the "status of experience" and when they had been absorbed fully within the literary texture. His theme, in short, would derive from the comprehension that there could be no theme. This evolving conception of the writer's task was based on the notion he had adopted from Ransom of a fundamental epistemological division between science and art. If science applied cold rationality to discover neat, precise, and verifiable truths about reality, art could claim its own version of the truth in the form of myth, which fused together historical actuality and metaphoric perception. Myth, like art, could never be dissected and analyzed without destroying its meaning: it had to be experienced directly, as, paradoxically, a "fiction, a construct, which expresses a truth and affirms a value." Myth was, one might say, a means for apprehending that irrationality inherent in modern existence that science could not come to terms with.[28]

As Warren was increasingly coming to realize, this belief in a distinct mode of artistic knowledge had important implications for the writer. For Ransom, as for many late Victorians, it had suggested the need to cultivate art for its own sake—not so much for epicurean reasons, but to preserve as large a realm as was possible for the imagination against the unremitting inroads of science. Originally Warren had shared this defensive attitude, but by 1935 he was taking a far more positive stance. Literature was valuable, he now claimed, "in so far as it conditions the total life and energy of the reader and refines his sensibility." To do so it must give the reader a heightened sense of the complexity of reality, undercutting his conventional assumptions through the use of paradox and keeping alive his mythological consciousness. The cool detachment of a Ransom or Cabell would thus no longer suffice; wit and irony could outline the predicament of modern man, but they could not by themselves redeem him from the Waste Land. For that, Warren believed, something more passionate, more experiential, was required.[29]

III

In 1936 chance again intervened to provide Warren a perfect opportunity to crystallize his developing beliefs. Herbert Agar, on his own initiative, had submitted "Prime Leaf" to a prize competition at the Houghton Mifflin Company. Soon afterward Warren received a contract to expand the short story into a novel. The appeal of the project was obvious: the tragedy of the Black Patch War, that most vivid memory of his childhood, was an ideal vehicle for combining actual history with personal experience, as his theory of fiction suggested. In addition, the subject gave Warren the chance to devise his own handling of political violence in contrast to the more romantic treatment accorded it by the writers of the proletarian school. As he later put it, "in some kind of a fumbling way I was aware, I guess, of trying to find the dramatic rub of the story at some point a little different from and deeper than the point of dramatic rub in some of the then current novels." Without ignoring the social and political issues involved, he would probe the human consequences of such action at the level of the individual activist. The result was *Night Rider*, a novel as modern in tone and thought as any that had come from the South to date.[30]

From the start, the novel was intended as a parable of the spiritual crisis of the twentieth century. The protagonist, Percy Munn, an ambitious young lawyer in the small Kentucky town of Bardsville, displays throughout the novel the intellectual and emotional characteristics that Warren associates with scientific naturalism. A "logical, skeptical scrutiny," Warren notes, is Munn's "natural attitude." To be sure, Munn is not drawn as a caricature of rationalism; he is capable on occasion of highly sensitive perceptions about himself and those around him. Indeed, that perceptiveness only serves to heighten his tragedy, for despite his efforts to save himself, Munn suffers from a certain hollowness, an incompleteness, and an isolation from his fellow human beings that ultimately consigns him to the abyss. Frequently he speculates on locating the "true and unmoved center of his being," but to no avail, for he has few secure ties to family, community, or history. Munn is modern atomistic man, bereft of identity, adrift on the turbulent waters of the present with no firm beliefs to guide him—and thus especially vulnerable to the buffeting of events and the force of dangerous impulses within himself.[31]

It is precisely his attempt to remedy this inner deficiency that leads to Munn's downfall. Always at the mercy of other people's promptings, he allows himself to be coaxed into serving on the board of directors of the Association of Growers of Dark Fired Tobacco because that organization seems to offer him a clear-cut cause and a sense of human community.

When trouble erupts, he becomes a night rider, in hopes of finding the clarity and finality he is searching for through acts of violence. He cannot, however, escape the confines of his rationality. He sees the association not as a movement to alleviate the concrete suffering of farmers, but as a mystic brotherhood held together by an abstract idea: "They [the members] were all webbed together by those strands, parts of their beings, which were their own, different each from each, coming together here, and becoming one thing. An idea—that was it—an idea seized parts of their individual beings and held them together and made them coalesce. And something was made that had not existed before." Before long the "idea of the Association" has become so important to Munn that, as he confesses to himself, he would gladly undertake coercion against his own neighbor for the movement's sake.[32]

The deeper Munn becomes involved in the association, the more he cuts himself off from genuine human feeling. As the violence escalates to beatings, barn-burnings, executions, and finally a massive dynamiting attack on the company warehouses, he is caught in a chain of events that rapidly move beyond his control. Soon his normal existence falls apart: his wife leaves him, his home is burned down, and, in the general chaos, he is indicted for a murder he did not commit. Reduced to the necessity of hiding in a cave by day and emerging only at night, he discovers his life completely enshrouded by darkness. By the end he realizes he has no identity apart from the association, and when that collapses, he is nothing. His death at the hands of a posse comes to him almost as a relief.[33]

The novel's title, then, carries a double meaning, for *Night Rider* comprises an unremitting portrait of Munn's journey into the engulfing blackness of the abyss. What is most striking about the narrative is the way Munn's faculty of self-analysis remains fully operative throughout his course of self-destruction, allowing him to puzzle over the sequence of events but not to comprehend it. He is aware, for example, of the pleasure he begins to take in torturing his wife by telling her of the violent happenings in the association, almost as if he were trying to "make her aware of the evil and instability in the world, to make her suffer." At times it seems that he has embarked on a psychological experiment, immersing himself in evil to test the results, exploring with perverse fascination the nature of man's inherent blackness:

> . . . then it came to him that all he knew was the blackness into
> which he stared and the swinging motion and the beat of the blood.
> But he was staring into blackness, a blackness external to him and
> circumambient, or was he the blackness, his own head of terrific
> circumference embracing, enclosing, defining the blackness, and

the effort of staring into the blackness a staring inward into himself, into his own head which enclosed the blackness and everything?

Munn can neither resist the chaos nor understand it; he is capable only of watching himself drown. In the late 1930s, with war clouds gathering over Europe and his personal circumstances still uncertain, Warren could imagine no better fate for twentieth-century man.[34]

To counterpoint Munn's plight, Warren introduces two characters who, in different ways, embody the moral integrity Munn cannot achieve. The first, Captain Todd, a former Confederate cavalry officer, represents the Cavalier heritage. Although he initially joins the association board, he also manages to preserve a "ripe, secret serenity . . . out of the swirl and reach of the general excitement." This independence of judgment leads him to resign when it becomes clear that night riders have taken over the movement. Munn admires Todd but cannot muster the strength to follow him; to Munn the Captain appears like a "great gray boulder, still unsubmerged, in the course of some violent, flooded stream" that would stay in place long after the waters subsided. "Perhaps," Munn speculates, "you could only get to be like Captain Todd if you lived through some firm conviction, some enveloping confidence, some time in your life; that is, if you were stout enough to come out on the other side of it afterward and still be yourself." But Todd's baptism by fire came during the Civil War, an event whose moral clarity and heroic proportions no longer seem attainable in the present age. Certainly the ragtag military raids of the night riders, undertaken out of economic self-interest, revenge, and desperation, offer no comparison. Todd's secret knowledge thus remains inaccessible to Munn. In fact, Captain Todd cannot even pass his wisdom to his own son, an innocent youth who meets a senseless death as a night rider.[35]

The alternate source of moral integrity in *Night Rider* is primitive Christianity, represented by Willie Proudfit, the simple hill farmer who provides Munn with a refuge. Once again such integrity stems from a previous initiation in violence. Willie's knowledge of human nature had come during his years as a buffalo hunter and Indian fighter out West as he watched his partner become obsessed with killing and greed and found the same tendencies rising in himself. "'They's a hoggishness in man, and a hogblindness,'" he observes. To save himself, Willie went to the mountaintop, leading a hermit-like existence for five years and ultimately experiencing a spiritual rebirth in the midst of a delirious fever. Transformed into a model of yeoman virtue, he had returned home to Kentucky and settled down to a peaceful life tilling the soil and practicing Christian precepts. But, like Todd, Willie Proudfit seems almost a chimera, living in isolation at the edge of the community, just as his story stands apart from the rest of the novel. Warren once admitted as much to Tate:

> Proudfit is a man who has been able to pass beyond his period of "slaughter" into a state of self-knowledge. If he is not at home in the world, practically (losing his place, etc.) he is at least at home with himself, has had his vision. It is an incommunicable vision, and is no solution for anyone but himself.

Warren was using mythical ideals of Cavalier and Christian yeoman to measure the desperate straits of ordinary men like Munn. But at the same time it was also clear that neither ideal was accessible to those caught in the maelstrom of the twentieth century.[36]

By the time he completed *Night Rider*, then, Warren had considerably refined his conception of the root causes of violence. No longer did he trace such behavior to personal failing or some special disposition to evil, as in *John Brown* or "Prime Leaf." Rather, he now believed, the cause lay in excessive rationality and a quest for false certainty, a quest that seemed especially seductive in an age as volatile as the present. Anyone who attempted to gain spiritual respite through an intense ideological commitment could easily fall prey. Perhaps no one understood this better than Frank Owsley, that battle-scarred warrior for Agrarianism, who noted with feeling how "Munn's involvement and inevitable destruction could be the fate of any of us." "Personally," Owsley added, "I have been involved . . . in things almost as dangerous, just as Munn was involved, step by step, each step seeming logical, inevitable and until too late, not evil." That was exactly the effect Warren had hoped to convey. For him there could be no substitute, no short-cut, for achieving genuine self-knowledge, especially in a time of crisis. The effort to circumvent cultural and social tensions by immersing oneself in an ideological movement— the expedient so many American intellectuals resorted to in the 1930s— was in his view a formula for disaster. Perhaps it was his own brief flirtation with Agrarianism that brought him to this insight; in any event, far more than any of his compatriots in that movement he came to recognize the perils, personal and artistic, of seeking forced answers to the dilemmas posed by Modernist culture.[37]

Warren does not, however, develop this theme as consistently in *Night Rider* as he would in later works. The reader is left unsure of many things, in particular of whether Munn's downfall is meant to have general symbolic significance, or whether Munn is in fact a special case, a social misfit, suffering from a weak character. Warren compounds the problem by suggesting on several occasions that his protagonist may have inherited a family inclination to loneliness and isolation, thus under-cutting the symbolism. The source of this confusion was probably War-ren's attempt to come to terms with his beloved grandfather Penn, who, on returning from the war, had lived in near-total isolation, maintaining no contact with the community save for commercial transactions and his one close relationship with his grandson. It was a "little bit odd," Warren would later recall, perhaps even "pathological." If much of Gabriel Penn's heroic character was embodied in Captain Todd, then, the less attractive side of him can be found in Munn. Warren's struggle to under-stand this contradictory man who represented for him the Cavalier past was still muddling his attempt to delineate his own thought.[38]

A similar confusion marks Warren's next novel, *At Heaven's Gate*. Though published in 1943, this book had actually been begun before *Night Rider*, but Warren had put it aside when Houghton Mifflin showed such interest in the tobacco wars. Although *At Heaven's Gate* was based on an actual incident—the collapse of the Nashville banking empire of Colonel Luke Lea in 1930—this time the events did not reside in War-ren's personal memory, with the result that he was forced to rely on extensive research. At one point, he informed Owsley, he had checked out every book in the Tennessee State Library on Sergeant Alvin York, the local war hero who would appear in the plot as Private Porsum. The consequence was a novel that, for all its skilled writing, falls curiously flat, its characters stereotyped and its social message riding close to the surface. A host of popular clichés from the 1920s parade through the narrative, foremost among them Jerry Calhoun, the son of a poor but proud yeoman farmer, who achieves fame as a star quarterback at the state university. Recruited by the finance manipulator Bogan Murdock (a modern Mephistopheles) to join his company, Calhoun finds himself the legal scapegoat when Murdock's bank fails, but he is ultimately wel-comed back by the salt-of-the earth family he had tried to repudiate. This sort of caricature might have lent itself well to comedy, but in attempting to make his belabored point through tragedy Warren ended up with a novel that all too often sounds like soap opera.[39]

Nonetheless, some further development of Warren's thought did take place in the writing of *At Heaven's Gate*. One finds the first appearance of a type of imagery that would recur constantly in Warren's later fiction, imagery that contrasted perfection with impurity, apparent health with signs of decay, smoothness with textured roughness—and, above all, the manners and control of the gentleman with the free emotional expression of the natural man. Within this metaphoric framework, Bogan Murdock, with his "brown, aquiline, handsome, unrevealing face," and his "per-fectly even, perfectly calm" voice, displays all the outward manifestations of the Cavalier. Never does he reveal the least trace of passion, always his actions are "balanced, lithe, and yet calculated . . . as of a force reined in its orbit." Yet it soon becomes clear that his gentlemanly restraint exists not to satisfy the aristocratic ideal but as a means of manipulating others in his decidedly ungentlemanly pursuit of profit. Whatever its value in the previous century, the Cavalier's code in Warren's view had now been appropriated by modern business to do the devil's work.[40]

In opposition to Bogan stand the various characters who openly demonstrate real emotion and who evince some degree of personal integrity. What is striking is that all such persons in this novel, without exception, are severely handicapped or maimed in one fashion or another. They include Jerry's father, inarticulate and pathetically clumsy, his paralytic Aunt Ursula and cantankerous old Uncle Lew, and the clubfooted Duckfoot Blake. It is as if the physical wound (and here Warren's own bout with possible blindness may be of significance) represents the piercing of the outward shield of innocence and perfection that must occur before a person's elemental humanity can shine through. Put another way, maturity must be won through some fateful confrontation with nature, through disease, death, ugliness, and decay. These attributes of human imperfection and mortality were coming to constitute the main basis of art for Warren. As one of his characters puts it,

> . . . the successful man offers only the smooth surface, like an egg. In so far as he is truly successful, he has no story. He is pure. But poetry is concerned only with failure, distortion, imbalance—with impurity. And poetry itself is impurity. . . . Poetry is the impurity which an active being secretes to become pure. It is the glitter of pus, richer than Ind, the monument in dung, the oyster's pearl.

Earlier writers in the region's literary renaissance had portrayed the ugliness in southern life, but chiefly for reasons of realism or sensationalism. Warren, however, had a deeper philosophic purpose here: like Flannery O'Connor, Walker Percy, and others who would come afterward, he had embraced the Modernist paradox that meaning could best be found through suffering and beauty through decay. He was becoming, in effect, an existentialist.[41]

IV

"Existence is prior to essence." What Jean-Paul Sartre's famous dictum implies is that man enters a world devoid of prior meaning. If man wishes to surmount this moral anarchy and establish an "essence" of his being—or, in other terms, an identity he can live by—he must create it himself. Not abstract reasoning, but the continuous lessons of experience must be his guide. This is the premise that brings existentialists so quickly to the problem of knowledge. For them the only real truth is that which each individual discovers through an unending struggle with both his environment and the irrational forces inside himself. As one writer puts it, the "whole man, and not only his intellect or reason, is caught up and involved. His emotions and his will must be aroused and engaged so that he can live the truth he sees." Existentialism, then, attempts to posit a new kind of knowledge based on the reintegration of man's intelligence with his emotions and sensibilities—a fact that makes existentialism the culminating philosophic expression of Modernism, as idealism was for Victorian culture.[42]

For some time, Warren had been moving toward an existentialist position. His literary theory was founded on the premise of a modern dissociation of sensibility, which the metaphoric vision of art could best help to heal. Ever since his attack on Puritanism in *John Brown*, the perils of embracing an abstract ideology had been a constant refrain in his thought. In Percy Munn he had created a character who, in the manner of European existentialist literature, stared directly into the abyss—although Munn had been unable to proceed further to a new state of self-knowledge (indeed had been swallowed by the abyss).

Among the many forces helping to shape Warren's existentialist vision was the performance of the theater of the absurd being enacted before his eyes during these years. As a member of the English department at Louisiana State University from 1933 on, he was in a strategic location to observe the antic regime of Huey P. Long and its aftermath. He had watched with fascination as the spoilsmen invaded the university, bringing with them largesse and corruption both. Warren himself had benefited from that patronage in 1935 when he and Cleanth Brooks received a substantial sum of money to launch the *Southern Review*. Yet, as so often was the case for intellectuals of that day, the comparison with contemporary events in Europe seemed inescapable. The world he saw "of pretentiousness, of bloodcurdling struggles for academic preferment, of drool-jawed grab and arrogant criminality" was, he later wrote, "all too suggestive, in its small-bore, provincial way, of the airs and aspirations that the newspapers attributed to that ex-champagne salesman Von Ribbentrop." These impressions gathered steadily in Warren's consciousness. Then, one day in the fall of 1937, while sitting on a friend's porch, he observed a squad of motorcycle police roar by. The spectacle of raw power appears to have provided just the catalyst he needed. In rapid order the material that would become *All the King's Men*, his first truly existential novel, took shape in his mind.[43]

His initial attempt to tell the story came in "Proud Flesh," a verse play written in 1938 about a character named Willie Talos, a politician whose dream, like that of Long, was to build a hospital that supplied free medical care to the people of his state. Although he seems to wield great power, Talos is intended to represent the blind force of history; his power in fact derives from his ability to ride the crest of events. The play is built around the polar opposition between the "practical" world of Talos and the world of the "idea," symbolized by the surgeon Adam Stanton—a polarity reinforced by two Greek-style choruses, one composed of motorcycle policemen and the other of surgeons, who comment on the action. Recruited by Talos to direct the new hospital, Stanton is appalled by the graft and corruption he finds, described by Warren in terms of "rot" and "pus." When he discovers that his sister Anne is having an affair with Talos, he attempts to remove the source of corruption at one fell stroke by shooting Willie down, only to be killed himself. At the outset Warren had great hopes for this play, but by the time he finished it he was clearly dissatisfied. The format was far too rigid and abstract for his taste, its thematic purpose was unclear, and besides, it lacked any sense of historical context. In 1941 he decided to turn the play into a novel and to undertake some research on the real Huey Long.[44*]

From this point onward the novel seems virtually to have written itself, as most exceptional works of literature tend to do. Realizing that his story was becoming so complicated that he would need a narrator, Warren turned to Jack Burden, a newspaper reporter and boyhood friend of Adam Stanton who had made a brief appearance in the verse play. The more Warren worked on the manuscript, the more Burden's personal development overshadowed the original concern with political corruption. Indeed, in the end the tale of Willie Stark (as the governor had been renamed) and his hospital had become meaningful only as it was reflected in Burden's consciousness. For Burden's story was no longer merely a

---

*Warren would always maintain that, as he once put it, "I never did one minute's research on Long, not one minute." His letter to Lambert Davis in 1941, however, makes clear that this is not exactly true. One suspects that what he really meant by such an emphatic statement is that he did not do research on Long in order to turn up an idea for a novel. Rather, the research represented an attempt to fill out the historical detail after his subject was already firmly in hand. See, for example, his remarks to Ralph Ellison: "Once you are engaged by a subject, are in your book, have your idea, you may or may not want to do some investigating. But you ought to do it in the same spirit in which you'd take a walk in the evening air to think things over. You can't research to get a book. You stumble on it. Or hope to. Maybe you will, if you live right." Ellison and Walter, "Art of Fiction," in Longley, *Warren*, 42.

technical device to give coherence to the plot; it represented nothing less than a repetition of Warren's own intellectual odyssey, as well as a summation of the process of change southern intellectual life in general had undergone in the past two decades.[45]

Like Warren himself, Burden enters the scene a stellar specimen of post-Victorian skepticism. Descended from a wealthy Delta family and endowed with traditional Cavalier ideals, he has felt compelled to reject his past in order to make contact with reality. Rather than attending Princeton as his mother desires, he has chosen to work his way through the state university. Instead of becoming a lawyer as his father once was, he has ended up a hard-bitten political reporter and eventually a personal aide to Willie Stark. A persistent instinct has guided him away from his sheltered existence and toward the sordid and brutal world of politics. What he has discovered in that world is the capricious character of the universe and man's essential helplessness within it. Throughout his narrative Burden is forever imagining calamities—sudden fatal traffic accidents, or the possibility of being caught on a train in the midst of an earthquake. Life to him seems no better than a game of cards, governed by a "perfectly arbitrary system of rules and values," in which the individual cards have no meaning outside the game. Given this basic outlook, Burden remains more an observer than a participant. Feeling powerless, he attaches himself passively to Willie's power. "I never tell anybody anything," he insists, "I just listen."[46]

It soon becomes apparent, however, that this persona of a professional cynic has been devised to cover up a residual core of innocence below. That innocence lingers on from his protected childhood, when "little Jack Burden . . . used to go out in his boat in the afternoon on the bay to fish, and come home and eat his supper and kiss his beautiful mother good night and say his prayers and go to bed at nine-thirty." Everything then appeared orderly, predictable, carefree, and good. That sense of false security had begun to dissipate when his childhood sweetheart, Anne Stanton, sister of Adam Stanton, inexplicably left him; that was the point when Burden decided he would need to learn more about the workings of the world. Though he has since made his way to an environment where corruption and blackmail are daily occurrences, a part of him still clings to the idealized images of Anne and Judge Monty Irwin, the aristocratic neighbor who had always acted like a father to him. At the deepest level of his mind, these two figures symbolize an unshakeable purity and goodness that is almost mythical; they become the moral lodestars by which he steers in the tooth-and-claw jungle of politics. It is in this respect that Jack Burden at the beginning of the novel still retains an essentially nineteenth-century sensibility.[47]

Burden employs several defenses to ward off threats to this residuum of innocence. His first tactic had been Idealism, a philosophy he learned in college, which, he realizes, could prove invaluable in shielding oneself from the pain of reality. "If you are an Idealist it does not matter what you do or what goes on around you because it isn't real anyway," he explains. At other times, when severe crises arise unexpectedly, he takes refuge in the "Great Sleep," the functional equivalent of a return to the womb. Most frequently, though, Burden relies on an impenetrable barrier of skepticism to protect him against the arrows of outrageous experience. This defense does exact a price. As Anne Stanton constantly complains, it makes him a man seemingly devoid of emotion, a creature blocked in normal human feeling. Burden himself is conscious of this fact: "nothing happened to Jack Burden, for nothing ever happened to Jack Burden, who was invulnerable. Perhaps that was the curse of Jack Burden: he was invulnerable." Still, like James Branch Cabell's various protagonists, Burden cannot face life without the shield in place.[48]

It is not unfair to say that the main action in *All the King's Men* concerns Burden's struggle to shed his skeptical persona, open himself to experience, and thus attain a true Modernist consciousness. That process begins in his attempt to write a doctoral dissertation on his ill-fated antebellum cousin, Cass Mastern, whose diary has found its way into Burden's hands. The diary tells of the terrible "darkness and trouble" that had followed Mastern's affair with the wife of a friend. The husband had shot himself, a slave girl who had stumbled onto the truth had been sold into prostitution, and the wife had lost her mind in rage and grief. It was, Mastern wrote, "as though the vibration set up in the whole fabric of the world by my act had spread infinitely and with ever increasing power and no man could know the end." Arriving at a profound religious faith and self-understanding through his suffering, Mastern enlists in the Confederate infantry to share the "bitterness" of his people, but on principle will not fire his gun. Although he dies of war wounds in a decrepit military hospital, he has found a semblance of peace for himself through his commitment to accept the vicissitudes of history. Burden senses that this story holds an important meaning for him, and he studies it carefully. In the end, however, he cannot piece the facts together into a coherent interpretation, "not because he could not understand, but because he was afraid to understand." Instead he goes into the Great Sleep.[49]

The Cass Mastern narrative serves as a prelude to Burden's second attempt at historical research, one in which he cannot escape the consequences of the knowledge he unearths because the issues have such immediate personal significance to him. Assigned by Willie Stark to find blackmail on Judge Irwin, Burden proceeds on the assumption that his investigation will only prove the Judge innocent. "There is always something," Willie warns him, and, sure enough, before long Jack has turned up a bribe the Judge had accepted at the start of his career, an act with repercussions that include the suicide of a lowly bookkeeper. At first Jack thinks of destroying the documents, but he cannot resist finding out how the Judge will respond when confronted with them:

> I had to know. . . . For the truth is a terrible thing. You dabble your foot in it and it is nothing. But you walk a little farther and you feel it pull you like an undertow or a whirlpool. First there is the slow pull so steady and gradual you scarcely notice it, then the acceleration, then the dizzy whirl and plunge to blackness.

Further repercussions follow swiftly from Jack's decision: Irwin chooses the course of honor and kills himself; Jack's mother reveals that the judge had in fact been Jack's father; Anne Stanton, on learning that her father as governor had condoned the bribe, becomes Willie's mistress; and Adam Stanton, tortured by these revelations, is driven to assassinate Willie, then is shot down himself. As in *Night Rider*, events take on a dynamic of their own, which, once set in motion, will not stop.[50]

Caught in this vortex, Jack finds himself virtually torn apart. His conscious mind remains a "nice, cool, steel filing cabinet with alphabetical cards" that allows him to function day by day, but below there is a boiling "kettle of pitch" he can barely keep from spilling over. What torments him most is the loss of the illusion of Anne Stanton's innocence, an "idea of mine which had had more importance for me than I had ever realized." That was why, he now comes to understand, he had refused at the last moment to make love to her when they were teenagers, lest he "plunge her into the full, dark stream of the world." Also lost are his illusions concerning Judge Irwin, whom Jack had admired much as Warren did his grandfather Penn. Like Captain Todd and Joseph Hardin before him, the judge represents character, learning, and stability, along with the only viable intellectual tradition the South has bequeathed to Jack's generation. Yet Jack also recognizes the limitations of that tradition, summarized by Willie's maxim that "there ain't anything worth doing a man can do and keep his dignity." And "doing something" is important to Jack. "Did you ever stop to think," Jack asks in anger, "what a mess your fine, God-damned, plug-hatted, church-going, Horace-quoting friends like Stanton and Irwin left this state in? At least the Boss does something, but they—they sat on their asses."[51]

With his skeptical persona fast breaking down, Jack searches in desperation for some other means of anesthetizing himself against experience. His solution is to declare himself a behaviorist, a believer in the "Great Twitch." For if there "was only the pulse in the blood and the twitch of the nerve," he tells himself, then "nothing was your fault or anybody's fault, for things are always as they are." With this "secret knowledge" he can look down, Cabell-like, "with benign pity on the sweat and striving." Behaviorism, then, offers, or seems to offer, an instant shortcut to the resolution of his ambivalence. It is the "dream that solves all problems," "the dream of our age."[52]

In addition to Burden, three other characters in the novel provide examples of men bent unsuccessfully on evading existential knowledge. One is Adam Stanton, the modern scientist, who, with his "clear, deep-set, ice-water-blue abstract eyes" maintains his purity by isolating himself from all meaningful human relations. Despite his great success as a surgeon, he lives alone, sees few people socially besides his sister and old friends, and carefully suppresses his emotions. When first approached to become the director of Willie's new hospital, he refuses because, as he puts it, he will not touch "filth." Only after Anne pleads with him to take the job does he change his mind. But, as one might expect in Warren, this willed innocence serves Stanton poorly when his inevitable time of disillusionment sets in, and his perfect self-control explodes into violence. His defeat could not be more total: when Jack sees him just before the assassination, Adam is covered with "mud and filth" up to his knees.[53]

Another man who falsely believes he can remove himself from evil is Ellis Burden, the man Jack calls the "Scholarly Attorney" and whom Jack originally believed to be his father. Cuckolded by his best friend, Judge Irwin, the Scholarly Attorney has abandoned his law practice in Burden's Landing, moved to a city slum, and devoted himself to spreading orthodox religion among the downtrodden. In contrast to Adam Stanton, who dreams of isolating and eliminating corruption on earth through science, the Scholarly Attorney has given up all hope for the natural world. He espouses spiritualism—the doctrine that spiritual entities alone are real—and counsels Jack to join him in renouncing material existence. "I will not touch the world of foulness again," he declares, "that my hand shall come away with the stink on my fingers." This advice provides no help for Jack, who regards the Scholarly Attorney as a pathological case. No longer, it would seem, did Warren look upon primitive Christianity as a potential source of modern salvation.[54]

Finally, there is Willie Stark himself. Prior to *All the King's Men*, southern intellectuals had generally treated Huey Long with scorn, painting him as a vulgar, simplistic demagogue who exploited the rabble. Warren's fictional surrogate for Long, however, is a highly complex figure. He begins his career as a local reformer, but quickly shifts gears after learning that the statehouse ring has used him as a decoy to draw votes from another rural candidate. Aware that his innocence has blinded him to political reality, he falls back on the lessons he learned in Calvinist Sunday School. "Man is conceived in sin and born in corruption and he passeth from the stink of the didie to the stench of the shroud," he periodically proclaims. At the same time Willie borrows freely from the evolutionary pragmatism of William James. His moral relativism is based squarely on Darwin and is concerned above all with the need for releasing human vitalities:

> When your great-great-grandpappy climbed down out of the
> tree, he didn't have any more notion of good or bad, or right or
> wrong, than the hoot owl that stayed up in the tree. Well, he
> climbed down and he began to make Good up as he went along.
> He made up what he needed to do business. . . . I'm not deny-
> ing there's got to be a notion of right to get business done, but by
> God, any particular notion at any particular time will sooner or later
> get to be just like a stopper put tight in a bottle of water and thrown
> in a hot stove the way we kids used to do at school to hear the bang.
> The steam that blows the bottle and scares the teacher to wet her
> drawers is just the human business that is going to get done, and it
> will blow anything you put in it if you seal it tight, but you put it
> in the right place and let it get out in a certain way and it will
> run a freight engine.

In short, Willie assumes that moral standards remain in constant flux depending on historical circumstances. He sees himself as an agent of this evolutionary process, an initiator of change regardless of its outcome. He is Talos become conscious of his role.[55]

These relativistic premises justify Willie's frequent excursions outside the law. Because of the overriding importance of bringing about change, he does not hesitate to use graft and blackmail. Nor does he flinch from employing the services of pure animality in the person of his bodyguard, Sugar Boy, or the pure avarice of political parasites like Tiny Duffy. The momentum that Willie establishes allows him to control, temporarily at least, these creatures of the nether world and to direct their energies toward political reform. In Reinhold Niebuhr's terms, he becomes a child of light utilizing the methods of the children of darkness. Or, as Willie prefers to put it, "You can't make bricks without straw, and most of the time all the straw you got is secondhand straw from the cowpen."[56]

But Warren is not prepared to endorse sheer relativism divorced from the achievement of true Modernist self-knowledge. Willie's logic turns out to have a fatal flaw: it leads him to become a persistent reductionist, forever operating on the belief that the only dependable reality is primordial "dirt." "A diamond ain't a thing in the world but a piece of dirt that got awful hot," he explains, "And God-a-Mighty picked up a handful of dirt and blew on it and made you and me and George Washington and mankind blessed in faculty and apprehension." As the action proceeds, however, it becomes apparent that this reductionism is in fact a cover for the large residuum of original innocence that has survived in Willie, much as skepticism serves as a cover for Jack's innocence. Beneath it all, Willie continues to cling to the old standard of purity. That is why he holds himself sharply above Tiny Duffy and why he will not allow any corruption in the construction of the magnificent hospital he is determined to leave as his principal legacy—a monument, one might say, to man's achievement in surmounting his "dirt" origins. "I'm not going to let those bastards muck with it," he tells Jack. Although he wavers briefly in this resolve, it is his decision finally to stick by it that ushers in his death and ironically installs Duffy as governor.[57]

These are the examples—Willie Stark, Adam Stanton, and the Scholarly Attorney—who pass before Jack Burden's gaze in his refuge of cosmic detachment. From their interlocking tragedies and that of Cass Mastern he slowly undergoes the transformation of consciousness that allows him to reenter the world shorn of his former innocence. The moment of revelation comes when he is informed that he is Judge Irwin's sole heir and will inherit the estate rescued by that long-ago bribe, "that act for which I, as the blameless instrument of justice, had put the pistol to his heart." Moreover, he now realizes, Irwin's decision not to marry Jack's mother had probably stemmed from the judge's sense of prior obligation to his ailing invalid wife. Sin, love, honor, guilt, and innocence were all hopelessly tangled together. Understanding this for the first time in an emotional, as opposed to a cerebral, way, Jack weeps uncontrollably. "It was like the ice breaking up after a long winter," he observes. "And the winter had been long."[58]

The knowledge Jack arrives at, and on which his new consciousness is based, is specifically historical knowledge. Instead of appearing as a jumble of unrelated fragments the world now seems to him an "enormous spider's web," which, when touched, even if inadvertently, carries vibrations to its "remotest perimeter." This principle of interrelatedness applies throughout historical time, for "all times are one time, and all those dead in the past never lived before our definition gives them life, and out of the shadow their eyes implore us." One almost suspects Warren responding here to the quandary Tate posed in his "Ode to the

Confederate Dead." For Tate, modern man seemed irrevocably alienated from the past, which was the repository of heroism and grandeur. For Warren, with his existentialist vision, the past exists only as it is recreated in our consciousness, and its claim to virtue is no greater than that which the present is willing to invest it with. Where Tate saw—or tried to see—history as tradition, a relatively static entity with moral values firmly embedded in it, Warren regarded it as process from whose workings man must tentatively construct his knowledge: "reality is not a function of the event as event, but of the relationship of that event to past, and future, events. . . . this only affirms what we must affirm: that direction is all. And only as we realize this do we live, for our own identity is dependent upon this principle." Nothing could be further from the old Victorian conception of a universe composed of timeless, abstract truths.[59]

In Warren's view history itself supplies no help in creating moral values. "Process as process is neither morally good nor morally bad," Jack Burden explains. "We may judge results but not process." In other words, although history contains no inherent meaning—as the late Victorians first discovered—man can and must impose a meaning on it by reflecting on his experience. The moral lessons he derives will necessarily be provisional and must of course be framed within the contours of historical change. No clearcut moral divisions will be possible. "What we students of history always learn," Jack tells Anne, "is that the human being is a very complicated contraption and that they are not good or bad but are good and bad and the good comes out of the bad and the bad out of the good, and the devil take the hindmost." Yet, although his morality will always be steeped in paradox, man does have a continuing obligation to search for values if he is to transcend the essential chaos of nature—in other words, to escape the fate of a Percy Munn or Willie Stark. That is what Jack Burden (and, by proxy, Warren himself) concludes from his study of history.[60]

All the King's Men, then, can be seen as the drama of a young southerner attaining a Modernist sensibility. It is a novel explicitly based upon the Modernist reconstruction of man as Warren understood it. This is why the book stands as a landmark in the region's intellectual history. By the mid-1940s the solidity of Victorian knowledge had become a relic of the past for Warren; all the king's men couldn't put it together again. Instead of the firm categories established by the nineteenth-century moral dichotomy, there was only Jack Burden's spider web: seamless, all-encompassing, but liable to come apart at the first touch. Within this new definition of the cosmos the existential struggle to overcome innocence and achieve knowledge could never stop. So Jack Burden reflects when

15. Robert Penn Warren in 1949
Photograph from Look Magazine courtesy of
University of Minnesota Archives

he comes home late one night to find an unexpected telegram waiting for him and debates whether or not to open it:

> the clammy, sad little foetus which is you way down in the dark
> which is you too lifts up its sad little face and its eyes are blind, and
> it shivers cold inside you for it doesn't want to know what is in
> that envelope. It wants to lie in the dark and not know, and be warm
> in its not-knowing. The end of man is knowledge, but there is one
> thing he can't know. He can't know whether knowledge will
> save him or kill him. There's the cold in your stomach, but you
> open the envelope, you have to open the envelope, for the end
> of man is to know.[61]

This constitutes, in its way, a heroic conception of human nature, and one not easy to sustain. One might even ask if it is too heroic. For what is most striking about the Modernist system of belief is its essential loneliness, its insistence (strangely reminiscent of orthodox Calvinism) that the individual must find salvation through self-knowledge almost entirely alone. That is the price the twentieth century has paid to throw off the fetters of nineteenth-century culture. Although free to retrieve the energies and fulfillments once suppressed, one must do so in a world where the only guideposts are those one creates through one's own thought and actions. According to the ideal formulation of this culture, one must define oneself, rather than find a definition of one's identity already provided by society. If most people living in post-1945 America have not felt the full force of that culture, certainly the intellectuals have. They most of all have had to live without certainty; they have been the prime beneficiaries and victims of the culture they helped bring into being.

Indeed, this tension is evident in *All the King's Men* during those moments when Warren himself appears to be slipping into a backdoor attempt to revive traditional Christian belief. One senses this, for instance, at the very end of the book, when the Scholarly Attorney delivers a disquisition on man's sin as the "awful index of God's omnipotence" and Jack Burden nods his head in agreement. "I did so," Jack remarks parenthetically, "to keep his mind untroubled, but later I was not certain but that in my own way I did believe what he had said." Warren's decision to set the sentence off in parentheses, the tentative quality of the diction ("I was not certain but that"), and the ambiguity of the key phrase ("in my own way") indicate the strength of Warren's yearning for religious affirmation. Unlike his friends Ransom and Tate, Warren was not prepared to make a definitive gesture to staunch that yearning; he was Modernist enough to know it would not work. Early in life he had stopped going to church, and he never maintained a formal religious affiliation. But the temptations he felt in this direction were powerful. Their presence in the background of *All the King's Men* suggests the intensity of the struggle Warren endured to reach the insights attributed to Jack Burden.[62]

CODA

For any who still doubted it, the triumph of southern Modernism was demonstrated in 1941 with the publication of Wilbur J. Cash's *The Mind of the South*. Surely the great significance of that work lay in the knockout blow it delivered to the Cavalier myth. Gathering the insights of the new generation of southern writers, Cash presented the Old South as a frontier society dominated by the "hard, energetic, horse-trading type of man" who attempted to disguise his crudeness by posing as an aristocrat. For Cash, the post-Reconstruction South was even more cutthroat and individualistic. Indeed, ugliness, conflict, and brutality abounded in his portrait. Relying heavily on his understanding of Freud, Cash posited a near-schizophrenic split within the southern psyche, between a voracious hedonism and an equally powerful Puritan guilt, a split that led to all sorts of pathological behavior from miscegenation to lynching. The final impression left was not that of a civilized society, but rather of one governed, to use Cash's own phrase, by a "savage ideal." *The Mind of the South*, in short, represented a complete reversal of the vision of the region's history once offered by New South writers—it read like a compendium of those aspects of the South they had deliberately screened out.[1]

What was remarkable was the rapidity with which this distinctly unflattering description of the region found general acceptance, not only in the North but among southern intellectuals as well. Save for Donald Davidson's harsh attack in the *Southern Review* and one other unfavorable notice, no dissenting voices were raised against Cash's work. On the contrary, the book became an instant classic, thereby testifying to the firm hold the Modernist viewpoint had gained among the South's educated elite. What would have been regarded as an unpublishable scandal a quarter century earlier was now largely accepted as a conventional truth.[2]

In fact, it is probably not unfair to say that Cash's South of conflict and depravity was, ironically, coming to enjoy the mythological status that had once characterized the innocent and genteel South of the nineteenth century. From Erskine Caldwell to Tennessee Williams, from

C. Vann Woodward to Marshall Frady, southern authors carried the critical spirit to its logical extreme, until Americans living outside the region formed a picture of southern society as one immense Tobacco Road. In doing this writers were simply following one of the basic dynamics of Modernist culture, with its rebellion against the practice of deliberate evasion. Cash himself was shrewd enough to recognize that the debunking he and others were engaged in represented a "sort of reverse embodiment of the old sentimentality." There should be no surprise in this: cultures typically take their shape in reaction to the culture being rejected, and their excesses often arise by way of correcting the excesses of their predecessors. Beyond doubt the false optimism and complacent self-deception of Victorianism needed correction, and that is precisely what the new generation accomplished.[3]

Perhaps the clearest articulation of these tendencies in the 1940s appeared in the writings of Lillian Smith, who, more than anyone else, brought the issues of race and segregation into the open. With her, the assault against the Victorian ethos reached maturity. Her account of the psychic forces sustaining segregation identified the Victorian dichotomy, with its separation of mind and body, as the chief culprit:

> Not only Negroes but everything dark, dangerous, evil must be pushed to the rim of one's life. Signs put over doors in the world outside and over minds seemed natural enough to children like us, for signs had already been put over forbidden areas of our body. The banning of people and books and ideas did not appear more shocking than the banning of our wishes which we learned early to send to the Dark-town of our unconscious.

Smith's entire crusade was pitched against this compartmentalization that her inherited culture had depended upon. Her goal was to establish a new culture based upon the opening of "doors" and the recapture of previously forbidden human energies. For her, "integration" meant more than a racial strategy; it meant the effort to restore man's "wholeness" in the deepest Modernist sense.[4]

Yet the striking thing is that, as bold as these pronouncements sounded in the late 1940s, today they have about them the ring of the commonplace. At the time Lillian Smith wrote, the Supreme Court's historic decision on school desegregation was still more than five years away, and the ensuing civil rights movement was beyond the imagination of most southerners. Now the so-called Second Reconstruction appears to be over; legal segregation has been banished, and the cultural battle Smith waged has largely been won. As a result, her description of southerners as repressed, violent, and perverted strikes readers of the 1980s as extravagant and overdramatic, much as Cash's critique of the South does. Her contention that blacks possess a unique culture that permits them a "marvelous love of life and play, a physical grace and rhythm and a psychosexual vigor," is now greeted with suspicion. Above all, her prescriptions for psychic health and liberation, radical as they seemed at first, evince a certain stilted quality for the present-day reader. We have long since passed this stage of the cultural debate, with the result that Smith's insights have become stale.[5]

Perhaps the fact that the main battle was over, that the transition to Modernist culture was essentially completed among southern writers, helps account for the noticeable drop in the intensity of intellectual activity in the region since the 1950s. One almost senses that southerners had little new to say about their society. Those sociologists who focused on the region continued the work of the Odum school, but their work, however competent, was not original or exciting. A high level of craftsmanship also distinguished southern journalism, with many newspapers earning Pulitzer Prizes during the civil rights struggle. However, from the standpoint of intellectual content their editorials in most instances repeated the themes set forth by the Regionalists. And in literature the shadows of Faulkner, Tate, and Warren loomed mightily over their successors: the Modernist mode had become a tradition. Tragedy, paradox, heroic endurance—those flashes of literary fire that had lit up the southern landscape during the interwar era—all became the staples of the new established mythology.[6]

By the 1960s, a few writers, among them William Styron, Eudora Welty, and Walker Percy, were beginning to reexamine the new mythology or at least were carrying its inner logic to the point where some of its contradictions stood revealed. In *The Last Gentleman,* for example, Percy created a character who attempts to carry out the Modernist search for meaning and integrity only to find the world gone totally mad. Like Warren's Jack Burden, Will Barrett is engaged on a quest that is fundamentally religious, though he has rejected any formal ties to a church. Rather, he seeks to plunge himself into everyday reality, opening himself up fully to experience in order to discover his true identity. Barrett's problem, though, is that his Modernist perceptivity has become so keen, his ability to see through appearances so great, that the world seems constantly to slip away from him. In this dilemma he instinctively tries to recapture what he can of his heroic Cavalier heritage. On one occasion he goes so far as to blow up a plaque on the Princeton campus commemorating the Union dead. Unfortunately for Barrett's purposes the plaque was hidden behind shrubbery, and no one discovers his deed. On returning to his hometown in Mississippi he finds himself in the midst of a racial confrontation and recalls the brave acts of his forebears in keeping racial peace. But this time all the characters involved in the confrontation are busy playing theatrical roles that have little connection to the moral issues at stake. Indeed, all of life becomes a theater for Barrett, a theater of the absurd. He reflects, "there [are] no clear issues anymore. Arguments are spoiled. Clownishness always intervenes."[7]

In his search for a route back to the heroic, Barrett attaches himself to Sutter Vaught, a failed young physician from Alabama, whose quest for existential meaning has taken him to the New Mexico desert. By stripping his existence down to a bare minimum, by reducing it to little more than the pleasures of the flesh, Vaught has endeavored to find a core to life that is both authentic and durable. "I accept the current genital condition of human relations," he explains, "and try to go beyond it. I may sniff like a dog but then I try to be human rather than masquerade as human and sniff like a dog. I am a sincere, humble, and even moral pornographer." What attracts Barrett is precisely this commitment of Sutter's to achieve heroism within a Modernist frame of values. Sutter has gone into the desert alone, suffered his personal Gethsemane, yet somehow survived. Unlike the heroic Cavalier, however, Sutter cannot share his vision with anyone; he can civilize no one, not even himself. All he can (or will) do for Barrett is pose questions:

> Which is the best course for a man: to live like a Swede, vote for the candidate of your choice, be a good fellow, healthy and generous, do a bit of science as if the world made sense, enjoy a beer and a good piece (not a bad life!). Or: to live as a Christian among Christians in Alabama? Or to die like an honest man?

Neither Barrett nor Sutter can answer these questions, and *The Last Gentleman* ends appropriately in total ambiguity, leaving no hint of how the two will resolve their lives.[8]

This was the quandary to which Modernist culture had brought southern writers by the mid-1960s. If one followed its mode of perception consistently and looked relentlessly beneath "appearances," one was lost in a world of paradox and moral relativism. Returning to the apparent stability of the nineteenth century was not an option: we are reminded of this by the plight of Barrett's father, a man of imposing self-certainty who blasts his head off with a shotgun, thus revealing the impasse of concealed agony the Victorians had come to. The twentieth century had at least brought these tensions into the open. Yet the price for liberation has been high, and perhaps it is now time for a liberation from liberation itself. Having freed the individual from the old moral code and reinstated the animal part of his being, Modernist culture may have reached its furthest limits. A new source of guidance has to be found. Surely the South, with its acute sense of loss of the old certainties, will have a role to play in that quest.

NOTES

This book was planned and written to appeal to the general reader as well as to the historian. Accordingly, the scholarly apparatus is presented as simply as possible. To keep the text uncluttered, the sources for quotations and other items are summarized in notes at the end of each paragraph. Sources in each note are given in the order in which the information appears in the text. By matching text and notes, the reader should be able to discern readily the source for any particular item.

INTRODUCTION

1. R. Jackson Wilson, *In Quest of Community*, 26–27.

2. Richard Hofstadter, *The Progressive Historians*, 86. Accounts of the prewar rebellion can be found in Henry F. May, *The End of American Innocence*, and Morton White, *Social Thought in America*. For an excellent study of the same intellectual transition in England that contains many insights applicable to the American scene, see Samuel Hynes, *The Edwardian Turn of Mind*.

3. Lionel Trilling, *Beyond Culture*, 3, 19–25; Irving Howe, *The Decline of the New*, 3–5, 9–10, 21–25; Daniel Bell, *The Cultural Contradictions of Capitalism*, xxi, 46–47; Berman, "All that is Solid," 54.

4. Peter Gay, *Freud, Jews and Other Germans*, 21–26, 70–71. For similar views, see the introduction to Richard Ellmann and Charles Feidelson, Jr., eds., *The Modern Tradition*, v–vi; and Louis Kampf, *On Modernism*, 16–30. Gay observes that "the historian of Modernist culture may best begin his revision of current, clearly inadequate interpretations by enlarging the territory of Modernism." That is exactly the approach adopted in the present study.

5. Raymond Williams, *Culture and Society, 1780–1950*, xiv–xv, discusses the shift in the meaning of "culture." For a more extended discussion of the Victorian dichotomy, see chap. 1.

6. H. Stuart Hughes, *Consciousness and Society*, charts the impact of Darwin, Freud, and Marx, although it would be inaccurate to attribute to him the formulation I have adopted here. See also Hayden White, "The Forms of Wildness," in Edward J. Dudley and Maximillian E. Novak, eds., *The Wild Man Within*, esp. 34–35.

7. Alfred L. Kroeber, "Eighteen Professions," 283–88; George W. Stocking, Jr., *Race, Culture, and Evolution*, 159, 267–68; Miklos Szabolcsi, "Avante-garde, Neo avante-garde, Modernism," 58.

8. Stocking, *Race*, 225–29; Clifford Geertz, "Ideology as a Cultural System," in David E. Apter, ed., *Ideology and Discontent*, 62; Erik H. Erikson, *Childhood and Society*, 285.

9. Steven Marcus, *The Other Victorians*, passim.

10. Lionel Trilling, *Sincerity and Authenticity*, 6–13, 141–44; May, *End of Innocence*,

398; Christopher Lasch, *The New Radicalism in America, 1889–1963*, 254. Much has been written about innocence as a distinctive trait of American national character—especially by writers in the American Studies tradition such as Richard W. B. Lewis in *The American Adam*. What is striking, however, is that these accounts almost always focus on American culture in the nineteenth century, a fact that suggests that what they are really talking about is American Victorianism. Certainly it is hard to make the case for an enduring national innocence relying on the literature of the 1920s onward.

11. Bell, *Contradictions*, xxi; Trilling, *Beyond Culture*, 79. It should also be stressed that one cannot make self-identification as a Modernist a means of determining whether a particular writer is in fact Modernist. Even though most twentieth-century American intellectuals, at least since the First World War, fall readily within the Modernist camp, few would describe themselves this way, primarily because of the prevalent error of viewing Modernism as an exotic movement within the arts rather than as a comprehensive culture. Bell and Trilling themselves supply cases in point—they would doubtless agree that their basic intellectual premises differ radically from those regnant in the nineteenth century, and one suspects that they would hardly be inclined to return to Victorian doctrine, no matter what their criticisms of the culture of their time. Moreover, in their reliance on post-Freudian psychological assumptions, their candid critical temperaments, their anthropological conceptions of culture, and their relativist scales of value, both men display the hallmarks of Modernism.

12. Paul Gaston, *The New South Creed*, 6–8, 160–62.

13. Wilbur J. Cash, *The Mind of the South*, 97.

14. Throughout this study I have employed the narrowest possible definition of the South, limiting it solely to the eleven states of the former Confederacy. Maryland, West Virginia, Kentucky, Missouri, and Oklahoma are *not* included in my definition of the South (although exceptions are made for Allen Tate and Robert Penn Warren, both born in Kentucky just over the Tennessee border). I have done this to insure that there be no question that the individuals I deal with are indeed southern. For the same reason I have chosen only those persons who were born, raised, and received most of their education in the South (at least through college) in deciding who should qualify as a southern intellectual.

CHAPTER 1

1. Robert Toombs, quoted in Marshall W. Fishwick, *Virginia*, 196; William R. Taylor, *Cavalier and Yankee*, 320.

2. Louis B. Wright, *The First Gentlemen of Virginia*, 2, 38–39, 51; Carl Bridenbaugh, *Myths and Realities*, 13, 17–18, 51–53; Fishwick, *Virginia*, 119. On the balance between the "aristocratic" and "democratic" elements in eighteenth-century Virginian political ideology, see Charles S. Sydnor, *American Revolutionaries in the Making*, 61–73. It is true that the rice planters of South Carolina did develop strong aristocratic pretensions of a European character during the eighteenth century, but as Bridenbaugh has shown, at century's end they were still a rather crude lot of men on the make, and besides they represented only a tiny fraction of the southern planter class. See his *Myths and Realities*, 61–62, 65, 72–73, 98–99.

3. Charles S. Sydnor, *The Development of Southern Sectionalism, 1819–1848*, 7–8, 13–14.

4. Ibid., 14–15; Clement Eaton, *The Growth of Southern Civilization, 1790–1860*, 151, 153; Taylor, *Cavalier*, 69; H. J. Eckenrode, *Jefferson Davis*, 29–30.

5. Rollin G. Osterweis, *Romanticism and Nationalism in the Old South*, 41–45, 51, 87;

Clement Eaton, *The Mind of the Old South*, 182–83; Wilbur J. Cash, *The Mind of the South*, 73.

6. Taylor, *Cavalier*, 74–75; David J. Rothman, *The Discovery of the Asylum*, 114.

7. Taylor, *Cavalier*, 75; Rothman, *Asylum*, 69–71, 119, 128.

8. Rothman, *Asylum*, xviii–xix, 133, 285. For the connection between the development of political parties and Jacksonian social anxieties, see Marvin Meyers, *The Jacksonian Persuasion*, esp. chaps. 4 and 6.

9. Sydnor, *Development of Sectionalism*, 91–94. A small reform movement did arise in the South at this time, but it was limited mainly to intellectuals in Virginia and South Carolina, it focused primarily on revamping southern agricultural practices (which the reformers regarded as a moral cause), and it was soon preoccupied with the defense of slavery. Nevertheless, Drew Faust has pointed out many similarities between this movement and the more conservative wing of northern reform. See her *A Sacred Circle*, 89–90, 129–31.

10. Taylor, *Cavalier*, 29; Hugh Swinton Legaré, quoted in William W. Freehling, *Prelude to Civil War*, 15.

11. Edgar T. Thompson, "The South in Old and New Contexts," in John C. McKinney and Edgar T. Thompson, eds., *The South in Continuity and Change*, 458; Edgar T. Thompson, "God and the Southern Plantation System," in Samuel S. Hill, Jr., ed., *Religion and the Solid South*, 67–69. On the dearth of public schools, see Sydnor, *Sectionalism*, 62–63, 304–5.

12. Kenneth S. Lynn, *Mark Twain and Southwestern Humor*, 5.

13. Mark Schorer, "The Necessity of Myth," in Henry A. Murray, ed., *Myth and Mythmaking*, 355–56; Richard V. Chase, *Quest for Myth*, 96–102; Jerome S. Bruner, *On Knowing*, 32, 35; Richard S. Slotkin, *Regeneration through Violence*, 6–14, 18–19, 558–63.

14. Taylor, *Cavalier*, 69, 124, 301–2.

15. George Fitzhugh, "Sociology for the South," in Eric L. McKitrick, ed., *Slavery Defended*, 35–37, 46–47.

16. George Fitzhugh, "Sociology for the South," in Harvey Wish, ed., *Ante Bellum*, 57; Taylor, *Cavalier*, 154.

17. Lynn, *Mark Twain*, 52–54, 60–63, 70, 118. A good general discussion of southern violence can be found in F. Sheldon Hackney, "Southern Violence," in Hugh Graham Davis and Ted Robert Gurr, eds., *Violence in America*, 479–97.

18. Lynn, *Mark Twain*, 61–64, 68. For a sampling of Southwest humor, see the selections in Kenneth S. Lynn, ed., *The Comic Tradition in America*.

19. Lynn, *Mark Twain*, 62, 115; Freehling, *Prelude*, 12; Clement Eaton, *Freedom of Thought in the Old South*, 52–53, 163.

20. Louis Hartz, *The Liberal Tradition in America*, 149.

21. C. Vann Woodward, *Origins of the New South, 1877–1913*, 154–57.

22. Paul M. Gaston, *The New South Creed*, 67–69, 86.

23. Gaston, *New South Creed*, 107–8, 114, 116.

24. Woodward, *Origins*, 154–55; Gaston, *New South Creed*, 160, 162, 206; Henry W. Grady, "The New South," 84–85, 87.

25. Gaston, *New South Creed*, 191–92; Gaston, "The 'New South,'" in Link and Patrick, *Writing Southern History*, 319–21.

26. Walter E. Houghton, *The Victorian Frame of Mind, 1830–1870*, 184, 189–91, 266, 305–9; G. M. Young, *Victorian England*, 32; David D. Hall, "The Victorian Connection," 563.

27. Houghton, *Victorian Frame*, 28; Young, *Victorian England*, 1–5.

28. Woodward, *Origins*, 144–48; Bruce Clayton, *The Savage Ideal*, 17–18, 161. Even

writers like George W. Cable who would not seem at first glance a part of this movement shared the values of moral uplift and progress. See Arlin Turner, *George W. Cable*, 48–50, on Cable's journalistic career.

29. Edward K. Graham, *Education and Citizenship and Other Papers*, 9, 73–77. For a sketch of Graham, see Louis R. Wilson, *The University of North Carolina, 1900–1930*, 179–291.

30. Graham, *Education*, 5–6.

31. Clayton, *Savage Ideal*, 32–33; William P. Trent, quoted in William S. Knickerbocker, "Trent at Sewanee," 146.

32. Peter L. Thorslev, Jr., "The Wild Man's Revenge," in Dudley and Novak, *The Wild Man Within*, 282–83; Roy Harvey Pearce, *Savagism and Civilization*, 139–55; Michael Timko, "The Victorianism of Victorian Literature," 613–15; Canon Charles Smyth, "The Evangelical Discipline," in *Ideas and Beliefs of the Victorians*, 98.

33. Houghton, *Victorian Frame*, 162; Peter T. Cominos, "Late-Victorian Sexual Respectability and the Social System," 23–24; Timko, "Victorianism," 627.

34. John Stuart Mill, "Civilization: Signs of the Times," in George L. Levine, ed., *The Emergence of Victorian Consciousness*, 87–88, 91–92, 99; Matthew Arnold, *Culture and Anarchy*, 37, 47, 55–58.

35. Houghton, *Victorian Frame*, 410, 233–36; Robert Louis Stevenson, *Dr. Jekyll and Mr. Hyde*, 90–91, 29, 101–3, 108; Masao Miyoshi, *The Divided Self*, 298–99.

36. Gertrude Himmelfarb, *Victorian Minds*, 305; Houghton, *Victorian Frame*, 353; John Morely, quoted in Houghton, *Victorian Frame*, 368; Cominos, "Sexual Respectability," 22, 24–25; James Turner, *Reckoning with the Beast*, 68; John S. Haller and Robin M. Haller, *The Physician and Sexuality in Victorian America*, 92–96, 112, 125–29.

37. Young, *Victorian England*, 2; Arnold, *Culture and Anarchy*, 69–70, 203–4; Raymond Williams, *Culture and Society, 1780–1950*, 104–9, 124–25; G. Kitson Clark, *The Making of Victorian England*, 48, 60–64; Daniel Walker Howe, "American Victorianism as a Culture," 528.

38. Hayden White, "The Forms of Wildness," in Dudley and Novak, *Wild Man Within*, 34–35.

39. Clayton, *Savage Ideal*, 214, 123; George W. Cable, quoted in Morton D. Sosna, *In Search of the Silent South*, 2.

40. Clayton, *Savage Ideal*, 131–32, 157. Dodd and Daniels both warmly supported Bryan in 1896. Wayne Mixon reports that Joel Chandler Harris also dissented from New South thought in favoring the "plain folk," though his affection for them seems to have been somewhat ambivalent and did not, in any event, extend to the poorest classes. See Mixon, "Joel Chandler Harris, the Yeoman Tradition, and the New South Movement," 309–12.

41. Clayton, *Savage Ideal*, 88, 123, 81–82; John C. Kilgo, "An Inquiry Concerning Lynchings," 7–8, 12–13; Edwin Mims quoted in Michael O'Brien, "Edwin Mims," 208.

42. Kilgo, "An Inquiry," 13; Edgar Gardner Murphy, *Problems of the Present South*, 87; Clayton, *Savage Ideal*, 163.

43. Murphy, *Problems*, 114, 26–27, 271. On Murphy himself, see Hugh C. Bailey, *Edgar Gardner Murphy*.

44. Murphy, *Problems*, 72–74. On the movement for "industrial education" for blacks generally, see Elizabeth Jacoway, *Yankee Missionaries in the South*.

45. Murphy, *Problems*, 284.

PART ONE

1. Louis D. Rubin, Jr., *No Place on Earth*, 45.

CHAPTER 2

1. Richard Hofstadter, "U. B. Phillips and the Plantation Legend," 109–10; Stanley M. Elkins, *Slavery*, 10; Wendell H. Stephenson, *The South Lives in History*, 75.

2. Eugene D. Genovese, "Race and Class in Southern History," 345, 355. On the dispute over the dedication of *Transportation in the Eastern Cotton Belt*, see William H. Carpenter to Phillips, October 16, 1907, Ulrich B. Phillips Papers.

3. Paul M. Gaston, "The New South," in Link and Patrick, *Writing Southern History*, 318–19, 321–22; Holland Thompson, *The New South*, 203–4. See also Philip A. Bruce, *The Rise of the New South*.

4. Gaston, "The New South," in Link and Patrick, *Writing Southern History*, 320; Bruce Clayton, *The Savage Ideal*, 68–70.

5. Ulrich B. Phillips, "The Economics of the Plantation," 232.

6. Ulrich B. Phillips, "Conservatism and Progress in the Cotton Belt," 7.

7. Ulrich B. Phillips, *Life and Labor in the Old South*, 123; Stephenson, *South Lives in History*, 60–64; Wood Gray, "Ulrich Bonnell Phillips," in William T. Hutchinson, ed., *The Marcus W. Jernegan Essays in American Historiography*, 355–57; Ulrich B. Phillips, "Georgia and States Rights," 2:3–224.

8. Wendell Holmes Stephenson, *Southern History in the Making*, 179; Ulrich B. Phillips to Henry [?], February 27, 1903, Frank L. Owsley Papers. According to Gerald M. Capers, a former student of Phillips at Yale University, one of the main reasons why Phillips did not return to the South was the strong objections of his New York-born wife to living in the region. Interview with Gerald M. Capers, January 15, 1980.

9. Gray, "Phillips," 357; Ulrich B. Phillips, introduction to *Plantation and Frontier Documents*, vol. 1 of *A Documentary History of American Industrial Society*, 3, 5. On Phillips as a Progressive, see the introduction by C. Vann Woodward to Ulrich B. Phillips, *Life and Labor in the Old South*, iii–iv; and Genovese, "Race and Class," 355.

10. David Bertelson, *The Lazy South*, 180; Ulrich B. Phillips, "The Origin and Growth of the Southern Black Belts," 803–5; Ulrich B. Phillips, *American Negro Slavery*, 273; Phillips, *Life and Labor*, 366.

11. Phillips, *American Negro Slavery*, 228, 398; Phillips, *Life and Labor*, 132–33.

12. Phillips, *American Negro Slavery*, 232. For additional passages of this sort, see ibid., 205–60; and Phillips, *Life and Labor*, 112–31.

13. Phillips, *American Negro Slavery*, 206–7, 167, 249–52; Phillips, *Life and Labor*, 116–18, 121–23.

14. Phillips, "The Economics of the Plantation," 233–36; Ulrich B. Phillips, "Plantations with Slave Labor and Free," 750.

15. Genovese, "Race and Class," 349–51, 357–58.

16. Phillips, *American Negro Slavery*, 301, 287, 385; Phillips, "Plantations with Slave Labor and Free," 742; Kenneth M. Stampp, "Reconsidering U. B. Phillips: A Comment," 366–68.

17. Phillips, *Life and Labor*, 293–96, 260–61, 285.

18. Phillips, *American Negro Slavery*, 307; Ulrich B. Phillips, "The Plantation as a Civilizing Factor," 264.

19. Phillips, "The Plantation as a Civilizing Factor," 264.

20. Idus A. Newby, *Jim Crow's Defense*, xi, 58–59; Elkins, *Slavery*, 11–13. For an extended treatment of Progressive racism, see John Higham, *Strangers in the Land*, 131–93.

21. Newby, *Jim Crow's Defense*, 29, 49, 64–65, 70–79; George M. Fredrickson, *The Black Image in the White Mind*, 314.

22. Newby, *Jim Crow's Defense*, ix, 69, 130; Fredrickson, *Black Image*, 221–22, 262, 275–81.

23. Fredrickson, *Black Image*, 210, 283–95.

24. Phillips, "Conservatism and Progress in the Cotton Belt," 9.

25. Ulrich B. Phillips, *The Slave Economy of the Old South*, 43; Phillips, *American Negro Slavery*, vii–ix, 8.

26. Phillips, *American Negro Slavery*, 432.

27. Ibid., 449, 474–76, 484; Phillips, *Slave Economy*, 60.

28. Phillips, *American Negro Slavery*, 3–4; Newby, *Jim Crow's Defense*, 27–29.

29. Phillips, "The Plantation as a Civilizing Factor," 257–67; Phillips, *Slave Economy*, 26; Phillips, *American Negro Slavery*, 342–43; Phillips, *Life and Labor*, 199–200.

30. Phillips, *American Negro Slavery*, 291; Phillips, *Life and Labor*, 163, 195; Phillips, *Slave Economy*, 51, 248–49.

31. Phillips, "The Plantation as a Civilizing Factor," 258, 265–66.

32. Ulrich B. Phillips, *The Course of the South to Secession*, 152, 165.

33. Stephenson, *South Lives in History*, 17–18; Phillips, *American Negro Slavery*, 202; Phillips to Carl R. Fish, May 19, 1926, Phillips Papers.

34. Genovese, "Race and Class," 350; Phillips, *American Negro Slavery*, 395–97; Ulrich B. Phillips, "The Economic Cost of Slaveholding in the Cotton Belt," 264–69, 271–75.

35. Phillips, *American Negro Slavery*, 396–97; Phillips, *Life and Labor*, 179, 185; Phillips, "The Economic Cost of Slaveholding in the Cotton Belt," 266–69, 271–74; Phillips, *Slave Economy*, 146, 150.

36. Phillips, *American Negro Slavery*, 337–39; Phillips, "Conservatism and Progress in the Cotton Belt," 3–4; Hofstadter, "U. B. Phillips," 122.

37. Phillips, *Slave Economy*, 247–49; Phillips, *Life and Labor*, 99–101; Phillips, *American Negro Slavery*, 399; Ulrich B. Phillips, "Transportation in the *Ante-Bellum* South," 451.

38. Phillips, *American Negro Slavery*, 289–90, 309, 314, 84; Phillips, *Slave Economy*, 437; Phillips, *Life and Labor*, 207.

39. Stephenson, *South Lives in History*, x; Phillips, "The Economics of Plantations," 236; Phillips, *American Negro Slavery*, 514; Phillips, "Conservatism and Progress in the Cotton Belt," 3.

40. Phillips, *American Negro Slavery*, 514, 401; Phillips, *Life and Labor*, 354–66; Phillips, *Slave Economy*, 34.

41. Phillips et al., *American Industrial Society*, 1:4–7; Phillips, *American Negro Slavery*, 78, 331, 512.

42. Phillips, *Life and Labor*, 107–11, 348, 351.

43. Phillips, *Course of the South to Secession*, 3–4, 31, 72, 95–97.

44. Ibid., 165.

CHAPTER 3

1. Paul M. Gaston, "The 'New South,'" in Link and Patrick, *Writing Southern History*, 321–24.

2. Oral History Memoir of Broadus Mitchell, Oral History Collection, 1, 23–24, 27, 56.

3. Ibid., 8, 10–12, 22.

4. Daniel W. Hollis, *University of South Carolina*, 2:249–62; Mitchell Memoir, 60–66.

5. Mitchell Memoir, 76–77.

6. Ibid., 76, 78; Mitchell to his mother, July 19, 1917, January 4, 1919, Samuel Chiles Mitchell Papers (hereafter cited as SCM Papers), Series B.

7. Wendell H. Stephenson, *The South Lives in History*, 1–2, 5; Mitchell Memoir, 75–76.

8. Mitchell to his mother, n.d. [November 1916], n.d. [1919], and September 15, 1918, SCM Papers, Series B; Morton White, *Social Thought in America*, 76–77.

9. Mitchell Memoir, 86–87, 90–91; Mitchell to his mother, December 6, 1920, SCM Papers, Series A.

10. Broadus Mitchell to S. C. Mitchell, March 24, 1917, May 27, 1917, SCM Papers, Series B; Mitchell to his mother, n.d. [April 1917], ibid. Incidentally, there is no evidence whatsoever to indicate that Mitchell had plans to use the *Record* for tactical advantage—i.e., as a forum to lecture southern mill owners against child labor. If that had been on his mind, he certainly would have mentioned it to his parents, with whom he was exceedingly candid; but he did not.

11. Broadus Mitchell to S. C. Mitchell, November 22, 1918, May 25, 1919, and n.d. [1920], SCM Papers, Series B; Mitchell to his mother, November 14, 1919, and August 9 [1920], ibid.

12. Broadus Mitchell, *The Rise of Cotton Mills in the South*, 95, 96n.

13. Ibid., 18, 102–4, 132; Mitchell, "Cotton Mills in Southern Civilization," in Broadus Mitchell and George S. Mitchell, *The Industrial Revolution in the South*, 247.

14. Mitchell, *Rise of Cotton Mills*, 47–48, 127, 105n, 273, vii–viii.

15. Ibid., 132n, 263, 265, 200.

16. Ibid., 273, 104, 108n, 151, 148; Mitchell, "Two Industrial Revolutions," in Mitchell and Mitchell, *Industrial Revolution*, 93, 108–11; Mitchell, "The Impact of Industry in the South," ibid., 128; Mitchell, "Southern Spindles," ibid., 57.

17. Gerald W. Johnson, "Service in the Cotton Mills," 220–21; Wilbur J. Cash, *The Mind of the South*, 180–81. For an interpretation opposite to Mitchell's, see C. Vann Woodward, *Origins of the New South, 1877–1913*, esp. 133–35, 223–27. Looking back in 1971, Mitchell generously allowed that Woodward's view was probably closer to the truth than his own. "The only thing I can offer as an apology for myself," he added, "is that I'd done it 50 years earlier, and there wasn't the wealth of critical material or basic material that has been developed since. It was a pioneering kind of experimental thing and you did the best you could" (Mitchell Memoir, 97).

18. Mitchell to his mother, September 16, 1916, SCM Papers, Series B.

19. Mitchell to his mother, n.d. [March 1915], SCM Papers, Series B; Mitchell, *Rise of Cotton Mills*, 104, 104–5n.

20. Mitchell, *Rise of Cotton Mills*, 161–62, 172, 90.

21. Mitchell, "Cotton Mills in Southern Civilization," 238.

22. Broadus Mitchell, *Frederick Law Olmsted*, 120.

23. Ibid., 141, 127–28, 102, 68, 45, 71, 105. For Olmsted's views on slavery see Laura Wood Roper, *FLO*, 84–89; and Arthur M. Schlesinger's introduction to Frederick L. Olmsted, *The Cotton Kingdom*, ix–lvi.

24. For the insanity plea as a conventional New South tactic, see chap. 1.

25. Mitchell, "Slippers and Old Sorrel" in Mitchell and Mitchell, *Industrial Revolution*, 281–85; Mitchell Memoir, 13–14.

26. Broadus Mitchell, *William Gregg*, ix.

27. Ibid., 44, 6–7, 221, 23, 146–47, 174. For a less flattering portrait of Gregg, see Eugene D. Genovese, *The Political Economy of Slavery*, 180–220. Genovese views Gregg as

a fundamentally weak man who allowed himself to be co-opted by the slaveholders instead of forcefully defending the rights of manufacturing.

28. Mitchell, *William Gregg*, 82, 76.

29. Ibid., 76, 82–85, 200–201, 60. Mitchell employed the same feudal imagery in reference to the mill villages of the 1880s. See *Rise of Cotton Mills*, 187n.

30. Mitchell, *William Gregg*, 259; Broadus Mitchell to William Terry Couch, June 18, 1928, in "Mitchell, *William Gregg*" file, University of North Carolina Press Papers, Southern Historical Collection (hereafter cited as SHC).

31. Mitchell, "The End of Child Labor," in Mitchell and Mitchell, *Industrial Revolution*, 218–24, 232; Mitchell, "Two Industrial Revolutions," 111.

32. Mitchell, "Fleshpots in the South," in Mitchell and Mitchell, *Industrial Revolution*, 33–37.

33. Ibid., 27–28, 35, 40, 46.

34. Broadus Mitchell to S. C. Mitchell, March 19, 1927, SCM Papers, Series A; John W. Arrington to James Southall Wilson, April 11, 1927, Mitchell to his mother, n.d. [April 1927], SCM Papers, Series B; Mitchell to Wilson, March 29, 1927, *Virginia Quarterly Review* Papers; Couch to Wilson, April 6, 1927, Couch to Mitchell, April 6, 1927, in "Mitchell, *William Gregg*" file, University of North Carolina Press Papers, SHC.

35. Howard W. Odum to Gerald W. Johnson, November 24, 1924, Howard Washington Odum Papers; William T. Couch to Kenneth Chorley, April 6, 1927, in "Laura Spelman Rockefeller Memorial" file, University of North Carolina Press Papers, SHC; David Clark to Bessie Z. Zaban, October 1, 1928, in "Mitchell: *William Gregg*" file, ibid.

36. Broadus Mitchell to Stringfellow Barr, February 23, 1932, *Virginia Quarterly Review* Papers; Mitchell to his mother, September 15, 1918, SCM Papers, Series B (his italics); Mitchell to his mother, January 5, 1922, SCM Papers, Series A.

37. Clarke A. Chambers, *Seedtime of Reform*, 6, 17, 63; Broadus Mitchell to S. C. Mitchell, June 6, 1930, June 18, 1930, SCM Papers, Series B. For more on Mitchell's attitude toward politics, see *Rise of Cotton Mills*, 29; and *Olmsted*, 120.

38. Mitchell to his mother, December 19, 1920, November 18, 1920, SCM Papers, Series A; Broadus Mitchell to S. C. Mitchell, n.d. [April 24, 1920], SCM Papers, Series B; background sheet submitted by Broadus Mitchell, n.d., in "*Culture*: Contributors" file, University of North Carolina Press Papers, SHC. See also his *How to Start Workers' Study Classes*.

39. Mitchell, "The Present Situation in the Southern Textile Industry," in Mitchell and Mitchell, *Industrial Revolution*, 18, 20–23; Mitchell, "The Cotton Mills Again," ibid., 186–87; Harriet L. Herring, "The South Goes to the Bindery," 429.

40. Mitchell to his mother and father, July 6, 1933, Mitchell to his mother, November 7, 1934, SCM Papers, Series B; Mitchell Memoir, 146–49; Broadus Mitchell to S. C. Mitchell, October 9, 1937, SCM Papers, Series A.

41. Albert S. Keister, Review of Broadus Mitchell, *General Economics*, 435; Mitchell Memoir, 150.

42. Broadus Mitchell, "American Radicals Nobody Knows," 394–95, 397; Broadus Mitchell, "Hamilton and Jefferson Today," 407.

43. Mitchell Memoir, 119–22, 126–29, 132, 157; Broadus Mitchell, *Alexander Hamilton*; and *Depression Decade*.

44. Mitchell to his mother, November 14, 1919, SCM Papers, Series B.

CHAPTER 4

1. The best accounts of the southern rebellion appear in Fred C. Hobson, Jr., *Serpent in Eden*, and George B. Tindall, *The Emergence of the New South, 1913–1945*, chap. 9; on the prewar rebellion see Henry F. May, *The End of American Innocence*. John M. Bradbury, *Renaissance in the South*, provides a helpful overview, as do the two fine collections of essays edited by Louis D. Rubin, Jr., and Robert D. Jacobs, *South* and *Southern Renascence*.

2. May, *End of Innocence*, 254–57, 294–97, 328–29; Louise S. Cowan, *The Fugitive Group*, 43; C. Hugh Holman, *Three Modes of Southern Fiction*, 8.

3. Frank Durham, "South Carolina's Poetry Society," 277–79, 281; Tindall, *The Emergence*, 292–93; Josephine Pinckney, "Charleston's Poetry Society," 52–55; John Crowe Ransom, "Modern with the Southern Accent," 189. See also the lament in Du Bose Heyward to James Southall Wilson, December 27, 1925, James Southall Wilson Papers. "My efforts have been fruitless so often when I have tried to get our people to back up the things that the South is trying to do in a literary way," Heyward confessed.

4. Francis Jean Bowen, "The New Orleans *Double Dealer*, 1921–1926," 443–48; James K. Feibleman, "Literary New Orleans between the Wars," 702–5; "The Function of the Wrecker," 287; Emily Tapscott Clark, *Innocence Abroad*, 111.

5. Hobson, *Serpent in Eden*, 14; H. L. Mencken, "The Sahara of the Bozart," 136–38; Mencken, "God Help the South!," 141–44; Mencken, "Morning Song in C Major," 1–5; Douglas C. Stenerson, *H. L. Mencken*, 216–17; May, *End of Innocence*, 210, 214–15.

6. Hobson, *Serpent in Eden*, 48; Gerald Langford's introduction to Emily Clark, *Ingenue among the Lions*, xviii–xix; Clark, *Innocence*, 59; Emily Clark to Joseph Hergesheimer, October 26, 1921, June, 1923, and February, 1923, all in Clark, *Ingenue*, 29, 156, 121.

7. Lambert Davis, "The Reviewer," 618–19; Mary Wingfield Scott, "The Provincetown Players Invade Broadway," 16; Emily Clark, "French Art Notes," 50–53; Mary Newton Stanard, "Poe as Temperance Preacher," 44; Clark, *Innocence*, 28, 18.

8. Emily Clark to Joseph Hergesheimer, January 11, 1922, May 23, 1922, February, 1923, and October 26, 1921, all in Clark, *Ingenue*, 48, 63, 110, 28; Clark, *Innocence*, 235. By contrast the *Virginia Quarterly Review* in the late 1920s was extremely interested in attacking southern topics in a critical fashion. See especially James Southall Wilson to Louis I. Jaffe, April 7, 1928, and Wilson to Robert Lathan, April 8, 1928, *Virginia Quarterly Review* Papers.

9. Vernon L. Parrington, *Main Currents in American Thought*, 3:345. For the contemporary estimate of Cabell, see also Carl Van Doren, H. L. Mencken, and Hugh Walpole, *James Branch Cabell*. For a more recent defense, see Edmund Wilson, "The James Branch Cabell Case Reopened," 129–56; along with Desmond Tarrant, *James Branch Cabell*. Tarrant unfortunately is long on opinion and short on perceptive analysis.

10. James Branch Cabell, *Beyond Life*, 50–51; David Daiches, *Some Late Victorian Attitudes*, 9–11, 90.

11. James Branch Cabell, *Jurgen*, 131; William James, *A Pluralistic Universe*, 319.

12. Daiches, *Late Victorian Attitudes*, 66–69. For another southern stoic of this generation, see Richard H. King, "Mourning and Melancholia," 250–51.

13. Joe Lee Davis, *James Branch Cabell*, 42–44; Louis D. Rubin, Jr., "Two in Richmond," in Rubin and Jacobs, *South*, 132–34; Dorothy B. Schlegel, "James Branch Cabell and Southern Romanticism," in Rinaldo C. Simonini, Jr., ed., *Southern Writers*, 127–28.

14. Davis, *Cabell*, 57; Arvin R. Wells, *Jesting Moses*, 26; Hobson, *Serpent*, 139–40.

15. Wells, *Jesting Moses*, 12–13, 46.

16. Ibid., 16, 43–45; Cabell, quoted in Edd W. Parks, "James Branch Cabell," in Rubin and Jacobs, *Southern Renascence*, 252; Cabell, *Beyond Life*, 19, 25–26, 45; Tarrant,

Cabell, 72. On Cabell's appeal to the young in the early 1920s, see, for example, the unsigned editorial in *The Double Dealer*, "Mr. Cabell of Virginia," 5–7. Even the members of the Fugitive group in Nashville regarded Cabell as little less than a god; see Jesse E. Wills to Allen Tate, January 20 [1920], December 13 [1922], and February 7, 1923, in the Allen Tate Papers.

17. Davis, *Cabell*, 71; Parks, "Cabell," in Rubin and Jacobs, *Southern Renascence*, 259; Masao Miyoshi, *The Divided Self*, 331, 311, 320; Cabell, *Jurgen*, 69, 54–55, 75; Katherine Anne Porter, "The Grave," in her *The Old Order*, 60.

18. Cabell, *Jurgen*, 75.

19. Ellen Glasgow, *A Certain Measure*, 11–12; Ellen Glasgow to Bessie Zaban Jones, January 8, 1935, in Glasgow, *Letters of Ellen Glasgow*, 171–72.

20. Frederick P. W. McDowell, *Ellen Glasgow and the Ironic Art of Fiction*, 15; Glasgow, *Certain Measure*, 8, 113–14.

21. Ellen Glasgow, quoted in McDowell, *Ellen Glasgow*, 28; E. Stanley Godbold, Jr., *Ellen Glasgow and the Woman Within*, 133; John Edward Hardy, "Ellen Glasgow," in Rubin and Jacobs, *Southern Renascence*, 240; Louis D. Rubin, Jr., *No Place on Earth*, 13, 47.

22. Julius R. Raper, *Without Shelter*, 15–19, 31; McDowell, *Ellen Glasgow*, 12–13; Godbold, *Ellen Glasgow*, 96.

23. Raper, *Without Shelter*, 22, 28–30; Godbold, *Ellen Glasgow*, 27.

24. McDowell, *Ellen Glasgow*, 14–15; Glasgow, *Certain Measure*, 16.

25. Raper, *Without Shelter*, 42–43, 46–47.

26. Edwin G. Boring, "The Influence of Evolutionary Theory upon American Psychological Thought," in Stow Persons, ed., *Evolutionary Thought in America*, 284; Raper, *Without Shelter*, 45–46; Winthrop D. Jordan, *White Over Black*, 217–20, 189–90; Michael Timko, "The Victorianism of Victorian Literature," 615–19.

27. Robert Scoon, "The Rise and Impact of Evolutionary Ideas," in Persons, *Evolutionary Thought*, 19; Raper, *Without Shelter*, 45–46. See also John Dewey, *The Influence of Darwinism on Philosophy*, 1–19.

28. Glasgow, *Certain Measure*, 60–61.

29. Ibid., 90–91; Ellen Glasgow, *Virginia*, 35, 5; Raper, *Without Shelter*, 244.

30. Glasgow, *Virginia*, 327, 319–20.

31. Ibid., 442, 486–87, 496.

32. Glasgow, *Certain Measure*, 79–80; Rubin, "Two in Richmond," in Rubin and Jacobs, *South*, 128; Glasgow, *Virginia*, 396, 379–81.

33. Glasgow, *Virginia*, 327–29, 379, 172, 375.

34. Ibid., 402, 410, 426–31, 500.

35. Ibid., 414–15.

36. Glasgow, *Certain Measure*, 94.

37. Ellen Glasgow, *Barren Ground*, 358; Glasgow, *Certain Measure*, 218; McDowell, *Ellen Glasgow*, 34–35.

38. Godbold, *Ellen Glasgow*, 108–9, 119–22.

39. McDowell, *Ellen Glasgow*, 32, 38; Glasgow, *Certain Measure*, 54, 15; Ellen Glasgow to Irita Van Doren, September 8, 1933, and n.d. [September 1933], in Glasgow, *Letters*, 143–44.

40. Glasgow, *Barren Ground*, v–vi, 311; Ellen Glasgow to Daniel Longwell, July 12, 1932, in Glasgow, *Letters*, 118.

41. Glasgow, *Barren Ground*, 6–7, 10, 44, 408.

42. Ibid., 98, 14, 117, 228, 185, 84.

43. Godbold, *Ellen Glasgow*, 36; McDowell, *Ellen Glasgow*, 13; Glasgow, *Certain Measure*, 221; Glasgow, *Barren Ground*, 367, 75.

44. Richard Hofstadter, *Social Darwinism in American Thought*, 10. On this point, see also George Santayana, *Character and Opinion in the United States*, 17, 20, 29.

45. Glasgow, *Barren Ground*, 48, 156, 195, 218.

46. Ibid., 367, 398, 327.

47. Ibid., 368, 375, 261.

48. Ibid., 227. Cf. Joan Foster Santas, *Ellen Glasgow's American Dream*, 9–11, 16.

49. Godbold, *Ellen Glasgow*, 9; Glasgow, *Certain Measure*, 141.

50. Paul Green, "A Plain Statement about Southern Literature," 71–75. The two writers Green refers to as "no more Southern than national" are likely Mark Twain and Edgar Allan Poe.

PART TWO

1. For similar observations on transitional intellectuals in Great Britain, see Raymond Williams, *Culture and Society, 1780–1950*, 161–62.

2. Wilbur J. Cash, *The Mind of the South*, 371–72.

CHAPTER 5

1. "Do You Know Your South? . . . The Editors Answer Their Own Questions," 110; Jonathan Daniels, *A Southerner Discovers the South*, 140.

2. Rupert B. Vance and Katharine Jocher, "Howard W. Odum," 203–17. The best available bibliography of Odum is in Howard W. Odum, *Folk, Region, and Society*, 455–69.

3. George B. Tindall, "The Significance of Howard W. Odum to Southern History," 307.

4. Wayne D. Brazil, "Howard W. Odum: The Building Years, 1884–1930," 4–6, 9–12. I am heavily indebted to Dr. Brazil not only for the information I have gleaned from his biography of Odum, but for the insights he has shared with me during our many discussions of Odum and twentieth-century southern thought.

5. Ibid., 10, 13–16, 20–27, 47–51, 55–57, 179.

6. Ibid., 72–74, 114–18.

7. Ibid., 120–24, 197, 225–27, 282–89, 292–96, 304.

8. Ibid., 310–12, 315, 317–18, 324–25, 328–30, 336–37; Bishop Warren A. Candler, quoted in Rupert B. Vance, "Howard W. Odum and the Case of the South," 2.

9. Louis R. Wilson, *The University of North Carolina, 1900–1930*, 446–49; Brazil, "Odum," 338, 347–48; interview with Louis R. Wilson, Chapel Hill, October 15, 1970; Howard W. Odum to Albert Bushnell Hart, March 20, 1920, Howard W. Odum Papers.

10. Wilson, *University of North Carolina*, 220–21, 464; Samuel H. Hobbs, Jr., "Developing a State Through Student Club Work," 48–49; Eugene C. Branson, "Wealth, Welfare, and Willingness," unpublished address, n.d. [1917], Eugene Cunningham Branson Papers; Dewey W. Grantham, *The Regional Imagination*, 155; Howard W. Odum to H. L. Mencken, September 24, 1926, Odum Papers. Branson's two most important articles by far are "Farm Tenancy in the Cotton Belt" and "Farm Tenancy in the South." See also his *Farm Life Abroad*, one of the best-selling books the University of North Carolina Press published in the 1920s.

11. Brazil, "Odum," 349–50, 354–60; Vance, "Odum," 1; Gerald W. Johnson, "Mr.

Babbitt Arrives at Erzerum," 207; Harry W. Chase, quoted in Wilson, *University of North Carolina*, 447.

12. Howard W. Odum to Harry W. Chase, March 17, 1920, May 3, 1920, and May 17, 1920, Odum to Francis Sage Bradley, November 9, 1920, Odum Papers; Brazil, "Odum," 348–53; Wilson, *University of North Carolina*, 449. See also Thomas J. Woofter, Jr., "The Teaching of Sociology in the South," 71.

13. Wilson, *University of North Carolina*, 462–67.

14. Howard W. Odum, Memorandum for the Board of Governors, Institute for Research in Social Science, April 13, 1927, University Papers. A bibliography of the Institute's publications and unpublished manuscripts through 1944 appears in *Social Forces* 23, no. 3 (March 1945): 305–28; a slightly more complete, annotated version is available at the Institute's office in Chapel Hill. The work of Odum's disciples will be discussed in greater detail in chap. 10.

15. Howard W. Odum, "Editorial Notes," 56–61; Odum to William F. Ogburn, May 1, 1922, Odum to Gerald W. Johnson, February 15, 1923, Odum Papers; Brazil, "Odum," 386–87, 389–93.

16. Brazil, "Odum," 390–94; Howard W. Odum, "The Search After Values," 639; Gerald W. Johnson to Odum, February 28, 1923, Odum Papers.

17. Howard W. Odum to Ora L. Hatcher, October 18, 1924, Odum Papers; Odum, "G. Stanley Hall," 145; Odum, "Democracy and the KKK," 179; Odum, "A Southern Promise," in Howard W. Odum, ed., *Southern Pioneers in Social Interpretation*, 17, 10, 21; Odum, "A More Articulate South," 732; George W. Cable, *The Silent South*. "A Southern Promise" also appeared as an editorial in *Social Forces* 3, no. 4 (May 1925): 739–46.

18. Howard W. Odum, "Industrial Democracy," 317–19; Odum, "Editorial Notes," 60–61; Odum, "Democracy and the KKK," 180.

19. Odum, "A Southern Promise," 15–16.

20. Ibid., 18, 8; Odum, "A More Articulate South," 732, 734; Odum, "G. Stanley Hall," 146.

21. Howard W. Odum to Gerald W. Johnson, November 28, 1922, February 15, 1923, and November 23, 1923; Odum to Harry W. Chase, January 7, 1924, December 19, 1924, Odum to H. L. Mencken, October 25, 1924, Odum Papers. Regarding David Clark's diatribes, Odum wrote Chase: "Personally I am glad to have this kind of an editorial. The more extreme they are the less harm, and the sooner we can get into common discussions of these common interests by all the groups the better it will be for us."

22. Harry Elmer Barnes, "Sociology and Ethics," 212–31; Luther L. Bernard, "The Development of the Concept of Progress," 207–212; Brazil, "Odum," 430–32.

23. Brazil, "Odum," 415–16, 419, 429–30; Willard B. Gatewood, Jr., *Preachers, Pedagogues, and Politicians*, 114–18; J. O. Guthrie to the editor, Raleigh *Times*, March 4, 1925; Gerald W. Johnson, "Chase of North Carolina," 187.

24. Howard W. Odum to Harry E. Barnes, February 4, 1924, Odum Papers; Brazil, "Odum," 420–24.

25. Brazil, "Odum" 436–43; Howard W. Odum to Rev. W. C. Barrett, March 5, 1925, Odum to Governor Angus W. McLean, March 10, 1925, Odum to the editor, February 20, 1925, Odum to Rev. D. V. Howell, February 23, 1925, Odum Papers; Gatewood, *Preachers*, 188–19.

26. Howard W. Odum to Rev. W. C. Barrett, March 5, 1925, Odum to Rev. M. T. Plyler, February 12, 1925, Odum to Josephus Daniels, February 12, 1925, Odum to the editor, February 20, 1925, Odum to Luther L. Bernard, March 7, 1925, Odum to Frank H. Hankins, March 23, 1925, Odum Papers.

27. Howard W. Odum to Luther L. Bernard, March 7, 1925, Odum Papers.

28. George S. Mitchell to his mother, n.d. [July 12, 1931], SCM Papers, Series A; Oral History Memoir of Arthur F. Raper; 42–43; Edwin Mims, *The Advancing South*, 123. Richard H. King also attributes Odum's dense prose to his desire for obfuscation; see *A Southern Renaissance*, 154.

29. Howard W. Odum to Gerald W. Johnson, November 4, 1929, Odum Papers.

30. Howard W. Odum to Herschel Brickell, May 1, 1930, Odum Papers.

31. Ibid., August 4, 1930, ibid.

32. Howard W. Odum to Gerald W. Johnson, December 8, 1926, June 18, 1929, Odum to Beardsley Ruml, March 27, 1928, Odum to Edmund E. Day, May 23, 1930, Odum Papers; Odum, "Notes on the Study of Regional and Folk Society," 170.

33. Brazil, "Odum," 241–44, 265–69; Dorothy Ross, "The Development of the Social Sciences," in Alexandra Oleson and John Voss, eds., *The Organization of Knowledge in Modern America, 1860–1920*, 114–15; Richard Hofstadter, *Social Darwinism in American Thought*, 36–42; Howard W. Odum, *An American Epoch*, 314; Odum to Gerald W. Johnson, November 4, 1929, Odum Papers.

34. Odum, *American Epoch*, x.

35. Jerome S. Bruner, "Art as a Mode of Knowing," in his *On Knowing*, 62–63; Odum, *American Epoch*, 283, 103; Brazil, "Odum," 267. Shrewd Odum-watchers like John Donald Wade and Gerald W. Johnson spotted this artistic bent from the start. By disguising himself as a sociologist, Johnson wrote in 1930, Odum had "almost entirely escaped detection as the artist he really is." Similarly, Wade discerned "a sensitiveness to beauty" in Odum "that was too keen for him to keep quiet about." Gerald W. Johnson, "The South Faces Itself," 153; John Donald Wade, review of *An American Epoch*.

36. Odum, *American Epoch*, 330–31. Interestingly, Barry D. Karl comes to a strikingly similar evaluation of the final report of the President's Research Committee on Social Trends, of which Odum was assistant research director: "As an attempt at a photograph of a moment in time, it succeeded to a remarkable degree in the literate, often sensitive conveying of detail about problems which past generations had sought to resolve and future generations would face" ("Presidential Planning and Social Science Research," 404).

37. George W. Stocking, Jr., *Race, Culture, and Evolution*, 73–74, 83, 105, 210; Josiah Morse to Samuel Chiles Mitchell, February 2, 1924, SCM Papers, Series A.

38. Stocking, *Race*, 159, 225–27.

39. Richard H. Pells, *Radical Visions and American Dreams*, 113.

40. Howard W. Odum, *Southern Regions of the United States*, 507; Odum to Gerald W. Johnson, October 25, 1927, Odum Papers; Odum, *American Epoch*, 313. On his early exposure to the ideas of Boas, see Brazil, "Odum," 211–12, 216–22.

41. Odum, *American Epoch*, 34–38. A nearly identical passage appears in *Southern Regions*, 23.

42. Odum, *American Epoch*, 45–52; Odum to H. L. Mencken, September 10, 1923, Odum Papers. In a letter to W. J. Cash, written at the same time as *An American Epoch*, Odum expressed similar views on the Old South, observing that "many . . . who were reputed to have a plantation and leisure still ate dinner in their shirtsleeves and washed on the back porch and let the chickens roost in the top of the trees in the yard. Or did they?" Cash was apparently struck by this imagery, for a decade later he put it to good use in *The Mind of the South*, esp. 14–16. Odum to W. J. Cash, November 20, 1929, Odum Papers.

43. Odum, *American Epoch*, 342.

44. Ibid., 3, 60–61, 220; Brazil, "Odum," 253–57; Odum, *Southern Regions*, 229, 531.

45. Odum, *American Epoch*, 19; Odum, *Southern Regions*, 227; Odum, "Modern Equivalents for Early Rural Pioneering Forces," 112–14. For his treatment of white southern folk music, see *American Epoch*, chaps. 13 and 14.

46. Odum, *American Epoch*, 70, 132–33, 321; Odum to Benjamin B. Kendrick, March 1, 1930, Odum Papers.

47. Brazil, "Odum," 120–24, 126, 158–59. For Bailey's views see his *Race Orthodoxy in the South, and Other Aspects of the Negro Question*; on scientific racism, the best study is Idus A. Newby, *Jim Crow's Defense*, 19–51.

48. Howard W. Odum, *Social and Mental Traits of the Negro*, 283, 13–14, 19.

49. Ibid., 150, 39, 166–67.

50. Ibid., 296, 260–61, 242–43, 270, 245, 286–89; Stocking, *Race, Culture, and Evolution*, 117.

51. Brazil, "Odum," 231–32, 489–90, 500–503; Stocking, *Race, Culture, and Evolution*, 177–78, 191; Odum to E. M. Taylor, October 3, 1925, Odum Papers.

52. Howard W. Odum and Guy B. Johnson, *The Negro and His Songs*, xvii–xviii, 12, 159; Odum and Johnson, *Negro Workaday Songs*, 34, 22; Johnson, Oral History Memoir, 61–62. Odum and Johnson did omit several songs because of their "vulgar and indecent character," a practice some reviewers objected to. See the notice by Arthur Kyle Davis, Jr., in *Virginia Quarterly Review* 2, no. 2 (April 1926): 296.

53. Howard W. Odum to D. L. Chambers, May 14, 1930, Odum to H. L. Mencken, June 19, 1925, D. L. Chambers to Odum, October 26, 1931 (gives sales figures for trilogy), Odum Papers; Odum and Johnson, *Negro Workaday Songs*, 208; Oral History Memoir of Rupert B. Vance, 65.

54. Howard W. Odum to D. L. Chambers, January 6, 1927, Odum to Gerald W. Johnson, January 4, 1928, Odum Papers; Nathan I. Huggins, *Harlem Renaissance*, 103, 95.

55. Howard W. Odum to D. L. Chambers, October 19, 1927, Odum Papers; Odum, *Rainbow Round My Shoulder*, 316, 67, 98–100, 83, 93, 5; Odum, *Social and Mental Traits*, 260.

56. Odum, *Rainbow*, 254, 153; Odum to D. L. Chambers, December 5, 1927, Odum Papers.

57. Howard W. Odum, *Cold Blue Moon*, 271, 158, 48–49.

58. Ibid., 211, 51, 197, 234; Howard W. Odum to Beardsley Ruml, March 27, 1928, Odum Papers. For a fuller and most excellent discussion of *Cold Blue Moon*, see Brazil, "Odum," 579–83. Although vitiated by several lapses of sentimentality, the book still deserves to be ranked among Odum's best.

59. Odum, *American Epoch*, 266–67; Odum, *Southern Regions*, 479–83. I am indebted to Professor Joel Williamson of The University of North Carolina at Chapel Hill for suggesting the term "ultimate integrationist."

60. Howard W. Odum to V. E. Daniel, April 7, 1936, Odum Papers.

61. Howard Odum to Herschel Brickell, May 1, 1930, Odum Papers; Odum, *American Epoch*, 23–26, 314.

62. Stocking, *Race, Culture, and Evolution*, 253–57, 265.

63. Odum, *American Epoch*, 25, 327; Odum, *Southern Regions*, 505–7; Stocking, *Race, Culture, and Evolution*, 247.

64. Odum, *Southern Regions*, 191, 253–59; Odum, *American Epoch*, 333; Odum, "Regionalism vs. Sectionalism in the South's Place in the National Economy," 338–39; Odum to Sydnor H. Walker, October 27, 1930, Odum Papers.

65. Odum, *Southern Regions*, 255, 580, 1, 331; Odum, "The Case for Regional-National Social Planning," 6-11; Odum to Arthur Kellogg, February 16, 1934, Odum Papers. On the vogue of planning in the 1930s and the diverse motives behind it, see Pells, *Radical Visions*, 69–75.

66. Donald Davidson to John Donald Wade, March 3, 1934.

67. Howard W. Odum to Sydnor H. Walker, June 17, 1933, Odum to Charles S.

Johnson, September 21, 1938, November 16, 1938, Odum to Herman C. Nixon, November 16, 1938, Odum to A. R. Mann, October 24, 1938, Odum Papers; Donald Davidson, "Social Science Discovers Regionalism," in his *The Attack on Leviathan*, 39–64.

For a view that takes Odum's dispute with the supposed "sectionalists" more seriously, see Michael O'Brien, *The Idea of the American South, 1920–1941*, 55–59. O'Brien in general portrays Odum as "the southern intellectual become organization man," as an expert at milking northern foundations whose decision to start studying the South intensively in 1927 came as the result of a "new mandate" from the General Education Board. Surely this is an inaccurate view of Odum. At the outset, it was true, Odum's institute represented the only southern social science research center that the Rockefeller Foundation and Social Science Research Council could support with any enthusiasm. By the mid-1930s, when other southern universities began to compete seriously for such grants, Odum retained his fair share only with great difficulty. The archival evidence suggests that, although foundation officers were often personally fond of Odum, they regarded his constant flow of memoranda and correspondence as something of an embarrassing nuisance; certainly they were not taken in by his transparent techniques. Hence it was more the peculiarities of the situation, and not, as O'Brien suggests, Odum's magic touch, that was responsible for the initial flow of money from New York in the 1920s and early 1930s.

As for the claim that Odum turned to research on the South only at the foundation's behest in 1927, anyone reading his editorials on the South in *Social Forces* in the early 1920s or his *Southern Pioneers in Social Interpretation* of 1925 could hardly agree that his interest in the region was contrived or sudden in 1927. O'Brien also errs in suggesting that Odum regarded the failure of his School of Public Welfare to renew its sustaining grant that year as a personal debacle. On the contrary, Odum by that time had come to see the school as an incubus diverting him from the research projects he cared most about, which is why he failed to give it sufficient attention. The incident, moreover, is a good indication of Odum's basic ineptitude in the art of grantsmanship. See O'Brien, *The Idea of the South*, 32, 45–47.

68. Howard W. Odum to H. L. Mencken, January 11, 1934, Odum to Harry E. Barnes and Frank H. Hankins, October 5, 1925, Odum to Gerald W. Johnson, July 18, 1931, Odum Papers. Odum, *Southern Regions*, 211–13, 587, 235; Odum, "Regionalism vs. Sectionalism," 341.

69. Will W. Alexander to Howard W. Odum, March 1, 1927, Odum to Alexander, March 4, 1927, September 14, 1933, and October 2, 1937, Miles Mark Fisher to Odum, January 24, 1933, Odum to Frank P. Graham, February 21, 1934, April 27, 1936, Odum to A. R. Mann, May 27, 1939, Odum to Jesse F. Steiner, October 29, 1941, Odum Papers; Odum, Address to the Commission on Interracial Cooperation, October 3, 1940, copy in Odum Papers.

70. Howard W. Odum to French Strother, March 13, 1930, Odum Papers; Tindall, "The Significance of Odum," 306; Grantham, *Regional Imagination*, 179–80.

CHAPTER 6

1. Howard W. Odum, "On Southern Literature and Southern Culture," in Rubin and Jacobs, *Southern Renascence*, 97.

2. Paula Snelling, "Southern Fiction and Chronic Suicide," 27.

3. David L. Cohn, *God Shakes Creation*, 15.

4. Jean Stein, "William Faulkner: An Interview," in Frederick J. Hoffman and Olga W. Vickery, eds., *William Faulkner*, 68; Faulkner quoted in Malcolm Cowley, *The Faulkner-Cowley File*, 114.

5. Conrad Aiken, "William Faulkner: The Novel as Form," in Robert Penn Warren, ed., *Faulkner*, 48; Walter J. Slatoff, *Quest for Failure*, 79, 83, 86.

6. C. Hugh Holman, *Three Modes of Southern Fiction*, 45; F. Garvin Davenport, Jr., *The Myth of Southern History*, 121; Aiken, "William Faulkner," in Warren, *Faulkner*, 48.

7. Robert Penn Warren, "Faulkner: Past and Present," in his *Faulkner*, 14–15.

8. Joseph L. Blotner, *Faulkner*, 1:759; William Faulkner to Horace Liveright, January 11, 1927, in William Faulkner, *Selected Letters of William Faulkner*, 34; Davenport, *Myth of Southern History*, 83–84. Faulkner in fact possessed an enormous library; see Joseph L. Blotner, ed., *William Faulkner's Library–a Catalogue*.

9. Blotner, *Faulkner*, 1:92, 101, 110, 146, 161–64, 203, 208, 299, 352; Michael Millgate, *The Achievement of William Faulkner*, 288–91; Faulkner, "An Introduction for *The Sound and the Fury*," 708–9.

10. Charles Chadwick, *Symbolism*, 2–4, 13, 22; Edmund Wilson, *Axel's Castle*, 13, 20–22; H. Edward Richardson, *William Faulkner*, 47–115; Blotner, *Faulkner*, 1:184–86, 264–65; Faulkner, "Verse Old and Nascent: A Pilgrimage," in his *Early Prose and Poetry*, 117. In respect to the motif of pastoral innocence sustained in his early poetry, it is significant that Faulkner was especially drawn to Paul Verlaine, the Symbolist who, as James R. Lawler points out, spoke always with a voice of "conscious naiveté." Lawler, *The Language of French Symbolism*, 67, 70.

11. William Faulkner, "Books & Things," in Faulkner, *Early Prose*, 84; Millgate, *Achievement of Faulkner*, 290, 66.

12. William Faulkner, *Soldier's Pay*, 23, 131–35, 137, 144; Frederick J. Hoffman, *The Twenties*, 88–90, 93.

13. William Faulkner, *Mosquitoes*, 153, 55, 45; Blotner, *Faulkner*, 1:418, 514–16; Hoffman, *The Twenties*, 236–37.

14. Blotner, *Faulkner*, 1:320, 428, 500; Faulkner, *Mosquitoes*, 154, 39–40.

15. Faulkner, "Verse Old and Nascent," in Faulkner, *Early Prose*, 116. The full meaning of the quotation becomes clearer if one substitutes "competition" for "contact" in the second sentence.

16. William Faulkner, autobiographical fragment, n.d. [1930 or 1931], William Faulkner Papers, Yale University, also available in Joseph L. Blotner, ed., "William Faulkner's Essay on the Composition of *Sartoris*," 124.

17. The sad story of how almost one-fourth of *Flags in the Dust* was cut over Faulkner's strenuous objections is told by Blotner in *Faulkner*, 1:580–84, and by Douglas Day in his introduction to the first uncut publication of the novel (1973). As all writers on Faulkner must do hereafter, I have relied on the novel as Faulkner actually wrote it. There is one problem, however—*Flags in the Dust* as we now have it is based on Faulkner's composite typescript as deposited at the University of Virginia Library, a typescript that seems to represent the next-to-final draft (the final draft was presumably used for the cutting). To help correct for this situation, I have felt free to use those passages in *Sartoris* not found in *Flags* on the assumption that they must either have appeared in the final draft or have been added by Faulkner at the galley-proof stage.

18. Irving Howe, *William Faulkner*, 34.

19. Faulkner, *Flags in the Dust*, 76, 126, 282, 291, 351–53.

20. Ibid., 331, 94, 432, 72.

21. Ibid., 14–15, 240, 279; Faulkner, *Sartoris*, 170.

22. Sigmund Freud, "On Narcissism: An Introduction," in his *General Psychological Theory*, 57; Otto Fenichel, *The Psychoanalytic Theory of Neurosis*, 40; Faulkner, *Flags*, 126, 351, 76.

23. Jack Falkner, quoted in Blotner, *Faulkner*, 1:105; ibid., 1:15–16, 21–22, 24, 27,

35–36, 42–44, 46–47, 50. The description of the monument appears in *Flags in the Dust*, 427–28. On the tendency of Faulkner and other southern writers of his generation to venerate their grandfathers and great-grandfathers and to associate them with the Cavalier mythology, see Richard H. King, *A Southern Renaissance*, 34–35, 77–85, 91–98.

24. Blotner, *Faulkner*, 1:9–10, 14–17, 31–32, 38–39, 24 (notes section).

25. Faulkner, *Sartoris*, 20; Faulkner, *Flags in the Dust*, 6, 263–64.

26. Faulkner, *Flags in the Dust*, 72–73, 76, 407–8; Blotner, *Faulkner*, 1:690–91.

27. Faulkner, *Flags in the Dust*, 177–79, 191–92, 31, 185–86, 158.

28. Ibid., 176, 79, 278, 77, 334, 370, 431.

29. Faulkner, *Flags in the Dust*, 170, 186, 190–91; Millgate, *Achievement of Faulkner*, 84; Cleanth Brooks, *William Faulkner*, 105–6.

30. Freud, "On Narcissism," in Freud, *Psychological Theory*, 70–71; Faulkner, *Flags in the Dust*, 341.

31. Faulkner, *Flags in the Dust*, 196, 223, 208, 191, 187, 202–3, 337–38; Joseph Conrad, *Lord Jim*, 214.

32. Carvel Collins, "A Note on *Sanctuary*," condensed in Warren, *Faulkner*, 290–91; Blotner, *Faulkner*, 1:492–93; Faulkner, *Sanctuary*, 52; Hyatt H. Waggoner, *William Faulkner*, 100.

33. Cleanth Brooks, *The Hidden God*, 25; Blotner, *Faulkner*, 1:674–75; Richard P. Adams, *Faulkner*, 66–67.

34. Faulkner, *Sanctuary*, 67, 71–74, 102, 149, 159–60; Panthea Reid Broughton, *William Faulkner*, 146. Millgate, in *Achievement of Faulkner*, 119, finds additional meaning in these names. The novel's "total inversion of official values," he writes, is "ironically underlined by the fact that *Lee* Goodwin and Ruby *Lamar*, those victims of southern society, bear two such honoured Southern names"—those of Robert E. Lee and Lucius Quintus Cincinnatus Lamar.

35. Faulkner, *Sanctuary*, 11–13, 68, 72. Several critics have followed the notion first put forth by Dr. Lawrence S. Kubie, a psychoanalyst writing on the novel in 1934, who claims that Horace harbors incestuous feelings toward Little Belle and that the crisis he experiences stems from his efforts to evade these "unacceptable" sexual desires within himself. But the evidence on which Kubie bases this theory is slim indeed, and, besides, the whole issue is really gratuitous to the central meaning of the book—Horace's loss of his ability to separate good and evil into watertight categories. If it does have any substance, the incest theme is at best an added dimension to Horace's already-tragic plight. See Kubie, "William Faulkner's *Sanctuary*," in Warren, *Faulkner*, 143, and Brooks's intelligent discussion of this point in *William Faulkner*, 129.

36. Faulkner, *Sanctuary*, 91, 94–95, 122, 126; Brooks, *William Faulkner*, 129.

37. Olga W. Vickery, "Crime and Punishment: *Sanctuary*," in Warren, *Faulkner*, 135; Faulkner, *Sanctuary*, 160, 162–63, 125.

38. Faulkner, *Flags in the Dust*, 431.

39. William Faulkner, *The Sound and the Fury*, 6; Henry Nash Smith, "Three Southern Novels," iv; William Faulkner, *Faulkner in the University*, 61; Blotner, *Faulkner*, 1:578–79; Faulkner, "An Introduction for *The Sound and the Fury*," 710; Waggoner, *William Faulkner*, 60.

40. Faulkner, "An Introduction for *The Sound and the Fury*," 710; Faulkner, "An Introduction to *The Sound and the Fury*," in *A Faulkner Miscellany*, 159–60 [Note: this is an alternate draft of the unpublished 1933 introduction]; Faulkner, *Sound and Fury*, 93; Jean Stein, "Faulkner: An Interview," in Hoffman and Vickery, *William Faulkner*, 73–74. For a somewhat different account of the composition of *The Sound and the Fury*, see Millgate, *Achievement of Faulkner*, 89–90, which is based on certain offhand remarks Faulkner

made during a visit to Japan in 1955. The 1933 documentary evidence, which Faulkner corroborated in countless subsequent interviews (as Millgate acknowledges) would seem more reliable.

41. Erik H. Erikson, *Identity and the Life Cycle*, 23, 53, 112, 26, 126–27.

42. Faulkner, *Sound and Fury*, 95, 99, 102–4.

43. Amos N. Wilder, "Vestigial Moralities in *The Sound and the Fury*," in J. Robert Barth, ed., *Religious Perspectives in Faulkner's Fiction*, 93, 97; John W. Hunt, *William Faulkner*, 50, 54; Brooks, *William Faulkner*, 335–36; Faulkner, *Sound and Fury*, 123, 95, 247, 276.

44. On isolation as an ego defense mechanism, see especially Anna Freud, *The Ego and the Mechanisms of Defense*, 37–38, and Fenichel, *Psychoanalytic Theory*, 155–60; Faulkner, *Sound and Fury*, 188.

45. Faulkner, *Sound and Fury*, 134, 131, 168, 44, 81, 191.

46. Ibid., 176.

47. Ibid., 167, 38–39, 135, 167; Millgate, *Achievement of Faulkner*, 96; Lawrance Thompson, "Mirror Analogues in *The Sound and the Fury*," in Warren, *Faulkner*, 118.

48. Faulkner, *Sound and Fury*, 135, 166, 197.

49. Faulkner, *Faulkner in the University*, 17; Erikson, *Identity and Life Cycle*, 96; Faulkner, *Sound and Fury*, 17.

50. Faulkner, *Sound and Fury*, 16, 271–72, 212; Millgate, *Achievement of Faulkner*, 101; Brooks, *William Faulkner*, 337; Erikson, *Identity and Life Cycle*, 69–70.

51. Faulkner, *Sound and Fury*, 253, 258, 224, 124; Erik H. Erikson, *Identity*, 107–8.

52. Faulkner, *Sound and Fury*, 319, 329.

53. Ibid., 290, 24, 30, 188–89.

54. Millgate, *Achievement of Faulkner*, 86; Evelyn Scott to Harrison Smith, May 10, 1929, William Faulkner Papers, University of Virginia; Stein, "Faulkner: An Interview," in Hoffman and Vickery, *William Faulkner*, 74; Thompson, "Mirror Analogues," in Warren, *Faulkner*, 112–13; Waggoner, *William Faulkner*, 44.

55. Faulkner, *Sound and Fury*, 335.

56. Waggoner, *William Faulkner*, 30; Faulkner, *Soldier's Pay*, 221.

57. Wilbur J. Cash, *The Mind of the South*, 321, 370; George B. Tindall, *The Emergence of the New South, 1913–1945*, 412; William Faulkner, *Light in August*, 191.

58. Blotner, *Faulkner*, 1:701, 765; Sterling A. Brown, "Negro Character as Seen by White Authors," 194–96; Brooks, *William Faulkner*, 49–50; Robert Penn Warren, "Faulkner: The South, the Negro, and Time," in his *Faulkner*, 259; Waggoner, *William Faulkner*, 101, 103.

59. Erik H. Erikson, *Childhood and Society*, 241–43; Erikson, *Identity*, 304; Robert D. Jacobs, "William Faulkner: The Passion and the Penance," in Rubin and Jacobs, *South*, 159–60.

60. Faulkner, *Light in August*, 328–29, 105–7.

61. Ibid., 128–30, 135–36, 139–40.

62. Ibid., 161–65, 137–38, 150, 178, 180.

63. Ibid., 195–97.

64. Ibid., 208, 205; Millgate, *Achievement of Faulkner*, 126.

65. Faulkner, *Light in August*, 241–44, 247; Fenichel, *Psychoanalytic Theory*, 78.

66. Faulkner, *Light in August*, 251, 255, 294, 306, 302.

67. Waggoner, *William Faulkner*, 106, 101; Alfred Kazin, "The Stillness of *Light in August*," in Warren, *Faulkner*, 151; Faulkner, *Light in August*, 322.

68. Faulkner, *Light in August*, 393, 407; Faulkner, *Faulkner in the University*, 72; Brooks, *William Faulkner*, 49.

69. Millgate, *Achievement of Faulkner*, 155; Hunt, *William Faulkner*, 106.

70. Blotner, *Faulkner*, 1:491, 696–98, 828–29; Faulkner, "Evangeline," in Faulkner, *The Uncollected Stories of William Faulkner*, 584.

71. Brooks, *William Faulkner*, 298; William Faulkner, *Absalom, Absalom!*, 11, 188, 8, 43, 16, 20; Davenport, *Myth of Southern History*, 99. One gets an idea of how highly charged Faulkner's demolition of the Cavalier myth still was for southerners in the late 1930s by reading George Marion O'Donnell's famous essay on Faulkner—one of the first important extended pieces of Faulkner criticism—which appeared in 1939. Incredibly, O'Donnell lumps Sutpen together with the Sartorises as exemplars of the old aristocratic tradition; he seems totally oblivious to Sutpen as a frontier entrepreneur. See his "Faulkner's Mythology," in Warren, *Faulkner*, 26–27.

72. Faulkner, *Absalom*, 221–22, 226; Brooks, *William Faulkner*, 297, 426; Adams, *Faulkner*, 188.

73. Faulkner, *Absalom*, 234–35; Helen Merrell Lynd, *On Shame and the Search for Identity*, 27, 34, 49–50.

74. Faulkner, *Absalom*, 242; Faulkner quoted in Blotner, *Faulkner*, 1:493.

75. Ilse D. Lind, "The Design and Meaning of *Absalom, Absalom!*," in Hoffman and Vickery, *William Faulkner*, 279; Faulkner, *Absalom*, 347–48.

76. Faulkner, *Absalom*, 119–20, 67.

77. Ibid., 120, 43, 96, 109.

78. Ibid., 250, 74, 104, 96.

79. Ibid., 95–99, 108, 323–24, 79.

80. Ibid., 89. Andrew Nelson Lytle, another prominent southern novelist of Faulkner's generation, was also drawn to the metaphor of incest in portraying the South. "For many years," he writes, "it has seemed to me that incest was a constant upon the Southern scene." By this, he explains, he means not only actual incest (which he suspects was more widespread in the South than elsewhere), but especially "the incest of the spirit," which "inhered within the family itself" and was manifest in "an intimacy and constancy of association in work and play which induced excessive jealousy against intrusion from the outside." Though not precisely the same, this is fairly close to Faulkner's use of the metaphor. See Lytle, "The Working Novelist and the Mythmaking Process," in Murray, *Myth and Mythmaking*, 147.

81. Cash, *The Mind*, 113. For a similar interpretation of Faulkner's use of incest, see Irwin, *Doubling and Incest*, 59.

82. Faulkner, *Absalom*, 72–73, 21; Faulkner, *Flags in the Dust*, 432; J. Robert Barth, "Faulkner and the Calvinist Tradition," in his *Religious Perspectives*, 16, 25.

83. Jacobs, "Faulkner: The Passion and Penance," in Rubin and Jacobs, *South*, 188; Lind, "The Design and Meaning," in Hoffman and Vickery, *William Faulkner*, 295.

84. Jean Pouillon, "Time and Destiny in Faulkner," in Warren, *Faulkner*, 80–84; Broughton, *Faulkner*, 116; Davenport, *Myth of Southern History*, 118.

85. Blotner, *Faulkner*, 1:845–47, 901, 2:951, 965; Faulkner to Morton Goldman, n.d. [August, 1934], in Faulkner, *Selected Letters*, 84; Millgate, *Achievement of Faulkner*, 165.

86. William Faulkner, *The Unvanquished*, 170–71, 175; Myra Jehlen, *Class and Character in Faulkner's South*, 47–49, 51, 54. For a defense of the novel, see Brooks, *William Faulkner*, 77, 84; Waggoner, *William Faulkner*, 171, 180; and James B. Meriwether, "Faulkner and the South," in Simonini, *Southern Writers*, 156. For the opposite conclusion and a discussion of the controversy, see Millgate, *Achievement of Faulkner*, 167–70.

87. Faulkner, *Unvanquished*, 188, 175. This is the same Bayard Sartoris, it should be noted, who appears as "Old Bayard" in *Flags in the Dust*.

88. William Faulkner, *Intruder in the Dust*, 71; Warren, "Faulkner," in Warren, *Faulk-*

ner, 17; Richard W. B. Lewis, "William Faulkner: The Hero in the New World," in Warren, *Faulkner*, 209; Jehlen, *Class and Character*, 55–56.

89. Faulkner, *Absalom*, 80.

CHAPTER 7

1. Twelve Southerners, *I'll Take My Stand*, xix.

2. Louis D. Rubin, Jr., "Southern Literature: The Historical Image," in Rubin and Jacobs, *South*, 39; "Foreword," *Fugitive* 1, no. 1 (April 1922): 2; Harriet Monroe, "The Old South," 91; "Merely Prose," *Fugitive*, 2, no. 7 (June–July 1923): 66; Allen Tate, quoted in Louis D. Rubin, Jr., *The Curious Death of the Novel*, 213.

3. Louise Cowan, *The Fugitive Group*, 42, 45, 169; Alec B. Stevenson to Allen Tate, August 27, 1933, Allen Tate Papers; Donald Davidson, *Southern Writers in the Modern World*, 18–23.

4. Allen Tate, *Memoirs and Opinions, 1926–1974*, 29, 25; Davidson, *Southern Writers*, 12–13; Cowan, *Fugitive Group*, 17–18; John L. Stewart, *The Burden of Time*, 54–66.

5. Donald Davidson to Allen Tate, March 29, 1926, March 21, 1927, Tate to Davidson, January 5, 1927, March 17, 1927, April 28, 1927, all in John Tyree Fain and Thomas Daniel Young, eds., *The Literary Correspondence of Donald Davidson and Allen Tate*, 162, 183, 195–96, 198; Tate to Davidson, May 31, 1927, Donald Davidson Papers; John Crowe Ransom to Tate, April 3 and 13 [dated "1926" by Tate but should be 1927], Tate Papers; Donald Davidson, "Stonewall Jackson's Way," in his *The Spyglass: Views and Reviews, 1924–1930*, 201.

Great confusion exists as to the year the symposium was first brought up, primarily as a result of an error Davidson made in dating his March 21, 1927, letter to Tate (cited above). For some unknown reason (most likely haste—Davidson closes the letter "Yours as ever hurrahing"), Davidson wrote "1926" instead of "1927." That the latter year is unmistakably correct can be determined by three things: (1) in the letter Davidson mentions his forthcoming review of Hart Crane's *White Buildings*, a book published in 1927 and reviewed by Davidson in the Nashville *Tennessean* on April 3, 1927; (2) Davidson speaks of revising the manuscript of "The Tall Men," a poem not completed until late 1926; (3) Davidson's letter is patently a response to Tate's of March 17, 1927, in which Tate first suggests a southern symposium.

Davidson's misdated letter apparently led Tate to observe in his personal account of the movement that the first discussion of *I'll Take My Stand* commenced in 1926 and to misdate Ransom's key letter of "April 3 and 13" (cited above) as 1926. See Tate, *Memoirs*, 34. These errors in turn have thrown a long list of writers on the Agrarians off the track; see, for example, Thomas D. Young, *Gentleman in a Dustcoat*, 490n. Most important, the dating errors have led historians of the movement to connect its origins with the Scopes trial of 1925, when in fact two years passed between the trial and the initial plans for the symposium.

6. Donald Davidson, "The Artist as Southerner," 781–83; Davidson to Tate, May 21, 1925, March 29, 1926, in Fain and Young, *Literary Correspondence*, 139, 163. On the tie between the Scopes trial and Agrarianism, see Stewart, *Burden of Time*, 114–19; Virginia Rock, "The Making and Meaning of *I'll Take My Stand*," 206–10; Richard Gray, *The Literature of Memory*, 41.

7. Davidson, "The Artist," 782–83; Davidson to Tate, March 4, 1927, in Fain and Young, *Literary Correspondence*, 193.

8. Lewis P. Simpson, *The Man of Letters in New England and the South*, 248.

9. Cowan, *Fugitive Group*, 71.

10. John Crowe Ransom, *God Without Thunder*, ix; Young, *Gentleman in a Dustcoat*, 7, 13, 60; Tate, *Memoirs*, 40, 43.

11. Young, *Gentleman in a Dustcoat*, 50–51, 96–99, 104–5; John Crowe Ransom, "Mixed Modes," 28–29.

12. Rock, "Making and Meaning," 177n; Oral History Memoir of Robert Penn Warren, 144; Young, *Gentleman in a Dustcoat*, 60; Tate to Davidson, January 16, 1923, Davidson Papers; Tate, *Memoir*, 42.

13. John Crowe Ransom, *Poems About God*, vi–vii, 4–5; Vivienne Koch, "The Achievement of John Crowe Ransom," in Thomas D. Young, ed., *John Crowe Ransom*, 116; Louis D. Rubin, Jr., *The Wary Fugitives*, 17–18, 20.

14. John Crowe Ransom, "Bells for John Whiteside's Daughter," "Dead Boy," "Captain Carpenter," "Old Mansion," and "Necrological," in his *Poems and Essays*, 10, 5, 33–37, 8–9; Isabel G. MacCaffrey, "Ceremonies of Bravery: John Crowe Ransom," in Rubin and Jacobs, *South*, 214–15.

15. John Crowe Ransom to Allen Tate, n.d. [Spring, 1926?], Tate Papers; "Necrological," in Ransom, *Poems and Essays*, 8–9; Cowan, *Fugitive Group*, 60; Ransom, preface to *Chills and Fever*, quoted in Robert Penn Warren, "John Crowe Ransom," 105.

16. Young, *Gentleman in a Dustcoat*, 50–57, 104–5; Ransom to Tate, December 17, 1923, April 3 and 13 [1927], Tate Papers; Ransom, "A Doctrine of Relativity," 93.

17. Ransom to Tate, April 3 and 13 [1927], Tate Papers; Ransom, "The Future of Poetry," 3; John Edward Hardy, "Poets and Critics," in Rubin and Jacobs, *South*, 267; Young, *Gentleman in a Dustcoat*, 135–36.

18. Ransom's most important critical pieces appear in *The World's Body* (1938), *The New Criticism* (1941), and *Poems and Essays* (1955).

19. Ransom to Tate, n.d. [February, 1923?], December 17, 1923, April 15, [1924], May 6, [1924], Tate Papers; Ransom, "Editorial," 68; Ransom, "Future of Poetry," 2–3.

20. Stewart, *Burden of Time*, 260–61; William J. Handy, *Kant and the Southern New Critics* (Austin, Texas, 1963), 10–12, 28, 34–36; Ransom to Tate, September 5 [1926?], Tate Papers; Ransom, *World's Body*, x–xi.

21. Ransom to Tate, September 5, [1926?], February 20, 1927, Tate Papers.

22. Ransom to Tate, n.d. [Spring?, 1926], September 5 [1926?], Tate Papers; Ransom, "Thoughts on the Poetic Discontent," 63–64; Handy, *Kant and the New Critics*, 7–9.

23. Ransom, "The Equilibrists," in *Poems and Essays*, 66; Cowan, *Fugitive Group*, 214; Michael O'Brien, *The Idea of the American South, 1920–1941*, 120–21; Ransom to Tate, February 20, 1927, Tate Papers; Ransom to Merrill Moore, November 27, 1929 [1927?], Merrill Moore Papers; Young, *Gentleman in a Dustcoat*, 173–74. In his 1935 essay on his former teacher, Robert Penn Warren also locates the center of Ransom's work in the striving for a "harmonious adjustment, or rather unified function, of thought and feeling." Ransom's irony, Warren contends, derives from the discrepancy between this goal of an integrated consciousness and the actual dissociation of sensibility that the characters in Ransom's poems manifest. Although he notes that Ransom himself does not "necessarily" enjoy an integrated consciousness, Warren does imply that Ransom may come closer to such integration because he is at least aware of his predicament. My quarrel with Warren is a minor one of degree: I do not think Ransom clearly understood his dilemma, with the result that his irony was less sharp and penetrating than, for example, Warren's own. Perhaps Warren, a full-fledged Modernist by the mid-1930s, was reading back his own ability to integrate thought and emotion into Ransom. See Warren, "Ransom," 100–104, 110–12.

24. Ransom to Tate, February 20, 1927, n.d. [Marked "?Fall" 1927, but almost certainly

March, 1927], April 3 and 13 [1927], Tate Papers; Tate to Davidson, March 17, 1927, in Fain and Young, *Literary Correspondence*, 195; Robert Buffington, *The Equilibrist*, 93–95; Ransom to John James Ransom, November 3, 1913, quoted in Young, *Gentleman in a Dustcoat*, 77. On "Antique Harvesters," cf. Rubin, *Wary Fugitives*, 38–42.

25. Ransom to Tate, April 3 and 13 [1927], January 5, 1929, Tate Papers.

26. Ransom to Tate, April 3 and 13 [1927], Tate Papers; Ransom, "Reconstructed But Unregenerate," in Twelve Southerners, *I'll Take My Stand*, 7–16.

27. Ransom, "Reconstructed," in Twelve Southerners, *I'll Take My Stand*, 22–27; Leo Marx, *The Machine in the Garden*, 170–74.

28. Ransom, *God Without Thunder*, 3–5; Rubin, *Wary Fugitives*, 55–56; Ransom to Tate, July 4, 1929, Tate Papers.

29. Ransom, *God Without Thunder*, 95, 54, 145, 31, 177, 217; Ransom to Tate, n.d. ["?Fall", 1927], Tate Papers.

30. Ransom, *God Without Thunder*, 26–27, 11, 111–14, 65, 83–85.

31. Ibid., 66, 86, 92–93, 103; Davidson, *Southern Writers*, 11–13; Cowan, *Fugitive Group*, 17–20; Rubin, *Wary Fugitives*, 13–14.

32. Ransom, *God Without Thunder*, 140–45, 155, 157.

33. Ibid., 208–10, 83, 258–61; Ransom to James Southall Wilson, November 3, 1926, Wilson to Ransom, October 29, 1929, Editorial Correspondence, *Virginia Quarterly Review* Papers; Alexander Karanikas, *Tillers of a Myth*, 127.

34. Ransom, *God Without Thunder*, 210–14, 217, 268–69.

35. Ibid., 307, ix–x, 325–28.

36. Young, *Gentleman in a Dustcoat*, 197–200; Kenneth Burke to Allen Tate, December 2, 1930, Tate Papers; Warren Memoir, 75; O'Brien, *Idea of the South*, 126. Years later Burke retracted his harsh initial opinion of *God Without Thunder*, but one wonders how much the retraction was really a homage to Ransom. See Burke, *The Philosophy of Literary Form*, 154–55.

37. Young, *Gentleman in a Dustcoat*, 270–72.

38. Rubin, *Wary Fugitives*, 267; Ransom, "Humanists and Schoolmasters," unpublished essay enclosed with Ransom to Tate, January 25, 1930, Tate Papers, 3, 5–7.

39. Rubin, *Wary Fugitives*, 268–69; Ransom to Tate, November 23, 1932 [1931?], May 19, [1932], October 25, [1932], Tate Papers; Ransom, "Happy Farmers," 516–17, 528–31; Ransom, "Land! An Answer to the Unemployment Problem," 219–23; Ransom, "The South Is a Bulwark," 300–302.

40. Ransom, "South Is a Bulwark," 300–301; Ransom, "A Capital for the New Deal," 136–41; Tate to Davidson, December 10, 1932, in Fain and Young, *Literary Correspondence*, 279.

41. Ransom, "What Does the South Want?," in Herbert Agar and Allen Tate, eds., *Who Owns America?*, 178–93; Rubin, *Wary Fugitives*, 254, 286. Ransom formally repudiated his Agrarianism in "Art and the Human Economy," 683–88.

42. Ransom to Tate, February 20, 1927, September 17, 1936, n.d. [September, 1936], Tate Papers.

43. Ransom, "Thoughts on the Poetic Discontent," 64; Stewart, *Burden of Time*, 189.

44. Ransom to Tate, n.d. [Spring?, 1926], Tate Papers; Young, *Gentleman in a Dustcoat*, 264; Ransom, "The Concrete Universal: Observations on the Understanding of Poetry," in *Poems and Essays*, 162.

45. Thomas D. Young and M. Thomas Inge, *Donald Davidson*, 17–18; Davidson to Tate, July 29, 1929, in Fain and Young, *Literary Correspondence*, 227; Rubin, *Wary Fugitives*, 153.

46. Davidson to Tate, July 2, 1922, August 13, 1922, August 29, 1922, June 26, 1923,

June 4, 1924, in Fain and Young, *Literary Correspondence*, 10–11, 32–33, 43, 73, 118; Davidson to Tate, July 25, 1922, October 6, 1922, Tate Papers; Tate to Davidson, July 31, 1922, in Fain and Young, *Literary Correspondence*, 27; O'Brien, *Idea of the South*, 187–88; Donald Davidson, "First Fruits of Dayton, 896–907.

47. Young and Inge, *Davidson*, 42–43, 51–52; Cowan, *Fugitive Group*, 160–61; Davidson, "Naiad," in his *An Outland Piper*, 39–40; Davidson to Tate, July 25, 1922, August 13, 1922, Tate to Davidson, June 15, 1924, in Fain and Young, *Literary Correspondence*, 25, 32, 121.

48. Rubin, *Wary Fugitives*, 152; Davidson, "The Artist as Southerner," 782–83; Davidson to Tate, August 13, 1922, in Fain and Young, *Literary Correspondence*, 32–33; Davidson, "Certain Fallacies in Modern Poetry," 67; Davidson, "Two Ways of Poetry," 95.

49. Davidson, "Swan and Exile," 80.

50. Davidson, *The Tall Men*; Randall Stewart, "Donald Davidson," in Rubin and Jacobs, *South*, 252; O'Brien, *Idea of the South*, 186–87. On Davidson's pioneer ancestry, see Young and Inge, *Davidson*, 17–19.

51. Davidson, *Tall Men*, 4–5, 43; Davidson to R. N. Linscott, April 9, 1927, Davidson Papers.

52. Davidson, *Tall Men*, 100–101; Rubin, *Wary Fugitives*, 182.

53. Tate to Davidson, May 14, 1926, December 29, 1926, January 5, 1927, Davidson to Tate, January 21, 1927, all in Fain and Young, *Literary Correspondence*, 166–67, 181–83, 185. See also Davidson to Tate, January 27, 1928, in ibid., 206, in which Davidson admitted that his own initial adverse reaction to Tate's "Ode" may have reflected "unconscious wrath" over Tate's "denunciatory remarks" on *The Tall Men*.

54. Davidson to Tate, November 29, 1925, February 23, 1927, March 4, 1927, May 9, 1927, in Fain and Young, *Literary Correspondence*, 151–52, 191, 193, 202; Stewart, *Burden of Time*, 119; O'Brien, *Idea of the South*, 188–89.

.55. Davidson to Tate, July 29, 1929, December 29, 1929, Tate to Davidson, December 12, 1929, in Fain and Young, *Literary Correspondence*, 227–28, 244–45, 249; Davidson to Ransom, July 5, 1929, Davidson Papers; O'Brien, *Idea of the South*, 187.

56. Stewart, *Burden of Time*, 158; Davidson, "A Mirror for Artists," in Twelve Southerners, *I'll Take My Stand*, 37–38, 34, 41–42, 39, 51, 60.

57. Davidson, "Mirror," in Twelve Southerners, *I'll Take My Stand*, 30, 52–53, 59; Andrew Nelson Lytle, "The Hind Tit," in Twelve Southerners, *I'll Take My Stand*, 244.

58. Davidson, "Southern Literature: A Partisan View," in William T. Couch, ed., *Culture in the South*, 208, 190–93, 197, 199.

59. Davidson to Tate, April 14, 1931, December 19, 1931, January 16, 1932, Tate Papers; Tate to John Gould Fletcher, December 3, 1930, John Gould Fletcher Papers; Ransom to Tate, n.d. [probably February 15, 1930], February 22, 1930, November 6, 1930, January 3, 1932, Tate Papers.

60. O'Brien, *Idea of the South*, 190–92, 195.

61. Davidson, *The Attack on Leviathan*, 9, 21–27, 236, 127, 40–41, 118–19, 235. For a time, Davidson even welcomed the Tennessee Valley Authority, but by 1936 he changed his mind. See Edward Shapiro, "The Southern Agrarians and the Tennessee Valley Authority," 802–5.

62. Davidson, *Leviathan*, 114–15, 185–89, 210, vi.

63. Ibid., 162–63, 252, 84, 333, 74, 176, 180.

64. Ibid., 176–77, 342–43.

65. Davidson to Tate, July 21, 1930, July 27, 1930, Tate Papers; Rock, "Making and Meaning," 362–63; Davidson to Frank L. Owsley, August 3, 1936, Frank L. Owsley Papers; Davidson to James Southall Wilson, March 14, 1937, James Southall Wilson Papers;

Donald Davidson, "Mr. Babbitt at Philadelphia," 700; Davidson, "Mr. Cash and the Proto-Dorian South," 19; Warren Memoir, 89; O'Brien, *Idea of the South*, 208–9; Rubin, *Wary Fugitives*, 257.

66. O'Brien, *Idea of the South*, 194; Tate to Davidson, March 27, 1936, Davidson to Tate, February 23, 1940, in Fain and Young, *Literary Correspondence*, 298, 323–24.

CHAPTER 8

1. Richard Gray, *The Literature of Memory*, 94; Donald Davidson to Allen Tate, October 26, 1929, in Fain and Young, eds., *Literary Correspondence*, 237; Andrew Nelson Lytle to Tate, November 16, 1932, Allen Tate Papers; Virginia Rock, "The Making and Meaning of *I'll Take My Stand*," 242.

2. Radcliffe Squires, *Allen Tate*, 14–18; Allen Tate, *Memoirs and Opinions, 1926–1974*, 39–40, 8–9; Rock, "Making and Meaning," 21, 537–38.

3. Tate, *Memoirs*, 39, 5–7, 17, 21; Louise Cowan, *The Fugitive Group*, 36–37n; Louis D. Rubin, Jr., *The Wary Fugitives*, 69–70.

4. Cowan, *Fugitive Group*, 35; Tate, *Memoirs*, 24.

5. Cowan, *Fugitive Group*, 35–36; Tate, "Whose Ox?," 99; Tate to Davidson, July 21, 1922, December 7, 1922, in Fain and Young, *Literary Correspondence*, 20, 57.

6. Oral History Memoir of Robert Penn Warren, 74–75; Tate, *Memoirs*, 30; Tate to Davidson, July 5, 1922, July 12, 1922, July 31, 1922, February 20, 1927, in Fain and Young, *Literary Correspondence*, 13, 16–17, 26–27, 189.

7. Tate to Davidson, August 8, 1922, December 7, 1922, July 25, 1925, in Fain and Young, *Literary Correspondence*, 30, 58, 143.

8. Tate to Davidson, July 25, 1925, August 8, 1922, August 17, 1922, June 23, 1925, in Fain and Young, *Literary Correspondence*, 142–43, 29, 36–37, 140; Tate, "One Escape From the Dilemma," 35–36.

9. Squires, *Allen Tate*, 46; Tate to Davidson, August 27, 1923, September 7, 1923, June 5, 1924, June 8, 1924, June 15, 1924, November 9, 1924, December 17, 1924, December 30, 1924, January 16, 1925, November 26, 1925, in Fain and Young, *Literary Correspondence*, 84, 89, 119–21, 127–29, 132–34, 136–37, 148–49; Robert Penn Warren to Tate, n.d. [Early Spring, 1924], Tate Papers.

10. John L. Stewart, *The Burden of Time*, 376–77; Squires, *Allen Tate*, 59; Tate to Davidson, January 3, 1926, in Fain and Young, *Literary Correspondence*, 156–57.

11. Tate, "Ode to the Confederate Dead," in his *Poems: 1928–1931*, 50; Tate to Davidson, April 12, 1928, in Fain and Young, *Literary Correspondence*, 212.

12. Tate, "Ode," in *Poems*, 50; Tate, "Narcissus as Narcissus," in his *The Man of Letters in the Modern World*, 336–38; Rubin, *Wary Fugitives*, 105–8.

13. Tate, "Ode," in *Poems*, 52; Tate, "Narcissus," in *Man of Letters*, 338–39. Louis Rubin offers a different reading of the conclusion to the "Ode"; see his *Wary Fugitives*, 115–16.

14. Tate to Davidson, May 5, 1927, March 17, 1927, January 19, 1928, in Fain and Young, *Literary Correspondence*, 199–200; Tate to John Gould Fletcher, July 20, 1927, August 27, 1927, John Gould Fletcher Papers.

15. Tate to Davidson, April 28, 1927, in Fain and Young, *Literary Correspondence*, 198; Tate, *Stonewall Jackson*, 110, 271–72, 32–33; Stewart, *Burden of Time*, 322.

16. Tate to Davidson, June 26, 1926, in Fain and Young, *Literary Correspondence*, 174; Tate, *Stonewall Jackson*, 38–40, 234, 303, 51.

17. Tate, *Stonewall Jackson*, 64, 68, 116–17, 171.

18. Michael O'Brien, *The Idea of the American South, 1920–1941*, 143.

19. Caroline Gordon Tate to Virginia Lyne Tunstall, September 30, 1928, Virginia Lyne Tunstall Papers; Squires, *Allen Tate*, 84–88; Rubin, *Wary Fugitives*, 121–25.

20. Tate to Davidson, October 24, 1928, February 18, 1929, August 10, 1929, Davidson to Tate, July 29, 1929, in Fain and Young, *Literary Correspondence*, 217–18, 223, 230, 227; Tate to John Gould Fletcher, November 21, 1928, March 5, 1929, Fletcher Papers.

21. Tate, *Jefferson Davis, His Rise and Fall*, 301, 87.

22. Ibid., 53, 55, 33–34, 38, 51, 44; Eugene D. Genovese, *The World the Slaveholders Made*, 121, 148, 162, 199.

23. Tate, *Jefferson Davis*, 51, 55–56.

24. Ibid., 18, 48.

25. Ibid., 12, 132, 79, 127, 94–95, 69.

26. Tate to Fletcher, July 31, 1929, Fletcher Papers; Tate to Davidson, August 10, 1929, in Fain and Young, *Literary Correspondence*, 229–34.

27. Squires, *Allen Tate*, 100–101; Rock, "Making and Meaning," 19; Tate to Fletcher, November 4, 1930, Fletcher Papers; Robert Shafer, "Humanism and Impudence," 489, 496; Tate, "The Same Fallacy of Humanism," 31–36; Tate to Davidson, January 18, 1930, January 24, 1930, February 9, 1930, Donald Davidson Papers; Tate to John Peale Bishop, n.d. [probably June, 1931], John Peale Bishop Papers.

28. Tate to Davidson, July 27, 1930, August 1, 1930, Davidson to Mr. [Eugene F.] Saxton, August 14, 1930, Davidson Papers; Tate to Davidson, n.d., quoted in Rock, "Making and Meaning," 288.

29. Tate, "Remarks on the Southern Religion," in Twelve Southerners, *I'll Take My Stand*, 156–62.

30. Tate to Fletcher, December 3, 1930, November 21, 1928, Fletcher Papers; Tate to John Crowe Ransom, July 27, 1929, "Tate" file, Davidson Papers; Tate, "The Fallacy of Humanism," in C. Hartley Grattan, ed., *The Critique of Humanism*, 160–64; J. David Hoeveler, Jr., *The New Humanism*, 168.

31. Tate, "Remarks on Southern Religion," 163.

32. Ibid., 166–68, 173; Tate to John Crowe Ransom, July 27, 1929, Davidson Papers ("Tate" file).

33. Tate, "Remarks on Southern Religion," in Twelve Southerners, *I'll Take My Stand*, 169, 171–72.

34. Ibid., 173–74.

35. T. S. Eliot to Tate, October 28, 1930, Tate Papers; Tate, "Remarks on Southern Religion," in Twelve Southerners, *I'll Take My Stand*, 174–75; Louis D. Rubin, Jr., *The Writer in the South*, 90; Tate to John Gould Fletcher, December 3, 1930, Fletcher Papers. On the controversy concerning Tate's alleged Fascist leanings, see Albert E. Stone, Jr., "Seward Collins and the *American Review*," 12–18. It is just possible that Tate may have been unconsciously echoing H. L. Mencken, whose persistent advice on the way to revive southern culture was that "the thing must be done with violence"—by which he meant tough, unsentimental criticism. See Fred C. Hobson, Jr., *Serpent in Eden*, 35.

36. Tate to the Contributors to the Southern Symposium, July 24, 1930, Tate to Davidson, September 7, 1930, in Fain and Young, *Literary Correspondence*, 406, 254–55; Davidson to Tate, n.d. [July-August, 1930], Tate Papers; Tate, "Remarks on Southern Religion," in Twelve Southerners, *I'll Take My Stand*, 155.

37. Tate to John Peale Bishop, n.d. [probably June, 1931], Bishop Papers.

38. Tate, "A Traditionalist Looks at Liberalism," 735–36, 739; Tate, "Spengler's Tract against Liberalism," 41, 46–47; Tate, "The Profession of Letters in the South," 171; Tate to John Peale Bishop, April 7, 1933, Bishop Papers; Squires, *Allen Tate*, 106–8; Edward S.

Shapiro, "Decentralist Intellectuals and the New Deal," 938–41; Tate to Eugene F. Saxton, November 17, 1933, Davidson Papers.

39. Tate to Warren and Davidson, December 10, 1931, Tate to Davidson, December 17, 1931, Davidson Papers; Davidson to Tate, December 15, 1931, Tate Papers; Tate, "A View of the Whole South," 418, 425, 421; Tate to Eugene F. Saxton, November 17, 1933, Davidson Papers.

40. Tate to John Peale Bishop, April 7, 1933, Bishop Papers; Tate, "Where Are the People?," 233–34, 231; Tate, "View of the Whole South," 420; Tate, "Notes on Liberty and Property," in Herbert Agar and Allen Tate, eds., *Who Owns America?*, 81, 86; Malcolm Cowley to Tate, April 23, 1936, Tate Papers.

41. Tate, "Where Are the People?," 236–37; Tate, "Notes on Liberty," in Agar and Tate, *Who Owns America?*, 83–85, 91–93; Tate to Davidson, January 18, 1936, in Fain and Young, *Literary Correspondence*, 295; Edward Shapiro, "The Southern Agrarians and the Tennessee Valley Authority," 791–99, 805–6. See also Edward S. Shapiro, "The American Distributists and the New Deal."

42. Tate to Davidson, December 12, 1929, in Fain and Young, *Literary Correspondence*, 244–45; Tate, "Regionalism and Sectionalism," 160–61; Tate to Davidson, April 16, 1931, February 5, 1933, Davidson Papers; Tate, "Ezra Pound," in Tate, *Man of Letters*, 262–63.

43. Tate, "John Peale Bishop," in Tate, *Man of Letters*, 276; Tate, "Poetry and the Absolute," 46, 48–50; Tate, "Emily Dickinson," 622.

44. Tate, "Emily Dickinson," in Tate, *Man of Letters*, 217–18, 212–13, 220–21, 223; Tate, "A Note on Donne," in ibid., 238–39.

45. Tate, "Narcissus as Narcissus," in Tate, *Man of Letters*, 333–36; Tate, "Emily Dickinson," in Tate, *Man of Letters*, 217; Tate, "Tension in Poetry," in ibid., 70–72.

46. Tate, "The Profession of Letters in the South," 175–76; Tate, "The New Provincialism," in Tate, *Man of Letters*, 330–31; Tate, *Memoirs*, 32–33; Richard H. King, *A Southern Renaissance*, 71.

47. Davidson to Tate, April 14, 1931, Malcolm Cowley to Tate, April 20, 1934, Robert Penn Warren to Tate, February 4, 1935, Tate Papers; Maxwell Perkins to Tate, July 9, 1931, "Scribner's" file, Tate Papers; Tate to John Peale Bishop, February 11, 1932, October 30, 1933, Bishop Papers; Tate to Ellen Glasgow, May 31, 1933, Ellen Glasgow Papers; Tate to Davidson, April 16, 1931, October 9, 1932, May 4, 1938, July 31, 1938, Davidson Papers.

48. Squires, *Allen Tate*, 146, 14; Tate, *The Fathers*, 29, 268.

49. Tate, *The Fathers*, 131–32; Rubin, *Wary Fugitives*, 323.

50. Tate, *The Fathers*, 134–35, 121, 28, 98, 278–79, 80–81, 121, 123–24, 177.

51. Ibid., 6–7, 179, 131–33, 44, 149, 179, 185, 250; Gray, *Literature of Memory*, 87; David Riesman et al., *The Lonely Crowd*, chaps. 5 and 6.

52. Tate, *The Fathers*, 179–80.

53. Frank Kermode, "Old Orders Changing (Tate and Lampedusa)," in Radcliffe Squires, ed., *Allen Tate and His Work*, 141–43; King, *Southern Renaissance*, 109; Tate, *The Fathers*, 22–23, 135, 183, 266–68, 283, 179, 17.

54. Tate, *The Fathers*, 185–86, 210; Tate to Bishop, November 19, 1938, Bishop Papers.

55. Tate, *The Fathers*, 5, 218–19, 254, 271; Rubin, *Wary Fugitives*, 320–21.

56. Tate to Bishop, November 19, 1938, Bishop Papers; Tate to Fletcher, May 31, 1933, March 4, 1935, Fletcher Papers.

57. Tate, *The Fathers*, 51, 73, 258; Robert Penn Warren, *All the King's Men* (New York, 1946), 438, 429. On Warren as a Modernist writer, see chap. 11.

58. Tate to Frank L. Owsley, May 18, 1939, November 20, 1939, November 26, 1939, Frank L. Owsley Papers; Rubin, *Wary Fugitives*, 324–26.

59. Tate, "Fallacy of Humanism," in Grattan, *Critique of Humanism*, 132.

PART THREE

1. James Agee and Walker Evans, *Let Us Now Praise Famous Men*, 207.

CHAPTER 9

1. Oral History Memoir of William Terry Couch, 138; interview with Louis Round Wilson, October 15, 1970.

2. Paul Green, introduction to Edward C. L. Adams, *Congaree Sketches*, x–xii, xvi–xvii; Couch Memoir, 134–35; Howard W. Odum to Beardsley Ruml, June 27, 1927, Howard W. Odum Papers.

3. Couch Memoir, 139.

4. Ibid., 136–37, 141; Couch to Irita van Doren, April 30, 1927, in "Adams, *Congaree Sketches*" file, University of North Carolina Press Papers, Southern Historical Collection (hereafter cited as UNCPP); Couch to Nell Battle Lewis, June 8, 1927, William Terry Couch Papers.

5. Couch to Edward C. L. Adams, June 20, 1927, James Weldon Johnson to Henry R. Fuller, July 13, 1927, in "Adams, *Congaree Sketches*" file, UNCPP; anonymous review in the Columbia (S.C.) *State*, June 5, 1927; "The Literary Lantern," Charlotte *Observer*, July 17, 1927; Couch Memoir, 142.

6. Couch Memoir, 308, 171; Couch to Walter Lippmann, June 7, 1927, Gertrude Weil to Couch, June 12, 1927, Couch Papers.

7. Couch Memoir, 1–12, 23, 45–46, 53–54, 57, 68.

8. Bruce Clayton, *The Savage Ideal*, 32.

9. Couch Memoir, 60, 68–69, 76, 79–80.

10. Couch to Erskine Caldwell, June 21, 1932, in "*Culture in the South*: Miscellaneous" file, UNCPP.

11. Couch Memoir, 109–10, 115–16; interview with Louis Wilson, October 15, 1970.

12. "Preliminary Plan for Organization," n.d. [September or October, 1921], in minutes of the Board of Governors of the University of North Carolina Press (in the possession of the UNC Press, Chapel Hill), 8–10. I am grateful to the press for allowing me to inspect these minutes. On the organization's beginnings, see also Louis R. Wilson, *The University of North Carolina, 1900–1930*, 484–92. At the time the University of North Carolina Press started up, publishing in the South was confined to the printing houses run by the various religious denominations in Nashville, a university press at the University of the South whose sole function was to issue the *Sewanee Review*, and a moribund press at Trinity College (later Duke University), which would not come alive until the 1930s.

13. UNC Press Board of Governors minutes, December 17, 1923, January 4, 1924; Louis R. Wilson to Fabian Franklin, January 9, 1924, in "Franklin" file, UNCPP; Louis R. Wilson, "Publishing in the South: The Next Twenty Years," unpublished lecture delivered to the American Association of University Presses, n.d. [1950], 9–10, Louis R. Wilson Papers; interview with Wilson, October 15, 1970. See also Chester Kerr, *A Report on American University Presses*, 26.

14. Couch Memoir, 140; Couch to Louis R. Wilson, July 1, 1927, in "L. R. Wilson: General Correspondence" file, UNCPP; Willard B. Gatewood, Jr., *Preachers, Pedagogues, and Politicians*, 112–13.

15. Couch Memoir, 114, 122; Couch to Pierce Matthews, September 2, 1926, Couch to William Louis Poteat, March 7, 1927, in "Poteat, *Can a Man*" file, UNCPP; Couch to Herschel Brickell, December 7, 1926, in "Odum and Johnson, *Negro Workaday Songs*" file,

UNCPP; Louis R. Wilson to Couch, March 28, 1927, in "L. R. Wilson: General Correspondence" file, UNCPP. A typescript of the Lewis article on Poteat, entitled "North Carolina's Leading Liberal," can be found in the "Poteat" file, UNCPP.

16. Couch to Nell Battle Lewis, January 16, 1927, Couch Papers.

17. "Comments on Cason: Below the Potomac," memorandum enclosed with Couch to Clarence Cason, September 19, 1934, in "Cason" file, UNCPP. Wilson remained director of the press officially until 1932, and Couch assistant director, but as early as 1927 Odum was under the belief that Couch was in "active charge." See Odum to Couch, March 30, 1927, Couch Papers.

18. Couch to Spencer Murphy, September 20, 1927, in "Wilson, *Southern Exposure*" file, UNCPP; Couch to John Selby, April 11, 1941, in "Wood, *First the Fields*" file, UNCPP; Couch to Wade H. Harris, December 8, 1932, in "Dabney, *Liberalism*" file, UNCPP.

19. A full listing of books published by the UNC Press under Couch can be found in *Books from Chapel Hill: A Record and Catalogue of Twenty-four Years of Publishing, 1923–1945*. For statistical information on the output and finances of the press, see Couch's introduction to this volume, esp. xvi–xviii.

20. Couch Memoir, 285; Oral History Memoir of Arthur F. Raper, 53. When asked if it made a difference to have his books of the 1930s published in the South, Raper answered: "Yes. Yes. Yes. Yes. Yes. See, it made a difference that I was a Southerner—yea, thousands of times I've been asked, when somebody's listened to what I said and didn't take it quite well, 'Where were you born?' 'I was born in North Carolina.' 'Who did you marry?' 'I married Martha Jarrell of Georgia.' 'Where did you go to school?' 'I went to the University of North Carolina and to Vanderbilt.' So every time they tested me, I was pathologically Southern. . . . 'Where did you publish your books?' 'University of North Carolina Press.'"

21. Couch to Richard C. Rothschild, October 4, 1941, in "Finances: 1941 Plans" file, Box 35, UNCPP; Couch to Will W. Alexander, October 23, 1936, in "Finances: New York Trip: November, 1936" file, Box 35, UNCPP; Couch, "A University Press in the South," 198–99; clipping from Mobile (Ala.) *Press Register*, n.d. [1935?], in "T. J. Cauley" file, UNCPP.

22. Allan Nevins to Couch, May 21, 1934, in "Cate" file, UNCPP; Henry Steele Commager to Couch, April 12, 1939, in "Harris, *Purslane*" file, UNCPP; Joseph A. Brandt, "A Pioneering Regional Press," 27–28. Brandt includes the University of Oklahoma Press along with Yale and Chapel Hill as a pioneer of the modern concept of scholarly publishing. However, Oklahoma, founded in 1928, did not begin active operations until the early 1930s, well after Couch's revolution at Chapel Hill had been launched. Part of Brandt's confusion may stem from the fact that he incorrectly dates the founding of the North Carolina Press at 1927—an understandable mistake.

23. Couch Memoir, 124, 448; Kerr, *American University Presses*, 28, 32; UNC Press Board of Governors minutes, November 23, 1939. On Couch's fear of competition from other southern presses, see also his letters to Robert Lester, May 24, 1941, in "Finances: 1941 Plans" file, and to Ralph Wager, May 15, 1934, in "Emory U. Publications" file, UNCPP.

24. "Comments on Cason: Below the Potomac," enclosed with Couch to Clarence Cason, September 19, 1934, in "Cason" file, UNCPP; William Stott, *Documentary Expression and Thirties America*, 132–34; Couch to Broadus Mitchell, April 6, 1927, in "Mitchell: *William Gregg*" file, UNCPP.

25. Couch, "The University Press as an Aid to Scholarship," 139; Couch to Donald Davidson, May 6, 1932, in "Culture Below the Potomac A-E" file, UNCPP; Couch, "Report on Chadbourn: Lynching and the Law," January 13, 1933, in "Chadbourn" file, UNCPP.

26. On the "Old and New South" series, see Addison Hibbard to James Southall Wilson, July 25, 1929, December 11, 1929, and April 19, 1930, all with enclosures, in James Southall Wilson Papers. For some reason these documents do not appear in the UNC Press Papers.

27. Couch to Virginius Dabney, October 12, 1932, in "Dabney, V." file, UNCPP. The folder also contains numerous clippings of reviews of Dabney's book. See also Couch Memoir, 209, and Couch to Lewis Gannett, February 4, 1933, in "Dabney" file, UNCPP.

28. Couch to Virginius Dabney, March 29, 1932, May 31, 1932, June 8, 1932, June 14, 1932, Dabney to Couch, June 12, 1932, in "Dabney, V." file, UNCPP; typescript, "Insert B," enclosed with Dabney to Couch, August 11, 1932 (apparently typed by Couch with Dabney's handwritten corrections), ibid.; Dabney, *Liberalism in the South*, 256–58, 331.

29. Typescript, "Suggestion for a new book to be published by the University Press," n.d. [late 1928], Couch to Howard W. Odum, November 27, 1928, Couch to Howard Mumford Jones, January 10, 1929, Jones to Couch, January 11, 1929, Couch Papers. It appears that the original idea for the book was suggested by a local North Carolina iconoclast named Charles L. Snider; see Couch to Snider, February 27, 1932, in "*Culture in the South*: Miscellaneous" file, UNCPP.

30. Couch to George Stevens, December 5, 1930, December 30, 1930, February 5, 1931, in "W. W. Norton" file, Box 37, UNCPP; Couch to Stevens, December 16, 1930, December 18, 1930, Howard Mumford Jones to Couch, October 20, 1930, December 27, 1930, January 26, 1931, Couch to Jones, December 18, 1930, December 30, 1930, February 12, 1931, in "*Culture in the South*: Miscellaneous" file, UNCPP; Couch Memoir, 211–14. That Jones's editorship was sloppy is beyond dispute. Will W. Alexander had sent Jones a rough draft for a chapter on race relations and was most surprised when Jones accepted it as a finished piece. See Alexander to Howard W. Odum, May 1, 1933, Odum Papers.

31. Couch to John Donald Wade, February 18, 1931, May 10, 1932, in "*Culture in the South*: O-W" file, UNCPP; Couch to George Stevens, April 7, 1931, in "*Culture in the South*: Miscellaneous" file, UNCPP; Couch to Herman C. Nixon, April 14, 1932, in "*Culture in the South*: G-N" file, UNCPP.

32. Couch to Erskine Caldwell, June 21, 1932, Couch to Ellen Glasgow, March 1, 1932, in "*Culture in the South*: Miscellaneous" file, UNCPP; Couch to George Fort Milton, April 14, 1932, in "*Culture in the South*: G-N" file, UNCPP.

33. Couch to John Donald Wade, June 23, 1932, in "*Culture in the South*, O-W" file, UNCPP; Couch to Charles L. Snider, March 9, 1932, in "*Culture in the South*: Miscellaneous" file, UNCPP; Couch to H. C. Brearley, September 22, 1932, in "*Culture in the South*: A-E" file, UNCPP.

34. Couch to Herman C. Nixon, April 7, 1932, in "*Culture in the South*: G-N" file, UNCPP; Couch to Edd W. Parks, July 23, 1932, in "*Culture in the South*, O-W" file, UNCPP; Couch to Robert Lathan, February 8, 1932, Lathan to Couch, March 11, 1932, in "*Culture in the South*: Miscellaneous" file, UNCPP; Couch to John D. Allen, May 17, 1932, October 18, 1932, Allen to Couch, May 19, 1932, in "*Culture in the South*: A-E" file, UNCPP. See also John D. Allen, "Journalism in the South," in Couch, ed., *Culture in the South*, 126–58.

35. Allen Tate, "A View of the Whole South," 411–32; Benjamin B. Kendrick, review of *Culture in the South*, 218–19; Jonathan Daniels, "The Aspiring South"; Constance Rourke, review of *Culture in the South*; Hamilton Basso, "A Spotlight on the South," 287–88.

36. Couch Memoir, 331–33, 367; Couch to Henry G. Alsberg, April 22, 1938, Couch Papers; Couch to Olive Tilford Dargan, July 5, 1932, in "*Culture in the South*: Miscellaneous" file, UNCPP; Couch to Frank P. Graham, June 5, 1940 [marked "not sent"], in "FWP Difficulties" file, UNCPP. Although interested in the book, Couch was also highly critical of

You Have Seen Their Faces, calling Caldwell's text "sentimental slush," inaccurate, and out of date. See his review, "Landlord and Tenant," 309–12.

37. Couch, "Instructions to Writers," in *These Are Our Lives*, 417–18; Stott, *Documentary Expression*, 204–6. The materials collected in the life histories project, incidentally, are presently located in the Federal Writers' Project Papers, Southern Historical Collection, University of North Carolina Library, Chapel Hill. Totaling over a thousand case histories, they represent a mother lode of raw data for the social historian working on the depression-era South. Thirty additional life histories have recently been published; see Tom E. Terrill and Jerrold Hirsch, eds., *Such As Us: Southern Voices of the Thirties* (Chapel Hill, 1978).

38. Couch, editor's preface to *These Are Our Lives*, ix–xii; Couch to Arthur Goldschmidt, April 27, 1939, Couch to Paul Kellogg, April 10, 1939, Couch to Ellsworth Faris, July 21, 1939, and August 3, 1939, in "FWP: *These Are Our Lives*" file, UNCPP; Couch to Guy B. Johnson, November 15, 1939, in "Mangum, *Legal Status of the Negro*" file, UNCPP.

39. Couch to "To Whom It May Concern in WPA," November 28, 1939, in "FWP Difficulties" file, UNCPP; Couch Memoir, 341, 351–56, 332; Ellsworth Faris to Couch, July 29, 1939, Couch to Paul Kellogg, July 20, 1939, in "FWP: *These Are Our Lives*" file, UNCPP.

40. Couch, preface to *These Are Our Lives*, xiii.

41. Howard W. Odum to Couch, August 4, 1932, in "Dabney, *Liberalism*" file, UNCPP; Harry W. Chase, draft of statement sent to Odum, Dudley D. Carroll, and Frank P. Graham, March 6, 1928, Odum Papers. There are indications that Chase's statement troubled Odum, especially the passage quoted above. See Odum to Chase, April 6, 1928, Odum Papers.

42. Couch to the editor, Durham (N.C.) *Morning Herald*, April 17, 1927, pt. 1, p. 4; Louis R. Wilson to Couch, April 19, 1927, Eugene C. Branson to Couch, May 4, 1927, Couch Papers; Couch Memoir, 232–33.

43. Couch to Bessie Zaban Jones, April 18, 1939, Couch to Mrs. Clyde Hoey, April 19, 1939, in "Harris, *Purslane*" file, UNCPP; Couch, "Comments on Cason," 2, 6, 9, in "Cason" file, UNCPP; Couch to Frank L. Owsley, March 14, 1935, Couch Papers; Couch, "American Peasants," 637–38.

44. Couch to the editor, *Nation*, April 12, 1927, Couch Papers; Couch to Walter Wilson, March 28, 1933, in "Steiner and Brown" file, UNCPP; Couch, "Comments on Cason," 3–4, in "Cason" file, UNCPP.

45. Couch to Henry Fuller, January 2, 1932, Couch Papers; Dan T. Carter, *Scottsboro*, 107–8; Couch and Josiah O. Bailey, "Dynamite in Burlington," 18–21; Couch, "For a New Southern Economy," typescript of prospectus for unwritten book, n.d. [1934?], Couch Papers; Couch, "An Agrarian Programme for the South," 321–24.

46. Howard W. Odum to A. R. Mann, December 8, 1939, Odum Papers.

47. Francis P. Miller to Frank P. Graham, November 13, 1934, Frank Porter Graham Papers; Herman C. Nixon to Couch, July 25, 1935, in "Johnson: *Collapse*" file, UNCPP; Miller, "Memorandum on Proposed Conference," n.d., enclosed with Miller to Couch, December 20, 1935, in "Miller, *Southern Policy Papers*" file, UNCPP; remarks by H. C. Nixon in minutes of the Institute on Southern Regional Development and the Social Sciences, June 25, 1936, Odum Papers. The best sources for ascertaining what actually went on at the 1936 SPA meeting are Francis P. Miller, ed., *Second Southern Policy Conference Report*; Couch to Frank W. Prescott, November 10, 1937, Couch Papers; and George Fort Milton, "What Are Democratic Institutions?"

48. S. R. McCulloch, "Red-Baiting in a Big Way in New Orleans," 1–3; McCulloch, "Red-Baiting," 1; editorial, "Tulane and Sedition"; Herman C. Nixon to Couch, September 30, 1936, November 22, 1936, December 15, 1936, Couch to Nixon, October 5, 1936, October 12, 1936, in "Miller, *Southern Policy Papers*" file, UNCPP; Nixon to Couch, December 6, 1936, National Policy Committee Records, Box 2, Library of Congress, Washington, D.C.; Couch Memoir, 391–92. It should be noted that Couch was not using the press for narrow partisan purposes. The same grant that helped finance Nixon's *Forty Acres and Steel Mules* (Chapel Hill, 1938) was also used to underwrite the publication of Donald Davidson's *The Attack on Leviathan* (Chapel Hill, 1938), which took a diametrically opposite point of view.

49. Thomas A. Krueger, *And Promises to Keep*, 22–24, 26, 29; George B. Tindall, *The Emergence of the New South, 1913–1945*, 636–37; press release, Southern Conference for Human Welfare, n.d. [October 15, 1938], folder 1938–76, Graham Papers; Couch, "Southerners Inspect the South," 168; Couch Memoir, 393–94; Herman C. Nixon to Francis P. Miller, September 16, 1938, National Policy Committee Records, Library of Congress.

50. Couch, "Southerners Inspect," 169; Krueger, *Promises to Keep*, 29–30, 32, 38; Couch Memoir, 395, 397; Herman C. Nixon to Frank P. Graham, January 18, 1939, and enclosure [includes text of the antisegregation resolution], Folder 1939–61, Graham Papers. On reaction to the resolution, see Mark Ethridge to Graham, November 30, 1938, Folder 1938–78 and Clarence Poe to Graham, December 10, 1938, Folder 1938–80, Graham Papers; Jonathan Daniels to Frank E. Winslow, December 13, 1938, Jonathan Daniels Papers.

51. Krueger, *Promises to Keep*, 75–83; Francis P. Miller to Howard A. Kester, November 25, 1938, Kester to Frank P. Graham, December 11, 1939, Howard A. Kester Papers; Herman C. Nixon to Graham, May 11, 1939, Folder 1939–64, Graham Papers.

52. Couch Memoir, 261; Couch to Paul Green, November 8, 1928, Couch Papers; Couch to Virginius Dabney, September 13, 1933, in "Dabney, V." file, UNCPP; Couch to H. C. Brearley, January 21, 1941, in "Brearley" file, UNCPP.

53. Couch to John B. Holt, in "Holt" file, UNCPP; Couch to Henry Fuller, January 2, 1932, Couch to Ruth Wind, October 12, 1938, Couch Papers; Couch to Allen Tate, December 7, 1939, in "FWP: *These Are Our Lives*" file, UNCPP. On liberal reaction to the pact, see Norman H. Pearson, "The Nazi-Soviet Pact and the End of a Dream," in Daniel Aaron, ed., *America in Crisis*, 327–48, and Frank A. Warren III, *Liberals and Communism*, 69–70, 84–86, 193–94.

54. Couch to Tarleton Collier, February 4, 1941, in "Raper and Reid, *Sharecroppers*" file, UNCPP; Couch to Henry Fuller, April 15, 1941, in "Markham, *Wave of the Past*" file, UNCPP.

55. Couch to Reuben H. Markham, February 6, 1941, Couch to Ruth Benedict, April 26, 1941, April 30, 1941, Couch to Struthers Burt, May 10, 1941, in "Markham, *Wave of the Past*" file, UNCPP; Couch, "Statement on War," n.d., enclosed with Edd W. Parks to Couch, June 5, 1940, in "Parks" file, UNCPP; Couch to Norman Foerster, February 29, 1940, in "Feibleman, *Positive Democracy*" file, UNCPP; Couch to Ernest Seeman, February 20, 1940, Couch to Virginia Durr, March 18, 1940, March 21, 1940, Durr to Couch, n.d. [March, 1940], in "ACLU" file, Box 35, UNCPP; Couch Memoir, 422–23, 398–407; Couch to Frank P. Graham, April 12, 1940, Folder 1940–78, Graham Papers.

56. Couch to Frank P. Graham, April 15, 1940, and enclosure [text of resolution], Folder 1940–79, Graham Papers; Couch Memoir, 412–21; Oral History Memoir of Rupert B. Vance, 1. Cf. Krueger, *Promises to Keep*, 62–63.

57. Memorandum, Guy B. Johnson to Couch, January 22, 1942, Couch to Rayford W. Logan, March 26, 1943, March 31, 1943, November 9, 1943, in "Logan, *What the Negro Wants*" file. UNCPP.

58. Couch, "The Negro in the South," in Couch, *Culture in the South*, 474–76, 461–62, 457, 455, 467; Will W. Alexander to Howard W. Odum, May 1, 1933, May 10, 1933, Odum Papers; Carter, *Scottsboro*, 107–8.

59. Howard W. Odum to Couch, June 28, 1929, Odum Papers; Couch to Benjamin Brawley, August 8, 1934, Anson Phelps Stokes to Brawley, November 1, 1934, in "Brawley, *Early Negro American Writers*" file, UNCPP; UNC Press Board of Governors minutes, July 18, 1936; Sterling A. Brown to the University of North Carolina Press, August 19, 1938, in "Redding, *To Make a Poet Black*" file, UNCPP.

60. Couch Memoir, 47, 51, 281; Couch to Erskine Caldwell, August 31, 1926, in "Puckett, *Folk Beliefs*" file, UNCPP; Couch, "Negroes and the University," unpublished typescript, February 21, 1939, Couch Papers.

61. Couch to Rayford W. Logan, October 8, 1943, November 9, 1943, November 17, 1943, in "Logan, *What the Negro Wants*" file, UNCPP.

62. Couch to Rayford W. Logan, December 14, 1943, January 19, 1944, Logan to Couch, December 18, 1943, January 14, 1944, Couch to Virginius Dabney, December 20, 1943, Dabney to Couch, January 10, 1944, in "Logan, *What the Negro Wants*" file, UNCPP.

63. N. C. Newbold to Couch, October 23, 1943, November 15, 1943, Couch to Newbold, December 23, 1943, in "Logan, *What the Negro Wants*" file, UNCPP; Couch, "Publisher's Introduction" to Rayford W. Logan, ed., *What the Negro Wants*, ix, xv–xix.

64. Couch, "Publisher's Introduction," in Logan, *What the Negro Wants*, x–xi, xv; Couch, "The Achievement of the Negro in America," unpublished address, n.d. [probably 1932 or 1933], Couch Papers.

65. Virginius Dabney to Couch, February 28, 1944, Mark Ethridge to Couch, April 11, 1944, Gerald W. Johnson to Couch, October 9, 1944, Fletcher M. Green to Couch, December 27, 1944, Allen Tate to Couch, October 10, 1944, Avery Craven to Couch, March 6, 1945, Couch to Dabney, February 15, 1944, in "Logan, *What the Negro Wants*" file, UNCPP.

66. Couch to Jackson Davis, February 4, 1944, in "Logan, *What the Negro Wants*" file, UNCPP.

CHAPTER 10

1. Thomas J. Woofter, Jr., "The Teaching of Sociology in the South," 71; Howard W. Odum to Jackson Davis, April 21, 1936, Howard W. Odum Papers.

2. Edgar T. Thompson, "Sociology and Sociological Research in the South," 360, 364–65.

3. Ibid., 365; "History of Institute for Research in the Social Sciences," n.d. [1949?], Institute for Research in the Social Sciences Papers; Oral History Memoir of Rupert B. Vance, 72. On the Virginia institute's accomplishments, see especially Wilson Gee, "Annual Report to Dr. Joseph H. Willitts," July 1, 1940, Institute Papers, which contains a full listing of staff, projects, and publications from 1926 to 1940.

4. Gerald W. Johnson, "North Carolina in a New Phase," 846; Nell Battle Lewis, "North Carolina," 40; Gerald W. Johnson, "Chase of North Carolina," 186–87, 189–90; Oral History Memoir of Frank Porter Graham, 11, 15.

5. Gerald W. Johnson to Odum, October 21, 1922, November 12, 1922, Harriet L. Herring to Odum, June 4, 1924, July 1, 1924, Odum to Herring, July 2, 1924, Odum, "Memorandum for Institute Meeting," December 17, 1924, Odum Papers; Nell Battle Lewis, "The University of North Carolina Gets Its Orders," 114–15.

6. Harriet L. Herring, *Welfare Work in Mill Villages*, 11, 32–34, 46–57, 229; Odum to Broadus Mitchell, January 17, 1928, Odum to Gerald W. Johnson, June 18, 1929, Odum Papers; Herring, "12 Cents, the Troops and the Union," 199–202, one of the finest pieces written on southern labor conflicts in the 1920s; Herring, "The Southern Mill System Faces a New Issue," 351, 353–59; Herring, "The Social Problem of Labor Organization Casualties," 271–73; Herring, "Social Development in the Mill Village," 269–71; Herring, "Cycles of Cotton Mill Criticism," 124–25; Herring, "Tracing the Development of Welfare Work in the North Carolina Textile Industry," 598; Arthur Evans Woods, review of *Welfare Work in Mill Villages*, 667–68.

7. Joseph L. Blotner and Frederick L. Gwynn, eds., *Faulkner in the University*, 275; Vance Memoir, 2–4, 7, 57.

8. Vance Memoir, 5–6, 11, 14.

9. Ibid., 11–12, 9, 17, 25–28, 46–47.

10. Ibid., 55–58, 48.

11. Ibid., 58–59; Vance, *Human Factors in Cotton Culture*, 295–97, 1–4, 252, 300–301; Vance, "Cotton Culture and Social Life and Institutions of the South," 51; Vance, "The Concept of the Region," 208–9.

12. Vance, *Human Factors*, 118–19, 149, 237–40, 305–7, 113; Vance, "Cotton Culture," 57.

13. Vance, *Human Factors*, 219–30, 249–50, 253–65, 302–3, 157; Odum to Bedford Moore, January 28, 1928, Odum Papers.

14. Vance, *Human Factors*, 49–51, 64, 71–79, 178. On Phillips, see chap. 2 above, and Vance Memoir, 62.

15. Vance, *Human Factors*, 140–47, 149, 180–81, 198, 185.

16. Vance, *Human Geography of the South*, 4, 59–62, 482, 22, 45n, 71–76; Vance Memoir, 62.

17. Vance, *Human Geography*, 75, 194–98, 184–85, 230–32, 154–55.

18. Ibid., 275, 308, 279–80, 296–98, 442.

19. Ibid., 446–60, 467, 356–57, 360–66, 368.

20. Vance Memoir, 58; Vance, *Human Geography*, 192–93, 462–63, 379–80, 388, 391, 403, 436, 439–41.

21. Vance, *Human Geography*, 483, 495–96, 498; Vance, "What of Submarginal Areas in Regional Planning?," 318, 324–27; Vance, "Little Man, What Now?," 564.

22. Vance Memoir, 93–97; Vance, "Is Agrarianism for Farmers?," 46, 54–55; Vance, "The Economic Future in the Old Cotton Belt," 85–86, 90–92; Vance, *Research Memorandum on Population Redistribution within the United States*, 34–35, 55–61; Vance, *All These People*, 471–76.

23. Vance, Memorandum, "Manuscript on American Regionalism," January 21, 1938, Odum Papers.

24. George M. Fredrickson, *The Black Image in the White Mind*, 329–30; Idus A. Newby, *Jim Crow's Defense*, 50–51; Nathan I. Huggins, *Harlem Renaissance*, 89, 91–92.

25. Thomas J. Woofter, Jr., *The Basis of Racial Adjustment*, 5–7. Morton D. Sosna provides an account of southern racial liberalism of this era in his *In Search of the Silent South*; however his treatment fails to take into sufficient account the inner tensions southern liberals felt about maintaining segregation.

26. Newbell N. Puckett, *The Magic and Folk Beliefs of the Southern Negro*, vii and passim; Newman I. White, "Racial Traits in the Negro Song," 397–400, 404; White, "Racial Feeling in Negro Poetry," 15, 18–20, 28.

27. Oral History Memoir of Guy B. Johnson, 1–4, 6–10, 13–20, 23, 25–28, 30–33.

28. Ibid., 30, 34–38.

29. Ibid., 42–44, 48–49.

30. Ibid., 44; Guy B. Johnson, "A Sociological Interpretation of the New Ku Klux Movement," 440–45; Guy B. Johnson, "The Race Philosophy of the Ku Klux Klan," 269–70. As Johnson notes in his memoir, the *Social Forces* article represented a synopsis of his master's thesis; hence all quotations used above are drawn from it.

31. Guy B. Johnson Memoir, 45–46.

32. Ibid., 58–59, 61–65; Odum and Guy B. Johnson, *The Negro and His Songs*; Odum and Guy B. Johnson, *Negro Workaday Songs*; Guy B. Johnson, "A Study of the Musical Talent of the American Negro." On the collaboration between Johnson and Odum, see chap. 5.

33. Johnson Memoir, 107–8; Leonard Outhwaite to Odum, May 20, 1926, Odum Papers; Guy B. Johnson, "Background Studies," 662–63.

34. Guy B. Johnson, "Newspaper Advertisements and Negro Culture," 707–9; Guy B. Johnson, "Double Meaning in the Popular Negro Blues," 12–13, 15–18.

35. Odum to H. L. Mencken, June 9, 1925, June 19, 1925, Odum Papers; Guy B. Johnson Memoir, 72–74, 86; Guy B. Johnson, *John Henry*, 4–5, 8–12, 53, 70–71, 87, 89–137, 140.

36. Guy B. Johnson Memoir, 75–78; Thomas J. Woofter, Jr. to Odum, February 13, 1928, Odum Papers.

37. Guy B. Johnson Memoir, 77, 80–84; Guy B. Johnson, *Folk Culture on St. Helena Island, South Carolina*, 74–78, 90, 94–115, 129, 6–10, 52–53; Guy B. Johnson, "The Negro Spiritual," 157, 160–67; Guy B. Johnson, "The Speech of the Negro," 346, 351–58. In a review of a collection of St. Helena spirituals written before his research on the island, Johnson noted how "the music does not show the influence of a constant contact with white music"; clearly his views changed dramatically as a result of his firsthand observations. See his "Recent Contributions to the Study of American Negro Songs," 789.

38. Guy B. Johnson Memoir, 82–84; Melville J. Herskovits, *The Myth of the Negro Past*, 263–64, 291; Lorenzo Dow Turner, *Africanisms in the Gullah Dialect*, 12 and passim; J. R. Peery, review of Odum and Guy B. Johnson, *The Negro and His Songs*; Guy B. Johnson, "Some Factors in the Development of Negro Social Institutions in the United States," 334–35.

39. Guy B. Johnson Memoir, 93–96; Dan T. Carter, *Scottsboro*, 257–58; Virginius Dabney, "The Voice of Reaction in Tarheelia."

40. Guy B. Johnson, "Does the South Owe the Negro a New Deal?," 94.

41. Guy B. Johnson, "The Negro and the Depression in North Carolina," 103, 111–15; Odum, *Southern Regions of the United States*, 485; Guy B. Johnson, "Race Relations: The Negro in American Life," radio talk delivered April 22, 1941, in "Raper: *Sharecropper* Reviews" file, UNCPP; minutes of the Institute on Southern Regional Development and the Social Sciences, Chapel Hill, 8th session, June 22, 1936, pp. 2–10, 15th session, June 25, 1936, pp. 1–4, Odum Papers.

42. Guy B. Johnson, "Education, Segregation, and Race Relations," 90–94; Guy B. Johnson, "Some Methods of Reducing Race Prejudice in the South," 275–76, 278; Guy B. Johnson, "Negro Racial Movements and Leadership in the United States," 67–71; Guy B. Johnson, "Isolation or Integration?," 89; Guy B. Johnson, autobiographical note, n.d., in "*Culture*: Contributors" file, UNCPP.

43. Horace R. Cayton and George S. Mitchell, *Black Workers and the New Unions*; Arthur F. Raper and Ira De A. Reid, *Sharecroppers All*; Charles S. Johnson, *Shadow of the Plantation* and *Growing Up in the Black Belt*; Richard Wright, *Native Son*, 367. The fact that Wright chose to use a white lawyer as his spokesman in the novel reveals how far black consciousness still had to go in the early 1940s. On Rayford W. Logan, ed., *What the Negro Wants*, see chap. 9.

44. Lillian E. Smith, "Southern Defensive—II," 43–45; Guy B. Johnson, "Southern Offensive," 91; Guy B. Johnson Memoir, 125–27, 130–32.

45. Gunnar Myrdal, *An American Dilemma*, 1:470–71, 2:831, 1405; Guy B. Johnson Memoir, 140–41, 147, 159. On desegregation in Chapel Hill and Johnson's role in it, see John Ehle, *The Free Men*, 75, 202–3, 237–42, 316–17.

46. Guy B. Johnson Memoir, 166–67.

47. Oral History Memoir of Arthur F. Raper, 39.

48. Ibid., 1–4. On the Moravians generally, see Gillian L. Gollin, *Moravians in Two Worlds*; on the Moravians in North Carolina, the best sources are Adelaide L. Fries, *The Road to Salem*, and Hunter James, *The Quiet People of the Land*.

49. Raper Memoir, 12–14, 22–23.

50. Ibid., 23, 25 –30, 32.

51. Ibid., 33–36, 41, 51; Jessie F. Steiner, *The American Community in Action*, 264–78; Odum to Will W. Alexander, September 14, 1926, Odum Papers.

52. Raper Memoir, 99–105. On the Interracial Commission, see Edward F. Burrows, "The Commission on Interracial Cooperation in the South," and Wilma Dykeman and James Stokely, *Seeds of Southern Change*.

53. William T. Couch to Raper, April 28, 1933, Couch to Roger Baldwin, September 19, 1933, in "Raper: *Tragedy*" file, UNCPP; Oral History Memoir of William Terry Couch, 268, 277–78; Dykeman and Stokely, *Seeds of Change*, 140–41; Raper Memoir, 90.

54. Will W. Alexander to Odum, August 7, 1930, Alexander to George Fort Milton, September 24, 1930 [copy], Alexander to Members of the Southern Commission for the Study of Lynching, September 5, 1930, Odum Papers; Raper Memoir, 86–87, 82–83.

55. Arthur F. Raper, *The Tragedy of Lynching*, 88, 111–15, 146–60; Raper Memoir, 88–89.

56. Walter White, *Rope and Faggot*, 56, 82, 153, 21.

57. Raper to Odum, March 21, 1932, Odum Papers; Raper, *Tragedy*, i, 166–71, 193–96, 5; White, *Rope and Faggot*, 40–48, 155. Raper did find some exceptions to the correlation between the incidence of lynching and the presence of community institutions. In Maryville, Missouri, where a black prisoner was chained to a pole and burned to death, there was an abundance of schools, welfare agencies, strong churches, and a thriving two-party political system. But, Raper also discovered, the fabric of community life had recently started to unravel due to the effects of the severe economic depression. See *Tragedy*, 439–40.

58. William T. Couch to Raper, February 23, 1934, Raper to Couch, March 26, 1934, in "Raper: *Preface*" file, UNCPP; Raper Memoir, 55–57, 60–65, 69–71.

59. Arthur F. Raper, *Preface to Peasantry*, 4–5, 149, 171. On Phillips, see chap. 2.

60. Raper, *Preface*, 23, 313–18, 324–27, 371; Raper Memoir, 97.

61. Donald Davidson, *The Attack on Leviathan*, 304, 286; Herman C. Nixon to William T. Couch, December 6, 1936, in "Dabney: *Liberalism*" file, UNCPP; Raper and Reid, *Sharecroppers All*, 246, 263–64.

62. Couch to Raper, May 10, 1938, in "Raper: *Sharecroppers*" file, UNCPP; Raper to Odum, February 23, 1938, August 10, 1938, Odum Papers; Raper and Reid, *Sharecroppers All*, v.

63. Samuel H. Hobbs, Jr., to Couch, March 16, 1939, Judge Orville A. Park to Couch, April 6, 1939, Odum to Couch, March 29, 1939, Will W. Alexander to Couch, April 14, 1939, Lucy R. Mason to Couch, June 22, 1939, Margaret J. Hagood, memorandum on *Sharecroppers All*, February 8, 1940, Raper to Couch, March 24, 1939, in "Raper: *Sharecroppers*" file, UNCPP.

64. Raper and Reid, *Sharecroppers All*, 209, 248, 217–18, 210, 180, 215.

65. Herman C. Nixon, *Forty Acres and Steel Mules*, especially 31–37; C. Vann Woodward, *Tom Watson*; Raper and Reid, *Sharecroppers All*, 244, 138.

66. Raper Memoir, 128, 142, 146–61; Raper, *Tenants of the Almighty*, 206–10, 358–61; Raper, "A Case Study of Democratic Procedures in Rural Development—A Personal Document" (East Lansing, Michigan, 1965), copy in Arthur F. Raper Papers.

67. Raper Memoir, 162.

CHAPTER 11

1. In a revealing passage, Warren once pointed up the apolitical character of Faulkner's work: "It is really strange that in his vast panorama of society in a state where politics is the blood, bone, sinew, and passion of life, and the most popular sport, Faulkner has almost entirely omitted, not only a treatment of the subject, but references to it" (Warren, "Faulkner: Past and Present," in Warren, *Faulkner*, 17).

2. Ellington White, "Robert Penn Warren," in Rubin and Jacobs, *South*, 199.

3. Leonard Casper, *Robert Penn Warren*, 3–4, 181; L. Hugh Moore, Jr., *Robert Penn Warren and History*, 69.

4. Oral History Memoir of Robert Penn Warren, 25–26; Louise Cowan, *The Fugitive Group*, 107–9; Allen Tate to Donald Davidson, April 17, 1924, May 24, 1924, May 26, 1924, Donald Davidson Papers.

5. John L. Stewart, *The Burden of Time*, 80, 437; Warren, "Death Mask of a Young Man," 69; Warren, review of *Sunrise Trumpets*, 29; Warren Memoir, 41–42.

6. Warren Memoir, 1–3, 6–13, 16. Warren has provided an excellent sketch of his grandfather, Gabriel Telemachus Penn, in his short story "When the Light Gets Green." On the accuracy of the sketch, see Warren Memoir, 12.

7. Warren Memoir, 17, 32–33, 50–51; Warren to Allen Tate, March 21, 1924, Jessie F. Wills to Tate, May 22, 1924, Allen Tate Papers.

8. Warren Memoir, 50–51. On the "unreasonable wound" and its connection with the rise of Modernist writing in America, see Frederick J. Hoffman, *The Twenties*, 88–97.

9. Warren Memoir, 43–44; Cowan, *Fugitive Group*, 216; Warren to Donald Davidson, August 21, 1925, Davidson Papers; Warren to Tate, February 6, 1926, May 26, 1926, n.d. [Spring, 1927], Tate Papers.

10. Warren Memoir, 49, 67.

11. Tate to Davidson, April 11, 1928, May 28, 1929, Davidson Papers; Warren Memoir, 47–48. For examples of the attack on *John Brown*, see Moore, *Warren and History*, 27–28, and Casper, *Warren*, 91. The flippant, often sarcastic, style of *John Brown* suggests that Warren's model may well have been Wade's biography of Augustus Baldwin Longstreet. Indeed, John Brown heading for Kansas Territory as Warren portrays him seems strikingly reminiscent of Ransy Sniffle going to Georgia to see if anything might turn up.

12. Warren, *John Brown*, 107–9, 162–65, 352–81.

13. Warren Memoir, 3, 101–2. The best account of the events surrounding the Dark-Fired Tobacco Association remains John G. Miller, *The Black Patch War*, although the account was written by the lawyer chiefly responsible for prosecuting the night riders.

14. Warren Memoir, 60–62, 14.

15. Warren, *John Brown*, 101–2, 141, 155, 350–51, 446, 226–27, 129; Casper, *Warren*, 91–92.

16. Warren, *John Brown*, 90, 136, 218; Cowan, *Fugitive Group*, 247; Charles H. Bohner, *Robert Penn Warren*, 30.

17. Warren, *John Brown*, 245–46. In a review for the *New Republic* written at this time, Warren again took aim at Emerson, accusing him of dissipating through his rationalism "any tragic possibilities" available to the New England writer. See Warren, "Hawthorne, Anderson and Frost," 400.

18. Warren to Herbert Agar, April 15, 1937, *Southern Review* Papers; Warren to Allen Tate, n.d. [Fall, 1929], May 19, 1930, Tate Papers; Warren Memoir, 82; Ralph Ellison and Eugene Walter, "The Art of Fiction XVIII: Robert Penn Warren" (interview with Warren first published in the *Paris Review*, Spring–Summer 1957), in John L. Longley, Jr., ed., *Robert Penn Warren*, 22, 27.

19. Warren to Donald Davidson, February 16, 1930, Davidson to Warren, March 17, 1930, Davidson Papers; Warren, "The Briar Patch," in Twelve Southerners, *I'll Take My Stand*, 250–58, 262.

20. Lyle Lanier to Allen Tate, July 21, 1930, August 1, 1930, Tate Papers; Tate to Donald Davidson, July 22, 1930, July 27, 1930, Davidson to Warren, March 17, 1930, October 1, 1930, Davidson Papers; Virginia J. Rock, "The Making and Meaning of *I'll Take My Stand*," 262–67.

21. Ellison and Walter, "Art of Fiction," in Longley, *Warren*, 21–22; Warren Memoir, 65–67, 97.

22. Warren, "Prime Leaf," in his *The Circus in the Attic and Other Stories*, 233–37, 252–59, 268–72.

23. Stewart, *Burden of Time*, 173–74, 451; Warren Memoir, 11, 51, 72.

24. Warren Memoir, 100, 105; Warren, "The Apple Tree," unpublished manuscript, Robert Penn Warren Papers, 27.

25. Warren, "God's Own Time," unpublished manuscript, Warren Papers, chap. 2, p. 12, chap. 3, pp. 2 and 8, chap. 5, p. 4, and chap. 6, p. 10.

26. Ibid., chap. 2, pp. 1 and 8, chap. 3, p. 8. Warren continued to be caught up by the mystery of the characters of Elsie Beaumont and her daughter Helen, seemingly ordinary women who proved unusually vulnerable to the flood of passion. See his short stories "The Love of Elsie Barton: A Chronicle" and "Testament of Flood," in *Circus in the Attic*, 143–69. The stories were culled (with much revision) from "God's Own Time."

27. Warren, "Some Recent Novels," 625–27, 629–31; Warren, "T. S. Stribling," 477–80.

28. Warren, "Some Recent Novels," 626; Warren, "The Blind Poet," 38; Warren, "John Crowe Ransom," 95–96, 98; Casper, *Warren*, 22; Moore, *Warren and History*, 20, 26–28.

29. Warren, "Some Recent Novels," 631–32; Warren, "Ransom," 111–12.

30. Warren Memoir, 101; Warren to Herbert Agar, October 20, 1937, *Southern Review* Papers; Warren to Allen Tate, n.d. [late 1938], Tate Papers; Ellison and Walter, "Art of Fiction," in Longley, *Warren*, 21.

31. Warren, *Night Rider*, 14, 37, 130; Warren Memoir, 120.

32. Warren, *Night Rider*, 17, 25, 34, 117; Warren Memoir, 117.

33. Warren, *Night Rider*, 267, 368.

34. Ibid., 104–5, 89–90, 169.

35. Ibid., 37–40, 145–46, 86, 196.

36. Ibid., 304, 326–30, 334, 338–41; Warren to Allen Tate, n.d. [late 1938], Tate Papers; Casper, *Warren*, 104, 106. It is noteworthy that both Tate and the publisher advised Warren

to cut the Willie Proudfit material from the novel, but Warren, after much reflection, insisted on leaving it in. See Warren to Tate, n.d. [late 1938], Tate Papers.

37. Frank L. Owsley to Warren, April 13, 1939, *Southern Review* Papers. On receiving Owsley's comments on *Night Rider*, Warren told his friend that "your analysis of the basic motivation and development [of the novel] . . . hits the nail on the head as regards my intentions—far more accurately than any reviewer has done." Warren to Owsley, n.d. [marked "ca 1938" but probably 1939], Frank L. Owsley Papers.

38. Warren, *Night Rider*, 146, 171–74; Warren Memoir, 12–15, 102–3. Critics have often described Munn as no more than a victim of weak character; see Alvin S. Ryan, "Robert Penn Warren's *Night Rider*: The Nihilism of the Isolated Temperament," in Longley, *Robert Penn Warren*, 52, and Moore, *Warren and History*, 60.

39. Warren Memoir, 100–101, 126; Warren to Frank Owsley, November 11, 1939, November 13, 1939, and n.d., Owsley Papers. For examples of Warren's clumsiness in handling his clichéd subject, see especially the descriptions of Murdock's firm, the "Happy Valley Hunt Club," and Slim Sarrett's soirees in Warren, *At Heaven's Gate*, 67–68, 128–30, 201–4. For an opposite, more favorable, interpretation of the novel, see John L. Longley, Jr., "Self Knowledge, The Pearl of Pus, and the Seventh Circle: The Major Themes in *At Heaven's Gate*," in his *Warren*, 60–74.

40. Warren, *At Heaven's Gate*, 223, 268, 178, 11, 6.

41. Ibid., 40, 44–45, 196; Stewart, *Burden of Time*, 436.

42. Jean-Paul Sartre, *Existentialism and Humanism*, 24–26, 28; David C. Roberts, *Existentialism and Religious Belief*, 6–8, 334; William Barrett, *Irrational Man*, 64, 36, 244.

43. Warren Memoir, 106–7, 138; Warren, "*All the King's Men*: The Matrix of Experience," in Longley, *Warren*, 77.

44. Warren Memoir, 123–25, 138; Warren, "Proud Flesh," unpublished manuscript, Allen Tate Papers; Casper, *Warren*, 119–20; Warren to Lambert Davis, December 17, 1941, in "Letters (unidentified)" file, *Southern Review* Papers.

45. Louis D. Rubin, Jr., *Writers of the Modern South*, 107.

46. Warren, *All the King's Men*, 120, 1, 76, 99, 79; Warren Memoir, 134.

47. Warren, *All the King's Men*, 40, 118.

48. Ibid., 30, 106, 159.

49. Ibid., 164–78, 186–89; Moore, *Warren and History*, 57–58.

50. Warren, *All the King's Men*, 215, 49, 343, 248–53.

51. Ibid., 325, 309–11, 125, 342, 38, 202. Jack's complaint about the slow pace of political reform reflected Warren's views on the situation in Louisiana. As Warren once put it, "if the government of the state had not previously been marked by various combinations of sloth, complacency, incompetence, corruption, and a profound lack of political imagination, there would never have been a Senator Huey P. Long" ("Matrix of Experience," in Longley, *Warren*, 79).

52. Warren, *All the King's Men*, 310–11, 315.

53. Ibid., 101, 246–47, 396.

54. Ibid., 151, 198–201.

55. Ibid., 12–17, 60–69, 81, 337, 49, 257–58; Warren Memoir, 141. On the reaction of southern intellectuals to Long, see, for example, Hamilton Basso, "Huey Long and His Background," 663–73; or Harnett Kane, *Louisiana Hayride*.

56. Warren, *All the King's Men*, 136–37; Reinhold Niebuhr, *The Children of Light and the Children of Darkness*, 41.

57. Warren, *All the King's Men*, 415, 155, 233, 260, 364.

58. Ibid., 354, 351.

59. Ibid., 189–90, 228, 384. On Tate, see chap. 8.

60. Ibid., 394, 436, 248; Moore, *Warren and History*, 18–20, 69, 99.

61. Warren, *All the King's Men*, 9; Barrett, *Irrational Man*, 62.

62. Warren, *All the King's Men*, 437; Warren Memoir, 77–78.

CODA

1. Wilbur J. Cash, *The Mind of the South*, 153, 60, 197, 327.

2. C. Vann Woodward, *American Counterpoint*, 261–63; Richard King, *A Southern Renaissance*, 146–50; Donald Davidson, "Mr. Cash and the Proto-Dorian South," 1–20.

3. Cash, *Mind of the South*, 387.

4. Lillian Smith, *Killers of the Dream*, 75–76, 98, 210.

5. Ibid., 99–100.

6. The one new direction in the recent sociological study of the South can be found in John Shelton Reed, *The Enduring South*, a work that treats "southern-ness" as an independent variable and attempts to measure its strength and characteristics using public opinion surveys. One hopes that more work will be done along these lines.

7. Walker Percy, *The Last Gentleman*, 267–68, 313–14, 318–26, 55, 234.

8. Ibid., 281, 379.

BIBLIOGRAPHY

MANUSCRIPT COLLECTIONS

CHAPEL HILL, NORTH CAROLINA
Southern Historical Collection,
University of North Carolina
Eugene Cunningham Branson Papers.
William Terry Couch Papers.
Jonathan Worth Daniels Papers.
Frank Porter Graham Papers.
Howard A. Kester Papers.
Samuel Chiles Mitchell Papers.
Howard Washington Odum Papers.
Ulrich Bonnell Phillips Papers.
Southern Tenant Farmers Union Papers.
University Papers.
University of North Carolina
Press Papers.
Louis R. Wilson Papers.
University of North Carolina Press
Minutes of the Board of Governors
(in possession of the Press).
CHARLOTTESVILLE, VIRGINIA
Edwin A. Alderman Library,
University of Virginia
F. Stringfellow Barr Papers.
Emily Tapscott Clark Papers.
Virginius Dabney Papers.
Ellen Glasgow Papers.
William Faulkner Papers.
Institute for Research in
Social Science Papers.
Southern Writers' Conference Papers.
Virginia Lyne Tunstall Papers.
Virginia Quarterly Review Papers.
James Southall Wilson Papers.

DURHAM, NORTH CAROLINA
Duke University Library
William Watts Ball Papers.
Journal of Southern History Archives.
Lucy Randolph Mason Papers.
South Atlantic Quarterly Papers.
Wendell Holmes Stephenson Papers.
FAYETTEVILLE, ARKANSAS
University of Arkansas Library
John Gould Fletcher Papers.
NASHVILLE, TENNESSEE
Vanderbilt University Library
Donald Davidson Papers.
Frank Lawrence Owsley Papers.
NEW HAVEN, CONNECTICUT
Yale University Library
William Faulkner Papers.
Southern Review Papers.
Robert Penn Warren Papers.
PRINCETON, NEW JERSEY
Princeton University Library
John Peale Bishop Papers.
William Faulkner Papers.
Allen Tate Papers.
Thomas F. Wertenbaker Papers.
RALEIGH, NORTH CAROLINA
North Carolina State Archives
Nell Battle Lewis Papers.
Clarence Poe Papers.
Wautauga Club Papers.
WASHINGTON, D.C.
Library of Congress
George Fort Milton Papers.
Merrill Moore Papers.
National Policy Committee Records.

INTERVIEWS

CHAPEL HILL, NORTH CAROLINA
Lambert Davis, February 8, 1972.
Louis R. Wilson, October 15, 1970, December 2, 1970.
NEW HAVEN, CONNECTICUT
C. Vann Woodward, November 13, 1971.
NEW YORK, NEW YORK
Columbia Oral History Collection, Columbia University Library
William Terry Couch, October 22, 1970, November 11, 12, and 21, 1970.
Jonathan W. Daniels, March 22 and 30, 1972.
Guy B. Johnson, December 14, 1971, April 13, 19, and 25, 1972.
Broadus Mitchell, November 11, 1971, December 29, 1971.
Arthur F. Raper, January 18, 1971.
Rupert B. Vance, September 3, 1970, December 5, 1970.
Robert Penn Warren, October 16, 1974.

PUBLISHED WORKS: PRIMARY SOURCES

Abernethy, Thomas Perkins. *From Frontier to Plantation in Tennessee: A Study in Frontier Democracy.* Chapel Hill, 1932.
Adams, Edward C. L. *Congaree Sketches.* Chapel Hill, 1927.
Agar, Herbert, and Tate, Allen, eds. *Who Owns America? A New Declaration of Independence.* Boston, 1936.
Agee, James, and Evans, Walker. *Let Us Now Praise Famous Men.* Boston, 1941.
Allen, John D. "Disunion in Dixie: A Symposium of Opinion Concerning *The Attack on Leviathan.*" *North Georgia Review* 3, no. 1 (Spring 1938): 3, 23–24.
Arnett, Alex M. *The Populist Movement in Georgia: A View of the "Agrarian Crusade" in the Light of Solid South Politics.* New York, 1922.
———, and Kendrick, Benjamin M. *The South Looks at Its Past.* Chapel Hill, 1935.
Arnold, Matthew. *Culture and Anarchy.* Edited by J. Dover Wilson. Cambridge, England, 1971.
Bailey, Thomas P. *Race Orthodoxy in the South, and Other Aspects of the Negro Question.* New York, 1914.
Ball, William Watts. *The State That Forgot: South Carolina's Surrender to Democracy.* Indianapolis, 1932.
Barnes, Harry E. "Sociology and Ethics: A Genetic View of the Theory of Conduct." *Social Forces* 3, no. 2 (January 1925): 212–31.
Barr, F. Stringfellow. "No North, No South!" *Nation,* January 21, 1931, pp. 67–68.
———. "A Reconstructed South." *Virginia Quarterly Review* 10, no. 2 (April 1934): 275–79.
———. "Shall Slavery Come South?" *Virginia Quarterly Review* 6, no. 4 (October 1930): 480–94.
———. "The Uncultured South." *Virginia Quarterly Review* 5, no. 2 (April 1929): 192–200.
Basso, Hamilton. "The Future of the South." *New Republic,* November 8, 1939, pp. 70–74.
———. "Huey Long and His Background." *Harper's Monthly Magazine,* May 1935, pp. 663–73.

_____. "Letters in the South." *New Republic*, June 19, 1935, pp. 161–63.

_____. "A Spotlight on the South." *New Republic*, April 18, 1934, pp. 287–88.

Bernard, Luther L. "The Development of the Concept of Progress." *Social Forces* 3, no. 2 (January 1925): 207–12.

Blackwell, Gordon W. "The Displaced Tenant Farm Family in North Carolina." *Social Forces* 13, no. 1 (October 1934): 65–73.

Blanshard, Paul. "Communism in Southern Cotton Mills." *Nation*, April 24, 1929, pp. 500–501.

_____. "One-Hundred Per Cent Americans on Strike." *Nation*, May 8, 1929, pp. 554–56.

Bond, Horace Mann. *The Education of the Negro in the American Social Order*. New York, 1934.

_____. *Negro Education in Alabama: A Study in Cotton and Steel*. Washington, D.C., 1939.

_____. "A Negro Looks at His South." *Harper's Monthly Magazine*, June 1931, pp. 98–108.

Books from Chapel Hill: A Record and Catalogue of Twenty-four Years of Publishing, 1923–1945. Chapel Hill, 1946.

Branson, Eugene Cunningham. *Farm Life Abroad: Field Letters from Germany, Denmark, and France*. Chapel Hill, 1924.

_____. "Farm Tenancy in the Cotton Belt: How Farm Tenants Live." *Social Forces* 1, no. 3 (March 1923): 213–21.

_____. "Farm Tenancy in the South: The Social Estate of White Farm Tenants." *Social Forces* 1, no. 4 (May 1923): 450–57.

Brawley, Benjamin. "The Lower Rungs of the Ladder." *Reviewer* 5, no. 4 (October 1925): 78–86.

_____. *The Negro Genius: A New Appraisal of the Achievement of the American Negro in Literature and the Fine Arts*. New York, 1937.

_____. "A Southern Boyhood." *Reviewer* 5, no. 3 (July 1925): 1–8.

Brearley, Harrington Cooper. "Ba-ad Nigger," *South Atlantic Quarterly* 38, no. 1 (January 1939): 75–81.

_____. *Homicide in the United States*. Chapel Hill, 1932.

_____. "The Negro and Homicide." *Social Forces* 9, no. 2 (December 1930): 247–53.

Brown, Roy M. *Public Relief in North Carolina*. Chapel Hill, 1928.

_____, and Steiner, Jesse F. *The North Carolina Chain Gang: A Study of County Convict Road Work*. Chapel Hill, 1927.

Brown, Sterling A. "Negro Character as Seen by White Authors." *Journal of Negro Education* 2, no. 2 (April 1933): 179–203.

_____. *The Negro in American Fiction*. Washington, D.C., 1937.

Bruce, Philip A. *The Rise of the New South*. Philadelphia, 1905.

Cabell, James Branch. *Beyond Life: Dizain des Demiurges*. New York, 1919.

_____. *The Cream of the Jest*. New York, 1922.

_____. *Jurgen: A Comedy of Justice*. New York, 1919.

Cable, George W. *The Silent South*. New York, 1885.

Caldwell, Erskine. *God's Little Acre*. New York, 1933.

_____. *Tobacco Road*. New York, 1932.

_____, and Bourke-White, Margaret. *You Have Seen Their Faces*. New York, 1937.

Cash, Wilbur J. "Jehovah of the Tar Heels." *American Mercury*, July 1929, pp. 310–18.

_____. "The Mind of the South." *American Mercury*, October 1929, pp. 185–92.

_____. *The Mind of the South*. New York, 1941.

Cason, Clarence. *90° in the Shade*. Chapel Hill, 1935.

_____. "The Red Japonica." *Sewanee Review* 42, no. 2 (April–June 1934): 135–43.

Cayton, Horace R., and Mitchell, George S. *Black Workers and the New Unions*. Chapel Hill, 1939.

Clark, Emily Tapscott. "Eve and Mr. Cabell:—and the Archbishop." *Virginia Quarterly Review* 4, no. 1 (January 1928): 114–19.

_____. "French Art Notes." *Reviewer* 1, no. 2 (March 1, 1921): 50–53.

_____. *Ingenue among the Lions: The Letters of Emily Clark to Joseph Hergesheimer*. Edited with an introduction by Gerald Langford. Austin, 1965.

_____. *Innocence Abroad*. New York, 1931.

_____. *Stuffed Peacocks*. New York, 1928.

Cohn, David L. *God Shakes Creation*. New York, 1935.

Conrad, Joseph. *Lord Jim*. New York, 1921.

Couch, William Terry. "An Agrarian Programme for the South." *American Review* 3, no. 3 (June 1934): 313–26.

_____. "The Agrarian Romance." *South Atlantic Quarterly* 36, no. 4 (October 1937): 419–30.

_____. "American Peasants." *Virginia Quarterly Review* 10, no. 4 (October 1930): 636–40.

_____. Introduction to *What the Negro Wants*, edited by Rayford W. Logan, pp. ix–xxiii. Chapel Hill, 1944.

_____. "Landlord and Tenant." *Virginia Quarterly Review* 14, no. 2 (Spring 1938): 309–12.

_____. "Mr. Beals' American Earth Quakes." *Southern Review* 5, no. 4 (Spring 1940): 633–41.

_____. "Reflections on the Southern Tradition." *South Atlantic Quarterly* 35, no. 3 (July 1936): 284–97.

_____. "Southerners Inspect the South." *New Republic*, December 14, 1938, pp. 168–69.

_____. "The Southern Mind." *Virginia Quarterly Review* 17, no. 3 (Summer 1941): 465–69.

_____. "The University Press as an Aid to Scholarship." *Journal of Proceedings and Addresses of the Association of American Universities* 36 (October 1934): 136–49.

_____. "A University Press in the South." *Southwest Review* 19, no. 2 (Winter 1934): 195–204.

_____, ed. *Culture in the South*. Chapel Hill, 1934.

_____, ed. *These Are Our Lives: As Told by the People and Written by Members of the Federal Writers' Project of the Works Progress Administration in North Carolina, Tennessee, and Georgia*. Chapel Hill, 1939.

_____, and Bailey, Josiah O. "Dynamite in Burlington." *Carolina Magazine* (April 1935): 18–21.

Craven, Avery O. *Edmund Ruffin, Southerner: A Study in Secession*. New York, 1932.

_____. *Soil Exhaustion as a Factor in the Agricultural History of Virginia and Maryland, 1606–1860*. Urbana, Ill., 1926.

Dabney, Virginius. *Below the Potomac: A Book about the New South*. New York, 1942.

_____. "Civil Liberties in the South." *Virginia Quarterly Review* 16, no. 1 (Winter 1940): 81–91.

_____. *Liberalism in the South*. Chapel Hill, 1932.

_____. "Southern Employers and Labor Reform." *Southern Review* 2, no. 2 (1935): 279–88.

_____. "The Voice of Reaction in Tarheelia." Richmond *Times-Dispatch*, September 18, 1932.

Daniels, Jonathan Worth. "The Aspiring South." *Raleigh News and Observer*, February 5, 1934.

———. "Democracy Is Bread." *Virginia Quarterly Review* 14, no. 4 (Autumn 1938): 481–90.

———. *A Southerner Discovers the South*. New York, 1938.

Davidson, Donald. "The Artist as Southerner." *Saturday Review of Literature*, May 15, 1926, pp. 781–83.

———. *The Attack on Leviathan: Regionalism and Nationalism in the United States*. Chapel Hill, 1938.

———. "Certain Fallacies in Modern Poetry." *Fugitive* 3, no. 3 (June 1924): 66–68.

———. "First Fruits of Dayton: The Intellectual Evolution in Dixie." *Forum* 79, no. 6 (June 1928): 896–907.

———. "Mr. Babbitt at Philadelphia." *Southern Review* 6, no. 4 (Spring 1941): 695–705.

———. "Mr. Cash and the Proto-Dorian South." *Southern Review* 7, no. 1 (Summer 1941): 1–20.

———. *An Outland Piper*. Boston, 1924.

———. *Southern Writers in the Modern World*. Athens, Ga., 1958.

———. *The Spyglass: Views and Reviews, 1924–1930*. Edited by John Tyree Fain. Nashville, 1963.

———. "Swan and Exile." *Fugitive* 3, no. 3 (June 1924): 80.

———. *The Tall Men*. Boston, 1927.

———. "Two Ways of Poetry." *Fugitive* 4, no. 3 (September 1925): 94–95.

Dewey, John. *The Influence of Darwinism on Philosophy*. New York, 1910.

Dollard, John. *Caste and Class in a Southern Town*. New Haven, 1937.

"Do You Know Your Own South? . . . The Editors Answer Their Own Questions." *North Georgia Review* 5, nos. 1–4 (Winter 1941): 47–128.

Faulkner, William. *Absalom, Absalom!* 1936. Reprint. New York, 1951.

———. *As I Lay Dying*. 1930. Reprint. New York, 1946.

———. *Early Prose and Poetry*. Edited by Carvel Collins. Boston, 1962.

———. *Faulkner in the University: Class Conferences at the University of Virginia, 1957–1958*. Edited by Frederick L. Gwynn and Joseph L. Blotner. New York, 1965.

———. *Flags in the Dust*. Edited by Douglas Day. New York, 1973.

———. *Go Down, Moses*. 1942. Reprint. New York, 1955.

———. "An Introduction for *The Sound and the Fury*," edited by James B. Meriwether. *Southern Review*, n.s. 8, no. 4 (October 1972): 705–10.

———. "An Introduction to *The Sound and the Fury*" (alternate draft). In *A Faulkner Miscellany*, edited by James B. Meriwether, pp. 156–61. Jackson, Miss., 1974.

———. *Light in August*. 1932. Reprint. New York, 1959.

———. *Mosquitoes*. 1927. Reprint. New York, 1965.

———. *Sanctuary*. 1931. Reprint. New York, 1954.

———. *Sartoris*. 1929. Reprint. New York, 1953.

———. *Selected Letters of William Faulkner*. Edited by Joseph L. Blotner. New York, 1977.

———. *Selected Short Stories of William Faulkner*. New York, 1962.

———. *Soldier's Pay*. 1926. Reprint. New York, 1951.

———. *The Sound and the Fury*. 1929. Reprint. New York, 1946.

———. *The Uncollected Stories of William Faulkner*. Edited by Joseph L. Blotner. New York, 1979.

———. *The Unvanquished*. 1938. Reprint. New York, 1959.

———. "William Faulkner's Essay on the Composition of *Sartoris*," edited by Joseph L.

Blotner. *Yale University Library Gazette* 37, no. 3 (January 1974): 121–24.

————, and Spratling, William. *Sherwood Anderson and Other Famous Creoles: A Gallery of Contemporary New Orleans*. New Orleans, 1926.

"The Function of the Wrecker." Unsigned editorial. *Double Dealer* 3, no. 18 (June 1922): 286–87.

Gaines, Francis Pendleton. *The Southern Plantation: A Study in the Development and Accuracy of a Tradition*. New York, 1924.

Gee, Wilson. "The Contribution of the Country-Side." *South Atlantic Quarterly* 23, no. 3 (July 1924): 211–17.

————. "The Distinctiveness of Southern Culture." *South Atlantic Quarterly* 38, no. 2 (April 1939): 119–29.

————. *The Place of Agriculture in American Life*. New York, 1930.

————. *Research Barriers in the South*. Chapel Hill, 1932.

————. "The Rural South." *Social Forces* 2, no. 5 (September 1925): 713–17.

Glasgow, Ellen. *Barren Ground*. 1925. Reprint. New York, 1957.

————. *A Certain Measure*. New York, 1943.

————. *Letters of Ellen Glasgow*. Edited by Blair Rouse. New York, 1958.

————. *The Romantic Comedians*. Garden City, N.Y., 1926.

————. *The Sheltered Life*. Garden City, N.Y., 1932.

————. *They Stooped to Folly*. Garden City, N.Y., 1929.

————. *Vein of Iron*. New York, 1935.

————. *Virginia*. Garden City, N.Y., 1913.

Grady, Henry W. "The New South." In *Joel Chandler Harris' Life of Henry W. Grady, Including His Writings and Speeches*. Edited by Joel Chandler Harris. New York, 1890.

Graham, Edward Kidder. *Education and Citizenship and Other Papers*. Edited by Louis R. Wilson. New York, 1919.

Green, Fletcher M. *Constitutional Development in the South Atlantic States, 1776–1860*. Chapel Hill, 1930.

Green, Paul. *The Lord's Will and Other Carolina Plays*. New York, 1925.

————. "A Plain Statement about Southern Literature." *Reviewer* 5, no. 1 (January 1925): 71–76.

Haardt, Sara. "Alabama," *American Mercury* 6, no. 21 (September 1925): 85–91.

————. "The Southern Lady Says Grace." *Reviewer* 5, no. 4 (October 1925): 57–63.

Hall, Grover C. "We Southerners." *Scribner's Magazine*, January 1928, pp. 82–88.

Heer, Clarence. *Income and Wages in the South*. Chapel Hill, 1930.

Herring, Harriet L. "The Beginnings of Industrial Social Work." *Social Forces* 5, no. 2 (December 1926): 317–24.

————. "Cycles of Cotton Mill Criticism." *South Atlantic Quarterly* 28, no. 2 (April 1929): 113–25.

————. "The Outside Employer in the Southern Industrial Pattern." *Social Forces* 18, no. 1 (October 1939): 115–26.

————. "Social Development in the Mill Village: A Challenge to the Mill Welfare Worker." *Social Forces* 10, no. 2 (December 1931): 264–71.

————. "The Social Problem of Labor Organization Casualties." *Social Forces* 9, no. 2 (December 1930): 267–73.

————. *Southern Industry and Regional Development*. Chapel Hill, 1940.

————. "The Southern Mill System Faces a New Issue." *Social Forces* 8, no. 3 (March 1930): 350–59.

————. "The South Goes to the Bindery." *Social Forces* 9, no. 3 (March 1931): 428–29.

———. "Tracing the Development of Welfare Work in the North Carolina Textile Industry." *Social Forces* 6, no. 4 (June 1928): 591–98.

———. "12 Cents, the Troops, and the Union." *Survey*, November 15, 1927, pp. 199–202.

———. *Welfare Work in Mill Villages: The Story of Extra-Mill Activities in North Carolina*. Chapel Hill, 1929.

Herskovits, Melville J. *The Myth of the Negro Past*. New York, 1941.

———. "Negro Art: African and American." *Social Forces* 5, no. 2 (December 1926): 291–98.

Heyward, Du Bose. *Porgy*. New York, 1925.

Hibbard, Addison. "Literature South—1924." *Reviewer* 5, no. 1 (January 1925): 52–58.

Hobbs, Samuel H., Jr. "Developing a State Through Student Club Work." *Social Forces* 2, no. 1 (November 1924): 48–49.

———. *North Carolina: Economic and Social*. Chapel Hill, 1930.

Irish, Marion D. "Proposed Roads to the New South, 1941: Chapel Hill Planners vs. Nashville Agrarians." *Sewanee Review* 49, no. 1 (January–March 1941): 1–27.

James, William. *A Pluralistic Universe*. New York, 1909.

Jenkins, William S. *Pro-Slavery Thought in the Old South*. Chapel Hill, 1935.

Johnson, Charles Spurgeon. *Growing Up in the Black Belt: Negro Youth in the Rural South*. Washington, D.C., 1941.

———. "The Present Status and Trends of the Negro Family." *Social Forces* 16, no. 2 (December 1937): 247–57.

———. "The Present Status of Race Relations with Particular Reference to the Negro." *Journal of Negro Education* 8, no. 3 (July 1939): 323–35.

———. *Shadow of the Plantation*. Chicago, 1934.

———; Embree, Edward R.; and Alexander, Will W. *The Collapse of Cotton Tenancy: Summary of Field Studies and Statistical Surveys, 1933–1935*. Chapel Hill, 1935.

Johnson, Gerald W. "Chase of North Carolina." *American Mercury*, June 1929, pp. 183–90.

———. "The Congo, Mr. Mencken." *Reviewer* 3, nos. 11 and 12 (July 1923): 887–93.

———. "Critical Attitudes North and South." *Social Forces* 2, no. 4 (May 1924): 575–79.

———. "Greensboro, or What You Will." *Reviewer* 4, no. 3 (April 1924): 169–75.

———. "The Horrible South." *Virginia Quarterly Review* 11, no. 2 (April 1935): 201–17.

———. "Issachar Is a Strong Ass." *Social Forces* 2, no. 1 (November 1924): 5–9.

———. "Journalism Below the Potomac." *American Mercury*, September 1926, pp. 77–82.

———. "Mr. Babbitt Arrives at Erzerum." *Social Forces* 1, no. 3 (March 1923): 206–9.

———. "North Carolina in a New Phase." *Current History* 27, no. 6 (March 1928): 843–48.

———. "Onion Salt." *Reviewer* 5, no. 1 (January 1925): 60–63.

———. "Service in the Cotton Mills." *American Mercury*, June 1925, pp. 219–23.

———. "The South Faces Itself." *Virginia Quarterly Review* 7, no. 1 (January 1931): 152–57.

———. *The Wasted Land*. Chapel Hill, 1937.

Johnson, Guy B. "Background Studies." *Social Forces* 5, no. 4 (June 1927): 662–65.

———. "Does the South Owe the Negro a New Deal?" *Social Forces* 13, no. 1 (October 1934): 100–103.

———. "Double Meaning in the Popular Negro Blues." *Journal of Abnormal and Social Psychology* 22, no. 1 (April–June 1927): 12–20.

————. "Education, Segregation, and Race Relations." *Quarterly Review of Higher Education Among Negroes* 3, no. 2 (April 1935): 89–94.

————. *Folk Culture on St. Helena Island, South Carolina.* Chapel Hill, 1930.

————. "Isolation or Integration?" *Journal of Negro Life* 13, no. 3 (March 1935): 89–90.

————. *John Henry: Tracking Down a Negro Legend.* Chapel Hill, 1929.

————. "The Negro and the Depression in North Carolina." *Social Forces* 12, no. 1 (October 1933): 103–15.

————. "The Negro Migration and Its Consequences." *Social Forces* 2, no. 4 (May 1924): 404—8.

————. "Negro Racial Movements and Leadership in the United States." *American Journal of Sociology* 43, no. 1 (July 1937): 57–71.

————. "The Negro Spiritual: A Problem in Anthropology." *American Anthropologist* 33, no. 2 (April–June 1931): 157–71.

————. "Newspaper Advertisements and Negro Culture." *Social Forces* 3, no. 4 (May 1925): 706–9.

————. "Personality in a White-Indian-Negro Community." *American Sociological Review* 4, no. 4 (August 1939): 516–23.

————. "The Race Philosophy of the Ku Klux Klan." *Opportunity* 1, no. 9 (September 1923): 268–70.

————. "Recent Contributions to the Study of American Negro Songs." *Social Forces* 4, no. 4 (June 1926): 788–93.

————. "A Sociological Interpretation of the New Ku Klux Movement." *Social Forces* 1, no. 4 (May 1923): 440–45.

————. "Some Factors in the Development of Negro Social Institutions in the United States." *American Journal of Sociology* 40, no. 3 (November 1934): 329–37.

————. "Some Methods of Reducing Race Prejudice in the South." *Southern Workman* 64, no. 9 (September 1935): 272–78.

————. "Southern Offensive." *Common Ground* 4, no. 4 (Summer 1944): 87–93.

————. "The Speech of the Negro" and "Folk Values in Recent Literature on the Negro." In *Folk-Say*, vol. 2, pp. 346–72. Norman, Okla., 1930.

————. "A Study of the Musical Talent of the American Negro." Ph.D. dissertation, University of North Carolina, 1927.

Jones, Howard Mumford. "The Future of Southern Culture." *Southwest Review* 16, no. 2 (January 1931): 141–63.

————. "Is There a Southern Renaissance?" *Virginia Quarterly Review* 6, no. 2 (April 1930): 184–97.

Jones, M. Ashby. "The Negro and the South." *Virginia Quarterly Review* 3, no. 1 (January 1927): 1–12.

Kane, Harnett T. *Louisiana Hayride: The American Rehearsal for Dictatorship, 1928–1940.* New York, 1941.

Keister, Albert S. Review of *General Economics*, by Broadus Mitchell. *Social Forces* 17, no. 3 (March 1939): 435–36.

Kendrick, Benjamin B. "Research by Southern Social Science Teachers." *Social Forces* 9, no. 3 (March 1931): 362–69.

————. Review of *Culture in the South*, edited by William T. Couch, *Annals of the American Academy of Political and Social Science*, 173 (May 1934): 218–19.

————. "A Southern Confederation of Learning." *Southwest Review* 19, no. 2 (Winter 1934): 182–95.

Kilgo, John C. "An Inquiry Concerning Lynchings." *South Atlantic Quarterly* 1, no. 1 (January 1902): 4–13.

Lanier, Lyle H., and Peterson, Joseph. *Studies in the Comparative Abilities of Whites and Negroes*. Baltimore, 1929.

Lewis, Nell Battle. "North Carolina." *American Mercury*, May 1926, pp. 36–43.

————. "North Carolina at the Cross-Roads." *Virginia Quarterly Review* 6, no. 1 (January 1930): 37–47.

————. "The University of North Carolina Gets Its Orders." *Nation*, February 3, 1926, pp. 114–15.

Logan, Rayford, W., ed. *What the Negro Wants*. Chapel Hill, 1944.

Lumpkin, Katharine Du Pre. *The South in Progress*. New York, 1940.

Lytle, Andrew Nelson. "The Backwoods Progression." *American Review* 1, no. 4 (September 1933): 409–34.

————. "John Taylor and the Political Economy of Agriculture." *American Review* 3, no. 4 (September 1934): 432–47.

McCulloch, S. R. "Red-Baiting." *New Orleans Item*, January 20, 1937, p. 1.

————. "Red-Baiting in a Big Way in New Orleans." *St. Louis Post Dispatch*, November 22, 1936, sec. 1, pp. 1–3.

MacDonald, Lois. *Southern Mill Hands: A Study of Social and Economic Forces in Certain Textile Mill Villages*. New York, 1928.

McIlwaine, Shields. *The Southern Poor White: From Lubberland to Tobacco Road*. Norman, Okla., 1939.

Mencken, H. L. "God Help the South!" In *Prejudices, Sixth Series*, pp. 141–44. New York, 1927.

————. "Morning Song in C Major." *Reviewer* 2, no. 2 (October 1921): 1–5.

————. "The Sahara of the Bozart." In *Prejudices: Second Series*, pp. 136–38. New York, 1920.

Miller, Francis P., ed. *Second Southern Policy Conference Report*. Southern Policy Papers, no. 8. Chapel Hill, 1936.

Miller, John G. *The Black Patch War*. Chapel Hill, 1936.

Milton, George Fort. "Democracy—Whither Bound?" *Virginia Quarterly Review* 2, no. 1 (January 1926): 17–30.

————. "The Duties of an Educated Southerner." *Sewanee Review* 38, no. 1 (January 1930): 61–70.

————. "The Impeachment of Judge Lynch." *Virginia Quarterly Review* 8, no. 2 (April 1932): 247–56.

————. "What Are Democratic Institutions?" *Chattanooga News*, May 12, 1936, p. 4.

Mims, Edwin. *The Advancing South: Stories of Progress and Reaction*. Garden City, N.Y., 1926.

————. "The Function of Criticism in the South." *South Atlantic Quarterly* 31, no. 2 (April 1932): 133–49.

"Mr. Cabell of Virginia." Unsigned editorial. *Double Dealer* 1, no. 1 (January 1921): 5–7.

Mitchell, Broadus. *Alexander Hamilton: Youth to Maturity*. New York, 1957.

————. "American Radicals Nobody Knows." *South Atlantic Quarterly* 34, no. 4 (October 1935): 394–401.

————. *Depression Decade: From New Era through New Deal, 1929–1941*. New York, 1955.

————. "Employers Front!" *Virginia Quarterly Review* 6, no. 4 (October 1930): 495–506.

————. *Frederick Law Olmsted: A Critic of the Old South*. Baltimore, 1924.

————. "Hamilton and Jefferson Today." *Virginia Quarterly Review* 10, no. 3 (July 1934): 394–407.

————. *How to Start Workers' Study Classes: A Primer to Promote Workers' Education.* New York, 1925.

————. *A Preface to Economics.* New York, 1932.

————. *The Rise of Cotton Mills in the South.* Baltimore, 1921.

————. *William Gregg: Factory Master of the Old South.* Chapel Hill, 1928.

————, and Mitchell, George S. *The Industrial Revolution in the South.* Baltimore, 1930.

Mitchell, George Sinclair. "The Labor Union Problem in the Southern Textile Industry." *Social Forces* 3, no. 4 (May 1925): 727–32.

————. "The Negro in Southern Trade Unionism." *Southern Economic Journal* 2, no. 3 (January 1936): 26–33.

————. *Textile Unionism and the South.* Chapel Hill, 1931.

Monroe, Harriet. "The Old South." *Poetry: A Magazine of Verse* 22, no. 2 (May 1923): 89–92.

Morse, Josiah. "The Outlook for the Negro." *Sewanee Review* 28, no. 2 (April 1920): 152–59.

————. "A Social Interpretation: South Carolina." *Social Forces* 4, no. 4 (June 1926): 690–701.

————. "The University Commission on Southern Race Questions." *South Atlantic Quarterly* 19, no. 4 (October 1920): 302–10.

Murchison, Claudius T. *King Cotton Is Sick.* Chapel Hill, 1930.

Murphy, Edgar Gardner. *Problems of the Present South.* New York, 1904.

Myrdal, Gunnar. *An American Dilemma: The Negro Problem and Modern Democracy.* 2 vols. New York, 1944.

National Emergency Council. *Report on Economic Conditions of the South.* Washington, D.C., 1938.

Nixon, Herman Clarence. "The Changing Background of Southern Politics." *Social Forces* 11, no. 1 (October 1932): 14–18.

————. "The Changing Political Philosophy of the South." *Annals of the American Academy of Political and Social Science* 153 (January 1931): 246–50.

————. "Farm Tenancy to the Forefront." *Southwest Review* 22, no. 1 (October 1936): 11–15.

————. *Forty Acres and Steel Mules.* Chapel Hill, 1938.

O'Donnell, George Marion. "Portrait of a Southern Planter: 1920–1932." *American Review* 3, no. 5 (October 1934): 608–20.

Odum, Howard Washington. *An American Epoch: Southern Portraiture in the National Picture.* New York, 1930.

————. "The Case for Regional-National Social Planning." *Social Forces* 13, no. 1 (October 1934): 6–23.

————. *Cold Blue Moon: A Novel of the Old South.* Indianapolis, 1931.

————. "Democracy and the KKK." *Social Forces* 1, no. 2 (January 1923): 178–83.

————. "The Discovery of the People." *Social Forces* 4, no. 2 (December 1925): 414–17.

————. "The Duel to the Death." *Social Forces* 4, no. 1 (September 1925): 189–94.

————. "Editorial Notes." *Social Forces* 1, no. 1 (November 1922): 56–61.

————. "The Errors of Sociology." *Social Forces* 15, no. 3 (March 1937): 327–42.

————. *Folk, Region, and Society: Selected Papers of Howard W. Odum.* Arranged and edited by Katharine Jocher, Guy B. Johnson, George Lee Simpson, Jr., and Rupert B. Vance. Chapel Hill, 1964.

————. "From Sections to Regions." *Saturday Review of Literature*, June 12, 1937, p. 5.

————. "Fundamental Problems Underlying Interracial Cooperation." *Social Forces* 1, no. 3 (March 1923): 282–85.

———. "G. Stanley Hall: Pioneer in Scientific Social Exploration." *Social Forces* 3, no. 1 (November 1924): 139–46.

———. "Industrial Democracy." *Social Forces* 1, no. 3 (March 1923): 315–20.

———. "Lynching, Fears, and Folkways." *Nation*, December 30, 1931, pp. 719–20.

———. "Modern Equivalents for Early Rural Pioneering Forces." *Social Forces* 2, no. 1 (November 1924): 111–14.

———. "A More Articulate South." *Social Forces* 2, no. 5 (September 1924): 730–35.

———. "New Frontiers of American Life." *Southwest Review* 18, no. 4 (July 1933): 418–29.

———. "Notes on the Study of Regional and Folk Society." *Social Forces* 10, no. 2 (December 1931): 164–75.

———. *Rainbow Round My Shoulder: The Blue Trail of Black Ulysses*. Indianapolis, 1928.

———. "Regionalism vs. Sectionalism in the South's Place in the National Economy." *Social Forces* 12, no. 3 (March 1933): 338–54.

———. "Regional Portraiture." *Saturday Review of Literature*, July 27, 1929, pp. 1–2.

———. "The 'Scientific-Human' in Social Research." *Social Forces* 8, no. 3 (March 1929): 350–62.

———. "The Search After Values." *Social Forces* 2, no. 5 (September 1924): 638–39.

———. *Social and Mental Traits of the Negro: Research into the Conditions of the Negro Race in Southern Towns*. New York, 1910.

———. "A Southern Promise." *Social Forces* 3, no. 4 (May 1925): 739–46.

———. *Southern Regions of the United States*. Chapel Hill, 1936.

———. "The State of Sociology in the United States and Its Prospect in the South." *Social Forces* 17, no. 1 (October 1938): 8–14.

———. "University Training and Research in Social Science." *Social Forces*, 3, no. 3 (March 1925): 518–24.

———, ed. *Southern Pioneers in Social Interpretation*. Chapel Hill, 1925.

———, and Johnson, Guy B. *The Negro and His Songs: A Study of Typical Negro Songs in the South*. Chapel Hill, 1925.

———, and Johnson, Guy B. *Negro Workaday Songs*. Chapel Hill, 1926.

Olmsted, Frederick L. *The Cotton Kingdom: A Traveller's Observations on Cotton and Slavery in the American Slave States*. Edited with an introduction by Arthur M. Schlesinger. New York, 1953.

Owsley, Frank L. "A Key to Southern Liberalism." *Southern Review* 3, no. 1 (1937): 28–38.

———. "Scottsboro, the Third Crusade: The Sequel to Abolition and Reconstruction." *American Review* 1, no. 3 (June 1933): 257–84.

———. "The Soldier Who Walked with God." *American Review* 4, no. 4 (February 1935): 435–59.

Parks, Edd W. *Segments of Southern Thought*. Athens, Ga., 1938.

Parrington, Vernon L. *Main Currents in American Thought*. 3 vols. New York, 1927–30.

Peery, J. R. Review of *The Negro and His Songs: A Study of Typical Negro Songs in the South*, by Howard W. Odum and Guy B. Johnson. *Memphis Commercial-Appeal*, September 27, 1925.

Peterkin, Julia. *Black April*. Indianapolis, 1927.

———. *Scarlet Sister Mary*. New York, 1928.

Phillips, Ulrich Bonnell. *American Negro Slavery: A Survey of the Supply, Employment, and Control of Negro Labor as Determined by the Plantation Regime*. New York, 1918.

————. "The Central Theme of Southern History." *American Historical Review* 34, no. 1 (October 1928): 30–43.

————. "Conservatism and Progress in the Cotton Belt." *South Atlantic Quarterly* 3, no. 1 (January 1904): 1–10.

————. *The Course of the South to Secession.* Edited by E. Merton Coulter. New York, 1964.

————. "The Economic Cost of Slaveholding in the Cotton Belt." *Political Science Quarterly* 20, no. 2 (June 1905): 257–75.

————. "The Economics of the Plantation." *South Atlantic Quarterly* 2, no. 3 (July 1903): 231–36.

————. "Fifteen Vocal Southerners." *Yale Review* 20, no. 3 (March 1931): 611–13.

————. "Georgia and States Rights: A Study of the Political History of Georgia from the Revolution to the Civil War, with Particular Regard to Federal Relations." *Annual Report of the American Historical Association.* 2 vols. Washington, D.C., 1902.

————. *Life and Labor in the Old South.* Boston, 1929.

————. "The Origin and Growth of the Southern Black Belts." *American Historical Review* 11, no. 4 (July 1906): 798–816.

————. "The Perennial Negro." *Yale Review* 21, no. 1 (September 1931): 202–4.

————. "The Plantation as a Civilizing Factor." *Sewanee Review* 12, no. 3 (July 1904): 257–67.

————. "Plantations with Slave Labor and Free." *American Historical Review* 30, no. 4 (July 1925): 738–53.

————. *The Slave Economy of the Old South: Selected Essays in Economic and Social History.* Edited by Eugene D. Genovese. Baton Rouge, 1968.

————. "The Slave Labor Problem in the Charleston District." *Political Science Quarterly* 22, no. 3 (September 1907): 416–39.

————. "Transportation in the *Ante-Bellum* South: An Economic Analysis." *Quarterly Journal of Economics* 19, no. 3 (May 1905): 434–51.

————; Commons, John R.; Gilmore, Eugene A.; Sumner, Helen L.; and Andrews, John B.; eds. *Documentary History of American Industrial Society.* 10 vols. Vol. 1: *Plantation and Frontier Documents.* Cleveland, 1910–11.

Pipkin, Charles W. *Social Legislation in the South.* Southern Policy Paper, no. 3. Chapel Hill, 1936.

————. "The Southern Philosophy of States' Rights: The Old Sectionalism and the New Regionalism." *Southwest Review* 19, no. 2 (Winter 1934): 175–82.

Porter, Katherine Anne. *The Old Order: Stories of the South.* New York, 1958.

Powdermaker, Hortense. *After Freedom: A Cultural Study in the Deep South.* New York, 1939.

President's Research Committee on Social Trends. *Recent Social Trends in the United States.* Washington, D.C., 1933.

President's Special Committee on Farm Tenancy. *Farm Tenancy.* Washington, D.C., 1937.

Puckett, Newbell Niles. *The Magic and Folk Beliefs of the Southern Negro.* Chapel Hill, 1926.

Ransom, John Crowe. "The Aesthetic of Regionalism." *American Review* 2, no. 3 (January 1934): 290–310.

————. "Art and the Human Economy." *Kenyon Review* 7, no. 41 (Autumn 1945): 683–88.

————. "A Capital for the New Deal." *American Review* 2, no. 2 (December 1933): 129–42.

————. "A Doctrine of Relativity." *Fugitive* 4, no. 3 (September 1925): 93–95.

———. "Editorial." *Fugitive* 1, no. 3 (1922): 66–68.

———. "The Future of Poetry." *Fugitive* 3, no. 1 (February 1924): 2–4.

———. *God Without Thunder: An Unorthodox Defense of Orthodoxy.* New York, 1930.

———. "Happy Farmers." *American Review* 1, no. 5 (October 1933): 513–35.

———. "Hearts and Heads." *American Review* 2, no. 5 (March 1934): 554–71.

———. "Land! An Answer to the Unemployment Problem." *Harper's Monthly Magazine*, July, 1932, pp. 219–23.

———. "Mixed Modes." *Fugitive* 4, no. 1 (March 1925): 28–29.

———. "Modern with the Southern Accent." *Virginia Quarterly Review* 11, no. 2 (April 1935): 184–200.

———. *The New Criticism.* New York, 1941.

———. *Poems About God.* New York, 1919.

———. *Poems and Essays.* New York, 1955.

———. "Sociology and the Black Belt." *American Review* 4, no. 2 (December 1934): 147–54.

———. "The South Is a Bulwark." *Scribner's*, May 1936, pp. 299–303.

———. "Thoughts on the Poetic Discontent." *Fugitive* 4, no. 2 (June 1925): 63–64.

———. *The World's Body.* New York, 1938.

Raper, Arthur Franklin. "Gullies and What They Mean." *Social Forces* 16, no. 2 (December 1937): 201–7.

———. *Preface to Peasantry: A Tale of Two Black Belt Counties.* Chapel Hill, 1936.

———. *Tenants of the Almighty.* New York, 1943.

———. *The Tragedy of Lynching.* Chapel Hill, 1933.

———, and Reid, Ira De A. "Old Conflicts in the New South." *Virginia Quarterly Review* 16, no. 2 (Spring 1940): 218–29.

———, and Reid, Ira De A. *Sharecroppers All.* Chapel Hill, 1941.

Rhyne, Jennings J. *Some Southern Mill Workers and Their Villages.* Chapel Hill, 1933.

Rourke, Constance. "The Land and Its People in a Living Alliance." Review of *Culture in the South*, edited by William T. Couch. *New York Herald-Tribune*, February 4, 1934, p. 4.

Sanders, Wiley B. *Negro Child Welfare in North Carolina.* Chapel Hill, 1933.

Santayana, George. *Character and Opinion in the United States.* 1920. Reprint. New York, 1967.

Scott, Mary Wingfield. "The Provincetown Players Invade Broadway." *Reviewer* 1, no. 1 (February 15, 1921): 15–19.

Shafer, Robert. "Humanism and Impudence." *Bookman* 70, no. 5 (January 1930): 489–98.

Shields, James W. "Woes of a Southern Liberal." *American Mercury* 34, no. 133 (January 1935): 73–79.

Simkins, Francis Butler. *Pitchfork Ben Tillman: South Carolinian.* Baton Rouge, 1944.

———. *The Tillman Movement in South Carolina.* Durham, N.C., 1926.

Smith, C. Alphonso. *Southern Literary Studies.* Chapel Hill, 1927.

Smith, Henry Nash. "Culture." *Southwest Review* 13, no. 2 (Winter 1928): 249–55.

———. "Three Southern Novels." *Southwest Review* 15, no. 1 (Autumn 1929): iii–v.

Smith, Lillian E. *Killers of the Dream.* New York, 1949.

———. "Southern Defensive—II." *Common Ground* 4, no. 3 (Spring 1944): 43–45.

Snelling, Paula. "Ellen Glasgow and Her South." *North Georgia Review* 6, nos. 1–4 (Winter 1941): 26–27.

———. "Southern Fiction and Chronic Suicide." *North Georgia Review* 3, no. 2 (Summer 1938): 3–6, 25–28.

Southern Policy Committee. *Southern Policy Papers 1–10.* Chapel Hill, 1936.

Stanard, Mary Newton. "Poe as Temperance Preacher." *Reviewer* 1, no. 2 (March 1, 1921): 41–45.

Steiner, Jessie F. *The American Community in Action: Case Studies of American Communities.* New York, 1928.

Stevenson, Robert Louis. *Dr. Jekyll and Mr. Hyde.* 1886. Reprint. New York, 1972.

Tannenbaum, Frank. *Darker Phases of the South.* New York, 1924.

Tate, Allen. *Collected Essays.* Denver, 1959.

———. "Emily Dickinson." *Outlook*, August 15, 1928, pp. 621–23.

———. "The Fallacy of Humanism." In *The Critique of Humanism: A Symposium*, edited by C. Hartley Grattan, pp. 131–66. New York, 1930.

———. *The Fathers.* New York, 1938.

———. *Jefferson Davis: His Rise and Fall.* New York, 1929.

———. *The Man of Letters in the Modern World: Selected Essays, 1928–1955.* New York, 1955.

———. *Memoirs and Opinions, 1926–1974.* Chicago, 1975.

———. "One Escape from the Dilemma." *Fugitive* 3, no. 2 (April 1924): 34–36.

———. *Poems: 1928–1931.* New York, 1932.

———. "Poetry and the Absolute." *Sewanee Review* 35, no. 1 (January 1927): 41–52.

———. "The Problem of the Unemployed: A Modest Proposal." *American Review* 1, no. 2 (May 1933): 129–49.

———. "The Profession of Letters in the South." *Virginia Quarterly Review* 11, no. 2 (April 1935): 161–76.

———. *Reactionary Essays on Poetry and Ideas.* New York, 1936.

———. *Reason in Madness: Critical Essays.* New York, 1941.

———. "Regionalism and Sectionalism." *New Republic*, December 23, 1931, 158–61.

———. "The Same Fallacy of Humanism: A Reply to Mr. Robert Shafer." *Bookman* 71, no. 1 (March 1930): 31–36.

———. "Spengler's Tract against Liberalism." *American Review* 3, no. 1 (April 1934): 41–47.

———. *Stonewall Jackson: The Good Soldier.* New York, 1928.

———. "A Traditionist Looks at Liberalism." *Southern Review* 1, no. 4 (Spring 1936): 731–44.

———. "A View of the Whole South." *American Review* 2, no. 4 (February 1934): 411–32.

———. "Where Are the People?" *American Review* 2, no. 2 (December 1933): 231–37.

———. "Whose Ox?" *Fugitive* 1, no. 4 (December 1922): 99–100.

Thompson, Edgar T. "The Planter in the Pattern of Race Relations in the South." *Social Forces* 19, no. 2 (December 1940): 244–68.

Thompson, Holland. *The New South: A Chronicle of Social and Industrial Evolution.* New Haven, 1919.

"Tulane and Sedition." Editorial in *New Orleans Item*, January 20, 1937.

Turner, Lorenzo Dow. *Africanisms in the Gullah Dialect.* 1949. Reprint. New York, 1969.

Twelve Southerners. *I'll Take My Stand: The South and the Agrarian Tradition.* New York, 1930.

Vance, Rupert Bayless. *All These People: The Nation's Human Resources in the South.* Chapel Hill, 1945.

———. "Aycock of North Carolina." *Southwest Review* 18, no. 3 (April 1933): 288–306.

———. "Braxton Bragg Comer: Alabama's Most Audacious." *Southwest Review* 19, no. 3 (April 1934): 245–64.

———. "The Concept of the Region." *Social Forces* 8, no. 2 (December 1929): 208–18.

————. "Cotton Culture and Social Life and Institutions of the South." *Publications of the American Sociological Society* 23, (1929): 51–59.

————. "The Economic Future in the Old Cotton Belt." *Southern Workman* 65, no. 3 (March 1936): 85–92.

————. "The Geography of Distinction: The Nation and Its Regions, 1790–1927." *Social Forces* 18, no. 2 (December 1939): 168–79.

————. *Human Factors in Cotton Culture: A Study in the Social Geography of the American South.* Chapel Hill, 1929.

————. *Human Geography of the South: A Study in Regional Resources and Human Adequacy.* Chapel Hill, 1932.

————. "Is Agrarianism for Farmers?" *Southern Review* 1, no. 1 (1935): 42–57.

————. "Little Man, What Now?" *Southern Review* 1, no. 3 (1935): 560–67.

————. "Planning the Southern Economy." *Southwest Review* 20, no. 2 (January 1935): 111–23.

————. "Rebels and Agrarians All: Studies in One-Party Politics." *Southern Review* 4, no. 1 (Summer 1938): 26–44.

————. *Regionalism and the South: Selected Papers of Rupert B. Vance.* Edited by John S. Reed and Daniel J. Singal. Chapel Hill, 1982.

————. *Research Memorandum on Population Redistribution within the United States.* New York, 1938.

————. *The South's Place in the Nation.* New York, 1936.

————. "Tennessee's War of the Roses." *Virginia Quarterly Review* 16, no. 3 (Summer 1940): 413–24.

————. "What of Submarginal Areas in Regional Planning?" *Social Forces* 12, no. 3 (March 1933): 315–29.

————, and Danilevsky, Nadia. "Population and the Pattern of Unemployment in the Southeast, 1930–1937." *Southern Economic Journal* 7, no. 2 (October 1940): 187–201.

————, and Wynne, Waller, Jr. "Folk Rationalizations in the 'Unwritten Law.'" *American Journal of Sociology* 39, no. 4 (January 1934): 483–92.

Wade, John Donald. *Augustus Baldwin Longstreet: A Study of the Development of Culture in the South.* New York, 1924.

————. Review of *An American Epoch: Southern Portraiture in the National Picture*, by Howard W. Odum. *Knoxville Journal*, November 2, 1930. (Copy in Odum Papers.)

Warren, Robert Penn. *All the King's Men.* New York, 1946.

————. *At Heaven's Gate.* New York, 1943.

————. "The Blind Poet: Sidney Lanier." *American Review* 2, no. 1 (November 1933): 27–45.

————. *The Circus in the Attic and Other Stories.* New York, 1947.

————. "The Fiction of Caroline Gordon." *Southwest Review* 20, no. 2 (January 1935): 5–10.

————. "Hawthorne, Anderson, and Frost." *New Republic*, May 16, 1928, pp. 399–401.

————. *John Brown: The Making of a Martyr.* New York, 1929.

————. "John Crowe Ransom: A Study in Irony." *Virginia Quarterly Review* 11, no. 1 (January 1935): 93–112.

————. "Katherine Anne Porter: Irony with a Center." *Kenyon Review* 4, no. 1 (Winter 1942): 29–42.

————. *Night Rider.* Boston, 1939.

————. "A Note on Three Southern Poets." *Poetry Magazine* 40, no. 2 (May 1932): 103–13.

————. "Not Local Color." *Virginia Quarterly Review* 8, no. 1 (January 1932): 153–60.

————. Review of *Sunrise Trumpets*, by Joseph Auslander. *Fugitive* 4, no. 1 (March 1925): 29–30.

————. "The Second American Revolution." *Virginia Quarterly Review* 7, no. 2 (April 1931): 282–88.

————. *Selected Poems, 1923–1943*. New York, 1944.

————. "T. S. Stribling: A Paragraph in the History of Critical Realism." *American Review* 2, no. 4 (February 1934): 463–86.

————. "When the Light Gets Green." *Southern Review* 1, no. 4 (1935): 799–806.

White, Newman I. "Racial Feeling in Negro Poetry." *South Atlantic Quarterly* 21, no. 1 (January 1922): 14–29.

————. "Racial Traits in the Negro Song." *Sewanee Review* 28, no. 3 (July 1920): 396–404.

White, Walter F. *A Man Called White: The Autobiography of Walter F. White*. New York, 1948.

————. *Rope and Faggot: A Biography of Judge Lynch*. New York, 1929.

Wilson, Louis R. "North Carolina—Publisher or Reader?" *Social Forces* 3, no. 2 (January 1925): 385–87.

Woods, Arthur Evans. Review of *Welfare Work in Mill Villages: The Story of Extra-Mill Activities in North Carolina*, by Harriet L. Herring. *American Journal of Sociology* 35, no. 4 (January 1930): 667–68.

Woodward, C. Vann. *The Burden of Southern History*. Baton Rouge, 1960.

————. *The South in Search of a Philosophy*. Gainesville, Fla., 1938.

————. *Tom Watson: Agrarian Rebel*. New York, 1938.

Woofter, Thomas J., Jr. *The Basis of Racial Adjustment*. Boston, 1925.

————. *Black Yeomanry: Life on St. Helena Island*. New York, 1930.

————. *Landlord and Tenant on the Cotton Plantation*. Washington, D.C., 1936.

————. "The Teaching of Sociology in the South." *Social Forces* 4, no. 1 (September 1925): 71–72.

Work, Monroe N. "Problems of Adjustment of Race and Class in the South." *Social Forces* 16, no. 1 (October 1937): 108–17.

————. "Racial Factors and Economic Forces in Land Tenure in the South." *Social Forces* 15, no. 2 (December 1936): 205–15.

————. "The South's Labor Problem." *South Atlantic Quarterly* 19, no. 1 (January 1920): 1–8.

Wright, Richard. *Native Son*. New York, 1940.

PUBLISHED WORKS: SECONDARY SOURCES

Aaron, Daniel. *Writers on the Left*. New York, 1961.

————, ed. *America in Crisis*. New York, 1952.

Adams, Agatha Boyd. *Paul Green of Chapel Hill*. Chapel Hill, 1951.

Adams, Richard P. *Faulkner: Myth and Motion*. Princeton, 1968.

Apter, David E., ed. *Ideology and Discontent*. New York, 1964.

Bailey, Hugh C. *Edgar Gardner Murphy: Gentle Progressive*. Coral Gables, Fla., 1968.

Bailey, Kenneth K. *Southern White Protestantism in the Twentieth Century*. New York, 1964.

Barrett, William. *Irrational Man: A Study in Existential Philosophy*. Garden City, N.Y., 1962.

Barth, J. Robert, ed. *Religious Perspectives in Faulkner's Fiction: Yoknapatawpha and Beyond.* Notre Dame, Ind., 1972.

Bell, Daniel. *The Cultural Contradictions of Capitalism.* New York, 1978.

Berger, Peter; Berger, Brigitte; and Keller, Hansfried. *The Homeless Mind: Modernization and Consciousness.* New York, 1973.

Berman, Marshall. "'All that is Solid Melts into Air': Marx, Modernism, and Modernization." *Dissent* 25, no. 1 (Winter 1978): 54–73.

Bertelson, David. *The Lazy South.* New York, 1967.

Blotner, Joseph. *Faulkner: A Biography.* 2 vols. New York, 1974.

———. ed. "William Faulkner's Essay on the Composition of *Sartoris*," *Yale University Library Gazette* 37, no. 3 (January 1974): 121–24.

———, ed. *William Faulkner's Library—a Catalogue.* Charlottesville, Va., 1964.

Bohner, Charles H. *Robert Penn Warren.* New York, 1964.

Bowen, Francis Jean. "The New Orleans *Double Dealer*, 1921–1926." *Louisiana Historical Quarterly* 39, no. 4 (October 1956): 443–56.

Bradbury, John M. *Renaissance in the South: A Critical History of the Literature, 1920–1960.* Chapel Hill, 1963.

Brandt, Joseph A. "A Pioneering Regional Press." *Southwest Review* 26, no. 1 (Autumn 1940): 26–36.

Brazil, Wayne D. "Howard W. Odum: The Building Years, 1884–1930." Ph.D. dissertation, Harvard University, 1975.

Bridenbaugh, Carl. *Myths and Realities: Societies of the Colonial South.* New York, 1968.

Brooks, Cleanth. *The Hidden God.* New Haven, 1963.

———. *William Faulkner: The Yoknapatawpha Country.* New Haven, 1963.

Broughton, Panthea Reid. *William Faulkner: The Abstract and the Actual.* Baton Rouge, 1974.

Bruner, Jerome S. *On Knowing: Essays for the Left Hand.* Cambridge, Mass., 1962.

Buckley, Jerome H. *The Victorian Temper: A Study in Literary Culture.* Cambridge, Mass., 1951.

Buffington, Robert. *The Equilibrist: A Study of John Crowe Ransom's Poems, 1916–1963.* Nashville, 1967.

Burn, W. L. *The Age of Equipoise: A Study of the Mid-Victorian Generation.* New York, 1965.

Burrows, Edward F. "The Commission on Interracial Cooperation in the South." Ph.D. dissertation, University of Wisconsin, 1955.

Carter, Dan T. *Scottsboro: A Tragedy of the American South.* Baton Rouge, 1969.

Cash, Wilbur J. *The Mind of the South.* New York, 1941.

Casper, Leonard. *Robert Penn Warren: The Dark and Bloody Ground.* Seattle, 1960.

Chadwick, Charles. *Symbolism.* London, 1971.

Chambers, Clarke A. *Seedtime of Reform: American Social Service and Social Action, 1918–1933.* Ann Arbor, 1967.

Chase, Richard V. *Quest for Myth.* Baton Rouge, 1949.

Clark, G. Kitson. *The Making of Victorian England.* New York, 1966.

Clayton, Bruce. *The Savage Ideal: Intolerance and Intellectual Leadership in the South, 1890–1914.* Baltimore, 1972.

Cohn, David L. *Where I Was Born and Raised.* Boston, 1948.

Cominos, Peter T. "Late-Victorian Sexual Respectability and the Social System." *International Review of Social History* 8, no. 1 (1963): 18–48.

Conrad, David E. *The Forgotten Farmer: The Story of Sharecroppers in the New Deal.* Urbana, Ill., 1965.

Cowan, Louise. *The Fugitive Group: A Literary History.* Baton Rouge, 1959.

Cowley, Malcolm. *The Faulkner-Cowley File: Letters and Memories, 1944–1962.* New York, 1966.

Daiches, David. *Some Late Victorian Attitudes.* London, 1969.

Davenport, F. Garvin, Jr. *The Myth of Southern History: Historical Consciousness in Twentieth-Century Southern Literature.* Nashville, 1970.

Davis, Joe Lee. *James Branch Cabell.* New York, 1962.

Davis, Hugh Graham, and Gurr, Ted Robert, eds. *Violence in America: Historical and Comparative Perspectives.* New York, 1969.

Davis, Lambert. "The Reviewer." *Virginia Quarterly Review* 7, no. 4 (October 1931): 617–20.

Degler, Carl N. *The Other South: Southern Dissenters in the Nineteenth Century.* New York, 1974.

Dudley, Edward J., and Novak, Maximillian E., eds. *The Wild Man Within: An Image in Western Thought from the Renaissance to Romanticism.* Pittsburgh, 1972.

Durham, Frank. "South Carolina's Poetry Society." *South Atlantic Quarterly* 52, no. 2 (April 1953): 277–85.

Dykeman, Wilma, and Stokely, James. *Seeds of Southern Change: The Life of Will Alexander.* Chicago, 1962.

Eaton, Clement. *Freedom of Thought in the Old South.* Durham, N.C., 1940.

————. *The Growth of Southern Civilization, 1790–1860.* New York, 1961.

————. *The Mind of the Old South.* Baton Rouge, 1964.

Eckenrode, H. J. *Jefferson Davis: President of the South.* New York, 1923.

Ehle, John. *The Free Men.* New York, 1965.

Elkins, Stanley M. *Slavery: A Problem in American Institutional and Intellectual Life.* New York, 1963.

Ellmann, Richard, and Feidelson, Charles, Jr., eds. *The Modern Tradition: Backgrounds of Modern Literature.* New York, 1965.

Erikson, Erik H. *Childhood and Society.* New York, 1963.

————. *Identity and the Life Cycle.* New York, 1959.

————. *Identity: Youth and Crisis.* New York, 1968.

Fain, John Tyree, and Young, Thomas Daniel, eds. *The Literary Correspondence of Donald Davidson and Allen Tate.* Athens, Ga., 1974.

Fallwell, Marshall, Jr., ed. *Allen Tate: A Bibliography.* New York, 1969.

Faust, Drew G. *A Sacred Circle: The Dilemma of the Intellectual in the Old South, 1840–1860.* Baltimore, 1977.

Feibleman, James K. "Literary New Orleans between the Wars." *Southern Review*, n.s., 1, no. 3 (July 1965): 702–19.

Fenichel, Otto. *The Psychoanalytic Theory of Neurosis.* New York, 1945.

Fishwick, Marshall W. *Virginia: A New Look at the Old Dominion.* New York, 1959.

Fredrickson, George M. *The Black Image in the White Mind: The Debate on Afro-American Character and Destiny, 1817–1914.* New York, 1971.

Freehling, William W. *Prelude to Civil War: The Nullification Controversy in South Carolina, 1816–1836.* New York, 1966.

Freidel, Frank. *F. D. R. and the South.* Baton Rouge, 1965.

Friedman, Lawrence J. *The White Savage: Racial Fantasies in the Postbellum South.* Englewood Cliffs, N.J., 1970.

Freud, Anna. *The Ego and the Mechanisms of Defense.* New York, 1946.

Freud, Sigmund. *General Psychological Theory.* Edited by Philip Rieff. New York, 1963.

Fries, Adelaide L. *The Road to Salem.* Chapel Hill, 1944.

Furniss, Norman F. *The Fundamentalist Controversy.* New Haven, 1954.

Gaston, Paul M. *The New South Creed: A Study in Southern Mythmaking.* New York, 1970.

Gatewood, Willard B., Jr. *Preachers, Pedagogues, and Politicians: The Evolution Controversy in North Carolina, 1920–1929.* Chapel Hill, 1966.

Gay, Peter. *Freud, Jews and Other Germans: Masters and Victims in Modernist Culture.* New York, 1978.

Genovese, Eugene. *The Political Economy of Slavery: Studies in the Economy and Society of the Slave South.* New York, 1965.

——————. "Race and Class in Southern History: An Appraisal of the Work of Ulrich Bonnell Phillips." *Agricultural History* 41, no. 4 (October 1967): 345–58.

——————. "Ulrich Bonnell Phillips and His Critics." Introduction to *American Negro Slavery,* by Ulrich B. Phillips. Baton Rouge, 1966.

——————. *The World the Slaveholders Made: Two Essays in Interpretation.* New York, 1969.

Godbold, E. Stanley, Jr., *Ellen Glasgow and the Woman Within.* Baton Rouge, 1972.

Gollin, Gillian L. *Moravians in Two Worlds: A Study of Changing Communities.* New York, 1967.

Gossett, Thomas F. *Race: The History of an Idea in America.* Dallas, 1963.

Grantham, Dewey W. *The Regional Imagination: The South and Recent American History.* Nashville, 1979.

Gray, Richard. *The Literature of Memory: Modern Writers of the American South.* Baltimore, 1977.

Gray, Wood. "Ulrich Bonnell Phillips." In *The Marcus W. Jernegan Essays in American Historiography,* edited by William T. Hutchinson, pp. 354–73. Chicago, 1937.

Hackney, F. Sheldon. "Southern Violence." In *Violence in America: Historical and Comparative Perspectives,* edited by Hugh Graham Davis and Ted Robert Gurr. New York, 1969.

Hall, David D. "The Victorian Connection." *American Quarterly* 27, no. 5 (December 1975): 561–74.

Haller, John S., and Haller, Robin M. *The Physician and Sexuality in Victorian America.* New York, 1977.

Handy, William J. *Kant and the Southern New Critics.* Austin, 1963.

Hartz, Louis. *The Liberal Tradition in America.* New York, 1955.

Higham, John. *Strangers in the Land: Patterns of American Nativism, 1860–1925.* New York, 1963.

Hill, Samuel S., Jr. *Religion and the Solid South.* Nashville, 1972.

Himmelfarb, Gertrude. *Victorian Minds.* New York, 1968.

Hobson, Fred C., Jr. *Serpent in Eden: H. L. Mencken and the South.* Chapel Hill, 1974.

Hoeveler, J. David, Jr. *The New Humanism: A Critique of Modern America, 1900–1940.* Charlottesville, 1977.

Hoffman, Frederick J. *The Twenties: American Writing in the Postwar Decade.* New York, 1962.

——————, and Vickery, Olga W., eds. *William Faulkner: Three Decades of Criticism.* New York, 1960.

Hofstadter, Richard. *The Progressive Historians.* New York, 1968.

——————. *Social Darwinism in American Thought.* Boston, 1955.

——————. "U. B. Phillips and the Plantation Legend." *Journal of Negro History* 29, no. 2 (April 1944): 109–24.

Hollis, Daniel W. *The University of South Carolina.* 2 vols. Columbia, S.C., 1951–56.

Holman, C. Hugh. *Three Modes of Southern Fiction: Ellen Glasgow, William Faulkner, Thomas Wolfe*. Athens, Ga., 1966.

Houghton, Walter E. *The Victorian Frame of Mind, 1830–1870*. New Haven, 1957.

Howe, Daniel Walker. "American Victorianism as a Culture." *American Quarterly* 27, no. 5 (December 1975): 507–32.

Howe, Irving. *The Decline of the New*. New York, 1968.

―――――. *William Faulkner: A Critical Study*. New York, 1962.

Huggins, Nathan I. *Harlem Renaissance*. New York, 1971.

Hughes, H. Stuart. *Consciousness and Society: The Reorientation of European Social Thought, 1890–1920*. New York, 1958.

Hunt, John W. *William Faulkner: Art in Theological Tension*. Syracuse, N.Y., 1965.

Hutchinson, William T., ed. *The Marcus W. Jernegan Essays in American Historiography*. Chicago, 1937.

Hynes, Samuel. *The Edwardian Turn of Mind*. Princeton, 1968.

Ideas and Beliefs of the Victorians. New York, 1966.

Irwin, John T. *Doubling and Incest/Repetition and Revenge: A Speculative Reading of Faulkner*. Baltimore, 1975.

Jacoway, Elizabeth. *Yankee Missionaries in the South: The Penn School Experiment*. Baton Rouge, 1979.

James, Hunter. *The Quiet People of the Land*. Chapel Hill, 1976.

Jehlen, Myra. *Class and Character in Faulkner's South*. New York, 1976.

Jordan, Winthrop D. *White Over Black: American Attitudes toward the Negro, 1550–1812*. Chapel Hill, 1968.

Kampf, Louis. *On Modernism: The Prospects for Literature and Freedom*. Cambridge, Mass., 1967.

Karanikas, Alexander. *Tillers of a Myth: Southern Agrarians as Social and Literary Critics*. Madison, Wis., 1966.

Karl, Barry D. "Presidential Planning and Social Science Research: Mr. Hoover's Experts." *Perspectives in American History* 3 (1969): 347–409.

Kerr, Chester. *A Report on American University Presses*. Washington, D.C., 1949.

Key, V. O., Jr. *Southern Politics in State and Nation*. New York, 1949.

King, Richard H. "Mourning and Melancholia: Will Percy and the Southern Tradition." *Virginia Quarterly Review* 53, no. 2 (Spring 1977): 248–64.

―――――. *A Southern Renaissance: The Cultural Awakening of the American South, 1930–1955*. New York, 1980.

Knickerbocker, William S. "Trent at Sewanee." *Sewanee Review* 48, no. 2 (April–June 1940): 145–52.

Kroeber, Alfred L. "Eighteen Professions." *American Anthropologist* 17 (1915): 283–88.

Krueger, Thomas A. *And Promises to Keep: The Southern Conference for Human Welfare, 1938–1948*. Nashville, 1967.

Lasch, Christopher. *The New Radicalism in America, 1889–1963: The Intellectual as a Social Type*. New York, 1965.

Lawler, James R. *The Language of French Symbolism*. Princeton, 1969.

Levine, George L., ed. *The Emergence of Victorian Consciousness: The Spirit of the Age*. New York, 1967.

Lewis, Richard W. B. *The American Adam: Innocence, Tragedy, and Tradition in the Nineteenth Century*. Chicago, 1955.

Link, Arthur S., and Patrick, Rembert W., eds. *Writing Southern History: Essays in Historiography in Honor of Fletcher M. Green*. Baton Rouge, 1965.

Longley, John L., Jr., ed. *Robert Penn Warren: A Collection of Critical Essays*. New York, 1965.

Lynd, Helen M. *On Shame and the Search for Identity*. New York, 1961.

Lynn, Kenneth S. *Mark Twain and Southwestern Humor*. Boston, 1959.

———, ed. *The Comic Tradition in America*. Garden City, N.Y., 1958.

McKinney, John C., and Thompson, Edgar T., eds. *The South in Continuity and Change*. Durham, N.C., 1965.

McKitrick, Eric L., ed. *Slavery Defended: The Views of the Old South*. Englewood Cliffs, N.J., 1963.

Marcus, Steven. *The Other Victorians: A Study of Sexuality and Pornography in Mid-Nineteenth-Century England*. New York, 1966.

Marx, Leo. *The Machine in the Garden: Technology and the Pastoral Ideal in America*. New York, 1964.

May, Henry F. *The End of American Innocence: A Study of the First Years of Our Own Time, 1912–1917*. New York, 1959.

McDowell, Frederick P. *Ellen Glasgow and the Ironic Art of Fiction*. Madison, Wis., 1960.

Meriwether, James B., ed. *A Faulkner Miscellany*. Jackson, Miss., 1974.

Meyers, Marvin. *The Jacksonian Persuasion: Politics and Belief*. Stanford, Calif., 1957.

Miller, John G. *The Black Patch War*. Chapel Hill, 1936.

Millgate, Michael. *The Achievement of William Faulkner*. New York, 1966.

Miyoshi, Masao. *The Divided Self: A Perspective on the Literature of the Victorians*. New York, 1969.

Mixon, Wayne. "Joel Chandler Harris, the Yeoman Tradition, and the New South Movement." *Georgia Historical Quarterly* 61, no. 4 (Winter 1977): 308–17.

Moore, L. Hugh, Jr. *Robert Penn Warren and History: "The Big Myth We Live."* The Hague, 1970.

Murray, Henry A., ed. *Myth and Mythmaking*. Boston, 1960.

Newby, Idus A. *Jim Crow's Defense: Anti-Negro Thought in America, 1900–1930*. Baton Rouge, 1965.

Niebuhr, Reinhold. *The Children of Light and the Children of Darkness*. New York, 1944.

O'Brien, Michael. "Edwin Mims: An Aspect of the New South Mind Considered." *South Atlantic Quarterly* 73, no. 2 (April 1974): 199–212.

———. *The Idea of the American South, 1920–1941*. Baltimore, 1979.

Oleson, Alexandra, and Voss, John, eds. *The Organization of Knowledge in Modern America, 1860–1920*. Baltimore, 1979.

Osterweis, Rollin G. *Romanticism and Nationalism in the Old South*. New Haven, 1949.

Pearce, Roy Harvey. *Savagism and Civilization: A Study of the Indian and the American Mind*. Baltimore, 1965.

Pells, Richard H. *Radical Visions and American Dreams: Culture and Social Thought in the Depression Years*. New York, 1973.

Persons, Stow, ed. *Evolutionary Thought in America*. New Haven, 1950.

Pierson, Mary B. *Graduate Work in the South*. Chapel Hill, 1947.

Pinckney, Josephine. "Charleston's Poetry Society." *Sewanee Review* 38, no. 1 (January 1930): 50–56.

Raper, Julius R. *Without Shelter: The Early Career of Ellen Glasgow*. Baton Rouge, 1971.

Reed, John Shelton. *The Enduring South: Subcultural Persistence in Mass Society*. Chapel Hill, 1972.

Richardson, H. Edward. *William Faulkner: The Journey to Self-Discovery*. Columbia, Mo., 1969.

Riesman, David; Denney, Reuel; and Glazer, Nathan. *The Lonely Crowd: A Study of the Changing American Character*. Garden City, N.Y., 1955.

Roberts, David C. *Existentialism and Religious Belief*. New York, 1959.

Rock, Virginia. "The Making and Meaning of *I'll Take My Stand*: A Study in Utopian-Conservatism, 1925–1939." Ph.D. dissertation, University of Minnesota, 1961.

Roper, Laura Wood. *FLO: A Biography of Frederick Law Olmsted*. Baltimore, 1974.

Rothman, David J. *The Discovery of the Asylum: Social Order and Disorder in the New Republic*. Boston, 1971.

Rubin, Louis D., Jr. *The Curious Death of the Novel*. Baton Rouge, 1967.

_____. *No Place on Earth: Ellen Glasgow, James Branch Cabell, and Richmond-in-Virginia*. Austin, 1959.

_____. *The Wary Fugitives: Four Poets and the South*. Baton Rouge, 1978.

_____. *The Writer in the South*. Athens, Ga., 1972.

_____. *Writers of the Modern South: The Faraway Country*. Seattle, 1963.

_____, and Jacobs, Robert D., eds. *South: Modern Southern Literature in Its Cultural Setting*. Garden City, N.Y., 1961.

_____, and Jacobs, Robert D., eds. *Southern Renascence: The Literature of the Modern South*. Baltimore, 1953.

_____, and Kilpatrick, James J., eds. *The Lasting South: Fourteen Southerners Look at Their Home*. Chicago, 1957.

Santas, Joan Foster. *Ellen Glasgow's American Dream*. Charlottesville, Va., 1965.

Sartre, Jean-Paul. *Existentialism and Humanism*. Translated by Philip Mairet. London, 1948.

Sellers, Charles G., Jr., ed. *The Southerner as American*. New York, 1966.

Shapiro, Edward S. "The American Distributists and the New Deal." Ph.D. dissertation, Harvard University, 1968.

_____. "Decentralist Intellectuals and the New Deal." *Journal of American History* 58, no. 4 (March 1972): 938–57.

_____. "The Southern Agrarians and the Tennessee Valley Authority." *American Quarterly* 22, no. 4 (Winter 1970): 791–806.

Simonini, Rinaldo C., Jr., ed. *Southern Writers: Appraisals in Our Times*. Charlottesville, Va., 1964.

Simpson, Lewis P. *The Man of Letters in New England and the South: Essays on the History of the Literary Vocation in America*. Baton Rouge, 1973.

Slatoff, Walter J. *Quest for Failure: A Study of William Faulkner*. Ithaca, N.Y., 1960.

Slotkin, Richard S. *Regeneration through Violence: The Mythology of the American Frontier, 1600–1860*. Middletown, Conn., 1973.

Smith, Henry Nash. *Virgin Land: The American West as Symbol and Myth*. Cambridge, Mass., 1950.

Sosna, Morton, D. *In Search of the Silent South: Southern Liberals and the Race Issue*. New York, 1977.

Squires, Radcliffe. *Allen Tate: A Literary Biography*. New York, 1971.

_____, ed. *Allen Tate and His Work: Critical Evaluations*. Minneapolis, 1972.

Stampp, Kenneth M. "Reconsidering U. B. Phillips: A Comment." *Agricultural History* 41, no. 4 (October 1967): 365–68.

Stenerson, Douglas C. *H. L. Mencken: Iconoclast from Baltimore*. Chicago, 1971.

Stephenson, Wendell H. *Southern History in the Making*. Baton Rouge, 1964.

_____. *The South Lives in History: Southern Historians and Their Legacy*. Baton Rouge, 1955.

Stewart, John L. *The Burden of Time: The Fugitives and Agrarians*. Princeton, 1965.

Stewart, Randall. "Tidewater and Frontier." *Georgia Review* 13, no. 3 (Fall 1959): 296–307.

Stocking, George W., Jr. *Race, Culture, and Evolution. Essays in the History of Anthropology*. New York, 1968.

Stone, Albert E., Jr. "Seward Collins and the *American Review*: Experiment in Pro-Fascism, 1933–1937." *American Quarterly* 12, no. 1 (Spring 1960): 3–19.

Stott, William. *Documentary Expression and Thirties America*. New York, 1973.

Sydnor, Charles S. *American Revolutionaries in the Making: Political Practices in Washington's Virginia*. New York, 1965.

––––––. *The Development of Southern Sectionalism, 1819–1848*. Baton Rouge, 1948.

Szabolcsi, Miklos. "Avante-garde, Neo avante-garde, Modernism: Questions and Suggestions." *New Literary History* 3, no. 1 (Autumn 1971): 49–70.

Tarrant, Desmond. *James Branch Cabell: The Dream and the Reality*. Norman, Okla., 1967.

Taylor, William R. *Cavalier and Yankee: The Old South and American National Character*. Garden City, N.Y., 1963.

Thompson, Edgar T. *Plantation Societies, Race Relations, and the South: The Regimentation of Populations*. Durham, N.C., 1975.

––––––. "Sociology and Sociological Research in the South." *Social Forces* 23, no. 3 (March 1945): 360–65.

Timko, Michael. "The Victorianism of Victorian Literature." *New Literary History* 6, no. 3 (Spring 1975): 607–27.

Tindall, George B. "The Benighted South: Origins of a Modern Image." *Virginia Quarterly Review* 40, no. 2 (Spring 1964): 281–94.

––––––. *The Emergence of the New South, 1913–1945*. Baton Rouge, 1967.

––––––. "The Significance of Howard W. Odum to Southern History: A Preliminary Estimate." *Journal of Southern History* 24, no. 3 (August 1958): 285–307.

Tomsich, John. *A Genteel Endeavor: American Culture and Politics in the Gilded Age*. Stanford, Calif., 1971.

Trilling, Lionel. *Beyond Culture: Essays on Literature and Learning*. New York, 1968.

––––––. *Sincerity and Authenticity*. Cambridge, Mass., 1972.

Turner, Arlin. *George W. Cable: A Biography*. Baton Rouge, 1966.

Turner, James. *Reckoning with the Beast: Animals, Pain, and Humanity in the Victorian Mind*. Baltimore, 1980.

Vance, Rupert B. "Howard W. Odum and the Case of the South." Paper delivered before the Southeastern Meeting of the American Studies Association, April 11, 1970.

––––––, and Jocher, Katharine. "Howard W. Odum." *Social Forces* 33, no. 3 (March 1955): 203–17.

Van Doren, Carl; Mencken, H. L.; and Walpole, Hugh. *James Branch Cabell: Three Essays*. Port Washington, N.Y., 1967.

Waggoner, Hyatt H. *William Faulkner: From Jefferson to the World*. Lexington, Ky., 1959.

Warren, Frank A., III. *Liberals and Communism: The "Red Decade" Revisited*. Bloomington, Ind., 1966.

Warren, Robert Penn. *Faulkner: A Collection of Critical Essays*. Englewood Cliffs, N.J., 1966.

––––––. "Some Recent Novels." *Southern Review* 1, no. 3 (1935): 624–49.

Wells, Arvin R. *Jesting Moses: A Study in Cabellian Comedy*. Gainesville, Fla., 1962.

White, Morton. *Social Thought in America: The Revolt against Formalism*. Boston, 1957.

Williams, Raymond. *Culture and Society, 1780–1950*. New York, 1958.

Wilson, Edmund. *Axel's Castle: A Study in the Imaginative Literature of 1870–1930*. New York, 1931.

————. "The James Branch Cabell Case Reopened." *New Yorker*, April 21, 1956, pp. 129–56.

Wilson, Louis R. *The University of North Carolina, 1900–1930: The Making of a Modern University*. Chapel Hill, 1957.

Wilson, R. Jackson. *In Quest of Community: Social Philosophy in the United States, 1860–1920*. New York, 1968.

Wish, Harvey, ed. *Ante Bellum*. New York, 1960.

Woodward, C. Vann. *American Counterpoint: Slavery and Racism in the North-South Dialogue*. Boston, 1971.

————. *Origins of the New South, 1877–1913*. Baton Rouge, 1951.

Wright, Louis B. *The First Gentlemen of Virginia: Intellectual Qualities of the Early Colonial Ruling Class*. San Marino, Calif., 1940.

Young, G. M. *Victorian England: Portrait of an Age*. London, 1936.

Young, Thomas Daniel. *Gentleman in a Dustcoat: A Biography of John Crowe Ransom*. Baton Rouge, 1976.

————, ed. *John Crowe Ransom: Critical Essays and a Bibliography*. Baton Rouge, 1968.

————, and Inge, M. Thomas. *Donald Davidson*. New York, 1971.

INDEX

ACKNOWLEDGMENTS

The author is grateful for permission to reproduce the following:

Donald Davidson, "Naiad," "Swan and Exile," and "The Tall Men." Reprinted by permission of Mary Davidson Bell.

John Crowe Ransom, "Bells for John Whiteside's Daughter" and "The Equilibrists," in his *Selected Poems*, Third Edition, Revised and Enlarged, copyright © 1969 by Alfred A. Knopf, Inc.

Daniel Joseph Singal, "Ulrich B. Phillips: The Old South as the New," *Journal of American History*, LXIII (March 1977), 871–891.

Daniel Joseph Singal, "Broadus Mitchell and the Persistence of New South Thought," *Journal of Southern History*, XLV (August 1979), 353–380.

Allen Tate, "Ode to the Confederate Dead," in Allen Tate, *Collected Poems, 1919–1976*, published in 1977 by Farrar, Straus & Giroux, Inc. Copyright © 1952, 1953, 1970, 1977 by Allen Tate. Copyright © 1931, 1932, 1937, 1948 by Charles Scribner's Sons. Copyright renewed © 1959, 1960, 1965 by Allen Tate.